GAY NEW YORK

Gay
NEW YORK

Gender, Urban Culture,
and the Making of the
Gay Male World,
1890—1940

GEORGE CHAUNCEY

BasicBooks
A Division of HarperCollinsPublishers

Designed by Jessica Shatan

Library of Congress Cataloging-in-Publication Data
Chauncey, George.
  Gay New York : gender, urban culture, and the making of the gay male world,
1890–1940 / George Chauncey
    p. cm.
  Includes bibliographical references and index.
  ISBN 0–465–02633–8
  1. Gay men—New York (N.Y.)—History—20th century. 2. Homosexuality,
Male—New York (N.Y.)—History—20th century.
HQ76.2.U52N53   1994
305.38'9664'097471—dc20   94–4542
                                                              CIP

94 95 96 97 ❖/HC 9 8 7 6 5 4 3 2

To My Parents

CONTENTS

Acknowledgments   *ix*
Introduction   *1*

PART I
MALE (HOMO)SEXUAL PRACTICES AND IDENTITIES IN THE EARLY TWENTIETH CENTURY

Chapter 1 The Bowery as Haven and Spectacle   *33*
Chapter 2 The Fairy as an Intermediate Sex   *47*
Chapter 3 Trade, Wolves, and the Boundaries of
     Normal Manhood   *65*
Chapter 4 The Forging of Queer Identities and the Emergence of
     Heterosexuality in Middle-Class Culture   *99*

PART II
THE MAKING OF THE GAY MALE WORLD

Chapter 5 Urban Culture and the Policing of
     the "City of Bachelors"   *131*
Chapter 6 Lots of Friends at the YMCA: Rooming Houses,
     Cafeterias, and Other Gay Social Centers   *151*
Chapter 7 "Privacy Could Only Be Had in Public":
     Forging a Gay World in the Streets   *179*
Chapter 8 The Social World of the Baths   *207*
Chapter 9 Building Gay Neighborhood Enclaves:
     The Village and Harlem   *227*

PART III
THE POLITICS OF GAY CULTURE

Chapter 10 The Double Life, Camp Culture, and the
     Making of a Collective Identity   *271*
Chapter 11 "Pansies on Parade": Prohibition and the
     Spectacle of the Pansy   *301*
Chapter 12 The Exclusion of Homosexuality from the Public
     Sphere in the 1930s   *331*

Epilogue: The Strange Career of the Closet   *355*
Note on Sources   *365*
Notes   *373*
Index   *459*

ACKNOWLEDGMENTS

THIS BOOK HAS BEEN A LONG TIME IN THE MAKING AND WOULD NOT HAVE been possible without the help of many people. It is a pleasure to thank them.

The book began as a dissertation in the History Department of Yale University. I was fortunate to be in a graduate program with Eric Arnesen, Jeanne Boydston, Ann Braude, Ileen DeVault, Dana Frank, Lori Ginzberg, Carol Karlsen, Regina Kunzel, Molly Ladd-Taylor, David Scobey, Amy Stanley, and other students who became my friends and teachers and made Yale a wonderfully collegial and stimulating place to study American history. Many of us were privileged to have Nancy Cott as an advisor. Her enthusiasm for my work, her perceptive criticisms of it, and her breathtaking insights into the problems it addressed, as well as the model of her own scholarship, meant more to me than she could know. John Boswell's scholarship, his counsel, and even his disagreements with me inspired, facilitated, and sharpened my work at every stage. David Montgomery profoundly influenced the way I thought about working-class history.

At a time when the federal government denied funding to gay-related research and art, I was fortunate to receive the support of several private foundations and research centers. The Danforth Foundation, the Bush Center in Child Development and Social Policy, the Woodrow Wilson Foundation, the Mrs. Giles Whiting Foundation, and the New York University School of Law made my studies at Yale and the completion of the dissertation possible. A postdoctoral fellowship year at the Rutgers Center for Historical Analysis in 1989–90 allowed me to begin rethinking the dissertation in a stimulating and collegial environment. I am grateful to Robert Nye, Barbara Sicherman, Jennifer Terry, Edward and Dorothy Thompson, Jacquelyn Urla, and especially John Gillis, the Center's leader, for creating that environment and commenting on my work. A fellowship from the American Council of Learned Societies for recent recipients of the Ph.D., as well as the support of the History Department and the Social Sciences Division of the University of Chicago, gave me the freedom of a year's leave of absence in which to finish the manuscript. I am particularly grateful to John Coatsworth, Edward Laumann, and John Boyer for making that year possible.

One of my greatest debts is to the more than seventy men who let me interview them. Although I was able to spend only a few hours with many of them, others became enduring friends. I am deeply grateful to them all for sharing their memories and reflections with me. I have referred to particular interviews only when citing an actual quote or a particular point an interviewee made, but the cumulative experience of having listened to so many men has influenced every line of this book. I am also grateful to Senior Action in a Gay Environment (SAGE), which let me listen to several of the interviews their oral history committee volunteers had recorded, and to Ray Gerard Koskovich for letting me use his interview with Edouard Roditi.

The assistance of numerous librarians was also essential, and I especially want to thank Douglas Freeman at the Kinsey Institute Library and Melanie Yolles at the Manuscript Collection of the New York Public Library, both of whom pointed me toward valuable sources; Kenneth Cobb at the New York Municipal Archives, who cheerfully put up for a full year with my twice-weekly visits in search of sodomy case records; and John Hammond at the International Gay Archives, who let me examine his important collection before it was transferred to the New York Public Library. The Kinsey Institute Library in Bloomington, Indiana, is an extraordinarily rich resource for historians of sexuality, and I am very grateful to the Institute's director, June Reinisch, for giving me permission to examine and quote from the papers of Thomas Painter and the pseudonymous "Will Finch." Donna Anderson graciously gave me permission to study and quote selected unpublished papers of Charles Tomlinson Griffes; and Charles Boultenhouse, executor of the Parker Tyler estate, kindly let me read and quote some of Parker Tyler's unpublished letters. I am also indebted to Ed Egan, Dick Leitsch, Boris Maysel, and the late Ermanno Stingo for sharing their priceless collections of books and newspaper clippings with me and/or granting me permission to examine and quote from their personal papers.

Allan Berube, John D'Emilio, Martin Duberman, John Gagnon, Bruce Kellner, David Levering Lewis, the late Michael Lynch, Edward Maisel, Joan Nestle, Esther Newton, Laurence Senelick, Jonathan Weinberg, and especially Eric Garber and Timothy Gilfoyle generously shared sources and research leads. My colleagues in the History Department at the University of Chicago have been generous in their support and their criticism, and have had a real influence on this book. Chad Heap provided invaluable research assistance during the last year and a half of this project; and Andrew Gillings spent several weeks reading newspapers for me. My friends Ed Cohen, William Cronon, Andrew Dolkart, Gert Hekma, Elizabeth Kennedy, Stanley Kurtz, Christopher Looby, William Nelson, William Novak, David Scobey, Anthony Stellato, Randolph Trumbach, Martha Vicinus, Kenneth Warren, and Jeffrey Weeks provided insightful criticisms of individual chapters and/or provocative discussions of ideas.

I am deeply grateful to Eric Arnesen, Kathleen Neils Conzen, David Halperin, James Schultz, Michael Sherry, and Judith Walkowitz for providing helpful readings of substantial portions of the manuscript at a late stage of revision. After I interviewed him about gay life in post–World War II New York, Joel Honig offered to read the entire manuscript, and I am grateful for his corrections, his suggestions, and his affirmation when he thought I had "gotten it right."

Susan Rabiner, who had faith in this book from the beginning, has been a terrific editor: full of shrewd advice and encouraging and insistent in just the right measure. Anne Montague was a superb copyeditor, and the staff of Basic Books, from the publisher on down, moved mountains on behalf of the book. Mike Mueller, Bill Davis, Kermit Hummel, Helena Schwarz, Mark Pensavalle, and Ellen Levine all deserve thanks. It's been a genuine pleasure to work with them.

Michael Sherry, James Schultz, and Kathleen Neils Conzen deserve special thanks for their unwavering support and good counsel during the final stages of this project. I also thank Leora Auslander, Steven Dubin, Kate Ellis, Shelley Fried, Susan Johnson, Stuart Michaels, Drew Minter, Catrina Neiman, Ken Rabb, Melissa Roderick, Daniel Walkowitz, Evan Wolfson, Jenny Wriggins, and especially David Hansell for the combination of intellectual stimulation, encouragement, prodding, and practical support that only true friends would provide. I also want to thank and honor the memory of Jack Winkler, Harry Scott, Michel Rey, and the other dear friends for whom I wrote this book and who did not live to see it.

Finally, I dedicate this book to my parents. I thank them for their support, even when my life took unexpected turns and my decisions seemed risky, and for the risks they have taken. Their love and the example of their moral vision and courage have been the greatest of gifts.

Drag balls were the largest communal events of prewar gay society, and the drag queens and other "fairies" spotlighted at them were its most visible representatives. In a sign of how gay life was integrated into African-American life, Harlem's leading photographer, James VanDerZee, produced this formal portrait of a drag queen, "Beau of the Ball," in 1927. *(Copyright © 1985 by Donna Mussenden-VanDerZee.)*

INTRODUCTION

I

IN THE HALF-CENTURY BETWEEN 1890 AND THE BEGINNING OF THE SECOND World War, a highly visible, remarkably complex, and continually changing gay male world took shape in New York City. That world included several gay neighborhood enclaves, widely publicized dances and other social events, and a host of commercial establishments where gay men gathered, ranging from saloons, speakeasies, and bars to cheap cafeterias and elegant restaurants. The men who participated in that world forged a distinctive culture with its own language and customs, its own traditions and folk histories, its own heroes and heroines. They organized male beauty contests at Coney Island and drag balls in Harlem; they performed at gay clubs in the Village and at tourist traps in Times Square. Gay writers and performers produced a flurry of gay literature and theater in the 1920s and early 1930s; gay impresarios organized cultural events that sustained and enhanced gay men's communal ties and group identity. Some gay men were involved in long-term monogamous relationships they called marriages; others participated in an extensive sexual underground that by the beginning of the century included well-known cruising areas in the city's parks and streets, gay bathhouses, and saloons with back rooms where men met for sex.

The gay world that flourished before World War II has been almost entirely forgotten in popular memory and overlooked by professional historians; it is not supposed to have existed. This book seeks to restore that world to history, to chart its geography, and to recapture its culture and politics. In doing so, it challenges three widespread myths about the history of gay life before the rise of the gay movement, which I call the myths of isolation, invisibility, and internalization.

The myth of isolation holds that anti-gay hostility prevented the development of an extensive gay subculture and forced gay men to lead solitary lives in the decades before the rise of the gay liberation movement. As one exceptionally well informed writer and critic recently put it, the 1969 Stonewall rebellion not only marked the beginning of the militant gay movement but was

> the critical . . . event that unleashed a vast reconstitution of gay society: gay bars, baths, bookstores, and restaurants opened, gay softball teams, newspapers, political organizations, and choruses proliferated. Gay groups of all sorts popped up while gay neighborhoods emerged in our larger, and many of our smaller cities. This was and is a vast social revolution . . . a new community came into being in an astonishingly short period of time.[1]

This has become the common wisdom for understandable reasons, for the policing of the gay world before Stonewall was even more extensive and draconian than is generally realized. A battery of laws criminalized not only gay men's narrowly "sexual" behavior, but also their association with one another, their cultural styles, and their efforts to organize and speak on their own behalf. Their social marginalization gave the police and popular vigilantes even broader informal authority to harass them; anyone discovered to be homosexual was threatened with loss of livelihood and loss of social respect. Hundreds of men were arrested each year in New York City alone for violating such laws.

But the laws were enforced only irregularly, and indifference or curiosity—rather than hostility or fear—characterized many New Yorkers' response to the gay world for much of the half-century before the war. Gay men had to take precautions, but, like other marginalized peoples, they were able to construct spheres of relative cultural autonomy in the interstices of a city governed by hostile powers. They forged an immense gay world of overlapping social networks in the city's streets, private apartments, bathhouses, cafeterias, and saloons, and they celebrated that world's existence at regularly held communal events such as the massive drag (or transvestite) balls that attracted thousands of participants and spectators in the 1920s. By the 1890s, gay men had made the Bowery a center of gay life, and by the 1920s they had created three distinct gay neighborhood enclaves in Greenwich Village, Harlem, and Times Square, each with a different class and ethnic character, gay cultural style, and public reputation.*

Some men rejected the dominant culture of the gay world and others passed through it only fleetingly, but it played a central role in the lives of many others. Along with sexual camaraderie, it offered them practical support in negotiating the demands of urban life, for many people used their gay social circles to find jobs, apartments, romance, and their closest friendships. Their regular association and ties of mutual dependence fostered their allegiance to one another, but gay culture was even more important to them for the emotional support it provided as they developed values and identities significantly different from those prescribed by the dominant culture. Indeed, two New Yorkers who conducted research on imprisoned working-class homosexuals in the 1930s expressed concern about the effects of gay men's participation in homosexual society precisely because it made it possible for them to reject the prescriptions of the dominant culture and to forge an alternative culture of their own. "The homosexual's withdrawal, enforced or voluntary, into a world of his own tends to remove him from touch with reality," they warned in 1941, almost thirty years before the birth of the gay liberation movement at Stonewall. "It promotes the feeling of homosexual solidarity, and withdraws this group more and more from conventional folkways . . . and confirms them in their feeling that they compose a community within the community, with a special and artificial life of their own."[2] Once men discovered the gay world, they knew they were not alone.

The myth of invisibility holds that, even if a gay world existed, it was kept invisible and thus remained difficult for isolated gay men to find. But gay men were highly visible figures in early-twentieth-century New York, in part because gay life was more integrated into the everyday life of the city in the prewar decades than it would be after World War II—in part because so many gay men boldly announced their presence by wearing red ties, bleached hair, and the era's other insignia of homosexuality. Gay men gathered on the same street corners and in many of the same saloons and dance halls that other working-class men did, they participated in the same salons that other bohemians did, and they rented the same halls for

*The "gay world" actually consisted of multiple social worlds, or social networks, many of them overlapping but some quite distinct and segregated from others along lines of race, ethnicity, class, gay cultural style, and/or sexual practices. I have nonetheless referred to the making of "a" gay world because almost all the men in those networks conceived of themselves as linked to the others in their common "queerness" and their membership in a single gay world, no matter how much they regretted it. The relationship different groups of men imagined themselves to have to one another is discussed at greater length later in the book.

parties, fancy balls, and theatrical events that other youths did. "Our streets and beaches are overrun by . . . fairies," declared one New Yorker in 1918,[3] and nongay people encountered them in speakeasies, shops, and rooming houses as well. They read about them in the newspapers, watched them perform in clubs, and saw them portrayed on almost every vaudeville and burlesque stage as well as in many films. Indeed, many New Yorkers viewed the gay subculture's most dramatic manifestations as part of the spectacle that defined the distinctive character of their city. Tourists visited the Bowery, the Village, and Harlem in part to view gay men's haunts. In the early 1930s, at the height of popular fascination with gay culture, literally thousands of them attended the city's drag balls to gawk at the drag queens on display there, while newspapers filled their pages with sketches of the most sensational gowns.

The drag queens on parade at the balls and the effeminate homosexual men, usually called "fairies," who managed to be flamboyant even in a suit were the most visible representatives of gay life and played a more central role in the gay world in the prewar years than they do now. But while they made parts of the gay world highly visible to outsiders, even more of that world remained invisible to outsiders. Given the risks gay men faced, most of them hid their homosexuality from their straight workmates, relatives, and neighbors as well as the police. But being forced to hide from the dominant culture did not keep them hidden from each other. Gay men developed a highly sophisticated system of subcultural codes—codes of dress, speech, and style—that enabled them to recognize one another on the streets, at work, and at parties and bars, and to carry on intricate conversations whose coded meaning was unintelligible to potentially hostile people around them. The very need for such codes, it is usually (and rightly) argued, is evidence of the degree to which gay men had to hide. But the elaboration of such codes also indicates the extraordinary resilience of the men who lived under such constraints and their success in communicating with each other despite them. Even those parts of the gay world that were invisible to the dominant society were visible to gay men themselves.

The myth of internalization holds that gay men uncritically internalized the dominant culture's view of them as sick, perverted, and immoral, and that their self-hatred led them to accept the policing of their lives rather than resist it. As one of the most perceptive gay social critics has put it, "When we hid our homosexuality in the past, it was not only because of fear of social pressure but even more because of deeply internalized self-hatred . . . [which was] very pervasive. . . . Homosexuals themselves long resisted the idea of being somehow distinct from other people."[4] But many gay men celebrated their difference from the norm, and some of them organized to resist anti-gay policing.

From the late nineteenth century on, a handful of gay New Yorkers wrote polemical articles and books, sent letters to hostile newspapers and published their own, and urged jurists and doctors to change their views. In the 1930s, gay bars challenged their prohibition in the courts, and gay men and lesbians organized groups to advocate the homosexual cause. A larger number of men dressed and carried themselves in the streets in ways that proclaimed their homosexuality as boldly as any political button would, even though they risked violence and arrest for doing so.

Most gay men did not speak out against anti-gay policing so openly, but to take this as evidence that they had internalized anti-gay attitudes is to ignore the strength of the forces arrayed against them, to misinterpret silence as acquiescence, and to construe resistance in the narrowest of terms—as the organization of formal political groups and petitions. The history of gay resistance must be understood to extend beyond formal political organizing to include the strategies of everyday resistance that men devised in order to claim space for themselves in the midst of a hostile society. Given the effective prohibition of gay sociability and the swift and certain consequences that most men could expect if their homosexuality were revealed, both the willingness of some men to carry themselves openly *and* the ability of other gay men to create and hide an extensive gay social world need to be considered forms of resistance to overwhelming social pressure. The full panoply of tactics gay men devised for communicating, claiming space, and affirming themselves—the kind of resistant social practices that the political theorist James Scott has called the tactics of the weak—proved to be remarkably successful in the generations before a more formal gay political movement developed.[5] Such tactics did not directly challenge anti-gay policing in the way that the movement would, but in the face of that policing they allowed many gay men not just to survive but to flourish—to build happy, self-confident, and loving lives.

One striking sign of the strength of the gay male subculture was its ability to provide its members with the resources necessary to reject the dominant culture's definition of them as sick, criminal, and unworthy. Some gay men internalized the anti-homosexual attitudes pervasive in their society. Many others bitterly resented the dominant culture's insistence that their homosexuality rendered them virtual women and despised the men among them who seemed to embrace an "effeminate" style. But the "unconventional folkways" of gay culture noted by the two 1930s researchers were more successful in helping men counteract the hostile attitudes of their society than we usually imagine. Many gay men resisted the medical judgment that they were mentally ill and needed treatment, despite the fact that medical discourse was one of the most powerful anti-gay forces in American culture (and one to which some recent social theories have attributed almost limitless cultural power). Numerous doctors reported their astonishment at discovering in their clinical interviews with "inverts" that their subjects rejected the efforts of science, religion, popular opinion, and the law to condemn them as moral degenerates. One doctor lamented that the working-class "fags" he interviewed in New York's city jail in the early 1920s actually claimed they were "*proud* to be degenerates, [and] do not want nor care to be cured."[6] Indeed, it became the reluctant consensus among doctors that most inverts saw nothing wrong with their homosexuality; it was this attitude, they repeatedly noted, that threatened to make the "problem" of homosexuality so intractable.

All three myths about prewar gay history are represented in the image of the closet, the spatial metaphor people typically use to characterize gay life before the advent of gay liberation as well as their own lives before they "came out." Before Stonewall (let alone before World War II), it is often said, gay people lived in a closet that kept them isolated, invisible, and vulnerable to anti-gay ideology. While it is hard to imagine the closet as anything other than a prison, we often blame people in the past for not having had the courage to break out of it (as if a powerful system were not at work to keep them in), or we condescendingly assume they had internalized the prevalent hatred of homosexuality and thought they deserved to be there. Even at our most charitable, we often imagine that people in the closet kept their gayness hidden not only from hostile straight people but from other gay people as well, and, possibly, even from themselves.

Given the ubiquity of the term today and how central the metaphor of the closet is to the ways we think about gay history before the 1960s, it is bracing—and instructive—to note that it was never used by gay people themselves before then. Nowhere does it appear before the 1960s in the records of the gay movement or in the novels, diaries, or letters of gay men and lesbians.[7] The fact that gay people in the past did not speak of or conceive of themselves as living in a closet does not preclude us from using the term retrospectively as an analytic category, but it does suggest that we need to use it more cautiously and precisely, and to pay attention to the very different terms people used to describe themselves and their social worlds.

Many gay men, for instance, described negotiating their presence in an often hostile world as living a double life, or wearing a mask and taking it off.[8] Each image has a valence different from "closet," for each suggests not gay men's isolation, but their ability—as well as their need—to move between different personas and different lives, one straight, the other gay, to wear their hair up, as another common phrase put it, or let their hair down.[9] Many men kept their gay lives hidden from potentially hostile straight observers (by "putting their hair up"), in other words, but that did not mean they were hidden or isolated from each other—they often, as they said, "dropped hairpins" that only other gay men would notice. Leading a double life in which they often passed as straight (and sometimes married) allowed them to have jobs and status a queer would have been denied while still participating in what they called "homosexual society" or "the life." For some, the personal cost of "passing" was great. But for others it was minimal, and many men positively enjoyed having a "secret life" more complex and extensive than outsiders could imagine. Indeed, the gay life of many men was so full and wide-ranging that by the 1930s they used another—but more expansive—spatial metaphor to describe it: not the gay closet, but the *gay world*.

The expansiveness and communal character of the gay world before World War II can also be discerned in the way people used another familiar term, "coming out." Like much of campy gay terminology, "coming out" was an arch play on the language of women's culture—in this case the expression used to refer to the ritual of a debutante's being formally introduced to, or "coming out" into, the society of her cultural peers. (This is often remembered as exclusively a ritual of WASP high society, but it was also common in the social worlds of African-Americans and other groups.) A gay man's coming out originally referred to his being formally presented to the largest collective manifestation of prewar gay society, the enormous drag balls that were patterned on the debutante and masquerade balls of the dominant culture and were regularly held in New York, Chicago, New Orleans, Baltimore, and other cities. An article published in the *Baltimore Afro-American* in the spring of 1931 under the headline "1931 DEBUTANTES BOW AT LOCAL 'PANSY' BALL" drew the parallel explicitly and unselfconsciously: "The coming out of new debutantes into homosexual society," its first sentence announced, "was the outstanding feature of Baltimore's eighth annual frolic of the pansies when the Art Club was host to the neuter gender at the Elks' Hall, Friday night."[10]

Gay people in the prewar years, then, did not speak of *coming out of* what we call the "gay closet" but rather of *coming out into* what they called "homosexual society" or the "gay world," a world neither so small, nor so isolated, nor, often, so hidden as "closet" implies. The Baltimore debutantes, after all, came out in the presence of hundreds of straight as well as gay and lesbian spectators at the public hall of the fraternal order of Elks. Their sisters in New York were likely to be presented to thousands of spectators, many of whom had traveled from other cities, in some of the best-known ballrooms of the city, including the Savoy and Rockland Palace in Harlem and the Astor Hotel and Madison Square Garden in midtown.

Although only a small fraction of gay men actually "came out" at such a ball or in the presence of straight onlookers, this kind of initiation into gay society served as a model for the initiation—and integration—into the gay world for other men as well.*

II

How did we lose sight of a world so visible and extensive in its own time that its major communal events garnered newspaper headlines and the attendance of thousands?

We lost sight of that world in part because it was forced into hiding in the 1930s, '40s, and '50s. The very growth and visibility of the gay sub-culture during the Prohibition years of the 1920s and early 1930s precip-itated a powerful cultural reaction in the 1930s. A new anxiety about homosexuals and hostility toward them began to develop, which soon became part of the more general reaction to the cultural experimentation of the Prohibition era that developed in the anxious early years of the Depression. A host of laws and regulations were enacted or newly enforced in the 1930s that suppressed the largest of the drag balls, cen-sored lesbian and gay images in plays and films, and prohibited restau-rants, bars, and clubs from employing homosexuals or even serving them. Anti-gay policing intensified during the Cold War, when Senator Joseph McCarthy warned that homosexuals in the State Department threatened the nation's security, and the police warned that homosexuals in the streets threatened the nation's children. Federal, state, and local

---

*The meaning of coming out has changed several times over the course of the twentieth century. In the 1920s it referred to initiation into the gay world, and even when "coming out" was used in a narrower sense, to refer to the process by which someone came to recognize his sexual interest in other men, it referred to something other than a solitary experience. Indeed, before the war this process was more commonly described by saying that someone was "brought out," which nec-essarily implied he had been initiated into homosexual practices by someone else, than by saying he "came out," something he could, at least grammatically, have done on his own. Writing in 1941, Gershon Legman noted that "this locution is losing its original connotation of initiation by another person, and circumstances or fate are coming to be considered the initiatory agents."[11] The meaning of the phrase continued to change. By the 1950s, gay men usually used "coming out" in a narrower sense to refer exclusively to their first sexual experience with another man. "I remember someone who was a total virgin but ran to the bars every week-end with makeup and screamed and shrieked and camped like crazy," one man recalled, "and everybody would ask, 'For God's sake, when is he going to come out?'" By the 1970s, its meaning had changed again. It could still be used to refer to a person's first homosexual experience, but it more commonly referred to announcing one's homosexuality to straight friends and family. The critical audi-ence to which one came out had shifted from the gay world to the straight world.

governments deployed a barrage of new techniques for the surveillance and control of homosexuals, and the number of arrests and dismissals escalated sharply.[12] Hundreds of gay men were arrested in New York City every year in the 1920s and 1930s for cruising or visiting gay locales; thousands were arrested every year in the postwar decade.

The primary purpose of this new wave of policing was not to eradicate homosexuality altogether, a task the authorities considered all but impossible, but to contain it by prohibiting its presence in the public sphere, the city's cafés, bars, streets, theaters, and newspapers, where authorities feared it threatened to disrupt public order and the reproduction of normative gender and sexual arrangements.[13] The effort was unsuccessful in many respects, for the gay world continued to thrive and became even more extensive in the 1940s and 1950s than it had been before the war. But gay life did become less visible in the streets and newspapers of New York, gay meeting places did become more segregated and carefully hidden, and the risks of visiting them increased. To use the modern idiom, the state built a closet in the 1930s and forced gay people to hide in it.

The periodization I propose here is counterintuitive, for despite the cautionary work of historians such as John D'Emilio, Allan Berube, and Lillian Faderman, and the events of recent memory (such as the anti-gay backlash that began in the late 1970s and intensified in the wake of AIDS), the Whiggish notion that change is always "progressive" and that gay history in particular consists of a steady movement toward freedom continues to have appeal.[14] This book argues instead that gay life in New York was *less* tolerated, *less* visible to outsiders, and *more* rigidly segregated in the second third of the century than the first, and that the very severity of the postwar reaction has tended to blind us to the relative tolerance of the prewar years.

A second reason the prewar gay subculture disappeared from historical memory is that, until recently, nobody looked for it. One of the most enduring legacies of the intellectual and social retrenchment precipitated by the Cold War was its censorship of inquiry into gay culture.[15] For decades, the general prejudice against gay people deterred research by effectively stigmatizing and trivializing historians of homosexuality as well as homosexuals themselves. Even professional historians with an interest in such inquiry dared not undertake it and warned their graduate students away from it; it is not surprising that some of the earliest, groundbreaking works of gay and lesbian history were written by nonacademic historians such as Jonathan Katz and Joan Nestle.[16] In recent years there has been a dramatic decline in prejudice and an equally dramatic increase in interest in gay culture outside the academy, as well as an explosion of work within it on the social history of other subaltern groups: women and workers, African-Americans and immigrants. Even now, though, any historian writing about homosexuality cannot help being cognizant of the potential professional consequences of working on a subject that continues to be marginalized within the discipline. Still, a door has been opened, and the gay world is beginning to be seen through it.

A third reason we have failed to see the prewar gay world is that it took shape in such unexpected places and was so different from our own that we have often not even known where to look or what to look for. As in any new field of study, historians first turned to the more easily accessible records of the elite before grappling with the more elusive evidence of the ordinary. This sometimes meant they looked in relatively unrevealing places: the *New York Times* instead of the African-American press and the tabloids, white middle-class culture instead of working-class culture, elite medical or juridical discourse instead of popular culture. The old dogma that the gay male world originated as an essentially middle-class phenomenon, which only white middle-class men had the resources to create, and the newer dogma that it was created in the pages of elite medical journals, have had continuing influence.[17] But the most visible gay world of the early twentieth century, as the headlines in the *Baltimore Afro-American* suggest, was a working-class world, centered in African-American and Irish and Italian immigrant neighborhoods and along the city's busy waterfront, and drawing on the social forms of working-class culture. Even the gay and lesbian enclave that developed in Greenwich Village in the 1910s and 1920s, which constituted the first visible middle-class gay subculture in the city, sprang up in the midst of a working-class Italian immigrant neighborhood and was populated largely by poorer youths from the outer boroughs, even though its middle-class and bohemian members are better remembered. The fact that the working-class gay world took different forms and defined itself in different terms from those of middle-class culture and from those that would develop in the postwar years should lead us not to exclude it from our inquiry, but to redefine the very boundaries of that inquiry.

A final reason we have failed to see the gay subculture that existed before World War II is that it has been obscured by the dramatic growth of the gay subculture *after* the war. As the groundbreaking work of Allan Berube and John D'Emilio has shown, the war "created something of a nationwide coming out experience." By freeing men from the supervision of their families and small-town neighborhoods and placing them in a single-sex environment, military mobilization increased the chances that they would meet gay men and explore their homosexual interests. Many recruits saw the sort of gay life they could lead in large cities and chose to stay in those cities after the war. Some women who joined the military, as well as those on the homefront who shared housing and worked in defense industries with other women, had similar experiences.

As a result, the war made it possible for gay bars and restaurants to pro-
liferate and for many new gay social networks to form.[18]

The recognition of the significance of the war has shattered the myth
that the gay movement and the gay world alike were invented virtually
overnight after the Stonewall rebellion in 1969; historians have shown
that a political movement preceded Stonewall by two decades and had its
origins in a gay subculture that expanded during the war. But the massive
evidence that a generation of men constructed gay identities and communities during the war does not in itself demonstrate that the war generation was the first generation to do so. The war was an epochal event for
its generation: almost every gay man who was young during the war (like
almost every heterosexual man) remembers it as a critical turning point
in his life, and given their age, it was almost inevitable that the war
should serve as the backdrop to their first sexual experiences and efforts
to live outside the family nexus. Moreover, it is clear that the war
enabled many men to participate in the gay world who otherwise would
not have done so and led many more to have the only homosexual experiences of their lives. But this does not mean that the war generation was
the *first* generation to leave the constraints of family life and watchful
neighbors, nor that it was first during the war that an urban gay subculture took shape.

Although the war did precipitate an immense social upheaval, prewar
American society had hardly been stable or immobile. The United States
has always been a nation of transients. The nineteenth century witnessed
the mass migration of Europeans to the United States, of newly freed
African-Americans throughout the South, and of people of every sort
from the East to the West. Every nineteenth-century city and town studied
by historians, from Eastern metropolis to frontier trading post, saw at
least half its adult residents move away during any given decade.[19] Forty
percent of New York City's residents in 1910 had immigrated to the city
from foreign lands, and although restrictive federal legislation severely
curtailed immigration from southern and eastern Europe in the 1920s,
internal migration continued apace as rural depression, agricultural mechanization, and environmental catastrophe pushed millions of farmers off
the land and the Great Depression forced millions of urban families and
single men alike to leave their homes in search of work. Throughout the
half-century before World War II, New York was full of single men and
women who had left their families in southern Europe or the American
South or whose work on the seas made New York one of their many temporary home ports. Countless men had moved to New York in order to
participate in the relatively open gay life available there, and the waterfront, the Bowery, Times Square, and other centers of transient workers
had become major centers of gay life.

Thus the many soldiers who discovered a gay world while passing through New York during the war had been preceded by at least two generations of men (and possibly more, as future research may show).[20] That subculture did grow immensely after the war, and its character also changed in significant ways. But it did not begin then. Moreover, while New York's prewar gay subculture may have been unusually large, its existence was hardly unique. Paris and Berlin hosted gay and lesbian subcultures even larger than New York's in the early twentieth century.[21] While little research has been conducted yet on other American cities, scattered evidence nonetheless indicates that Chicago, Los Angeles, and at least a handful of other cities hosted gay subcultures of considerable size and complexity before the war, and that many small towns also sustained gay social networks of some scope.[22]

Moreover, the work of Randolph Trumbach, Michel Rey, Alan Bray, Theo Van Der Meer, and a host of other historians has demonstrated that "sodomitical subcultures" had emerged in major European cities by the eighteenth century, and it is possible that similar subcultures took root in the ports of the American colonies, although their appearance may well have depended on the later growth of those cities. (In either case, the precise terms by which men involved in such subcultures understood themselves and distinguished themselves from others must be analyzed with care; threads of historical continuity may link the "molly houses" Alan Bray and Randolph Trumbach have located in eighteenth-century London with the Bowery resorts in late-nineteenth-century New York, but much more work will need to be undertaken before we can establish their existence or analyze their significance.)[23] As one American observer noted as early as 1889, there was "in every community of any size a colony of male sexual perverts . . . [who] are usually known to each other and are likely to congregate together."[24] It will take another generation of research before we will understand much about those "colonies," or be able to judge the distinctiveness of New York's gay world or develop a more comprehensive view of the development of American sexual subcultures. But we should never presume the absence of something before we have looked for it.

III

Although the gay male world of the prewar years was remarkably visible and integrated into the straight world, it was, as the centrality of the drag balls suggests, a world very different from our own. Above all, it was not a world in which men were divided into "homosexuals" and "heterosexuals." This is, on the face of it, a startling claim, since it is almost impossible today to think about sexuality without imagining that it is organized along an axis of homosexuality and heterosexuality; a person is either one or the other, or possibly both—but even the third category of "bisexuality" depends for its meaning on its intermediate position on the axis defined by those two poles. The belief that one's sexuality is centrally defined by one's homosexuality or heterosexuality is hegemonic in contemporary culture: it is so fundamental to the way people think about the world that it is taken for granted, assumed to be natural and timeless, and needs no defense.[25] Whether homosexuality is good or bad, chosen or determined, natural or unnatural, healthy or sick is debated, for such opinions are in the realm of ideology and thus subject to contestation, and we are living at a time when a previously dominant ideological position, that homosexuality is immoral or pathological, faces a powerful and increasingly successful challenge from an alternative ideology, which regards homosexuality as neutral, healthy, or even good. But the underlying premise of that debate—that some people are homosexuals, and that all people are either homosexuals, heterosexuals, or bisexuals—is hardly questioned.

This book argues that in important respects the hetero–homosexual binarism, the sexual regime now hegemonic in American culture, is a stunningly recent creation. Particularly in working-class culture, homosexual behavior per se became the primary basis for the labeling and self-identification of men as "queer" only around the middle of the twentieth century; before then, most men were so labeled only if they displayed a much broader inversion of their ascribed gender status by assuming the sexual and other cultural roles ascribed to women. The abnormality (or "queerness") of the "fairy," that is, was defined as much by his "woman-like" character or "effeminacy" as his solicitation of male sexual partners; the "man" who responded to his solicitations—no matter how often—was not considered abnormal, a "homosexual," so long as he abided by masculine gender conventions. Indeed, the centrality of effeminacy to the representation of the "fairy" allowed many conventionally masculine men, especially unmarried men living in sex-segregated immigrant communities, to engage in extensive sexual activity with other men without risking stigmatization and the loss of their status as "normal men."

Only in the 1930s, 1940s, and 1950s did the now-conventional division of men into "homosexuals" and "heterosexuals," based on the sex of their sexual partners, replace the division of men into "fairies" and "normal men" on the basis of their imaginary gender status as the hegemonic way of understanding sexuality. Moreover, the transition from one sexual regime to the next was an uneven process, marked by significant class and ethnic differences. Multiple systems of sexual classification coexisted throughout the period in New York's divergent neighborhood cultures: men socialized into different class and ethnic systems of gender, family life, and sexual mores tended to understand and organize their homosexual practices in different ways. Most significantly, exclusive heterosexuality became a precondition for a man's identification as "normal" in middle-class culture at least two generations before it did so in much of Euro-American and African-American working-class culture.

One way to introduce the differences between the conceptual schemas by which male sexual relations and identities were organized in the first and second halves of the twentieth century (as well as this book's use of terminology) is to review the changes in the vernacular terms used for homosexually active men, and, in particular, the way in which *gay* came to mean "homosexual". This does not mean reconstructing a lineage of static meanings—simply noting, for instance, that *gay* meant "prostitute" before it meant "homosexual." In keeping with the methodology of the study as a whole, it means instead reconstructing how men *used* the different terms *tactically* in diverse cultural settings to position themselves and negotiate their relations with other men, gay and straight alike.

Although many individuals at any given time, as one might expect, used the available terms interchangeably and imprecisely, the broad contours of lexical evolution reveal much about the changes in the organization of male sexual practices and identities. For many of the terms used in the early twentieth century were not synonymous with *homosexual* or *heterosexual*, but represent a different conceptual mapping of male sexual practices, predicated on assumptions about the character of men engaging in those practices that are no longer widely shared or credible. *Queer, fairy, trade, gay*, and other terms each had a specific connotation and signified specific subjectivities, and the ascendancy of *gay* as the preeminent term (for gay men among gay men) in the 1940s reflected a major reconceptualization of homosexual behavior and of "homosexuals" and "heterosexuals." Demonstrating that such terms signified distinct social categories not equivalent to "homosexual" and that men used many of them for themselves will also explain why I have employed them throughout this study, even though some of them now have pejorative connotations that may initially cause the reader to recoil.

Gay emerged as a coded homosexual term and as a widely known term for homosexuals in the context of the complex relationship between men known as "fairies" and those known as "queers." According to Gershon Legman, who published a lexicon of homosexual argot in 1941, *fairy* (as a noun) and *queer* (as an adjective) were the terms most commonly used by "queer" and "normal" people alike to refer to "homosexuals" before World War II.[26] Regulatory agents—police, doctors, and private investigators alike—generally used technical terms such as *invert, pervert, degener-*

ate, or, less commonly, *homosexual* (or *homosexualist,* or simply *homo*), but they also knew and frequently used the vernacular *fairy* as well. In 1917, for instance, an agent of an anti-vice society reported to his supervisor on a "crowd of homosexualists, commonly known as 'fairies.'"[27] Another agent of the society reported ten years later that he had noticed a "colored pervert" in a subway washroom, but added that in identifying the "pervert" to another man in the washroom he had used the more commonplace term: "I said, 'He is a fairy.'"[28]

While most gay men would have understood most of the terms in use for homosexual matters, some terms were more likely to be used in certain social milieus than others. *Fag* was widely used in the 1930s, but almost exclusively by "normals" (the usual word then for those who were not queers); gay men used the word *faggot* instead, but it was used more commonly by blacks than whites. An investigator who visited a "woman's party" at a 137th Street tenement in Harlem in 1928, for instance, reported that one of the women there told him "'Everybody here is either a bull dagger [lesbian] or faggot.'"[29] The investigator, a black man working for an anti-vice society, appears to have believed that the term was less well known than *fairy* to the "normal" white population. When he mentioned in another report that two men at a Harlem restaurant were "said to be 'noted faggots,'" he quickly explained to his white supervisor this meant they were "fairies."[30] While gay white men also used the term *faggot* (although less often than blacks), they rarely referred to themselves as being "in the life," a phrase commonly used by black men and women.[31]

Most of the vernacular terms used by "normal" observers for fairies, such as *she-man, nance,* and *sissy,* as well as *fairy* itself, emphasized the centrality of effeminacy to their character. In the 1920s and 1930s, especially, such men were also often called *pansies,* and the names of other flowers such as daisy and buttercup were applied so commonly to gay men that they were sometimes simply called "horticultural lads." ("Ship me home," said a "nance" to a florist in a joke told in 1932. "I'm a pansy.")[32] The flamboyant style adopted by "flaming faggots" or "fairies," as well as its consistency with outsiders' stereotypes, made them highly visible figures on the streets of New York and the predominant image of *all* queers in the straight mind.

Not all homosexual men in the prewar era thought of themselves as "flaming faggots," though. While the terms *queer, fairy,* and *faggot* were often used interchangeably by outside observers (and sometimes even by the men they observed), each term also had a more precise meaning among gay men that could be invoked to distinguish its object from other homosexually active men. By the 1910s and 1920s, the men who identified themselves as part of a distinct category of men primarily on the basis of their homosexual interest rather than their womanlike gender status usually called themselves *queer*. Essentially synonymous with "homosexual," *queer* presupposed the statistical normalcy—and normative character—of men's sexual interest in women; tellingly, queers referred to their counterparts as "normal men" (or "straight men") rather than as "heterosexuals." But *queer* did not presume that the men it denoted were effeminate, for many queers were repelled by the style of the fairy and his loss of manly status, and almost all were careful to distinguish themselves from such men. They might use *queer* to refer to any man who was not "normal," but they usually applied terms such as *fairy, faggot,* and *queen* only to those men who dressed or behaved in what they considered to be a flamboyantly effeminate manner. They were so careful to draw such distinctions in part because the dominant culture failed to do so.[33]

Many fairies and queers socialized into the dominant prewar homosexual culture considered the ideal sexual partner to be "trade," a "real man," that is, ideally a sailor, a soldier, or some other embodiment of the aggressive masculine ideal, who was neither homosexually interested nor effeminately gendered himself but who would accept the sexual advances of a queer. While some gay men used the term *trade* to refer only to men who insisted on payment for a sexual encounter, others applied it more broadly to any "normal" man who accepted a queer's sexual advances. The centrality of effeminacy to the definition of the fairy in the dominant culture enabled trade to have sex with both the queers and fairies without risking being labeled queer themselves, so long as they maintained a masculine demeanor and sexual role. Just as significantly, even those queers who had little interest in trade recognized that trade constituted a widely admired ideal type in the subculture and accepted the premise that trade were the "normal men" they claimed to be.

Ultimately men who detested the word *fairy* and the social category it signified were the ones to embrace *gay* as an alternative label for themselves. But they did not initiate its usage in gay culture. The complexity of the emergence of the term's homosexual meanings is illustrated by a story told by a gay hairdresser, Dick Addison, about an incident in 1937 when he was a fourteen-year-old "flaming faggot" in a Jewish working-class section of New York:

A group of us hung out at a park in the Bronx where older boys would come and pick us up. One boy who'd been hanging out with us for a while came back once, crying, saying the boy he'd left with wanted him to suck his thing. "I don't want to do *that*!" he cried. "But why are you hanging out with us if you aren't gay?" we asked him. "Oh, I'm *gay*," he exclaimed, throwing his hands in the air like an hysterical queen, "but I don't want to do *that*." This boy liked the gay life—the clothes, the way people talked and walked and held themselves—but, if you can believe it, he didn't realize there was more to being gay than that![34]

Gay, as the story indicates, was a code word. Gay men could use it to identify themselves to other gays without revealing their identity to those not in the wise, for not everyone—certainly not the boy in this story (unless he was simply using the word's protean character to joke with the group)—knew that it implied a specifically sexual preference. But it did not simply mean "homosexual," either. For all the boys, the "gay life" referred as well to the flamboyance in dress and speech associated with the fairies. Indeed, it was the fairies (the especially flamboyant gay men), such as the ones Addison associated with, who used the word most in the 1920s and 1930s. Will Finch, a social worker who began to identify himself as "queer" while in New York in the early 1930s, recalled in 1951 that the word *gay* "originated with the flaming faggots as a 'camp' word, used to apply to absolutely everything in any way pleasant or desirable (not as 'homosexual'), . . . [and only began] to mean 'homosexual' later on."[35]

The earliest such uses of *gay* are unknown, but the "flaming faggots" Finch remembered doubtless used the word because of the host of apposite connotations it had acquired over the years. Originally referring simply to things pleasurable, by the seventeenth century *gay* had come to refer more specifically to a life of *immoral* pleasures and dissipation (and by the nineteenth century to prostitution, when applied to women), a meaning that the "faggots" could easily have drawn on to refer to the homosexual life. *Gay* also referred to something brightly colored or someone showily dressed—and thus could easily be used to describe the flamboyant costumes adopted by many fairies, as well as things at once brilliant and specious, the epitome of camp.[36] One can hear these meanings echo through the decades in Finch's comment in 1963 that he still "associate[d] the word with the hand waving, limp-wristed faggot, squealing 'Oh, it's *gay*!'"[37] One hears them as well in the dialogue in several novels written in the late 1920s and early 1930s by gay men with a camp sensibility and an intimate knowledge of the homosexual scene. "I say," said Osbert to Harold in *The Young and Evil*, perhaps the campiest novel of all, "you look positively gay in the new clothes. Oh, said Harold, you're lovely *too*, dear, and gave him a big kiss on the forehead, much to Osbert's dismay."[38] A chorus boy gushed to his friend in another, rather more overwritten 1934 novel, "'I'm lush. I'm gay. I'm wicked. I'm everything that flames.'"[39] And Cary Grant's famous line in the 1938 film *Bringing Up Baby* played on several of these meanings: he leapt into the air, flounced his arms, and shrieked "I just went gay all of a sudden," *not* because he had fallen in love with a man, but because he was asked why he had put on a woman's nightgown. The possibility of a more precisely sexual meaning would not have been lost on anyone familiar with fairy stereotypes.*

The word's use by the "flaming faggots" (or "fairies"), the most prominent figures in homosexual society, led to its adoption as a code word by "queers" who rejected the effeminacy and overtness of the fairy but nonetheless identified themselves as homosexual. Because the word's use in gay environments had given it homosexual associations that were unknown to people not involved in the gay world, more circumspect gay men could use it to identify themselves secretly to each other in a straight setting. A properly intoned reference or two to a "gay bar" or to "having a gay time" served to alert the listener familiar with homosexual culture. As one gay writer explained in 1941,

Supposing one met a stranger on a train from Boston to New York and wanted to find out whether he was "wise" or even homosexual. One might ask: "Are there any gay spots in Boston?" And by slight accent put on the word "gay" the stranger, if wise, would understand that homosexual resorts were meant. The uninitiated stranger would never suspect, inasmuch as "gay" is also a perfectly normal and natural word to apply to places where one has a good time. . . . The continued use of such *double entendre* terms will make it obvious to the initiated that he is speaking with another person acquainted with the homosexual argot.[41]

Will Finch provided a similar example in 1946, when he described how a young man tried to determine whether Finch's friend Edward,

---

*This line has been noted by several historians.[40] It has not been noted, however, that Grant followed the quip (which apparently he made up on the spur of the moment) with an equally significant line: "I'm just sitting in the middle of Forty-second Street waiting for a bus." The line has doubtless not been noticed because its homosexual connotations have now been forgotten, but it seems likely that Grant used it precisely because those connotations amplified the homosexual meaning of his first line. In the late 1930s, when the film was made, Forty-second Street, as chapter 7 shows, was the primary cruising strip for the city's male prostitutes, including transvestite prostitutes, as Grant almost surely would have known. One of the reasons it acquired this status was that it was a heavily trafficked street and transportation hub, where men loitering would not draw particular notice—it was, in other words, the sort of place where a man who was cruising could quip that he was just waiting for a bus to anyone who inquired about his purpose.

whom he had just met, was also homosexual. The youth, obviously very interested in Edward, "acts all right," Finch reported, by which he meant the youth did not act like a fairy and make it clear he was homosexual by camping, "but throws in a few words like 'gay' for Edward to follow the lead on, but Edward plays dumb."[42] And in the early 1930s a speakeasy on East Twenty-eighth Street seeking gay patronage noted suggestively that it was located "in the Gay 20's." Similarly, in 1951 the Cyrano Restaurant let gay men know they were welcome while revealing nothing to others by advertising itself as the place "Where the Gay Set Meet for Dinner."[43]

While such men spoke of "gay bars" more than of "gay people" in the 1920s and 1930s, the late 1930s and especially World War II marked a turning point in its usage and in their culture. Before the war, many men had been content to call themselves "queer" because they regarded themselves as self-evidently different from the men they usually called "normal." Some of them were unhappy with this state of affairs, but others saw themselves as "special"—more sophisticated, more knowing—and took pleasure in being different from the mass. The term *gay* began to catch on in the 1930s, and its primacy was consolidated during the war. By the late 1940s, younger gay men were chastising older men who still used *queer,* which the younger men now regarded as demeaning. As Will Finch, who came out into the gay world of Times Square in the 1930s, noted in his diary in 1951, "The word 'queer' is becoming [or coming to be regarded as] more and more derogatory and [is] less and less used by hustlers and trade and the homosexual, especially the younger ones, and the term 'gay' [is] taking its place. I loathe the word, and stick to 'queer,' but am constantly being reproved, especially in so denominating myself."[44]

Younger men rejected *queer* as a pejorative name that others had given them, which highlighted their difference from other men. Even though many "queers" had also rejected the effeminacy of the fairies, younger men were well aware that in the eyes of straight men their "queerness" hinged on their supposed gender deviance. In the 1930s and 1940s, a series of press campaigns claiming that murderous "sex deviates" threatened the nation's women and children gave "queerness" an even more sinister and undesirable set of connotations. In calling themselves *gay,* a new generation of men insisted on the right to name themselves, to claim their status as men, and to reject the "effeminate" styles of the older generation. Some men, especially older ones like Finch, continued to prefer *queer* to *gay,* in part because of *gay*'s initial association with the fairies. Younger men found it easier to forget the origins of *gay* in the campy banter of the very queens whom they wished to reject.

Testimony given at hearings held by the State Liquor Authority (SLA) from the 1930s to the 1960s to review the closing of bars accused of serving homosexuals provides striking evidence of the growing use of the word *gay*. At none of the hearings held before the war did an SLA agent or bar patron use the word to refer to the patrons. At a hearing held in 1939, for instance, one of the Authority's undercover investigators testified that the bar in question was patronized by "homosexuals or fairies, fags commonly called." Another investigator also called the bar's patrons "fags," but noted that the "fags" preferred to call themselves "fairies." A few moments later he referred to a group of "normal" people having a good time at a party as "people that were gay," indicating that the term, in his mind, still had no homosexual connotations.[45] Twenty years later, however, SLA agents casually used *gay* to mean homosexual, as did the *gay* men they were investigating. One agent testified in 1960 that he had simply asked a man at a suspected bar whether he was "straight or gay." "I am as gay as the Pope" came the knowing reply. ("Which Pope?" asked the startled investigator. "Any Pope," he was assured.)[46]

Once the word was widely diffused within the gay world, it was introduced to people outside that world by writers who specialized in familiarizing their readers with New York's seamier side. Jack Lait and Lee Mortimer, for instance, confided to the readers of their 1948 *Confidential* guide to the city that "not all New York's queer (or, as they say it, 'gay') people live in Greenwich Village."[47] In 1956, the scandal magazine *Tip-Off* played on the expectation that some of its readers would understand the term—and others would want to—by putting a report on homosexuals' supposed "strangle-hold on the theatre" under the headline, "WHY THEY CALL BROADWAY THE 'GAY' WHITE WAY."[48] By 1960, liquor authority attorneys prosecuting a gay bar were so certain a bartender in a heavily gay neighborhood such as Greenwich Village could be expected to understand the word that they used one bartender's claim that he was unsure of its meaning as a basis for questioning his candor. "You live only a few blocks from . . . the heart of Greenwich Village," an attorney demanded incredulously, "and you are not familiar with the meaning of the word gay?"[49] The word had become familiar to hip New Yorkers and others fully a decade before the gay liberation movement introduced it to the rest of the nation, and parts of the "respectable" press began using it in the late 1960s and early 1970s.

The ascendancy of *gay* as the primary self-referential term used within the gay world reflected the subtle shifting occurring in the boundaries drawn among male sexual actors in the middle decades of the century. Earlier terms—*fairy, queer,* and *trade* most commonly—had distinguished various *types* of homosexually active men: effeminate homosexuals, more conventional homosexuals, and masculine heterosexuals who would accept homosexual advances, to use today's nomenclature. *Gay* tended to group all these types together, to deemphasize their differences by emphasizing the *similarity* in character they had presumably demonstrated by their choice of male sexual partners. This reconfiguration of sexual categories occurred in two stages.

First, gay men, like the prewar queers but unlike the fairies, defined themselves as gay primarily on the basis of their homosexual interest rather than effeminacy, and many of them, in a break with older homosexual cultural norms, adopted a new, self-consciously "masculine" style. Nonetheless, they did not regard all men who had sex with men as gay; men could still be trade, but they were defined as trade primarily on the basis of their purported heterosexuality rather than their masculinity (though modified as "rough" trade, the term still emphasized a man's masculine character). A new dichotomous system of classification, based now on sexual object choice rather than gender status, had begun to supersede the old.

In the second stage of cultural redefinition, trade virtually disappeared as a sexual identity (if not as a sexual role) within the gay world, as men began to regard *anyone* who participated in a homosexual encounter as "gay," and, conversely, to insist that men could be defined as "straight" only on the basis of a total absence of homosexual interest and behavior. Alfred Gross, publicly a leader in psychological research and social work related to homosexuals in New York from the 1930s through the 1960s and secretly a gay man himself, derided the distinction between homosexuals and trade in a speech he gave in 1947. Fairies, he contended, "are preoccupied with getting and holding their 'man.'" But, he remonstrated, they refuse "to recognize that the male, no matter how roughly he might be attired, how coarse his manners, how brutal or sadistic he may be, if he be willing to submit regularly to homosexual attentions, is every whit as homosexual as the man who plays what is considered the female role in the sex act."[50]

A growing number of gay men subscribed to this more limited view of the behavior allowed men if they were to be labeled "straight"; by the 1970s, most regarded a self-proclaimed "piece of trade" who regularly let homosexuals have sex with him not as heterosexual but as someone unable to recognize, or accept, or admit his "true nature" as a homosexual. A complaint voiced by Dick Addison, who had come out in the 1930s, about the rejection of the trade–gay distinction by subsequent generations reflects the conflict between the two interpretive systems:

Most of my crowd [in the 1930s and 1940s] wanted to have sex with a straight man. There was something very hot about a married man! And a lot of straight boys let us have sex with them. People don't believe it now. People say now that they must have been gay. But they weren't. They were straight. They wouldn't look for [it] or suck a guy's thing, but they'd let you suck theirs. If you want to say they were gay because they had sex with a man, go ahead, but I say only a man who *wants* to have sex with a man is gay.[51]

Addison's complaint also suggests that "trade," as a practical matter, had become harder to find in the 1960s, a change in sexual practice that suggests "straight" men as well as gay had redefined the boundaries of normalcy. It had become more difficult for men to consider themselves "straight" if they had *any* sexual contact with other men, no matter how carefully they restricted their behavior to the "masculine" role, or sought to configure that contact as a relationship between cultural opposites, between masculine men and effeminate fairies. This narrowing of the limits "straight" men placed on their behavior was also noted by another man, since 1940 a bartender at gay bars, who observed in 1983 that he and his friends had for some years found it "a lot harder to find straight guys to do it with."[52] The bartender himself suggested one reason for the shift: he bitterly criticized the "gay lib movement" for having made straight guys "afraid" to have sex with him—afraid, that is, they would be labeled gay themselves. But whether we attribute this change in attitude to the success of the movement's ideological offensive, as the bartender complained, or regard the gay movement as simply the symbol—or embodiment—of a generational rejection of his view of the sexual world, the cultural potency of the change it represented for him is clear. Over the course of a generation, the lines had been drawn between the heterosexual and homosexual so sharply and publicly that men were no longer able to participate in a homosexual encounter without suspecting it meant (to the outside world, and to themselves) that they were gay. The change the bartender had noticed was not just in the way people "thought" about sexuality but in the way that ideology was manifest in the rules that governed their everyday erotic practices.

The ascendancy of *gay* reflected, then, a reorganization of sexual categories and the transition from an early twentieth-century culture divided into "queers" and "men" on the basis of gender status to a late-twentieth-century culture divided into "homosexuals" and "heterosexuals" on the basis of sexual object choice. Each set of terms represented a way of defining, constituting, and containing male "sexuality," by labeling, differentiating, and explaining the character of (homo)sexually active men. Any such taxonomy is necessarily inadequate as a measure of sexual behavior, but its construction is itself a significant social practice. It provides a means of defining the deviant, whose existence serves both to delineate the boundaries of acceptable behavior for all men and to contain the threat of deviance, at once stigmatizing it and suggesting that it is confined to a "deviant" minority.[53]

IV

This book reconstructs the gay world that existed before the hetero–homosexual binarism was consolidated as the hegemonic sexual regime in American culture—before, that is, the decline of the fairy and the rise of the closet. It ends around 1940, when the boundaries between the straight and gay worlds and between "normal" and "abnormal" men were beginning to change. Cultural transformations as fundamental as these occurred neither suddenly nor definitively, of course, and traces of the prewar sexual regime and gay world persisted in the postwar years and into our own era (in the continuing association of effeminacy with male homosexuality, for instance).[*] But the centrality of the fairy in gay culture and in the dominant culture's representation of gay men, the visibility of the gay world and its integration into the straight world, and, most significantly, the different configuration of the boundaries between the normal and abnormal made the prewar gay world this book describes a world distinctly different from the one existing today. A second volume, currently in preparation, will chart the making of the modern gay world—the rise of the modern sexual regime and the rise and fall of the closet—from the 1940s to the 1970s.

This book maps two distinct but interrelated aspects of what I call the sexual topography of the gay world in the half-century before the Second World War: the spatial and social organization of that world in a culture that often sought to suppress it, and the boundaries that distinguished the men of that world from other men in a culture in which many more men engaged in homosexual practices than identified themselves as queer. The first project of the book, then, is to reconstruct the topography of gay meeting places, from streets to saloons to bathhouses to elegant restaurants, and to explore the significance of that topography for the social organization of the gay world and homosexual relations generally. It analyzes the cultural conditions that made it possible for some gay meeting places to become well known to outsiders and still survive, but it pays more attention to the tactics by which gay men appropriated public spaces not identified as gay—how they, in effect, reterritorialized the city in order to construct a gay city in the midst of (and often invisible to) the normative city.[54] Indeed, while the book analyzes the complex interaction of social conventions and government policies that endeavored to sup-

---

[*]Given these continuities, I have occasionally used illustrative material from the postwar decade in this book when it is consistent with prewar evidence.

press the gay world, it focuses even more on the everyday tactics gay men developed to forge a collective social world in the face of that opposition. Gay men's tactical use of the term *gay* to secretly identify gay places, events, and people to each other in the 1920s and 1930s is indicative of the linguistic and cultural stratagems they used to keep the gay world hidden from the straight while rendering it visible to the gay. By describing this book as a study of *gay* New York, I seek to evoke those tactical considerations and that different cultural and political context, even though the homosexual meaning of the term is now widely recognized, and to signal my intention to map the prewar gay city that gay men themselves would have known.

The second project of the book is to map the boundaries of the gay world under a sexual regime in which many homosexually active men did not identify themselves as a part of it.* Many men who identified themselves as queer lived double lives and participated in the gay world only irregularly, even if it was quite important to them when they did so. Given the centrality of the fairy to gay New York, many more homosexually active men refused (or saw no reason) to identify themselves as queer at all. This book charts the shifting boundaries drawn between queers and normal men, as well as among queers themselves, in the decades before the meaning of *gay* had broadened to incorporate almost all homosexually active men under its rubric. It does not offer a theory of the formation of sexual subjectivities or of the constitution of sexual desire, theoretical projects in which others are engaged. Instead, it develops an ethnographic account of the social organization and cultural meaning of sexual practices and of the dominant cultural categories by which sexually active men had to measure themselves as they constructed their identities.[55]

Although the boundaries between the highly visible fairies and the more covert queers were permeable and both distinguished themselves from "normal" men, the strategies they adopted for negotiating their presence in the city and their relations with "normal" men often clashed. Because the highly contested relationship between them was central to the experience of each group and reveals much about the organization of the gay world more generally, it is one of the central concerns of this book. While I identify and distinguish men as queers or fairies when it is analytically appropriate to do so, I also often refer to them as gay men, since they did perceive themselves to be related to each other as queers and to be part of the same world (different from the straight world),

---

*I do not use "homosexually active" to refer to men who played the so-called active (or "masculine") role in homosexual relations, but to men who engaged in sexual relations of any sort with other men.

even if they contested the terms and significance of that relationship. It is a usage they would have understood by the 1920s and 1930s. I do not, however, use *gay* to refer to men who merely engaged in sexual activity with other men, even if they did so on a regular basis, if they did not consider themselves to be "queer."

This book is not, however, about the making of the gay male world alone, for in mapping the boundaries of the gay world it necessarily maps the boundaries of the "normal world" as well. The prewar gay world was a subculture whose character reveals much about the dominant culture in which it took shape. To call it a "subculture" is not to minimize its vibrancy, but simply to acknowledge that it developed in relationship to a more powerful culture that defined the parameters of its existence in manifold implicit and explicit ways.[56] The men who organized the massive drag balls of the 1920s and 1930s, for instance, were appropriating rituals of the dominant culture—debutante and masquerade balls—and investing them with new meaning. Much of gay culture consisted of this sort of *bricolage*: the manipulation and revaluation of the signs and practices available to gay men in the historically specific parameters of their culture. As this suggests, the relationship between the gay subculture and the dominant culture was neither static nor passive: they did not merely coexist but constantly created and re-created themselves in relation to each other in a dynamic, interactive, and contested process. Not only did the "queer folk" of the gay subculture define themselves by their difference from the dominant culture, but the "normal people" of the dominant culture defined *themselves* by their difference from the gay subculture: they constituted themselves as "normal" only by eschewing anything that might mark them as "queer."[57]

The process by which the normal world defined itself in opposition to the queer world was manifest in countless social interactions, for in its policing of the gay subculture the dominant culture sought above all to police its own boundaries. Given the centrality of gender nonconformity to the definition of the queer, the excoriation of queers served primarily to set the boundaries for how normal men could dress, walk, talk, and relate to women and to each other. At times this took official and precise form, as when the state's ban on gay bars and other sites of gay public sociability produced a set of gender regulations that, as we shall see, literally codified the permissible speech patterns, dress, and demeanor of men and women who wished to socialize in public. But the threat of extralegal sanctions—of ostracism and the loss of jobs, family, and social respect—was a much more potent threat than the threat of judicial sanctions. Indeed, the policing of queer ways, and thus of normal ways, was most commonly effected through the informal policing of the streets, in gossip and in the jeers and manhandling visited on men whom other men regarded as queer. In defining the queer's transgressions against gender and sexual conventions, "normal" men defined the boundaries of acceptable behavior for anyone who would be normal; in attacking the queer they enforced those boundaries by reminding everyone of the penalties for violating them. While most people did not encounter such policing directly or even take special note of it, it effectively served as a warning to all.

This book is not just about the making of the gay male world, then, but also about the making of the normal world: about how the normal world constituted itself and established its boundaries by creating the gay world as a stigmatized other. Examining the boundaries drawn between queers and normal men in the early twentieth century illuminates with unusual clarity—and startling effect—the degree to which the social definition of a "normal man" has changed in the last century. For the erotic behavior allowed "normal" men three generations ago simply would not be allowed "heterosexual" men today. Heterosexuality, no less than homo-sexuality, is a historically specific social category and identity.

As my focus on the street-level policing of gender suggests, another of the underlying arguments of this book is that histories of homosexual-ity—and of sex and sexuality more generally—have suffered from their overreliance on the discourse of the elite. The most powerful elements of American society devised the official maps of the culture: inscribing meaning in each part of the body, designating some bodily practices as sexual and others as asexual, some as acceptable and others as not; des-ignating some urban spaces as public and others as private. Many histo-ries of sex and sexuality have focused on those official maps, the ones drawn up by doctors, municipal authorities, the police, religious figures, and legislators, the ones announced at city council meetings and in med-ical journals. Those maps require attention because they had real social power, but they did not guide the practices or self-understanding of everyone who saw them.[58] While this book pays those maps their due, it is more interested in reconstructing the maps etched in the city streets by daily habit, the paths that guided men's practices even if they were never published or otherwise formalized.[59] It argues that maps of meaning not only guide social practices but inhere in and constitute those practices, and it argues for the significance of such socially structured and socially meaningful everyday practices in the construction of identities.

Moreover, a periodization of sexual practices and meanings based on those announced by the elite seriously misrepresents their historical development.[60] This book challenges the assumption, for instance, that nineteenth-century medical discourse constructed the "homosexual" as a personality type, and that the appearance of the homosexual in medical discourse should be taken as indicative of or synonymous with the homosexual's appearance in the culture as a whole. I have argued in previous work that the medical literature was more complex than this and represented simply one of several powerful (and competing) sexual ideologies.[61] This book seeks to analyze the power of medical discourse by situating it in the context of the changing representation of homosexuality in popular culture and the street-level social practices and dynamics that shaped the ways homosexually active men were labeled, understood themselves, and interacted with others. It argues that the invert and the normal man, the homosexual and the heterosexual, were not inventions of the elite but were popular discursive categories before they became elite discursive categories.

Similarly, while the study's ethnography of sexual subcultures confirms several of Michel Foucault's most speculative and brilliant insights, it modifies the periodization based on those insights by giving equal weight to working-class culture. Most significantly, it shows that the "modern homosexual," whose preeminence is usually thought to have been established in the nineteenth century, did not dominate Western urban industrial culture until well into the twentieth century, at least in one of the world capitals of that culture. The homosexual displaced the "fairy" in middle-class culture several generations earlier than in working-class culture; but in each class culture each category persisted, standing in uneasy, contested, and disruptive relation to the other.[62]

Two other parameters of the study need explanation. The book focuses on men because the differences between gay male and lesbian history and the complexity of each made it seem virtually impossible to write a book about both that did justice to each and avoided making one history an appendage to the other.[63] The differences between men's and women's power and the qualities ascribed to them in a male-dominated culture were so significant that the social and spatial organization of gay male and lesbian life inevitably took very different forms. As in many societies, for instance, gay men in New York developed a more extensive and visible subculture than lesbians did, in large part because men had access to higher wages and greater independence from family life. Gay men as men also enjoyed greater freedom of movement than lesbians did as women, since many of the public spaces where gay men met, from street corners to bars, were culturally defined as male spaces. Moreover, the different sexual and emotional characters ascribed to men and women meant that the boundaries between "normal" and "abnormal" intimacies, both physical and affective, were also drawn differently for men and women. Given the centrality of gender inversion to the culture and representation of both lesbians and gay men, it will ultimately prove important to theorize their historical development in conjunction, but it may take another generation of research on each before an adequate basis for such theories exists.

Even though this study focuses on men, however, it ignores neither women nor gender, but seeks instead to build on the insights of women's historians into the social construction of gender by examining the construction of masculinity, sexual identities, and patterns of male sociability. It argues that the construction of male homosexual identities can be understood only in the context of the broader social organization and representation of gender, that relations *among* men were construed in gendered terms, and that the policing of gay men was part of a more general policing of the gender order. This book is centrally concerned with the shifting boundaries between sex, gender, and sexuality, and demonstrates that sexual desire itself was regarded as fundamentally gendered in the early twentieth century.

The book focuses on New York, which homosexuals regarded as the "gay capital" of the nation for nearly a century, for several reasons. Focusing on a single city makes it possible to study broad questions with a greater degree of precision and specificity than would otherwise be possible: questions about changes in sexual practices, the interaction between men across lines of class, ethnicity, and neighborhood, the changing uses of urban space, the logic of the territorial organization of the gay world, and the changing focus and character of policing and resistance. It has been necessary to situate the history of the gay world in the context of the broadest social and cultural history of New York City, for the history of that world—from the development of gay enclaves in particular neighborhoods at particular times to the emergence of gay speakeasies and drag balls—can be understood only in the context of more general changes in the social geography of the city, the shifting sites and conventions of commercial culture and urban sociability, and the cultural organization of urban space. The complexity of New York's social structure makes it an ideal subject (if one also fraught with difficulties, as any historian of New York will know) because it facilitates the investigation of a wide range of questions concerning the history of sexuality, such as the extent of class and ethnic differences in the social organization and cultural meaning of sexual practices. Moreover, the city's historic role as a national center of intellectual, cultural, and political ferment has meant that its artists, journalists, physicians, jurists, prison reformers, critics, and activists have had a disproportionate influence on national culture.

I do not claim that New York was *typical*, because the city's immense size and complexity set it apart from all other urban areas. It is particularly important that readers not assume that the periodization I have developed for the gay history of New York is necessarily applicable to the rest of the country. Nonetheless, New York may well have been *prototypical*, for the urban conditions and cultural changes that allowed a gay world to take shape there, as well as the strategies used to construct that world, were almost surely duplicated elsewhere. Only future studies will allow us to determine the representativeness of New York's experience with any certainty, and to test the analysis and periodization proposed here.

PART 1

*Male (Homo)sexual Practices
and Identities in the Early
Twentieth Century*

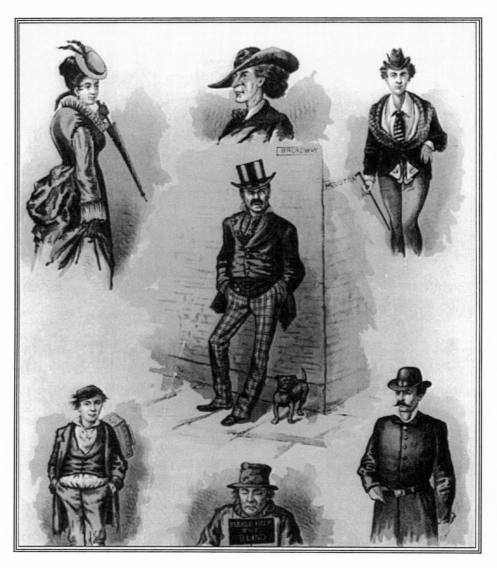

Figure 1.1. Fairies were already fixtures in the streets of New York City's working-class neighborhoods by the late nineteenth century. This map appeared in a book published in the 1870s to familiarize visiting Latin American businessmen with New York's neighborhoods. The social figures it shows populating the section of lower Manhattan now known as Soho include the prostitute (upper left), the shoeshine boy, the beggar, the cop on the beat—and the fairy (upper right). *(From the private collection of David Kahn, Executive Director, Brooklyn Historical Society.)*

Chapter 1

THE BOWERY AS HAVEN AND SPECTACLE

AT THE END OF THE 1890S, COLUMBIA HALL (BETTER KNOWN AS PARESIS Hall), on the Bowery at Fifth Street, was, by all accounts, the "principal resort in New York for degenerates" and well known as such to the public.[1] An investigator who visited the place several times in 1899 noted that he had "heard of it constantly" and that it made no attempt to disguise its "well-known" character as a "resort for male prostitutes." Like other men, he found it easy to gain admittance to the Hall, despite the spectacle to be found within:

> These men . . . act effeminately; most of them are painted and powdered; they are called Princess this and Lady So and So and the Duchess of Marlboro, and get up and sing as women, and dance; ape the female character; call each other sisters and take people out for immoral purposes. I have had these propositions made to me, and made repeatedly.[2]

An officer of the Reverend Charles Parkhurst's City Vigilance League, who had visited the place fully half a dozen times in April and May, added that the "male degenerates" there worked the tables in the same manner female prostitutes did: "[They] solicit men at the tables, and I believe they get a commission on all drinks that are purchased there."[3]

But if Paresis Hall was the principal such establishment in the red-light district centered in the working-class neighborhoods south of the Rialto (Fourteenth Street) at the turn of the century, it was hardly the only one. One well-informed investigator claimed in 1899 that there were at least six such "resorts" (saloons or dance halls) on the Bowery alone, including one called Little Bucks located across the street from Paresis. New York's chief of police added Manilla Hall, the Palm Club of Chrystie Street, and the Black Rabbit at 183 Bleecker Street to the list. North of the Rialto, on West Thirteenth Street between Fifth and Sixth Avenues, stood Samuel Bickard's Artistic Club, whose patrons were summarily arrested and fined for disorderly conduct on several occasions.[4] Five years later, just before a crackdown closed most of the resorts, the Jumbo and several other halls on the Bowery still functioned as "notorious degenerate resorts," according to the men who organized the crackdown, while the "chief attraction" of several places on Bleecker and Cornelia Streets was said to be "perversion."[5]

This chapter sets the stage for our investigation of male (homo)sexual practices, cultures, and identities in the early twentieth century by offering a brief tour of the Bowery fairy resorts, an introduction to the neighborhood in which they developed, and an overview of the different places occupied by queer life in working- and middle-class culture. As the antivice crusaders who sought to reform the moral order of turn-of-the-century American cities discovered, gay male society was a highly visible part of the urban sexual underworld and was much more fully and publicly integrated into working-class than middle-class culture. The subculture of the flamboyantly effeminate "fairies" (or "male degenerates") who gathered at Paresis Hall and other Bowery resorts was not the only gay subculture in the city, but it established the dominant public images of male sexual abnormality. Other men from different social milieus crafted different kinds of homosexual identities, as we shall see. But the prominence of the Bowery fairies and their consistency with the gender ideology of the turn of the century meant their image influenced the manner in which all homosexually active men understood their behavior.

It is not surprising that the Bowery was the center of the city's best-known sites of homosexual rendezvous at the turn of the century, for it was a center of other "commercialized vice" as well. Since early in the nineteenth century the Bowery, a wide boulevard cutting diagonally through the center of Manhattan's Lower East Side, had been the epicenter of a distinct working-class public culture, with its own codes of behavior, dress, and public sociability. When Italians, Jews, and other new immigrant groups replaced the Irish, Germans, and native-born white "Americans" as the largest working-class communities in that area of New York near the end of the century, the Bowery continued to play that role. The boulevard and surrounding streets were alive with theaters, dime museums, saloons, and dance halls, where men and women found relief from their jobs and crowded tenement homes.

To the horror of respectable but politically powerless Jews and Italians living nearby, the Bowery (along with an area known as the Tenderloin, which stretched up Broadway and Sixth Avenue from Twenty-third Street to Fortieth) was also a center of the city's institutions of "commercialized" sex.[6] Next to the theaters and amusement halls stood the tenement brothels and assignation hotels that served the sexual interests of the large numbers of unmarried workingmen and married immigrants, unaccompanied by their wives, who lived in the neighborhood during their sojourn in this country. Along Broadway, Allen Street, Second Avenue, Fourteenth Street, and the Bowery itself, female prostitutes congregated to ply their trade. They made no effort to disguise their purpose, and the children who grew up on the Lower East Side quickly learned to identify them. The left-wing Jewish writer Mike Gold recalled of his street that "on sunshiny days the whores sat on chairs along the sidewalks. . . . [They] winked and jeered, made lascivious gestures at passing males . . . call[ing] their wares like pushcart peddlers. At five years I knew what it was they sold."

He and his contemporaries also learned to recognize the fairies (as they were called) who congregated on many of the same streets. As one man complained in 1899, not only were there "male degenerates upon the Bowery in sufficient number to be noticeable," but "boys and girls get into these dance halls on the East Side [referring to Paresis and Manilla Halls], . . . [and] watch these horrible things." In 1908, when he was fifteen, Jimmy Durante got a job as a pianist at a Coney Island dive, where the customers included "the usual number of girls," by which he meant prostitutes, and the "entertainers were all boys who danced together and lisped." He insisted that none of this bothered him. On "the Bowery, where I was brought up," he boasted, "I had seen enough to get acclimated to almost anything."[7]

But if the Bowery, like the Tenderloin, was an area where working-class men and women could engage in sexually charged encounters in public, it also took on particular significance in bourgeois ideology and life in the late nineteenth century as a so-called red-light district. Sociability was, in most respects, more privatized and ritualized in the city's middle-class neighborhoods. Higher incomes bought apartments or townhouses that provided greater privacy than was imaginable in the tenements, and socializing tended to take place at home, in restaurants, or in private clubs rather than on the stoop or in saloons open to the street.[8] Indeed, men and women of the urban middle class increasingly defined themselves as a class by the boundaries they established between the "private life" of the home and the rough-and-tumble of the city streets, between the quiet order of their neighborhoods and the noisy, overcrowded character of the working-class districts. The privacy and order of their sexual lives also became a way of defining their difference from the lower classes. Sexual reticence and devotion to family became hallmarks of the middle-class gentleman in bourgeois ideology, which presumed that middle-class men conserved their sexual energy along with their other resources. The poor and working classes, by contrast, were characterized in that ideology by their lack of such control; the apparent licentiousness of the poor, as well as their poverty, was taken as a sign of the degeneracy of the class as a whole.[9] Middle-class ideology frequently interpreted actual differences in sexual values and in the social organization of middle-class versus working-class family life that grew out of their quite different material circumstances and cultural traditions as evidence of working-class depravity. It also tended to interpret even those working-class strategies adopted to sustain the integrity of the family as evidence of flagrant disregard for family values. Working-class families often took in boarders as a way to help preserve the family household by allowing women to stay at home with their children while also contributing to the family income, for instance. But middle-class observers condemned the practice as invasive of the privacy of the home and as a threat to the mother's sexual purity.[10]

In this ideological context, the red-light district provided the middle class with a graphic representation of the difference between bourgeois reticence and working-class degeneracy. The spatial segregation of openly displayed "vice" in the slums had both practical and ideological consequences: it kept the most obvious streetwalkers out of middle-class neighborhoods, and it reinforced the association of such immorality with the poor. If the Bowery resorts served the interests of some working-class men and women and also appalled others of the same class who felt powerless to eliminate them, the red-light district also came to represent the sexual immorality of the working class as a whole in bourgeois ideology. This representation could take quite tangible form. Going slumming in the resorts of the Bowery and the Tenderloin was a popular activity among middle-class men (and even among some women), in part as a way to witness working-class "depravity" and to confirm their sense of superiority. Mary Casal, a woman who took the tour, recalled years later that "it was considered very smart to go slumming in New York" in the 1890s, and many of her friends "were anxious to go again and again." But she went only once, she said, for she was stunned by "the ugliness of the displays we saw as we hurried from one horrid but famous resort to another in and about the Bowery," many of them full of male "inverts."[11]

But if most slummers were suitably scandalized by what they saw, many were also titillated. Slumming gave men, in particular, a chance to cultivate and explore sexual fantasies by opening up to them a subordinate social world in which they felt fewer constraints on their behavior. It allowed them to escape the norms of middle-class propriety and, in particular, to shed the constraints they felt imposed on their conduct by the presence of respectable women of their own families or class. Resorts competed to offer them the most scandalous shows as well as music, drink, dancing, and, for a price, access to women and fairies of the lower classes with whom they could engage in ribald behavior inconceivable in their own social worlds.[12]

At a time when New York was famous for being a "wide-open town," some clubs went so far as to stage live sexual performances, some of them designed to startle and engage their audiences by their transgression of normal racial and gender boundaries. In 1904, for instance, three hundred men, most of them apparently middle class, paid $2.50 (a fee high enough to exclude most laborers) to crowd into the back room of a saloon on Thirty-third Street between First and Second Avenues known as Tecumseh Hall & Hotel, which unions hired for their meetings on other nights. The lure was a live sex show that included sex between a black man and a white woman, between two women, and between a woman and a man in women's clothes.[13] The employees arrested in 1900 in a raid on another club, the Black Rabbit on Bleecker Street, included the French floorman, known as the "Jarbean Fairy"; a twenty-year-old woman called a "sodomite for pay" by the anti-vice crusader Anthony Comstock (she had apparently engaged in sodomy with two men as part of the floor show); and a third person Comstock called a hermaphrodite, who had displayed her/his genitalia as part of the show.[14]

A number of resorts made "male degenerates" pivotal figures in their portrayal of working-class "depravity." Billy McGlory had realized as early as the late 1870s that he could further the infamy of Armory Hall, his enormous dance hall on Hester Street at the corner of Elizabeth, by hiring fairies—powdered, rouged, and sometimes even dressed in women's clothes—as entertainers. Circulating through the crowd, they sang, danced, and sometimes joined the best-paying customers in their curtained booths to thrill or disgust them with the sort of private sexual exhibitions (or "circuses") normally offered only by female prostitutes.[15] By 1890, several more halls had added fairies as attractions, and the Slide, Frank Stevenson's resort at 157 Bleecker Street, had taken Armory Hall's place as New York's "worst dive" because of the fairies he gathered there (see figure 1.2).

The fairies' presence made such clubs a mandatory stop for New Yorkers out slumming and for the urban entrepreneurs who had made a business out of whetting and then satisfying the urge of men visiting the city to see the spectacle of the Sodom and Gomorrah that New York seemed to have become. As a *New York Herald* reporter observed in 1892:

It is a fact that the Slide and the unspeakable nature of the orgies practised there are a matter of common talk among men who are bent on

AT MIDNIGHT IN "THE SLIDE."

HERE, MR. NICOLL, IS A PLACE TO PROSECUTE.

Witness the Scenes in "the Slide"
as the Herald Describes Them
to You, and Straightway
Begin Your Work
of Reform.

MOST INFAMOUS OF ALL "DIVES."

Depravity of a Depth Unknown in the
Lowest Slums of London or Paris
Can Here Be Found.

ORGIES BEYOND DESCRIPTION.

The Police Profess Ignorance of Its
Existence, but They Can Easily Secure the Evidence Necessary
for a Conviction.

Figure 1.2. When the *New York Herald* launched a campaign against a "degenerate resort" called the Slide, it published this drawing of limp-wristed young men entertaining the resort's other customers. *(From the* New York Herald, *January 5, 1892.)*

taking in the town, making a night of it. . . . Let a detective be oppor-
tuned by people from a distance to show them something *outre* in the
way of fast life, the first place he thinks of is the Slide, if he believes the
out-of-towner can stand it.[16]

A retrospective account of slumming agreed. In 1915 a lawyer recalled
the "Famous Old Time Dives [whose] Nation-Wide Evil Reputation
Nightly Drew Throngs of 'Spenders'": "No visitor ever left New York
feeling satisfied unless he had inspected the mysteries of [Chinatown],"
the heart of any city's red-light district, he claimed, but on his way back
uptown the visitor almost always stopped on Bleecker Street to visit the
Slide,

> one of the most vile, vulgar resorts in the city, where no man of decent
> inclinations would remain for five minutes without being nauseated.
> Here men of degenerate type were the waiters, some of them going to
> the extent of rouging their necks. In falsetto voices they sang filthy dit-
> ties, and when not otherwise busy would drop into a chair at the table
> of any visitor who would brook their awful presence.[17]

As the *Herald* story suggests, New Yorkers did not need to leave their
armchairs to go slumming in the Bowery, for a new kind of metropolitan
press had emerged in the city in the 1880s and 1890s that constructed a
mass audience by focusing the public's attention on precisely such manifestations of urban culture. Joseph Pulitzer's *World* and William Randolph
Hearst's *Journal* pioneered in those years a new style of journalism that
portrayed itself as the nonpartisan defender (and definer) of the "public
interest," waged campaigns on behalf of moral and municipal reform, and
paid extravagant attention to local crimes, high-society scandals, and the
most "sensational" aspects of the urban underworld. Their low prices and
nonpartisan character allowed these newspapers to build a mass market to
which advertisers could sell products; their journalistic voyeurism turned
urban life itself into a commodity to be hawked at a penny a copy and
helped mark the boundaries of acceptable public sociability. Fairies were
not a staple of the new journalism's press campaigns, but they appeared
regularly enough in the pages of New York's newspapers to alert any
reader to their existence. The 1892 *Herald* story about the Slide, to take
one example, included an extensive description of the resort, which must
be regarded as an effort to titillate readers by supplying them with fulsome
detail even as the paper asserted its own respectability by adopting a tone
of reproach. "Here, Mr. Nicoll, Is a Place to Prosecute," the paper
announced to the district attorney and the public in the headline it placed
over the story.[18]

But what the *Herald* reporter identified as evidence of depravity also points to the importance of the Bowery resorts to men who were fairies, for he made it clear that the Slide was a place where they felt free to socialize with their friends and to entertain not only the tourists but also the saloon's regulars and one another with their campy banter and antics. The night the reporter visited, he saw a group of men "bandying unspeakable jests with other fashionably dressed young fellows, whose cheeks were rouged and whose manner," he noted, using an expression normally reserved for describing female prostitutes, "suggested the infamy to which they had fallen." He later saw "half a score of the rouged and powdered men" sitting at a table on a raised dais in the center of the barroom, where they normally ensconced themselves to "amuse the company with their songs and simpering requests for drinks." One of them, either suspicious of the reporter's motives or interested in including him in the merriment, actually approached him (or "minced up to me and lisped," as the reporter put it) and asked for a drink.[19]

While the reporter at least feigned outrage at the request, the other men present, as his account suggests, did not. Moreover, the record of another man's conversation with a "degenerate type" at the Slide also indicates that the men who were made part of the spectacle at such resorts nonetheless managed to turn them into something of a haven, where they could gather and find support. Charles Nesbitt, a medical student from North Carolina who visited the city around 1890, took the slummer's tour with a friend. As he later recalled, he visited several beer gardens on the Bowery where "male perverts, dressed in elaborate feminine evening costumes, 'sat for company' and received a commission on all the drinks served by the house to them and their customers." Such men dressed in male attire at the Slide, he discovered, but still sat for company as their transvestite counterparts did elsewhere. Intrigued, Nesbitt asked one of the men, known as "Princess Toto," to join his table; to his surprise, he found the fellow "unusually intelligent" and sophisticated. Princess Toto, he quickly decided, was "the social queen of this group" and "had pretty clear cut ideas about his own mental state and that of his fellows." Nature had made him this way, Toto assured the young medical student, and there were many men such as he. He indicated his pride in the openness of "my kind" at places like the Slide, calling them "superior" to the "perverts in artistic, professional and other circles who practice perversion surreptitiously." "Believe me," the student remembered him commenting, "there are plenty of them and they are good customers of ours."[20]

Sensing the medical student's interest, Toto invited him to attend a ball at Walhalla Hall, one of the most prominent of the many Lower East

Side halls that neighborhood social clubs rented to hold their affairs. Nesbitt went and discovered some five hundred same-sex male and female couples in attendance, "waltzing sedately to the music of a good band." Along with the male couples there were "quite a few . . . masculine looking women in male evening dress" dancing with other women, many of whom seem to have impressed the student as being of "good" background. "One could quite easily imagine oneself," he recalled with amused incredulity, "in a formal evening ball room among respectable people."[21]

As the medical student discovered, the Bowery resorts were only the most famous element of an extensive, organized, and highly visible gay world. The men who sat for company at the Slide were part of a subculture that planned its own social events, such as the Walhalla ball, and had its own regular meeting places, institutions, argot, norms and traditions, and neighborhood enclaves. To worried anti-vice investigators and newspaper reporters, the Slide was an egregious manifestation of urban disorder and degeneracy. But to the men who gathered there, it served as a crucial institution in which to forge an alternative social order. Although middle-class gay men participated in the gay world, its public sites were restricted at the turn of the century to the working-class neighborhoods of the Bowery and waterfront, their very existence contingent on the ambivalent tolerance afforded them by working-class men.

The institutions and social forms of the gay subculture were patterned in many respects on those of the working-class culture in which it took shape: the saloons, small social clubs, and large fancy-dress balls around which fairy life revolved were all typical elements of working-class life. The core institutions of the gay subculture were a number of Lower East Side saloons, a few of them famous among slummers as "resorts" but most of them not on the slummers' map.

The role of the saloons is hardly surprising, since they were central to the social life of most working-class men, although their precise character varied among immigrant and other cultural groups. Located on every block in some tenement districts, saloons served as informal labor exchanges, where men could learn of jobs and union activities. Saloons cashed paychecks and made loans to men who had little access to banks, and they provided such basic amenities as drinking water and toilet facilities to men who lived in tenements without plumbing. Above all, they became virtual "workingmen's clubs," where poor men could escape crowded tenements, get a cheap meal, discuss politics and other affairs of the day, and in a variety of ways sustain their native cultural traditions of male sociability. Saloons were often attached to large public halls, which saloonkeepers made available for meetings of unions or social clubs, whose members returned the favor by patronizing the bar. Most saloons also had smaller, more private back rooms, behind the public front barroom, where unmarried women and prostitutes sometimes were allowed to meet men and where patrons could engage in more intimate behavior than would be possible in the front.[22]

Although saloons of varying degrees of affluence could be found throughout the city, they played a particularly critical role in those neighborhoods where social life was likely to be conducted on a sex-segregated basis and where housing was so crowded and inadequate that men had no alternative but to seek out such public spaces in which to socialize. In such neighborhoods these most public of establishments also afforded a degree of privacy unattainable in the patrons' own flophouses and tenements; many of the saloons even rented private rooms on an hourly basis to prostitutes and their customers and to other couples.

"Normal" men and "fairies" intermingled casually at many saloons, some of which were well known as "fairy places" in their neighborhoods. At some of them, fairies and their partners used the back rooms for sexual encounters, just as mixed-sex couples did. The Sharon Hotel, on Third Avenue just above Fourteenth Street, for instance, was known in the neighborhood as "Cock Suckers Hall," and investigators found a room behind the first-floor saloon where a dozen or more youths waited on male customers. "The boys have powder on their faces like girls and talk to you like disorderly girls talk to men," one investigator reported in the summer of 1901. He even observed several men having sex in the back room. On one occasion two of the fairies sat at a stout man's table, had him buy them drinks, and then unbuttoned his trousers and masturbated him "in front of everybody who was in the place."[23] Five blocks north on Third Avenue at Twentieth Street stood Billy's Hotel, which investigators called "without a doubt . . . one of the worst houses of perverts in NYC." Seventy-five "Fairies" were found in the back room one evening in the spring of 1901, "dressed as women, [with] low neck dresses, short skirts, [and] blond wigs." Fairies who met men in the saloon could take them to rooms upstairs or to the basement, where they had keys to a row of bathhouse-like closets in which they could "carry on their business."[24]

Although anti-vice investigators focused on the saloons' role as a site for sexual assignations, the saloons also functioned as important social centers for gay men, just as they did for other working-class men. They provided a place for gay men to meet, socialize, and enjoy one another's company. At Paresis Hall, for instance, Ralph Werther, a student living in New York in the 1890s and 1900s who later wrote an account of his experiences, discovered a whole society of "men of my type," for whom the hall was not the degenerate resort seen by slummers but a center of community and source of support.[25] The fairies' appropriation of the resources available at

Paresis Hall was emblematic of the way gay men appropriated and transformed the practices and institutions of their natal cultures as they forged their own. Many youths in the tenement districts, for instance, organized informal social clubs that rented rooms, often connected to saloons, as places for unsupervised gatherings, and that periodically sponsored larger parties or dances serving both to entertain the club's members and to raise funds for other outings.[26] The Cercle Hermaphrodits, which Werther learned some of the men at Paresis Hall had organized, was such a club. It permanently rented a room above the bar, where members could gather by themselves and store their personal effects, since the laws against transvestism and the hostility of some men made it dangerous for them to be seen on the Bowery in women's attire. A "small colony of pederasts" said to exist on the Lower East Side in 1902 may have been another such social club, whose members organized social events and entertained other men at a saloon. "The members of this band," a surgeon reported having been told, "have a *théâtre comique*, where they perform and have their exclusive dances; they also 'pair off,' living together as husband and wife."[27]

Such loosely constituted clubs and other gay social networks fostered and sustained a distinctive gay culture in a variety of ways. In addition to organizing dances and other social activities, the men who gathered at saloons and dance halls shared topical information about developments affecting them, ranging from police activity to upcoming cultural events. They assimilated into the gay world men just beginning to identify themselves as fairies, teaching them subcultural styles of dress, speech, and behavior. The clubs also strengthened the sense of kinship such men felt toward one another, which they expressed by calling themselves "sisters." Perhaps most important, they provided support to men ostracized by much of society, helping their members reject some of the harsh judgments rendered against them by many of their contemporaries. According to Ralph Werther, many of the fairies at Paresis Hall disparaged the implications of the slang name the slummers had given their meeting place, officially named Columbia Hall; *paresis* was a medical term for insanity, which outsiders thought men might acquire at the hall from syphilis or simply from associating with the fairies. Werther and his associates, by contrast, defended the hall as "the headquarters for avocational female-impersonators of the upper and middle classes." "Culturally and ethically," he emphasized in his account of the place, "its distinctive clientele ranked high." Werther also recorded numerous conversations among club members about the humiliations and harassment they had suffered at the hands of slummers, the police, and young toughs, but his reports also suggested that the conversations helped the men resist internalizing such hostility.[28]

While the Bowery resorts and other saloons served as meeting places primarily for working-class men, gay and "normal" alike, they were also visited by middle-class men, and not only by uptown "sporting men" keen to spend an uninhibited night out on the town. Many uptown gay men visited them as well in order to escape the restrictions imposed on their conduct in their own social circles. Werther lived such a "double life," as he called it. At least once a week he left his respectable routine as a student at an uptown university (probably Columbia) in order to visit the streets and resorts of the Lower East Side, exchanging his normal gentleman's garb for more feminine attire. He took extravagant precautions to avoid being seen by his everyday acquaintances on the train or on the Bowery, for fear that "even my best friend would be likely to get me thrown out of my economic and social position" if he learned of Werther's life as a fairy.[29] Werther and the other middle-class men he met on the Bowery went there because they found working-class men to be more tolerant of their kind than their middle-class colleagues and acquaintances were. Since "the 'classy,' hypocritical, and bigoted Overworld considers a bisexual [by which he meant an "intermediate type" or fairy] as monster and outcast," Werther claimed, "I was *driven* to a career in the democratic, frank, and liberal-minded Underworld." Drawing on the same imagery of heights and depths and light and shadow that many middle-class writers used to characterize the different class worlds and moral orders coexisting in the city, he added: "While my male soul was a leader in scholarship at the university uptown, my female soul, one evening a week, flaunted itself as a French doll-baby in the shadowy haunts of night life downtown."[30] He quoted another middle-class man who claimed that he revealed his character only on the Bowery, and not in his own social circles, because "the world [by which he meant his own, middle-class world] thinks female-impersonation disgraceful, [and] I had to spare my family all risk."[31]

As even this brief tour suggests, the gay world had become part of the spectacle of the Bowery by the 1890s. At a time when New York was a notoriously "wide-open" city, "degenerate resorts" and "fairy back room saloons" were a highly visible feature of the city's sexual underworld, spotlighted by the press and frequented by out-of-town businessmen and uptown slummers alike. The gay world was, moreover, remarkably integrated into the life of the working-class neighborhoods in which it took shape. Gay men not only modeled their own social clubs and events on those of other working-class men, but socialized extensively and overtly with "normal" workingmen as well. Most of the saloons they frequented were patronized by a mixed crowd of gay and straight men. This was not because there were too few gay men to support a separate gay saloon culture. One investigator reported seeing some seventy-five fairies at a single saloon in 1901, after all, and a decade earlier a medical student had seen hundreds of same-sex couples dancing at a masquerade ball. The number of "mixed" saloons reveals instead the degree to which gay culture was tolerated by—and integrated into—working-class culture and the degree to which social and sexual interactions between "queer" and "normal" men were central to gay life. Gay men, as we shall see, sometimes had to fight to claim their place in working-class neighborhoods, but there was room for them in working-class culture to claim such a place.

Indeed, the saloons and other resorts where gay and straight men interacted were a highly revealing part of male sexual culture at the turn of the century, complex institutions playing varying roles for different constituencies and capable of multiple cultural meanings. In keeping with their working-class origins, they were the most commercialized and visible sites of gay sociability in the city; middle-class gay culture, as we shall see, tended to be more circumspect, as was middle-class culture generally at the turn of the century. A source of scandal and titillation for uptown slummers, the resorts were also a source of support and communal ties for middle- and working-class fairies alike. And to the horror of middle-class reformers—and the great curiosity of latter-day historians—they were a central site of a distinctly working-class male culture in which "fairies" and "normal" men publicly—and sexually—interacted with remarkable ease.

Figure 2.1. Three cartoons published in a New York tabloid in the early 1930s illustrate the prevailing conception of fairies as men who thought they were women. *(From* Broadway Brevities: *"No Difference," December 14, 1931; "All at Sea," February 29, 1932; "Swish!" June 6, 1932.)*

Chapter 2

THE FAIRY AS AN INTERMEDIATE SEX

THE STRIKING IMAGE OF THE "MALE DEGENERATES" OR "FAIRIES" CONGRE-gating at Paresis Hall and the other Bowery resorts forcefully undermines the familiar presumption that homosexuals were isolated from one another and that homosexuality itself was all but invisible in turn-of-the-century New York. But it also presents us with a picture of male sexual identities and practices different from the one predominant at our end of the century. The "female impersonators" on display at the Bowery resorts were the most famous symbols of gay life, and the impression of that life they conveyed was reinforced by the countless other effeminate men who were visible in the streets of the city's working-class and amusement districts in the early decades of the century. As Mary Casal recalled of her tour of the Bowery resorts, "Seeing hundreds of male inverts . . . gathered together in a group made it easy to recognize them on any occasion where we might meet or see them, and so avoid any contact."[1] They were not the only homosexually active men in New York, but they constituted the primary image of the "invert" in popular and elite discourse alike and stood at the center of the cultural system by which male–male sexual relations were interpreted. As the dominant pejorative category in opposition to which male sexual "normality" was defined, the fairy influenced the culture and self-understanding of *all* sexually active men. The fairy thus offers a key to the cultural archaeology of male sexual practices and mentalities in this era and to the configuration of sex, gender, and sexuality in the early twentieth century.[2]

The determinative criterion in the identification of men as fairies was not the extent of their same-sex desire or activity (their "sexuality"), but rather the gender persona and status they assumed.[3] It was only the men who assumed the sexual and other cultural roles ascribed to women who identified themselves—and were identified by others—as fairies. The fairies' sexual desire for men was not regarded as the singular characteristic that distinguished them from other men, as is generally the case for gay men today. That desire was seen as simply one aspect of a much more comprehensive gender role inversion (or reversal), which they were also expected to manifest through the adoption of effeminate dress and mannerisms; they were thus often called *inverts* (who had "inverted" their gender) rather than *homosexuals* in technical language. In the dominant turn-of-the-century cultural system governing the interpretation of homosexual behavior, especially in working-class milieus, one had a *gender* identity rather than a *sexual* identity or even a "sexuality"; one's sexual behavior was thought to be necessarily determined by one's gender identity. (Or, to put it in other words, since the language is notoriously ambiguous here, one had an identity based on one's gender rather than on one's "sexuality," which was not regarded as a distinct domain of personhood but as a pattern of practices and desires that followed inevitably from one's masculinity or femininity.) Sexual desire for men was held to be inescapably a woman's desire, and the inverts' desire for men was not seen as an indication of their "homosexuality" but as simply one more manifestation of their fundamentally womanlike character. The fundamental division of male sexual actors in much of turn-of-the-century working-class thought, then, was not between "heterosexual" and "homosexual" *men*, but between conventionally masculine males, who were regarded as men, and effeminate males, known as fairies or pansies, who were regarded as virtual women, or, more precisely, as members of a "third sex" that combined elements of the male and female. The heterosexual–homosexual binarism that governs our thinking about sexuality today, and that, as we shall see, was already becoming hegemonic in middle-class sexual ideology, did not yet constitute the common sense of working-class sexual ideology.

The numerous treatises on sexual inversion prepared by doctors and gay intellectuals at the turn of the century help explicate (even if they did not determine) the terms of the cultural system by which homosexual behavior was understood. The centrality of gender inversion to the culture's understanding of what we would now term homosexual desire is evident in the explanations they offered for men who sexually desired other men. For instance, Dr. William Lee Howard argued in 1904 that the inverts' "sexual desire for their—apparent—own sex" was "really a *normal* sexual feeling," because the inverts were actually *women* (who naturally desired men) even though they *appeared* to be men (for whom

such desire would have been perverted). He explained this apparent para-
dox by asserting that although the inverts had male bodies, they had
female brains, and by reminding his readers that the brain, rather than
the anatomy, was "the primary factor" in classifying the sex of a person.[4]
Most of the other doctors writing about inversion in the late nineteenth
and early twentieth centuries adopted a related approach by conceptualizing fairies (as well as lesbians or "lady lovers") as a "third sex" or an
"intermediate sex" between men and women, rather than as men or
women who were also "homosexuals."[5]

Most gay intellectuals writing in Europe and the United States shared
this perspective. In the 1860s, Karl Ulrichs, the first German writer (and
for decades the only openly "inverted" man) to discuss inversion in a
public forum, did not define it in the same terms now used for homosexuality, but characterized the *Urning* (his term for an invert) as representing a "woman's spirit in a man's body." At the turn of the century, many
of the next generation of gay intellectuals, including Edward Carpenter
in Britain and Magnus Hirschfeld in Germany, adopted a version of this
theory, claiming that they were best characterized as a "third sex" or an
"intermediate sex" (the loose but popular translation of Ulrich's phrase,
sexuelle Zwischstufe), hermaphroditically combining psychic qualities of
both the male and female. This was also the distinction made by Marcel
Proust in his classic account of inversion, the *Sodom and Gomorrah* volume of *Remembrance of Things Past*.[6]

This mode of conceptualizing the character of inverts was strikingly
indicated by the meaning such writers gave the term *bisexual*. By the mid-
twentieth century, when a system categorizing people on the basis of their
sexual object-choice had largely replaced one categorizing them on the
basis of gender style, the word referred to individuals sexually attracted to
both men and women. At the turn of the century, however, *bisexual*
referred to individuals who combined the physical and/or psychic attributes of both men and women. A bisexual was not *attracted* to both males
and females; a bisexual *was* both male and female.[7]

The prominence of the fairy in turn-of-the-century New York and his
consistency with the hegemonic gender ideology of the era made him the
dominant—and most plausible—role model available to boys and men
trying to make sense of vague feelings of sexual and gender difference.
The model of the fairy offered many men a means of constructing public
personas they considered more congruent with their "inner natures" than
conventional masculine ones, but that were also consistent with the terms
of the dominant gender culture in which they had been socialized and
that had, therefore, helped constitute those "inner natures." Taking on

the role of the fairy, that is, allowed them to reject the kind of masculinity prescribed for them by the dominant culture, but to do so without rejecting the hegemonic tenets of their culture concerning the gender order. As we shall see, many men rejected the role of the fairy as inconsistent with their male identities (or as too dangerous to their status as men), or only identified themselves as fairies before discovering there were alternative ways of being gay. But many other men embraced the identity because it embodied a way of understanding how they, as men, could have the feelings their culture ascribed exclusively to women.

THE SEMIOTICS OF INVERSION: EFFEMINACY AS A CULTURAL STRATEGY

The feminine character ascribed to the fairies is shown most clearly by the highly gendered—and engendering—signs that others used to identify them. When an anti-vice agent who investigated Paresis Hall in 1899 wished to illustrate the effeminacy of the "degenerates" he had seen there, he cited a wide range of womanlike characteristics as particularly revealing: not only did the men there solicit normal men—such as the investigator himself—for "immoral purposes," but they were "painted and powdered," used women's names, and displayed feminine mannerisms (or "aped the female character").[8] The adoption of these signs was critical to the process whereby many men transformed their self-identity—or at least their public persona—into that of a fairy. Some men embraced such styles as more "natural" to them than conventional masculine styles, so they help explain how men who had been raised to be "normal" used the role of the fairy to come to terms with their sense of sexual difference from other men. Other men adopted such signs as part of a cultural strategy that allowed them to negotiate the terms of their relationships with other men, and they highlight the dynamics of that strategy. Their centrality to gay culture and their utility as a means of identifying "fairies" suggests they provide an unexpected prism for viewing the cultural construction of gender in the era.

Like the men at Paresis Hall who called themselves "Princess this and Lady So and So and the Duchess of Marlboro," most fairies adopted women's names as part of the process by which they constructed a gay persona. Many men chose campy, flamboyant women's names or nicknames (such as Queen Mary, Salome, Cinderella, Violet, Blossom, Edna May, and Big Tess), feminine nicknames that highlighted a personal characteristic (such as Dixie, Gaby, Chuckles), names that played on their own names (Max might become Maxine), or the names of well-known women performers. By the 1910s and 1920s, they often borrowed the names of movie stars whose images resonated in some way with gay culture, each name evoking the particular feminine persona associated with the actress. Some men, for instance, adopted the name of Theda Bara, the classic vamp in the films of the mid-1910s, who portrayed erotically aggressive women capable of enervating the strongest of men. In the succeeding two decades, Gloria Swanson, an actress known for both her numerous marriages and her wardrobe, was perhaps the most popular of drag personas, and was taken as the *nom de drag* by the best-known African-American drag queen of the 1930s (see chapter 9). Mae West was a popular drag name by the early thirties.[9]

Adopting a woman's name not only announced a man's gay identity and perhaps something about the persona he sought to cultivate, but marked his transition from the straight world to the gay as well. Some men who permanently joined the sexual underworld, such as entertainers and full-time prostitutes, left their masculine birthnames behind and became known exclusively by their women's names (or camp names). Others, who moved back and forth between the gay world and the straight, used their feminine names only in gay circles, as a way of marking their temporary transition into the gay world; having two names emblematized their participation in a double life. Some of them adopted such pseudonyms when they ventured into the sexual underworld for the same reason many prostitutes did, to conceal and protect their identities in the straight world.[10] For fear of blackmail if his status in the straight world were discovered, "Ralph Werther" (a part-time fairy who later wrote about his experiences) was as careful to hide his straight life from his Bowery associates as he was his gay life from his university colleagues, even giving a false name when asked on the Bowery what his masculine name was. He went by "Jennie June" there (using the pen name of one of the nineteenth century's most famous female journalists), telling his working-class associates that Werther was his legal name, and he authored his first book under yet another pseudonym, Earl Lind.[11] Even in later decades, many men went by "bar names" or "camp names" at gay bars or parties, some using them only occasionally and in jest, others using them constantly in order to conceal their straight identities.[12]

Although fairies were known as "female impersonators," transvestism was not central to their self-representation. Relatively few men wore women's clothes, and, given the laws against transvestism (see chapter 10), even most men who wished to don a woman's full wardrobe dared do so only in relatively secure settings, such as a few of the Bowery resorts.[13] But dressing entirely as a woman was hardly necessary to indicate that one was a fairy. In the right context, appropriating even a single feminine—or at least unconventional—style or article of clothing might signify a man's identity as a fairy. Thus a much larger number of men adopted more subtle, but still telling, clothing cues; the essential ingredient of a fairy's dress, as Ralph Werther explained, was that it be "as fancy and flashy as a youth dare adopt." He recalled that he "proclaimed myself" as a fairy to working-class youth on Fourteenth Street in the 1890s simply by wearing "white kids [gloves] and [a] large red neck-bow with fringed ends hanging down over my lapels."[14]

Writing in the late 1930s or around 1940, a gay man named Thomas Painter described a system guided by similar principles, although adapted in its particulars to contemporary male fashions. He counted "green suits, tight-cuffed trousers, flowered bathing trunks, and half-lengthed flaring top-coats" as distinctively homosexual attire, along with such accessories as "excessively bright feathers in their hat-bands." Dark brown and gray suede shoes were "practically a homosexual monopoly."[15] Writing at about the same time, another gay man, Gershon Legman, included "cosmetics . . . flamboyant clothes and suede or high-heeled shoes" as the insignia of the "flaming queen . . . who attempts thus to attract attention and drum up trade."[16]

Some clothes, such as a green suit, were so bold that few dared wear them. Other items of apparel, which sent the same message more subtly, were worn more commonly. Perhaps the most famous of these in the early years of the century was the red tie. By 1916 a physician in Chicago had heard that "male perverts in New York . . . are known as 'fairies' and wear a red necktie," even though, he added, "inverts are generally said to prefer green."[17] Still, the red tie was famous only in certain circles; it was a subtle signal likely to be understood in some contexts more than others. A man wearing a red necktie on a well-known New York cruising street such as Riverside Drive or Fourteenth Street, for instance, was likely to be labeled a fairy. In the early 1910s a New York "invert" explained that "to wear a red necktie on the street is to invite remarks from newsboys and others. . . . A friend told me once that when a group of street boys caught sight of the red necktie he was wearing they sucked their fingers in imitation of *fellatio*."[18] But a man wearing the same tie in a social setting in which people were less alert to such signs might just be considered odd. An unconventional choice in an era of conservative colors, a red tie announced unorthodox tastes of another sort only to those in the know.

Styles of dress, demeanor, and physicality varied among ethnic cultures at any given time. Behavior or attire that signified sexual abnormality in one group might well signify normality—and even affiliation with the group—in another. One man might further the impression of effeminacy by wearing a "necklace"; another might signify his status as a "rough," highly masculine working-class youth by wearing a chain with a cross around his neck. Styles also changed over time. One man

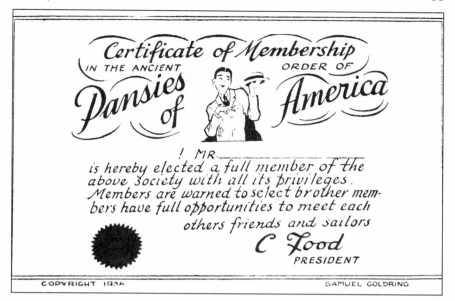

Figure 2.2. This "certificate" circulated among gay men in the 1930s. It can be read as a spoof of pansies or as an assertion *by* those pansies of their membership in a social group—or both. The "C Food" signature draws on gay slang ("seafood" referred to sailors as sex objects) to make an insider's joke about the desirability—and availability—of sailors. *(From Yale Collection of American Literature, Beinecke Rare Books and Manuscripts Library, Yale University.)*

active in New York's gay world since the 1930s noted in the summer of 1951 that the straight white working-class youths from South Brooklyn with whom he associated had suddenly started wearing chartreuse and fuchsia shirts, "for which they would have been hooted off the street and the shirt off their backs, with comments like 'pansy,' years ago." In the meantime, gay men had adopted other styles. Choice in color was not just a marker of gender or sexuality, however. According to the same man, such colors were embraced only by men from certain ethnic backgrounds in the early 1950s. Many Irish youth, he noted a year later, rejected color in male attire in part because "they considered it Latin, or, more to the point, Negro, to effect color." Whatever the actual patterns of dress, the presumed differences in attitudes toward color in dress became a way Irish and German youths distinguished themselves from Italians, African-Americans, and Puerto Ricans as well as from gay men.[19]

Observers often considered the unusual—even fairylike—dress of entertainers, artists, and other professionally colorful personalities to be just another sign of their special status rather than a sign of their sexual deviance. As a result, however, describing someone as "artistic" could be a coded way of calling him homosexual, and observers often played on the ambiguity in their criticisms of artists. A 1933 *Daily News* profile of the entertainer Harry Richman, full of innuendo that Richman was sexually eccentric, furthered the impression by remarking that Richman had "gone in for gay colored suits recently. He even owns and wears a green suit . . . likes bright underwear and wears only silk . . . [and] likes sapphires and odd-shaped jewelry."[20]

Gay men, like most men and women, also sought to engender their bodies by molding them in ways that approximated the ideal gender types of their cultural group. Like other people, in other words, they undertook artificial means to cultivate the shape, density, carriage, and texture of their bodies, which they nonetheless continued to regard as the natural repository and signifier of their "sex."[21] Every aspect of their bodies' appearance was densely gendered, but they paid particular attention—like their "normal" counterparts, but with different goals in mind—to the ways they cut, styled, and colored their hair, painted and scented their faces, and grew, shaved, penciled, or tore out their eyebrows and other facial hair, as well as to the ways they walked, sat, spoke, moved their eyes, and carried their heads, hands, arms, and legs.

Perhaps most commonly, men used unconventional styles in personal grooming to signal their anomalous gender status. "Plucked eyebrows, rouged lips, powdered face, and marcelled, blondined hair" were the essential attributes of the fairy, one straight observer noted in 1933, succinctly summarizing the characteristics at least two generations of New Yorkers had used to identify such men.[22] In his 1934 painting *The Fleet's In*, the gay painter Paul Cadmus signaled the sexual character of a male civilian offering a cigarette to a sailor by giving him precisely such features—as well as a red tie (as shown in figure 3.1). The fairies' "painted and powdered" faces were usually the first thing visitors to the Bowery resorts commented on in the 1890s, and Ralph Werther identified several "low class fairies" in a Bowery saloon in the same period partly on the basis of their "hair a la mode de Oscar Wilde (that is, hanging down in ringlets over the ears and collar)."[23] In 1922 a seventeen-year-old Italian boy told of being arrested with a friend in Prospect Park when a detective "took off our hats and saw that our eyebrows were tweezed [and] said, 'You are fairies.'"[24] That the detective's surmise about the meaning of tweezed eyebrows was widely shared was confirmed not only by the boys' efforts to hide their telltale eyebrows with hats but also by an eighteen-year-old's assertion, a few years later, that it was "common knowledge" among the boys in his Italian Harlem neighborhood that "men with full faces, long delicate fingers, tweezed eyebrows and well shaped lips are inverts."[25]

As investigators' descriptions of Paresis Hall and other gay resorts suggest, some gay men reinforced the image conveyed by their grooming by
using a variety of other gender codes in their carriage, demeanor, and
speech, which identified them as gay to straight and gay men alike. In
explaining how he identified homosexuals at the bars he investigated,
one government agent noted in the 1930s that "the most striking feature
[of homosexuals] would be the fact that although they represent and are
dressed as one sex they act and impersonate the opposite sex . . . by gesture, voice inflection, manner or mode of speech, or walk, and in general
[they] impersonate all of the other characteristics of a female that they
can possibly assume."[26]

While his use of such stereotypical signs to identify homosexuals might
seem incredible to the present reader, gay men used them as well. Ralph
Werther immediately discerned that a group of men he met in 1895 were
fairies on the basis of "the timbre of their voices . . . and their feminesque
mannerisms."[27] The way men walked and carried their arms and hands
were also taken as clues to their sexual identities. A limp wrist or an
exaggerated swivel-hipped, mincing walk—known as "swishing" in the
gay world—was regularly caricatured on the vaudeville stage and occasionally seen on the street as a sign of the "true" fairy. But more subtle
stances were also read as gender-specific. Whereas a "normal" man
rarely stood with his hands on his hips, according to a gay writer in
1941, when he did so it was "with his thumbs back and his fingers forward, his elbows straight out or somewhat backward." By contrast, he
thought, a "very effeminate homosexual" was more likely to adopt such
a pose, and to place "his thumbs *forward* and his fingers back, his shoulders hunched somewhat forward, and his head facing to one side."[28] A
gay sailor, pressed in 1919 to explain how he identified someone as
"queer," pointed to less precise but similarly subtle indications of effeminacy: "He acted sort of peculiar; walking around with his hands on his
hips. . . . [His] manner was not masculine. . . . The expression with the
eyes and the gestures. . . . "[29]

To dismiss such signs as mere stereotypes is to misapprehend their significance. They *were* stereotypes, to be sure. But the fact that men were
identified as fairies on the basis of such minimal and "stereotypical" deviations from the conventions of masculine demeanor and dress indicates
the narrow range of deviation from normative gender styles allowed *most*
men. It also suggests the extraordinary sensitivity of men to subtle markers of gender status, thus highlighting the pervasive character of gender
surveillance in working-class street culture. Furthermore, it confirms what
I have already suggested about the articulation of the boundaries of gender and sexuality in the era, for it indicates that an inversion of any one
aspect of one's prescribed gender persona was presumed to be sympto-

matic of a much more comprehensive inversion, which inevitably would manifest itself in abnormal sexual object-choice as well.

More significant, in this context, is that the effectiveness of such signs suggests the extraordinary plasticity of gender assignment in the culture in which the fairies operated, and the remarkable ease with which men could construct a public persona as a quasi-woman or fairy. Many more gay men adopted such effeminate mannerisms then than do today because they were so central to the dominant role model available to them as they formed a gay identity. But many men switched the mannerisms on and off as easily as they changed from feminine to more masculine attire, and were able to manipulate such symbols to avoid being labeled fairies. By wearing conventional masculine attire and carrying themselves with a "masculine" demeanor, most men could pass as straight, even if they chose to camp it up when in a secure gay environment.

Perhaps more unexpectedly, many men deliberately *used* such markers in order to signal their sexual character to other gay men and to straight men in public contexts. Effeminacy was one of the few sure means they had to identify themselves to others. As a man who moved to New York from Michigan in the 1920s recalled, "Back in the early twenties, people had to be quite effeminate to be identified, at least that was true in my case."[30] His statement implied that he could avoid being identified by avoiding any sign of effeminacy, but his point was that he *chose* to be effeminate precisely because he wanted to identify himself to other men. Another gay man made the same point with a somewhat different emphasis when he commented in the 1920s that the men he knew "talk and act like women, have feminine ways . . . [and] use rouge and pow-der . . . *in order to attract men.*"[31]

For many men, then, adopting effeminate mannerisms represented a deliberate cultural strategy, as well as a way of making sense of their sense of sexual difference. It was a way to declare a gay identity publicly and to negotiate their relationship with other men. The fairies' effeminacy helped them attract men not only by signaling their interest but also by establish-ing the cultural script that would govern their social and sexual interac-tions and reaffirm the cultural distance between them and the men they sought.[32] By taking on the role of women and making their violation of gender conventions consistent—by insisting, for instance, that men refer to them with women's names and pronouns—they reaffirmed those conven-tions in a way that allowed men to interact with them as if they *were* women, even though all parties understood that anatomically they were males. An agent investigating an African-American speakeasy in the base-ment of a Harlem brownstone in 1928 was approached by a man using just this strategy. "[He] said to me in a very high pitched voice 'Oh come, let's dance, I am a B[itch] like those others sitting over there,' indicating a group of women."[33]

One indication of the extent to which men became accustomed to thinking of fairies as pseudo-women was provided in 1939 by a State Liquor Authority investigator who casually referred to a fairy (who went by a woman's name but dressed in conventional male attire) as "she," even though he was testifying at a formal hearing of the Authority. "We did get in a conversation with Beverly," he testified, "and she stated she liked us very much." When asked by an attorney whether he meant "she" or "he," he explained that the fairies "address themselves by these effeminate names and refer to one another in the effeminate terms," and promptly continued: "She [the fairy] made a date with Mr. Van Wagner and myself for Saturday night."[34]

Much evidence suggests that the fairy, so long as he abided by the conventions of this cultural script, was tolerated in much of working-class society—regarded as an anomaly, certainly, but as more amusing than abhorrent, and only rarely as a threat to the gender order. He was so obviously a "third-sexer," a different species of human being, that his very effeminacy served to confirm rather than threaten the masculinity of other men, particularly since it often exaggerated the conventions of deference and gender difference between men and women. The fairies reaffirmed the conventions of gender even as they violated them: they behaved as no man should, but as any man might wish a woman would.[35] Their representation of themselves as "intermediate types" made it easier for men to interact with them (and even have sex with them) by making it clear who would play the "man's part" in the interaction.

The conventions governing such interactions were so well established and their meaning so well understood that gay men did not always need to engage in an elaborate performance to signal their character and establish the terms of their interaction with other men. A 1929 account by the young writer Parker Tyler in a letter to a gay friend of his encounter with several men one evening in the Village suggests both the extraordinary effectiveness of these conventions in structuring such interactions and gay men's ability to play with them:

[A friend] and I were in a speakeasy and four young [men] (I think they were newsreel cameramen) tried to make me, asking to be taken to my apartment. But they were frightfully vulgar; they called me Grace or something, until I insisted on Miss Tyler. It was really amusing, for one made a date with me quite anxiously and quite seriously, just as though I were a girl. You know the type he is: W - o - l - f. But I stood him up, of course—the little prick!

The young men's interaction with one of Tyler's friends indicates the degree to which the fairy's reconstruction of his gender through his gay cultural style outweighed the physical evidence of his body in determining the men's response to him. "Jules, being drunk, camped with them too, and they tried to date him—even after feeling his muscle: he could have laid them all low: really it's as wide as this paper."[36]

The presence of fairies at the Bowery resorts in the late nineteenth century provides one sign that they were tolerated by and integrated into working-class culture. Even more significant is the fact that fairies were also tolerated at many working-class dance halls and other meeting places where they were not made an official part of the "show," but interacted more casually with other patrons, albeit often still serving as an informal source of entertainment. At a dance hall opposite Jackson Avenue Park in Brooklyn in 1912, an anti-vice agent witnessed two fairies known as Elsie and Daisy carrying on with a group of young women, borrowing their powder puffs and acting in a "conspicuous way." When many of the men and women moved to the saloon next door after the hall closed at midnight, Elsie and Daisy entertained them with songs "which were obscene to the farthest limit," according to the agent, and later danced together, imitating "the action of committing sodomy," much to the delight of the other youths, who engaged in their own suggestive styles of dancing.[37]

To say that fairies were tolerated in much of working-class society, however, is not to say that they were respected. The men who became fairies did so at the cost of forfeiting their privileged status as men. Indeed, if working-class gender culture created an opening for fairies, it was a highly contested one, and men had to struggle to claim their place as fairies in the neighborhood. While some men, like Elsie and Daisy, managed to establish a place for themselves in their own neighborhoods, many others sought to minimize the risks involved in carrying themselves as fairies by doing so only in parts of town distant from their homes, where being brutalized or mocked would at least have fewer long-term consequences. The seventeen-year-old Italian mentioned previously, for instance, adopted a conventional persona in his own neighborhood, carrying himself as a fairy (by taking off his hat to reveal his tweezed eyebrows) only in another part of town.

Mockery and contempt often colored the public interactions between men and fairies in the streets and Bowery resorts, although gay men sometimes contested the conventions of ridicule. A 1928 report by an undercover investigator illustrates this, while also revealing how visible gay men were in working-class neighborhoods and how casually other men interacted with them. In the course of a conversation with the agent, the proprietor of a speakeasy on West Seventeenth Street mentioned the fairies who frequented an Italian restaurant down the street, and the agent asked to see them. The proprietor readily agreed to take him to the restaurant. "It's fun," he declared. "I've been up there lots of times and kidded them along." But he also indicated that the fairies were willing to let the kidding go only so far; "some sure can fight," he added, indicating his respectful recognition that the fairies were prepared to defend themselves if the kidding got out of hand.[38] Jimmy Durante's recollection of the "queer entertainers" at the Bowery and Coney Island saloons where he got his start at the turn of the century indicates they had adopted a similar stance: "Some of them were six feet tall and built like Dempsey," he later noted, "so it was never very healthy to make nasty cracks."[39]

Not all fairies were built like Dempsey, though, and the threat of physical assaults on them was an abiding one. If fairies and other homosexuals were widely recognized as social types in the streets of working-class neighborhoods, they were also regarded as easy marks by the gangs of youths who controlled much of the traffic on those streets. "Go[ing] after fags" was an easy way to make money, observed one nineteen-year-old in an Italian Harlem gang in the early 1930s. The "fags" sometimes paid the boys and young men they met for quick sexual encounters in the parks and movie theaters; even better, they sometimes took the young men home to their apartments. Once they "bring you to an apartment," the nineteen-year-old added, "you just clean it out." The social researcher who interviewed him while studying East Harlem considered "the common practice of exploiting homosexuals" to be as characteristic of such boys' lives as the poolroom and petty thievery.[40] Even Ralph Werther, who waxed rhapsodic in his memoirs about his playful relationships with Irish and Italian youths in the 1890s and 1900s, repeatedly deplored the fact that such youths felt justified in brutalizing fairies. "The thievishly inclined regularly prey on androgynes," he noted, because they knew the latter were considered "outlaws" by the authorities and thus would not dare complain to the police for fear of drawing attention to themselves. Werther blamed the boys' behavior on the hatred preached against his kind by clergymen and doctors, the professional men to whom his memoir was addressed. Charles Nesbitt also noted the "peculiar type of savage violence to which [such men] were subjected by the non-sympathetic in their own social stratum," in his memoir concerning his trip to New York around

1890.[41] The fairies' conventionally feminine behavior also led thieves to expect little resistance from them. Two undercover agents discovered this in 1920 when three thieves tried to rob them "because they thought we were a couple fairies" and that it would thus be "a soft job."[42]

Such violence often served a more instrumental purpose in reinforcing the boundaries between fairies and other men. Some men beat or robbed their effeminate male sexual partners after sex as if to emphasize that they felt no connection to them and had simply "used" them for sexual release. Although not a regular phenomenon, this happened often enough that many gay men interested in sex with straight men sought to avoid the situations in which it could happen most easily.[43]

In some cases the violence directed against fairies may have represented an intersection of gender and class hostilities. Werther reported that he had been subjected to gang rapes by several of the Irish and Italian youth gangs he approached.[44] In this his fate was no different from that of women whom men considered sexually available; if fairies were tolerated because they were regarded as women, they were also subject to the contempt and violence regularly directed against women. Fairies, like women who crossed certain lines (even such narrow ones as daring to walk down certain streets alone, without male guardianship), were considered fair game by many gangs. Werther's situation was complicated by the fact that it must have been obvious to such gangs that he was not a "fairy of the slums," but an uptown gentleman out slumming. One suspects that he became a convenient target for working-class men's resentment of the upper-class gentlemen who visited their neighborhood for purposes of slumming and using "their" women. If working-class men often tried to claim a certain gender superiority over effete gentlemen on the basis of their supposed greater masculinity, they could ritually enact and enhance that sense of superiority by their sexual subjection and brutalization of the homosexual gentlemen who came their way.[45]

The mixture of tolerance, desire, and contempt with which men regarded fairies also resulted from the particular *kind* of feminine role they adopted. Although I have argued that fairies were considered womanlike in their behavior and self-representation, that is really too imprecise a formulation. For no single norm governing "feminine" (or "masculine") behavior existed at the turn of the century; such normative injunctions varied along class lines and among immigrant groups and, indeed, became one of the standards by which such groups constituted themselves and distinguished themselves from others. In crucial respects the fairies' style was comparable not so much to that of some ideal category of womanhood as to that of a particular subgroup of women or cultural type: prostitutes and other so-called "tough girls."[46] The fairy's sexual aggressiveness in his solicitation of men was certainly inconsistent with the sexual passivity expected of a respectable woman, but it was entirely in keeping with the sexual character ascribed to tough girls and prostitutes. That gay men themselves shared this identification accounts, in part, for the popularity of "strong" or "tough" women, such as Mae West, as gay icons and drag personas: they were regarded as women who disdained convention, were determinedly and overtly sexual in character, and did what they needed to get what they wanted.

Moreover, both fairies and prostitutes congregated in many of the same locales and used some of the same techniques to attract attention; the fairy's most obvious attribute, his painted face, was the quintessential marker of the prostitute.[47] And while fairies, like prostitutes, played the so-called woman's part in sexual relations with men, both groups engaged in certain forms of sexual behavior, particularly oral sex, which many working-class and middle-class women alike rejected as unbecoming to a woman, "dirty," and "perverted."[48] (Anti-vice investigators called prostitutes who performed fellation "perverts," the same term they applied to the men who performed it.)[49] The fairies' style, then, was not so much an imitation of women as a group but a provocative exaggeration of the appearance and demeanor ascribed more specifically to prostitutes. As a result, many men seem to have regarded fairies in the same terms they regarded prostitutes. This conflation may have made it easier for them to distance themselves from fairies and to use them for sexual purposes in the same way they used female prostitutes.[50]

The men who adopted the styles of the fairy boldly announced to the world that they were sexually different from other men and that they sexually desired other men. They made their existence obvious to everyone in the city and provoked a range of responses from "normal" men: desire, contempt, fascination, abuse. Becoming a fairy offered men a way to make sense of their feeling sexually different from other men and to structure their relations with other men. Because the fairy was the central pejorative category against which men had to measure themselves as they developed their gender and sexual style, all men had to position themselves in relation to it. Some men who desired other men, as we shall see, rejected the style and identity of the fairy altogether, but that style and identity had numerous meanings even to the men who embraced it. Some men, like Ralph Werther, identified with the image of the fairy completely; becoming a fairy seemed a "natural" way to express their "true" feminine natures. Many other men had a more complicated and distant relation to the persona of the fairy, adopting it in a more calculated and strategic manner in order to negotiate their relations with other men. Using the style of the fairy allowed them to announce their identities to gay and straight men alike in the settings in which they wished to do so. It also allowed them to attract "normal" men who would interact with them publicly only if they behaved in a manner that was appealing and that made it clear to onlookers who would play the "woman's part" in their sexual relations.

Gay men themselves believed that such effeminacy was more natural to some men than others. "If not naturally, we tried to walk very effeminately, talk very effeminately, look effeminate, use rouge and make-up, etc., to impersonate a female," commented one man, to whom such effeminacy did not come so "naturally" as it did to others, in the early 1920s.[51] Parker Tyler noted the strategic purposes served by such styles more directly: as he wrote to a gay friend in 1931, he only adopted them in order to avoid "insulting" a group of "inferior males all dying except certain ones to believe i am dying for them."[52]

The very ability of gay men to act this way—to transform themselves into fairies or quasi-women by changing their dress or demeanor—both highlights and can only be understood in the context of the plasticity of gender assignment in the rough working-class culture in which the fairies operated. As one gay man explained in the mid-1920s: "It is well known fact"—widely believed, apparently, in his circles, at least—

> that the secret of a woman's appeal to man is not so much her sex as her effeminacy. . . . The attitude of the average man to the homosexual is determined by the degree of effeminacy in the homosexual. Your writer has observed that nine out of ten [men] take favorably to the homosexual. Of course, they seek the eternal feminine in the homosexual . . . [and] feminine homosexuals naturally have the greater number of admirers.[53]

He, in other words, not only imagined that cultural gender could be disassociated from anatomical sex, but that the former was more significant in erotic attraction and in everyday social interactions than the latter. His comment, which is echoed by many others, also suggests that the working-class men with whom he interacted were more capable of distinguishing cultural gender from anatomical sex than their middle-class contemporaries were; the latter were more likely to object to homosexual men of any sort. To explain why workingmen found it easier to interact with fairies than middle-class men did, we need to explore the distinctive sexual cultures of working-class and middle-class men in the early twentieth century.

Figure 3.1 *The Fleet's In* (1934), a painting by the gay artist Paul Cadmus, depicts the efforts of women and gay men alike to seduce sailors. The man offering a cigarette to the sailor has the typical markers of a fairy: bleached hair, tweezed eyebrows, rouged cheeks, and red tie. The sailor's eyes suggest he knows exactly what is being offered along with the smoke. *(Courtesy of Navy Art Collection; detail from painting shown.)*

Chapter 3

TRADE, WOLVES, AND THE BOUNDARIES OF NORMAL MANHOOD

THE MOST STRIKING DIFFERENCE BETWEEN THE DOMINANT SEXUAL CULTURE of the early twentieth century and that of our own era is the degree to which the earlier culture permitted men to engage in sexual relations with other men, often on a regular basis, without requiring them to regard themselves—or to be regarded by others—as gay. If sexual abnormality was defined in different terms in prewar culture, then so, too, necessarily, was sexual normality. The centrality of the fairy to the popular representation of sexual abnormality allowed other men to engage in casual sexual relations with other men, with boys, and, above all, with the fairies themselves without imagining that they themselves were abnormal. Many men alternated between male and female sexual partners without believing that interest in one precluded interest in the other, or that their occasional recourse to male sexual partners, in particular, indicated an abnormal, "homosexual," or even "bisexual" disposition, for they neither understood nor organized their sexual practices along a hetero–homosexual axis.

This sexual ideology, far more than the other erotic systems with which it coexisted, predominated in working-class culture. It had particular efficacy in organizing the sexual practices of men in the social milieu in which it might be least expected: in the highly aggressive and quintessentially "masculine" subculture of young and usually unmarried sailors, common laborers, hoboes, and other transient workers, who were a ubiquitous presence in early-twentieth-century American cities. After demonstrating how widely it was assumed that "normal" men could engage in sexual relations with other men and the role of this sexual ideology in organizing the sexual world of "rough" working-class men, this chapter explores the basis of that ideology in working-class gender ideology and in the deeper logic of the association of fairies with prostitutes. For the complex conventions governing the social interactions of fairies and normal workingmen established the terms of their sexual relations as well, and reveal much about the organization of gender, sex, and sexuality in working-class culture.

THE SISTERS AND THEIR MEN: TRADE AND THE CONCEPTUALIZATION OF MALE SEXUAL RELATIONS IN WORKING-CLASS CULTURE

The strongest evidence that the relationship between "men" and fairies was represented symbolically as a male–female relationship and that gender behavior rather than homosexual behavior per se was the primary determinant of a man's classification as a fairy was that it enabled other men to engage in sexual activity with the fairies—and even to express publicly a strong interest in such contacts—without risking stigmatization and the undermining of their status as "normal." So long as they maintained a masculine demeanor and played (or claimed to play) only the "masculine," or insertive, role in the sexual encounter—so long, that is, as they eschewed the style of the fairy and did not allow their bodies to be sexually penetrated—neither they, the fairies, nor the working-class public considered *them* to be queer. Thus a private investigator reported in 1927 that a Mr. Farley, owner of a newsstand in the basement of the Times Square Building at Forty-second Street and Broadway, complained to him that "whenever the fleet comes into town, every sailor who wants his d— licked comes to the Times Square Building. It seems to be common knowledge among the sailors that the Times Square Building is the place to go if they want to meet any fairies." He was unhappy about the commotion so many unruly sailors caused around his newsstand and disapproved of their actions. In no way, however, did he indicate that he thought the sailors looking for sex with the fairies were themselves fairies or otherwise different from most sailors. The investigator himself observed "two sailors . . . in the company of three men who were acting in an effeminate manner." He labeled the effeminate men "fairies" even though it was the sailors who were "making overtures to these men to go to their apartments [and the men] declined to go."[1]

Even men working for state policing agencies categorized men in these terms. New York State Liquor Authority agents investigating a sailors' bar in Brooklyn in October 1938 reported that shortly after midnight, "several males who were apparently 'fags' enter[ed] the premises in groups of twos and threes." They later observed "sailors leaving with some girls, and some men in uniform leaving with the fags." To make it clear that they thought the sailors were leaving with the fags for the same sexual reason that other sailors left with female prostitutes, they added: "In particular it was observed that two marines left with two of the fags and remained in the dark street under the railroad trestle." The investigators did not regard the marines who left with the "fags" as "fags" themselves, nor did they otherwise question the marines' status as men. Indeed, their final report recommended that the state close the bar precisely because it "permitt[ed] prostitutes to congregate with male customers . . . [and] permitt[ed] 'fags' to congregate on the premises and solicit males for immoral purposes."[2] They gave no indication that they found it shocking or unusual that the "fags" should have as much success picking up sailors as female prostitutes did. On the contrary, they regarded the sailors' response to the solicitations of "fags" as no different in kind from their responses to those of female prostitutes.

The acceptance of men's relations with fairies as proper manifestations of the male quest for pleasure and power was indicated even more strikingly by the structure of male prostitution in the late nineteenth and early twentieth centuries. By the 1910s and 1920s, it was increasingly common for both gay- and straight-identified men to sell sexual services to gay-identified men. But at the turn of the century the predominant form of male prostitution seems to have involved fairies selling sex to men who, despite the declaration of desire made by their willingness to pay for the encounters, identified themselves as normal. Indeed, while the term *fairy* generally denoted any flamboyantly effeminate homosexual man (whose self-presentation resembled that of a female prostitute), numerous references in the early twentieth century make it clear that the word was sometimes used specifically to denote men who actually worked as prostitutes selling sexual services to "normal" men.[3] Fairies still appeared in this role in several novels published in the 1930s about New York–based homosexual characters. One 1933 novel, for instance, referred to "the street corner 'fairy' of Times Square" as a "street-walker," invariably "rouged, lisping, [and] mincing." And in Kennilworth Bruce's *Goldie,* also published in 1933, a working-class youth from New Jersey explained "the ways and wiles of the twilight world in New York" to the protagonist, whom the youth had identified as a fairy: "He told him about the 'fairies' and the 'wolves' that frequent the streets of New York . . . around the Times Square section. . . . 'The fairies pull down big dough, too. . . . There's the actors and musicians when the shows break; there's the gamblers and guys with small-time rackets; and there's the highbrow sots when they leave the speakeasies in the wee hours. Fairies work up a regular trade.'"[4]

Numerous accounts of turn-of-the-century homosexual prostitution confirm that it commonly involved men paying fairies for sex, while still considering themselves to be the "men" in the encounter. This, after all, was the premise of the Lower East Side resorts, such as Paresis Hall and the Slide, where female prostitutes also gathered and where many of the fairies were not only called "male prostitutes" but (in the language of the day) "sat for company," having the men who joined their tables buy them drinks, just as female prostitutes did. Significantly, in prostitutes' slang a "slide" denoted an "establishment where male homosexuals dress[ed] as women and solicit[ed] men," a meaning apparently known to the officials involved in a state investigation of police corruption in 1894. A Captain Ryan testified he had "closed up every disorderly-house, every gambling-house and policy office, and every slide and dives [sic] in the precinct [within] three months [of taking command]." When asked if he were sure he knew what a slide was, he reminded his questioner that "we had one of the most notorious slides in the world in Bleecker street when I had command of that precinct." His comment both confirms the fame of the Slide, which he had shut down in 1892, and suggests that the resort's management had deliberately used the slang term in naming the club in order to announce its character (even though, in fact, the fairies there did not dress as women).[5] Moreover, the very existence of the slang term suggests that other such resorts existed, as indeed they did.

There were also brothels where men could meet fairies more privately, as the Reverend Charles Parkhurst discovered in 1892 when he took his famous tour of New York's underworld (his own form of slumming) to gather evidence for his assault on Tammany Hall corruption. His guide took him to a brothel on West Third Street, the Golden Rule Pleasure Club, where the basement was divided into cubicles, each occupied by "a youth, whose face was painted, eye-brows blackened, and whose airs were those of a young girl, . . . [who] talked in a high falsetto voice, and called the others by women's names," each youth waiting for a man to hire his services.[6] It should be remembered that neither the fairies at the Slide nor those at the Pleasure Club were dressed as women; no customer seeking their services could have mistaken them for "normal" women.

This pattern was not restricted to such brothels and saloons. Fairy prostitutes, usually dressed as men but using their hair, makeup, and demeanor to signal their character, worked along the Bowery, Riverside Drive, Fourteenth Street, and Forty-second Street, and in Bryant Park and Prospect Park, as well as in the back rooms of saloons on Elizabeth Street and Third Avenue. (These street patterns are discussed at greater length in chapter 7.) One fairy, for instance, a female impersonator from a poor neighborhood in Brooklyn where he was known as Loop-the-loop, a suggestive play on the name of a popular ride at Coney Island, reported to a doctor in 1906 that he regularly plied his trade "chiefly for the money there is in it" (see figure 3.2). Loop-the-loop often worked in his neighborhood as well as in Prospect Park, where, he reported, he and the other prostitutes paid off the patrolmen so that they could wear dresses. His efforts at female impersonation would not have persuaded any of his clients that they were having sex with a woman, given the inartfulness of his costume and the heavy growth of hair on his legs and arms (he complained of the hair himself, but added that "most of the boys don't mind it").[7] But his costume and demeanor, like those of the fairies at Paresis Hall, *did* signify to "the boys" that he was not a normal man, either, but rather a third-sexer, with whom they could have sex without complicating their understanding of their own sexual character.

The relationship between a fairy prostitute and his male customers emblematized the central model governing the interpretation of male–male sexual relationships. The term *trade* originally referred to the customer of a fairy prostitute, a meaning analogous to and derived from its usage in the slang of female prostitutes; by the 1910s, it referred to any "straight" man

Figure 3.2 Loop-the-loop, a fairy prostitute from Brooklyn who was married to another man, as photographed in 1906. *(From the* American Journal of Urology and Sexology *13 [1917]: 455.)*

who responded to a gay man's advances. As one fairy put it in 1919, a man was trade if he "would stand to have 'queer' persons fool around [with] him in any way, shape or manner."[8] *Trade* was also increasingly used in the middle third of the century to refer to straight-identified men who worked as prostitutes serving gay-identified men, reversing the dynamic of economic exchange and desire implied by the original meaning. Thus the term *trade* sometimes referred specifically to "straight" male prostitutes, but it also continued to be used to refer to "straight" men who had sex with queers or fairies for pleasure rather than money. The sailors eagerly seeking the sexual services of fairies at the Times Square Building, like those who left the Happy Hour Bar & Grill with the "fags," were considered trade, whether or not money was part of the transaction. So long as the men abided by the conventions of masculinity, they ran little risk of undermining their status as "normal" men.

Although it is impossible to determine just how common such interactions were in the early twentieth century or precisely how many men were prepared to engage in homosexual behavior on these or any other terms, Alfred Kinsey's research suggests that the number may have been large. Published in 1948, *Sexual Behavior in the Human Male* was based on the sexual life histories Kinsey and his associates gathered from men in the 1930s and 1940s, and thus offers an overview of sexual patterns among men in the half-century preceding World War II. Although most recent commentary on the Kinsey Report has focused on (and criticized) its supposed estimate that 10 percent of the population were homosexuals, Kinsey himself never made such an estimate and argued explicitly that such estimates could not be based on his findings. His research is much more helpful if used, as Kinsey intended, to examine the extent of occasional homosexual behavior among men who may or may not have identified themselves as "homosexual." Only 4 percent of the men he interviewed reported having been exclusively homosexual in their behavior throughout their lives, but 37 percent acknowledged having engaged in at least one postadolescent homosexual encounter to the point of orgasm, and fully a quarter of them acknowledged having had "more than incidental homosexual experience or reactions" for at least three years between the ages sixteen and fifty-five.[*] Clearly some cultural mechanism was at work that allowed men to engage in sexual relations with other men without thinking of themselves as abnormal.

Kinsey's own remarks about the proper interpretation of his findings

---

[*]Alfred Kinsey, Wardell Pomeroy, and Clyde Martin, *Sexual Behavior in the Human Male* (Philadelphia: W. B. Saunders, 1948), 650–51. Kinsey's statistical methods were subject to criticism almost from the moment of their publication, and this criticism has mounted in recent years in the wake of several new studies

suggest the prevalence at the time of the interpretation of homosexual relations outlined here. They indicate that many of the men he interviewed believed their sexual activity with other men did not mean they were homosexual so long as they restricted that behavior to the "masculine" role. (Indeed, his commentary is probably more useful to historical analysis than his statistical claims.) He presumably singled out for comment those notions that his interviews had revealed to be particularly widespread in the culture. His comments are not now generally noted, since the hetero–homosexual binarism has become hegemonic and the ideas against which he argued no longer have credibility. But it is significant that in the 1940s he still believed he needed to take special care to dispute interpretations of homosexual relations that regarded only one of the men involved in them as "genuinely homosexual" (and possibly not genuinely a man) and the other as not homosexual at all. It was absurd to believe, he argued, that "individuals engaging in homosexual activity are neither male nor female, but persons of mixed sex," or that "inversion [by which he meant a man playing the roles culturally ascribed to women] is an invariable accompaniment of homosexuality."[10] Equally untenable (and, apparently, common), he thought, were the claims of men who allowed themselves to be fellated but never performed fellation on other men that they were really "heterosexual," and the popular belief that "the active male in an anal relation is essentially heterosexual in his behavior, and [only] the passive male . . . homosexual."[11]

To argue that the fairy and his man emblematized the dominant conceptual schema by which homosexual relations were understood is not to argue, however, that it was the only schema or that all men were equally

---

that have produced lower estimates of the incidence of homosexual behavior.[9] It is not necessary to defend Kinsey's sampling methodology or to assert the infallibility of his estimates, however, to object on historical grounds to the effort by recent critics to prove Kinsey was "wrong" by contrasting his figures with the lower figures produced in recent studies. The fact that a certain percentage of the population engaged in homosexual practices in the 1990s does not mean that the same percentage did so fifty years earlier, when Kinsey conducted his study. It is precisely the argument of this book that such practices are culturally organized and subject to change, and that the prewar sexual regime would have made it easier for men to engage in casual homosexual behavior in the 1930s than in the 1980s, when such behavior would ineluctably mark them as homosexual. Kinsey's methodology makes his precise statistical claims unreliable, but the fact that they are higher than those produced by recent studies does not by itself demonstrate they are wrong. Moreover, Kinsey's study had the merit of trying to measure the incidence of homosexual activity rather than presuming that there was a clearly defined population of "homosexuals" whose size he could measure. Even if Kinsey's study overestimated the incidence of homosexual activity twofold or threefold, his numbers are still astonishingly high.

prepared to engage in sexual relations with other men on those terms. The image of the fairy was so powerful culturally that it influenced the self-understanding of all sexually active men, but men socialized into different class and ethnic systems of gender, family life, and sexual mores nonetheless tended to understand and organize their sexual practices in significantly different ways. Several sexual cultures coexisted in New York's divergent neighborhoods, and the social locus of the sexual culture just described needs to be specified more precisely. As the next chapter will show, middle-class Anglo-American men were less likely to accept the fairy–trade interpretive schema Kinsey reported, and even their limited acceptance of it declined during the first half of the century. It was, above all, a working-class way of making sense of sexual relations.

Among working-class men there were also ethnic differences in the social organization and tolerance of homosexual relations. Unfortunately, the evidence is too fragmentary to support a carefully delineated or "definitive" characterization of the predominant sexual culture of any of the city's immigrant or ethnic groups, and, in any case, no single sexual culture existed in any such group since each of them was divided internally along lines of gender, class, and regional origin. Nonetheless, the limited evidence available suggests that African-Americans and Irish and Italian immigrants interacted with "fairies" more extensively than Jewish immigrants did, and that they were more likely to engage in homosexual activity organized in different terms as well. Certainly, many Anglo-American, Jewish, and African-American gay men thought that "straight" Italian and Irish men were more likely to respond to their sexual advances than straight Jewish men were, and police records tend to support the conclusions of gay folklore.[12]

The contrast between Italians and Jews, the two newest and largest groups of immigrants in New York at the turn of the century, is particularly striking. A 1921 study of men arrested for homosexual "disorderly conduct," for instance, reported that "the Italians lead" in the number of arrests; at a time when the numbers of Italians and Jews in New York were roughly equal, almost twice as many Italians were arrested on homosexual charges.[13] More significant is that turn-of-the-century investigators found a more institutionalized fairy subculture in Italian neighborhoods than in Jewish ones. The Italian neighborhood of the Lower East Side had numerous saloons where fairies gathered interspersed among the saloons where female prostitutes worked. In 1908, Vito Lorenzo's saloon, located at 207 Canal Street (near Baxter), was charged by the police with being a "fairy place."[14] In 1901, agents conducting a systematic survey of "vice conditions" on the Lower East Side found male prostitutes working in two Italian saloons on the block of Elizabeth Street between Hester and Grand, the same block where the Hotel Zaza's manager hired rooms to female prostitutes who stood at the windows in "loose dresses and call[ed] the men upstairs."[15] One investigator noted that the Union Hall saloon was crowded with old Italian men and several young fairies on the night of March 5; a few doors up the street, at 97 Elizabeth, stood a saloon where the fairies, aged fourteen to sixteen, could "do their business right in [the] back room." A month later the same saloon was said to have "5 boys known as [*finocchio*, or fairies] about 17 to 25 years of age."[16]

Strikingly, the same investigators found no such open "fairy resorts" in the Lower East Side's Jewish section, located just a few blocks to the east, even though they discovered numerous tenements and street corners where female prostitutes worked. The police periodically discovered men soliciting other men in a less organized fashion in the Jewish neighborhood's streets, tenements, and even synagogues, to be sure. Two policemen, for instance, arrested a twenty-two-year-old Jewish immigrant for soliciting men from the window of 186 Suffolk Street, at Houston, in 1900.[17] But they arrested far fewer Jews than Italians on such charges, and the sites of homosexual rendezvous were less stable and commercialized, less well known, and thus, presumably, less tolerated in the Jewish neighborhood than in the Italian.

It is difficult to assess the reasons for the apparent differences in the social organization of and larger community's tolerance of male homosexual relations in Italian versus Jewish immigrant enclaves, particularly given the absence of more extensive ethnographic studies of the overall sexual culture of either group. But three interrelated factors seem particularly crucial: the sexual cultures the Jews and Italians brought with them to the States from Europe, the different circumstances of their immigration , and the ways gender relations were organized in their communities.

The sexual cultures of immigrants in the United States were clearly shaped in large part by the gender and sexual cultures of their homelands, each of which was, in turn, significantly differentiated internally along regional and class lines. Northern Italians brought to the United States a set of cultural assumptions about sex different from those of Sicilians, for instance; middle-class Italians were likely to organize gender relations differently from peasants or workers.*

Although both Catholic and Jewish religious authorities condemned homosexual relations, Catholic teaching, especially, focused on the moral dangers posed by sexual contact between men and women to such a

---

*Unfortunately, no ethnographic studies have been made of the social organization of homosexual relations in southern Italy or the Jewish Pale of Settlement in Russia at the turn of the century, for example, that might shed light on the behavior of

degree that it may implicitly have made sexual contact between men seem relatively harmless. One man who grew up in an Italian neighborhood recalled that "homosexuality just wasn't regarded as a mortal sin, it wasn't seen as that bad." Perhaps more significant is that immigrant Italians were well known for their rejection of church teaching on a wide range of moral matters, and the anti-gay religious injunction was much less effective among them than among Jewish men. Kinsey singled out Orthodox Jewish men for their "phenomenally low" rates of homosexual activity.[18]

By the late nineteenth century, southern Italian men had a reputation in northern Italy and in the northern European gay world for their supposed willingness to engage in homosexual relations. Although this reputation doubtless resulted in part from the propensity of dominant cultural groups to try to differentiate and stigmatize subordinate groups by attributing "immoral" or "bizarre" sexual practices to them, considerable evidence nonetheless suggests that such practices were both more common and more accepted in southern Italy than in the north. Numerous British and German gay men traveled to southern Italy at the turn of the century in search of a more tolerant climate; forty years later, during World War II, many gay American soldiers were startled to discover the frequency and overtness of homosexual solicitation there. On the basis of his own observations during a research trip to Europe in 1955 and the reports he received from several of his most trusted informants, Alfred Kinsey also concluded that southern Italian men were considerably more open to homosexual relations than northern Europeans were. Many Italian youths adopted an instrumental attitude toward their bodies before marriage and did not consider it shameful to use them to secure cash or advancement, observers reported, and even many married men were willing to engage in homosexual relations so long as they took the "manly part." Only the adult male who took the "woman's part" was stigmatized.

The patterns of homosexual behavior noted in Sicily appear to have persisted in modified form in the Italian enclaves on the Lower East Side, in Greenwich Village, and in East Harlem. Although more research would need to be done to substantiate the point, it seems likely that an important part of the homosexual culture of fairies and their sex partners visible in turn-of-the-century New York represented

---

immigrants from those regions. As a result, my comments here must remain highly tentative and can only suggest directions for future research by historians of Europe as well as of American immigrants. Such research would not only help us understand the social organization and cultural meaning of same-sex relations in those cultures, but would also offer a revealing new vantage point for thinking more generally about gender relations in each group.

the flowering in this country of a transplanted Mediterranean sexual culture.[19]

The relative acceptance of homosexual relations in Italian immigrant communities was related as well to the demographics of Italian immigration to the United States, which were strikingly different from those of eastern European Jews. Given the escalation of anti-Semitic violence and the draconian restrictions placed on Jewish economic and social activities in eastern Europe in the late nineteenth century, most Jewish immigrants to New York had decided to leave their villages for good with as many of their family members as possible. But the great majority of the city's Italian immigrants were single men or married men unaccompanied by their families who planned to return to Italy after earning funds to invest there. Eighty percent of the Italians who entered the United States from 1880 to 1910 were males, and the great majority of them were in their prime working years, from fourteen to forty-four years old. So many of them came to work on a seasonal basis or for only a year or two that 43 Italians left the United States for every 100 who arrived in the mid-1890s, and 73 left for every 100 who arrived in the peak immigration years of 1907–11. By contrast, only 21,000 Jews left the United States in 1908–12, while 295,000 arrived; 42 percent of Jewish immigrants were females in the 1890s—twice the proportion of Italian females—and a quarter were children under fourteen, compared to only 11 percent of the Italians.[20] Italian men may have been more responsive to homosexual overtures than Jewish men in part simply because far fewer of them were living with their wives.

Italian men also tended to have less contact with women than Jewish men did because of the greater gender segregation of Italian neighborhoods, a cultural difference only accentuated by the demographics of southern Italian immigration. Not only did more Jewish men live with their families, they centered their social lives in their apartments as well as in their synagogues, union halls, and other communal meeting places. Young Jewish men and women had their own gender-segregated groups and young women bore heavy responsibilities at home, but they were also likely to socialize in mixed-gender groups and at the dance halls, movie theaters, and other commercial amusements that abounded in their neighborhoods. Although they expected to be asked for permission, Jewish parents tended to allow their daughters to go to dances or take walks with young men. The high degree of interaction between young Jewish men and women stood in sharp contrast to the gender segregation of Italian neighborhoods, as many contemporary observers noted. The social investigator Sophonisba Breckinridge commented in 1921, "Most immigrant parents, except those from southern Italy, recognize the impossibility of maintaining the old rules of chaperonage and guardianship of the girls . . . [but] Italian parents . . . try to guard their girls almost as closely as they did in Italy."[21]

Although many Italian men in New York also lived with their families and many others boarded with families, a large number of them lived in rooming houses, where they organized surrogate, all-male families with other Italian men. Even those men who boarded with families spent much of their time outside their cramped accommodations, in the neighborhood's streets, poolrooms, and saloons; young men living with their parents spent most of their time in similar locales. As the historian Robert Orsi notes, "Men significantly outnumbered women in the first decades of Italian Harlem . . . [and] they lived in a largely male world."[22]

In this all-male social world, clubs or "gangs" of various sorts formed, usually with loosely defined memberships that fluctuated as people moved in and out of the neighborhood. Walking down four short blocks of Mulberry Street, the chief thoroughfare of the Italian Lower East Side, around 1920, John Mariano counted signs announcing the existence of at least thirty such clubs, each of them drawing young men from the immediate neighborhood, often a single block. He described the members of one of them as American-born truckers, dockworkers, and the like, who ranged in age from twenty to thirty. Employed irregularly in seasonal labor markets that made it impossible for most of them to establish even a modicum of economic security, they prided themselves on their rejection of the unrealizable "American" work ethic. "When they desire to be facetious," he noted disapprovingly, "they call themselves 'the Sons of Rest.'" Not only were two-thirds of these men in their twenties unmarried, but the third who were married nonetheless spent a great deal of their leisure time in the all-male group.[23]

THE BACHELOR SUBCULTURE

As men who (whether married or not) spent most of their time in a largely male social world, these first- and second-generation Italian immigrants were prototypical members of what several historians and sociologists have rather ambiguously termed a "bachelor subculture." This subculture was the primary locus of the sexual dyad of fairies and trade, and its dynamics help explain the sexual culture not only of Italian immigrants but also of many Irish, African-American, and Anglo-American working-class men. The bachelor subculture played a significant (though relatively little studied) role in American cities from the mid-nineteenth century until the mid-twentieth, when about 40 percent of the men over fifteen years old were unmarried at any given time. It was really a series of distinct but overlapping subcultures centered in the poolrooms and saloons where many workingmen spent their time, in the cellar clubrooms and streets where gangs of boys and young men were a ubiquitous presence,

and in the lodging houses that crowded the Bowery and the waterfront.*
It was a highly gender-segregated social world of young, unmarried, and
often transient laborers, seamen, and the like, the "rough" working-class
men, that is, whom we have already seen at the Times Square newsstand
and the Brooklyn sailors' bar and whom Ralph Werther, for one, identified as particularly receptive to his advances.

Many of the young men of the bachelor subculture would later go on
to marry. Many were immigrants (such as the Italians) planning to work
in the States only a short while before returning to their families in
Europe. The Irish contributed disproportionate numbers of men to this
subculture as well. Irish-American men, like their compatriots in Ireland
itself, tended to marry only in their early thirties, if at all, and much of
their social life was consequentially organized around all-male groups.
Indeed, the high rates of lifelong bachelorhood among the Irish provoked periodic discussions in the Irish and Catholic press of the danger
of Irish "race suicide."[24] The bachelor subculture also included native-
born Anglo-Americans who either had not yet married or planned never
to do so, as well as immigrants who had left home precisely in order to
escape the pressure to marry. It also included married men from many
backgrounds who chose to spend most of their time in the company of
other men and moved regularly between the bachelor world of "rough"
workingmen and the more family-oriented world of "respectable" workingmen.

The working-class bachelor subculture drew heavily from three sometimes overlapping occupational cultures: sailors, merchant marines, and
other seamen; transient workers who spent time in the city between stints
in the countryside as agricultural laborers, lumberjacks, construction
workers, and ice cutters; and common laborers based in New York, who

---

*These men have received remarkably little attention in recent studies of immigration
and working-class culture. In response to an older historiographical and sociological
tradition that viewed social "disorganization" and instability as the inevitable consequences of immigration, a generation of historians has sought to document the social
cohesiveness of the extended kinship systems of immigrants and their central role in
organizing migratory networks and settlement patterns. In response to older studies
that made universal claims about the process of immigration on the basis of men's
experience alone, a generation of historians has offered a finely nuanced analysis of
the role of women and families in immigration. These studies have corrected and
deepened our understanding of immigration in significant ways, but an inadvertent
consequence of their focus has been to ignore the ubiquitous presence of unattached
men in immigrant neighborhoods and to limit inquiry into the social worlds they created. Although such men often migrated to the United States to serve the interests of
a larger family-oriented and family-determined economic strategy (to raise capital for
investment in land in southern Italy, for instance), once in this country many of them
moved in an all-male world.

worked on the waterfront, in construction, and in other heavy manual-labor jobs. The highly irregular and unpredictable work of many of them on shipboard, in agriculture, or in construction often took them out of the city on a seasonal basis and made it difficult for them to support or maintain regular ties with a family. The native-born among them, especially, were part of the immense army of migrant laborers, usually known as hoboes or tramps, who constituted a significant part of the American workforce in the decades before the 1920s.

The sailor, seen as young and manly, unattached, and unconstrained by conventional morality, epitomized the bachelor subculture in the gay cultural imagination. He served for generations as the central masculine icon in gay figure pornography, as the paintings of Charles Demuth and Paul Cadmus (see figure 3.1) from the early decades of the century and the photographs produced by gay pornographers in its middle decades attest.[25] But as the records of anti-vice investigators show, his role in the gay subculture was not simply an object of fantasy. He was a central figure in the subculture, and his haunts became the haunts of gay men as well. He was, however, usually not "of" that culture, since he typically declined to identify himself as other than normal and in sexual encounters almost always took the role of the "man."

The members of the bachelor subculture were a ubiquitous presence in New York in 1900, when two of every five men in Manhattan aged fifteen years or older were unmarried. They were especially evident in parts of Harlem, in the Italian and Irish districts, along the bustling waterfront, and along the Bowery, long known as the "main stem," or center, of the city's "Hobohemia." Their world began to disappear in the 1920s, when the sex ratios of immigrant communities started to stabilize after the strict new federal immigration laws passed in that decade made it difficult for immigrant workers to enter the United States for brief periods of work. The number of seamen in the city began to decline as New York's port declined, and the number of transient workers (or hoboes) dropped throughout the country in the 1920s, as economic and technological developments, such as refrigeration, the mechanization of agricultural production, and the expansion of auto transport, reduced the need for them.[26] The men of the working-class bachelor subculture continued to play a significant role in the city's life throughout the half-century before World War II, however, and it was in their social world that the interaction of fairies and trade took its most visible and highly developed form.

The bachelor subculture, as several historians have shown, shared many of the characteristics of working-class male culture as a whole, but it also had certain distinctive elements that made it particularly amenable to the presence of fairies.[27] The dominant working-class ideology made the ability and willingness to undertake the responsibility of supporting a family two of the defining characteristics of both manliness and male "respectability." But many of the men of the bachelor subculture, either because their irregular and poorly paid work made supporting a family difficult or because they had deliberately chosen to avoid such family encumbrances, forged an alternative definition of manliness that was predicated on a rejection of family obligations. Although many of the men would eventually marry, they tended to remain isolated from women and hostile to the constraints of marriage during the many years they were involved in the bachelor subculture. (They were also considerably more open to advances of fairies before their marriages; Ralph Werther, for instance, noted that most of his young Italian and Irish sex partners went on to marry women.)[28] Indeed, not only their disengagement from the conventions of family life and domesticity but their decided rejection of them were central elements of their culture; they were considered "rough" not simply because many of them rejected family life per se, but more precisely because they scorned the manners associated with the domesticating and moralizing influence of women.

Some of the descriptions of "rough" working-class life provided by hostile middle-class observers in the 1900s and 1910s suggest the extent to which the observers considered the rejection of the feminine domestication of male behavior, the casual mingling of men and fairies, and open displays of homosexuality to be characteristic of such life. An agent investigating the Subway Cabaret on East Fourteenth Street for a moral-reform society in 1917 cited such mingling, along with men refusing to doff their hats (a sign of their lack of domestication), in order to illustrate the "lowergrade" character of the place to his supervisor:

> For instance, at one table one sees three or four tough looking fellows . . . who have to be requested to keep their hats off. At another table one sees a sailor, sitting drinking with two other fellows in civilian clothes, the sailor with his arm around the other fellows neck. The proprietor had to make the sailor behave himself. The sailor was constantly going out with one of the other fellows to the lavatory. I went out also a couple of times but they would just stand there and talk while I was there, and thus I was cheated out of witnessing a little homosexuality.[29]

Embodying a rejection of domesticity and of bourgeois acquisitivism alike, the bachelor subculture was based on a shared code of manliness and an ethic of male solidarity. The solidarity it celebrated was expressed in the everyday ties built at work on the waterfront or in construction; it was symbolized by the rituals of saloon conviviality that expressed mutual regard and reciprocity, perhaps most commonly through the custom of treating one's fellows to rounds of drinks. A man's "manliness" was signaled in part by his participation in such rituals and by his behavior on the job, but it was demonstrated as well by his besting of other men in contests of strength and skill in all-male arenas such as the boxing ring, poolroom, and gambling den. Sexual prowess with women was another important sign of manliness, but such prowess was significant not only as an indication of a man's ability to dominate women but also as evidence of his *relative* virility compared to other men's; manliness in this world was confirmed by other men and in relation to other men, not by women.[30]

The way the men in this social milieu constructed their manliness allowed other men to construct themselves as something other than men. The men in this culture regarded manhood as a hard-won accomplishment, not a given, and as a continuum, not an absolute value or characteristic. Even as they celebrated their masculine camaraderie and commitment to fraternity, they constantly had to prove their manhood and often sought to demonstrate that they were more manly than their rivals. To be called a "man" or a "regular guy" was both the highest compliment in this world and the most common. But the very repetitiveness of such praise implied that men were in danger of being called something else: unmanly, a mollycoddle, a sissy, even a pansy. Whereas manhood could be achieved, it could also be lost; it was not simply a quality that resulted naturally and inevitably from one's sex. The calculated character of the everyday rituals of male sociability, solidarity, and competition by which men enacted their manliness and demonstrated their relative virility suggests the remarkable degree to which they regarded their manliness as a kind of ongoing performance, to use Erving Goffman and Judith Butler's term. It also reveals the degree to which relations in this all-male environment were gendered.[31] It was both this self-consciousness about the performativity of gender and the gendering of relations among men that allowed some males to turn themselves into "she-men," so long as they did not question other men's status as men, and allowed other males to confirm their own "he-manliness" by subordinating them. The very theatricality of the fairies' style not only emphasized the performative character of gender but evoked an aura of liminality reminiscent of carnivals at which the normal constraints on men's behavior were suspended, making it easier for men to interact with them without considering it consequential.[32]

One of the reasons fairies were tolerated by tough working-class men and often had remarkably easygoing relations with them was the care they took to confirm rather than question the latter's manliness. Fairies related to men as if they themselves were women—though often the "tough" women who dared venture into the social spaces dominated by tough men—and they did so in a manner that confirmed the complex social conventions of gender deference, inequality, and power character-istic of gender relations in that culture. But some gangs of men regarded fairies, like women, as fair game for sexual exploitation. Sexually using a fairy not only could be construed and legitimized as a "normal" sexual act but could actually provide some of the same enhancement of social status that mastering a woman did.

That this dynamic sometimes influenced the meaning ascribed to homosexual encounters is suggested by the experience of one Italian youth around 1920. He was sexually active with other men (almost always, he said, "act[ing] as a woman"), but he tried to protect his repu-tation by developing a conventionally masculine style in the other spheres of his life. He did not carry himself as a fairy and sought to establish his masculinity with the other youths he met at a neighborhood gymnasium by deliberately "talk[ing] about women" with them. Participating in the collective sexualization and objectification of women was one of the ritu-als by which he established himself as a man. At the gym he met a twenty-five-year-old boxer to whom he was attracted, and he eventually agreed to let the boxer, who had sensed his interest, anally penetrate him. To the boy's horror, the boxer promptly went to the gym and told everyone what he had done; the boy, humiliated, concluded he could never go there again.[33] A man who allowed himself to be used sexually as a woman, then, risked forfeiting his masculine status, even if he were otherwise con-ventionally masculine; in this case, the boy's shame clearly derived from his perception that he had been made a fairy in the eyes of his comrades. The story also illustrates the belief among men in this world that so long as they played the "man's" role, they remained men. The most striking aspect of the story is the confidence the boxer felt that reporting the encounter would not endanger his status among his friends, that, indeed, having sexually subordinated the boy would enhance it. If a man risked forfeiting his masculine status by being sexually passive, he could also establish it by playing the dominant role in an encounter with another man. Sexual penetration symbolized one man's power over another.

Men's sexual relations with fairies were also fundamentally influenced by the character of their sexual relations with women, particularly the prostitutes and other "tough girls" who were the only women with whom many men in the bachelor subculture interacted. The very social organiza-tion and meaning of their sexual relations with women made it relatively unobjectionable for them to substitute fairies when such women could not be found. Numerous reports by undercover agents investigating female prostitution in the early decades of the century make it clear that in those social milieus dominated by young, single laborers and seamen, it was understood that men in search of women sexual partners might be willing to make just that substitution. It was not thought that all men *would*, but it was not considered remarkable when any man *did*.

One evening in the fall of 1927 two agents in search of female prostitutes were taken by a sailor to an Italian restaurant on West Seventeenth Street, where sailors and "hardened neighborhood girls" congregated. After failing to lure any of the women away from the sailors (but, presumably, having succeeded in demonstrating their sexual interest in women), they asked their waitress if she knew where they could find a "sporting girl." The woman said she did not, but immediately added that "there is a fairy [who] comes in here," and called him over. One might expect that the fairy was pimping for female prostitutes, but the agents' response indicates they believed they were being offered the fairy in place of a prostitute. Quickly taking advantage of the unexpected opportunity, they "tried to make an appointment with [him] . . . and [made] an effort . . . to learn where he resided or took his trade." The fairy begged off, citing a previous appointment.[34] The fairy's disinclination to cooperate meant that the agents—and we—learned nothing more of his life, but the fact that the waitress referred the agents to him in the first place tells us much about the understanding of male sexuality she had developed while working in a milieu dominated by sailors and Italian laborers. It evidently seemed plausible—even likely—to her that a man anxious for sexual satisfaction would accept it from a fairy if a woman were unavailable.

The Italian waitress was not the only one who believed this. The general secretary of the city's major anti-prostitution society warned in 1918 that opponents of his anti-prostitution campaign might use the "apparent increase of male perversion" during World War I as "evidence to sustain their argument that vice driven out of one form will appear in another."[35] (The campaign is discussed in chapter 5.) His fear that such reasoning would seem plausible was well founded. One of his own investigators had used it to explain the homosexual liaisons he had observed on the streets surrounding the Brooklyn Navy Yard late one summer night in 1917, when no women were to be found:

> The streets and corners were crowded with the sailors all of whom were on a sharp lookout for girls. . . . It seemed to me that the sailors were sex mad. A number of these sailors were with other men walking arm in arm and on one dark street I saw a sailor and a man kissing each other. . . . It looked like an exhibition of mail [sic] perversion showing itself in the absence of girls or the difficulty of finding them. Some of the sailors told me that they might be able to get a girl if they went 'up-town' but it was too far up and they were too drunk to go way up there.[36]

The belief that fairies could be substituted for female prostitutes—and were virtually interchangeable with them—was particularly prevalent among men in the bachelor subculture whose opportunities for meeting "respectable" women were limited by the moral codes, gender segregation, or unbalanced sex ratios of their ethnic cultures. Indeed, many of these men found the sexual services of fairies to be both easier and cheaper to secure than those of women. They could be found around the Navy Yard and along the waterfront, on well-known streets and in many saloons frequented by sailors and workingmen, and even in many subway washrooms, where a man could find quick release on the way home from work merely by presenting himself. A finely calibrated map of the sexual geography of the neighborhood was usually part of men's gender-specific "local knowledge." Many workingmen knew precisely where to go to find fairies with whom, if they chose, they need not exchange a word to make their wishes clear.[37]

Still, the relative accessibility of fairies to men isolated from women hardly explains the latter's willingness to turn to them. After all, thousands of women were working as prostitutes in the city, and workingmen often *did* have recourse to them; the immense number of single men in the city with few other means of meeting women supported the business of prostitution on a scale that would never be repeated after the 1920s.[38] If men had risked being stigmatized as queer on the basis of a single homosexual encounter, most of them would have sought sex exclusively with such women.

But the very character of their sexual relations with prostitutes and other "tough" women made it possible for them to turn to fairies as well. The moral codes governing the sexual practices of many men in the bachelor subculture (as in the larger culture of men) divided the world into "pure women," with whom men did not expect sexual contact until after marriage, and "impure women" or "whores," whom men felt free to pursue aggressively for sexual purposes.[39] In the eyes of such men, the simple willingness of a woman to enter the saloons, poolrooms, and other social spaces they dominated was a sign that she was a prostitute. In a culture in which men regarded themselves as highly lustful creatures whose health would be impaired if their explosive sexual needs did not find release (or, as they usually termed it, "relief" or "satisfaction")[40], a phallocentric economy of sexual pleasure governed relations with such women. Sex was something a man did *to* them, not *with* them: a man's phallic dominance and "satisfaction" were his paramount concern. A man might have a close romantic relationship with one woman, whom he hoped to marry and treated with affection and respect, but still feel free to use a prostitute to satisfy his immediate sexual needs. Few men would ever even imagine substituting a fairy for their beloved (although they might develop feelings of affection for some fairies, just as they did for some prostitutes, and might even find it easier to relate to fairies than to prostitutes because they found it easier to relate to men than to women).* But many men did find it relatively easy to substitute a fairy for a prostitute, since both offered immediate sexual satisfaction, as well as the pleasures and amusements of bawdy "female" companionship. In a world in which "every woman is just another place to enter," as one Italian teenager described the attitude of men at his neighborhood pool hall in 1930, the body to enter did not necessarily have to be a woman's.[42]

Gang rapes and other phallocentric sexual practices highlighted the cultural logic that allowed men to substitute fairies for women as objects of sexual penetration. Loop-the-loop, the fairy prostitute mentioned previously, reported to a doctor in 1906 that on a single day he had had sex with "no fewer than twenty-three men . . . one immediately after the other . . . in a room in Brooklyn."[43] His boast is more plausible than it may at first seem, for he would have engaged in a well-established practice when he had sex with a line of men, even if he exaggerated the number. "Line-ups," in which men ("anywhere from three to seventeen," by one account from an Italian neighborhood in the late 1920s) formed a queue to have intercourse, one after another, with a single woman, were not uncommon. Some line-ups constituted nothing less than gang rapes (in which the women "were the victims of a planned scheme on the part of the men," according to the same account). In a smaller number of cases, the women had enough control of the situation to stop it when they chose and to charge the men for the encounter. Every line-up allowed men to find sexual satisfaction and to enact their solidarity with other men by establishing their collective difference from and dominance of the woman they used. In a similar manner, groups of young men and boys sometimes forced younger boys to provide them with sexual "relief," either by submitting to anal penetration, or, when the number of boys was too large, by masturbating the older boys, one after another.[44] The very structure of such encounters and the interchangeability of fairies, women, and boys in them highlights the degree to which

---

*Will Finch, a middle-class gay man who had pursued and constantly associated with straight working-class men since the 1930s, believed that the homosocial character of "rough" working-class culture gave gay men an advantage over women in one respect: "We can be *buddies* of men, whereas a woman never can." For most of the unmarried working-class men he knew, women were for sex, men for "companionship," a situation, Finch thought, comparable to that in classical Greece. One of his sex partners, whom Finch wryly christened "the voice of the urban proletariat," had commented, typically enough, "that he is not at ease with a girl socially and intellectually and emotionally, but only with other males. But girls are lots of fun to fuck."[41]

men were simply using the body of the fairy and sometimes the body of a boy, just as they might use the body of a woman, as a vehicle for phallic satisfaction and manly solidarity.

The phallocentric presumption that a man's sexual satisfaction was more significant than the gender or character of the person who provided that satisfaction allowed gay men to make certain arguments in their approach to "normal" men that would seem utterly incredible in the absence of that presumption. Most commonly, gay men simply offered to perform certain sexual acts, especially fellation, which many straight men enjoyed but many women (even many prostitutes) were loath to perform. In such cases it was the particular phallocentric pleasure, rather than the gender of the person providing the pleasure, that men found appealing, although fairies, who were commonly called "cocksuckers," were especially known for this service, in part because so many women refused to provide it. As one gay man observed of the Irish and Italian young men from South Brooklyn with whom he associated in the 1940s and 1950s, they "do not (necessarily) despise fellators—including these 'nice' Brooklyn boys. Or especially they. They find the fellator desirable. . . . The same with sailors."[45] But even though men found the queer man's services desirable, they also believed that a man lost status if he fellated another man. This was not simply a matter of his losing gender status, however, for women also lost status by performing fellation, which is one reason so many women refused to do it. The act itself—a nonreproductive sexual act whether performed by man or woman and thus "unnatural" by the tenets of a reproductively oriented sexual ideology—was considered perverted for men and women alike to do. Its transgressive character was, indeed, part of its appeal, whether performed by men or women.

Some gay men interested in sex with "straight" men also portrayed themselves as less dangerous than women by arguing that there was no chance they would infect the men with the venereal diseases women were thought to carry. Their success with this remarkable line becomes more understandable when one considers the focus of the highly publicized education campaigns launched to curb venereal disease during World War I. The campaigns, controlled by officials concerned with preserving the sexual morality of young men from rural homes as much as with protecting their health, had tried both to heighten men's fear of venereal disease and to use that fear to persuade them to shun contact with prostitutes or the other "loose" women they might encounter in the nation's port cities and training camps. Some educational materials explained that condoms could protect men from venereal disease (and a measure of their success was that condoms came to be called "protectors" in the slang of the 1920s). But most leaflets and posters identified sex with a woman, rather than sex without a condom, as the source of venereal disease.[46] Ironically, one quite unintentional effect of such moralistic campaigns was to reinforce the traditional belief among men that they could catch syphilis or gonorrhea *only* from female prostitutes or other women, whereas sexual contacts with another man were safe—a misconception men interested in seducing other men were quick to seize upon. An investigator posing as a seaman recounted the following conversation with a thirty-year-old Swede employed by the United Fruit Line, in a waterfront cafeteria's washroom in 1931:

> I was about to leave and he said "It smells like a c . . . house. Did you have a woman lately?" I said "No, I am looking for one. Do you know a place?" He said "Wouldn't it be much safer to have it blown?" I said "Do you know a woman who would do that?" He said "Why do you want a woman, they are not safe." I said, "I want only a woman." He then took hold of my arm and said, "Let's get inside. I'll do it for you."[47]

This view was shared by the police as well. A crackdown on homosexual activity after World War I came to an end, in part, because the chief of the vice squad grew concerned that the campaign had diverted too much attention from the squad's efforts against prostitutes, who, he apparently feared, posed a medical, as well as moral, danger to their customers, and through them to their families. Telling his men that "one prostitute was more dangerous than five degenerates," he ordered them to give more attention to the former, a shift in priorities soon reflected in the squad's arrest statistics.[48] Concern about the relative health risk posed by sexual relations with fairies and prostitutes was possible only because it was presupposed that men could substitute fairies for women without undermining their masculine status. Indeed, men's ability to calculate the relative rewards and risks involved in each kind of encounter provides the most powerful evidence possible that the hetero–homosexual axis did not govern their thinking about sexual practices. In the right circumstances, almost any man might choose to experiment with the queer pleasures of sex with a fairy.

HUSBANDS, WOLVES, AND PUNKS

If every workingman was thought to have the capacity to respond to the advances of a fairy, it was nonetheless the case, as gay men themselves realized, that some men were more interested in sexual contacts with fairies and boys than others were. And although some men treated fairies in the same way they treated prostitutes, not every relationship between a man and a fairy was brief, coercive, or loveless, nor did all men orchestrate the relationships in a way that established their distance from the fairies. Some men sought love and even marriage with fairies, and others at least made no bones about their sexual preference for them. Parker Tyler found many of the Italian men who lived in the Village to be responsive to his charms, for instance, but in his 1929 account of his interaction with the cameramen in a Village speakeasy (see chapter 2), he regarded the one who seemed the most anxious about the meeting and who made the most earnest entreaties *to him* as a more distinctive character: a "wolf."

Such men, known as "husbands," "wolves," and "jockers" (terms sometimes used interchangeably, sometimes for different groups of men in different social milieus), occupied an ambiguous position in the sexual culture of the early twentieth century. They abided by the conventions of masculinity and yet exhibited a decided preference for male sexual partners. From a late-twentieth-century perspective they might be regarded as homosexuals more easily than the men just described, since they engaged in homosexual activity on a more exclusive basis than most men who were trade. But the fact that neither they nor their peers regarded them as queer, even if they sometimes regarded them as *different* from other "normal" men, highlights the degree to which gender status superseded homosexual interest as the basis of sexual classification in working-class culture.

Some men involved in marriages with fairies were so confident of their status as "normal" men that they readily acknowledged their relationships to others. One such man, a band musician, told a doctor in 1906 that he did not limit himself to brief, anonymous, and infrequent sexual encounters with other men, but considered himself the "husband" of a fairy (the prostitute Loop-the-loop), with whom he was involved in an ongoing relationship. He "apparently [did] not care an iota," Dr. Shufeldt reported, "whether I was aware of his sex relations with [the fairy] or not," an impression strengthened by the man's willingness to confide to the doctor, man to man as it were, that Loop-the-loop was "the most passionate mortal he had ever heard of, and one of the most difficult to satisfy." Given the doctor's middle-class and professional background, his response to the man was ambivalent. By remarking on the man's nonchalance, the doctor implied that he, in contrast to his subject, considered the arrangement noteworthy and somewhat objectionable. He also expressed his "surprise [that] he was an intelligent young man," although his surprise was probably due at least in part to the fact that he would have predicted a less respectable husband for the fairy, whom he considered "very uncouth." But he did not feel compelled to comment directly on the man's sexual character, and clearly did not regard him in the same terms as he regarded the fairy. The relationship reproduced the conventions of a highly role-differentiated marriage between a man and a woman, and the "husband," since he played the conventional masculine role, even though with a wife who was anatomically male, did not seem so "abnormal."[49]

The male partners of men such as the musician were not always fairies, nor were the relationships always so close. Indeed, some sexual relationships were organized on the basis of a power and status hierarchy dictated by age rather than by gender (although that age hierarchy was sometimes thematized as one of gender) and sometimes took on a more coercive edge. Known as "active pederasts" or, most commonly, "wolves," the term Tyler used, such men acknowledged having a particular predilection for playing the "man's role" in sex with fairies and, more typically, youths, the latter usually referred to as "punks." *Punk* generally denoted a physically slighter youth who let himself be used sexually by an older and more powerful man, the wolf, in exchange for money, protection, or other forms of support.

The punk's sexual character was ambiguous: he was often neither homosexually interested nor effeminate himself, but was sometimes equated with women because of his youth and his subordination to the older man. He was regarded by some men as simply a young homosexual, by others as the victim of an aggressive older man, and by still others as someone whose sexual subordination was merely an aspect of his general subordination to a dominant older man.[50] In a west Pennsylvania prison in 1892, for instance, an older prisoner explained the meaning of *punk* to the anarchist Alexander Berkman in the following manner: "Ever read Billy Shakespeare? Know the place, 'He's neither man nor woman; he's punk.' Well, Billy knew. A punk's a boy that'll . . . give himself to a man. . . . It's done in every prison, an' on th' road [by which he meant among hoboes], everywhere." This may have been the original derogatory meaning of *punk,* which only later passed into underworld and then more general slang as an epithetic diminutive without specifically sexual connotations.[51]

The erotic system of wolves and punks was particularly widespread (and tended to take somewhat different form) among three groups of men who were exceptionally disengaged from the family and neighborhood systems that regulated normative sexuality: seamen, prisoners, and the immense number of transient workers (or hoboes) who passed through American cities before the 1920s. That the wolves regarded themselves as something other than queer attests both to the absence of a sharp hetero–homosexual binarism in their culture, which would inevitably have classified them as homosexual, and to the centrality instead of effeminacy to the definition of sexual abnormality among workingmen. Their behavior in prison or on shipboard could be dismissed as a product of the situation (the absence of women) rather than of predisposition (a preference for boys or fairies), but such explanations became implausible when the

behavior persisted in settings where women were available. Wolves combined homosexual interest with a marked masculinity. None of them
behaved effeminately or took feminine nicknames, and few played the
"woman's part" in sexual relations—and then only secretly. On the contrary, their very appellation, *wolf,* evoked the image of the predatory
man-about-town intent on seducing young women, and their masculine
dominance over punks was further emphasized by the fact that the latter
were also referred to as *lambs* and *kids.* Wolves generally did not seek
sexual encounters with other "men," in which they might have been
forced into sexual roles that would have compromised their own masculine identification, but only with punks or fairies, males ascribed lower
status because of their youth or effeminacy.[52]

Thus a seaman blithely explained to an undercover agent whom he
met on the lower Manhattan waterfront in 1931 that he liked sex with
"fairies or c . . . s . . . . . . ," particularly fifteen- and sixteen-year-old
boys he called "punks." "I had one of those punks living with me at the
[Seamen's Church] Institute for quite some time," the man bragged. "He
was a young kid about 15 years old, [and] pretty." The fact that he
found a boy attractive, regularly had sex with him, and supported him
financially did not make the older man, in his own mind or in the opinion of the investigator, a fairy or queer. Critical to both was the fact that,
in the seaman's version of the relationship, the boy "satisfied me the
same as a woman." At the same time, the seaman appears to have
believed that some men—possibly including the investigator—were more
likely than others to take an interest in punks; he mentioned his relations
with the punks only after learning that the investigator had not visited
the "sporting houses" (tenement brothels) that he had previously shown
him.[53] Indeed, their interaction suggests that having recourse to a punk
or fairy did not have the same reputability in this milieu that going to a
prostitute did. When the seaman introduced the agent to a punk prostitute, the agent was able to put off meeting with him by indicating he did
not want to make an appointment in front of his friend. This concern
evidently seemed plausible to the boy, who accepted the excuse but
assured the agent that he could find him anytime around the Seamen's
Church Institute.[54] Nonetheless, the seaman's willingness to boast about
his relationship with a punk to a man he barely knew suggests that he
did not expect to lose much, if any, status because of it. If one man might
be reticent about admitting such interests (as he might be about any sexual matter), they were acceptable enough that another man could take
pride in commenting on them.

The seaman's interest in punks and fairies was not unusual, nor were
such interactions kept carefully hidden. The investigator accompanied
the man to Battery Park, whose benches were filled with young men

waiting to be picked up by sailors. The punk to whom the seaman introduced him, a sixteen-year-old named Julius, assumed he wanted a rendezvous and immediately offered to find a room in a lodging house in
Chatham Square. He also offered a straightforward account of his prices:
along with the room, which cost a dollar, he charged 50 cents for oral
sex and 75 cents for anal sex. The investigator frequently saw punks and
fairies talking with seamen at the Institute, in nearby lunchrooms, and in
the park; on one occasion a seaman identified fifteen male prostitutes in
the park, sitting "on separate benches, always leaving room for a [man]
to sit down."[55] Although the openness and even the existence of such
men was news to the investigator, it must have been common knowledge
among workers and residents of the waterfront.

Long-term relationships or "marriages" between wolves and punks
seem to have been even more common among hoboes, although precisely
how many hoboes participated in such relationships is, of course, impossible to determine. A study of a hundred "vagrants" in New York City in
1916 identified a quarter of them as "perverts"; studies conducted in
other cities produced lower figures, although any such estimates need to
be regarded with suspicion.[56] The prevalence of homosexual relations
was so "generally assumed to be true among hoboes," wrote the sociologist and former hobo Nels Anderson in a 1931 hobo handbook, "that
whenever a man travels around with a lad he is apt to be labeled a
'jocker' or a 'wolf' and the road kid is called his 'punk,' 'preshun,' or
'lamb.' It has become so that it is very difficult for a good hobo to enjoy
the services of an apprentice."[57]

As Anderson's comment suggests, partnerships between older and
younger men on the road were common, and while they were presumed
to have a sexual element, many did not. In both sexual and nonsexual
partnerships, the older man usually took responsibility for teaching his
apprentice the arts of the road as well as providing for his material
needs. The younger man performed a host of services for his mentor,
including shaving him, and also contributed to their supply of cash. In
many respects their relationship reproduced the sexual roles, division of
labor, and conventions of mutual dependence that were characteristic of
husbands and wives in the dominant culture. In his classic 1923 sociological study of hoboes, Anderson noted that "it is not uncommon to
hear a boy who is seen traveling with an older man spoken of as the
'wife' or 'woman.'"[58] As with heterosexual marriages, the quality of the
partnerships varied widely: some were brutal and coercive, others were
close and affectionate, and still others simply instrumental.

The character of such relationships needs to be explored more fully by
historians, but it seems likely that the widespread existence of hobo partnerships made it easier for men in sexual relationships to fit into the

social world that took shape in rural hobo camps and in urban "hobo-hemias," the districts, such as the Bowery, where many transient workers spent the winter. Some men doubtless entered into such relationships only because of the circumstances in which they found themselves, but other men must have sought out such circumstances precisely because they made it possible for them to engage in homosexual intimacies.*

Another locus of relations between wolves and punks, the New York City Jail on Welfare Island, deserves scrutiny because the organization of sexual relations in it illuminates the boundaries drawn between different kinds of men who engaged in homosexual practices. Although the homo-sexual world that took shape among prisoners was a peculiar one, it was not so exceptional as is often thought. Nor does the culturally blind con-cept of "situational homosexuality" offer an adequate framework for analyzing that world. In a remarkable study of homosexual relations in an American prison in the 1970s, Wayne S. Wooden and Jay Parker showed that the social organization of such relations varied among Chicanos, African-Americans, and Euro-Americans. Men did not react to being deprived of other sexual contacts by engaging in homosexual practices in a spontaneous and unstructured way, but organized those relations in accordance with the sexual norms they brought to the prison from their own cultures.[60] Similarly, the homosexual world that evolved in the New York City Jail in the early twentieth century, rather than being a singular world cut off from wider cultural patterns, was pro-foundly shaped by those patterns. It drew especially on the patterns of the bachelor subculture, whose members, as the men least socialized into the dominant social order, were disproportionately represented in the jail.

The dominant pre–World War II conceptualizations of homosexuality were inscribed in the spatial organization of prisons and in the everyday interactions of prisoners. The central position of the fairy in the dominant cultural conception of homosexuality was signaled by the decision of prison authorities not only to segregate homosexual prisoners from other men but to classify as "homosexuals" only those men who exhibited the typical markers of effeminacy. It is not clear when this policy was initiated, but it had become a well-established practice by the 1910s. All prisoners

*Indeed, homosexual relationships appear to have been so widespread among sea-men and hoboes that historians need to recognize the desire to live in a social milieu in which such relationships were relatively common and accepted—or to escape the pressure to marry in a more family-oriented milieu—as one of the motives that sent men on the road or to sea. More work needs to be done on the patterns of same-sex relations in all-male work settings where "hoboes" and other transient laborers worked, such as lumber camps, cattle ranges, and many mining camps.[59]

who had been convicted of homosexual solicitation or transvestism were incarcerated in this unit, of course, but the majority of inmates identified as "perverts" had been convicted of drug use or other nonsexual offenses; the authorities segregated any man whose dress or mannerisms suggested he might be homosexual. Segregation from the other prisoners was complete. "Fags" were confined to the prison's South Annex, the most isolated and secure section of the prison; they ate separately, saw movies separately, and worked in separate work gangs, which were assigned "women's work" in the prison laundry and in the warden's home (see figure 3.3). Within the South Annex (which many prisoners called the Fag Annex), men were informally allowed to wear long hair, wigs, makeshift dresses, and homemade rouge and lipstick. Guards and other prisoners alike usually referred to them by their camp names—"Greta Garbo," "Lillian Russell," "Broadway Rose"—and at Christmas the South Annex inmates staged a bawdy show called the "Fag Follies" for a select audience of guards and well-connected prisoners. Normally the only contact between the "fags" and other prisoners came when the former were marched past the latter on their way to the mess hall.[61]

If the basis on which the authorities segregated homosexual prisoners confirms how widely the fairy was regarded as a distinct social type, the reasons they gave for segregating them confirm how widely it was believed that any man might be attracted to a fairy. Most authorities did not think that men isolated from women would randomly engage in homosexual behavior, but they did assume that such men would be susceptible to the fairies. When a new administrator took over the jail in 1934 he announced that he would force the fairies with long hair to get "military hair cuts," in order, he explained to the press in a revealing comment, to "cut down their attractiveness."[62] Although most prison authorities found inmates' having sex with fairies to be reprehensible, they hardly considered it unusual. Indeed, their fear was not just that fairies would induce other men to engage in homosexual practices but that rivalries between men for a fairy's attentions would escalate into violent confrontations. "Perverts, frank and under cover, stimulate tortured men to indulge in perversion, often by direct solicitation," one prison doctor and reform advocate warned in 1934. "The constitutional type, the one the man in the street recognizes under the optimistic title of 'fairy,' should be segregated in colonies, such as now utilized for mental defectives; only in this way can their moral leprosy be prevented from spreading."[63]

Prison officials generally refused to acknowledge the existence of homosexual activity in their prisons, but reformers brought it to the attention of the public in 1934. Shortly after the newly elected mayor, Fiorello La Guardia, appointed his own commissioner of corrections,

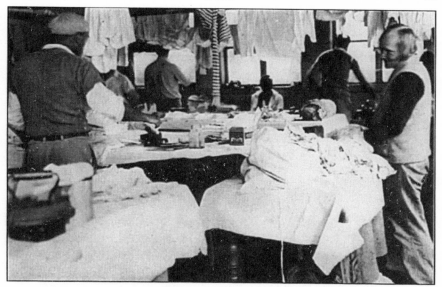

Figure 3.3 The original caption for this photo, published in a 1934 prison study, announced: "In the penitentiary at Welfare Island, New York, are confined a daily average of 75 members of the 'third sex.'" Gay prisoners were segregated from other prisoners and assigned "women's work" in the prison laundry. *(From Joseph F. Fishman,* Sex in Prison *[New York: National Library Press, 1934].)*

Austin H. MacCormick, the commissioner conducted a raid of Welfare Island. His purpose was both to seize control of the prison from the crime-boss inmates who exercised effective suzerainty within it—running numbers rackets, selling liquor, and leading as luxurious a life as prison conditions would allow—and to discredit both the old prison administration that had allowed such conditions to develop and the Tammany Hall mayoral administration preceding La Guardia's.[64] The raid produced sensational newspaper stories that destroyed the credibility of the old administration. Some of the most lurid stories concerned the homosexual segregation unit. The new administrators used the "freedoms" granted homosexuals as well as gang lords to attack the old administration; when they invited the press to tour the prison on the day of the raid, they pointed to the spectacle of homosexual depravity to demonstrate the depths to which the prison had sunk.

The *New York Herald Tribune* cooperated fully in the effort. It described the scene witnessed by the crusading commissioner on the day of the raid when the "sex perverts" entered the mess hall: "These men appeared for lunch, some of them heavily rouged, their eye brows painted, their lips red, hair in some instances hanging to the shoulder, and in most cases hips swinging and hands fluttering. . . . Mr. MacCormick

Figure 3.4 The day after authorities raided the New York City penitentiary, a newspaper published this artist's depiction of corrupt jail conditions, which spotlighted the liberties supposedly given homosexual prisoners. A drawing of someone who appeared to be a woman dancing in front of another inmate was captioned: "We have a few of the boys entertaining." *(From the* New York Daily Mirror, *January 26, 1934. Courtesy of State Historical Society of Wisconsin.)*

[said] he could see no reason 'for permitting them to flaunt themselves in front of the rest of the prisoners in this way,'" and he "intimated" that this was "but a slight example of the liberties this group had previously had in the prison." The *Daily Mirror* offered a fuller account of their "liberties" when it noted they "had been permitted by the prison bosses to roam the Island, visiting various buildings and cell-tiers 'in drag'—or female costume," although even it only hinted at the sordid purpose of their visits. When the raiding party entered the South Annex, the *Herald Tribune* continued, it was "greeted by cries and howls in high falsetto voices. . . . Inside the cells were found every conceivable article of women's wearing apparel. Dozens of compacts, powder puffs, and various types of perfume were found, while silk step-ins, nightgowns and other bits of negligee were strewn about the cells." The paper also described the dramatic scene as "one man . . . clung desperately to a set of false eyelashes, which he did not want disturbed," in an apparent effort to turn the confiscation of the false eyelashes into a symbol of the reformers' struggle to restore order to the New York City Jail.[65] The sensational

news articles were soon followed by a flurry of more "authoritative" studies by prison doctors and reformers with titles like *Sex in Prison* and *Revelations of a Prison Doctor*.[66]

The segregation of "fags" hardly put an end to homosexual liaisons in the city jail, though. As numerous reformers and prisoners themselves testified, the jail was the quintessential home of the "wolf" and the "punk," and the treatment accorded the wolf by inmates and prison authorities alike attests to the degree to which he was regarded as a "normal" man. The wolf's behavior led him to lose little status among other prisoners; if anything, he gained stature in many men's eyes because of his ability to coerce or attract a punk. Prison authorities did not try to segregate the highly masculine and aggressive older wolves by confining them in the "degenerate" unit in which they segregated the effeminate fairies, primarily because they did not think it was possible to distinguish wolves from other prisoners.

Whether the wolf could be distinguished from the other inmates was subject to debate. Some prison reformers, such as Thomas Mott Osborne, thought that "'wolves,' who by nature or practice prefer unnatural to what we may call natural vice," should be distinguished from other homosexually active men "who have no liking for unnatural vice [and] outside of prison would never be guilty of it." Several reformers recommended that wolves be segregated from vulnerable youths.[67] But most prisoners, like the prison authorities, seem to have regarded the wolves as little different from other men; their sexual behavior may have represented a moral failure, but it did not distinguish them from other men as the fairy's gender status did. As one prisoner wrote in 1933, "The 'wolf' (active sodomist), as I have hinted before, is not considered by the average inmate to be 'queer' in the sense that the oral copulist, male or female, is so considered. While his conduct is felt to be in some measure depraved, it is conduct which many a prisoner knows that he himself might resort to under certain special circumstances." The "special circumstances" he envisioned were not so special after all and presumed that any prisoner might be attracted to a youth. "If the prisoner can find a good-looking boy, and the opportunity, and is sufficiently 'hard up' for sexual satisfaction," he explained, "he will not usually disdain to make use of him for purposes of relief."[68] The line between the wolf and the normal man, like that between the culture of the prison and culture of the streets, was a fine one indeed.

The ability of many workingmen to alternate between male and female sexual partners provides powerful evidence that the hetero–homosexual axis—the dichotomy between the "homosexual" and the "heterosexual"—governed neither their thinking about sexuality nor their sexual practices. While fairies, trade, wolves, and punks all engaged in what we would define as homosexual behavior, they and the people who observed them were careful to draw distinctions between different modes of such behavior: between "feminine" and "masculine" behavior, between "passive" and "active" roles, between desire for sex with a man and desire for sex. The organization of the relationships between fairies or punks and their husbands, trade, wolves, and customers (sometimes overlapping groupings of men) serves to highlight the cultural presumption that the men in such relationships were defined by their *differences*—manifested in their different sexual roles or their differently gendered modes of self-presentation—rather than by their *similarities*—their shared "homosexuality." Even evidence of persistent and exclusive interest in sexual relations with another man did not necessarily put a man in the same category as his partner. The band musician's marriage to Loop-the-loop did not turn him into a fairy, after all, but into the husband of a fairy. While today we might regard all of them equally as "homosexuals," they recognized no "homosexual" category in which they all could be placed. In the very different sexual culture that predominated at the turn of the century, they understood themselves—and were regarded by others—as fundamentally different kinds of people. To classify their behavior and identities using the simple polarities of "homosexual" and "heterosexual" would be to misunderstand the complexity of their sexual system, the realities of their lived experience.

As this chapter's ethnography of sexual practices and identities demonstrates, men did not just use different categories to think about a sexuality that, despite appearances, was fundamentally the same as that of men today, for those different cultural categories governed and were manifest in men's everyday social practices. Even in the terms of the late-twentieth-century hetero–homosexual axis, in other words, it would be difficult to argue that the "normal" men who had sex with fairies were *really* homosexuals, for that would leave inexplicable their determined pursuit of women sexual partners. But neither could they plausibly be regarded as heterosexuals, for heterosexuals would have been incapable of responding sexually to another male. Nor were they bisexuals, for that would have required them to be attracted to both women as women and men as *men*. They were, rather, men who were attracted to womanlike men or interested in sexual activity defined not by the gender of their partner but by the kind of bodily pleasures that partner could provide.

Not all men in working-class New York had the same degree of interest in sex with a fairy (and many had none at all), just as not all men had the same degree of interest in sex with a dark-skinned woman or a middle-aged woman or a blue-eyed woman. But almost all workingmen—from the liquor authority agents who watched "fags" trying to pick up sailors at the Happy Hour Bar to the newsstand owner who watched sailors trying to pick up fairies at the Times Square Building—considered it unremarkable that a man might go with a fairy and as little revelatory about his sexual identity as his preference for one kind of woman over another. A man's occasional recourse to fairies did not prove he had homosexual desire for another man, as today's hetero–homosexual binarism would insist, but only that he was interested in the forms of phallic pleasure a fairy could provide as well as a female prostitute could. Men's identities and reputations simply did not depend on a sexuality defined by the anatomical sex of their sexual partners. Just as the abnormality of the fairy depended on his violation of gender conventions, rather than his homosexual practices alone, the normality of other men depended on their conformity to those conventions rather than on an eschewal of homosexual practices which those conventions did not require. Heterosexuality had not become a precondition of gender normativity in early-twentieth-century working-class culture. Men had to be many things in order to achieve the status of normal men, but being "heterosexual" was not one of them.

A CASE OF SEXUAL INVERSION, PROBABLY WITH COMPLETE SEXUAL ANÆSTHESIA.

By Austin Flint, M. D., LL. D.,
New York,

Professor Emeritus of Physiology in the Cornell University Medical College.

In 1894 I was the medical member of a commission appointed by the governor of the State of New York to investigate certain alleged abuses in the management of the Elmira Reformatory. During this investigation, which extended over several months, I had the opportunity to observe a number of sexual perverts such as are usually found in penal institutions for males only. It seemed to me that there was something in the physiognomy and manner of these unfortunates that was easily recognizable, especially when the abnormity was congenital.

In the following summer (1895), on making a visit to Bellevue Hospital, I noticed a young man who was being questioned by the house staff and who gave me the idea, by his manner and gestures, even at a considerable distance, that he was affected with sexual abnormity. I was informed that he had been arrested in the Central Park for masquerading in feminine dress and had been sent to the hospital for examination into his mental condition. When I saw him he was dressed as a boy; but in a hand bag belonging to him were found a woman's gown, corsets, a skirt, women's drawers, long stockings and garters, and women's shoes, in which clothing he was attired when arrested.

I was then visiting at what is now called the Psychopathic Ward, and I directed that he be sent there for examination. The general appearance of this individual, in his woman's dress, is shown in Fig. 1. The facial expression is certainly some-

Figure 4.1. In the late nineteenth century, doctors began to make the "sexual perverts" they encountered in New York's streets and prisons a subject of medical inquiry. (*From* New York Medical Journal, *December 2, 1911.)*

THE FORGING OF QUEER IDENTITIES AND THE EMERGENCE OF HETEROSEXUALITY IN MIDDLE-CLASS CULTURE

THE EFFEMINATE "FAIRY," PUT ON STAGE AT THE BOWERY RESORTS IN THE 1890s and at massive drag balls in the 1910s, '20s, and '30s, and highly visible on the streets of New York throughout this period, came to represent all homosexuals in the public mind. "Any mention of the subject [of sexual intermediacy]," one doctor observed in 1918, "usually conjures up visions of 'fairies'—the male prostitute of the streets, about whom is centered a whole jargon unknown to many sexologists."[1] The same point was made by the gay author of a 1933 novel, *Better Angel,* which offered one of the decade's few wholly sympathetic depictions of a gay character. The protagonist, a musician and teacher, "sensitive" but not otherwise "feminine," protests "the strange vindictiveness the normal man has toward our sort. We're all, to him, like the street corner 'fairy' of Times Square—rouged, lisping, mincing . . . [a] streetwalker."[2]

As his lament suggests, not all gay men in the prewar era thought of themselves as "flaming faggots" or "third-sexers," nor did all of them adopt the fairies' highly visible style. The fairy represented the primary role model available to men forming a gay identity, and many men found in it both a way of understanding themselves and a set of guidelines for organizing their self-presentation and relations with other men. But while the culture of the fairies provided remarkable support to men who rejected the gender persona and sexual roles prescribed to them by the dominant culture, it also alienated many others who were repelled by the fairy's flamboyant style and his loss of manly status. "By the time I was eighteen I began to think I was different from other boys," recalled one office clerk in the mid-1930s. "I had heard about fairies and I began to be alarmed. I would cringe at the thought that I was one of them, although there was always some man I desired. . . . Men who speak with an effeminate voice, who refer to each other as 'she' or who make feminine gestures, are repugnant to me."[3]

In a culture in which becoming a fairy meant assuming the status of a woman or even a prostitute, many men, like the clerk, simply refused to do so. Some of them restricted themselves to the role of "trade," becoming the nominally "normal" partners of "queers" (although this did not account for most such men). Many others simply "did it," without naming it, freed from having to label themselves by the certainty that, at least, they were not fairies. But many men aware of sexual desires for other men, like the clerk, struggled to forge an alternative identity and cultural stance, one that would distinguish them from fairies and "normal" men alike. Even their efforts, however, were profoundly shaped by the cultural presumption that sexual desire for men was inherently a feminine desire. That presumption made the identity they sought to construct a queer one indeed: unwilling to become virtual women, they sought to remain men who nonetheless loved other men.

The efforts of such men marked the growing differentiation and isolation of sexuality from gender in middle-class American culture. Whereas fairies' desire for men was thought to follow inevitably from their gender persona, queers maintained that their desire for men revealed only their "sexuality" (their "homosexuality"), a distinct domain of personality independent of gender. Their homosexuality, they argued, revealed nothing abnormal in their gender persona. The effort to forge a new kind of homosexual identity was predominantly a middle-class phenomenon, and the emergence of "homosexuals" in middle-class culture was inextricably linked to the emergence of "heterosexuals" in that culture as well. If many workingmen thought they demonstrated their sexual virility by playing the "man's part" in sexual encounters with either women or men, normal middle-class men increasingly believed that their virility depended on their exclusive sexual interest in women. Even as queer men began to define their difference from other men on the basis of their homosexuality, "normal" men began to define their difference from queers on the basis of their renunciation of any sentiments or behavior that might be marked as homosexual. Only when they did so did "normal men" become "heterosexual men." As Jonathan Katz has suggested, heterosexuality was an invention of the late nineteenth century.[4] The "heterosexual" and the "homosexual" emerged in tandem at the turn of the century as powerful new ways of conceptualizing human sexual practices.

FORGING A QUEER IDENTITY

By the 1910s and 1920s, men who identified themselves as different from other men primarily on the basis of their homosexual interest rather than their womanlike gender status usually called themselves "queer." "Queer wasn't derogatory," one man active in New York's gay world in the 1920s recalled. "It wasn't like kike or nigger. . . . It just meant you were different."[5] While some men regretted the supposed aberration in their character that *queer* denoted, others regarded their difference positively and took pleasure in being different from the norm. (As one associate of the writer Carl Van Vechten quipped, "Who wanted to be 'normal' and *boring?*")[6] Many queers considered *faggot* and *fairy* to be more derogatory terms, but they usually used them only to refer to men who openly carried themselves in an unmanly way. It was the effeminacy and flagrancy, not the homosexuality, of the "fairies," "faggots," or "queens" that earned them the disapprobation of queers.

While less visible than the fairies on the streets of New York, queer men constituted the majority of gay-identified men in New York in the early decades of the century. This chapter seeks to introduce some of the ways queer men saw themselves in relation to (and distinguished themselves from) the predominant images of male sexual abnormality in their culture, particularly the fairy, as well as the "normal" men of the working and middle classes, in ways that subsequent chapters will explore more fully.

Some men, like the clerk quoted above, refused from the beginning to accept the loss of dignity and self-respect that identifying themselves as fairies would entail. As one man who moved to New York from Germany in 1927 remembered, *fairy* and *queer* were the words he most commonly heard used for and by homosexual New Yorkers, but "I used 'homosexual' about myself." He found the ubiquity of fairy styles in New York's gay world deeply troubling: "I resented 'fairy' . . . and men speaking of another man as 'Mary' or 'she.' I resent that. I'm a *male.*"[7]

Jeb Alexander, another, more charitable young gay man, wrote in 1927:

[Effeminacy] is one thing that I do not like in a man. Of course I am not narrow-minded about it in any way. I realize that effeminacy was born with [some men] and sympathize with [their] handicap. I like gentleness, love it in a youth or man, but effeminacy repels me. Thank God I have been spared that. Homosexuality may be curse enough (though it has its wonderful compensations and noble joys) but it is a double curse when one has effeminate ways of walking, talking, or acting.[8]

But many other queer men embraced the style of the fairies before rejecting it: becoming a fairy was the first step many men took in the process of making sense of their apparent sexual and gender difference and reconstructing their image of themselves. A disproportionate number of the most flamboyant fairies, by most accounts, were young men; most of the men who attended the city's drag balls in women's clothes, for instance, were only in their twenties or early thirties.[9] Given the sexual culture of the Bowery, some of them believed that behaving like a fairy was the only way to be gay and to attract men. Others found in the style of the fairy a way to express dramatically the "feminine side" they had long suppressed. "Coming out flaming" by becoming a fairy allowed men to break decisively with their old ways of life and to reconstruct their self-image and social relations. Some men sustained the difficult project of being a fairy throughout their lives, but for many it represented only a transitional stage in the project of self-reconstruction. Many young fairies became more circumspect as they grew older. Some did so because once they entered the gay world they discovered there were other ways of being gay and more satisfying ways of negotiating their social and sexual relations. Others did so because they realized that their professional advancement depended on their giving up the styles associated with fairies, or at least restricting their expression to gay settings. One man recalled in the mid-1930s that for many years he had fought his attraction to other men and acceded to his family's wishes that he continue his father's work as a banker, but at age twenty-seven he broke with the conventional structures that bound him. He "went to the other extreme," as he put it, "designing dresses and associating constantly with obvious homosexuals. As a result, I was socially ostracized by my former friends and alienated from my family," but also "happier than I had ever been in my life." After about a year he moved to New York to begin yet another life, in which he continued to work as a designer and to have homosexual liaisons, but kept those liaisons hidden from his "conventional friends" and reestablished relations with his family. He had made a decisive break with his old life, but his interest in leading a less "messy" life eventually led him to become more discreet.[10]

In general, then, the style of the fairy was more likely to be adopted by young men and poorer men who had relatively little at stake in the straight middle-class world, where the loss of respect the fairy style entailed could be costly indeed. Most men who were more involved in that world sought to pass in it by adopting the style of queers, who typically displayed their homosexuality only in more private settings or by using signals that were less easily recognized by outsiders than those of the fairy. While they rejected the flamboyance of the fairy as a strategy for positioning themselves in relation to the dominant society, however, they, too, had to come to terms with the status assigned to them by the dominant culture as non-men or pseudo-women because of their desire for men.

The fact that the fairy constituted the dominant public image of the male homosexual during this period had ambiguous consequences for other gay men. On the one hand, the flamboyant stereotype diverted attention from other, more guarded men, and made it relatively easy for them to pass as straight. As a result of the straight world's ignorance of the existence of a hidden middle-class gay world—a world that did not fit the fairy stereotype—police harassment posed considerably less threat to that world than it did to the fairy resorts. As the writer and tattoo artist Samuel M. Steward recalled of the 1920s, '30s, and '40s, "Those of us who could maintain our secret lived under an extraordinary protective umbrella: the ignorance and naiveté of the American public. . . . We existed under the shadow and cover of such naiveté."[11] A man who interviewed numerous homosexuals in the late 1930s about their lives in the 1910s and 1920s reported that "everybody gave me the feeling that they were not haunted by the police, that there was a thriving subculture. [The public] didn't realize much was going on, [gay] things were not suspected [of being gay], and so people didn't get in trouble."[12]

Nonetheless, many queers not only refused to endure the indignities suffered by fairies, but resented the men who did, for they believed it was the flagrant behavior of the fairies on the streets that had given the public its negative impression of all homosexuals. "I don't object to being known as homosexual," insisted one man, an artist, in the mid-1930s, "but I detest the obvious, blatant, made-up boys whose public appearance and behavior provoke onerous criticism." With the fairy as the homosexual's representative, he added, "I don't begrudge normal people their feeling against homosexuals."[13]

If the image of the fairy was so powerful that it normally blinded people to the presence of other gay men, it also threatened to overwhelm the other images people had of men whom they discovered to be homosexual.[14] A young middle-class man living in Washington, D.C., Jeb Alexander often confessed his fear that casual observers might identify him as "a fairy." "Then, out on the streets, the old trouble," he wrote in his diary one day in 1924. "I was seized with that hideous feeling that every person I passed was inwardly mocking me, saying, There goes a fairy, or something worse. It started from the tiniest of things—a look, a gesture—in fact I don't know how it started." A year later he wrote: "Walking out of the store I saw a handsome boy and girl. . . . The girl looked at me calmly and impersonally, as she might have glanced at a lamp-post, and said audibly, 'That's a fairy. . . . ' If I weren't so sensitive. But I struggled and didn't suffer from it as I might."[15]

The resentment many gay men felt toward the fairies, though, may have resulted as much from the *affinity* they felt with them as from the *difference* in their styles. The fact that many men referred to "flaming faggots" or "swishes" as "obvious types" or "extreme homosexuals" suggests the extent to which they saw themselves as part of a continuum linking them to the public stereotype, a continuum on which they represented merely a "less extreme" form of the fairy.[16] The clerk who refused as a youth to become a fairy did so with such vehemence only because he recognized the possibility of such an identification. His comment "I would cringe at the thought that I was one of them, although there was always some man I desired" indicates he initially feared he *must* be one since this was the only way he knew how to interpret his desires. While most men could elaborate the ways in which they were *different* from the fairies, they needed to do so only because the similarities seemed so frighteningly apparent.

Indeed, the cultural system of gender emblematized by the fairy had enormous influence on the way even most queers understood themselves and structured their encounters. Most significantly, the belief that desire for a man was inherently a woman's desire led even many of those queers who regarded themselves as normally masculine in all other respects to regard their homosexual desire as a reflection of a feminine element in their character. In 1925, when F. O. Matthiessen, the noted Harvard literary historian and critic, was still a graduate student at Oxford, he wrote to his lover, the painter Russell Cheney, "We are complex—both of us—in that we are neither wholly man, woman, or child." In another letter he noted: "Just as there are energetic active women and sensitive delicate men, so also there are . . . men, like us, who appear to be masculine but have a female sex element."[17] Matthiessen's self-conception was thus different from that of many fairies, because he distinguished the sexual "element" from other elements of his gender persona and did not believe that the inversion of his sexual desire meant his entire gender character was inverted. Nonetheless, he did believe that his love for Cheney, as the sexological treatises written by Havelock Ellis explained and his grounding in his culture affirmed, must be a "female" love, even if he otherwise appeared to be masculine.

Other men rejected this reasoning altogether, however, and argued that their love for men was more *masculine* than love for women. Walt Whitman was heralded as a prophetic spokesman by many such men, who regarded Whitman's celebration of "the manly love of comrades" as an affirmation of the nobility of their love. As a young man living in Washington in the 1920s, Jeb Alexander frequently invoked Whitman in his diary and in his conversations with other gay men. When a former lover confessed to pursuing women as well as men, Alexander reacted negatively. "I don't like his interest in girls," he noted in his diary. "The 'manly love of comrades' is nobler and sweeter and ought to be sufficient." After reading the Calamus poems in Whitman's *Leaves of Grass,* he added: "What a noble, lovable man old Walt was! Often I yearn toward Walt as toward a father, look up at his picture, then close my eyes and feel him beside me, rugged and strong with his gentle hands caressing and comforting me." Whitman stood for a noneffeminate gentleness, a love for other men that was unquestionably masculine.[18]

From the perspective of outsiders, though, many of the gay men who rejected the "crude" effeminacy of the fairies would hardly have seemed "masculine" in their interests or demeanor, as some queers realized all too well. The boundaries between the styles of fairies and queers were permeable, not only because both groups sometimes engaged in similar forms of behavior but also because queer culture encouraged a style of dress and demeanor and an interest in the arts, decor, fashion, and manners that were often regarded by outsiders as effete, if not downright effeminate. Many queers liked to behave in ways not so different from those of the fairies when they were in secure settings—adopting feminine camp names, using feminine pronouns, and burlesquing gender conventions with a sharp and often sardonic camp wit. Although queers sometimes viewed the fairies' effeminacy as a sign of their constitutional makeup and of their biological difference from themselves—as "a handicap" that some men were "born with," as Jeb Alexander put it in 1927—they were equally capable of viewing it as merely a style that a man could adopt or discard at will. But almost all queers agreed with the artist quoted previously that it was the fairy's *public* display of the most "extreme forms" of gay cultural style that violated the social conventions of hetero-normativity and thus antagonized "normal" people.

Many middle-class queers blamed anti-gay hostility on the failure of fairies to abide by straight middle-class conventions of decorum in their dress and style. In their censure, they were not unlike the many German-American Jews who believed that the "foreignness" (or reluctance to assimilate) of the eastern European Orthodox Jews who immigrated to the United States in large numbers at the turn of the century had provoked American anti-Semitism, or the many middle-class African-American residents of Northern cities who blamed the resurgence of Northern white racism on the "backwardness" of the uneducated rural black Southerners who migrated north a few years later.[19] Some gay men drew the parallel explicitly, associating themselves with the "assimilated" middle-class members of other stigmatized groups. "As the cultured, distinguished, conservative Jew or Negro loathes and deplores his vulgar, socially unacceptable stereotype, plenty of whom unfortunately are all too visible," wrote one man who had begun to identify himself as queer in the 1930s, "so does their homosexual counterpart resent *his* caricature in the flaming faggot. . . . The general public [makes no distinction], and the one is penalized and ostracized for the grossness and excesses of the other."[20]

As this man's remarkable comment implies, the queers' antagonism toward the fairies was in large part a *class* antagonism. Not all queers were middle class, by any means, just as not all fairies were of the working class. But if the fairy as a cultural "type" was rooted in the working-class culture of the Bowery, the waterfront, and parts of Harlem, the queer was rooted in the middle-class culture of the Village and the prosperous sections of Harlem and Times Square, as the following chapters will show. Many working-class men defined themselves as queers and eschewed the style of the fairy because they found such styles inexpressive or objectionable or because they simply refused to suffer the indignities of being a fairy. But the cultural stance of the queer embodied the general middle-class preference for privacy, self-restraint, and lack of self-disclosure, and for many men this constituted part of its appeal. Similarly, one source of middle-class gay men's distaste for the fairy's style of self-presentation was that its very brashness marked it in their minds as lower class—and its display automatically preempted social advancement.

Given the heightened sensitivity that marginalization sometimes fosters, queers often had an acute perception of the degree to which gender and class status were interdependent and mutually constituted in their culture—of the degree to which gender styles were taken as markers of class status, and class styles were read in gendered terms. Forms of speech, dress, or demeanor that might be ridiculed as womanly, effeminate, or inappropriate to a "real" man in one cultural group might be valued as manly, worldly, or appropriate to a "cultured" (or "sensitive") man in another. This made it possible for men to try to recast gay cultural styles that might be read as signs of effeminacy as signs instead of upper-class sophistication.

Thus while many fairies created a place for themselves in working-class culture by constructing a highly effeminate persona, many other gay men created a place in middle-class culture by constructing a persona of highly mannered—and ambiguous—sophistication. One element of this persona was the pronounced Anglophilia (which, more precisely, was a reverence of the elegance and wit attributed to the English gentry) that became a significant tendency in portions of middle-class gay male culture.[21] While the fairy intended his style to mark him as a sexual invert, however, the queer intended his style to deflect such suspicions. The adoption of such styles did not entirely protect queers from ridicule for gender nonconformity, but it did allow them to recast, denigrate, and dismiss such ridicule as a sign of lower-class brutishness. "In no way [did] anything indicat[e] his intimate life was other than the so-called normal," one friend commented in 1938 about the manner of Charles Tomlinson Griffes, a noted modernist composer of the 1910s, whom he knew to be gay. He added immediately, though, "Of course [Griffes] was refined and had the manners of a man of cultural development," in an implicit acknowledgment of the relationship often presumed to exist between effete styles and effeminacy, between cultural development and sexual degeneracy. "In the army," Griffes's friend continued, at once acknowledging and seeking to dismiss such presumptions, "I have often seen [such manners] taken by those [men] of the lower classes as 'sissy.' Charles had none of this."[22]

Such styles gave some gay men a place in middle-class culture, but only so long as they exploited them to disguise their homosexuality. They needed to do so because as queers they suffered far more social hostility from middle-class men than fairies faced from working-class men. Griffes, for instance, felt no shame in his homosexuality but decided that as a struggling young composer he should hide it from his professional associates in the music world and from many of his friends as well. As a music student in Berlin from 1903 to 1907, he had learned of the German homosexual emancipation movement led by Magnus Hirschfeld and had read the work of gay intellectuals such as Edward Carpenter, André Gide, and Oscar Wilde. He came to believe strongly that his homosexuality was "natural" and that anti-homosexual prejudice was unjust. When he moved to the New York area in the 1910s he developed a small circle of gay friends. Nonetheless, he took care not to let most of his "normal" friends know that he was homosexual, even going so far as to use coded expressions and shift into German when recording gay-related experiences in his diary, to make it more difficult for the casual snoop to understand their significance. When he finally told one close friend that he was gay, the man later recalled, he "expressed a fear of losing me." While "Charles had the belief that he was in every way natural," the friend noted, his fear of rejection led him to keep his homosexuality a secret from all of their acquaintances.[23]

Griffes found more casual acceptance in the world of workingmen; he also found workingmen more open to his sexual advances. Queers as a group were more likely than fairies to seek relationships with queer men like themselves, in part because they were more likely to regard themselves as manly and thus to believe that the queers they desired were manly as well. (In practice, fairies often had relationships with other fairies, but they were *expected*—and often themselves expected—to seek "men.") Some queers, however, like fairies, were attracted to men they regarded as their opposites, highly masculine "normal" men whose sexual partners were usually women, a phenomenon the gay writer Glenway Wescott referred to in the 1930s as the "cult of the normal young man of the people, that is, of the lower classes."[24] As Wescott's wry observation suggests, gay men typically looked for such men in the working class, both because they regarded workingmen's class status as a sign of their masculinity and because they found that "normal" workingmen were more likely than "normal" middle-class men to respond favorably to their approaches.

Griffes, for one, was infatuated with "normal" workingmen, even though he also had relationships with other middle-class gay men. As he repeatedly noted, it was the masculinity of such men that attracted him, a masculinity constituted as much by emblems of their class status, such as work uniforms, as by their physical appearance. On one occasion he even discovered that "I was rather disappointed with [a train conductor] in civilian clothes" after meeting him at a lunch he had arranged; while he still had a "masculine ... demeanor," Griffes thought, "he doesn't look nearly as attractive *this way*." A bit taken aback by the experience, Griffes remarked: "One can see by that how certain clothes, a uniform matter."[25] But in the eyes of most middle-class gay men it was not just the workingman's clothes that made the man. The same gendering of class styles that made the cultivated manners of some middle-class men seem "sissy" made the "rough" styles of speech, demeanor, and physicality of some workingmen seem emblems of their manliness.

Like many other middle-class queer men, Griffes was attracted to workingmen not just because he thought they were masculine but because he found them more responsive to his advances than "normal" middle-class men would have been, as the extraordinary diary he kept reveals. Griffes spent several summers in the 1910s in New York City, where he shared an apartment with a singing teacher. During the school year he visited the city as frequently as his duties as a music teacher at a private school in nearby Tarrytown, New York, would permit. He usually occupied himself on his trips into the city by striking up conversations with the train conductors and trying to make dates with them;[26] but he was particularly interested in pursuing the Irish policemen he met in the city. In the years before electric traffic lights were installed, policemen were to be found at major intersections directing traffic, and Griffes took every opportunity to approach them, seeking to become familiar enough with them to be able to make a date. He tracked the shifting stations of his favorites and filled his diary with the record of his efforts to approach them.

"I ... spoke to 43-5 for a few minutes," Griffes reported one day in the spring of 1914, referring to the officer stationed at the corner of Forty-third Street and Fifth Avenue, whose name he did not yet know, "and was very pleased with it because he seemed very friendly again and said 'good-bye' so pleasantly when I left." He stopped by 43-5's corner twice again on a single day two weeks later, and was pleased that the man "smiled so pleasantly and friendly." He continued to pass by the man's station, often while on his way to visit other policemen he was cultivating, and four months later he reported that "43-5 greeted me of his own accord," a milestone in such pursuits. Two days later "43-5 said hello of his own accord [again] and talked a bit to me. Later I walked by him again and he very nicely said 'good-night,' with a warm smile. . . . Now he really recognizes me." The following year, Griffes reported passing the next milestone with another policeman: "I talked for about 20 minutes with the policeman stationed at 42-5 in the evenings," a man he had been approaching for weeks. "He remembers me this time and was so responsive I asked him to go to the theater with me." Not only did the man agree to do so, but he and Griffes finally exchanged names, a turning point of almost equal significance. Judging the responsiveness of policemen was, however, a delicate process, fraught with anxiety. "This morning I talked to 39-5," Griffes noted worriedly one day in April 1914, "and maybe went too far because I asked him to go to the theater with me some evening. He didn't say no, but he told me that next week would be better. I felt that I had made a fool of myself and left. Did I make an error? He is always so friendly, but maybe he's like that with everybody." Despite his embarrassment, Griffes talked to the man again several weeks later and was relieved to discover "he isn't angry, as I had been afraid of. However," he added, "I was probably too hasty about the theater matter."[27]

Griffes found a remarkable number of policemen and train conductors, most of them Irish, some of them married, to be responsive to his advances. A good number of them, like the train conductor who showed up for lunch in civilian clothes, were lured by his queer charms. He eventually developed a long-term relationship with a married Irish policeman, who frequently visited Griffes at the West Forty-sixth Street apartment the composer maintained in the summer and occasionally even invited Griffes out to his home in Corona, Queens, to dine with his family. After one such dinner, Griffes commented that the wife "was very cordial and urged me to come out again." "He is a very dear man," Griffes once commented of his companion; "it was a perfectly beautiful time with [him] from beginning to end."[28]

Griffes was not the only gay man interested in policemen, nor was he the only one to succeed in pursuing them. On one occasion in the summer of 1916 he talked with his Corona companion about "the *many* invitations he gets that he doesn't accept and why he always accepted mine." Griffes also discussed the matter with other gay men who shared his attraction to policemen and sometimes passed on tips about particularly receptive ones. "F. told me about Policeman M. whom I then went to see on his beat at 6 o'clock," Griffes noted Thanksgiving week in 1914. "He seemed very responsive and open to the idea [*entgegendkommend und bereit*]." He was also, apparently, familiar with the rituals of courtship: "I was pleased with how he at once followed and understood." The next year, Griffes talked with another man, who claimed to have "had the greatest luck with policemen and knows, in New York alone, 53 in a homosexual way." Based on his more limited experience with the force, Griffes found the man's claim astonishing but plausible: "He appears to be *able* to do what I *want* to do."[29] The man's boast hardly provides definitive evidence of his success, but it does indicate that such pursuits were part of the folklore—and everyday practices—of more than one gay man.

Charles Griffes, Ralph Werther, and the newspapermen reporting on the Bowery resorts were not the only observers to remark that straight working-class men, including some of New York's finest, were more likely than straight middle-class men to tolerate gay men and respond to their advances. After interviewing thousands of men in the 1930s and 1940s, Alfred Kinsey was surprised to reach a similar conclusion. Men at the highest and lowest social strata, he found, were more likely than those in the middle classes to tolerate other men's homosexual activity. Even those men in the lower-status group who did not engage in homosexual activity themselves rarely tried to prevent other men from doing so. Kinsey attributed the tolerance of better educated men to the greater sophistication about human nature he also attributed to them, but was less sure how to explain the lower-status group's tolerance, except to note that many of them accepted homosexuality "simply as one more form of sex," which they, as a group, tended to consider simply a "natural" and therefore acceptable human need, not to be frustrated by moral injunctions.[30]

Even middle-class opinion was divided on the subject of homosexuality: while "many broad-minded, intelligent professional men and laymen" became "utterly disgusted . . . at [its] very mention," as one psychiatrist reported in 1913,[31] many others took little note of the phenomenon, and homosexuality rarely became a major public issue or special target of scrutiny before the 1930s (as chapter 12 will show). Nonetheless, it is clear that by the turn of the century, middle-class men as a group were more hostile and anxious about homosexuality than workingmen were.

Why should this have been the case? Why were most "normal" middle-class men less willing to respond to the advances of Griffes and other gay men than many workingmen were? What was the source of middle-class men's greater hostility toward men who violated the social conventions governing gender style and who expressed sexual desire for men? The relative hostility of middle-class men needs to be explained as much as the relative tolerance of working-class men, since neither is an "obvious" response. Addressing such questions requires an examination of the broader context of the changes in masculinity and sexuality in middle-class culture at the turn of the century.

THE EMERGENCE OF HETEROSEXUALITY IN MIDDLE-CLASS CULTURE

The growing antipathy of middle-class men toward both fairies and queers at the turn of the century was closely tied to their growing concern that the gender arrangements of their culture were in crisis. Their hostility was part of their response to the growing threats they perceived to their very status and prerogatives as men. On every front, it seemed, the social patterns and cultural expectations that had formed middle-class men's sense of themselves as men were being challenged or undermined.

Changes in the social organization and meaning of work were particularly significant. Men's participation in what they regarded as the male sphere of productive work, their ability to support families on the basis of that work, and, above all, their skill as entrepreneurs and their independence from other men had long been critical to their sense of themselves both as men and as members of the middle class. But the reorganization and centralization of the American economy in the late nineteenth century with the rise of large corporations transformed the character and meaning of the work performed by many middle-class men. Increasing numbers of men lost their economic independence as they became the salaried employees of other men; the number of salaried, nonpropertied workers grew eight times between 1870 and 1910.

In the new order, as the historian Anthony Rotundo puts it, "every businessman had to submit [to another man]—the successful one was the man who submitted to the fewest others." The great majority of middle-level employees working in the new corporate bureaucracies had little prospect of significant advancement, and much of the work they performed was fragmented and sedentary. "More important," as the historian Jackson Lears notes, "it isolated them from the hard, substantial reality of things."[32] More and more women began working at such firms as well, and although they took on different, and usually subordinate, tasks, their very presence in offices, as Rotundo observes, seemed to feminize the culture of the corporate workplace and to diminish its status as a masculine domain.

Many men believed that women were threatening the sanctity of other male domains as well and were trying to take control of the nation's culture. The women's suffrage campaign seemed the most direct challenge, for many men interpreted women's demand for the vote as a renunciation of men's prerogative to represent the women in their families in the (male) public sphere. But they regarded women's challenge to extend far beyond that single demand. As women came to dominate the ranks of elementary and secondary school teachers, they seemed to have eliminated the role of men in the socialization of youth and threatened to produce a generation of sissified boys. Even more strikingly, women seemed to be trying to control the lives of adult men as well. The Woman's Christian Temperance Union, founded in 1874, represented the best-known attempt; it had identified alcohol as a male vice and campaigned to shut down the saloons and private clubs where men gathered to socialize and drink. Other women's groups waged well-organized campaigns against men's rights to manly entertainments in the nation's boxing rings and red-light districts. On every front, women seemed to be breaching the division between the sexes' proper spheres and to be claiming or challenging the prerogatives of men.[*]

Threats to the masculinity of middle-class men came from other men as well as from women. As the "captains of industry" were reducing these men's independence, workingmen—who, increasingly, were immigrants who enacted their manliness in sometimes foreign ways—also seemed to be bringing middle-class men's masculinity into question. If middle-class men exerted power over the lives of workingmen (and claimed a degree of superiority) because they worked with their heads, not their hands, they recognized, as well, that the very physicality of workingmen's labor afforded them a seemingly elemental basis for establishing their manliness. Working-class men and boys regularly challenged the authority of middle-class men by verbally questioning the manliness of middle-class supervisors or physically attacking middle-class boys. As Charles Griffes's friend recalled, he had "often seen [middle-class cultivation] taken by those [men] of the lower classes as 'sissy.'"[33] The increasingly militant labor movement, the growing power of immigrant voters in urban politics, and the relatively high birthrate of certain immigrant groups established a worrisome context for such personal affronts and in themselves constituted direct challenges to the authority of Anglo-American men as a self-conceived class, race, and gender.

As middle-class men's anxieties about their manliness intensified, a

---

[*]I do not mean to sketch the lines of debate too starkly. Many middle-class men supported temperance as a way to control the immigrant working class, and many working-class organizers supported it as well because they thought the enticements of the saloon served to divert men from the workers' struggle. Nonetheless, many middle-class men regarded women's leadership of the campaign with suspicion and were opposed to its extension to middle-class clubs.

preoccupation with threats to manhood and with proving one's manhood became central to the rhetoric of national purpose. Theodore Roosevelt epitomized this tendency; the quest for manhood became the central metaphorical image in his speeches, which cast the struggle for national revitalization and international supremacy as a struggle for manhood itself. "If we . . . shrink from the hard contests where men must win at hazard of their lives," he declared in one famous 1899 address, "then the bolder and stronger peoples will pass us by, and will win for themselves the domination of the world. Let us therefore . . . [resolve] to do our duty well and manfully."[34] Roosevelt's effort to frame the national challenge as a manly one served both to mobilize male citizens by using some of the era's most effective and resonant rhetoric and to reinforce the claim that the public sphere of civic action was a distinctly male sphere.

In a similar vein, politicians, businessmen, educators, and sportsmen alike protested the dangers of "overcivilization" to American manhood and thus to American culture, in a not very oblique reference to the dangers of women's civilizing influence and the effeminization of men. The Spanish-American War of 1898 and the spirit of militarism it engendered were widely celebrated as the savior of American manhood. "The greatest danger that a long period of profound peace offers to a nation," one man wrote in the wake of "the short and glorious little war," was that it encouraged "effeminate tendencies in young men . . . especially in a country where the advancement of civilized methods of living has reached the point now touched by it in the United States."[35]

The growing concern about the danger of the overcivilization and feminization of American men had manifold practical ramifications for men's everyday lives—and for their attitude toward fairies and queers. In response to the threat they thought women posed to the manliness of the nation's boys, men organized a host of groups designed to restore the role of men in the socialization of youth: the Knights of King Arthur, the Sons of Daniel Boone, and, in 1912, the Boy Scouts of America. As work began to fail to confirm men's sense of themselves as manly, growing numbers of them turned to "strenuous recreation, spectator sports, adventure novels, and a growing cult of the wilderness" as a means of proving their manhood.[36] Theodore Roosevelt was the most famous advocate of the "strenuous life" of muscularity, rough sports, prizefighting, and hunting as an antidote to the overcivilization of American men, but the cause was taken up in newspapers, boys' clubs, and backyard lots throughout the nation. Rough sports became popular on college campuses, endorsed by educators and students alike as the optimal way to build character. Prizefighters, cowboys, soldiers, and sailors became popular heroes, heralded as paragons of virility. "Leave the close air of the office, the library, or the club and go out into the streets and the highway," insisted one writer in 1897. "Consult the teamster, the farmer, . . . or the drover. . . . From his loins, and not from those of the dilettante, will spring the man of the future."[37]

The glorification of the prizefighter and the workingman bespoke the ambivalence of middle-class men about their own gender status, for it suggested that they, too, regarded such men as more manly than themselves—more physical, less civilized, less effeminate. It also suggests that when middle-class gay men celebrated such workingmen as paragons of masculinity, they only followed the lead of other men of their class.

As the boundaries between men's and women's spheres seemed to blur, many men also tried to reinforce those boundaries by reconstructing their bodies in ways that would heighten their physical differences from women. What the historian Elliot Gorn has called a "cult of muscularity" took root in turn-of-the-century middle-class culture. Bodybuilding and prizefighting became immensely popular activities: one let boys and men develop their muscles, while the other let them express their admiration for men who literally embodied the new manly ideal of muscularity. Professional bodybuilders such as Eugene Sandow, who in the 1890s became the first professional to pose in the nude rather than in revealing classical costume, also became objects of adulation by middle-class men and boys.[38] Boys and young men displayed a growing concern about the development of their muscles as if in reaction to the threats posed by a muscular working class and loss of power elsewhere in their lives. Just as important, building manly bodies and focusing on the physical basis of manliness allowed men to emphasize their difference from women at a time when women seemed to be insisting on the similarity of the sexes. Indeed, descriptions of manly character in turn-of-the-century popular men's fiction increasingly focused on the physical attributes of manliness, as if men sought to root their difference from women in the supposedly immutable differences of the body at a time when other kinds of difference no longer seemed so certain.[39]

The attack on women's influence on American culture led to an attack on men who seemed to have accepted that influence by becoming "over-civilized," and men who did not do their part to uphold the manly ideal were subject to growing ridicule. Earlier in the nineteenth century, men had tended to constitute themselves as men by distinguishing themselves from boys: to become a man was to assume the responsibilities and maturity of an adult. To call someone a "boy"—as whites regularly addressed African-American men—was an insult. But in the late nineteenth century, middle-class men began to define themselves more centrally on the basis of their difference from women. As the historian John Higham has noted, *sissy, pussy-foot,* and other gender-based terms of derision became increasingly prominent in late-nineteenth-century

American culture, as men began to define themselves in opposition to all that was "soft" and womanlike.[40]

The scorn heaped on overcivilized men established the context for the emergence of the fairy as the primary pejorative category against which male normativity was measured. The fairy was not invented as a cultural type by fin de siècle male angst, but that angst—as well as the growth of the gay subculture—made the fairy a much more potent cultural figure, and one so prominent that it could serve to mark the boundaries of acceptable male behavior. As Rotundo has noted, the sexual implications of "Miss Nancy," "she-men," and other epithets became more pronounced around the turn of the century.[41] The frequency of such epithets suggests the degree to which men had come to define themselves in opposition to the fairy as well as to the woman. It also indicates the virulence with which they policed the gender performances of other men who, like the fairy, seemed to subvert the new masculine ideal.

The meanings ascribed to the figure of the fairy were, however, more complex than this. The fairy became one of the most prominent and volatile signs of the fragility of the gender order, at once a source of reassurance to other men and the repository of their deepest fears. On the one hand, men could use their difference from the fairy to reassure themselves of their own masculinity. The spectacle of the Bowery fairies became popular in the closing years of the century in part because the very extremity of the fairy's violation of gender conventions served to confirm the relative "normality" of other men.

But the fairy also provoked a high degree of anxiety and scorn among middle-class men because he embodied the very things middle-class men most feared about their gender status. His effeminacy represented in extreme form the loss of manhood middle-class men most feared in themselves, and his style seemed to undermine their efforts to shore up their manly status. His womanlike manner challenged the supposed immutability of gender differences by demonstrating that anatomical males did not inevitably become men and were not inevitably different from women. The fairy's feminization of his body seemed to ridicule and highlight the artificiality of the efforts of other men to masculinize theirs. Being called a fairy became a serious threat to middle-class men precisely because the boundaries between the she-man and the middle-class man seemed so permeable, despite men's best efforts to develop manly bodies and cultural styles.

The overtness of the fairy's sexual interest in men was even more unsettling, because it raised the possibility of a sexual component in other men's interactions. Once that possibility was raised, the very celebration of male bodies and manly sociability initially precipitated by the masculinity crisis required a new policing of male intimacy and exclusion of sexual desire for other men. Claiming that the fairy was different from normal men allowed normal men to claim that the fairy alone experienced sexual desire for men and thus to preclude the possibility that the normal man's gaze at the working-class male body had a sexual component. But the very existence of the fairy made manifest and drew attention to the potential sexual meaning of that gaze. To put this in the terms usefully suggested by Eve Sedgwick, middle-class men subscribed to both minoritizing and universalizing conceptions of gender inversion and homosexuality.[42] They simultaneously regarded each condition, that is, as safely contained in particular groups of people (a minority) but also as already present in, or capable of rapidly infecting, an entire population (and thus having a universalizing propensity).

Thus the fairy served to contain the threat of gender nonconformity and to free other men from any taint of it, for he alone was a real invert, but any man risked being stigmatized as a fairy if he displayed any of the signs of inversion. Similarly, the personality of the fairy or the queer served to contain the threat of homosexuality—by suggesting that it was limited to a deviant minority of men—but it also made it possible to conceive of men's solidarity as having a sexual component. Given the crisis in middle-class masculinity, many middle-class men felt compelled to insist—in a way that many working-class men did not—that there was no sexual element in their relations with other men.

Bernarr Macfadden, advocate of physical culture and publisher of bodybuilding magazines treasured by straight and gay men alike, could barely contain his loathing of the men who sexualized and perverted the male gaze at male bodies. His insistence that there could be no relationship between the healthy youngster's adoration of a barely clad exemplar of manly muscularity and the depraved sexual desires of a degenerate—and the fear that some might think there were a relationship—hovered behind his 1904 denunciation of "painted, perfumed, . . . mincing youths . . . ogling every man that passes." He praised the men who attacked such youths, but the very severity of his response to them betrayed his fear that he might somehow be identified with them. "There is nothing nasty, . . . vulgar, . . . [or] immodest in the nude," he regularly insisted in the pages of *Physical Culture,* a magazine he published that was full of male nudes. "The nastiness exists in the minds of those who view it, and those who possess such vulgar minds are the enemies of everything clean, wholesome, and elevating." The overt sexual interest of the fairy in men made the possibility that normal men's admiration of manly bodies might have a sexual component inescapable. It required men whose manliness was already suspect to assert their exclusive sexual interest in women in order to show they were not queer.[43]

The insistence on exclusive heterosexuality emerged in part, then, in response to the crisis in middle-class masculinity precipitated by the manly comportment of working-class men and the subversion of manly ideals and sexualization of male social relations by the fairy. But heterosexuality became even more important to middle-class men because it provided them with a new, more positive way to demonstrate their manhood. Sexual style had long been a crucial aspect of gender style; both sexual aggressiveness and sexual self-control—as well as the ability to propagate and support children—had served as markers of manliness among different groups of men. But by the late nineteenth century, sexual personality—or "sexuality"—had emerged as a distinct domain of personhood and an independent basis for the assertion of manliness. Middle-class men increasingly conceived of their sexuality—their heterosexuality, or exclusive desire for women—as one of the hallmarks of a real man. It was as if they had decided that no matter how much their gender comportment might be challenged as unmanly, they were normal men because they were heterosexual.

The growing heterosexual and heterosocial imperatives were, in any case, evident throughout middle-class culture in the first third of the century. In the 1910s and 1920s, as numerous historians have shown, older patterns of gender segregation among American youth (and their elders) gave way to a new emphasis on heterosocial—and often dyadic—relations. Single-sex (or homosocial) gave way to mixed-sex (or heterosocial) socializing, as the number of commercial amusements where young men and women could gather proliferated: amusement parks, movie theaters, cabarets, cafés, late-night restaurants, dance halls, and the like. The dance craze of the 1910s, which encouraged men and women to hold each other and move their bodies in more or less salacious ways, was one of the great markers of the "new freedom in morals and manners." The culture of the speakeasies in the Prohibition era of the 1920s, as we shall see, encouraged an even more casual atmosphere for mixed-sex socializing. Numerous observers suggested that unchaperoned dating had become a significant part of young people's lives in the 1910s and 1920s, and had, to some extent, replaced the single-sex group. The change affected young married men and women as well as young singles. Marriage manuals of the 1910s and 1920s, according to the historian Christina Simmons, asserted the need for men to develop "companionate marriages" to make marriage more attractive and satisfying to women. While the ability to support a family had been central to middle-class men's gender and class identities since the formation of the American middle class in the nineteenth century, the families of the early twentieth century put new emphasis on both the emotional intimacy and sexual satisfaction of husband and wife.[44]

The growing insistence on heterosociability and stigmatization of single-sex institutions was a response to women's autonomy as much as to peculiarly male anxieties, and it had dramatic effects on the lives of middle-class women. A generation of women in the late nineteenth century had forsworn marriage in order to pursue careers and work for social reform. Many women activists remained devoted to women and unmarried to men; as many as 50 percent of the graduates of some women's colleges in the late nineteenth century never married. Heterosexual marriage and motherhood, as constituted in their society, would have left them little opportunity to pursue their chosen work. But in the 1920s the age of first marriage dropped, the percentage of women who married increased, and many women left autonomous women's organizations to join the dominant (and male-dominated) political and professional organizations of their day.

The shifting patterns of women's sociability and women's political choices had many sources, as feminist historians such as Nancy Cott have shown. Many "new women" of the 1920s embraced the new possibilities of sexual subjectivity and joined in the attack on the older generation of women as "sexless spinsters" and prudes; many professional women thought that in order to advance women's cause it was important to work in the dominant professional organizations of their day, rather than in separate and unequal women's organizations. But the increasing stigmatization of women who lived without men undermined the middle-class women's culture that had sustained a generation of challenges to the male-dominated professions and social order. Given its effects on the women's movement, the sexual revolution of the 1910s and 1920s could equally be viewed as a heterosexual counterrevolution.[45]

Although there were increasing opportunities for men and women to socialize across gender lines in both middle- and working-class culture, heterosexuality became more important to middle-class than to working-class men. The establishment of heterosexuality as a precondition of male normativity in middle-class culture, as well as its continued absence in much of working-class culture, is strongly suggested by one of Kinsey's most striking—if virtually unnoticed—findings. His analysis of the way men's participation in homosexual activity varied along class lines in the 1910s, '20s, and '30s offers startling confirmation of the observation made by Griffes, Werther, and numerous other gay men of the era that working-men were more willing than middle-class men to engage in sexual practices with other men. Although Kinsey's methods did not produce accurate estimates of the aggregate frequency of sexual practices, they probably did produce a roughly accurate gauge of the differences in sexual patterns among different social groups. Common day laborers, he reported, engaged in more homosexual activity than any other group of men, followed by semi-skilled workers and men in low-status white-collar jobs, such as clerks in banks, offices, and stores, secretaries, and small entrepreneurs. The men he grouped together as having higher-status white-collar jobs, ranging from clergymen, actors, artists, and musicians to bank officials and owners of large stores, were less likely to engage in homosexual activity. Men in the professions, such as college teachers, physicians, and lawyers, were the least likely of all men to do so.[46]

Significantly, the class variations in the rate of participation in homosexual activity were consistent with a more general class pattern. Common laborers and semi-skilled workers engaged in the most nonmarital *heterosexual* intercourse as well as in the most homosexual, and professionals in the least. Several generations of middle-class men had considered sexual self-control to be crucial to their image as middle-class gentlemen and a means of distinguishing themselves from lower-class men. Kinsey's findings suggest that, as numerous historians have argued, middle-class men were more observant of the moral injunctions against nonmarital sexual behavior propagated by their class than working-class men were.[47]

But the reluctance of middle-class men to engage in sexual relations with other men also resulted, I would suggest, from their growing belief that anyone who engaged in homosexual activity was implicated as "being" a homosexual. It was easier for workingmen to engage in such activity because the conventions of their sexual culture tended to categorize only one of the men involved as "queer." This interpretation is supported by two of Kinsey's other findings, which he reported without commentary. First, while men at the lowest educational and class levels were more likely than other men to engage in homosexual activity throughout their lives, even after marriage, they were also *less likely* than men at higher class levels to be *exclusively* homosexual in their behavior. Second, they were also more likely to restrict the role they played in homosexual relations. While homosexually active middle-class men were almost equally likely to play either the active or passive role in fellation, a much higher percentage of lower-status men restricted their participation to the "masculine" role.[48] Common laborers, in other words, found it easier than middle-class men to alternate between sexual relations with men and relations with women (apparently without feeling that one precluded the other), so long as they played the "man's part" with both of them. Middle-class men, on the other hand, were more likely to organize their sexual practices—and to identify themselves—as "homosexuals," who engaged in a variety of sexual relations with men exclusively, or "heterosexuals," who avoided sexual encounters of any sort with men.

Two dramatic changes in middle-class culture between the mid-nineteenth century and the early twentieth century show that the division of the sexual world into heterosexuals and homosexuals was a new development: the decline of romantic friendships between men as they began to be stigmatized as homosexual and the emergence of the hetero–homosexual binarism in middle-class medical discourse.

The growing insistence in middle-class culture that, to be considered normal, men eschew any homosexual contact is particularly evident in the increased scrutiny middle-class men gave male friendships. As a number of historians have recently shown, young men in the first two-thirds of the nineteenth century frequently slept together and felt free to express their passionate love for each other. "Warmth [sometimes] turned into tender attachment, and closeness became romance," writes Anthony Rotundo, who has studied the diaries of dozens of nineteenth-century middle-class men. "These ardent relationships were common" and "socially accept-able." Devoted male friends opened letters to each other with greetings like "Lovely Boy" and "Dearly Beloved"; they kissed and caressed one another; and, as in the case of Joshua Stead and the bachelor lawyer Abraham Lincoln, they sometimes shared the same bed for years. Some men explicitly commented that they felt the same sort of love for both men and women. "All I know," wrote one man quoted by Rotundo, "is that there are three persons in this world whom I have loved, and those are, Julia, John, and Anthony. Dear, beloved trio." It was only in the late nineteenth century that such love for other men became suspect, as men began to worry that it contained an unwholesome, distinctly homosexual element.[49]

As Rotundo, Donald Yacovone, and other historians have argued, the men involved in such same-sex relationships should not retrospec-tively be classified as homosexual, since no concept of the homosexual existed in their culture and they did not organize their emotional lives *as* homosexuals; many of them were also on intimate terms with women and went on to marry. Nonetheless, the same historians persist in calling such men heterosexual, as if that concept *did* exist in the early nineteenth century.[50] In doing so they mistake the fact that men who passionately and physically expressed their love for other men were considered *normal* for their having been considered *heterosexual,* as if it were not the very inconsistency of their emotional lives with contemporary models of heterosexuality that made them seem curious to historians in the first place. If homosexuality did not exist in the early nineteenth century, then neither did heterosexuality, for each cate-gory depends for its existence on the other. The very capacity of men to shift between male and female love objects demonstrates that a differ-ent sexual regime governed their emotions. "Normal" men only became "heterosexual" men in the late nineteenth century, when they began to make their "normalcy" contingent on their renunciation of such intimacies with men. They became heterosexuals, that is, only when they defined themselves and organized their affective and physical relations to exclude any sentiments or behavior that might be marked as homosexual.

A second sign of the emergence of heterosexuality in middle-class culture at the turn of the century was its appearance in middle-class medical discourse. Doctors approached the issue of sexual inversion as members of a profession still struggling to secure a measure of cultural authority and power, and one that often sought to do so by claiming special expertise in the management of "problems" that had been defined by middle-class men as a whole, including the problem of gender. They also approached the issue as members of a professional class whose manliness seemed increasingly in question and for whom such problems were palpable. Although they claimed a unique, dispassionate perspective on the problem of sexual inversion and their thought had a distinct disciplinary cast, they shared the basic presumptions and anxieties of their gender and class.

Most of the doctors writing about inversion in the late nineteenth and early twentieth centuries adhered to the popular conceptualization of fairies as "inverts" whose desire for people of the—apparent—same sex was simply one feature of a more thoroughgoing gender inversion (see chapter 2). Their manner of explaining the character of "she-men" also adhered to the dominant popular conceptions of sex and gender as well as the dominant currents of scientific thought. Scientific writers regularly sought to reinforce existing social arrangements of race, class, and gender by asserting their biological determination and consequent inevitability. As the historians Carroll Smith-Rosenberg and Charles Rosenberg have argued, "Would-be scientific arguments were used in the rationalization and legitimization of almost every aspect of Victorian life, with particular vehemence in those areas in which social change implied stress in existing social arrangements."[51] It was thus incumbent upon such writers to search for a gender-based biological explanation that would account for the behavior of "inverts" in a way that confirmed the naturalness and consequent immutability of the gender arrangements their unmanly or unwomanly behavior threatened to call into question. Like legions of young bodybuilders, in other words, they sought to defend a particular social arrangement of gender by investing it with the timeless authority of the body itself. Thus one widely accepted medical theory argued that men who desired men simply were not the sex they first appeared to be, but were hermaphrodites, incorporating biological elements of both sexes.[52]

Women who challenged the sanctity of the male sphere were subject to particular scorn by physicians, who stigmatized them as biological misfits and inverts. In a direct attack on women who sought to curtail male sexual prerogatives, one doctor characterized them in 1916 as lesbian predators. "The androphobia [fear and hatred of men], so to speak, of the

deeply ingrained sex invert has led to her leadership in social purity movements and a failure to recognize inversion," he warned. "Such inverts see
no harm in [the] seduction of young girls while dilating on the impurity of
even marital coitus."[53] The same doctor's comments on the work of
another doctor suggest how frequently a link between sexual inversion
and women's activism was proposed. "As might be expected," he wrote in
1914, "Claiborne does not finish his paper [nominally on unusual hair
growth in women] without touching upon the influence of defective sexuality in women upon political questions. While, of course, he does not
think every suffragist an invert, yet he does believe that the very fact that
women in general of today are more and more deeply invading man's
sphere is indicative of a certain impelling force within them."[54] Other doctors were less restrained in proposing a literally organic relationship
between the women's movement and lesbianism. Dr. William Lee Howard
warned in 1900 that

> the female possessed of masculine ideas of independence; the viragint
> who would sit in the public highways and lift up her pseudo-virile
> voice, proclaiming her sole right to decide questions of war or religion,
> or the value of celibacy and the curse of women's impurity, and that
> disgusting anti-social being, the female sexual pervert, are simply dif-
> ferent degrees of the same class—degenerates.

By this account, the woman who "invaded man's sphere" was likely to
want the vote, have excessive, malelike body hair, smoke cigars, be able
to whistle, and take female lovers.[55]

Doctors' analysis of the character of men involved in same-sex relations
was somewhat more complex. They sought to explain—and at once stigmatize and contain—the unmanly behavior of some men by pointing to
biological defects that made those men literally less than men. They were
less sure how to deal with manly men who had sex with other men, however. While many of them reproduced the popular distinction between
fairies and trade, they also displayed a distinctly middle-class hostility
toward men in the trade category. Many doctors writing in the late nineteenth and early twentieth centuries regarded the fairy as an "intermediate
sex" between men and women, but they also believed that many men
engaged in homosexual activity without being inverts. A "fairy," they
thought, like a woman, was "naturally" attracted to his opposite, a conventionally masculine "normal" man, and weak-willed "normal" men
were capable of responding to his advances. They frequently distinguished
the two participants in such a relationship as "inverts" (who, as feminine
in character, were naturally attracted to men) and "perverts" (who, as conventionally masculine men, perverted their normal sexual drive when they

responded to the advances of someone who appeared anatomically to be another man, even if that person was actually an invert). While working-class sexual ideology tended to regard men who were trade neutrally, middle-class physicians were more likely to condemn the fairy's masculine partner as morally—if not physiologically—deficient, as the very term *pervert* implies.

In 1921, for instance, Dr. Perry Lichtenstein drew such distinctions in a report based on his study of hundreds of men segregated in the homosexual ward of the New York City penitentiary, where he worked as a physician. The fairies he dealt with there were "freak[s] of nature who in every way attempt to imitate woman," he explained. "They take feminine names, use perfume and dainty stationery which frequently is scented, and in many instances wear women's apparel." Lichtenstein implied that the fairies did not solicit sex with other fairies, but instead sought "normal" men, who responded to their advances not because of congenital need but because of willful perversity. He demeaned the effeminate fairies as "degenerates," but also evinced a certain proprietary sympathy for them, urging that treatment, rather than punishment, be attempted, in an effort to cure them of their malady, over which they surely had no control. But he showed no mercy at all toward the "normal" men with whom the fairies had sex and made no effort to argue that the medical profession should take over their management from the prisons: "Let us punish most severely the man who yields to the advances of these individuals," he insisted, "for such as he are worse than the pervert [the men most doctors called an 'invert'] and deserve no sympathy."[56]

The commentaries written by other doctors point to the emergence of an even more striking class difference in conceptions of male–male sexual relations. A growing number of doctors began to conceive of the inverts' sexual partners not just as morally lax but as tainted by homosexual desire. In 1913, for instance, A. A. Brill, the chief of the Clinic of Psychiatry at Columbia University, argued that homosexuality was not a sign of somatic or psychic hermaphroditism or bisexualism. While "in a great many cases" the invert "would feel like a woman and look for the man," he conceded, this did not "indicate the general character of inversion," which, he argued, had to account for *any* man who had sex with another man. In sharp contrast to popular working-class thought, he explicitly classified the "masculine" men who had sex with transvestite prostitutes and other effeminate men as "homosexuals," who "retain their virility and look for feminine psychic features in their sexual object." Citing Freud, he even classed men who "resorted to homosexuality [only] under certain conditions," such as prisoners with no access to women, as "occasional inverts" who were a distinct class of men, different from normal men, because of their capacity "to obtain sexual gratification from a person of the same sex."[57] Marking a sharp break with both working-class and earlier middle-class thought, Brill's grouping of fairies and trade together in the single category of the homosexual was predicated on the emerging notion that male normality depended not on a man's masculine comportment but on his exclusive heterosexuality. For all its allusions to psychological complexity, Brill's psychoanalytic article ignored the complex symbolic system of power and imaginary gender that governed the meaning of sexual penetration and the classification of sexual actors in working-class culture. It made the sex of the body with whom a man had sex the arbiter of his heterosexual normality or homosexual abnormality.

Freud was a key figure in the reconceptualization of male sexual actors. In the first of his *Three Essays on the Theory of Sexuality* (1905), he introduced the concepts of sexual aim and object. *Sexual aim,* in his view, referred to a person's preferred mode of sexual behavior, such as genital or oral sex, or passive or active roles. *Sexual object* referred to the object of sexual desire; children, animals, and persons of the same sex were "deviations in respect of the sexual object" rather than of sexual aim. Many earlier theories had not focused on sexual object or had viewed it as subordinate to sexual aim in the classification of men's sexuality. They maintained that a man who wished to play an inverted, passive sexual role would logically seek a male to play the active role, whereas a man who wished to play the active role was not "inverted" even if his passive partner were male instead of female. But in Freud's scheme, sexual object existed independently of sexual aim and became even more significant to sexual classification. "The most complete mental masculinity," he argued, "can be combined with male inversion [same-sex desire]."[58]

Freud was not the only theorist to distinguish homosexual desire from gender inversion. His sometime antagonist, the prominent British sexologist Havelock Ellis, also argued that sexual inversion, in the case of men, should be distinguished from transvestism and other forms of gender inversion, which he claimed were often practiced by heterosexual men. While he generally characterized female inverts as masculine, he told a meeting of the Chicago Academy of Medicine in 1913 that sexual inversion correctly referred "exclusively [to] such a change in a person's sexual impulses . . . that the impulse is turned towards individuals of the same sex, while all the other impulses and tastes may remain those of the sex to which the person by anatomical configuration belongs."[59] The homosexual man, defined solely by his capacity to find sexual satisfaction with another male, began to emerge as a distinct figure in medical discourse, different from the invert, who was still defined by a more thoroughgoing inversion of gender conventions, and from the heterosexual man, who could find sexual satisfaction only with a female.

The writings of doctors help explicate the shifting terms of sexual ideology in the early twentieth century. But such writers did not *create* the social category of the "invert" or the "homosexual," as some recent theories have proposed.[60] As Lichtenstein's description of the men he had encountered in the city jail demonstrates particularly clearly, their writings represent little more than an (often unsuccessful) effort to make sense of the male sexual culture they had observed or of which they were a part. The medical analysis of the different character of "inverts," "perverts," and "normal people" reflected a set of classificatory distinctions already widely recognized in the broader culture. The fairy, regarded as a "third-sexer," more womanly than manly, was a pivotal cultural figure in the streets of New York before he appeared in the pages of medical journals. The effeminacy doctors ascribed to the invert was emphasized by the common terms people already used for fairies, such as *buttercup, nance, pansy,* and *sissy;* and the gender-based distinction some doctors drew between "normal" (that is, conventionally masculine) men and "inverts" only reproduced the distinction drawn in the vernacular between "he-men" and "she-men."[61] Similarly, the new division of the sexual world by medical discourse into homosexuals and heterosexuals reflected a shift already evident more broadly in middle-class culture. The fairy and the queer, not the medical profession, forced middle-class men to consider the possibility of a sexual element in their relations with other men.

Until the mid-twentieth century, the medical discourse on homosexuality had only a limited effect on most individuals. While a few boys were diagnosed as homosexuals by doctors, many more were denounced as queers by the other boys on their street. Most men who escaped such denunciations did not begin to think they were fairies because they read about them in articles published in obscure medical journals, but because they met fairies in the streets and were confronted every day by the inconsistency between their desires and those proclaimed by the men and women around them. The fairy's position in the sex–gender system made sense to them not because it had been constructed (or explained) so carefully by elite writers, but because it seemed reasonable in terms of the social practices that constituted and reconstituted gender on an everyday basis. While doctors sometimes succeeded in articulating the cultural assumptions underlying those practices with exceptional clarity, they still had relatively little influence over them at the turn of the century.*

---

*Medical professionals had played a key role in the criminalization of abortion in the mid-nineteenth century and played a growing role in the regulation of prostitution and venereal disease in the early twentieth, but they did not play a major role in the state regulation of homosexuality until World War II.[62]

"Normal" middle-class men's growing resistance to any physical or affective ties redolent of homosexuality, and the insistence of middle-class "queer" men that it was their sexual desire, not gender inversion, that distinguished them from other men, mark the emergence of the "heterosexual" and the "homosexual" in middle-class culture. The emergence of each signals the consolidation of sexuality itself as a central component of identity in middle-class culture and tends to confirm Michel Foucault's insight that the construction of sexuality as a distinct field of personhood, linking affective desires and physiological responses in a matrix that was central to the definition of one's personhood, was initially a distinctly bourgeois production.[63]

The broad class differences discernible in early-twentieth-century gender and sexual ideology were never absolute differences. There were significant differences between "respectable" and "rough" working-class men, among workingmen from different ethnic subcultures, between established middle-class businessmen and professionals and the new middle class of white-collar clerks. Moreover, as the anthropologist Richard Parker has observed in a different context, any given individual was aware, to one degree or another, of the variety of competing sexual ideologies available in his culture, which gave him some room for maneuvering among them.[64] Some working-class men eschewed all sexual contact with other men as "perverse" and "abnormal," and others identified themselves as "queers" and insisted that their difference from other men resided not in their gender persona but in their sexuality alone. Some middle-class men experimented with sex with other men without believing that it ineluctably marked them as homosexual, while almost all self-identified middle-class gay men considered themselves marked, to some degree, as gender deviants as well as sexual deviants, even if they tried to recast that gender difference in terms of cultural sophistication or sensitivity.

Still, it would be wrong to imagine that each ideological system was free-floating and easily appropriated by any man, regardless of his social location. Every man had to position himself in relation to the ideology prevailing in the social worlds in which he was raised and lived. Every man had constantly to negotiate his relations with the men and women around him, that is, as well as with the legal, religious, and medical authorities who sought to enforce, with varying degrees of consistency and effectiveness, particular ideological positions. The predominant class locations of the queer, the fairy, the heterosexual, and trade illuminate the shifting relationship of sex, gender, and sexuality in different class cultures. The association of the homosexual and heterosexual with middle-class culture highlights the degree to which "sexuality" and the rooting of gender in anatomy were bourgeois productions, and the association of the fairy and trade with working-class culture highlights the degree to which gender governed the interpretation of sexual practices and manliness was self-consciously performative in that culture.

The transition from the world of fairies and men to the world of homosexuals and heterosexuals was a complex, uneven process, marked by substantial class and ethnic differences. Sex, gender, and sexuality continued to stand in volatile relationship to one another throughout the twentieth century, the very boundaries between them contested. It was in the context of this volatile matrix—the variety of modes of sexual categorization, and the complex mixture of fascination, revulsion, and desire evoked by the fairy and the homosexual—that a gay world took shape. It is to the making of that world that we now turn.

PART II

The Making of the Gay Male World

COMMERCIALIZED AMUSEMENT   12:30 to 1:10 AM #4

Manhattan Casino, 8th Av & 155th St.

    About 12:30 A.M. we visited this place and found approximately 5,000 people, colored and white, men attired in women's clothes, and vice versa. The affair, we were informed, was a "Fag/Masquerade Ball." (fairy) This is an annual affair where the white and colored fairies assemble together with their friends, this being attended also by a certain respectable element who go here to see the sights.

    While here, remaining about three-quarters of an hour, a certain amount of intoxication was observed. On three occasions it was seen where both men and women were intoxicated to the extent of being unable to walk unaided, and were taken from the hall by their friends. There was also a large number of uniformed patrol patrolmen seen both outside, and in the hall proper as well as plainclothesmen. Noticing that to remain here would be unproductive, we shortly departed.

    Prior to leaving B and 5 questioned some casuals casuals in the place as to where women could be met, but could learn nothing.

Read and found correct   *JK.*   ✳   ✍

H.K,

Figure 5.1. The Committee of Fourteen's undercover investigators filed thousands of reports such as this one during the almost thirty years they kept New York City's dance halls, saloons, and other "commercialized amusements" under surveillance. They rarely lingered when they came across gay events such as the annual Hamilton Lodge drag ball (described here) since they were more concerned about prostitution than homosexuality. *(From Committee of Fourteen Records, Rare Books and Manuscript Division, The New York Public Library, Astor, Lenox, and Tilden Foundations.)*

Chapter 5

URBAN CULTURE AND THE POLICING OF THE "CITY OF BACHELORS"

THE MEN WHO BUILT NEW YORK'S GAY WORLD AT THE TURN OF THE CENtury and those who sought to suppress it shared the conviction that it was a distinctly urban phenomenon. "Only in a great city," declared one man who had moved to New York in 1882, could an invert "give his overwhelming yearnings free rein *incognito* and thus keep the respect of his every-day circle. . . . In New York one can live as Nature demands without setting every one's tongue wagging."[1] In his hometown he had needed to conform at all times to the social conventions of the community, for he had been subject to the constant (albeit normally benign and unselfconscious) surveillance of his family and neighbors. But in the city it was possible for him to move between social worlds and lead a double life: by day to hold a respectable job that any queer would have been denied, and by night to lead the life of a fairy on the Bowery.

This freedom was precisely what troubled the Committee of Fifteen, an anti-vice society established in 1900 to suppress female prostitution in New York's saloons. It noted ominously that in the city

> the main external check upon a man's conduct, the opinion of his neighbours, which has such a powerful influence in the country or small town, tends to disappear. In a great city one has no neighbours. No man knows the doings of even his close friends; few men care what the secret life of their friends may be. . . . [T]he young man is left free to follow his own inclinations.[2]

The Committee was particularly concerned about the ease with which men developed liaisons with female prostitutes in New York, but it was distressed as well by other, more unconventional manifestations of such "freedom." Its agents visited saloons primarily in search of female prostitutes, but they repeatedly stumbled upon resorts where fairies gathered, such as Paresis Hall on the Bowery and Billy's Place on Third Avenue, which they believed would never have been tolerated in smaller communities.

To some observers, sympathetic and hostile alike, the fairy became an emblem of modernity and of the collapse of traditional forms of social control. Doctors who studied the problem of inversion inevitably associated it with the growth of cities and sometimes attributed it either to the cities' increasingly alien character or to the nervous exhaustion (or "neurasthenia") produced by the demands of urban industrial culture. In 1895, for instance, the American translator of a French article on inversion claimed that the "forms of vice" the article described were "as yet little familiar [to Americans], at least so far as concerns [our] native-born population."* But he warned that "the massing of our population, especially the foreign element, in great cities" would inevitably lead to an increase in inversion and similar vices.[3] Some theorists in the first generation of American urban sociologists, who echoed many of the concerns of the reformers with whom they often worked, expressed similar anxieties about the enhanced possibilities for the development of a secret homosexual life that urban conditions created. Urbanization, they warned, resulted in the breakdown of family and other social ties that kept an individual's behavior under control in smaller, more tightly organized and regulated towns. The resulting "personal disorganization," the sociologist Walter Reckless wrote in 1926, led to the release of "impulses and desires . . . from the socially approved channels," and could result "not merely in prostitution, but also in perversion."[4]

As the early sociologists suspected, the emergence of an extensive and multifaceted gay male world was made possible in part by the development of distinctive forms of urban culture. But the gay world was shaped as well by the efforts of those sociologists, the Committee of Fifteen, its successor, the Committee of Fourteen (established 1905), and a host of other authorities to understand and discipline that broader culture. The making of the gay world can only be understood in the context of the evolution of city life and the broader contest over the urban moral order.

Like the first generation of sociologists, many subsequent analysts have focused on the supposed anonymity of the city as the primary reason it became a center of unconventional behavior. To be sure, the relative

---

*The English tended to blame homosexuality on the French, and the French to blame it on the Italians, but the Americans blamed it rather more indiscriminately on European immigration as a whole.

anonymity enjoyed in Manhattan by gay tourists from the heartland—and even from the outer boroughs—was one reason they felt freer there than they would have at home to seek out gay locales and behave openly as homosexuals. But to focus on the supposed anonymity of the city (a quality that is, in any case, always relative and situational) is to imply that gay men remained isolated from (or "anonymous" to) one another. The city, however, was the site not so much of anonymous, furtive encounters between strangers (although there were plenty of those) as of an organized, multilayered, and self-conscious gay subculture, with its own meeting places, language, folklore, and moral codes. What sociologists and reformers called the social *disorganization* of the city might more properly be regarded as a social *reorganization*. By the more pejorative term, investigators actually denoted the multiplication of social possibilities that the massing of diverse peoples made possible. "Disorganization" also evoked the declining strength of the family, the neighborhood, the parish, and other institutions of social control, which seemed, in retrospect at least, to have enforced older patterns of social order in smaller communities.[5] But it ignored, or was incapable of acknowledging, the fact that new forms of social order were emerging in their place. Although the anonymity of the city was important because it helped make it possible for gay men to live double lives, it was only a starting point. It will prove more useful to focus on the ways gay men utilized the complexity of urban society to build an alternative gay social order.[*]

The complexity of the city's social and spatial organization made it possible for gay men to construct the multiple public identities necessary for them to participate in the gay world without losing the privileges of the

[*]Whether the processes described here should be regarded as an effect of urban culture or of industrial capitalism has been subject to debate. Both positions have merit. It clearly was not the massing of people or the spatial expansion of cities alone that facilitated the emergence of gay subcultures. Changes in urban social organization and in the role of particular cities in the broader economy were also critical. The decline of the system of household-based artisanal production in New York City in the nineteenth century, which resulted in a breakdown in preindustrial modes of social control, was equally significant, for instance. Thus there is considerable merit to the argument made by some urban theorists that "urban culture" is a misnomer for the forms of social organization characteristic of industrial capitalist culture. The latter conceptualization of the phenomenon, however, fails to account fully for the social and spatial complexity peculiar to cities even in an industrial capitalist society. Although limited gay social networks developed in rural areas, and even small towns usually had a handful of surreptitious gay meeting places by the early twentieth century—hotel men's bars, bus stations, and certain street corners or blocks, most commonly, as well as the homes of a few of the town's "confirmed bachelors"—only large cities had the social and spatial complexity necessary for the development of an extensive and partially commercialized gay subculture.[6]

straight: assuming one identity at work, another in leisure; one identity before biological kin, another with gay friends. The city, as the sociologist Robert Park observed in 1916, sustained a "mosaic of little [social] worlds," and their segregation from one another allowed men to assume a different identity in each of them, without having to reveal the full range of their identities in any one of them. "This [complexity] makes it possible for individuals to pass quickly and easily from one moral milieu to another," Park mused, which "encourages the fascinating but dangerous experiment of living at the same time in several different contiguous, but otherwise widely separated, worlds ... [and] tends ... to produce new and divergent individual types."[7] Though Park's model overestimated the cohesiveness and isolation of each "little world"—and underestimated the degree to which they were mutually constitutive and to which dominant social groups intervened in the social worlds of the subordinate—it captured some of the significance for gay men of the complexity of the city's social organization.

The extent to which men manipulated such possibilities—and the extent to which these possibilities concerned the enforcers of public morality—was emphasized by the comments of a district attorney prosecuting a sodomy charge filed in 1903. The defendant was a draftsman caught in a police raid on the Ariston Baths, where men gathered for sexual encounters (see chapter 8 for a discussion of gay bathhouses). He had secured character references from his employer and a number of distinguished colleagues, who insisted that the man they knew could not have been found having sex with other men in a bathhouse. In his response, the district attorney used the jury's presumption that a respectable man would—and *could*—hide his homosexual involvements from his everyday associates to undermine the character witnesses' testimony. "A man's friends," he reminded the jury, "would be the very last persons on earth who would know of a tendency of this kind entertained by anybody ... he would be very careful to conceal his perverted appetite from them." And while one character witness, an architect who had employed the draftsman, was "a well known gentleman," whose sincerity in praising the defendant ought not to be impugned, the attorney argued, it would be ridiculous to "suppose that this defendant would allow his employer to discover any such habit as this.... What one of you gentlemen, who employs people," the prosecutor, echoing the concerns of the Committee of Fifteen and of the early sociologists, demanded of the jury, "has really any accurate knowledge as to what his employees are doing, out of business hours, when they are away from you?"[8] Persuaded by the attorney's arguments and by the testimony of several undercover police investigators against the draftsman, the jury convicted him and he was sentenced to more than seven years in the state penitentiary. The severity of the punishment reminds us why men went to such lengths to hide their involvement in the gay world from their nongay associates.

It is impossible to determine how many men moved to New York at the turn of the century in order to participate in the gay life emerging there, but gay men and other contemporary observers believed the numbers were large. Case histories of "inverts" published in medical journals early in the century were peppered with accounts of men who came to New York because they were aware of homosexual interests they had to hide in their hometowns or because they were forced to flee when their secret was discovered. Numerous doctors not only identified inversion as a distinctly urban phenomenon but commented especially on the number of inverts in New York. As early as the 1880s, George Beard thought that many male inverts lived there, and in 1913 the psychiatrist A. A. Brill confidently estimated there were "many thousands of homosexuals in New York City among all classes of society."[9] Two researchers investigating homosexual life in the late 1930s found that most of the men they interviewed who had moved to New York from smaller towns had done so because "their local communities frowned upon homosexuality, and New York [seemed to them] to be the capital of the American homosexual world."* The researchers noted that many such migrants had indeed been able to find "work, a homosexual circle of acquaintance, [and] a definite social life."[11]

Whatever the numbers, gay men's migration was clearly part of the much larger migration of single men and women to the city from Europe and rural America alike. A disproportionate number of the people who moved to the cities were young and unmarried, and while for many of them migration was part of a carefully considered strategy designed to address the broader economic needs of their families, for many it also provided a welcome relief from family control.[12] The city was a logical destination for men intent on freeing themselves from the constraints of the family, because of its relatively cheap accommodations and the availability of commercial domestic services for which men traditionally would have depended on the unpaid household labor of women.

"For the nation's bachelors," the *New York Times Magazine* declared

---

*One native New Yorker commented to me that many of the men he knew in the 1940s and 1950s "had moved to New York from small towns, to get away from the hostility or to be more themselves. . . . [M]any left because if they stayed home they would have to do the marriage bit." In his study of homosexuals in Montreal in the early 1950s, the sociologist Maurice Leznoff found that three-quarters of the gay men he interviewed who had moved to Montreal from small towns had done so at least in part because it would be easier for them to develop a homosexual life there. He also learned of a man from Montreal who had moved to New York because he feared disgracing his family.[10]

in 1928, "this city is the Mecca. Not only is it the City of Youth, but it is the City of the Single," with some 900,000 unmarried men and 700,000 single women counted among its residents. "It is certain," the article continued, "they are not all in a [Madison Square] Garden line-up waiting for admission to the next fight, neither are they all concentrated in speakeasies and along the docks. . . . The city has something for every kind of bachelor."[13] Some of those bachelors were working-class immigrants crowded in the tenement districts and waterfront; others were American-born rural youths barely making enough to rent a furnished room; still others were successful entrepreneurs living in the city's luxurious new apartment hotels. Together the bachelors constituted 40 percent or more of the men fifteen years of age or older living in Manhattan in the first third of the century.*

The existence of an urban bachelor subculture facilitated the development of a gay world. Tellingly, gay men tended to gather in the same neighborhoods where many of the city's other unmarried men and women clustered, since they offered the housing and commercial services suitable to the needs of a nonfamily population. Gay male residential and commercial enclaves developed in the Bowery, Greenwich Village, Times Square, and Harlem in large part because they were the city's major centers of furnished-room housing for single men. Lesbian enclaves developed for similar reasons in the 1920s in Harlem and the Village, then the city's two primary centers of housing for single women. Rooming houses and cafeterias served as meeting grounds for gay men, facilitating the constant interaction that made possible the development of a distinctive subculture. To the horror of reformers, many small entrepreneurs ignored the "disreputable" character of their gay patrons precisely because they were patrons. A smaller number actively encouraged the patronage of openly gay men because it attracted other customers.

The expanding bachelor subculture in the city's furnished-room and tenement districts precipitated a powerful reaction by social-purity forces, which would have enormous consequences for the development of the gay world. The emerging bachelor subculture was only one of the ominous features of a changing urban landscape that many native-born middle-class Americans found increasingly threatening. The rapid growth in the num-

---

*The number of unmarried men and women in the city increasingly distinguished it from the nation as a whole. Immigrants were disproportionately young and single, but even the native-born Americans of the city were much less likely to marry than their rural counterparts. Only a third of the native-born white men aged twenty-five to thirty-four with American parents were unmarried in the nation as a whole in 1900, compared to half of those in Manhattan; only 15 percent of those aged thirty-five to forty-four were unmarried in the nation, versus 30 percent of those living in Manhattan.[14]

ber and size of cities in the late nineteenth century was itself a source of concern, but even more anxiety-provoking was their increasingly "alien" character. As America's greatest port, New York City had always been an immigrant metropolis. Even as early as 1860, Irish Catholic immigrants constituted a quarter of the city's white population, and the nineteenth century was punctuated by nativist reactions to them. Beginning in the 1880s, the national background of the immigrants began to shift from northern and western Europe—the historic source of the so-called old-stock Americans—to southern and eastern Europe. Germans and the Irish continued to migrate in large numbers, but by the 1890s the majority of people immigrating to New York, in particular, were from Italy or Russia (the latter primarily Russian Jews). Almost a third of Manhattan's residents in 1910 were foreign-born Jews or Italians and their children.[15]

This reconstitution of the population had vast ramifications for the city's politics and for the social organization and culture of class, nationality, and sexuality. The growing number of immigrants and their cultural difference from the northwestern Europeans who had already settled in the States led many Americans of "older stock" to fear that they would lose control of their cities and even the whole of their society. This provoked a generation of struggle over urban political and social power. These conflicts became inextricably linked to the class conflict of the late nineteenth century, for, to an astonishing extent, the industrial working class forged in the late-nineteenth-century United States was an immigrant class. The peasants and laborers who left their European homelands became the workhorses of the second industrial revolution in the United States. The sharp class conflict of the late nineteenth century, then, was construed in ethnic as well as class terms, and conflicts over political and cultural power became inextricably intertwined with conflicts of class, ethnicity, and race. The Anglo-American middle class increasingly defined its difference from immigrants in the interrelated—and mutually constitutive—terms of race and class. As immigrants seemed to overwhelm the nation's cities, growing numbers of Anglo-American middle-class families fled to suburbs such as Brooklyn. They increasingly feared, as the historian Paul Boyer has shown, that the city posed a threat not just to the morality of individuals but to the survival of American society as a whole.[16]

In the closing decades of the nineteenth century and the opening decades of the twentieth, an extraordinary panoply of groups and individuals organized to reform the urban moral order. Although their efforts rarely focused on the emerging gay world, most of them nonetheless had a significant effect on its development. Some sought to reconstruct the urban landscape itself in ways that would minimize the dissipating effects of urban disorder: reforming the tenements, putting up new residential hotels in which single men and women could lead moral lives, creating parks to reintroduce an element of rural simplicity and natural order to the city, building playgrounds and organizing youth clubs to rescue young people from city streets and gangs, and constructing grand boulevards and public buildings that would inspire a new order in the city itself and command respect for an orderly society.[17]

Other reform efforts had a more coercive edge. Native-born Americans usually controlled the state legislatures in which smaller towns and rural districts were disproportionately represented, but they could not count on locally controlled urban police forces to enforce the vision of moral order they had codified in state law. Indeed, the integration of New York City's police force into the local political structure, the subordination of individual officers to local ward bosses, and their role in enforcing the elaborate system of extortion and profiteering that allowed the Bowery resorts to exist were continuing sources of outrage and frustration to the reformers.[18]

Beginning in the 1870s, they responded to this problem by organizing a host of private anti-vice and social-purity societies to enforce the laws themselves and to institutionalize a new regime of surveillance and control. Sometimes working together, sometimes highly competitive, each society claimed the authority to combat a different threat to the city's moral order. At the height of its powers under the leadership of the Reverend Charles Parkhurst in the 1890s, the Society for the Prevention of Crime, founded in 1877, worked to compel the police to enforce anti-vice laws by exposing the links between police corruption and the vice resorts of the Bowery and Tenderloin. In later decades it focused its more limited resources on studying criminal behavior. The Society for the Suppression of Vice, which Anthony Comstock founded in 1872 under the auspices of the Young Men's Christian Association of New York and led until his death in 1915, fought to suppress stage shows and literature it deemed obscene. The Committee of Fourteen, founded in 1905, took the lead in the fight against prostitution; it was the largest and most effective of the groups until its demise at the onset of the Depression. The Society for the Prevention of Cruelty to Children, founded in 1872 by Eldridge Gerry as an offshoot of the Society for the Prevention of Cruelty to Animals, sought to protect children in general. It concentrated its efforts on "saving" children from immigrant parents who they thought neglected or abused them. In immigrant neighborhoods, as the historian Linda Gordon notes, it was known simply as "The Cruelty" because of its agents' reputation for taking children from homes it deemed undesirable.[19]

The policing of gay culture in the early twentieth century was closely tied to the efforts of these societies to police working-class culture more generally. The societies' efforts to control the streets and tenements and to eliminate the saloon and brothel were predicated on a vision of an ideal social order centered in the family. The reformers' targets reflected their growing anxiety about the threat to the social order posed by men and women who seemed to stand outside the family: the men of the bachelor subculture who gathered without supervision in the "dissipating" atmosphere of the saloons; the women whose rejection of conventional gender and sexual arrangements was emblematized by the prostitute; the youths of the city whose lives seemed to be shaped by the discordant influences of the streets rather than the civilizing influences of the home; and, on occasion, the gay men and lesbians who gathered in the niches of the urban landscape constructed by those groups. The reform campaigns constituted a sweeping assault on the moral order of working-class communities, and especially of single women and rough working-class men, although middle-class entrepreneurs and intellectuals also became their targets at times. The Anti-Saloon League, for instance, mounted a frontal attack on one of the central institutions of male sociability in many working-class neighborhoods. Similarly, the Committee of Fourteen defined "prostitution" more broadly than many working-class youths did. As the historian Kathy Peiss has shown, the Committee frequently regarded working-class conventions of treating as a form of prostitution, for it labeled women who were willing to offer sexual favors (of any sort) to men in exchange for a night on the town, or even as part of an ongoing relationship, as "amateur prostitutes."[20] Thus their campaign against "prostitution" led the reformers to attack not just brothels but saloons, cabarets, and other social venues where men and women transgressed Victorian gender conventions by interacting too casually.

The social-purity activists were also keen to prevent the violation of racial boundaries, which they imagined inevitably had a sexual element. W. E. B. Du Bois learned as much in 1912, when the Committee tried to close Marshall's Hotel on West Fifty-third Street, because, according to the Committee, it tolerated "that unfortunate mixing of the races which when the individuals are of the ordinary class, always means danger [that is, interracial sex]."[21] Similarly, the Society for the Suppression of Vice's definition of indecent literature was not limited to erotic photographic or written depictions of sexual acts, which even most opponents of suppression agreed were "indecent." Their targets also included birth control literature, medical studies of homosexuality, and plays and short stories with lesbian or other unorthodox sexual themes, which other people might classify as "scientific," "artistic," or "serious."[22] The reform societies' campaigns against "prostitution" and other "social evils," in other words, actually constituted much broader campaigns to reconstruct the moral world by narrowing the boundaries of acceptable sociability and public discourse.

Some of the organizations secured quasi-police powers from the state legislature in order to pursue their objectives; others used their connections with the city's business leaders to put economic pressure on tenement landlords, hotel operators, and the brewing companies to close clubs and saloons where men and women interacted too freely or women worked as prostitutes. Reformers hired agents who put the immigrant neighborhoods under surveillance: visiting the saloons, streets, and tenements where men and women gathered; reviewing the moral tenor of the films, stage shows, burlesque routines, and club acts seen by New Yorkers; attending the masquerade balls and other social events organized by the city's immigrant, bohemian, and gay social clubs to regulate the kinds of costumes worn and dancing allowed. They also monitored the police and devised elaborate administrative mechanisms to force them to uphold moral regulations they otherwise would ignore. Ironically, the records of the anti-vice societies serve as one of the richest sources for this study. Although requiring careful interpretation, they constitute some of the most comprehensive surveys available of the social and sexual life of the city's working-class districts from the 1870s (and especially the 1890s) until the 1920s, after which state agencies began to take greater responsibility for regulating the urban moral order.

The role of the anti-vice societies in enforcing the state's sodomy law is emblematic. A legacy of English statutes, laws against sodomy and the "crime against nature," had existed since colonial days, but the state had done little to enforce the sodomy law in the first century of independence. As the scholars Timothy Gilfoyle and Michael Lynch discovered, only twenty-two sodomy prosecutions occurred in New York City in the nearly eight decades from 1796 to 1873. The number of prosecutions increased dramatically in the 1880s, however. By the 1890s, fourteen to thirty-eight men were arrested *every year* for sodomy or the "crime against nature." Police arrested more than 50 men annually in the 1910s—more than 100 in 1917—and from 75 to 125 every year in the 1920s. Although the dramatic increase in arrests resulted in part from intensified concern among the city's elite about homosexuality and a new determination on the part of the police, much of it stemmed from the efforts of the Society for the Prevention of Cruelty to Children, which involved itself in the cases of men suspected of sodomy with boys in order to ensure their indictment and successful prosecution by the district attorney. The fragmentary court records available suggest that at least 40 percent—and up to 90 percent—of the cases prosecuted each year were initiated at the complaint of the SPCC. Given the SPCC's focus on the status of children in immigrant neighborhoods, the great majority of sodomy prosecutions were initiated against immigrants in the poorest sections of the city; in the 1940s and 1950s, African-Americans and

Puerto Ricans would become the primary targets of sodomy prosecutions for similar reasons.[23]

The role of the SPCC in the prosecution of men for sodomy exemplified the role of the other moral-reform groups in the policing of homosexuality before World War I. Although the SPCC had a tremendous impact on the number and character of sodomy prosecutions, it did not make homosexuals a special target. It was only in the course of its more general campaign to protect the city's children from assault that men were arrested for having sex with boys. The other societies also contributed substantially to the policing of homosexuality, but they, too, usually did so only in the course of pursuing some other, more central mission, and rarely focused on homosexuality per se. The Society for the Prevention of Crime and its allied organization, the City Vigilance League, investigated and denounced the male prostitutes of Paresis Hall in 1899, for instance, but only as part of their general campaign against the police corruption that allowed prostitution to flourish in New York. The superintendent of the Society reported to his board of directors in 1917 that one of its agents had been solicited by "a man of unnatural sexual desires" near its offices on Union Square and that "evidence of many such cases could probably be got." In response, the board instructed him to proceed against such cases only on an individual basis when they came to his attention and not to "enter upon [a] campaign against such vice."[24] Similarly, the sporadic efforts of the Committee of Fourteen to prevent men's use of the streets and saloons for homosexual trysts and social gatherings, while not insignificant, usually were only an incidental aspect of its more general effort to regulate the streets and commercial amusements that served as sites for sexual encounters or unchaperoned meetings between young men and women.[25] Until World War I, the societies did not identify homosexuality as a social problem so threatening that it merited more than incidental attention.

WORLD WAR I AND THE DISCOURSE OF URBAN DEGENERACY

World War I was a watershed in the history of the urban moral reform movement and in the role of homosexuality in reform discourse. The war embodied reformers' darkest fears and their greatest hopes, for it threatened the very foundations of the nation's moral order—the family, small-town stability, the racial and gender hierarchy—even as it offered the reformers an unprecedented opportunity to implement their vision. It also led them to focus for the first time on homosexuality as a major social problem. For the Committee of Fourteen and other social-purity groups, which had monitored New York's sexual underworld closely since the turn of the century, were convinced that the war had resulted in a substantial growth in the scale and visibility of gay life in the city.

Military mobilization had an enormous impact on New York, the major port of embarkation for the European theater. Hundreds of thousands of servicemen passed through the city during the war; one official estimated that five thousand to ten thousand soldiers from two camps on Long Island alone visited New York every day, and twice that many came on weekends.[26] The streets were filled with soldiers and sailors. "They were to be seen singly," one of the Committee of Fourteen's investigators reported in 1917, "or (and mostly) in couples, trios and quartettes walking about the streets either soliciting girls or being solicited by the girls and women. . . . There were many thousand . . . in the proportion of three soldiers to ten . . . civilians."[27] They congregated especially in the Union Square area, on Fourteenth Street near Third and Fourth Avenues, at Times Square, and on MacDougal Street in the Village, as well as in Riverside and Battery Parks and other waterfront areas— places known as cruising areas for gay men as well as prostitutes.[28]

The presence of so many soldiers from rural backgrounds in New York and other cities augured to purity crusaders a moral crisis of alarming proportions. The war to make the world safe for democracy threatened to expose hundreds of thousands of American boys from farms and small towns to the evil influences of the big city. The manner in which the reformers construed this crisis was profoundly shaped by the discourse of urban degeneracy that had been central to their moral vision throughout the Progressive Era. Indeed, the social disorganization, anomie, and unraveling of family ties associated with urbanism colored the responses to the war on every side, from the solemn pledge President Wilson made to the mothers of America that Uncle Sam would act in loco parentis, protecting their sons from urban evils, to the gleeful taunt of urban musicians (who viewed the change altogether more positively), "How You Gonna Keep 'Em Down on the Farm After They've Seen Paree?" The dominant wartime discourse portrayed American troops as naive rural boys, "innocents abroad," and depicted New York itself as a seductive big-city woman who threatened to infect those small-town boys with venereal diseases and unwholesome city ways. As a longtime social-purity activist warned at the moment of American entry into the war, soldiers who were not protected from temptation "not only will . . . bring back into the social structure a vast volume of venereal disease to wreck the lives of innocent women and children, but they will bring back into it other attitudes and practices which will destroy homes, cause misery, and degenerate society."[29] Urban immorality was a virulent plague threatening to invade the bodies and minds of the nation's youth, and, through them, the nation itself.

But if the war threatened to expose millions of rural youths to the moral perils of urban life, it also made it possible for the social-purity forces to implement their program of reform on an unprecedented scale. The anti-

German and anti-immigrant hysteria fostered by the war allowed the Anti-Saloon League and its allies to portray Prohibition as a decisive blow against the un-American culture of German brewers and immigrant saloons and to secure passage of the Prohibition Amendment in 1919. Wartime moral fervor also encouraged social-purity activists to launch an assault on that other quintessential symbol of urban degeneracy: the brothel. The anti-prostitution movement that had begun in New York City with the founding of the Committee of Fifteen in 1900 had gained strength throughout the nation in the subsequent fifteen years, as businessmen and reformers in more than a hundred cities established their own commissions to study the problem of prostitution and campaign for its eradication. By 1917 these groups were sufficiently well organized and influential at the national level to be able to persuade Congress and military leaders to wage a massive campaign against the threat posed to soldiers' health and morality by prostitution and venereal disease. Moreover, as the historian Allan Brandt has observed, "What began as an attempt to save the health and efficiency of the American fighting man was eventually transformed into a comprehensive program to rid the nation of vice, immorality, and disease."[30] Using the draconian laws made possible by the wartime emergency, they banned alcohol from the vicinity of military bases, suppressed most of the nation's red-light districts, and detained tens of thousands of women suspected of working as prostitutes. The Committee of Fourteen assumed primary responsibility for the anti-prostitution campaign in New York, but it was joined in its efforts by the American Social Hygiene Association, the Bureau of Social Hygiene, and other reform groups, as well as the military and police.[31]

The efforts of the anti-vice societies to curtail prostitution—or at least to push it underground—were largely successful in New York. But as the war progressed, the societies were astonished to detect "an apparent increase in male perversion." Agents reported seeing "perverts" approaching soldiers and sailors on the streets, in theaters, and in hotel lobbies, meeting them in bars, and taking them to assignation hotels. They saw suspicious-looking civilians inviting servicemen to join them in saloons and hotel bars (which were prohibited from selling liquor to men in uniform) where they surreptitiously passed them their drinks. Agents had noticed fairies fraternizing with sailors for years, but it was at the beginning of the war that they witnessed the spectacle of "sex mad" sailors near the Brooklyn Navy Yard "walking arm in arm and on one dark street . . . a sailor and a man kissing each other . . . an exhibition of mail [sic] perversion showing itself in the absence of girls."[32] At the moment of their triumph, the social-purity forces were confronted with mounting evidence that the war had somehow unleashed the most appalling of urban vices.

Seventy-five years later, it is difficult to assess the effects of World War I on gay life. Allan Berube and a handful of other historians have offered a compelling and detailed portrait of the effects of World War II on gay men and lesbians, but too little research has been conducted yet on its predecessor to allow a similarly conclusive analysis of its impact.[33] It is likely that the first war had a less dramatic effect than the second, in part because it led to the mobilization of a far smaller number of people for a shorter period of time, and in part because of the different social context in which it occurred. Nonetheless, the existing evidence suggests the First World War, like the Second, did serve to increase the scope and visibility of New York's gay world, and that it contributed to a new self-consciousness on the part of some gay New Yorkers.

The war not only took many Americans from their small towns, it sent them to Europe, where they were likely to encounter a cultural and political climate for homosexuals that was almost unimaginable at home. By the time of World War I, there existed in Paris and Berlin a highly developed gay commercial subculture that easily surpassed the scale of the gay world in New York. Gay Americans' perception of this world still needs to be explored, but it is already clear, for instance, that it constituted part of the attraction of Paris for some of the American expatriates who gravitated there in the 1920s.

Even more striking is that a movement for the rights of homosexuals had existed in Germany since the end of the nineteenth century, which at least some gay men, such as the writer Henry Gerber and the composer Charles Tomlinson Griffes, encountered while in Europe before or during the war. Inspired by such European models, Gerber organized a short-lived homosexual-rights group in Chicago in 1924, upon his return from the war (it was promptly suppressed by the police), and although Griffes did not take so dramatic a step, he told his New York friends about the work of the German homosexual emancipationist Magnus Hirschfeld and about how the German movement and Edward Carpenter's books had helped him think more positively about his homosexuality.[34] It is likely that thousands of American gay men were similarly affected by their encounter with a culture in which homosexuals experienced a greater degree of tolerance and had begun to speak and organize on their own behalf, much as thousands of African-American servicemen were politicized by their experience of living in a less racist society while fighting to defend "American democracy."[35] A decade after his return from Europe, and seven years after his fledgling Society for Human Rights had been crushed, Henry Gerber denounced American attitudes by contrasting them with those of a supposedly enlightened Europe. Many "homosexuals live in happy, blissful unions, especially in Europe, where homosexuals are unmolested as long as they mind their own business," he insisted in a 1932 essay published in the journal of opinion *Modern Thinker*, "and are not, as in England and in the United States, driven to the underworld of perversions and crime for satisfaction of their very real craving for love."[36]

But the political movements and more tolerant sexual mores of France and Germany had less of an impact on most men than the experience of military life itself. For military mobilization, by removing men from the supervision of their families and small-town neighborhoods and placing them in a single-sex environment, increased the chances that they would encounter self-identified gay men and explore their homosexual interests. An extensive investigation of homosexuality among the men stationed at the Naval Training Station in Newport, Rhode Island, conducted by naval officials immediately following the war revealed that numerous sailors there had begun to forge identities as fairies and queers after meeting other gay-identified sailors during the war, and that a much larger number of men who did not consider themselves homosexual had nonetheless become familiar with the gay world and had homosexual experiences. Many of these men believed they could continue their homosexual lives only with great difficulty and circumspection if they returned to their hometowns, both because of the need to hide their homosexuality from their parents and because of the limited gay life available in most small towns.[37]

Military mobilization also gave many recruits the chance to see the sort of gay life that large cities, especially New York, had to offer. Many of the gay sailors stationed in Newport had been taken by friends to places in New York "where the 'queens' hung out," or had at least heard of them from gay New Yorkers, and the anti-vice societies' own agents reported that many soldiers passing through New York had met gay men in the Village, Times Square, near the Brooklyn Navy Yard, and along the waterfront.[38] Indeed, it seems likely that the experiences of many of the soldiers who passed through the city simply replicated, on a vast scale, those of earlier migrants who had moved there in order to create a gay life, or who had begun to construct gay identities in the course of their encounter with its gay world. It is impossible to determine how many gay soldiers stayed in New York after the war, but the growing visibility of gay institutions in the city in the 1920s (which the following chapters document) suggests that many of them did so—that it was, indeed, hard to keep them down on the farm after they'd seen gay New York.

The moral-reform societies' perception that the war had precipitated an increase in "perversion" in the city led them to focus on homosexual vice—and on homosexuals—as a discrete social problem for the first time. The Committee of Fourteen devoted unprecedented resources to monitoring homosexual activity during the war. It sent agents to the major cruising streets—Broadway, Riverside Drive, Fifth Avenue, Central Park West—in search of gay men.[39] It also placed suspected restaurants under surveillance. Shortly after the end of the war, the Committee learned that Enrico's, a well-known Italian restaurant at 64 West Eleventh Street in the Village, had "a reputation of being a hangout for perverts." It sent an agent to the restaurant several times, even though she repeatedly had to report she could develop no conclusive evidence of their presence. On one visit the agent noticed two young men who were "extremely effeminate," but she ultimately decided they did nothing to conclusively "brand them as perverts"; the following week she noticed "several girls whom I suspected of being this type but they [also] made no definite motions or signs that they were such."[40] Suspected gay meeting places had never before been placed under such sustained observation.

The Society for the Suppression of Vice played the most active role in the wartime crusade against homosexuality. Even before the war, the SSV had devoted more attention to homosexual matters than the other societies. During the course of Anthony Comstock's forty-year-long leadership of the group, he had orchestrated police raids on clubs with gay performers and on shops with gay literature; he had even initiated prosecutions against individual "moral perverts" or "sodomers" and men who possessed indecent homosexual photos. At one such trial, in 1900, he claimed to "have had dealings with a great many [people] of this character."[41] But it was only during World War I, after Comstock's death, that the Society singled out homosexuality as a problem and began to devote significant resources to its eradication. The Society may have done so because it had been given no role in the anti-prostitution campaign jointly managed by the other societies and the government, either because of its historic focus on obscene literature or because of some now unknown estrangement from the other groups.

The issue of homosexuality seems, in any case, to have been a personal passion of John Sumner, who became the Society's leader in 1915 after Comstock's death. As the nation moved closer to war, he launched a campaign in cooperation with the police against the places where homosexuals gathered, including various theaters, bathhouses, streets, and saloons. From 1916 to 1919 he helped organize three raids on the Everard and Lafayette bathhouses (see chapter 8), and in 1920–21 his agents assisted in the arrest of two hundred men on charges of degenerate disorderly conduct by leading the police to movie theaters, subway washrooms, and restaurants where they had learned gay men congregated. Although the SSV ceased focusing on the city's gay underground at the end of 1921, it continued to attack theatrical representations of homosexuality for more than two decades, orchestrating campaigns against Broadway theaters offering "serious" dramas touching on gay or lesbian themes as well as burlesque shows with homosexual acts.[42]

The city's police force took up the anti-gay cause as well, partly at the prompting of the SSV, but largely, it would seem, of its own accord. The number of men convicted in Manhattan for homosexual solicitation leapt from 92 in 1916 to 238 in 1918 and to more than 750 in 1920—an eightfold increase in four years. Although the figures declined in 1921 when the chief of the vice squad instructed his men to refocus their efforts on female prostitutes, they continued to average more than 500 a year for the rest of the decade.[43] The anti-vice societies interpreted this increase as yet more evidence of the wartime growth in perversion.

The societies' intensifying concern about homosexuality led them to convene an unprecedented, high-level meeting devoted to the problem in the fall of 1921. Key figures from anti-vice societies that had played a significant role in the wartime cleanup of the city attended: Frederick Whitin, the general secretary of the Committee of Fourteen; Judge Corrigan, a municipal court judge known for his special interest in degeneracy cases; Dr. Salmon, the medical director of the National Committee for Mental Hygiene; and Messrs. Johnson and Worthington of the American Social Hygiene Association. (The SSV was not invited, despite its leadership in the anti-gay campaign; the reasons went unrecorded, but its absence furthers the impression of its estrangement from the other groups.) Whitin presented a memorandum that laid out some of the dimensions of the problem by reviewing the dramatic increase in arrests, the backgrounds of the men arrested and the kinds of places they met, and the challenges posed by the absence of a uniform court procedure for handling such cases.[44]

The theories advanced at the meeting to explain the apparent increase in homosexuality reveal much about the conferees' conceptualization of homosexual vice and its relationship to urban culture. The anti-vice organizers never even considered the possibility that some of the servicemen seen with homosexual civilians were themselves "perverts." Instead, they believed, like most people in their era, that "perverts" were naturally interested in sex with "normal" men and that in certain circumstances "normal" men (such as sex-starved soldiers on a military base) were entirely susceptible to the perverts' advances. The majority of the anti-vice crusaders feared that the soldiers were victims of the crusaders' very success in suppressing female prostitution; they believed that the recruits responded to the advances of degenerates only because prostitutes were unavailable. Several of them were concerned about the effects of young men being introduced to "perverse practices" in this manner, and a few warned that such exposure could have permanent consequences.[45]

But if the societies blamed themselves, in part, for the rise of homosexual activity, they also blamed the conditions of war, speculating that

"American boys undoubtably [sic] became familiar with perverse practices while in France or while at sea." The reformers' predisposition to blame France suggests a bit of wishful thinking about the absence of homosexuality in the United States as well as their often-voiced uneasiness about France's sexual culture.* But they did not think they could blame the problem entirely on the French. They also worried that many recruits had become familiar with homosexuality "to some extent while in the large cities of their own country," which seemed only to confirm their worst fears about the debilitating effects of urban life.

The group resolved to collect more information and to continue discussions about the desirability of taking action to reform the court procedures in homosexual cases. But even though reformers convened several more meetings to discuss the problem, they developed no joint plan of action, and their sense of urgency about the problem of homosexuality seems to have receded along with the memory of wartime conditions. This may have been because officials believed the problem was subsiding with the return to "normalcy." It is more likely, though, that their attention was deflected from the subject by the rapid growth, in the wake of Prohibition, of other problems more closely associated with their traditional concerns. Nonetheless, Prohibition soon made it possible for the gay world to expand and become considerably more visible than it had been during the war. As a result, the Committee of Fourteen and the Society for the Suppression of Vice both continued, more episodically, to place homosexual meeting places under surveillance and to initiate actions against them throughout the decade. They never again devoted the same degree of attention to gay meeting places as they had from 1916 to 1920, and it would not be until the 1930s, under new leadership, that a more powerful campaign against gay life would develop.

The efforts of the social-purity societies to eradicate vice from the city had an enormous effect on gay life throughout the years of their existence, even if it was usually only an incidental one. Much of gay life was centered in the same commercial institutions and neighborhoods where prostitutes were to be found and where other aspects of people's behavior violated middle-class notions of respectability. Crusades to reform such institutions and neighborhoods could not help but have consequences for gay men. The campaigns waged by the Society for the Prevention of Crime and Committee of Fourteen against police corruption and prostitution resulted

*It would be wrong to dismiss their reasoning as altogether fanciful. The French government had demonstrated its strikingly different attitude toward sexual matters by refusing to cooperate with the U.S. Army's effort to suppress prostitution near its French military bases, and, as we have seen, many Americans probably were affected by their encounter with the French gay subculture.[46]

in the closing of many Bowery resorts where "fairies" had gathered (and all of the most famous of them). On a longer-term if less spectacular basis, the success of the societies in forcing the police department to act more decisively against vice conditions on and off the streets led the police to take more action against gay men's uses of the streets. The surveillance of restaurants, cafeterias, cabarets, theaters, and other sites of "commercialized amusement" by both the police and the societies, and the legal actions they periodically initiated against them, also served to reinforce the disinclination of many managers to allow prostitutes or homosexuals to gather on their premises. In the course of establishing a place for themselves in the city, gay men constantly had to struggle with the public and private agencies of social control, as well as with popular hostility.

Figure 6.1. Gay men and lesbians made numerous cafeterias and restaurants their meeting places. This sketch of a supposed gay drinking party appeared in *Broadway Brevities* in 1924. *(Collection of Leonard Finger.)*

LOTS OF FRIENDS AT THE YMCA: ROOMING HOUSES, CAFETERIAS, AND OTHER GAY SOCIAL CENTERS

WHEN WILLY W. ARRIVED IN NEW YORK CITY IN THE 1940s, HE DID WHAT many newcomers did: he took a room at the Sixty-third Street YMCA. As was true for many other young men, the friends he made at the Y remained important to him for years and helped him find his way through the city. Most of those friends were gay, and the gay world was a significant part of what they showed him. He soon moved on, though, to the St. George Hotel in Brooklyn, which offered more substantial accommodations. The St. George, it seemed to him, was "almost entirely gay," and the friends he met there introduced him to yet other parts of the gay world. After living briefly in a rooming house on Fiftieth Street near Second Avenue, he finally took a small apartment of his own, a railroad flat on East Forty-ninth Street near First Avenue, where he stayed for years. He moved there at the invitation of a friend he had met at Red's, a popular bar on Third Avenue at Fiftieth Street that had attracted gay men since its days as a speakeasy in the 1920s. The friend had an apartment in the building and wanted Willy to take the apartment next to his. An elderly couple had occupied it for years, and, since the walls were rather thin, the friend had never stopped worrying that they heard him late at night with gay friends and had grown suspicious of the company he kept. When they moved out he wanted to make sure that someone more understanding would take their place. Willy was happy to do so, and as other apartments opened up in the building he invited other friends to move in. Several friends did, and some of the newcomers encouraged their own friends to join them. The building's narrow railroad flats, if not luxurious, were adequate and cheap; the location, near the gay bar circuit on Third Avenue in the East Fifties, was convenient;

and, most important, the other inhabitants were friendly and supportive. Within a few years, Willy remembered, "we took over." Gay men occupied fourteen of the sixteen apartments in the building.* Willy not only lived in a gay house, but in a growing gay neighborhood enclave, whose streets provided him with regular contact with other gay men. Although Willy's success in creating an almost completely gay apartment building was unusual, his determination to find housing that maximized his autonomy and his access to the gay world was not. In his movement from one dwelling to the next, Willy traced a path followed by many gay men in the first half of the century as they built a gay world in the city's hotels, rooming houses, and apartment buildings, and in its cafeterias, restaurants, and speakeasies. Gay men took full advantage of the city's resources to create zones of gay camaraderie and security.

BACHELOR HOUSING

Although living with one's family, even in a crowded tenement, did not prevent a man from participating in the gay world that was taking shape in the city's streets, many gay men, like Willy, sought to secure housing that would maximize their freedom from supervision. For many, this meant joining the large number of unmarried workers living in the furnished-room houses (also called lodging or rooming houses) clustered in certain neighborhoods of the city. No census data exist that could firmly establish the residential patterns of gay men, but two studies of gay men incarcerated in the New York City Jail, conducted in 1938 and 1940, are suggestive. Sixty-one percent of the men investigated in 1940 lived in rooming houses, three-quarters of them alone and another quarter with a lover or other roommates; only a third lived in tenement houses with their own families or boarded with others.[2] Court records from the first three decades of the century provide relatively few accounts of men apprehended for sexual encounters in rooming houses (itself indirect evidence of the relative security of such encounters), but they do abound in anecdotal evidence of men who lived together in rooming houses or took other men to their rooms, and whose relationships or rendezvous came to the attention of the police only because of a mishap.†

---

*This was not the only predominantly gay apartment building Willy remembered. In the 1950s a major apartment house at Number 405 in a street in the East Fifties was so heavily gay that gay men nicknamed it the "Four out of Five."[1]

†Such information most frequently came to the attention of the police when a man who had been brought home assaulted or tried to blackmail his host, when parents discovered that a man had invited their son home, when the police followed men to a furnished room from some other, more public locale, or when one of the tenants sharing a room with his lover was arrested on another charge.[3]

Usually situated in rowhouses previously occupied by single families, rooming houses provided tenants with a small room, a bed, minimal furniture, and no kitchen facilities; residents were expected to take their meals elsewhere. Such housing had qualities that made it particularly useful to gay men as well as to transient workers of various sorts. The rooms were cheap, they were minimally supervised, and the fact that they were usually furnished and were rented by the week made them easy to leave if a lodger got a job elsewhere—or needed to disappear because of legal troubles.[4] Rooming houses also offered tenants a remarkable amount of privacy. Not only could they easily move out if trouble developed, the tenants at most houses compensated for the lack of physical privacy by maintaining a degree of respectful social distance. (Inclined to dislike anything they saw in the rooming houses, housing reformers, somewhat contradictorily, were as distressed by the lack of interest roomers took in one another's affairs as by the lack of privacy the houses afforded.) One study conducted in Boston in 1906 reported that in addition to taking their meals outside their cramped quarters, most roomers also developed their primary social ties elsewhere, at cheap neighborhood restaurants, at their workplaces, and in saloons.[5] Moreover, the absence of a parlor (which usually had been converted into a bedroom) in most rooming houses, the respect many landladies had for their tenants' privacy, and, perhaps most important, the competition among rooming houses for lodgers led many landladies to tolerate men and women visiting each other's rooms and bringing in guests of the other sex. Numerous landladies in the 1920s, when queried by male investigators posing as potential tenants, said straightforwardly that they could have women in their rooms: "Why certainly, this is your home" was the reassuring reply of one.[6]

Some landladies doubtless tolerated known homosexual lodgers for the same economic reasons they tolerated lodgers who engaged in heterosexual affairs, and others simply did not care about their tenants' homosexual affairs. But most expected their tenants at least to maintain a decorous fiction about their social lives. The boundaries of acceptable behavior were, as a result, often unclear, and in many houses men felt constrained to try to conceal the gay aspects of their lives. The story of one black gay man who lived in the basement of a rooming house on West Fiftieth Street, between Fifth and Sixth Avenues, in 1919 suggests the latitude—and limitations—of rooming-house life. The tenant felt free to invite men whom he met on the street into his room. One summer evening, for instance, he invited an undercover investigator he had met while sitting on the basement stairs. But, as he later explained to his guest, while three "young fellows" had been visiting him in his room on a regular basis, he had finally decided to stop seeing the youths because they made too much noise, and he did not want the landlady "to get wise." Not only might he lose his room, he feared, but also his job as the house's chambermaid.[7] The consequences of discovery could be even more severe. In 1900 a suspicious boardinghouse keeper on East Thirteenth Street barged into the room taken only a few days earlier by two waiters, a twenty-year-old German and seventeen-year-old American. She caught them having sex, had them arrested, and eventually had the German sent to prison for a year.[8]

In general, though, the same lack of supervision in the rooming houses that so concerned moral reformers made the houses particularly attractive to gay men, who were able to use their landladies' and fellow tenants' presumption that they were straight in order to disguise their liaisons with men. A male lodger attracted less attention when a man, rather than a woman, visited his room, and a male couple could usually take a room together without generating suspicion.[9] Moreover, the privacy and flexibility such accommodations provided often helped men develop gay social networks. Young men new to New York or the gay life often met other gay men in their rooming houses, and these men sometimes served as their guides as they explored gay society. The ease with which men could move from one rooming house to another also allowed them to pursue and strengthen new social ties by moving in with new friends (or lovers) or moving closer to restaurants or bars where their friends gathered.[10]

Moral reformers expressed concern that the casual intermingling of strangers in furnished-room houses could "assume a dangerous aspect," especially when it introduced young men and women to people of ill repute. In response to this threat, some sought to offer more secure environments to young migrants to the city.[11] Various groups established special hotels at the turn of the century in order to provide men with moral alternatives to the city's flophouses, transient hotels, and rooming houses. Ironically, though, such hotels often became major centers for the gay world and served to introduce men to gay life. In an all-male living situation, in which numerous men already shared rooms, it was virtually impossible for management to detect gay couples. The Seamen's Church Institute, for instance, had been established as a residential and social facility by a consortium of churches in order to protect seamen from the moral dangers the churchmen believed threatened them in the lodging houses of the waterfront areas. But, as we have already seen, gay seamen and other gay men interested in seamen could usually be found in the Institute's lobby. Men involved in relationships also had no difficulty taking rooms together: one seaman told an investigator in 1931 that he had lived with a youth at the Institute "for quite some time," and he had apparently encountered no censure there.[12] Similarly, the two massive Mills Houses, built by the philanthropist Darius O. Mills, were intended to offer unmarried workingmen moral accommodation in thousands of small but sanitary rooms. (The first one was built in 1896 directly across Bleecker Street from the building that had housed the notorious fairy resort, the Slide, just a few years earlier, as if to symbolize the reestablishment of moral order on the block; the second was built on Rivington Street in 1897.) Its attractiveness as a residence for working-class gay men is suggested by the frequency with which its residents appeared in the magistrate's courts. In March 1920, for instance, at least three residents of the two Mills Houses were arrested on homosexual charges (not on the premises): a forty-three-year-old Irish laborer, a forty-two-year-old Italian barber, and a thirty-eight-year-old French cook.[13]

The residential hotels built by the Young Men's Christian Association provide the most striking example of housing designed to reform men's behavior that gay men managed to appropriate for their own purposes. The YMCA movement had begun in the 1840s and 1850s with the intention of supplying young, unmarried migrants to the city with an urban counterpart to the rural family they had left behind. Its founders had expressed special concern about the moral dangers facing such men in the isolation of rooming-house life. The Y organized libraries, reading groups, and gymnasiums for such men, and in some cities established residential facilities, despite some organizers' fear that they might become as depraved and degrading as the lodging houses.[14] The New York YMCA began building dormitories in 1896, and by the 1920s the seven YMCA residential hotels in New York housed more than a thousand young men, whose profiles resembled those of most rooming-house residents: primarily in their twenties and thirties, nearly half of them were clerks, office workers, and salesmen, while smaller numbers were "professional men," artisans, mechanics, skilled workers, and, especially in the Harlem branch, hotel, restaurant, and domestic-service employees.[15]

The fears of the early YMCA organizers were realized. By World War I, the YMCAs in New York and elsewhere had developed a reputation among gay men as centers of sex and social life. Sailors at Newport, Rhode Island, reported that "everyone" knew the Y was "the headquarters" for gay men, and the sailor's line in Irving Berlin's World War I show, *Yip, Yip, Yaphank,* about having lots of friends at the YMCA is said to have drawn a knowing laugh.[16] The reputation only increased in the Depression with the construction, in 1930, of two huge new YMCA hotels, which soon became famous within the gay world as gay residential centers. The enormous Sloane House, on West Thirty-fourth Street at Ninth Avenue, offered short-term accommodations to "transient young men" in almost 1,500 rooms, and the West Side Y, on Sixty-third Street at Central Park West, offered longer-term residential facilities as well. A man interviewed in the mid-1930s recalled of his stay at Sloane House:

> One night when I was coming in at 11:30 P.M. a stranger asked me to go
> to his room. They just live in one another's rooms although it's strictly
> forbidden. . . . This Y.M.C.A. is for transients but one further uptown
> [the West Side Y] is a more elegant brothel, for those who like to live in
> their ivory towers with Greek gods. If you go to a shower there is
> always someone waiting to have an affair. It doesn't take long.[17]

Such observations became a part of gay folklore in the 1930s, 1940s,
and 1950s, when the extent of sexual activity at the Ys—particularly the
"never ending sex" in the showers—became legendary within the gay
world. A man living in New Jersey remembered that he stayed at Sloane
House "many times, every chance I got . . . [because] it was very gay";
another man called it a "gay colony." Indeed, the Y had such a reputation for sexual adventure that some New Yorkers took rooms at Sloane
House for the weekend, giving fake out-of-town addresses. "It was just a
free for all," one man who did so several times recalled, "more fun than
the baths."[18]

While the sexual ambience of the Ys became a part of gay folklore, the
role of the Ys as gay social centers was also celebrated. Many gay New
Yorkers rented rooms in the hotels, used the gym and swimming pool
(where men swam naked), took their meals there, or gathered there to
meet their friends. Just as important—and more ironic, given reformers'
intentions—was the crucial role the hotels often played in introducing
young men to the gay world. It was at the Y that many newcomers to the
city made their first contacts with other gay men. Grant McGree arrived in
the city in 1941, not knowing anyone, intimidated by the size of the city,
and full of questions about his sexuality. But on his first night at the Y as
he gazed glumly from his room into the windows of other men's rooms he
suddenly realized that many of the men he saw sharing rooms were couples; within a week he had met many of them and begun to build a network of gay friends. As gay men used to put it, the letters Y-M-C-A stood
for "Why I'm So Gay."[19]

Donald Vining's diary of his move to New York in search of work in
the fall of 1942 provides a particularly detailed account of how the Y
and similar residential hotels could serve to introduce men to the gay
world. Upon arriving in New York, Vining took a room at Sloane
House, and within a week was startled to have someone approach him
in the shower room. Nothing happened that time, but, intrigued and
emboldened, he initiated contact with someone else in the shower room
a few days later. Within a week he had moved to the Men's Residence
Club (formerly a YMCA hotel), on West Fifty-sixth Street, which he
later wryly described as "a combination old men's home and whore-
house," where he continued to meet men. He soon took a job back at

Sloane House, where he worked with several other gay men at the front desk. Within weeks of his arrival in the city, his contacts at the Y and the Club had supplied him with a large circle of friends, with whom he took his meals, went to the theater, and explored the gay life of the city. Although he eschewed the dominant institutions of the gay world, particularly bars and private parties, he created an extensive gay social circle based on the contacts he made at work and at home.[20]

The response of the YMCA's managers to such activity was ambiguous. At some residences they took steps to restrict contact between certain groups of men (and thus, in effect, to restrict the possibilities for liaisons), such as assigning servicemen to certain floors, segregating the floors by age or by other criteria, and prohibiting residents from taking outsiders to their rooms. It is not clear why the management developed such regulations; many gay men believed they had been designed precisely in order to hamper their socializing, but this, of course, reveals more about the extent to which they viewed the Y as a gay arena than it does about the actual concerns of management. The upper echelon of the Y's management occasionally indicated its concern about the situation by ordering crackdowns on homosexual activity. In general, however, the fate of gay residents depended on the personal predilections of the lower-level security staff and desk clerks. Some of them were gay themselves; as one man recalled, "The job was considered a plum—[the] fox guarding the hen house!"[21] Many of them, whatever their own inclinations, appear to have had little interest in spending their time ferreting out homosexual activity or in punishing the occasional homosexual liaisons of which they became aware, so long as the participants observed certain rules of decorum.

While working as a desk clerk at Sloane House in June 1943, for instance (at a time, admittedly, when the pressure of wartime mobilization relaxed many standards), Donald Vining recorded in his diary that "a note was left [tonight] for 417, a vacated room, and when the new occupant read the note, he [laughed and] handed it to us. It was asking for a return assignation with 424." The head clerk simply threw it away, "without setting the house man to check on the guy who wrote it," which "gladdened my heart." On another occasion, when a man went far beyond the boundaries of discretion expected by the staff—several residents complained that he had entered their rooms while they were sleeping and attempted to initiate sexual contacts—he was asked to leave, but, significantly, he was not reported to the police.[22]

As in most housing situations, then, gay men at the Y constantly ran the risk of being discovered and penalized for their homosexual liaisons or simply for their status as homosexuals. But so long as they regulated their own behavior in accordance with the restrictions unofficially imposed on them, the risk of discovery and retribution was slight.

While both the YMCA and rooming houses offered a modicum of privacy to men of moderate means, the development of apartment hotels and houses in the last quarter of the nineteenth century made it possible for men with greater financial resources to acquire accommodations with greater privacy and respectability. Apartment hotels, originally introduced in the 1870s and built primarily in the late 1890s and 1900s, created new possibilities for independent living among unmarried men. A number of the earliest apartment hotels, such as the Bachelor Apartments, built at 15 East Forty-eighth Street in 1900, and the Hermitage Hotel, built in 1907 on Seventh Avenue just south of Forty-second Street, were specifically designed for well-off bachelors: they offered small but comfortable living quarters (without cooking facilities), a public restaurant, and communal lounging and writing rooms designed to resemble those of a gentlemen's club.

Although the superior social status of apartment *hotels* over rooming houses quickly allowed them to become respectable accommodations for middle-class bachelors, apartment *houses*, whose kitchen facilities made them more suitable for families, were initially eschewed by middle-class families. For most of the nineteenth century, a private rowhouse had been the mark of a successful family in a city whose immigrant masses were herded together in tenements, and most bourgeois families initially regarded the apartment house as little more than a better sort of tenement. The respectability and popularity of apartments grew in the last decade of the century, however, as the skyrocketing cost of land in desirable neighborhoods made individual home ownership unobtainable for all but the wealthy and as apartments became known for their size, convenience, and elegance. Middle-class New Yorkers began to accept them as the only way to live in desirable neighborhoods, and at the end of the depression of the mid-1890s, apartment construction commenced in earnest. By the 1920s, New York was well on its way to becoming a city of apartment dwellers.[23]

The increasing number and respectability of apartment houses and hotels helped make it possible for a middle-class gay male world to develop. At a minimum, they offered gay men greater privacy, space, and prestige than rooming houses. An employee-doorman, rather than an owner-landlady, observed their comings and goings, and residents generally sought to reproduce the privacy of an individual home by remaining aloof from the activities of their neighbors.* Such privacy allowed men

---

*One account of urban life in 1932 pointed to the still notable anonymity of life in the big midtown apartment buildings, "where your neighbor is just a number on the door." It illustrated its point with a description of an expensive building on West Fifty-sixth Street, whose two hundred apartments included not only the homes of "quiet families [who] know little or nothing about the activities of their neighbors," but also, it claimed, three flats on the ninth floor where lesbians lived, and another on the tenth occupied by a gay man.[24]

to bring gay friends home and allowed couples to live together. More important, the ample space of an apartment allowed gay men to entertain friends on a large scale, a resource of inestimable value at a time when police harassment restricted their ability to gather in more public spaces.[25] Finally, the apartment offered middle-class gay men the unquestioned aura of respectability that eluded residents of rooming houses and flophouses. The "bachelor flat" became an established form of accommodation, and this made it easier for men whose backgrounds and occupations would not have allowed them to live at the Y to live outside the family system.

As apartment living became more financially accessible and commonplace in New York in the early decades of the century, it became the accommodation of choice for gay men as for other New Yorkers. In the 1920s and 1930s, growing numbers of tenements and railroad flats, which previously had been occupied by entire families (or even several families), were turned into apartments occupied by a single resident or a couple. A middle-class gay residential enclave developed on the Upper East Side in the 1930s, 1940s, and 1950s. Many gay men moved into the railroad flats in the East Fifties and Sixties east of the Third Avenue elevated train, which allowed them to live close to the elegance of Park Avenue (as well as the gay bars of Third Avenue) at a fraction of the cost. At the same time, a less wealthy gay enclave developed in the Forties west of Eighth Avenue, as large groups of poorer gay men, often youths, crowded into flats in the old tenements of Hell's Kitchen (see chapters 11 and 12).

While some men were able to secure relatively private accommodations, many others had little space to themselves at home. This problem was hardly unique to gay men, for most poor people in the city, whether they rented a cot in one of the city's flophouses or lived with a dozen or more people in a tiny three-room tenement flat, had little access to the privacy that bourgeois ideology ascribed to the home. Couples living in the cramped quarters of working-class neighborhoods needed private space for sexual encounters, as did the prostitutes offering sexual services to the city's enormous population of single men; thus hotel and saloon proprietors found it profitable to rent their rooms by the hour to unmarried couples. The struggle between entrepreneurs and moral reformers over the provision of such accommodations in the early decades of the century was a key component in the campaign over the moral and spatial order of the city (see chapter 5). But if the provision of respectable residential accommodations for single men did little to prevent gay men from meeting, the more coercive campaigns aimed at closing the assignation hotels had even less effect on them.

The number of assignation hotels in New York grew dramatically after the state legislature enacted the Raines Law in 1896. Billed as a temperance measure, it required saloons to close on Sundays, one of their busiest days. That the law was designed to control working-class male sociability more than to encourage temperance was made clear by a provision that allowed bars attached to hotels, which generally served a class of male drinkers considered more respectable by the legislators, to remain open. Sunday was the only day off for many workingmen, however, and many liked to spend it relaxing with their friends in a saloon. In order to avoid losing the vitally important Sunday trade, more than a thousand saloons managed to convert themselves into "hotels" by renting ten adjoining rooms (the minimum number required for certification as a hotel) or, even more commonly, by renting a smaller number of rooms and partitioning them into ten spaces, each large enough for little more than a bed or cot. By 1906, officials estimated that fully 1,200 of the 1,400 hotels registered in Manhattan and the Bronx were such "Raines Law hotels," and that in the great majority of them the saloon proprietors had found it most profitable to rent each room several times a night to successive unmarried couples or to prostitutes and their customers.[26] They also discovered that several resorts forced to close in the crackdown following the revelations of the Parkhurst campaign in 1894, including Paresis Hall, had been able to reopen under the auspices of the Raines Law.[27]

Transforming a saloon into a Raines Law hotel became a common—and successful—business practice not only because it allowed proprietors to circumvent the Sunday closing law, but also because it allowed them to profit from the need for private quarters on the part of many unmarried men and women. Many saloons not only became assignation hotels for unmarried sweethearts, but also, in a bid to attract new customers and increase profitability, made sure that prostitutes were always available in the back room of the saloon itself. As a result, the law inadvertently encouraged the dispersion of prostitution into new neighborhoods of the city, and in certain quarters streetwalkers could be found outside saloons, soliciting men to accompany them inside.

It was in response to the appearance of the Raines Law hotels that moral reformers and shocked city businessmen founded the Committees of Fifteen and Fourteen. The Committee of Fifteen, founded in 1900, sent investigators to saloons throughout the city and published a study, *The Social Evil*, in 1902 that deplored the Raines Law hotels as dens of prostitution that had spread the vice throughout the city. Spurred on by its findings, a meeting in 1905 at the City Club, an elite businessmen's club, established the Committee of Fourteen for the Suppression of Raines Law Hotels in New York City, which launched a campaign against the hotels. In 1912 the Committee concluded that its efforts had been successful. But, asserting that cabarets and other centers of "commercialized amusements" had simply replaced the hotels as the sites of prostitution and unrestrained socializing between men and women, it reorganized itself as a general anti-prostitution society, which continued to be a major force in the city's anti-vice campaigns until it disbanded in 1932.[28]

Although the Committee's campaign led to the closing of the best-known Bowery resorts where "fairies" were on display, such as the Jumbo, its efforts had less effect on the use of the Raines Law hotels for sexual trysts by male couples than by heterosexual couples, precisely because of their focus on female prostitution. The Committee's main strategy was to close as many of the hotels as possible, with the cooperation of the brewers, and to prevent those it could not close from being used for assignations by prohibiting them from admitting women. By 1909, it had reduced the number of such hotels by half and had forced almost three-quarters of the remaining 690 hotels to agree to admit men only.[29] This forced a wholesale movement of prostitution out of such hotels and back into tenements and furnished-room houses, but it had little effect on male couples seeking accommodation.

The history of a hotel-saloon at 36 Myrtle Avenue, near the Brooklyn Navy Yard, illustrates the range of tactics used by the Committee as well as the unanticipated effects they could have for gay men. When the Committee's agents first investigated the hotel in 1910 or 1911, they determined that it was "a resort for prostitutes and their customers . . . a typical Raines Law hotel." The Committee persuaded the brewer backing the saloon to withdraw its support. This was the Committee's usual ploy and resulted in the closing of most offending saloons, since most proprietors were dependent on a brewer's financial support. The Myrtle Avenue saloon was able to stay open, however, by securing the backing of another brewer less susceptible to Committee pressure. Not to be outmaneuvered, the Committee and police counterattacked by sending plainclothesmen to the hotel to gather evidence of the hotel's hosting assignations, which they used in 1912 to secure the conviction of the hotel clerk for keeping a disorderly house. As a result of the conviction, the hotel's saloon lost its liquor license for a year, and after it reopened it was prohibited from admitting women. The proprietor, like hundreds of others, abided by this restriction. But, as the Committee subsequently learned, the exclusion of women from his hotel simply resulted in his developing an alternative market. In 1917, four years after the hotel had reopened, the police discovered that it regularly permitted known "male perverts" to take sailors and other men to their rooms for "immoral purposes."[30]

Even after the suppression of the Raines Law hotels, larger, more conventional hotels unconnected to saloons, some with as many as a hundred rooms, continued to serve the needs of those couples with no place else to meet. By one estimate forty such assignation hotels were operating in the city in 1915, and even after a concerted campaign to close them, twelve of them remained in 1918. They flourished again after the Committee's demise in the early thirties. Many of the hotels did not cater to prostitutes and their customers, which seemed too dangerous, but simply provided rooms to couples who had nowhere else to go.[31] Some of them, as well as a larger number of cheap lodging houses, made their rooms available on an hourly basis to male couples, about whose purposes they could have had no doubt. Most were clustered near streets and parks that served as meeting places for gay and straight couples alike. The young male prostitute (or "punk") who met a prospective customer in Battery Park in 1931, it will be recalled, explained they could easily rent a room for a dollar at one of the many Chatham Square lodging houses that served the Bowery's transient male population.[32] By the 1910s, assignation hotels and cheap transient lodging houses renting rooms to male couples existed near Union Square, Battery Park, and the Brooklyn Navy Yard, and by the 1930s—and possibly earlier—they could be found near Times Square and in the West Seventies near Central Park, as well as in Chatham Square.[33]

The Committee's campaign was remarkably successful. As its investigators repeatedly discovered, hotels wishing to retain a respectable reputation refused to allow men to take women other than their wives to their rooms, for fear that the Committee's agents would denounce them for colluding in the "immoral" use of their facilities. Wealthier gay men nonetheless had access to more respectable hotels that did not offer rooms by the hour and would not have allowed an unmarried heterosexual couple to rent one for the night. A male couple sharing a room, or a respectable-looking male hotel guest taking another man to his room for a few hours, aroused less suspicion on the part of desk clerks than a mixed couple, from whom he might require some proof of marriage. A few hotels, such as the St. George in Brooklyn, developed a reputation for their willingness to accommodate gay men on a short- or long-term basis, but gay men could use a larger number of them surreptitiously. On his visits into the city in the 1910s, for instance, Charles Tomlinson Griffes frequently stayed at the Hotel Longacre in the Times Square district, and he had no trouble taking the men he had met on the streets or in the baths back to his room there.[34] Similarly, a thirty-five-year-old man from Kentucky regularly invited men to his rooms at the Hotel Shelton on Lexington Avenue at Forty-ninth Street, where he resided for several months in 1929. He even felt free to give his hotel address to casual pickups. When he met an investigator at Grand Central Station one evening, he invited the man to visit him the next day at the nearby hotel, where he tried to seduce him and spoke of "quite a number of [other] friends who come to see me [in the hotel]."[35] The presumption that all "normal"-looking men were heterosexual and the related focus by the vice squad on suppressing female prostitution granted gay men an astonishing degree of mobility and freedom, which, nonetheless, they always had to exercise with great caution.

The campaigns to control assignation hotels illustrate the degree to which the anti-vice societies often neglected homosexuality because of their preoccupation with controlling female prostitution, as well as the ability of "normal"-looking gay men to manipulate observers' presumption that they were straight to their own advantage. But many of the hotels were available only to men of means, and, in any case, offered only temporary refuge to men who had met elsewhere. To participate in a collective gay life, men needed to visit other, more public spaces, and in many such locales investigators were more likely to notice male couples and to harass them as much—or more—than heterosexual couples.

CAFETERIA SOCIETY

Like most young, single residents of rooming houses, gay men took most of their meals at the cheap restaurants, cafeterias, and lunch counters that dotted the city's commercial and furnished-room districts. But such facilities took on special significance for many gay men. Most such men needed to manage multiple public identities and to present themselves as straight—or, at least, not gay—at work, at home, and in other consequential social settings. Numerous restaurants and cafeterias became important to them because they could "let their hair down" there and meet other gay people who accepted them as gay, even if they needed to guard against drawing the potentially hostile attention of other diners. Gay men turned many restaurants into places where they could gather with gay friends, gossip, ridicule the dominant culture that ridiculed them, and construct an alternative culture. They turned them into places where it did not seem queer to discuss opera or the latest Broadway show, to talk about an art show or a favorite torch singer, to laugh collectively about the morning paper's picture of the sailor with his arms wrapped around the cannon he was cleaning.[36] Restaurants became places, in short, where men branded as outsiders turned themselves into insiders by creating and sharing a gay reading of the world, a distinctive ironic, camp perspective that affirmed them and challenged the normativity of the world that branded them abnormal (a process discussed at length in chapter 10).

Particular restaurants served as the locus of particular gay social networks; overlapping groups of friends would meet regularly for dinner and camaraderie. The role of restaurants as social centers meant they often functioned as a crucial point of entry into the gay world for men just beginning to identify themselves as gay; for men already deeply involved in the gay world, they were a vital source of information about the gay scene, police activity, cultural events, and the like. The determination of gay men to claim space for themselves in the city's eating places—which they did boldly enough at some cafeterias to give them citywide reputations as "fairy hangouts," and surreptitiously enough at other places that they remained known only to other gay men—occasionally provoked a sharp reaction from social-purity forces. But gay men developed elaborate stratagems to protect such places, precisely because they played such an important role in their lives.

The number of cheap dining facilities increased rapidly in the late nineteenth and early twentieth centuries, in response to the growing number of unmarried clerks and shop workers living in the city. As more and more boardinghouses, whose landladies had provided meals for roomers, were converted into rooming houses, which served no meals and had no kitchen facilities, residents were forced to take meals elsewhere. The number of restaurants surged even further in the 1920s as Prohibition devastated their major sources of competition, closing both the saloons that had offered workingmen a free lunch and the businessmen's clubs that had offered more elegant fare, and making numerous suitable commercial spaces available for conversion into restaurants.[37]

The growth of such facilities is exemplified by the history of two of New York's most famous cafeteria chains, Childs and Horn & Hardart, both of which came to play major roles in the gay world. William and Samuel Childs opened the first of their many restaurants in 1889. Enormous, relatively inexpensive, and sparkling clean, they quickly became popular spots for white-collar workers to take their lunches, dinners, and after-theater suppers, and by 1898 there were nine Childs restaurants serving fifteen thousand to twenty thousand people a day. Childs sought to broaden its appeal further that year by introducing cafeteria-style eating to New York in a restaurant situated to pick up the lunch-hour business of Wall Street clerks. Following its success, the chain opened additional cafeterias throughout the city. By 1939, there were forty-four Childs cafeterias and restaurants in Manhattan, and several other chains, such as Bickford's, Schrafft's, Longchamps, and Caruso, had joined them in appealing to the ever-growing number of unmarried office workers and young families in which the wife continued to work before having children.[38] Following Childs' lead, Horn & Hardart opened its first Automat in New York in 1903. Quickly growing in number, the Automats reached the height of their popularity during the Depression, when more than forty of them could be found in Manhattan alone.[39]

The cafeterias and Automats were not just cheap places to take meals. Many people also used them as meeting places, where they gathered on an almost nightly basis. In the 1930s they were known as the salons of the poorer bohemians of the Village, who wryly called their social world "Cafeteria Society Downtown," in contrast to the wealthier "Café Society Uptown."[40] The Automats appealed primarily to working people and the unemployed, but a cafeteria's clientele could vary enormously. It "all depends on where the restaurant is located," observed one guide in 1925, and, it might have added, on the time of day. Most of the Childs cafeterias were "the feeding ground of obscure and lowly folk" during the day, as the guide put it, but some also attracted a more affluent trade late at night, after the theater and supper clubs had closed.[41] Similarly, restaurants that served lunch to businessmen and dinner to families or theatergoers could cater to a less respectable clientele later at night. Investigators repeatedly warned during World War I and the postwar years that prostitutes and their customers were gathering at two and three in the morning at the Childs restaurants near Union Square, Penn Station, Columbus Circle, and 125th Street.[42]

Some of these cafeterias, Automats, and lunchrooms catered to a gay clientele, while others were simply taken over by gay men, who were allowed to remain so long as they increased business without drawing the attention of the police. Many gay men also had jobs in the city's restaurants,* and some tested the limits of managerial tolerance in the boldness with which they welcomed gay customers. Parker Tyler described the scene in the fall of 1929 when he visited a Childs in Brooklyn with several friends: "Well my dear considering that I was in a huge fur coat of Clairmont's [one of his women companions] and must have looked very gorgeous, it isn't a surprise but that waiter started right in camping just as though there were *no law*!! And everybody in our party started camping after the waiter asked me: 'What will you have, gorgeous?', and I replied bitterly: 'Nothing you've got, dearie,' which really did upset everyone. And you can imagine how things went from bad to worse. So I concluded Brooklyn is wide open and N.Y. should be notified of its existence."[44]

Automats were among the safest refuges available to poorer gay men. They became even more secure during the Depression, when their rock-bottom prices and lack of supervision gave them a reputation as a sanctuary for social outcasts and the unemployed. The Automat on Forty-second Street across from Bryant Park became particularly well known as the site of raucous gatherings.[45]

---

*Of the two hundred men arrested on homosexual charges by the police in cooperation with the Society for the Suppression of Vice in 1920–21, thirty-nine were restaurant employees, by far the largest single occupational category represented. Frederick Whitin, general secretary of the Committee of Fourteen, surmised in 1921 that this might be related to the apparent move by homosexuals, like prostitutes, to turn restaurants into their major "resorts" after the closing of the saloons.[43]

While the Automats' clientele were particularly famous for their lack of inhibition, the atmosphere at even the large cafeterias in the very well established Childs chain could become astonishingly freewheeling, as Tyler's vignette suggests, particularly late at night, after the dinner hour, when managers tolerated a wide spectrum of customers and behavior in order to generate trade. Gay men quickly spread the word about which restaurants and cafeterias would let them gather without guarding their behavior. Several Childs cafeterias and restaurants located in heavily gay neighborhoods became known among gay men as meeting places; indeed, the campy antics of the more flamboyant among them became part of the draw for other customers. One gay man who lived in the city in the late 1920s recalled that the Childs restaurant in the Paramount Theater Building on Broadway at Forty-third Street was regularly "taken over" by "hundreds" of gay men after midnight. Even if his recollection exaggerates the situation, it suggests his sense of the extent to which gay men felt comfortable there; in any case, *Vanity Fair*'s 1931 guide to New York informed its readers that the Paramount Childs was particularly interesting because it "features a dash of lavender."[46]

The Paramount Childs was not the only restaurant in the chain to earn such a reputation. Two Childs located in the blocks of Fifth Avenue south of Central Park, which served as a major gay cruising area in the 1920s—one in the Falkenhayn apartment building on Fifth Avenue between Fifty-eighth and Fifty-ninth Streets and another on the Avenue near Forty-ninth Street—were also patronized by so many gay men that they became known in the gay world as meeting places.[47] But perhaps the most famous such rendezvous, christened "Mother Childs" by some, was the one on Fifty-ninth Street at Columbus Circle, close to Central Park cruising areas as well as to Broadway theaters. Numerous investigators in the early 1920s reported seeing "prostitutes, charity girls . . . cabaret performers [and] fairies" carrying on there, telling stories, camping, and moving from table to table to greet old friends and meet new ones.[48] A man who had moved to New York from a small town in North Dakota in 1922 recalled:

> After hours—you might say after the theater, [which brought] hordes of people together—Childs was a meeting place for gays and they would congregate and sit and have coffee and yak-yak and talk til three and four and five o'clock in the morning. . . . I was always there with friends, that was the social thing to do.[49]

The history of two cafeterias in the Village in the 1920s and 1930s, Stewart's and the Life Cafeteria, both located on Christopher Street at Sheridan Square, demonstrates even more clearly the extent to which gay men could be made part of the spectacle of an establishment, even as they turned it into a haven. Both cafeterias, like the turn-of-the-century Bowery resorts before them, seem to have premised their late-night operations on the assumption that by allowing lesbians and gay men to gather there they would attract sight-seers out to gawk at a late-night "fairy hangout." The 1939 *WPA Guide to New York City* almost surely described the Life when it delicately explained that "a cafeteria [at Sheridan Square], curiously enough, is one of the few obviously Bohemian spots [left] in the Village, and evenings the more conventional occupy tables in one section of the room and watch the 'show' of the eccentrics on the other side."[50] Several other guidebooks made the same (and usually equally coded) point about both Stewart's and the Life,* but in 1936 one man, outraged by the situation, described the "show" more explicitly. One of the largest cafeterias in town, "brilliantly lighted, [and] fully exposed to two streets [in the Village]," he charged in a medical journal, was the meeting ground for "exhibitionists and degenerates of all types":

> The Park Avenue deb with the Wall Street boy friend nibbles cheap pastry and stares and jibes at the "show.". . . Wide-eyed school girls and boys from neighboring parts of the city gape at the unbelievable sight—boys with rouge on!—and drunken parties end their carousing here. . . . Once I heard one [gay man] say: "That queen over there is camping for jam" [that is, for straights].[52]

Although gay men served as a tourist attraction at the Life, they were still able to make it their own, turning it into one of the few public spaces where their culture predominated and where they could anticipate meeting their friends. The openness of gay men at the Life also made it a point of entry into the gay world for young men just coming out. Because of its reputation as a "fairy hangout," it was easily found by isolated men searching for others like themselves as well as by tourists. Dick Addison, who first visited the Life Cafeteria in 1939

---

*The varying levels of explicitness with which other guides made the same point—as well as the longevity of Stewart's and the Life as gay rendezvous—are illustrated by two accounts from the 1930s. In 1935 a restaurant guide explained that Stewart's, an "innocent-enough looking cafeteria," was "the current hangout of Bohemia . . . [where] you may take a peek at the local crop of would-be Villons." In a coded (but easily understood) reference to the gay men and lesbians whom the tourist could see there, the author went on to compare the "heterogeneous crowd that infest Stewart's" to "the lillies of the field." Characteristically, *Broadway Brevities* was more explicit; in late 1933 it reported that a restaurant at Sheridan Square had become "a gathering spot for that nocturnal clan, the third sexers. Dykes, fags, pansies, lesbians, and others of that unfortunate ilk convene there nightly, parading their petty jealousies and affairs of the heart."[51]

when he was a sixteen-year-old from the Bronx, remembered its significance when he came out:

> The Life Cafeteria was a big hangout. Faggots from all over the coun-
> try would gather there. They'd just sit in the window, drinking coffee
> and smoking cigarettes and carrying on. It had huge plate glass win-
> dows so people on the street could see in, and tourists would pass by
> to see them, because they wore heavy makeup—blue eye shadow,
> rouge, mascara—and had long hair. It attracted young people coming
> out, like me. They would go there because they didn't know anywhere
> else to go. They'd go to the Village because they'd heard that was
> where the action was, and then see this cafeteria and go there. They
> could go in there and have a cup of coffee for a nickel, sit and occupy
> a table and laugh and talk all night long. It was a place where they
> could meet people.[53]

The dramaturgical language widely used to describe the "show" at
such cafeterias signals how unusual and noteworthy such public expressions of gay culture were considered, since "normal" people's antics
were rarely noticed as unusual. But it also points again to one of the central strategies deployed by gay men for claiming space in the city. They
regularly sought to emphasize the theatricality of everyday interactions
and to use their style to turn the Life and other such locales into the
equivalent of a stage, where their flouting of gender conventions seemed
less objectionable because it was less threatening. It let slummers experience the thrill of seeing the "perverts," while letting gay men themselves
adopt a style that mocked the conventions of heterosexuality. Nonetheless, gay men and lesbians who put on such "shows" always ran the
risk of harassment from other patrons, eviction by the management, or
arrest by the police, particularly when they did not limit their openness
to locales where they were clearly tolerated.

Many gay men and lesbians, in fact, especially younger people who
felt they had less social position to lose, regularly tested the limits on
their openness at restaurants, speakeasies, and other establishments, by
dancing together, speaking loudly about their affairs, and camping for
others. While at the Round Table in Greenwich Village one night in
1929, Parker Tyler was invited to join a group of lesbians and gay men
who were clearly unwilling to brook any restrictions on their evening's
fun: "Someone—Lesbian—rushed up and asked me to join their drinking party," Tyler wrote a gay friend, "and I did and someone who said
he had just been brought out began making drunken love to me but he
wasn't much and then someone—officially male—asked me to dance."
The management had tolerated the gay flirtation at Tyler's table, but

drew the line at same-sex dancing and promptly "ordered [them] off the floor." The woman who had invited him to join them dismissed the management's action by commenting curtly that "THEY DON'T UNDERSTAND OUR TYPE," as Tyler recalled in full capitals. Although Tyler sometimes declined invitations to dance for fear of such reprimands, he often tested the limits in precisely this way—and was almost as often told to stop dancing with men.[54]

Even Tyler, hardly reticent, was occasionally taken aback by how relentlessly some of his friends challenged hetero-normativity in their Village haunts—and by how insistently they demanded that he not present himself as anything other than gay. At a neighborhood speakeasy one night he found himself, somewhat to his surprise, beginning to neck with a woman he had just met. After a brief flirtation and "some drinks," he reported to a gay friend (in a reversal of the usual attempt to blame *homosexual* escapades on drink), "I found myself . . . kissing her madly." The fact that he was "kissing her madly" suggests the casual atmosphere of the place, though casual heterosexual interactions were usually treated more casually than homosexual. But his friends would have nothing of it, and turned his brief heterosexual flirtation into an occasion for asserting a gay presence in the speakeasy. "Who should come in about then," Tyler continued, "but Paula who exclaimed, 'What! Parker kissing a female!'" Tyler quieted his friend, but when he returned to the first woman and "started to kiss her again," a second friend, a gay man, "exclaimed in a booming voice: 'Parker! Why don't you tell this girl you're homosexual?'" Before Tyler could recover from his embarrassment, "who should positively BLOW in at that moment but a bitch named—(artist) who shouted at the top of his voice O HELLO MISS TYLER!" "And this was in a speakeasy," Tyler added immediately, as if even he found it astonishing that someone should be so overtly—and loudly—gay in such a space.[55] He had a similar reaction to the waiter at the Brooklyn Childs who "started right in camping just as though there were *no law*!!" For all his boldness, Tyler never forgot there *was* a law—informal as well as formal—against public expressions of gay culture, and it is doubtful that any other gay man did either. Nonetheless, many of them regularly tested the boundaries that law established.

Most managers, like the ones who stopped Tyler from dancing, never let matters get "out of hand." But when the informal injunction against gay visibility was successfully challenged by gay men and lesbians or gave way to public fascination with gay visibility, the formal agencies of the law—the police and social-purity organizations—sometimes stepped in to reestablish (the social) order. They sometimes did this with the connivance of skittish managers, who realized they had let things go "too far" by letting their gay clientele become too "obvious," as difficult as it might be to judge when that line had been crossed. In February 1927, for instance, after gay men had been congregating at the Forty-second Street Liggett's drugstore for some time, the management, perhaps sensing a temporary hardening of police attitudes or simply fearing for its reputation, suddenly called on the police to drive the men from its premises. The police raided the store and arrested enough men to fill two police vans.[56]

The state and social-purity groups intervened most commonly, though, against the wishes of managers who saw no harm and much profit in tolerating a gay presence. Some of those managers devised elaborate schemes to protect their businesses. The background to a raid on a Lower East Side cabaret in 1920 illustrates the strategies such establishments used to protect themselves and highlights the complex relationship between the social-purity societies, the police, the courts, and the entrepreneurs they sought to control, as well as the constraints affecting gay men who wished to socialize in public.

The Hotel Koenig, a small hotel and cabaret run by the German-born George Koenig on East Fourth Street near First Avenue, had developed a citywide reputation among gay men. Police records show that few of the men arrested there in a raid one night in 1920 were from the immediate neighborhood; most lived more than twenty blocks away, near Madison Square, in the midtown theater district, or in even more distant parts of Manhattan and Brooklyn, and two were visiting from Philadelphia. All were white and, like most of the city's bachelors, young: three-quarters were in their twenties, only a few were even in their thirties, and none was older. They seem to have taken care in choosing their housing and meeting places to ensure they could be openly gay, for about a quarter of them had come with roommates or live-in lovers. And they were quite open at Koenig's. One Committee of Fourteen investigator, who learned that fairies had begun to gather at the Koenig in the spring of 1920, reported that "most of the patrons paid more attention to the action of the fairies than to the cabaret performance." Koenig's tolerance of the men's flagrant campiness was consistent with his decision to permit prostitutes and other women to drink with the male patrons, "using vile language," according to the investigator, "and [not] behav[ing]." Koenig had clearly decided to cater to a rough crowd.[57]

While the Hotel Koenig was well known as a "fairy resort" to the cabaret's gay and straight patrons alike, court officials expressed surprise after the raid that such a place existed in the neighborhood at all, especially "without the knowledge of it being more general." As the Committee of Fourteen discovered in the course of its investigation, George Koenig had made arrangements to ensure that "knowledge of it" would be kept from the court, primarily by making his facilities freely available to a social club whose members included numerous patrolmen from the local precinct. On one occasion, for instance, the members, after taking in a burlesque show on West 125th Street, brought several female prostitutes and some of the "burlesque girls" down to the cabaret, where they drank and partied all night.

Such arrangements might have protected Koenig's indefinitely, had the Committee of Fourteen not become involved during its postwar anti-gay campaign. The precautions Koenig had taken certainly made the Committee's job more difficult, requiring it to bypass the local precinct and persuade the chief inspector of the First Inspection District, a division of the police department independent of the precincts, to send four plainclothesmen to investigate the cabaret. Once it had prevailed upon the inspector to raid the place, the Committee needed to investigate the court schedule to ensure that the raid would be conducted on a night when a sympathetic judge would hear the case; "by all means we want to stay away from [certain judges]," the committee cautioned the inspector. On the last Saturday night in July 1920, when the judge they wanted to hear the case was sitting, the inspector's officers raided the cabaret and arrested thirty patrons, the manager, and the waitress. Koenig was charged with "keeping a disorderly house," a "resort for degenerates," and all of the arrested patrons were charged with degenerate disorderly conduct. Gay men appear to have been the only customers arrested.

No law specifically prohibited gay men from assembling in a public place at the time of the raid in 1920, but the police charged the men at Koenig's with "degenerate disorderly conduct." Indeed, the sentences the men received suggest how dangerous it could be to assert a gay presence at any public establishment. Twenty-three of the men were sentenced to ten days in the workhouse, and the remaining seven were fined fifty dollars. These sentences were unusually severe for men charged with disorderly conduct; sixteen men with similar backgrounds who appeared in court just before the Koenig group on the same charge, but with no implication of "degeneracy," were fined only one or two dollars apiece. Both the judge and the Committee nonetheless lamented that the penalties were relatively light for men charged with "degenerate" disorderly conduct. They considered them the harshest they dare impose, however, since their case was so weak, dependent on a sympathetic judge for successful prosecution. "As individual complaints had not been drawn and the defendants were all tried together," the judge confided to the Committee, he "was afraid the record would not stand on an appeal." No one had been charged with engaging in sexual acts or with any other particular incidents of disorderly conduct, in other words; as the judge well knew, he had convicted them simply for being members of a group of gay men congregating in a public place. Both the judge and the committee settled on relatively light sentences because they feared that, with so many men involved, at least some would be provoked by a heavier sentence to make a successful appeal. None of the men did file an appeal, though, either because they realized they had gotten off *relatively* lightly—"only" ten days in the workhouse, compared to the sixty days often served by men convicted of degeneracy—or because they were simply too intimidated.

"Degenerate disorderly conduct," the offense for which the men at Koenig's were convicted, was the charge usually brought against gay men or lesbians found gathering on the streets or in public accommodations, or gay men trying to pick up other men. The use of the disorderly-conduct law against gay people was consistent with the intent of the law, which effectively criminalized a wide range of non-normative behavior in public spaces, as defined by the dominant culture, be it loitering, gambling, failure to hire oneself out to an employer, failure to remain sober, or behaving in a public space in any other manner perceived as threatening the social order. The disorderly-conduct law was one of the omnibus legal measures used by the state to try to impose a certain conception of public order on the city's streets, and, in particular, to control the large numbers of immigrants from Ireland and southern and eastern Europe, as well as African-American migrants from the South—the so-called "dangerous classes" many bourgeois Anglo-Americans found frightening. Its purview was so general and ill defined, especially before the statute's revision in 1923, that the interpretation of its scope was left largely in the hands of the police, and it gave them a rationale for arresting people for a wide range of behavior, even though the charges ultimately might be (and regularly were) dismissed by the courts in any particular case.

In the course of its general revision of the statute in 1923, the New York state legislature, for the first time, specified homosexual solicitation (a person "frequent[ing] or loiter[ing] about any public place soliciting men for the purpose of committing a crime against nature or other lewdness") as a form of disorderly conduct. In specifying the solicitation of men and a wide but unspecified range of "lewd" behavior, the new disorderly-conduct statute became the first law in the state's history to verge on specifying male homosexual conduct as a criminal offense. Even the statutes against sodomy and the crime against nature, which dated from the colonial era, had criminalized a wide range of nonprocreative sexual behavior between people of the same or different genders, without specifying male homosexual conduct or even recognizing it as a discrete sexual category. The criminalization of male homosexual conduct implicit in the wording of the law was made explicit in its enforcement, for Penal Law 722, section 8, "degenerate disorderly conduct," was used exclusively against men the police regarded as "degenerates." Although little evidence remains concerning the history of the legislature's decision, its timing surely reflects the degree to which the social-purity societies and the police had identified homosexuality as a distinct social problem during World War I.[58] The statute became one of the underpinnings of new state regulations after the repeal of Prohibition in 1933 that, for the first time, specifically and formally banned the assembly of gay people in a public space.

As the 1920 Koenig case and numerous other cases to be related in this book demonstrate, however, New York City's police and courts construed the disorderly-conduct statute to mandate a much broader ban on gay cultural practices than a narrow reading of its wording might suggest, both before and after its revision in 1923. They regularly used the statute to criminalize the assembly of gay men in a public place or their adoption of distinctive cultural styles, from camp behavior to dancing with people of the same gender or wearing clothes assigned to the other gender. The police and local courts construed such forms of "degenerate" conduct as *disorderly* conduct posing so dangerous a challenge to the social order that they merited imprisonment and fines, and for more than a decade before the law's revision in 1923, the authorities specified in their own records which disorderly-conduct arrests were for "degeneracy." Gay men managed to claim considerable space for themselves in the city's streets, cafeterias, and restaurants despite this policy, and the number of men actually arrested remained relatively small before the 1940s. But they had always to contend with the possibility of such penalties.*

Given both the lack of a specific legal prohibition against gay assembly before 1933 and the tolerant attitude toward gay men in certain quarters of the city, the use of the disorderly-conduct statute to arrest men gathering in a restaurant was episodic and depended to a large degree on the location of the restaurant and the strength of its political connections. Some smaller speakeasies, restaurants, and clubs that tolerated the open presence of lesbians and gay men flourished, but they were subject to the constant threat of harassment. An insider's review of the history of gay and lesbian meeting places in the 1920s, published in 1931, concluded that "it was not long before all the places were either raided or given up."[59]

---

*Lesbians arrested for assembling in a public place, dancing together, and the like were also often charged with disorderly conduct (although not with degenerate disorderly conduct). The revised 1923 statute did not specify lesbian conduct (by criminalizing the solicitation of women, for instance), but, as in the case of gay men before 1923, the police and courts did not need such a specific ban to construe lesbian visibility as a kind of disorderliness. The history of the police's enforcement of the degenerate-disorderly-conduct statute is documented in greater detail in the following chapter.

A cafeteria in a well-established chain with a citywide reputation, such as Childs, on the other hand, had greater political clout and was less susceptible to police interference and raids than a smaller establishment run by a solitary entrepreneur. Large cafeterias in certain neighborhoods could maintain gay reputations for years, as the extraordinary resilience of Stewart's and the Life Cafeteria—which together served as well-known gay meeting places in the Village for almost two decades—demonstrates. Nonetheless, the police did occasionally raid the large cafeterias and Automats where gay people gathered, when they or the anti-vice societies thought the places had become too uproarious or the management, perhaps fearing the authorities were about to reach that conclusion, decided it was time to use the police to eliminate their "fairy" trade. On such occasions, the police might arrest every gay customer at the cafeteria on disorderly-conduct charges. In the summer of 1926, for instance, many lesbians and gay men started gathering at the Childs restaurant on Forty-eighth Street, where they enjoyed "peace and quietude," according to one contemporary account, "until one bright August night, when the place was packed with Lesbians and Pansies, two patrol wagons drove up and arrested every one in the place."[60] On at least one occasion in the mid-1930s the police even raided Stewart's, arresting the "degenerates" who "loiter[ed]" there, after the normally tolerant manager, apparently sensing a temporary hardening in police opinion, had filed a complaint about their presence.[61]

Restaurants—and gay men—developed a variety of strategies for eluding police detection. Many, like Koenig's, simply bribed the police or made other arrangements to mollify them; in the early twentieth century, many small entrepreneurs considered this a regular part of doing business. Other restaurants sought to protect themselves while still retaining the patronage that a covert gay reputation could generate by permitting gay men to gather openly only in certain sections of the restaurant, where they would not be seen by other diners. Jack's Restaurant on Sixth Avenue at the corner of Twenty-sixth Street appears to have adopted such a policy in the early 1920s. More elegant than a cafeteria and drawing a more affluent (and circumspect) clientele, including numerous single men and women living in the area, Jack's had three dining rooms. "Unescorted women" (as women seen in public without men were usually called) and numerous mixed-gender couples sat in the first two rooms, but the management seated most male couples and unaccompanied men in the rear room. Late one night in 1921, just after Christmas, an investigator saw ten or fifteen men he identified as homosexuals (or, in his words, "degenerates") "of a better class or type" sitting at the tables in this room. The agent thought they "were acting and talking like fairys [sic] and anybody could tell who they were simply [by] looking at their actions": among other things, the men felt free to make eye contact and strike up conversations with strangers and to call them over to their tables. The management's collusion with the arrangement was confirmed when a waiter, upon questioning, admitted he knew the men were "fairys," although he protested that he personally "didnt [have] any use for them."[62]

More commonly, restaurants permitted the patronage of gay men only so long as they eschewed behavior that might mark them as gay. Most men were not directly affected by such regulations, it should be noted, because nothing in their demeanor would have signaled their homosexuality to outsiders. Indeed, most gay men mingled unobtrusively with other customers in restaurants that did not cultivate a gay crowd, eating alone or with small groups of gay friends. Charles Tomlinson Griffes and his gay friends regularly patronized Louis', Jouberts, and Rosini's in the mid-1910s without drawing attention to themselves.[63] One man who moved in the gay, artistic, and theater circles around the novelist Carl Van Vechten in the early twenties recalled that he "went very often with my friends [to] . . . a restaurant at Forty-third and Sixth Avenue, called Jack's [different from the Jack's mentioned above]. It was very well known. Mostly theater people went there, though they were very discreet."[64]

While gay men mixed unobtrusively with other customers at many of the city's restaurants, a number of restaurants attracted a predominantly gay clientele and developed a muted gay ambience without attracting much attention from outsiders. Louis' Restaurant on West Forty-ninth Street, and then Louis's second venture, the Jewel Restaurant on West Forty-eighth, both between Fifth and Sixth Avenues, were popular meeting places for successful gay men and women who lived and worked in the Times Square theater district. The restaurants became as well known in gay circles in the 1920s as the most famous Village spots. Several lesbian motion-picture stars and authors were said to patronize Louis' Restaurant, and a decade later, when it had moved to West Forty-fifth Street between Eighth and Ninth Avenues, it continued to be known as a major theatrical rendezvous, where people came to relax, get a cheap meal, and "see and be seen."[65]

Louis's restaurants eventually became known to anti-vice investigators as "hang-outs for fairies and lady lovers" and even received a 1924 mention in a Broadway gossip sheet as a rendezvous of "the queer smart trade," but they never achieved the notoriety of the city's other gay haunts. Even hostile observers acknowledged differences between the behavior of the gay patrons of Louis' and other quiet restaurants with a largely gay clientele, and those who frequented the more boisterous

Village spots. In 1924 one man described the scene at Louis' as a "far cry" from that at the Columbus Circle Childs, even though he still regarded its patrons with contempt. "It is orderly, for one thing, because the fairies who frequent it are a better type than the Village and Columbus Circle fags. . . . It is a place where aberrants dine before going to theatre or mayhap some other evening function. . . . The fairies dish the dirt there the same as they would if they were in a hovel in the Village or in Gertrude Stein's bizarre salon. But they seldom raise their voices."[66] A year later an investigator reported that while he had heard that "wild parties [are] suppose[d] to go on on [the restaurant's] upper floors," the behavior of the patrons in the main dining room on the first floor was unremarkable.[67] Indeed, Louis' hid its role as a major gay rendezvous from casual straight observers so successfully that a sedate 1925 restaurant guide recommended it to its readers, describing it—clearly without apprehending the full significance of its observation—as "one of the institutions of the neighborhood."[68]

Gay men pursued a variety of strategies as they negotiated their presence in the city's restaurants, cafeterias, and speakeasies. Some of them boldly claimed their right to gather in public, speaking loudly about gay matters, dancing with their friends, even putting on a "show" for the other customers. Most men did not make themselves so noticeable, but they nonetheless claimed space in a large number of restaurants on a regular basis, meeting friends, talking about whatever they wanted, and noticing—and sometimes trying to gain the notice of—the other gay men around them. The latter group of men could meet in small, intimate restaurants and huge, impersonal cafeterias alike. The former group of men were more likely to be branded as "fairies" and restricted to the cafeterias or to restaurants located in sections of town with large concentrations of gay residents, such as the Village, Times Square, and Harlem. Although such men made their presence known throughout the early decades of the century, their numbers and boldness grew in the 1920s during Prohibition.

Both groups were protected, in part, by the preoccupation of the social-purity forces with female prostitution, which usually kept them from paying as much attention to gay meeting places as the Committee of Fourteen did in the case of Koenig's. They were also protected by the absence of a formal ban on gay assembly, the laissez-faire attitude of many New Yorkers and, often enough, of the police, and the complex system of bribes and political connections in which most small businessmen, ward politicians, and policemen were enmeshed. Above all, they were protected by the dominant popular image of the fairy, which was more likely to provoke fascination than outrage on the part of many

New Yorkers, and, in any case, rendered most other gay men invisible to outsiders. The very brilliance of the fairy left most men safely in the shadows, and made it easier for them to meet their friends in restaurants throughout the city without provoking the attention of outsiders. Gay men seized the opportunities this portended.

Figure 7.1. One fairy gets his man at the expense of his rival, a prostitute, while another tries to get the attention of a sailor. As these cartoons suggest, Riverside Drive was a well-known cruising avenue for gay men, prostitutes, and sailors. *(From* Broadway Brevities: *"Little Accident," March 7, 1932; "Pickled Corned Beef," October 19, 1933.)*

Chapter 7

"PRIVACY COULD ONLY BE HAD IN PUBLIC": FORGING A GAY WORLD IN THE STREETS

ALTHOUGH NEW YORKERS OCCASIONALLY SAW GAY MEN IN RESTAURANTS and cafeterias, they encountered them more frequently in the city's streets, parks, and beaches, where they seemed to some to be an almost ubiquitous presence. In 1904, the bodybuilding publisher Bernarr Macfadden denounced "the shoals of painted, perfumed, Kohl-eyed, lisping, mincing youths that at night swarm on Broadway in the Tenderloin section, or haunt the parks and 5th avenue, ogling every man that passes and—it is pleasant to relate—occasionally getting a sound thrashing or an emphatic kicking." In the following decade, another New Yorker declared that "our streets and beaches are overrun by . . . fairies," and in the 1920s and 1930s one of the city's tabloids regularly published cartoons that caricatured the supposed efforts of fairies to accost sailors and other men on Riverside Drive (see figure 7.1).[1]

As these comments of observers attest, gay men claimed their right to enjoy the city's public spaces. It was in such open spaces, less easily regulated than a residential or commercial venue, that much of the gay world took shape. The city's streets and parks served as vital meeting grounds for men who lived with their families or in cramped quarters with few amenities, and the vitality and diversity of the gay street scene attracted many other men as well. Streets and parks were where many men— "queer" and "normal" alike—went to find sexual partners, where many gay men went to socialize, and where many men went for sex and ended up being socialized into the gay world.

Part of the gay world taking shape in the streets was highly visible to outsiders, but even more of it was invisible. As Macfadden's comment makes clear, gay men had to contend with the threat of vigilante anti-gay violence as well as with the police. In response to this challenge, gay men devised a variety of tactics that allowed them to move freely about the city, to appropriate for themselves spaces that were not marked as gay, and to construct a gay city in the midst of, yet invisible to, the dominant city. They were aided in this effort, as always, by the disinclination of most people to believe that any "normal"-looking man could be anything other than "normal," and by their access, as men, to public space.

Although gay street culture was in certain respects an unusual and distinctive phenomenon, it was also part of and shaped by a larger street culture that was primarily working-class in character and origin. Given the crowded conditions in which most working people lived, much of their social life took place in streets and parks. The gay presence in the streets was thus masked, in part, by the bustle of street life in working-class neighborhoods. Gay uses of the streets, like other working-class uses, also came under attack, however, because they challenged bourgeois conceptions of public order, the proper boundaries between public and private space, and the social practices appropriate to each.

CRUISING THE CITY'S PARKS

The city's parks were among the most popular—and secure—of New York's gay meeting places, where men gathered regularly to meet their friends and to search (or "cruise," as they called it by the 1920s) for sexual partners.* One of the ostensible purposes of parks, after all, was to offer citizens respite from the tumult of city life, a place where citizens could wander aimlessly and enjoy nature. This provided a useful cover for men wandering in search of others.[3] Few gay men stood out among the other couples, families, and groups of friends and neighbors who thronged the parks, socializing, playing sports, and eating their picnic suppers.

Cruising parks and streets provided many young men and newcomers to the city with a point of entry into the rest of the gay world, which was sometimes hidden from men looking for it by the same codes and subterfuges that protected it from hostile straight intrusions. "It was quite a handicap to be a young guy in the 1920s," remembered one man, who had moved to New York from Michigan. "It took an awfully long time

---

*In a 1929 letter that also confirms Fifth Avenue's significance as a cruising area, Parker Tyler wrote: "Took a walk on Fifth Ave. last Sunday night, just to see what it was like after over a year of absence. . . . Some 'cruisers' but all pretty stiff except undesirables."[2]

to learn of a gay speakeasy."[4] The parks and streets were perhaps the most common place for newcomers to meet men more familiar with that world, and these men became their guides to it. A German Jew who immigrated to New York in 1927, for instance, recalled that within two or three weeks of his arrival, "I found my way to Riverside Drive and the Soldiers and Sailors Monument." He still knew almost no one in the city, but his cruising quickly remedied that. "It was 1927, about two or three days before the big reception parade for Lindbergh after he came back from his flight to Paris, and the bleachers were already up there. I met a man there and we started talking. He was a Harvard man and taught ethical culture. And that was the best contact I made; he and I had a wonderful affair." The affair lasted two years, the friendship many more, and his Riverside Park pickup became his most important guide to the new world.[5]

The German immigrant was not the only man to begin a relationship with someone he met while cruising. Many relationships began through such contacts, and many friendships as well. "E. is a very sentimental lad," Parker Tyler wrote to Charles Ford in the summer of 1929. "The darling faun almost wept to me because tonight is the anniversary of our first meeting: 42nd St. and 5th Ave. = Fate."[6] The novelist Glenway Wescott recorded in his diary the story of N., who upon hearing of the Central Park cruising strip for the first time "hastened to it the next night, and there encountered his great love."[7]

The streets and parks were social centers for groups as well as individuals. Many groups of youths who could afford no other recreation gathered in the parks, and young men just coming out could easily find other gay men in them. Sebastian Risicato, an eighteen-year-old Italian-American living with his parents in the Bronx in 1938, for instance, heard about Bronx Park from the gay crowd he spent time with outside an older gay man's beauty salon on Gladstone Square. He went to the park and quickly became part of the gang of young "painted queens" who gathered near the 180th Street bridge. It was a "big social scene" as well as a cruising ground, he recalled. "We met and we dished [gossiped] . . . I would meet [my best friend], and the other sisters, and we'd go for a soda, then we'd come back, and cruise down and see if a number came by." At the park he learned about other places where gay men gathered and also met several people who became lifelong friends.[8]

Because of its central location, Bryant Park, a small park adjoining the Public Library on Forty-second Street near Times Square, became well known to straight and gay men alike as a meeting place for young "fairies" in the 1920s and 1930s. Brooklyn's Prospect Park, although less well known to the general public, served the same social role for somewhat older and more conventional-looking gay men. One high school teacher recalled that although he went to Prospect Park primarily to cruise, he became friendly with several of the other "regulars" who frequented the park and often took breaks from cruising with them, sharing information and casual conversation. Battery Park, on the southwest tip of Manhattan, was a popular rendezvous for seafaring men. Riverside Park, stretching along the western shore of Manhattan, where ships of all sorts were moored, was also a major cruising area and social center, especially for seamen and their admirers. Two landmarks in the park, Grant's Tomb at 122nd Street and the Soldiers and Sailors Monument at 89th Street, were especially renowned as meeting places in the gay world.[9]

Not surprisingly, Central Park, because of its location, vast stretches of unsupervised, wooded land, and heavy patronage, was especially renowned within the gay world both as a social center and as a cruising ground. At the turn of the century, men met each other next to the Belvedere Castle, on the west lawn near Sixty-third Street, and in other "secluded spots," according to trial records, and by the 1910s the benches at the southwest corner of the park at Columbus Circle—across the street from Mother Childs—had become a major pickup site.[10] In the 1920s so many men met on the open lawn at the north end of the Ramble that they nicknamed it the Fruited Plain. In the 1920s and 1930s, hundreds of gay men gathered every temperate evening in the park south of Seventy-second Street, on the benches at Columbus Circle, along the walk leading into the park from the Circle, and at the fountain and plaza by the lake. The greatest concentration of men could be found (packed "practically solidly," according to one account) on the unbroken row of benches that lined the quarter-mile-long walk from the southeastern corner of the park to the mall, a stretch nicknamed Vaseline Alley by some and Bitches' Walk by others. "You'd walk down and there'd be a lot of real obvious queens, and some closet queens, and sometimes guys would come down on their bikes," one man remembered; there was always lots of "socializing." "The nance element holds regular conventions in Paddies Lane," Variety reported in the fall of 1929. "Tis their rendezvous!"[11]

In the late 1930s, particularly after Mayor Fiorello La Guardia had closed most of the city's gay bars in a pre–World's Fair crackdown, hundreds of gay men gathered at the band concerts offered at the Central Park Mall on summer nights, meeting friends, socializing, and cruising. "They are so thick in the crowd," declared one gay man at the time, "that if one were to walk through with a strikingly handsome male friend, one would be conscious of creating something of a sensation—there would be whisperings, nods, suddenly turned heads, staring eyes."[12] Most nongay observers noticed only the most obvious "nance element" in the crowd and along the walks, but gay men themselves were fully aware of their numbers on such evenings and exulted in transforming Central Park into a gay park.

The enormous presence of gay men in the parks prompted a sharp response from the police. They regularly sent plainclothesmen to cruising areas to entrap men; in the grounds around the Central Park zoo in the first half of 1921 alone, they made thirty-three arrests. They periodically conducted sweeps and mass arrests of suspected homosexuals in the parks, either to increase their arrest statistics, to get some publicity, or to force men to remain more covert in their cruising. In 1943 the police arrested Donald Vining and several other men sitting on the benches by an entrance to Central Park simply because they were in a cruising area; a judge dismissed the charges, but only after the men had spent a night in jail. Four years later seventeen-year-old Harvey Milk was arrested in a similar sweep in a Central Park cruising area: the police arrested the shirtless men they found there whom they suspected were gay, charging them with indecent exposure. They ignored the family men standing nearby, with their shirts off but their children in tow.[13]

The parks endured as a locus of sexual and social activity for homosexual and heterosexual couples alike, despite police harassment, in part because the police found them challenging to regulate. They were physically more difficult to raid than an enclosed space, offered more hiding spaces than a street, and although La Guardia began closing Bryant Park at night in 1944 in order to "prevent undesirables from gathering," the larger parks, at least, were impossible to seal off.

Gay men also gathered on the city's beaches, which were enormously popular in the decades before air conditioning. More than a million people might crowd onto the Coney Island beach on a hot summer afternoon; photos of the scene portray a huge mass of bathers indiscriminately covering virtually every grain of sand, but the beach, too, had a more carefully delineated social geography. Different ethnic groups, sports groups, and other groups colonized sections of the beach and organized their use of its space in distinctive ways. While some gay men joined their ethnic compatriots, either individually or in groups, either blending in or making their gayness clear, other gay men claimed a certain section of the beach as their own and sometimes attracted notice for doing so. They sometimes put on for other beachgoers a "show" that outpaced even the shows at the Life and Mother Childs, turning their towels into dresses and fancy hats, swishing down the beach, kicking up their heels. Groups of friends from a neighborhood, bar, or cafeteria sometimes congregated in a subsection of the gay section of the beach. A large group of deaf gay men, for instance, regularly gathered on one of the city's beaches in the 1940s, according to several hearing men who saw them. Other, less obvious men found the beaches a good place to mingle with the crowd in search of sexual partners, and the muscle beach section was often a prime target. In the years after World War II the police sometimes arrested men at Riis Beach, in particular, but gay men seem to have faced little opposition earlier in the century.[14]

The confidence that men gained from their numbers and campiness on the beach—and from the absence of a strong reaction to their openness—led them to become remarkably bold on occasion. A male beauty contest held at Coney Island's Washington Baths in the summer of 1929, for instance, took an unexpected turn. To the surprise of a *Variety* reporter who served as one of the judges, most of the people who gathered to watch the contest were men. And to her further surprise, most of the men participating in the contest wore paint and powder. "[One] pretty guy pranced before the camera and threw kisses to the audience," she wrote. "One man came in dressed as a woman." Others had mascara on their eyelashes. "The problem," as she put it tongue-in-cheek, "became that of picking a male beaut who wasn't a floosie no matter how he looked." The judges settled on a contestant they knew to be married (which *Variety* reported just in case any of its readers had not yet realized who the other "floosies" were). On a packed beach on a hot summer afternoon, gay men had taken over a male beauty contest, becoming its audience, its contestants, its stars.[15]

THE SOCIAL ORGANIZATION OF THE STREETS
Along with the parks and beaches, the streets themselves served as a social center, cruising area, and assignation spot. Gay men interacted on streets throughout the city, but just as various immigrant groups predominated in certain neighborhoods and on certain streets, so, too, gay men had their own streets and corners, often where gay-oriented saloons and restaurants could be found and along which men strolled, looking for other men to pick up.

The streets could be dangerous, though, for men faced there the threat of arrest or harassment from the police and from anti-gay vigilantes. The police regularly dispatched plainclothes officers to the most popular cruising areas, and the results of their surveillance could be devastating. An arrest made in 1910 illustrates both the police's familiarity with gay haunts and the hazards the police could pose. At midnight on December 15, a forty-four-year-old clerk from Long Island had gone to Union Square, one of the city's best-known cruising areas at the time, and met a seventeen-year-old German baker who had walked over from his Park Row lodging house. They agreed to spend the night together and walked to a hotel on East Twenty-second Street at Third Avenue where they could rent a room. Both men had evidently known that the Square was a place where they could meet other men. So, too, had the police. Two detectives, apparently on the lookout for such things, saw them meet, followed them to the hotel, spied on them from the adjoining room through a transom, and arrested them after watching them have sex. The older man was convicted of sodomy and sentenced to a year in prison.[16]

The police action at Union Square was not an isolated event. Around 1910, the police department added the surveillance of homosexuals (whom they often labeled "male prostitutes") to the responsibilities of the vice squad, which already handled the investigations of female prostitutes.[17] Around 1915, the squad assigned one of its plainclothes officers, Terence Harvey, to "specialize in perversion cases." He patrolled the parks, theaters, and subway restrooms known as centers of homosexual and heterosexual rendezvous alike; he arrested some men after seeing them meet in gay cruising areas and following them home, and he entrapped others. He appears to have been quite effective, for he won the praise of the anti-vice societies and was responsible for almost a third of the arrests of men charged with homosexual activity in the first half of 1921.[18]

Most of the men he and the other members of the vice squad arrested were charged not with sodomy, a felony, but with disorderly conduct, a misdemeanor that was much easier to prove and did not require a trial by jury.[19] By the early 1910s, the police had begun to specify in their own records which of the men arrested for disorderly conduct had been arrested for "degeneracy."[20] As previously noted in chapter 6, the state legislature formalized this categorization in 1923 as part of its general revision of the disorderly-conduct statute. The statute, like the use of the vice squad to pursue homosexual cases, reflected the manner in which the authorities associated homosexual behavior with female prostitution, for it used wording strikingly similar to that used to prosecute female prostitutes in its definition of the crime as the "frequent[ing] or loiter[ing] about any public place soliciting men for the purpose of committing a crime against nature or other lewdness."[21] (On the ideological basis of this association, see chapter 2.) As a practical matter, the authorities generally interpreted this statute to apply only to the "degenerates" who solicited "normal" men for sex and not to the men who responded to such solicitations, just as prostitutes were charged but their customers' behavior remained uncensured. In most cases this was because the "normal" man was a plainclothes policeman (who, presumably, had responded only to the degree necessary to confirm the "degenerate's" intentions), but it also applied to some cases in which the police had observed "fairies" solicit men they regarded as "normal."* In other cases, the police labeled and arrested both the men involved as "degenerates."

Although the law was used primarily to prosecute men for trying to pick another man up (cruising), the police and sympathetic judges sometimes interpreted it loosely enough to encompass the prosecution of men who simply behaved in a campy, openly gay way, as in the case of men arrested when the police raided a cafeteria or bar homosexuals frequented. (For an example, see the discussion in chapter 6 of the police raid on the Hotel Koenig.) An exceptionally high percentage of the arrests on such charges resulted in convictions—roughly 89 percent in one 1921 study. Although different judges were likely to impose different sentences, the same study found that in general they were unusually harsh in such cases. Less than a quarter of the men convicted had their sentences suspended, while more than a third of them were sentenced to a period of days or even months in the workhouse, and a similar number were fined. An average of 650 men were convicted for degeneracy each year in Manhattan in the 1920s and 1930s.[23]

The police and the social-purity groups were not the only forces to threaten gay men's use of the streets. A variety of other groups also sought to ensure the maintenance of moral order in the city's streets on a more informal—but nonetheless more pervasive and, often, more effective—basis. The men who gathered at the corner saloon or poolroom often kept an eye on the street and discussed the events unfolding there, shopkeepers took an interest in the activities outside their stores, and mothers watched the movements of their children and neighbors from their stoops and windows. On most blocks in the tenement neighborhoods, gangs of youths kept "their" street under near-constant surveillance from their street-corner outposts. Although the first concern of such gangs was to protect their territory from the incursions of rival gangs, they also kept a close watch over other strangers who threat-

---

*In most cases the policeman let the accused put his hand "on [the officer's] person," which, as we shall see, usually would have happened only if the plainclothesman had indicated his willingness for it to happen. A smaller number of men were convicted for degeneracy on the basis of having verbally (or in some cases nonverbally) offered to "commit" or "permit" sodomy.[22]

ened the moral order of the block. These groups often disagreed among themselves about what that moral order properly was, but gay men had to contend with the threat of the popular sanctions any of them might impose against "inverts" and homosexuals, from gossip to catcalls to violence.

Gay men responded to the threat of both formal and informal sanctions by developing a variety of strategies for negotiating their way on the streets. Some of them boldly announced their sexual interests and created a visible gay presence by speaking, carrying themselves, and dressing in styles that the dominant culture associated with fairies, even though this could result in harassment from onlookers. In 1918 an agent witnessed the response of passersby to several fairies near Herald Square: they "mocked them and called in effeminate fashion after some of them and threw kisses at them." Agents witnessed groups of youths heckling fairies in Harlem as well, and Ralph Werther was attacked by several gangs near the Bowery, even though he was taken under the protection of others. In the 1920s, groups of family men who lived near Riverside Drive sometimes accosted men they thought to be gay and threatened them with violence if they did not leave the neighborhood. In 1930 Parker Tyler and a gay friend were chased by "quite a lot of sailors and civilians in their shirt sleeves" on Riverside Drive and were "saved" only by the sudden appearance of some policemen. When the police took one of the sailors and the two gay men to the station, Tyler felt he was in as much trouble as his assailant; as soon as he had a moment alone in the patrol car he spit on his handkerchief to wash off his telltale mascara. (The judge eventually dismissed the charges against all of them.)[24] Often fairies did not encounter such hostile reactions, but their willingness to risk them should be regarded as a form of defiance and resistance to a heterosexist cultural system. The intensity of the reaction their openness sometimes provoked indicates that many "normal" people regarded it as such.

Given the risks involved in asserting a visible presence in the streets, most gay people chose not to challenge the conventions of heterosexual society so directly. But they resisted and undermined them nonetheless by developing tactics that allowed them to identify and communicate with one another without alerting hostile outsiders to what they were doing. Such tactics kept them hidden from the dominant culture, but not from one another. Whereas fairies used codes that were intelligible to straights as well as to gays, such as flashy dress and an effeminate demeanor, other gay men (the "queers") developed codes that were intelligible only to other men familiar with the subculture, which allowed them to recognize one another without drawing the attention of the uninitiated, whether they were on the street, in a theater, or at a predominantly straight cocktail party or bar. They were so effective that medical researchers at the turn of the century repeatedly expressed their astonishment at gay men's ability to identify each other, attributing it to something akin to a sixth sense: "Sexual perverts readily recognize each other, although they may never have met before," one doctor wrote with some alarm in 1892, "and there exists a mysterious bond of psychological sympathy between them."[25]

The "mysterious bond" between gay men resulted in large part from their participation in the gay subculture and consequent knowledge of its codes and tactics, both almost wholly unfamiliar to the doctors. It resulted as well from their simple attentiveness to the signals that might identify like-minded men; most other city residents were preoccupied with other matters or remained deliberately oblivious to the surfeit of stimuli on the streets. Involvement in the gay world familiarized men with the styles of clothing and grooming, mannerisms, and conventions of speech that had become fashionable in that world but were not stereotypically associated with fairies. Those fashions served as signs, "neither masculine nor feminine, but specifically and peculiarly homosexual," observed the writer and gay activist Donald Webster Cory in the early 1950s; these were "difficult for [outsiders] to pinpoint," but enabled men to recognize one another even as they concealed their identities from others.[26]

Gay men also made tactical use of the gender conventions governing men's public interactions. They took full advantage of the cultural injunction against men looking at other men in the sexually assertive way they gazed at women; a "normal" man almost automatically averted his eyes if they happened to lock with those of a stranger, whereas a gay man interested in the man gazing at him returned his look." The eyes, the eyes, they're a dead giveaway," recalled one man who was introduced to the gay world during World War II when he stumbled upon a major cruising area in London, Leicester Square. "If someone looks at you with a lingering look, and looks away, and then looks at you again. If you looked at a straight man he wouldn't stare back, he'd look immediately away."[27] In order to confirm the interest indicated by eye contact, or as a way of initiating contact, men made use of a number of utterly conventional gestures. Perhaps the most common simply involved asking for a match or for the time of day. Thomas Painter joked in 1941 that asking for a match in New York had become the equivalent of accosting, and the gay novelists of the thirties delighted in parodying the interaction. The technique was so well known within the gay world (and to the police) that Max Ewing, a young writer who moved in both the gay and high-society circles centered around Carl Van Vechten, could satirize it (along with police entrapment and gay actors and chorus boys), in his 1933 novel, *Going Somewhere*. In one scene an actor who needed to get to the theater by eight "went up to a man who was standing in front of a clothing shop window and asked him if he knew what time it was. This man was a plain-clothes detective, so the boy was arrested, and sent to Welfare Island for seven weeks. Nothing could be done about it. The cast of the show regretted the episode, for the boy was 'an awfully nice kid.'"[28] The man who made such a request could rest assured that anyone unaware of its coded significance would simply respond to it straight-forwardly, since men often asked other men for such things, while a man interested in responding to its hidden meaning would start a con-versation.

Gay men used such subcultural codes to make contact and communi-cate with one another throughout the city, but they also made tactical decisions about the safest places to meet. Like other marginalized groups seeking a public presence, gay men had to hone their sense of the social dynamics governing various neighborhoods and the possibilities each pre-sented.[29] In constructing a gay map of the city, they had to consider the maps devised by other, sometimes hostile, groups, so a tactical logic gov-erned the location of gay cruising areas. They tended to be clustered in theater and retail shopping districts, where many gay men worked and where heavy pedestrian traffic offered cover, such as Union Square, Herald Square, and Harlem's Seventh Avenue and 135th Street; along the socially less desirable avenues darkened by elevated trains thundering overhead, particularly Third and Sixth Avenues, where few powerful interests would notice them; close to the parks where men gathered, such as Fifth Avenue in the twenty blocks south of Central Park (and, in later years, Central Park West in the Seventies); along Riverside Drive and other parts of the waterfront, where many seamen and other unmarried or transient workers were to be found; and, in general, in the same "vice" areas where other forms of disreputable sexual behavior, particularly prostitution, were tacitly allowed to flourish, or that for one reason or another provided a measure of privacy and "cover" to gay men seeking to meet.

As the historian Susan Porter Benson has observed, the elaborate dis-play windows that department stores began installing in the late nine-teenth century quickly became the locus of one of the few acceptable street cultures for middle-class women, who could stroll down the street looking at them and conversing with other browsers, "their loi-tering in public space," as Benson notes, "legitimized by its association with consumption." As men, gay men had less need to justify their

presence on the streets, but they took advantage of the same legitimizing conventions. One man who had indicated his interest in meeting
another might stop before a window and gaze at the display; the second could then join him at the window without attracting undue attention and strike up a conversation in which they could determine
whether they wanted to spend more time together.[30] "Fairies hang out
in the saloon opposite Bloomingdale's," a Macy's saleswoman claimed
in 1913, and, she added, the blocks of Third Avenue in the East Fifties,
a marginal retail strip under the El, were "their favorite beat."[31] A
study of arrests for homosexual activity in 1921 provides further evidence of the extent to which cruising was concentrated in retail shopping districts, for it revealed that the subway stations at Lexington and
Fifty-ninth Street (where Bloomingdale's stood), Union Square (the site
of numerous cheap retail outlets), and Herald Square (where Macy's,
Gimbels, and Saks–34th Street were located) each accounted for more
arrests than any other station, and together accounted for three-quarters of the arrests reported in all subway stations.[32]

The evolution of East Fourteenth Street between Third Avenue
and Union Square as one of the preeminent centers of working-class
gay life and of homosexual street activity in the city from the 1890s
into the 1920s illustrates the factors that encouraged the development of a cruising area. Known as the Rialto, Fourteenth Street had
once been at the heart of a fashionable entertainment and residential
district. But by the 1890s it had become an inexpensive retail strip
and a center of ribald entertainment for working-class men, where
"theatres, muse-ums for men only, drinking palaces, gambling
joints, and worse abounded."[33] Its legitimate theaters had turned
into vaudeville and burlesque houses, and its elegant restaurants had
given way to workingmen's saloons. It was also a center of female
street prostitution and, before the crackdowns of the early 1910s, of
brothels. It was in this context that Fourteenth Street had become
the "chief stamping-ground in the New York metropolitan district"
of fairies and other gay men in the 1890s.[34] Ralph Werther spent
many a night there, attracting the attention of young men as he
promenaded up and down the street in the flashy clothes that proclaimed his identity as a fairy. Twenty years later, in 1914, the
German homosexual emancipationist Magnus Hirschfeld (presumably on the word of his American informants) still described Union
Square as a center of homosexual activity in New York.[35] Arrest
records, novels, and diaries confirm that Fourteenth Street remained
an important cruising area, especially for male prostitutes and for

less obvious gay men, until the 1930s, when it was eclipsed by Times Square.*

The relationship between a neighborhood's changing social dynamics and its gay street scene can be seen even more clearly in Times Square, Union Square's successor. The shifting spatial and social organization of just one aspect of the Times Square's gay street culture—that of male prostitution—highlights the extent to which the apparent chaos of the most active street scenes masked a highly organized street culture, whose boundaries and conventions were well known to the initiated.

Times Square, already a busy center of female prostitution, became one of the city's most significant centers of male prostitution in the 1920s. Initially, two distinct groups of male prostitutes, whose interactions with customers were construed in entirely different ways, worked the Times Square area. Well-dressed, "mannered," and gay-identified hustlers serving a middle-class gay-identified clientele generally met their customers as the latter left the theater and walked home on the west side of Fifth Avenue from Forty-second to Fifty-ninth Streets. This was also a stretch where men who were not hustlers often met each other, and where hustlers could meet men walking to Central Park, another major cruising area (but not one where sexual contacts usually involved monetary exchange). Although a regular part of the Times Square scene, neither the hustlers nor their customers attracted much attention, since neither conformed to the era's dominant stereotypes of inverts. During the 1920s, a second group of male prostitutes came to dominate Forty-second Street itself between Fifth and Eighth Avenues: the effeminate (but not transvestite) "fairy prostitutes" who sold sexual services to other gay men and to men who identified themselves as "normal," including Italians and Greeks living to the west of the Square in Hell's Kitchen, as well as tourists from afar. The self-presentation of the prostitutes operating on the two streets differed markedly, as did the self-conception of their customers.[36] The proximity of the two groups points up the degree to which the Square's streets, like those in other parts of the city, were the site of multiple sexual systems, each with its own cultural dynamics, semiotic codes, and territories.

The transformation of Forty-second Street during the 1920s and early 1930s had enormous repercussions for the street's gay scene. Forty-second

---

*Charles Henri Ford and Parker Tyler's roman à clef, *The Young and Evil*, described Fourteenth Street as "a most vulgar street, invariably alive with the sex-starved," and included a scene in which a gay character makes eye contact with someone in a Fourteenth Street cafeteria and then follows him into Union Square in a taxi, ordering the cab to stop by the man so that he can pick him up (133–40).

Street was the site of the oldest theaters in the Times Square district, and the city's elite had regarded it as a distinguished address early in the century. By 1931, however, it had effectively become a working-class male domain. The conversion of two prominent Forty-second Street theaters, the Republic (later Victory) and Eltinge (later Empire), into burlesque houses in 1931 had both signified and contributed to the masculinization of the street. Not only the strippers inside but the large quasi-pornographic billboards and barkers announcing the shows outside intensified the image of the street as a male domain, threatening to women.[37] The masculinization of the street was confirmed by the conversion of the remaining theaters to a "grind" policy of showing male-oriented action films on a continuous basis and the opening of several men's bars and restaurants that catered to the increasing numbers of sailors, servicemen, and unemployed and transient men who frequented the street.

As the gender and class character of Forty-second Street changed, it became a major locus of a new kind of "rough" hustler and of interactions between straight-identified servicemen and homosexuals.[38] The deepening Depression of the 1930s led growing numbers of young men—many of them migrants from the economically devastated cities of Pennsylvania, Massachusetts, New York, and the South—to support themselves or supplement their income by hustling.[39] Not gay-identified themselves, many became prostitutes for the same reason some women did: the work was available and supplied a needed income. "In the Depression the Square swarmed with boys," recalled one man who became a customer in 1933. "Poverty put them there."[40] According to another account, 1932 was a critical year, when growing numbers of "transient boys . . . went to Times Square to 'play the queers.'"[41] They were joined by many soldiers and sailors, long attracted to the Square, who began hustling as well. These new hustlers, aggressively masculine in their self-presentation and usually called "rough trade" by gay men, took over Forty-second Street between Seventh and Eighth Avenues, forcing the fairy prostitutes to move east of Sixth Avenue, to Bryant Park.[42]

The precise locus of the hustlers' and gay men's activity on Forty-second Street shifted several times over the course of the 1930s. The details of the moves are unimportant in themselves, but they reveal something of the social organization of the streets in general, for they resulted largely from the changing geography of the gay bars and other commercial sites where men met. The corner of Broadway and Forty-second near the Times Building was popular in the late 1920s, when the building's basement arcade and the Liggett's drugstore upstairs functioned as meeting places.[43] Men gathered in the middle of the northern side of the block between

Seventh and Eighth Avenues in the mid-1930s, when it was the site of the Barrel House, the most famous sailor–prostitute–homosexual bar of the era. It was "wholly uninhibited . . . as to 'accosting,'" recalled one patron. "You could count a dozen [hustlers] lined up on the curb outside the Barrel House, in addition to the number inside who had the price of a beer to get in."[44] They moved to the south side of the street after the police closed the Barrel House and the Marine Bar & Grill took its place. During the war they settled near Sixth Avenue, where several cheap luncheonettes and sailor and hustler bars, such as the Pink Elephant, stood under the Elevated.[45]

The hustler scene followed the bars so closely in part because the bars attracted customers and offered shelter from the elements, but also because the streets and bars functioned as extensions of each other. Each site had particular advantages and posed particular dangers in men's constant territorial struggles with policing agents, as the men subject to that policing well knew. The purchase of a beer at a bar legitimized behavior involved in cruising that might have appeared more suspicious on the streets, including a man's simply standing about aimlessly or striking up conversations with strangers. But while the police periodically tried to clean up the streets by chasing hustlers and other undesirable loiterers away, they could not permanently close the streets in the way they could close a bar. In a heavily trafficked nonresidential area such as Forty-second Street, no one had the same interest in controlling pedestrians' behavior on behalf of the police that a bar owner threatened with the loss of his license had in controlling his customers. Whereas the police might harass men on the street simply for standing about with no apparent purpose, bars might evict them simply for touching, and plainclothesmen might arrest them for trying to pick up a man in either locale. The relative dangers of either site varied and depended on the momentary concerns of the police, and much of the talk on the streets was necessarily devoted to their shifting tactics. On more than one occasion in the 1930s and 1940s a man noted in his diary that all of the street's hustlers had suddenly disappeared, apparently aware of some danger their customers did not perceive.[46]

Although bars were the major gathering place for men after the repeal of Prohibition in 1933, the numerous cheap cafeterias, Automats, and lunchrooms that crowded the Times Square area had a similar symbiotic relationship with the "public" life of the street throughout the 1920s and 1930s. Thompson's Lunch Room on Sixth Avenue between Forty-second and Forty-third Streets was reputed to be a gay rendezvous in 1920, as was "a place on W 46 St [in 1921] where fairies [are] supposed to hang out and meet men."[47] Men also moved back and forth between the streets and the large cafeterias located in the Square, and according to one 1931 account, during the winter the Automat across Forty-second Street from Bryant Park became a favorite haunt of the men who gathered in the park during the summer.[48]

Numerous movie and burlesque theaters, especially those in gay cruising areas, also became a part of the gay circuit. The small, dark, and unsupervised nickelodeons that began to appear in working-class neighborhoods in the 1890s had immediately aroused the concern of social purists, who feared they would become the site of illicit mingling of the sexes. The theaters also developed an unsavory reputation in middle-class society at large, which the nascent movie industry overcame only by building huge, elegant theaters (appropriately known as movie palaces) in the 1910s and 1920s.[49] Even some of the palaces became known as trysting spots for heterosexual couples, however, and a few, particularly in less reputable areas, became places where gay men (as well as straight men simply interested in a homosexual encounter) could meet one another. Although men pursued other men in all sections of the theaters, the standing-room area and the balconies were particularly suitable as meeting places. Ushers, some of whom were gay themselves (and some of whom supplemented their income by introducing male patrons to female prostitutes working in the theaters), seem generally to have avoided the balconies (where heterosexual couples also often met) and left them free from surveillance.[50]

In the first six months of 1921, at least sixty-seven men were arrested for homosexual solicitation in movie theaters in Manhattan, including an astonishing forty-five men at a single theater at 683 Sixth Avenue, near Twenty-second Street. A city magistrate who had heard the cases of many of the men arrested there claimed that the theater had been "the resort of male degenerates" for the previous two or three years "to such an extent that from one to two policemen are detailed to sit in the audience almost constantly." The judge thought it had acquired a reputation among gay men "as a place where men of a certain class [that is, homosexual] will meet congenial spirits." He claimed to have tried the case of a tourist who had learned of the theater before visiting New York and gone there "within two hours of his arrival in the city."[51]

Since moviegoing was a perfectly legitimate way to spend the afternoon, theaters were places where young men could go to search out other gay men and begin to learn about the gay world. "I thought I was [the] only one like this until I reached High School," recalled one thirty-four-year-old black man in 1922. After learning a bit about the gay world from the other homosexuals he met in school, though, "I used to go to matinees, meet people like myself, get into conversation and [I] learned that this is a quite common thing. They put me wise."[52] Another man who frequented the Forty-second Street theaters during World War II met several men there who became his friends. He and his friends shared stories of their adventures there, suggesting that such venues were not just sites for anonymous, furtive encounters but could also serve valued social (and socializing) functions.[53] The theaters, like other locales, were subject to periodic crackdowns, and gay men depended on the grapevine to protect themselves. On one occasion in 1945 the man mentioned above stopped going to the Forty-second Street theaters for several weeks because gay friends had warned him that they were infested with plainclothesmen.[54]

FINDING PRIVACY IN PUBLIC: THE MULTIPLE MEANINGS OF "PUBLIC SEX"

Men used public spaces to meet their friends and to find potential sexual partners. But they also used them for sex. Poorer men, especially, had few alternatives. Unable to bring male partners home to crowded tenement quarters, unable to afford even an hour's stay at a Raines Law hotel or flophouse, they were forced to find secluded spots in the city's streets and parks where they could, for a moment, be alone with their partners. But they were joined there by other men as well, including middle-class men with access to more private quarters who found "public sex" exciting, and a variety of men who were not gay-identified but nonetheless used such sites for various purposes. The encounters in such "public" spaces thus had different meanings for different men—and suggest the complexity of the city's sexual topographies.

Sodomy-trial depositions from the 1890s and early 1900s record the range of spaces used by workingmen for sexual encounters: an Irish laborer and a schoolboy discovered by a suspicious patrolman in a covered wagon standing on a lower Manhattan street one night in 1889; two laborers caught in an ice wagon in an Italian immigrant neighborhood in 1896; a German deli worker and an Irish waiter seen on a loading platform on a deserted industrial street at 3 A.M. one night the same year; an Irish porter and an Italian laborer discovered in a recessed doorway another night; and, throughout the period, couples apprehended in vacant lots and in the nooks and crannies of the tenements—the outhouse in the backyard, the roof, the cellar, the darkened stairway.[55] The absence of private quarters forced men constantly to improvise, in other words, to seize whatever relatively hidden space they could find, whenever they found a sexual partner.

But they also developed a more finely calibrated sexual map of the city: certain streets, sections of parks, and public washrooms where men regularly went for sex and knew they were likely to find other men. They shared many of those sites with young heterosexual men and women, who sought privacy in them for the same reasons many gay men did. Both groups, for instance, found the city's parks particularly useful. They were dark at night, and the larger ones offered numerous secluded spots in the midst of bushes and trees where couples could find privacy in even so public a space. Police and anti-vice investigators regularly noted the troubling appearance of unsupervised heterosexual couples spooning on secluded benches and disappearing into the bushes in the city's numerous parks. "We didnt see anything else but couples laying on grass, or sitting on benches, kissing and hugging each other . . . especially [in] the dark sections which are poor lighted," an agent reported of Central Park in 1920.[56] Agents surveying the problem at Van Cortlandt Park in the Bronx late in the summer of 1917 observed a similar scene: soldiers met prostitutes and other women at the nearby subway station and walked into the park, where they hid in the bushes and near the boathouse. They also discovered that men interested in meeting other men took similar advantage of the park's hidden spaces, for they noticed "many soldiers in the dark spots on [the] way in [the] Park to the Inn, walking arm and arm hugging and kissing."[57] Police records suggest how common a practice it was for men to use the parks for sexual encounters. In the last five years of the nineteenth century, park police arrested men found having sex in the recesses of Central, Riverside, Mount Morris, City Hall, Tompkins Square, and Battery Parks, and by early in the twentieth century they had arrested men in Washington Square Park as well.[58]

Of all the spaces to which men had recourse for sexual encounters, none were more specific to gay men—or more highly contested, both within the gay world and without—than New York's public comfort stations and subway washrooms. The city had begun building the stations in the late nineteenth century in parks and at major intersections, partly in an effort to offer workingmen an alternative to the saloons, which until then had afforded virtually the only publicly accessible toilets in the city. By 1925, there were eighteen comfort stations in Manhattan.[59] A wave of arrests in 1896, shortly after the first stations opened, indicates that several of them, including the ones at Battery Park, City Hall Park, and Chatham Square, all near concentrations of cheap transient lodging houses, had quickly become regular homosexual rendezvous. The public comfort station at City Hall Park appears to have developed a particularly widespread reputation as a meeting ground, drawing men from throughout the city. A twenty-eight-year-old salesman from West Thirty-fourth Street met a twenty-four-year-old clerk from Brooklyn there one night in March 1896, for instance; later that year a porter living in a Bowery rooming house met a cook there who was visiting the city from Westport, Connecticut.[60]

As the city's subway system expanded in the early years of the century, its washrooms also became major sexual centers. Men who had met on the subway could retire to them easily, and men who wanted a quick sexual release on the way home from work learned that there were men at certain subway washrooms who would readily accommodate them. Encounters could take place at almost any station, but certain washrooms developed reputations for such activity. By the 1930s, the men's washroom in the Times Square subway station and the comfort station at Times Square were used so frequently for sexual encounters that they became widely known among gay men as the "Sunken Gardens" (possibly an allusion to the song by Beatrice Lillie about the fairies at the bottom of *her* garden), a name subsequently sometimes applied to other underground washrooms. Gay men dubbed all the restrooms (often called "t-rooms," short for "toilet-rooms," in early-twentieth-century slang) "tearooms," which allowed them to discuss their adventures surreptitiously in mixed company, and may also have been an arch comment on the rooms' significance as social centers. If "tearoom" normally referred to a gracious café where respectable ladies could meet without risk of encountering inebriated males, it could ironically name the less elegant locale where so many gay men met.[61]

Bourgeois ideology—and certainly the ideology that guided state regulation—regarded comfort stations as public spaces (of the most sordid sort, in fact, since they were associated with bodily functions even more stigmatized than sex), but the men who used them for sex succeeded in making them functionally quite private. As the sociologist Laud Humphreys's research in the 1960s revealed, public washrooms became a locus of homosexual encounters throughout the country not only because of their accessibility to men of little means, but also because it was easy to orchestrate sexual activity at even the most active of tearooms so that no one uninvolved in it would see it, thus providing the participants, as Humphreys put it, "privacy in public."*

The vice squad and other policing agents were well aware of men's abil-

---

*One man often served informally as a sentry who could warn the others about the approach of strangers, and, given the possible consequences of approaching the wrong man, even two strangers alone in an isolated washroom usually sought to confirm their mutual interest in an encounter through a series of nonverbal signs before overtly approaching each other. The most popular tearooms had elaborate and noisy entrances, which alerted men to the approach of another and gave them time to stop whatever they were doing. To reach one tearoom famous among gay men in the 1940s, located on the eighth floor of the RCA Building at Rockefeller Center, for instance, those arriving had to pass through several doors in a long corridor, thus providing the men in the room ample warning of their approach.[62]

ity to conceal their encounters. By the 1910s they had developed ways to circumvent the men's tactics and keep the tearooms under surveillance. Most commonly, the vice squad hid policemen behind the grill facing the urinals so that they could observe and arrest men having sex there or in the stalls. In 1912, agents of the Pennsylvania Railroad even cut holes in the ceiling of the men's room at their Cortlandt Street ferry house in order to spy on men using the facilities. The observers' need to hide was significant; as even the police admitted, the men they observed would have stopped having sex as soon as they heard someone beginning to open the outer door. The police also periodically sent plainclothesmen into the public comfort stations and subway washrooms to entrap men. In the earliest recorded incident, in 1914, a plainclothesman stationed at the Chatham Square comfort station got into a conversation with another man there, agreed to go with him and a third man to a secluded part of Battery Park, and then arrested both of them.[63] A 1921 study confirmed the risks these police tactics posed to the men who met in such locales: fully 38 percent of the arrests of men for homosexual activity that year were made in subway washrooms.[64] Nonetheless, enforcement efforts were only sporadic. The police could hardly monitor every subway station's washroom every day, and the tearooms continued to be widely used for decades.

Arrests could have catastrophic consequences. Conviction often resulted in a sentence of thirty to sixty days in the workhouse, but the extralegal sanctions could be worse. An arrest could result in a man's homosexuality being revealed to family members, employer, and landlord, either because the police called to "confirm" a man's identity, employment, or residence or because the man himself had to explain his incarceration. Augustus Granville Dill, an activist in the National Association for the Advancement of Colored People and the business manager of its magazine, *The Crisis*, was widely known and admired in Harlem circles. He had a reputation as a dandy, who always wore a bright chrysanthemum in his buttonhole and was known to engage in flamboyant behavior in public. In 1928 he was arrested in a subway washroom. W. E. B. Du Bois, the editor of *The Crisis*, promptly fired him.[65]

The men who used subway washrooms tended to be relatively poor and to have relatively little access to other kinds of private space, either because of their poverty or because their own homes were unavailable to them for homosexual trysts. Among other sources, two surveys in 1938 and 1940 of homosexual inmates at the city jail, many of whom would have been apprehended in the tearooms, suggest this. Almost half the inmates surveyed were laborers (another 13 percent had no job at all) and a third lived in tenement houses with families. Only 3 percent to 5 percent were professionals or lived in "superior" housing.[66] "Subways were *the* meeting place for everyone," recalled one black man of his days as a poor youth in Harlem in the 1920s and 1930s. "Every station had a restroom then and you could always meet people there. People who didn't have a place to stay could take the train up to the Bronx and always find someone who'd give them a place to stay and some money."[67]

It would be wrong, though, to suppose that *only* poor men frequented the tearooms, for many other men visited them as well. Indeed, the constant sexual activity in the city's public restrooms involved thousands of men for whom the encounters had widely varying meanings. Even among gay men, views about the propriety of such visits varied enormously. Some men, particularly those who were professionally successful in jobs that required them to pass as straight, found it astonishing that anyone in their circles would *risk* going to a tearoom, given the threat of arrest and the availability of alternatives to men highly integrated into gay society. Others were as likely as the anti-vice societies to regard such encounters as shameful, for they expected the same level of romanticism, monogamy, and commitment to be involved in gay relationships that bourgeois ideology expected of marriage. (The painter Russell Cheney sought to forswear his visits to comfort stations after falling in love with the literary critic F. O. Matthiessen in 1925, for instance; such escapades, previously so important to him, seemed inconsistent with the life his newfound love made him wish to lead.)[68] As a result, even many of the men who visited the tearooms were ashamed of the practice and never revealed them to their friends.

A different and perhaps more dominant strain of gay male culture valued sexual adventurism, experimentation, and variety. Men who shared this perspective were likely to regard tearooms more positively because of the unparalleled access they provided to a large and varied group of men. Some men found the very anonymity, unpredictability, and danger of encounters in public places to be sexually exciting. They took such encounters as a matter of course and many regaled their friends with stories of their tearoom exploits. Some men involved in long-term nonmonogamous relationships even took their lovers to see the particularly active sites they had discovered.[69]

Tearoom encounters' very lack of romanticism and emotional involvement made them particularly attractive to another group of men. If some men used tearooms because police harassment and poverty left them nowhere else to go, others used them because anti-homosexual social attitudes left them unable, emotionally, to go elsewhere. Pervasive anti-homosexual social attitudes kept many men who were interested in other men from fully acknowledging that interest to themselves, and many of them sought sexual encounters in spaces, such as public washrooms, that seemed to minimize the implications of the experiences by making them easy to isolate from the rest of their lives and identities. The association of tearooms with the most primal of bodily functions reinforced men's sense that the sexual experiences they had there were simply another form of release, a bodily function that implied nothing more about a man's character than those normally associated with the setting.

The same lack of commitment also made the tearooms attractive to straight men interested in a quick sexual release and to yet another group of men who acknowledged their homosexual interests to themselves, but dared not visit a bar or restaurant with a gay reputation because of their other public roles and identities. A brief stop at a subway tearoom did not seem to involve the risk of suffering the loss in status that identifying themselves as gay to their everyday associates would. Anonymous encounters with strangers were the only way some men conscious of distinctively homosexual desires felt safe satisfying them. The existence of places like the tearooms made it easier for men to move in and out of the gay world, and many who had sexual encounters there participated no further in that world. Indeed, some of them regularly returned from those encounters to their conventional lives as respected family men. A quarter of the men arrested for homosexual activity in 1920–21, for instance, were married and many of them had children—although for those family men, the illusion of security offered by the tearooms had been shattered.[70]

Men went to the tearooms for a variety of reasons, and their encounters could have radically different meanings for each participant. But the encounters often affected how even men little involved in other aspects of the gay world regarded that world. They reinforced the negative impressions of many men, for they seemed to offer vivid confirmation of the cultural association of homosexuality with degeneracy by putting homosexuality and homosexuals almost literally in the gutter. Even the men most attracted to the tearooms as sexual meeting grounds had to be influenced by a culture that regarded such locales and such practices with disgust.

But the tearooms also offered more positive insights into the character of the gay world. Even anonymous participation in the sexual underground could provide men with an enticing sense of the scope of the gay world and of its counterstereotypical diversity, which led some of them to decide to explore that world further. The sheer numbers of men they witnessed participating in tearoom sex reassured many who felt isolated and uncertain of their own "normality," especially since most of the participants were not "flaming queens" but "normal"-looking men of diverse backgrounds.* When a physician at the New York City Jail in the early 1920s asked gay prisoners, many of whom had been arrested for cruising tearooms and streets, to estimate the number of homosexuals in New York, some guessed there must be half a million, or at least a hundred thousand; even the more conservative put the figure at fifty thousand to a hundred thousand.[72] While such figures hardly constitute reliable estimates of the size of the city's gay population, they provide vivid evidence that men who frequented the streets and tearooms perceived themselves to be involved in an underworld of enormous dimensions. Such an impression could be particularly important to men just beginning to explore the gay world. "From the 'gay side' of the Astor Hotel bar to the bushes behind the Forty-second Street library [in Bryant Park]," recalled Martin Goodkin of his early forays into New York's gay underworld, "to the public tearoom right outside of Fordham University (where I was once arrested by entrapment . . .) to the eighth floor restroom in the RCA Building to the restroom across the street in the parking garage . . . and on and on and on, New York seemed to be one big cruising ground, especially to this teenager." It was an electrifying realization, he recalled, and a reassuring one, for it persuaded him that he had discovered and become part of a vast secret world, with its own territories and codes, whose existence would ensure he never felt isolated again.[73]

THE CONTESTED BOUNDARIES BETWEEN PUBLIC AND PRIVATE SPACE

The streets and parks had particular significance as meeting places for gay men because of the special constraints they faced as homosexuals, but they were hardly the only people to use these venues for socializing and even for sexual encounters in the early twentieth century. Indeed, gay street culture was in many respects simply part of a much larger working-class street youth culture and was policed as part of the policing of that larger culture. Many of the same forces drawing working-class gay men into the streets drew other young working-class men and women as well. The pull of social ties was important to both groups, who were keen to create a communal life in the streets and other public spaces. There women bargained with peddlers or socialized with their neighbors on the stoop, men met in nearby saloons, children played and searched for rags and other useful items. But there were material reasons for street life as well. The most important, as noted previously, was that most working-class men and women, gay and straight alike, lived in crowded

---

*Even the probation officers who investigated the backgrounds of some of the men arrested for homosexual solicitation in 1921 commented that "perhaps half did not impress [them] as [being] of the homo-sexual type," by which they presumably meant the men did not conform to the stereotypical image of the "pansy."[71]

tenements, boardinghouses, and lodging houses, which offered them few amenities and virtually no privacy. Young people in search of sex and romance discovered that "privacy could only be had in public," in the evocative phrase of Samuel Chotzinoff. As a result, recalled Chotzinoff, who was raised in a Jewish immigrant family on the Lower East Side, the streets of his neighborhood in the evening "were thick with promenading couples, and the benches around the fountain and in Jackson Street Park, and the empty trucks lined up at the river front, were filled with lovers who had no other place to meet."[74] Men interested in homosexual encounters were not the only people to make use of such so-called public spaces.

Nor were tenement-roof rendezvous the exclusive domain of gay men. A 1914 study of the working-class Irish and German youth of the Hell's Kitchen district west of Times Square found conditions there no different from those described by Chotzinoff. "The youth of the district and his girl" found "uses" for the "dark, narrow passages" of the tenement hallways, the report observed, and "certain roofs of the neighborhood [had] a name as a rendezvous for children and young couples for immoral practices."[75] Moreover, as noted previously, undercover agents surveying the sexual uses of the city's parks noted the presence of both same-sex and mixed-sex couples. Denied the privacy the home was ideally supposed to provide, in other words, young men and women throughout the tenement districts tried to construct some measure of privacy for themselves in spaces middle-class ideology regarded as "public."

The men who sought homosexual encounters in the streets, then, were participating in and expanding a street culture already developed by working-class youths seeking freedom from their families' supervision. That culture sustained a set of sexual values and a way of conceptualizing the boundaries between public and private space that paralleled those governing many aspects of gay men's behavior—and that middle-class ideology found almost as shocking in the case of heterosexual couples as in homosexual. The purposes and tactics of gay men out cruising resembled those of young men and women out looking for a date in many respects. The casual pickups men made on the streets were hardly unique to male couples in this era, for many young women depended on being picked up by men to finance their excursions to music halls and amusement parks, as the historians Kathy Peiss and Joanne Meyerowitz have shown. It was common on the streets for men to approach women with whom they were unacquainted to make a date. This distressed middle-class moral reformers, who considered casual pickups almost as undesirable as professional prostitution, if they distinguished the two at all.[76] The fact that these couples met in unsupervised public places and even had sex there was more shocking still to middle-class reformers, in part because it challenged the careful delineation between public and private space that was so central to bourgeois conceptions of public order.

The use of public spaces for sexual purposes was only one aspect of a more general pattern of class differentiation in the uses of the streets and in the norms of public sociability, a difference that troubled middle-class reformers deeply. Struggles over the proper social and sexual order were central to the process of class differentiation, constitution, and conflict in the Progressive Era. Those struggles were fueled by middle-class fears about the apparently pernicious social effects of urbanization, which were graphically represented by the disorderly, unregulated, and alien character of working-class street life. The 1914 Russell Sage Foundation study of the conditions of young people in Hell's Kitchen indicted the unruly culture of the streets as the source of the "lawlessness" of neighborhood boys, even as it painted a portrait of a working-class life starkly different from that of its readers. "Streets, roofs, docks, hallways,—these, then, are the West Side boy's playground, and will be for many years to come," observed the report, which warned that the boys' parents, "so long accustomed to the dangers of the streets, to the open flaunting of vice, drunkenness, and gambling on all sides . . . do not take into account the impression which these conditions are making upon young minds."[77] Although the dangers *these* conditions posed to the character of the young were not limited to the sexual, this was certainly a concern of the reformers. Appalled by the overt sexualization of public space and the public character of sexual interactions in working-class neighborhoods, the report observed that "children of both sexes indulge freely in conversation which is only carried on secretly by adults in other walks of life [middle-class adults]." And although it did not stress the point, it warned that the boys' unrestricted involvement in the life of the streets resulted in their becoming familiar with the "many sexual perverts" to be found in the neighborhood, whom they might otherwise have avoided, which led to "experimentation among the boys, and to the many forms of perversion which in the end make the degenerate. . . . Self-abuse is considered a common joke," it added, "and boys as young as seven or eight actually practice sodomy."[78]

The Progressive movement to construct parks, playgrounds, and after-school programs of organized recreation and education, which would "Americanize" immigrant children, reflected middle-class reformers' concerns about the corrupting influences of the street on working-class youth. So, too, did the escalation of campaigns by the forces of social purity against working-class street culture and sexual culture, which resulted in an expansion of the vice squad and in the campaigns against the Raines Law hotels, saloons, cabarets, and other commercial amusements, already chronicled, which had a powerful effect on gay life.

The efforts of the police to control gay men's use of public space, then, were part of a much broader effort by the state to (quite literally) police the boundaries between public and private space, and, in particular, to impose a bourgeois definition of such distinctions on working-class communities. Gay men's strategies for using urban space came under attack not just because they challenged the hetero-normativity that ordinarily governed men and women's use of public space, but also because they were part of a more general challenge to dominant cultural conceptions of those boundaries and of the social practices appropriate to each sphere. The inability of the police and reformers to stop such activity reflects their failure to impose a single, hegemonic map of the city's public and private spaces on its diverse communities.

Gay men developed a gay map of the city and named its landmarks: the Fruited Plain, Vaseline Alley, Bitches' Walk. Even outsiders were familiar with sections of that map, for the "shoals of painted, perfumed, . . . mincing youths that at night swarm on Broadway in the Tenderloin section, . . . the parks and 5th avenue" made the gay territorialization of the city inescapable to Bernarr Macfadden and many others. But even more of that map was unknown to the dominant culture. Gay men met throughout the city, their meetings invisible to all but the initiated and carefully orchestrated to remain so. Certain subway stations and public comfort stations, as well as more open locales such as parks and streets, were the sites of almost constant social and even sexual interactions between men, but most men carefully structured their interactions so that no outsiders would recognize them as such.

The boundaries of the gay world were thus highly permeable, and different men participated in it to different degrees and in different ways. Some passed in and out of it quickly, making no more than occasional stops at a subway tearoom for a quick sexual encounter that had little significance for their self-identity or the other parts of their life. Even those men who were most isolated from the organized gay world got a glimpse of its size and diversity through their anonymous encounters in washrooms and recessed doorways, however, and those encounters provided other men with entrée into a world much larger and more highly organized than they could have imagined. The streets and parks served them as social centers as well as sites of sexual rendezvous, places where they could meet others like themselves and find collective support for their rejection of the sexual and gender roles prescribed them. The "mysterious bond" between gay men that allowed them to locate and communicate with one another even in the settings potentially most hostile to them attests to the resiliency of their world and to the resources their subculture had made available to them.

Figure 8.1. Charles Demuth's painting *Turkish Bath* (1916) most likely depicts the Lafayette Baths, New York City's most popular gay bathhouse at the time. As his image of this relaxed and happy couple suggests, gay bathhouses offered men secure environments in which to find friendship and romance as well as sex. *(From a private collection, on loan to the Harvard University Art Museums. By permission of The Harvard University Art Museums.)*

THE SOCIAL WORLD OF THE BATHS

THE SAFEST, MOST ENDURING, AND ONE OF THE MOST AFFIRMATIVE OF THE settings in which gay men gathered in the first half of the twentieth century was the baths. None of the other open spaces or commercial establishments appropriated by gay men—streets, parks, speakeasies, restaurants—were theirs alone. In each of them, gay men had to contend with outsiders, who might ignore them, accept them, attack them, or turn them into a spectacle, but in any case had a direct and powerful influence on the way they carried and saw themselves. As a result, many gay men sought to gather in more private spaces, such as apartment parties, where they felt more secure and could relax their guard. It was only in the late 1930s and 1940s that bars patronized exclusively by gay men began to appear in New York, their development, as we shall see, in part an inadvertent consequence of the new state policing of commercial spaces introduced after the repeal of Prohibition. But decades earlier, gay men had begun to appropriate one traditional male space as their own: the city's bathhouses.

Gay bathhouses had appeared in New York by the turn of the century, and by World War I several of them had become institutions in the city, their addresses and distinctive social and sexual character known to almost every gay New Yorker and to many gay Europeans as well. The baths were a singular phenomenon, but their development and character were also emblematic of the development and character of the gay world more generally. They deserve scrutiny, therefore, for they reveal much about the evolution of gay commercial institutions in general and about the patterns of gay sociability. The transition from "mixed" (straight and gay) to exclusively gay bathhouses foreshadowed the arrival of other exclusively gay establishments. Moreover, analysis of the ways men used the bathhouses reveals much about the general character of the gay world: the permeability of its boundaries and the density of the social networks it sustained. For while the baths attracted men in the first instance because of the sexual possibilities they offered—and, indeed, fostered a distinctive sexual culture—they encouraged the cultivation of broader social ties as well. The baths exemplify the manner in which men built a social world on the basis of a shared marginalized sexuality.[1]

THE EVOLUTION OF GAY BATHHOUSES

There were three major categories of bathhouses in the city in the early twentieth century, each with a different purpose and serving a different constituency. Public baths were established by reformers to encourage cleanliness in the tenement districts; religious baths were established by Jewish authorities for purposes of ritual cleansing; and elegant Turkish, Roman, and Electric baths were established by entrepreneurs as virtual temples to the body for wealthier New Yorkers. They varied markedly in the quality and range of their facilities, the social class of patrons they attracted, and the social and sexual possibilities they offered gay men.

The New York Association for the Improvement of the Condition of the Poor had opened the first public bath in 1852, but it closed a few years later because of insufficient patronage. In the 1890s the Association began a new campaign for the construction of baths in New York's most densely populated tenement districts, where only one in forty families lived in a house or tenement with a bathroom. It opened a bath on the Lower East Side in 1891 and succeeded in making the need for such facilities an issue in the 1894 mayoral campaign that defeated Tammany Hall. In response to continuing pressure, the city built eleven public baths in Manhattan in the 1900s, and by 1915 there were sixteen. Such baths offered individual shower rooms connected to private changing booths, and could accommodate hundreds of bathers (male and female) a day. The last five baths to be built were more elaborate, including indoor swimming pools, gymnasiums, and laundry services among their facilities.[2]

The social organization of both the Jewish ritual bath (*mikvah*) and the public baths discouraged sexual activity, for they kept bathers under close supervision. The Jewish baths were community institutions, which offered no escape from one's neighbors.* The public baths, in contrast,

---

*The number of Jewish baths in the city grew sharply in the late nineteenth century as the number of Jewish immigrants increased. A 1902 survey found that only 8 percent of the city's Jewish families, who lived largely in the tenement wards, had private baths. The resulting practical need for communal baths in Jewish neighborhoods was reinforced by Jewish ritual requirements for cleanliness. Only one or two of the twenty-two bathhouses in the city in 1880 were Jewish; by 1897 over half of the city's sixty-two bathhouses were Jewish.[3]

were more impersonal, but they imposed a more formal regime of surveillance on their patrons. Men who met in the public baths could make
appointments to meet again elsewhere and sometimes managed to have
sex at the bath itself. But such baths offered only limited spaces for sexual encounters and discouraged lengthy stays (most limited showers to
twenty minutes), and thus remained relatively unattractive to men seeking sexual partners. Moreover, the staff at the baths kept a sharp eye on
their wards. One summer evening in 1910 at the Public Baths on Avenue
A at East Twenty-third Street, which had been in business just two years,
a bathhouse attendant noticed a sixteen-year-old errand boy from the
neighborhood and a thirty-eight-year-old porter from Brooklyn enter a
booth together. His suspicions aroused, the attendant entered the booth
and found the men having sex. He not only interrupted them but held
them for the police and had them charged with sodomy. Both men
pleaded guilty, and less than two weeks after the encounter the older
man found himself sentenced to three to five years in the state penitentiary.[4]

More amenable to the interests of gay men were the private Russian
and Turkish baths that dotted Manhattan. As the middle class's preoccupation with the body intensified at the turn of the century, such
baths became highly respectable and fashionable resorts by offering a
wide range of services. By the 1920s there were fifty-seven of them in
Manhattan, some located in the basements of hotels, others in their
own, often lavishly decorated buildings. It is likely that sexual encounters occurred occasionally at most private bathhouses, and that men
who met at them more often made arrangements to go elsewhere. But
gay patronage and sexual activity were concentrated at two kinds of
baths: baths visited by straight as well as gay men but whose management tolerated limited homosexual activity (which I have termed
"mixed" or "gay-tolerant" baths), and those that catered to gay men
by excluding nonhomosexual patrons and creating an environment in
which homosexual activity was encouraged and safeguarded (which
are properly termed "gay baths").

At gay-tolerant baths, men could and often did have sexual encounters,
but only if they could do so without drawing the attention of other
bathers. They usually did this only in the privacy of their dressing rooms
or, possibly, in the steam room, if it were sufficiently dark or hazy. The
management at such baths chose not to stop such sexual activity unless it
became too obvious. "Not a few of the places which cater to the public
demand for steam baths are glad to enjoy the patronage of pansies provided their actions do not result in police proceedings," stated one 1933
account, which pointed to the "fat tips" a manager supposedly could
receive from "his degenerate patrons."[5] Some of these mixed baths had a

reputation for being particularly homosexual in character at certain times of day or on certain days of the week. One gay man who had apparently visited New York in the early 1910s reported that "among the many Turkish baths in New York, one is frequently visited by homosexuals in the afternoon and one in the evening."[6] One gay man remembered a quite respectable hotel whose swimming pool and steam room were notoriously cruisy in the 1930s. He had friends from out of town who chose to stay there on visits to New York in order to make its facilities and sexual ambience part of their holiday. Because homosexual activity was tolerated but restricted at such establishments, their sexual ambience resembled that of the YMCAs on West Thirty-fourth and Sixty-third Streets, described in chapter 6. The degree of management regulation varied and depended on a variety of factors, ranging from the amenability of the staff in charge on a given night to the intensity of the concern expressed by external authorities such as the police. The Committee of Fourteen and the Society for the Suppression of Vice occasionally sent investigators into baths to monitor the extent to which management acquiesced in such behavior.[7]

The varying degrees of management regulation at the numerous baths at Coney Island epitomized the dynamics of a mixed and ambiguously gay-tolerant bath. Homosexuals frequented and occasionally made sexual contacts at most of the baths at Coney Island, including one where professional male models, bodybuilders, and their admirers gathered in the 1930s, and another where gay men could do little more than enjoy the company of "tough" working-class boys and young men. But two baths, Stauch's and Claridge's, achieved special fame as homosexual rendezvous. Stauch's three stories and its rooftop sundeck, originally part of a much larger entertainment complex, occupied a prominent place at the center of the amusement park, standing at the corner of the boardwalk and Stillwell Avenue, the main thoroughfare leading to the beach from the subway station. The gay scene at Stauch's—as in much of New York—was particularly unabashed during the Depression. Both Thomas Painter and a man who worked briefly at Coney Island in the 1930s recalled that gay men felt free to camp it up on the sundeck, and the latter man even recalled seeing men in drag there.[8] Painter described Stauch's in 1939–40:

> Coney Island [has] one truly amazing bath. . . . It gives the visitor the impression of being exclusively homosexual. If one visits the roof there is the spectacle of at least a hundred naked males practically all of them homosexuals, with a few hustlers and kept boys

about, lying around in the sun. . . . The more direct homosexual expression is reserved for the steam rooms. There, in an atmosphere murky with steam—so murky, indeed, that one cannot see more than a few feet ahead—with benches around the walls, fellation and pedication are not at all uncommon. . . . If one stumbles over a pair in the act, one mutters a hasty apology and goes on quickly in another direction.[9]

After the Second World War, when the police stepped up their anti-gay activity, Stauch's management took greater care to control its patrons' behavior, but with only limited success. Will Finch spent many Sunday afternoons in the 1950s soaking up the sun and the sights on the roofdeck, while other men pursued sexual partners in the cubicles below. "They had a private detective, and he would come in an old shirt and a bathing suit, and would sneak around the corners, trying to see two people going in the same little cubicle," one man recalled. If he saw something, he "would pound on the door, telling you 'Only one person in the booth!'" "He couldn't do it fast enough, though," another man remembered, laughing. "There were too many of us, it was a big place, and everybody knew who he was." As the result of management's efforts, Stauch's took on more of the appearance of a straight bath, but the gay presence persisted. As one of its patrons recalled, "All the old Jewish men would sit around taking steam, and the queens would sit around the bathhouse itself."[10]

More significant to the development of New York's gay society than the mixed baths were the gay baths, whose management excluded non-gay customers and safeguarded—rather than merely tolerated—homosexual activity. There was considerable financial incentive to do so, since developing a reputation as a gay bath increased patronage and lent a competitive edge, particularly as use of the baths began to wane in the general population.

It is not clear when the management of a New York bath first decided to cater to homosexuals. Edward Prime Stevenson, an expatriate American writing about the international homosexual scene around 1900, thought New York had several baths that served as "homosexual rendezvous" but at which men could do no more than make appointments to meet elsewhere.[11] He was either misinformed or the situation changed very quickly, for by no later than 1902 at least one bath in the city, the Ariston Baths, located in the basement of the twelve-story Ariston apartment hotel at the northeast corner of Broadway and West Fifty-fifth Street, had begun to cultivate a homosexual clientele. By early 1903, the bath's "very bad" reputation had reached the police, who discovered that it had served for at least a year (and possibly much longer) as "the resort of persons for the purpose of sodomy and that sodomy was regularly practiced there."[12] The police sent several undercover inspectors into the baths over a period of days to investigate the situation. On the basis of their reports, the police decided to raid the baths on a busy Saturday night, sending the agents back into the baths several hours before the raid to secure evidence against individuals engaged in sodomy. Their subsequent testimony depicted the spatial and social organization of an early gay bathhouse in unparalleled detail.[13]

The layout and organization of the Ariston were typical. A man entered the baths through a basement entrance on Fifty-fifth Street and, after paying a dollar and checking his valuables, was assigned a private dressing room and given a sheet to drape over his shoulders after he had undressed. The Ariston, like the other grand private baths of the era, offered a variety of services that made it much more luxurious than the gay baths of the 1940s and 1950s. On its staff were masseurs, a manicurist, and a chiropodist, and its facilities included a café where cigars and cool drinks were sold, a parlor with chairs and cots, a swimming pool, and a small gymnasium with dumbbells and other equipment, as well as a steam room and sauna, four cooling rooms with cots where men could rest after taking a steam bath, showers, and numerous private dressing rooms with cots.[14]

It should not be surprising that in an era of fairy resorts and back-room saloons, men were quite open in their sexual activity in those settings where it was permitted. The extent of the overt homosexual activity witnessed by the police at the Ariston makes it clear that the activity must have been countenanced by the management and that everyone who bathed there must have been aware of it. Men felt free to approach other men in the common rooms and hallways and to invite them back to their private dressing rooms (marked as A on the diagram of the Ariston Baths, figure 8.2).[15] But the homosexual character of the baths was made clearest by the amount of sexual activity that took place publicly in the dormitory and cooling rooms. The most active room was the southeast cooling room (B). In this long and narrow room, seven cots stood against one wall and only a two-foot-wide passageway separated them from the opposite wall. Men crowded into the room looking for partners, and one investigator testified that he saw almost two dozen sexual encounters in the room over the course of two hours, with at least one involving more than two men. Although there were no lights in the room, it was partially illuminated by the light of the gaslights in the next-door parlor (C), which streamed in through an open door. Voyeurism and exhibitionism were an important part of the sexual excitement in the resulting light and shadow: one officer testified that

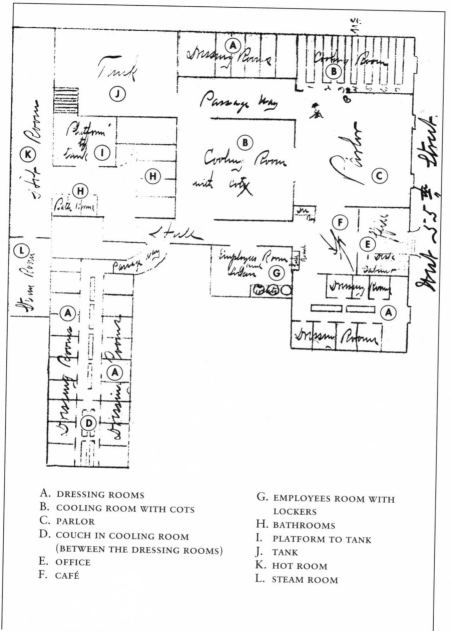

A. DRESSING ROOMS
B. COOLING ROOM WITH COTS
C. PARLOR
D. COUCH IN COOLING ROOM
   (BETWEEN THE DRESSING ROOMS)
E. OFFICE
F. CAFÉ

G. EMPLOYEES ROOM WITH
   LOCKERS
H. BATHROOMS
I. PLATFORM TO TANK
J. TANK
K. HOT ROOM
L. STEAM ROOM

Figure 8.2. This diagram of the Ariston Bathhouse, drawn by a policeman after a raid in 1903, shows the private dressing rooms (marked A) where men could take partners, and the larger common rooms (B and D) where men openly had sexual encounters. *(From Court of General Sessions, New York City, Records in the Case of People v. Kregal, 1903.)*

two men had sex while he stood less than a foot away from them, and that another eight or so men observed the pair while standing against the walls or lying on cots.[16] Widely understood (and therefore unspoken) conventions of conduct governed the men's sexual interactions. The officers observed a fifty-three-year-old Irish pantryman have sex with nine different men, most of whom indicated their interests with gestures.[17] This was not the only public sexual space; in another cooling room (D) officers saw two men have sex on a couch in the presence of ten or fifteen other men.[18]

The police raided the Ariston after midnight on Saturday night, February 21, 1903, several hours after the four investigators had entered the bath to gather evidence against individual bathers. When the raiding squad entered the baths, they blocked the exit and rounded up the staff and the seventy-eight patrons scattered through the facilities. The police denigrated the patrons as fairies; one man recalled them shouting, "Come out here, Maude," as they pounded on his dressing room door, and "Oh, here is the indignant lady," when he swung the door open.[19] The police had the men get dressed and assemble in the parlor (C), before leading them one by one into the café (F), where the four investigators who had been at the baths that night identified the ones against whom they had direct evidence of homosexual activity. The twenty-six men they identified were bundled into two paddy wagons and hustled down to the 22nd Precinct station, where they were locked up for the night before being arraigned. The other fifty-two men were let go with a warning. But before being released, the *New York Sun* reported, "each was required to furnish a full account of himself and to show some credentials proving the truth of his assertions." They were then "passed out at the door one at a time," and forced to walk through the crowd that had gathered outside, which "hooted and jeered" at them.[20]

The police were careful to arrest only the men against whom they had specific evidence of homosexual activity, because a series of scandals had recently diminished their credibility. Public mistrust of the police was so pervasive that the judge in one of the Ariston trials felt obliged to warn the jury not to presume that *every* police witness was "unworthy of belief and liable to commit perjury."[21] But the arresting officers were rewarded for their care. The results have been lost of the trials of the manager, who was charged with running a disorderly house and selling liquor without a license, and of the four bath attendants charged with violating the liquor laws. But the consequences of the raid for the baths' patrons can be ascertained. Six of them were charged only with disorderly conduct and fined five or ten dollars; the other sixteen were held on the more serious charge of sodomy, and twelve eventually faced trial. After a series of sensational trials held through the spring, the Irish pantryman who had been seen with nine sexual partners was sentenced to twenty years in the state penitentiary, two of his partners to seven years and two months, and a third to four years. Five of his partners escaped punishment (three because they forfeited bail), but two of the other defendants received prison terms of seven years and two months.[22]

None of the men arrested in subsequent raids on gay bathhouses were penalized as severely as those apprehended at the Ariston (like most men arrested for gay activity by the 1910s, they were usually charged with degenerate disorderly conduct, a misdemeanor, rather than sodomy, a felony). But some of the subsequent raids were more brutal. A man caught in 1929 in a raid on the Lafayette Baths (described below) bitterly recalled:

> [The] brutality [of the arresting officers] was simply indescribable. . . . Various people were struck, kicked down, kicked. . . . A Swede standing next to me was struck on the eye with a bunch of keys, and then he got hit in the back so [hard] that two of his ribs broke.[23]

Some of the raids also had more devastating effects. The manager of the Lafayette caught in an earlier raid in 1916 committed suicide before the conclusion of his trial, apparently because of his distress at the public revelation that he managed a homosexual rendezvous.[24]

But while raids could have tragic consequences, the police generally ignored the baths (presumably they were paid to do so). Three of the five raids on record from 1900 to 1930 involved (and were probably initiated by) the same private social-purity societies that were generally behind the police's periodic endeavors to enforce moral regulations. Even these organizations paid little attention to the baths, however, most likely because they did not constitute a particularly visible form of "public disorder"; at the baths, as elsewhere, men who made an effort to keep themselves hidden were relatively safe. The Society for the Prevention of Crime was involved in the raid on the Ariston in 1903, when reformers briefly controlled the mayor's office and the Society's influence was at its peak, but it expressed no further interest in eradicating homosexuality from the city's baths. When the Society's superintendent reported to the board of directors in 1917 that one of its agents had been solicited by a man near its offices on Union Square, he pointed out that the "Turkish baths are frequented considerably by this type of degenerate," but, as already noted, the board did not authorize him to "enter upon [a] campaign against such vice."[25] The only reason the board even considered such a campaign was that the Society for the Suppression of Vice had recently organized the raid on the Lafayette Baths as part of its wartime campaign against homosexual activity in the city, but not even the SSV expressed further interest in the baths after the war emergency had passed.

Because of their relative security, gay baths grew in number. It is not clear whether the Ariston continued to be a homosexual rendezvous after being raided, although this seems doubtful, given the notoriety of the trials and the severity of the sentences imposed on the patrons. Nor is it clear precisely which other baths took its place in the 1900s or already were (and continued to be) homosexual in character, although several accounts indicate that such baths existed.[26] But a decade later, the evidence becomes more precise, and shows that by the mid-teens several establishments functioned as gay bathhouses.

The most famous—and enduring—of the gay baths was the Everard, which provided gay men a refuge for more than half a century before a fire destroyed it in 1977. (A new Everard took its place until 1985, when the city closed it and other gay bathhouses as an anti-AIDS measure.) The Everard, originally a church, was converted into a bathhouse in 1888 by James Everard, a prominent financier, brewer, and politician. Its location at 28 West Twenty-eighth Street, just west of Broadway, put it in the heart of the Tenderloin entertainment district, where it was surrounded by famous theaters and restaurants and by infamous resorts such as the Haymarket and the French Madam's, as well as some of the city's largest brothels. In its early years it was known for its wealthy and middle-class clientele, and in the 1920s it was still considered one of the eight major Turkish bathhouses in Manhattan, offering well-appointed facilities and a variety of steam baths.[27]

It is not certain when gay men began patronizing the Everard, but they clearly had begun to do so by World War I. On January 5, 1919, the Society for the Suppression of Vice organized a raid on the Everard in which the manager and nine customers were arrested, and a year later the police raided the bath again, this time arresting fifteen men. The identities of those arrested tell us much about the clientele of the Everard. They were not all so well off as its reputation might suggest: they included two clerks, an unemployed butler, a sailor, and an art student, as well as a contractor and a journalist. But the one-dollar admission fee was sufficiently high to preclude visits by the great mass of workingmen, such as the errand boy and porter arrested at the public baths on Avenue A in 1910. None of the men arrested at the Everard in 1919 were manual laborers, and almost all of those convicted for degenerate disorderly conduct after the 1920 raid were able to pay a $25 fine in order to avoid a five-day jail term. All the men were white, and most were in their thirties (although a few were in their twenties or forties), which suggests that younger men found the place difficult to afford and older men found it inhospitable. The Everard's reputation apparently extended throughout the city and beyond. Men had come in from New Jersey on both nights, and in 1920 the customers hailed not only from Greenwich Village, Harlem, and midtown Manhattan, but also from Brooklyn, New Jersey, and even Philadelphia and Dayton, Ohio.[28] By 1927, the British actor and playwright Emlyn Williams recalled, the Everard's fame had extended to Europe's gay world; he visited it on a trip to New York that year after hearing from a French friend that "London, mon cher, is *nothing* compared to it. . . "[29]

In addition to the Everard, New York's gay bathhouses in the 1910s included the Produce Exchange Baths at 6 Broadway and the Lafayette Baths at 403–405 Lafayette Street, just south of Cooper Union.[30] The Lafayette was the more important, a favorite of the early modernist composer Charles Tomlinson Griffes and the painter Charles Demuth, and the victim of police raids in 1916 and 1929. The Lafayette drew men from the same social strata as the Everard, although its patrons were somewhat more diverse in background. On the night of the 1916 raid, they included four house servants, two clerks, two drivers, a watchman, a detective, a tailor, a milliner, a jeweler, a weaver, a teacher, a bartender, a cook—and sixteen men who refused to reveal their occupations. In both the 1916 and 1929 raids, about 70 percent of the customers were in their twenties or thirties, but a few were in their forties or fifties, and in 1929 two were in their sixties. All the men were white, but they were of disparate ethnic backgrounds, with native-born Protestants the single largest group but a third of the patrons foreign-born, and both foreign- and native-born Jews, Italians, Irish, and Scandinavians moderately represented.

Like the Everard, the Lafayette was part of a well-developed and self-conscious subculture, which facilitated the spread of its reputation. A German patron reported in 1929 that it was "very well-known . . . especially as a place where like-minded people meet (a quee[r']s place)." A fifth of the men arrested with the German in 1929 had come in from New Jersey, and several more from Long Island and the boroughs; Manhattanites accounted for only half the patrons. On the fateful night of the 1916 raid, almost three-quarters of the customers were from various Manhattan neighborhoods, but two visitors from Boston and Pittsburgh were also present.[31]

By the 1930s and 1940s, baths that did not cater to gay men had begun to decline in number and popularity as indoor plumbing and private bathing facilities became more widely available and as the elegance and social cachet previously associated with private bathhouses began to wane. The Ariston and Lafayette had closed by then, but several other baths, acutely aware of the need to develop a steady patronage in the face of a diminishing market, had taken their place as gay rendezvous. Most of them would survive, if in changed form, through the 1970s. Although the baths—whose customers were, after all, literally stripped of most class signifiers—continued to be more egalitarian in style than most other gay institutions and their clientele became more diverse, their customers continued to be differentiated along lines of race and increasingly along lines of sexual style. One man might enjoy visiting several different baths, as the mood struck him, but each of the baths established a reputation for catering to particular tastes and kinds of men.

The Everard, for example, had established itself by the 1930s as the "classiest," safest, and best known of the baths. Its efforts to exclude men not interested in homosexual encounters contributed to the security its patrons felt there. Persistent rumors that it was owned by the Police Athletic League enhanced its reputation as being safe from police harassment, making it the first choice of professional men concerned about the consequences of an arrest.[32]

Beginning in the 1920s, the Penn Post Baths, located only a few blocks away in the basement of a seedy assignation hotel on West Thirty-first Street near Eighth Avenue, offered a strikingly different sexual scene.[33] Like the Everard, it was busiest in the evening, especially after the bars closed, during lunch, and right after work, when it drew men from the many offices and depots in the neighborhood and from among the commuters who passed through Penn Station, just across the street. But because it was so cheap, its clientele was more diverse than the Everard's, and included poorer office and manual workers. It had none of the privacy or the elegance of the Everard, for its facilities consisted of little more than one large room, which held a dozen or so bunks and a few benches, plus a shower room and a tiny steam room, and its exhibitionistic sexual scene, as well as its "low-class" clientele, gave it a somewhat unsavory reputation among middle-class gay men.[34]

The Mount Morris Baths, located in Harlem on Madison Avenue at 125th Street, was the only gay bath in the city to admit African-American men. It had opened by 1893, but it is unclear when it became a gay bathhouse, since it escaped being raided before World War II (and thus left no records). Most of the other baths overtly excluded blacks until the 1960s. The Mount Morris was also visited by whites and, like the Penn Post, was known for its "rough trade." The St. Mark's Bath, in the East Village on St. Mark's Place near Third Avenue, had opened as a Jewish bathhouse by 1915. It continued to function as such during the day until the mid-1970s, but it had begun attracting gay men (though not an exclusively gay clientele) in the evenings by World War II.[35]

THE BATHHOUSE AS SEXUAL AND SOCIAL CENTER

As a sexual arena, the baths had distinct advantages over some of the other venues used by gay men, such as parks and washrooms. Perhaps most important, they were safer. As one man explained in 1913, "In general one can say that the Turkish baths of America are a very safe place for homosexuals. . . . The people one meets there have not come there to blackmail."[36] There was always the danger, as he implied, that a man taken home from the streets would try to rob or blackmail his host, or that a sexual encounter in a park would end in violence. Men who went to the baths avoided such dangers, for they were able to leave their valuables and identification papers stored safely in a locker and were surrounded by other gay men who could come to their assistance in the event of trouble. The baths' management realized that it was in its own interest to prevent incidents from occurring on the premises, so its staff kept each floor under surveillance and was ready to intervene to prevent fights or thefts. Just as important, men were relatively safe in the baths from the police; although plainclothesmen as well as thieves threatened them on the streets, they rarely entered the baths, nor did they raid them nearly as often as they raided the city's bars and other commercial venues.[37]

The baths were also more secure because the management sought to exclude straight men who might react angrily to a homosexual advance. As a result of this policy, the sexual climate of the gay baths was different from that of certain streets—and even of many Bowery resorts and waterfront dives—in several significant ways. First, it made it possible for men to disabuse themselves of negative feelings about their homosexuality, for although some of the other men at the baths might reject them as sexual partners, none would reject them simply for being homosexuals. It also meant that the baths became a rendezvous for those gay men who wished to have mutually satisfying sex with other gay men rather than to service "normal" men (the possibility of "servicing trade" was part of the appeal of mixed baths). The investigators at the Ariston Baths in 1903, for instance, observed a scene that would have been almost inconceivable to the fairies and "normal" men at the Bowery resorts: two men spent a considerable amount of time lying on a couch, embracing and kissing, and each played both "active" and "passive" roles.[38]

Although many interactions were more one-sided than this, the sexual culture of the baths—unlike that of certain streets—presumed that both (or more) partners desired whatever contact they had and to play whatever role they took. In sharp contrast to most social situations, which negated the body and homosexual desire, the baths affirmed them by facilitating public interactions, group encounters (or "mass sex," as it was usually called), and, at the least, overt expressions of homosexual interest. When a friend with "little experience but great desire" confided his homosexual longings to Charles Griffes in 1916, Griffes took him to the Lafayette so that he could meet other gay men and explore his sexual interests in a supportive environment; the friend was "astounded and fascinated" by what he saw there. The baths also encouraged more advanced forms of sexual experimentation. Griffes himself had had his first encounter with a man interested in sadomasochism at the Lafayette two years earlier (he found the man "interesting" but the experience unappealing), and several men interviewed in the mid-1930s referred to experimenting in the baths and learning of new pleasures.[39]

The homosexual character of the baths was reflected in the virtual absence of prostitution. Casual prostitution sometimes occurred, particularly at the mixed baths at Coney Island, where a youth might ask for   carfare home, but the organization and layout of exclusively gay baths   discouraged professional hustlers. The admission fee alone proved a disincentive—and sometimes an insurmountable barrier—to hustlers, especially since they could meet men on the streets at no expense and might even be treated to a drink at the bars. Moreover, it was difficult to enforce a financial agreement in a bath. As Thomas Painter wryly observed in 1941, "It is not convenient to try to collect a fee from a naked man," and it was virtually impossible for the hustler to get to a man's wallet held at the office. The man could easily call for help if a hustler followed him to his cubicle to demand payment, and it would have been foolhardy for a hustler to try to follow his customer to the office. Such practical obstacles might have been surmounted, however, but for the even greater impediment to the hustler's success posed by the sexual culture of the baths. Most men who visited the baths were more interested in sex with other gay men than with hustlers or "trade."[40]

For some men, the baths served as a refuge where they could pursue homosexual interests they had to hide in other settings. Some married men, for instance, found them a relatively safe and anonymous setting in which to satisfy their need for homosexual contact. Of the seventeen men arrested at the Lafayette in 1916 whose marital status was indicated, three were married, as were three of the nine men arrested at the Everard in 1919.[41] They were also a convenient rendezvous for men who dared not be seen at a cafeteria, a bar, or other more public gay establishments, which a nongay person was more likely to enter than a bathhouse. Charles Tomlinson Griffes, rather bold himself, attested to the baths' crucial role in such men's lives when he bitterly complained in 1914: "It always angers me that one cannot meet these people anywhere except there, but they always seem to be afraid."[42] Emlyn Williams's description of a man doffing his togalike bathsheet, getting dressed, and leaving the baths in 1927 captured the distance between the gay world and the straight—and how easily that distance was bridged: "Roman apparition transformed into business-man—hat, overcoat with velvet collar, spats, brief-case—to be seen on weekday evenings in his hundreds on the sidewalks, hailing a taxi to take him to Grand Central and home to his wife in Westchester County."[43]

But the baths should not be regarded as simply the scene of furtive encounters between men who had disguised their identities, for they also served to introduce gay men to one another and foster their sense of allegiance to other gay men. Some married men leading otherwise conventional lives patronized the baths not only for sexual encounters but also to visit with gay friends in a gay environment, and the baths became the center of their gay social lives. The baths also played an important role in the social lives of many men more fully integrated into the gay world, both in the early decades of the century, when relatively few other gay institutions existed, and in later years, when the streets and bars grew more dangerous because of increased police activity.

Some men made a particular bath their own and developed ties with its other regular patrons and staff. Charles Griffes, for instance, visited the Lafayette on a regular basis in the mid-teens, frequently running into men he had previously met there as well as friends from the outside; once he even complained that "there are almost always the same people there." After the police raid that closed the Lafayette in October 1916, Griffes started frequenting the Produce Exchange Baths in its stead, but he stopped by to talk with the Lafayette's new manager when the bath reopened in late December and subsequently began patronizing it again. (Though Griffes did not say so in his diary, they must have had an interesting conversation. The new manager was Ira Gershwin.)* An

---

*Griffes met the Lafayette's new manager on December 29, 1916, but did not name him in his diary. This was, however, the month the Gershwins took over the management of the Lafayette Baths. The possibility of a meeting between the two musical-giants-to-be is intriguing, but Griffes left no record of the conversation, which seems to have been a courtesy call and may have been designed to elicit information about the status of the bath in its new incarnation. Unfortunately it is impossible to determine precisely when he began frequenting the Lafayette again after his meeting with the new manager at the end of 1916, because he made virtually no reference to homosexual matters in his 1917 diary. Indeed, he wrote nothing at all in the 1917 diary until April 11 and subsequently made only occasional entries, most of which were short notes concerning his professional activities. We know that the Lafayette continued to function as a gay bath and that he continued to patronize it because he mentioned visiting it (and meeting another gay friend there) on October 27, 1917, the date of his diary's last entry, but it is possible that the Gershwins tried to keep it relatively quiet for a short while after reopening.

attendant at the Ariston testified that one man arrested there in 1903 had visited the bath once or twice a week for at least a year, often on the same night as a second man with whom the police had seen him in a passionate embrace, and the man himself later admitted he had been patronizing the bath since 1897.[44] A man arrested at the Lafayette in 1929 had already been there ten times since moving to New York, and several men interviewed about the 1930s, '40s, and '50s recalled having a favorite bath they regularly visited and to which they developed some loyalty. This loyalty was fostered by the bathhouse's staff, for whom it made good business sense to encourage regular patronage: an employee at the St. Mark's recalled getting to know dozens of regular customers by name and spending hours with them in the restaurant, as well as reserving rooms and performing other favors for them.[45] That the staff at the baths was relatively successful at screening out heterosexuals who unwittingly tried to visit is a testimony to their familiarity both with their regular customers and with the subcultural codes men used to signal their homosexuality.

Charles Griffes's diary record of his bathhouse visits provides a rich portrait of the baths' role as social centers. Griffes patronized the baths frequently on his trips to the city from the private boarding school in Tarrytown, New York, where he taught music. Although his first interest in the baths was always sexual, he met many men there who became good friends and with whom he visited outside the baths as well.[46] The seven hours he spent at the Lafayette one day in the summer of 1916 illustrates the range of contacts he made there. He met two men, apparently a couple, and arranged to spend the following day with both of them and for one of them to see him on a more intimate basis a few days later. (The couple kept the date and listened to Griffes perform several of his piano pieces in his apartment before joining him on an excursion to Coney Island, and in the following weeks he made several appointments to go to the baths with each   of them separately.) He also made an appointment for later that evening to see "the new Andrew," someone new to the baths who apparently had become a subject of conversation among his friends there; although Andrew accepted the invitation, he failed to show up. "Other than that," Griffes commented, "I was quite satisfied with the afternoon."[47] He frequently took men he met at the baths to Luchow's or some other restaurant so they could have a meal and get to know each other, and the men he met there entered into the web of his life in a variety of ways. On one occasion he met someone who called him the next day with information about an apartment he might rent for the summer. He eventually had something of a social circle based at the baths, and his visits there sometimes led to long conversations with old friends. One afternoon at the Lafayette in January 1916, he not only caught up with a friend he had not seen since the summer but also had a long, intimate discussion with a former lover "about myself and my character."[48]

The experiences of Griffes and of subsequent generations of gay men demonstrate that the baths were not only a venue for fleeting encounters but also an important setting for the development of social relationships among gay men. Thirty years after Griffes, for instance, Martin Goodkin also found that the baths facilitated the development of relationships, some confined to the baths and others assuming a life beyond their walls. He recalled having "steady sex partners over a period of three years [in the early 1950s] at the Everard baths. We came to know everything about each other [even though we] never did socialize outside." After leaving New York he corresponded with two of them for more than thirty years.[49]

Although some men were ashamed of their visits to the baths and refused to identify themselves when there or to talk about them when elsewhere, many others valued them highly and discussed them unabashedly in other gay settings. A fixture in gay life and culture, the baths became a part of gay folklore—hardly a likely development if all their patrons had remained isolated from one another and done no more than use the baths surreptitiously, never mentioning them. In an article published in Broadway Brevities in December 1924, a columnist recalled that "the Everard Baths were once raided, and—years before that—the Lafayette Baths (where Robt. L---K--- used to go) and, still other years before, the Ariston Baths, where Lillian Russell lived upstairs. The latter more than twenty years ago."[50] The fact that a columnist writing in 1924 knew of the raids on the Everard in 1919–20, the Lafayette in 1916, and the Ariston in 1903—and something as well of the lore of the baths, such as the putative Lillian Russell connection—is remarkable testimony both to his familiarity with the gay world and to the historical self-consciousness of the men in that world. Even in the first quarter of the century, they had created a subculture that sustained a collective memory and made the history of the baths a significant part of its folklore.

Gay baths were few in number and served a more limited—and generally more affluent—clientele than most of the other spaces gay men appropriated in the early twentieth century. But they constituted a singular gay environment. They were some of the first exclusively gay commercial spaces in the city. The most stable of gay institutions, they outlasted every gay bar and restaurant in the city and provided a place safe from police and vigilantes alike in which to meet other gay men. Forthrightly sexual in character, the baths were also important social centers, where gay men could meet openly, discuss their lives, and build a circle of friends. Their distinctive character fostered a sense of community among their patrons.

Although the baths were singular institutions, their development as social—as well as strictly sexual—spaces points to certain fundamental characteristics of the gay world in general. The experience of men at the baths highlights the way gay men built social ties on the basis of their sexual ties and created a social world on the basis of a shared and marginalized sexuality. For while many men used the baths simply as a convenient site for quick sexual encounters, others, who had also initially been drawn to them by their sexual interests, soon formed more elaborate social relationships with the men they met there, and came to depend on them in a variety of ways. Charles Tomlinson Griffes was drawn into the gay world by the baths not just because he had sex there, but because he met men there who helped him find apartments and otherwise make his way through the city, who appreciated his music, who gave him new insights into his character, and who became his good friends. The gay world became a central part of his everyday world, even though he kept it hidden from his nongay associates.

The different ways that different men used the baths also reveal the variety of ways men negotiated their involvement in the gay world as a whole. Some of the men who visited them were highly integrated into the larger gay world, for they frequented as well the cafeterias, restaurants, and streets where gay men gathered. But the baths also served as a haven for men who dared not risk being seen in such more easily accessible locales because they were married or had jobs that required enormous caution. Despite the fact that they limited their involvement in gay society to the highly circumscribed social arena offered by the baths, many of them made gay friends and developed extensive gay social ties within those limits.

The sharp division the latter group of men made between their gay lives at the baths and their straight lives outside was not typical for gay men, but in one respect it may be regarded as prototypical. For if the limits they imposed on their involvement in the gay world were more extreme than those most men imposed, their experience nonetheless exemplified the extent to which men could participate in gay life—and identify themselves with it—even as they hid any trace of that participation from their everyday associates. If the baths served as a kind of "closet" for those men, protecting them from the knowledge and hostility of outsiders, it was a very large closet indeed, filled with other people, with doors the police occasionally pried open but which, more often, they themselves opened and closed at strategic moments. In such closets, a gay world was built.

Figure 9.1. This 1932 cartoon plays on Greenwich Village's reputation as a center of lesbian and gay life by showing a bored male being ignored by the women at a club. A close look reveals that almost all of the couples depicted are same-sex, usually including one woman in a suit. (*From* Broadway Brevities, *June 6, 1932.*)

Chapter 9

BUILDING GAY NEIGHBORHOOD ENCLAVES:
THE VILLAGE AND HARLEM

THE GAY WORLD EVOLVED THROUGHOUT THE CITY, BUT IT TOOK ITS MOST developed and visible form in just a few neighborhoods. The Bowery had been a center of fairy life at the turn of the century; by the 1910s and 1920s, two other neighborhoods had become gay centers, attracting disproportionate numbers of gay residents and commercial establishments where gay men and lesbians set the tone. In the 1920s, Greenwich Village hosted the best-known gay enclave in both the city and the nation—and the first to take shape in a predominantly middle-class (albeit bohemian) milieu. By the late 1910s, a Village song included the line "Fairyland's not far from Washington Square," and by the early 1930s, the Village's gay reputation was so firmly established that a New York tabloid could quip that while a doctor had learned how to "switch the sex of animals, turning males into females, they beat the scientist to it in Greenwich Village!"[1] Gay men and women had to fight for space even in the Village, but its reputation for flouting bourgeois convention made it seem an inviting place and did in fact let them create a haven for homosexuals.

If the Village was considered the city's most infamous gay neighborhood by outsiders, many gay men themselves regarded Harlem as the most exciting center of gay life. In a segregated city, it was the *only* place where black gay men could congregate in commercial establishments, and they were centrally involved in many of the currents of Harlem culture, from the creative literary circles that constituted the Harlem Renaissance to the blues clubs and basement speakeasies where the poorest of Harlem's residents gathered. African-Americans organized the largest annual communal event of New York's gay society, the Hamilton

Lodge Ball, which attracted thousands of white as well as black partici-pants and spectators. Nonetheless, the men and women who built Harlem's gay world confronted the same challenges their white counter-parts did elsewhere. While the "faggots" who were highly visible in the neighborhood's streets and nightspots might earn a degree of grudging respect from others, they had no hope of respectability. Most middle-class gay Harlemites struggled to keep news of their homosexuality from spreading, lest it cause their social downfall.

New York's first substantial lesbian enclaves developed in the Village and Harlem at the same time gay male enclaves did. Although lesbians and gay men continued to move in largely separate social worlds, they both gathered at some of the same speakeasies, including several particu-larly prominent ones run by lesbians or featuring lesbian performers, and lesbians attended some of the drag balls organized by gay men. The limited convergence of lesbian and gay life in the 1920s, particularly through the appearance of commercial establishments attracting both men and women on the basis of their shared participation in the gay life, marked an important stage in the emergence of the social category of the homosexual.

Neither the Village nor Harlem could be said to have been a gay neigh-borhood in the 1920s, for in neither did homosexuals set the tone. But each neighborhood, for different reasons, allowed a gay enclave to take shape, and the differences between those enclaves highlight the degree to which particular gay subcultures were shaped by the dominant neighbor-hood (or parent) cultures in which they developed.

LONG-HAIRED MEN AND SHORT-HAIRED WOMEN: THE GAY WORLD OF VILLAGE BOHEMIA

The emergence of Greenwich Village as a gay center was closely linked to the development of the bohemian community there. Although the Village had originally been north of the city's borders, a refuge for the rich from urban disorder and disease, by 1900 most of its elite residents had departed and the Village itself had been physically incorporated into a city whose borders had long since pushed far beyond it to the north. At the turn of the century the area was known simply as the Ninth Ward, dominated by working-class Italian immigrants. Only when native-born bohemian writers, artists, and radicals began to move into the neighbor-hood in the 1900s did it begin to be called "the Village" again—and then only by the self-styled bohemian "Villagers" who moved there, not the Italian "Ninth Warders."

The newcomers to the Village were attracted by its winding streets and Old World charm, by its relative isolation from the rest of the city, and above all by the social life its cheap apartments and services made possible. "After college and the war," the writer Malcolm Cowley recalled of his generation of writers, "most of us drifted to Manhattan, to the crooked streets south of Fourteenth, where you could rent a furnished hall-bedroom for two or three dollars weekly or the top floor of a rickety house for thirty dollars a month. We came to the Village . . . because living was cheap."[2] Although the Village became the most famous bohemian community in the country in the 1910s and 1920s, subject to searching examination in the national press, similar residential districts were developing in large cities throughout the country. In many respects the Village was a prototypical furnished-room district, for it offered cheap rooms to unmarried men and women who wished to develop social lives unencumbered by family obligations and to engage in work likely to be more creative than remunerative.

Lesbians and gay men also found the cheap rents and cheap restaurants appealing, but greater attractions were the Village's reputation for tolerating nonconformity (or "eccentricity") and the impetus for social experimentation engendered in the district by the bohemians who originally settled there, for these held out the promise of making the Village a safe and even congenial place for homosexuals to live. Moreover, the particular forms of eccentricity allowed the "artistic types" made it unusually easy for gay men and lesbians to fit into Village society and also provided a cover to those who adopted flamboyant styles in their dress and demeanor.

Not only were many Villagers unmarried, but by becoming artists, free-lovers, and anti-materialists (if not always anti-capitalists), they had forsaken many of the other social roles and characteristics prescribed for their class and gender in ways stereotypically associated with homosexuals.[3] Indeed, the unconventional behavior of many bohemian men—ranging from their long hair, colorful dress, and interest in art to their decided lack of interest in the manly pursuits of getting married and making money—often led outsiders to consider all of them queer. Although not everyone thought their queer tastes extended to sexual matters, the bohemian men of the Village were often regarded as unmanly as well as un-American, and in some contexts calling men "artistic" became code for calling them homosexual.

The frequent references by critics to the "long-haired men" and "short-haired women" of the Village sometimes constituted precisely such accusations of perversity, only slightly veiled, since the gender reversal implied by such images directly evoked the semiotic codes that denoted sexual perversion. In 1929, for instance, a conservative Village paper attacked bohemian women for being "so ashamed of their sex that they do their best to appear like men, claiming, however, the privileges of womanhood just the same." It went on to charge that "the majority of that type manifestly endeavor to create a third sex."[4]

This overlapping of homosexual and bohemian characteristics threatened some straight members of the avant-garde, who often were not so tolerant of homosexuals as their reputation might suggest. Indeed, a considerable gap often existed between the *representation* and the *actuality* of Village life and mores. As the historians Ellen Kay Trimberger and Leslie Fishbein have shown, many of the leading self-identified male feminists of the Village remained deeply troubled or ambivalent about the independence of women and strove to protect their prerogatives and identities as men from the demands made by the ideologies of feminism and bohemianism.[5] In this context it is not surprising that many of them were also troubled by the insinuation that their unorthodox behavior meant they were "queer" in a specifically sexual sense. In his 1934 memoir, Malcolm Cowley acknowledged his fear that he and his fellow writers, intellectuals, and artists were being slandered as perverts. He recalled that *Broom*, the little magazine he worked on in the early 1920s, received letters at its 45 King Street office addressed to "45 Queer Street," and "mention[ing] Oscar Wilde." He added, "I came to believe that a general offensive was about to be made against modern art, an offensive based on the theory that all modern writers, painters and musicians were homosexual. . . . I began to feel harried and combative, like Aubrey Beardsley forced to defend his masculinity against whispers." His reaction, as he frankly admitted, was to "hate . . . pansipoetical poets." He claimed to have had drunken dreams of a writers' revolution in the Village, when "you would set about hanging policemen from the lamp posts, . . . and beside each policeman would be hanged a Methodist preacher, and beside each preacher a pansy poet."[6]

The artistic and political bohemian men of the Village discussed sex more explicitly than their middle-class contemporaries deemed proper, and their "modern," scientific views of homosexuality sometimes disturbed the guardians of the old order. But their "frank" consideration of homosexuality was not necessarily positive, and it often simply condemned homosexuality in scientific rather than more overtly moralistic terms. John Sumner, Anthony Comstock's successor as head of the Society for the Suppression of Vice, attacked *The Masses*, a radical magazine published by Villagers in the 1910s, for addressing the question of homosexuality, but its coverage was hardly always positive.

The Masses had long mocked the Society's censorious moralism. In one issue, it published a caricature of Comstock dragging a woman by her hair before a judge and charging, "Your Honor, this woman gave birth to a naked child!" Sumner retaliated in the summer of 1916, shortly after Comstock's death and just a year before the Post Office closed *The Masses* for good for circulating anti-war propaganda, by targeting the bookshop the magazine ran in the Village. The shop sold such classics of the new sexual thought as *Love's Coming of Age* by the British gay socialist Edward Carpenter and *The Sexual Question* by the Swiss sexologist Auguste Forel, and the magazine regularly filled its pages with ads for them. Sumner, charging that *The Sexual Question* was an "indecent book," raided the shop on August 31, arrested the circulation manager, and seized the magazine's September issue, which contained an advertisement for the book.

A few days before the raid, when Floyd Dell, the magazine's managing editor, happened to be minding the shop, Sumner had visited it to secure proof that it carried the book. As Dell later recalled, he had inquired as to why Sumner found the book so objectionable. "It was," Dell remembered, "because Forel expressed sympathy for homosexuals—or, as Sumner put it, 'approval,' which, as I remembered the book, was not true." Dell himself was hardly sympathetic to homosexuals. In his own book, *Love in the Machine Age*, he argued that homosexuality was characteristic of patriarchal societies in which women were subordinated to men, and, in the modern age of free love, was a social anachronism and sign of personal regression. He considered Forel's treatise "a very wise and good book," one of "the most enlightened books that existed upon the subject of sex," and, tellingly, he was correct in noting that it did not approve of homosexuality. It attacked the writings of Karl Heinrich Ulrichs, Magnus Hirschfeld, and other German homosexual crusaders as the work of "apologists," and argued that homosexuality was a perversion.[7] Sumner, it is clear, was disturbed that Forel considered homosexuality a medical rather than a moral problem, properly in the domain of physicians rather than clergymen and moral crusaders, a perspective Dell lauded as enlightened. But it seemed unobjectionable to Dell that, in contrast to the studies of Hirschfeld, Forel's enlightened approach to homosexuality should simply condemn it as evidence of biological rather than moral degeneration. A report on the raid in the November 1916 issue of *The Masses* recorded Sumner's claim that Forel's book "advocates sodomy!" before reassuring its readers that "it does, of course, nothing of the sort." If anything, the magazine suggested in an anti-homosexual aside, it was the minds of "our prominent vice-experts" that "really do not seem to us to be normal."[8]

Dell's critique and Cowley's anxiety hardly represented the entire range of bohemian opinion on the subject of homosexuality, however, and other bohemians—especially bohemian women—accepted the gay people in their midst with greater equanimity. The anarchist Emma Goldman, for one, defended the rights of homosexuals in some of her speeches. According to the historian Judith Schwarz, not only were numerous lesbians involved in the feminist club Heterodoxy, but the club's other mem-

bers accorded lesbian relationships the same respect they granted marriages.[9]

Even a cursory review of the intellectual and political ferment of the
1910s demonstrates that numerous homosexuals participated in the
bohemian milieu and that several played an important role in the construction of Village bohemia itself. Carl Van Vechten was a gay married man and a leading white critic and novelist of the 1910s and
1920s who helped introduce the white public to the Harlem
Renaissance. He played a key role in the 1910s in organizing Mabel
Dodge Luhan's famous salons on lower Fifth Avenue, at which social-
ists and anarchists, Freudians and free-lovers, artists and activists
debated the issues of the day. The lesbians in Heterodoxy were open
with heterosexual friends. Eugene O'Neill's companions in the Village
and Provincetown included the noted gay painters Charles Demuth
and Marsden Hartley, and, according to O'Neill's biographer Louis
Sheaffer, the playwright based Charles Marsden, the effete, implicitly
homosexual character in *Strange Interlude*, on them.[10] Margaret
Anderson and her masculinely attired lover, Jane Heap, published the
influential *Little Review* from the Village, gathering gay and nongay
writers around them.

As these few examples suggest, individual homosexuals were accepted
as friends by many Villagers in the 1910s, although they were scorned by
others. But gay people were initially drawn to the Village primarily as
bohemians rather than as homosexuals and had little apparent interest in
developing distinctively gay institutions. The development of a gay
enclave resulted from the expansion and reorganization of the Village
community during World War I and the postwar years, the loss of the
intimacy and small scale of the Village as it was integrated into the city
as a whole, and the development of a speakeasy demimonde in which
gay locales might develop.

The Changing Character of the Postwar Village

The rapid commercialization of the Village during and after World War I
altered its character. The construction of the subway routes along
Seventh Avenue in 1917 and along Sixth Avenue in 1927–30 and the
simultaneous widening and extension of both avenues transformed the
Village from a remote, self-contained backwater into one of the most
central and easily reached of the city's neighborhoods. Because the opening of the subway lines made the Village a more convenient place to live,
growing numbers of businessmen, attracted by the Village's Old World
charm, began to move there. They pushed rents up and some of the
struggling artists out, real estate developers began building new apartment complexes in prime locations, and newly established taxpayers'

associations launched campaigns to clean up some of the more disreputable aspects of the Village.[11]

Just as the Village became more accessible, the advent of Prohibition in 1920 made it a particularly attractive destination to men and women out on the town. The Italian restaurants, grocers, drugstores, and other shops that lined its streets were the city's major sources of homemade Italian wine, and people flocked to the Village for their liquor supplies.[12] The Village's national reputation as a center of "free love" and other unconventional behavior was just as intriguing to tourists. The tearooms to the west and south of Washington Square had already enjoyed a boom during the war, when they became a major attraction to the soldiers and sailors passing through the city. In the years following Prohibition, the area's speakeasies and clubs lured growing numbers of middle-class men and women out slumming, as well as men out to find the women known as "free-lovers of the Greenwich Village type."

Villagers complained that their less scrupulous compatriots had begun to cater to the tourist trade, decking themselves out in the costumes visitors expected of bohemians, selling their verse and etchings to the unsophisticated, and offering tours of a fabricated "Bohemia" to the gullible. Sheridan Square became known for the outlandish theatricality of its establishments. Don Dickerman's Pirate's Den featured "clanking chains, clashing cutlasses, ship's lanterns, and patch-eyed buccaneer waiters"; jazz clubs proliferated; and Julius', a particularly successful speakeasy at Waverly Place and Tenth Street, became known as the rendezvous of college men and "flappers."[13]

Most of the original Villagers, the political radicals and bohemian artists who self-consciously identified themselves as members of a small-scale experimental community, lamented these changes. In their eyes, the postwar Village seemed to have lost the intimacy, intellectual ferment, and genuinely bohemian aspect of its halcyon prewar days. The Village's incorporation into the city in the 1920s had turned it into another Coney Island, a cheap amusement center and playground for rich uptown slummers and poorer youths from the boroughs alike. The sociologist Caroline Ware, who published a study of the Village in 1935, reflected such misgivings when she dismissed the postwar generation of Villagers as "pseudo-Bohemians," interested less in intellectual creativity than in a mindless escape from the conventions of bourgeois society.[14]

Nonetheless, the condescension of contemporary observers toward the newcomers should not be allowed to obscure the fact that the Village's reputation as a center of unconventional behavior—particularly of unconventional sexual behavior—had made it a beacon not only for rich slummers but also for increasing numbers of disaffected youths from the city's outer boroughs who wished to escape the constraints of family and neighborhood supervision. The Village became an even more visible national symbol over the course of the twenties, as the cultural gap between Prohibition America and Jazz Age New York seemed to widen, with rural politicians pandering to prohibitionist and nativist constituencies by denouncing New York as the nation's Sodom and Gomorrah.

In this context the Village took on special significance for lesbians and gay men around the country, and disaffected New Yorkers were joined in the Village by waves of refugees from the nation's less tolerant small towns.[15] As one gay man wrote in 1924: "I have for the longest time tr[ied] so hard to make people understand me, and [it] was so very hard; my friends that I know don't care for people of that kind and I left them because I always thought they would find [me] out, then I went down to the Village and [met] plenty [of gay people]."[16] A hostile newspaper reporter made the same point when he asserted in 1931 that the people who flocked to Greenwich Village were "men and women taunted by their biologically normal companions in the small towns that ostracize those who neither eat nor sleep nor love in the fashion of the hundred percenters."[17] They fled to the Village, and in the 1920s they built an extensive gay world there.

If the Village's reputation for unconventional sexuality attracted lesbians and gay men, their growing visibility in the district soon made homosexuality almost as much a part of the Village's reputation as free love. The presence of "fairies" and "lady lovers" in the Village was already sufficiently well known to have elicited press comment and attracted slummers by the beginning of World War I, and the Village's reputation as a gay neighborhood solidified throughout the 1920s. One 1927 account of New York nightlife noted that two women dancing together in a Times Square club elicited no comment, while in the Village it would be taken as a sign of their lesbianism.[18] The "exposés" of the Village periodically published by the city's newspapers increasingly focused on the homosexual aspects of the neighborhood's "depravity." In 1931 one series spotlighted gay meeting places in its "initial [tour] of the innermost stations of Greenwich Village's sex, pollution, and human decay."[19] In 1936 even the staid medical journal *Current Psychology and Psychoanalysis* published an article on the "Degenerates of Greenwich Village," which announced that the Village, "once the home of art, [is] now the Mecca for exhibitionists and perverts of all kinds."[20]

The gay scene in the Village became so prominent that it even turned up in the movies. In the 1932 Clara Bow vehicle *Call Her Savage*, Bow's escort took her to a Greenwich Village dive patronized by artists, revolutionaries, and pairs of neatly dressed male and female couples, sitting in booths with their arms around each other. The waiters were two young men in frilly white aprons and maid's caps, each sashaying about holding a feather duster and singing: "If a sailor in pajamas I should see / I know he'll scare the life out of me / But on a great big battleship / We'd like to be / Working as chamber maids!"[21]

Caroline Ware noted the growing prominence of homosexual circles in the Village over the course of the twenties, although she dismissed it as a fad: "As sex taboos broke down all over the country and sex experimentation found its way to the suburbs, the Village's exoticism could no longer rest on so commonplace a foundation." The Jazz Age public's growing curiosity about homosexuality, she thought, simply provided the Village with a new angle: "The Village became noted as the home of 'pansies' and 'Lesbians,' and dives of all sorts featured this type." Villagers "pass[ed] on from free love to homosexuality . . . to mark the outposts of revolt."[22]

Throughout her study Ware regarded homosexual behavior and identity, particularly that of women, as nothing more than something that "normal" people experimented with as part of a general "revolt," rather than as part of a significant effort to shape a personal and collective identity. Indeed, she suggested that in the late 1920s, homosexuality, and especially lesbianism, had become chic among Villagers, including numerous heterosexual women (whom she derisively termed "pseudo-Lesbians," as though they were a subcategory of "pseudo-Bohemians") who behaved like lesbians simply because it seemed the thing to do. "By 1930, promiscuity was tame and homosexuality had become the expected thing. One girl who came nightly [to a speakeasy noted for its gay patronage] was the joke of the place because she was trying so hard to be a Lesbian, but when she got drunk she forgot and let the men dance with her."[23] Despite Ware's cynicism, however, her observations suggest that by the 1920s, homosexuality had become more acceptable in Village circles and that lesbians and gay men had seized the opportunities provided by the general bohemian rebellion to construct a sphere of relative cultural autonomy for themselves.

The history of the dances, or balls, held at Webster Hall on East Eleventh Street near Third Avenue illustrates how gay people used the openings created by bohemian culture to expand their public presence; it also points up the commercialization and homosexualization of the Village's reputation. The first and most prominent of the balls were thrown in the mid-teens by the Liberal Club to finance its operations. But the financial rewards of organizing a ball had soon become so evident that entrepreneurs unaffiliated with any community group began to sponsor them, competing to produce the most outlandish balls and attract the largest audiences.[24] Floyd Dell, one of the organizers of the Liberal Club's first ball, lamented that the club's success had "shown the more commercially enterprising among us another way to make money out of the bourgeoisie." The balls had "finished the process [of betraying the Village's original ideals] which the restaurants [that drew slummers] had begun."[25]

Reports submitted by Committee of Fourteen agents investigating "vice conditions" in the wartime Village confirm Dell's recollection that as the reputation of the Village as a bohemian enclave grew, increasing numbers of slummers from throughout the city visited the balls in order to get a taste of the unconventional life. As one agent reported in 1917: "Many of the people are advertising their dances as Greenwich Village dances in order to get the crowd, and it works."[26] In a later report he noted, "These dances are getting quite popular." The reason was obvious: "Most of those present at these dances being liberals and radicals, one is not surprised when he finds a young lady who will talk freely with him on Birth Control or sex psychology."[27]

"Free love" was an important part of the attraction of the Village balls, but so, too, was homosexuality. In 1918 the same investigator reported that an increasingly "prominent feature of these dances is the number of male perverts who attend them. These phenomenal men . . . wear expensive gowns, employ rouge[,] use wigs[,] and in short make up an appearance which looks for everything like a young lady."[28] In another report he confirmed how essential such "phenomenal men" were to the allure of the Village balls when he commented that a ball had attracted "the *usual crowd* who go expecting to find ['Homosexualists'] there. Some of the latter mocking [the 'Homosexualists'], others actually patronizing them, associating with them during the night and dancing with them. . . . I mean," he added, "*men* with *men*."[29]

Part of the attraction of an amusement district such as Greenwich Village, like that of Harlem, was that it constituted a liminal space where visitors were encouraged to disregard some of the social injunctions that normally constrained their behavior, where they could observe and vicariously experience behavior that in other settings—particularly their own neighborhoods—they might consider objectionable enough to suppress. The organizers of the balls were well aware of this phenomenon and welcomed the presence of flamboyant gay men—sometimes making them a part of the pageants they staged—precisely because they knew they enhanced the reputation and appeal of such events. At the Liberal Club's Golden Ball of Isis, attended by two thousand people in February 1917, Horace Mann (well known to the audience, apparently, as a "noted homosexualist") took the major role of the slave in love with the

Egyptian goddess Isis in the 1 A.M. pageant.[30] Some Villagers expressed
reservations about the presence of such men—in 1922 one Villager worried publicly that "the golden goose of Village ball promotion was
slowly being strangled by the admission of stags and certain mincing
undesirables from uptown who love to exhibit themselves in dainty efful-
gence"[31]—but bohemian ideology encouraged the toleration of unconventional forms of sexual expression and identity. Gay people clearly
capitalized on this tolerance to claim their right to participate in Village
affairs.

A Visible Gay Presence

By the early 1920s, the presence of gay men and lesbians in the Village
was firmly established. No longer were they simply visitors to the Liberal
Club's masquerade balls. They organized their *own* balls at Webster Hall
and appropriated as their own many of the other social spaces created by
the bohemians of the 1910s. Chief among these were the cheap Italian
restaurants, cafeterias, and tearooms that crowded the Village and served
as the meeting grounds for its bohemians. Gay men and lesbians seem to
have become noticeable in such locales during World War I, at about the
same time they began attracting attention at the Liberal Club's balls.[32] By
the end of the war, the gay presence seemed to some worried observers to
have become ubiquitous: an anti-vice agent investigating a MacDougal
Street restaurant in 1919 commented that "in this restaurant, *as in all
other Greenwich Village places*, there are all sorts of people among [the
customers], many obviously prostitutes and perverts, especially the latter."[33]

The gay presence became even more noticeable after the war, when lesbians and gay men began opening their own speakeasies and tearooms. In
the early 1920s at least twenty restaurants and tearooms "catering to the
'temperamental' element" were said to exist in the Village. Some were a
few blocks west of Washington Square Park on Christopher and Charles
Streets; others were located in the heart of the Village's bohemian commercial district just south and west of the Square, along MacDougal
Street to the south and along West Third and Fourth Streets as far west as
Sixth Avenue and Sheridan Square. The Flower Pot, run by Dolly Judge,
was described as a "gay and impromptu place where excitement reigned
from nine in the evening until the wee hours of the morning." Located at
the corner of Christopher and Gay Streets, it was not far from the Pirate's
Den, a straight tourist trap, and just around the corner from Trilby's,
another gay rendezvous. Charles Street was the home of the Red Mask, a
club run by the well-known gay impresario Jackie Mason, and a third
"ultra-ultra speak," which, one account noted, "isn't Ireland even if the
fairies may be seen there."[34]

The arrangements made for the Fourth of July party held in 1922 at the Jungle, a "hangout for fairies" at Cornelia Street and Sixth Avenue, indicate how secure gay men and lesbians felt in the area. The club advertised its party by distributing a handbill promising souvenirs, refreshments, a jazz band, and entertainment by "Rosebud" and the "Countess." Rosebud and the Countess were men—not female impersonators, but gay men, or "degenerates," as an investigator who had attended the event after seeing the notice described them—apparently with a local reputation big enough to draw a crowd. Their audience consisted primarily of unattached men and women, the investigator reported, most of them apparently "fairies," many of them seemingly wealthy, "lady lovers of [the] Greenwich Village type," and, apparently, a few interested heterosexuals. The club had obviously made arrangements to ensure police protection—and protection from the police. The investigator noted that "a uniformed patrolman who is stationed in here was sitting with some of these fairies at one table and conversing with them and also entertained by them. . . . It appeared that he took a great interest [in] this performance [by Rosebud and the Countess] and clapped his hands after [the] performance was over."[35]

Such arrangements could stave off the police for only so long, however. After receiving numerous complaints from real estate interests trying to "upgrade" the Village and from parents who had discovered their sons were frequenting the places surreptitiously, the police launched a series of crackdowns in 1924 and 1925. In the spring of 1925 they succeeded in having two of the proprietors convicted of keeping disorderly houses; one was sent to the penitentiary. By one account, they had closed all but three of the clubs by May. But several more soon opened.[36]

Many of the gay and lesbian clubs were modeled on the "personality clubs" that had played an important role in building the original Village community. The original clubs were run by gregarious men and women whose personalities set the tone for their establishments and attracted a following. Their restaurants and tearooms served as the salons of the Village intelligentsia. The proprietors made sure that new patrons were welcomed and introduced to regulars, they sponsored poetry readings, musicales, and discussion groups, and, above all else, they offered a congenial environment in which regulars could maintain ties with their friends and meet other like-minded people. The best known of such locales in the 1910s was Polly's Restaurant on MacDougal Street. Run by Paula Holladay with the assistance of her husband, the restaurant served as the unofficial dining club of the Liberal Club, which met in the rooms above it.[37]

When several gay men and lesbians such as Dolly Judge followed Holladay's lead by opening similar places in the 1920s, they quickly became leading centers of gay social life. Gay residents of the Village formed the core of their patronage, but these restaurants also provided a home-away-from-home for gay visitors from other parts of town, a place where people who had no private space of their own in the neighborhood could gather nightly and construct a social world for themselves. This function was especially important for poorer men and women; Caroline Ware noted that many would-be Villagers forced by high rents to live with their relatives or crowded with other youths in the outer boroughs had succeeded in making the Village their social center by spending their evenings in its restaurants and cafeterias, and their number surely included gay men and women. Although gay people were not the only patrons of the gay-run restaurants, they predominated and set the tone. By the late twenties, as Ware discovered, most of the personality clubs had closed, making it more difficult for newcomers to meet others and become a part of the Village community. But lesbian and gay clubs represented a notable exception to this trend; homosexuals, especially lesbians, found it easier than most other newcomers to find an entrée into the Village community.[38]

One of the best-known gay personality clubs in the Village in the 1920s was Paul and Joe's. It had opened as an Italian restaurant at the corner of Sixth Avenue and Ninth Street in 1912, and during the war years, when the Village was thronged with soldiers on leave, it was considered a "tough place," reputed to attract prostitutes who robbed their customers. Although some gay men and lesbians may have patronized it then, it did not have a gay reputation and seems to have begun cultivating a gay following only after the war, when it began hosting impromptu drag performances. The club gave several female impersonators their start, including Jackie Law, who opened his own place, the Studio Club on Fifteenth Street near Fifth Avenue, in the late twenties, and Gene Malin, whose nightclub act played a prominent role in the pansy craze of the early thirties (see chapter 11). By the early twenties, the restaurant had established itself as a major gay locale in the Village.

In an effort to escape the police crackdown in the Village in 1924, Paul and Joe moved their restaurant up Sixth Avenue to a building on the corner of Nineteenth Street, thus removing it from the Village proper. There they controlled the rooms upstairs, which patrons could rent for the evening for private parties. With the move, Paul and Joe consolidated their position, quickly becoming, by one account, the "headquarters for every well-known Lesbian and Queen in town," who felt no need to hide their homosexuality there and who were joined by numerous stage and screen celebrities, opera divas, and underworld figures. The restaurant also became identified publicly as a gay rendezvous. One gossip sheet mentioned its homosexual patrons several times in 1924, and in 1925 the writer and Village booster Bobby Edwards described it as the "hangout of dainty elves and stern women" in the pages of his magazine, the *Greenwich Village Quill*. It closed around 1927, possibly due to the efforts of the Committee of Fourteen.[39]

After the 1925 crackdown, the block of MacDougal Street south of Washington Square—the site of the Provincetown Playhouse and numerous bohemian restaurants, gift shops, and speakeasies—became the busiest, and certainly the best known, locus of gay and lesbian commercial establishments. Lesbians managed several of the speakeasies there in the twenties. The most famous of the lesbian proprietors was Eva Kotchever, a Polish Jewish émigré who went by the name Eve Addams (also spelled Adams), an androgynous pseudonym whose biblical origins her Protestant persecutors might well have found blasphemous. Called the "queen of the third sex" by one paper and a "man-hater" by another, after the police crackdown of 1925 she opened a tearoom at 129 MacDougal Street that quickly became popular with the after-theater crowd. A sign at the door announced "Men are admitted but not welcome."[40]

Addams's place soon aroused the ire of some of the neighborhood's bohemians, including Bobby Edwards, who ran a regular commentary on Village events and personalities in his *Greenwich Village Quill*. Although Eve's place stood directly across the street from his office, he failed to mention it or its weekly poetry readings, musicales, and discussions until the summer of 1926. In the June issue that year he listed the club in his Village guide. "Eve's Hangout," it announced, "Where ladies prefer each other. Not very healthy for she-adolescents, nor comfortable for he-men." Despite the ad, Edwards participated in a poetry reading at Eve's on June 15, which drew a number of other locally prominent poets, and he provided an unusually long account of it in his July issue, which noted that "the place [was] jammed." Two nights after the poetry reading, however, the police raided the club. Addams, charged with writing an "obscene" book, *Lesbian Love* (reportedly a collection of short stories about "the lesbian element"), as well as with disorderly conduct, was sentenced to a year in the workhouse and was deported the following December. (Upon her arrival in Paris, she was said to have opened a lesbian club in Montmartre.)

Edwards published no comment on the raid, noting in his September 1926 issue only that "Eve's place is gone," and that she had been replaced by a new, more commendable proprietor. Five years later, however, the raid on Eve Addams's place was still recalled bitterly by many Villagers, and at least one commentator contended that the police had been led to act by a campaign orchestrated by Edwards against the visibility of lesbians in the Village. Edwards seems to have been sensitive to such charges, for in the *Quill* published around the time of the raid he contended that while he had often "longed to cast out [from the Village] all radicals, Freudians, androgynes, narcissi, etc., . . . I was no Mussolini or Savonarola." But he concluded hopefully that "now it looks like we're going to have a real Village again," and in the following issue he reiterated his disdain for lesbians by commenting in an essay on the Village that "boys must be boys. But girls mustn't."

Addams was remembered fondly by many Villagers. In 1929, three years after her deportation, a Village theatrical group surreptitiously presented a play based on her *Lesbian Love* stories at the Play Mart, a cellar theater on Christopher Street. *Variety* reported that the two-week run drew "mainly an audience of queers," who asserted that recent lesbian- and gay-themed plays on Broadway, including *The Captive* and *Pleasure Man* (see chapter 11), seemed like "kindergarten stuff in comparison." The performers, who billed themselves as the Scientific Players and called the play *Modernity*, had planned a four-week run. But they abruptly closed the show after being tipped off that the police planned to raid it.[41]

In the late twenties and early thirties, Addams's tearoom was succeeded by several other ventures on the blocks of MacDougal just south of Washington Square. The Black Rabbit on MacDougal at the corner of Minetta, "one of the Village's gay stamping grounds," was as well known for its lesbians in overalls as for its rum concoctions before the police closed it around 1929. Louis' Luncheon, at 116 MacDougal, which attracted a varied crowd of writers and Ziegfeld Follies chorus girls, had a reputation as a lesbian and gay hangout in the early 1930s.[42] The Bungalow, a speakeasy run by a former prizefighter who called himself Battling Thompson, attracted some of the Black Rabbit's old customers—nothing but "lisping boys and deep-voiced girls," according to one scornful account in 1931. Next door stood Julian's, a cheap and popular "whole-in-the-wall [sic] lunch counter" run by "a mannishly attired lady." Julian, one of the major gay entrepreneurs of the period, subsequently opened the Left Bank, a restaurant on Wooster Street just south of the Square, whose announcement card sported a drawing of a sexually ambiguous couple (most likely two women, one femininely and the other mannishly attired) and the promise of entertainment by Eric, formerly the pianist at Tillie's, a Harlem restaurant patronized by homosexuals. Julian and a partner also organized a dinner dance and rumba revue on Sunday evenings at the Fullhouse Restaurant on West Fourth Street at Cornelia, near the old site of the Jungle.[43]

The unprecedented success of lesbians and gay men in claiming space in the Village was signaled by several developments in the Village press in the late twenties and early thirties. The underemployed writers and artists of the Village produced a number of small and usually short-lived neighborhood journals, particularly in the early years of the Depression. Most of them devoted attention to the gay scene. Some of them, like Bobby Edwards's *Quill*, were hostile. In its inaugural issue in 1929, *Greenwich Village: A Local Review*, one of the more conservative and overtly boosterish of the papers, ran a long diatribe against the bohemian women of the Village stigmatizing their behavior as lesbian-like.[44]

But other papers adopted a more benign perspective, and by the early thirties several columnists were presenting an unprecedentedly positive view of the gay presence in the Village. The *Greenwich Villager*, published weekly in 1933–34, included a reference to the "short-haired women and long-haired men [who] filled the streets" in its description of the changes brought about in the Village by the war, and casually included gay references in its gossip column and articles.[45] Billy Scully, a columnist for the *Greenwich Village Weekly News*, went further, supporting gay clubs and including complimentary references to prominent lesbian and gay personalities in his gossip column, "Village on Parade." His background is obscure, but he displayed an insider's knowledge of the history of the Village's gay community. In a 1931 column he praised the "brilliance" of the customers at Billie Champion's "lesbian hang-out" of the early 1920s, and he described Eve Addams's club, closed five years earlier by the police, as "one of the most delightful hang-outs the Village ever had."[46] He openly defended a lesbian musician (who remained unnamed, but presumably would have been known to those who followed the Village club scene or the newspapers' reviews) by attacking a "Broadway columnist" who criticized the musician's playing "because she prefers the attention of a certain girl to the unwanted affection showered on her by the writer and his brother."[47]

Scully and other pro-gay columnists assumed their readers were sophisticated in their knowledge of gay matters. Four years after Eva Kotchever was deported (and five years after her MacDougal Street tearoom was padlocked), a second columnist for the *Greenwich Village Weekly News* alluded to her famous pseudonym by noting that the gay novel Parker Tyler was "working like mad on" was "to be called something like 'Eve's Adam.'"[48] (It was finally called *The Young and Evil*, and, given its gay content and surrealist style, had to be published in Paris.) The papers these columnists wrote for were as short-lived as the others of their genre, but the fact that some of them were prepared to publish pro-gay comments by pro-gay writers, many of which seemed designed for a sophisticated gay audience with a sense of its history, indi-

cates the extent to which lesbians and gay men had established themselves in the Village.

The opposition that Addams's tearoom and the other gay-run clubs
that succeeded it on MacDougal Street encountered should not obscure
the more important fact that the very existence of such clubs in a middle-
class milieu was unprecedented. Before the development of the bohemian
community in the Village, middle-class gay life had always been conducted covertly, and commercial establishments publicly identified as gay
had been restricted to working-class entertainment districts such as the
Bowery. In the 1890s, when the notorious "degenerate resort" the Slide
stood on Bleecker Street, just two blocks south of Washington Square
and two blocks east of MacDougal, the neighborhood was occupied
largely by poor African-Americans and Italians. That gay life was more
open in working-class than middle-class society should not be surprising,
given the findings of other recent historical studies. Although historians
long assumed that change in attitudes concerning sexuality had begun in
the middle class in the 1910s and 1920s, and only later percolated down
to the more "rigid" working class, recent work has suggested that much
of the new "freedom in manners and morals" among middle-class
youths in the twenties was modeled on that of working-class youths,
who were generally more direct about sexual matters than bourgeois reticence allowed.[49]

But the growing toleration of homosexuality within the bohemian elements of middle-class society did not simply replicate older working-class
attitudes. Homosexually active men in the working class had hardly been
"free," as we have seen; rather, their behavior had simply been circumscribed by a different pattern of social regulation, which shaped them as
firmly as bourgeois propriety shaped their middle-class brethren. The gay
clubs of the bohemian Village seem to have tolerated a wider range of gender behavior on the part of gay men than the Slide; to use the terminology
of the era, they were open resorts for "queers" (who did not clearly demar-
cate their difference from "normal men" by their inversion of gender
norms) as well as for "fairies" (who did). Their clientele was "mixed," in
that, like the Slide, they attracted queer and straight men alike, but also
because, unlike the Slide, they attracted non-prostitute women as well as
men and were often *run* by women.

Moreover, the straight and queer men who interacted in the
MacDougal Street clubs, unlike those at the Slide, did not, as a rule, do
so as potential sexual partners. Some bohemian men might be willing to
experiment, but most of them, unlike the "normal" men at the Slide,
had begun to think of themselves as heterosexuals properly interested
only in the women they socialized with at the clubs. Queer and straight
men thus thought of themselves as sexually incompatible as well as sex-

ually different. They also often thought of themselves in other terms altogether, as bohemians united by their rejection of bourgeois convention. By the 1930s there were still relatively few commercial institutions where queers or fairies could openly socialize (with or without the presence of heterosexuals). The appearance of clubs in the Village patronized openly by queers and straights alike thus represented an unprecedented expansion in the possibilities for gay sociability and marked a decisive change from earlier patterns in both working-class and middle-class society.

The gay history of Greenwich Village suggests the extent to which the Village in the teens and twenties came to represent to the rest of the city what New York as a whole represented to the rest of the nation: a peculiar social territory in which the normal social constraints on behavior seemed to have been suspended and where men and women built unconventional lives outside the family nexus. Attracted by the Village's bohemian reputation, gay men and lesbians soon played a distinctive role in shaping both the image and reality of the Village, for they became part of the spectacle that defined the neighborhood's colorful character, even as they used the cultural space made available by that character to turn it into a haven. Although their numbers remained small and their fellow Villagers did not always live up to their reputation for open-mindedness, gay people in the 1920s seized the opportunity provided by Village culture to begin building the city's most famous gay enclave.

"IN THE LIFE" IN HARLEM

Although Greenwich Village's gay enclave was the most famous in the city, even most white gay men thought gay life was livelier and more open in Harlem than in the Village—"Oh, much more! Much more!" the artist Edouard Roditi declared.[50] "Harlem was wide open," a white female impersonator recalled. The clubs would "be open all night long. Some of them didn't *open* until midnight."[51] It was easier for white interlopers to be openly gay during their brief visits to Harlem than for the black men who lived there round the clock. But black gay men nonetheless turned Harlem into a homosexual mecca. Denied access to most of the segregated restaurants and speakeasies white gay men patronized elsewhere in New York, they built an extensive gay world in their own community, which in many respects surpassed the Village's in scope, visibility, and boldness. The Village's most flamboyant homosexuals wore long hair; Harlem's wore long dresses. The Village had cafés where poets read their verse and drag queens performed; Harlem had speakeasies where men danced together and drag queens were regular customers. The Village's Liberal Club ball was attended by scores of drag queens and hundreds of spectators; Harlem's Hamilton Lodge ball drew *hundreds* of drag queens and *thousands* of spectators. Among outsiders, Greenwich Village's reputation as a gay mecca eclipsed Harlem's only because it was a white, middle-class world—and because Harlem's singular reputation as a black metropolis took precedence over everything else.

Harlem had become Manhattan's major black neighborhood in the 1900s and 1910s. Most of the community's rowhouses had been built by speculative builders in the last years of the nineteenth century. A collapse in the area's real estate market around 1904—and the aggressive tactics of a handful of realtors—made those houses available to blacks just as they were being forced out of their old neighborhood in the West Thirties by the construction of Pennsylvania Station. By the mid-teens, more than 80 percent of Manhattan's African-Americans lived there, and by the early 1920s, Harlem was home to most of the city's major black churches and social organizations.[52]

Harlem consolidated its status as New York's leading black neighborhood just as World War I led tens of thousands of Southern blacks to migrate to New York and other Northern cities. The Great Migration, as historians have called it, was precipitated by the sudden availability of thousands of well-paying jobs in Northern industry due to the military mobilization of white workers and the cutoff of European immigration. Many blacks also viewed moving North as an act of political self-determination, tied to the elevation of the race as well as to individual improvement. To many southern migrants, the North seemed a land of freedom, where they could escape the grinding poverty, political powerlessness, and daily indignities to which they seemed forever condemned in the Jim Crow South. African-American newspapers, published in Northern cities and smuggled by Pullman car porters to blacks in Southern towns where the papers were banned by white officials, trumpeted the good wages and free life to be found outside the secessionist states. Some barbershop proprietors, small shopkeepers, churchwomen, and other local leaders organized the move North of whole communities, which re-created themselves on the blocks of Harlem and Chicago's South Side. The ferment of the Great Migration, the heated debate among blacks about whether they should support a racist government's war to "preserve democracy," and the bitter disappointment that resulted when scores of anti-black race riots broke out in the year following the war produced an unprecedented level of militancy in the immense new black neighborhoods spread across the North.[53]

The largest and most significant of these neighborhoods was Harlem. In the 1920s, Harlem became to black America what Greenwich Village became to bohemian white America: the symbolic—and in many respects, practical—center of a vast cultural experiment. A huge black metropolis unlike anything America had seen before, it was home to soaring black cathedrals, thriving businesses, a wide array of social clubs, and Marcus Garvey's militant black nationalist movement, to dozens of elegant nightclubs and hundreds of basement jazz clubs and speakeasies, and to the poets, artists, and novelists whose work produced the Harlem Renaissance. Above all, it was home to what African-Americans themselves called the New Negro, self-assured and determined to control his or her own destiny. Seventh Avenue from 110th to 148th Streets was "the crossroad of the Negro world," one Harlemite wrote in the 1930s, "where Black people from Africa, our own southern states, the West Indies, South America, parts of Asia and many of the half forgotten Islands of the East Indies meet."[54]

Harlem's elegant and lively nightlife also made it the Paris of New York, one of the city's most popular entertainment districts.[55] "Harlem was really jumpin'" in the 1920s, the singer Bricktop recalled. It "was the 'in' place to go for music and booze, and it seemed like every other building on or near Seventh Avenue from 130th Street to 140th was a club or a speakeasy. . . . Every night the limousines pulled up . . . and the rich whites would get out, all dolled up in their furs and jewels."[56] Pointing to its "sizzling cafes, 'speaks,' night clubs and spiritual seances," *Variety* declared in 1929 that Harlem's "night life now surpasses that of Broadway itself."[57]

The liquor and the sensational floor shows available at Harlem's clubs attracted white visitors. But so, too, did their growing curiosity about the vibrant African-American society taking shape in Harlem. The production of several musicals featuring black performers, especially *Shuffle Along*, which opened on Broadway in 1921, helped further the new interest in black culture. The publication in 1926 of *Nigger Heaven* by Carl Van Vechten provoked a storm of outrage among black intellectuals, who criticized its depiction of Harlem life as well as its title, but its very caricature of black lasciviousness only whetted white New Yorkers' interest in the neighborhood and reinforced their sexualized—and condescending—attitude toward the neighborhood's people.

Some whites went "slumming" to cabarets and small after-hours clubs in Harlem where blacks predominated. But most slummers felt safer visiting the enormous white-owned clubs that excluded blacks from the audience. There they could experience a highly contrived version of black culture by listening to jazz bands and watching elaborate (but "primitive" and sometimes salacious) floor shows. "One of the New York evening pastimes," a typical New York guidebook noted in 1925, "is to observe the antics of members of its enormous negro population, many of whom show great ability in song, dance and comedy performance. . . . Their unfailing sense of rhythm, their vocal quality, something primitive, animal-like and graceful in their movements," the guide explained in a stunning summary of the era's racist construction of blacks as primitive other, "combine to make their performances interesting to all who can put racial prejudice out of their minds." As the guide pointed out, "Most of these shows . . . try to establish a Southern illusion"; the Cotton Club, the Everglades, and other clubs adopted Southern names and motifs to evoke the history of black subordination and to emphasize the subordination of the African-American performers. The clubs thus played on their customers' desire to feel they were transgressing the conventional boundaries of race while resolutely confirming them.[58]

The ascendancy of Harlem's nightlife—particularly its speakeasies and brothels—also owed much to the willingness of city authorities to look the other way as a largely white-controlled "vice industry" took shape in a poor black neighborhood. Even the Committee of Fourteen devoted less effort to the moral regulation of Harlem than of white neighborhoods.[59] Although it advocated the eradication rather than the segregation of vice, it effectively colluded in the concentration of "vice" in Harlem by virtually ignoring the neighborhood. Only in 1928, at the height of the white invasion of Harlem, did the Committee temporarily hire an African-American investigator to study prostitution there. But after publishing a report indicting the district as a den of immorality, it turned its attention back to neighborhoods it cared about more.[60]

As the historian Eric Garber has shown, an extensive gay and lesbian social world developed in this complex cultural context.[61] Among the thousands of young men and women who flocked to the land of freedom were people who hoped Harlem would liberate them from the conformity imposed in small Southern communities. Although some evidence suggests that gay men were more accepted in rural black communities than in comparable white communities, moving to the city made it possible for them to participate in a gay world organized on a scale unimaginable in a Southern town. In 1930 three times as many African-American men aged thirty-five to forty-four were unmarried in Harlem as in South Carolina, one of the major sources of Harlem's migrants, and almost twice as many as in the nation as a whole.[62]

Harlem's gay world was perhaps the most complex in the city because segregation forced such a wide range of people to live side by side: successful professionals and wealthy businesspeople occupied the immaculate townhouses and apartment buildings of Sugar Hill and the elegant Italianate brownstones of Stiver's Row (138th and 139th Streets), while the poorest of new migrants crowded into tenements and subdivided rowhouses nearby. Gay life suffused the district, but the class and stylistic conflicts that divided the white gay world elsewhere in the city took on special force in Harlem, simply because so many people from such varied backgrounds were gathered together. Black gay life was also complicated by the number of white gay men visiting Harlem, who enjoyed a kind of freedom unavailable to their black hosts. Like the straight white slummers who made Harlem's jazz clubs and speakeasies their playground, gay white men visiting Harlem were leaving behind the communities and families who enforced the social imperatives that normally constrained their behavior. But unlike the white visitors, black gay men and lesbians had to negotiate their presence in the shops and churches of Harlem as well as its clubs.

Sissy Men in Working-Class Harlem

Although Harlem was best known to outsiders for its glamorous clubs, most Harlemites socialized at corner cabaret saloons, basement speakeasies, and tenement parties thrown to raise money for the rent.[63] There Harlem's poorest residents danced, drank, saw their friends, and claimed stature and respect in a cultural zone governed by their own social codes rather than those of white employers or the black bourgeoisie. Many of those locales attracted prostitutes, gamblers, and other "disreputable" folk who participated in what they called the "sporting life" or simply "the life." Lesbians and gay men were "in the life" as well, and they mixed easily with the other guests at many such gatherings.

At speakeasies where men and women engaged in sexually charged behavior, lesbians, gay men, and sometimes the latter's "normal" male friends were likely to do the same in the full view of the other patrons. Late one night in May 1928 the black investigator hired by the Committee of Fourteen was taken to a speakeasy in the basement of a building on West 136th Street, where he witnessed lesbians and gay men socializing with a larger number of straight people. In the front room men and women sat around drinking, talking, and laughing, but in a back room a larger group of people were dancing:

> Another woman was dancing indecently with a man. . . . Several of the men were dancing among themselves. Two of the women were dancing with one another going through the motions of copulation. One of the men [invited him to dance]. I declined to dance. I also observed two men who were dancing with one another kiss each other, and one sucked the other's tongue.[64]

Gay men were a fixture at many quieter places as well, recognized and accepted by other patrons. When the investigator visited the Blue Ribbon Chile Parlor in the basement of 72 West 131st Street, at two in the morning, he found a handful of men and women drinking. The women were prostitutes trying to make connections, and one of the patrons casually pointed out two of the men as "noted faggots."[65]

Some men carried themselves openly as fairies in the streets of other working-class neighborhoods, but perhaps nowhere were more men willing to venture out in public in drag than in Harlem. Drag queens appeared regularly in Harlem's streets and clubs. When Cyril Lightbody opened a café on Seventh Avenue in December 1930, its informal atmosphere immediately attracted "the artistic group, freethinkers, communists and thrill-seeking youths from downtown," according to Baltimore's *Afro-American*. "Sunday afternoon was its opening and we saw erotics, neuretics [sic], perverts, inverts and other types of abnormalities, cavorting with wild and Wilde abandon to the patent gratification of the manager and owner. . . . About two A.M., five horticultural gents came in 'in drag' as the custom of appearing in feminine finery is known."[66]

The casual acceptance of the drag queens at Cyril's Café and the frequency of their appearance in Harlem's streets suggest a high degree of tolerance for them in the neighborhood as a whole. Still, it took considerable courage for men to appear in drag, since they risked harassment by other youths and arrest by the Irish policemen who patrolled their neighborhood. Over the course of two weeks in February 1928 the police arrested thirty men for wearing drag at a single club, Lulu Belle at 341 Lenox Avenue near 127th Street. Five men dressed in "silk stockings, sleeveless evening gowns of soft-tinted crepe de chine and light fur wraps" were arrested on a single night.[67]

Some drag queens refused to cower before the police and defied them all the way to the courthouse. Two "eagle-eyed" detectives patrolling Seventh Avenue early one Sunday morning in 1928 enjoyed watching the amusing antics of four young women who "seemed well lit up and out for a glorious morning promenade" until they realized the "girls" were "pansies on parade." They quickly arrested the quartet and marched them to the 123rd Street police station; the next morning the men were sentenced to sixty days in the workhouse. Still defiant, the drag queens, aged eighteen to twenty-one, mocked the officers by shouting "Goodbye dearie, thanks for the trip as we'll have the time of our lives" as they were led out of the courtroom.[68]

Not all drag queens were so defiant. After a policeman casually looked at a twenty-one-year-old "woman" as they passed each other on 117th Street late one night in 1928, the "woman," fearful that the policeman had realized he was a female impersonator, began to run. Keen to learn what the "woman" had to hide, the patrolman chased her down the street, up some stairs, and across the rooftops until cornering her. Although later commenting that "'she' could run faster than any 'woman' he had ever chased," the policeman realized he had arrested a drag queen only when they got to the station. The queen had good reason to fear arrest. He had already been arrested twice, once for degenerate disorderly conduct and once for masquerading as a woman, and had served three months in the workhouse on the latter charge.[69] When in 1932 the police raided a Seventh Avenue apartment, perhaps a buffet flat, and arrested the twenty-seven men they found gambling and drinking there, one of them, a forty-two-year-old in women's clothes, leapt from the second-floor window, fracturing his skull and spine.[70]

Although "faggots" were casually integrated into many lower-class social settings, they also became part of the spectacle at some of the local resorts. They played a particularly prominent role in some of the neighborhood's buffet flats. As Eric Garber has explained, the flats were private apartments whose tenants made their rooms available to paying guests. They had originally developed to meet the needs of black travelers denied space at white hotels, but developed a wilder reputation in the 1920s, functioning as virtual speakeasies, where drinking, gambling, and other illegal activities could take place. The most notorious offered their customers live sex shows as well as prostitutes. The gay sex shows became part of the entertainment for Harlem's "lower" elements, much as the fairies and sex shows of the Bowery had been to an earlier generation of immigrants. It was "an open house, everything goes on in that house," recalled Ruby Smith of a Detroit-based flat she had visited with her aunt Bessie Smith.

> They had a faggot there that was so great that people used to come there just to watch him make love to another man. He was that great. He'd give a tongue bath and everything. By the time he got to the front of that guy he was shaking like a leaf. People used to pay good just to go in there and see him do his act.

A buffet flat featuring an immense female impersonator on 140th Street in Harlem was known as "The Daisy Chain" or the "101 Ranch."[71]

The place of gay men in the culture of black working-class migrants was captured by the blues, the primary expressive musical form of poorer blacks. The blues reflected the everyday experiences, disappointments, conflicts, and resolve of these migrant men and women in a racist society. Most blues singers were migrants themselves, who had joined touring vaudeville troupes to escape the South or had taken jobs in cellar speakeasies as an alternative to domestic service, and who identified more with the prostitutes and poor people who patronized their clubs than with respectable Harlemites. Many of them were lesbian or bisexual: Ma Rainey, Bessie Smith, Ethel Waters, Alberta Hunter, and, above all, Gladys Bentley, who performed in a tuxedo and top hat and married her white lesbian lover in a much discussed ceremony.[72] Some of their songs offered pungent critiques of the injustices migrants faced, while others evoked the personalities and everyday events of the "lowlife" milieu. Along with their songs about lonely separations from loved ones gone North and the need to put up with violent husbands and petty employers, they sang about "sissies" and "bulldaggers"—and about men who turned to sissies in place of their wives. Ma Rainey complained about her husband leaving her for a sissy man named "Miss Kate." Several male blues singers recorded "Sissy Man Blues," in which they demanded "If you can't bring me a woman, bring me a sissy man." The songs typically represented the sissy man as a fairy—a "lisping, swishing, womanish-acting man," in one of Bessie Smith's songs, which also referred to "a mannish-acting woman."[73] They did not celebrate such people, but they recognized them as a part of black working-class culture and acknowledged their potential sexual desirability to "normal" men.

A select group of "noted faggots" became famous in Harlem. Most famous of all, perhaps, was "Gloria Swanson" (nee Winston), a female impersonator who had already won a clutch of prizes at Chicago's drag balls and had run his own club there before moving to New York around 1930. He quickly found employment in New York as hostess at a popular cellar club on West 134th Street. "Here he reigned regally," one gay Harlemite noted, "entertaining with his 'hail-fellow-well-met' freedom, so perfect a woman that frequently clients came and left never suspecting his true sex." He sang "bawdy parodies," danced a bit, and appeared constantly in "net and sequins, velvet-trimmed evening-gown-skirts displaying with professional coyness a length of silk-clad limb." The press took note of his appearances at the neighborhood drag balls and clubs. "Gangsters and hoodlums, pimps and gamblers, whores and entertainers showered him with feminine gee-gaws and trappings; spoke of him as 'her,' and quite relegated him to the female's functions of supplying good times and entertainment."[74]

Swanson had moved to New York at an opportune moment. The late 1920s and early 1930s were the heyday of lesbian and gay clubs and performers in Harlem, as in much of the city (see chapter 11). As Bruce Nugent, a gay African-American writer explained, it was a time when

"male" and "female" impersonation was at its peak as night club entertainment. . . . The Ubangi Club had a chorus of singing, dancing, be-rib-
boned and be-rouged "pansies," and Gladys Bentley who dressed in
male evening attire, sang and accompanied herself on the piano; the
well-liked Jackie Mab[ley] was one of Harlem's favorite black-faced
comediennes and wore men's street attire habitually; the famous
Hamilton Lodge "drag" balls were becoming more and more notorious
and gender was becoming more and more conjectural.[75]

Many of the gay-oriented clubs were located in the area between Fifth
and Seventh Avenues, from 130th to 138th Street, where most of Harlem's best-known clubs were clustered. The Cotton Club, Connie's Inn,
Barron's, the Lenox, and other clubs that attracted a large (and sometimes exclusively) white trade were in this district, along with the Savoy
Ballroom, Small's Paradise, and other clubs welcoming a largely black or
interracial audience. Many of the district's most notorious speakeasies
and clubs lined a strip on 133rd Street between Lenox and Seventh
Avenues known as "The Jungle." Gay entertainers with large gay follow-
ings were featured at several of the district's clubs, including the Hot Cha
at 132nd Street and Seventh Avenue, where the well-known entertainer
and host Jimmie Daniels sang sophisticated tunes. A handful of clubs
catered to lesbians and gay men, including the Hobby Horse, Tillie's
Kitchen, and the Dishpan, and other well-known clubs, including Small's
Paradise, welcomed their presence.[76]
Although many gay entertainers included songs with sophisticated
double-entendre in their repertoire, few were open to outsiders about
their homosexuality. In the late 1920s and early 1930s, though, several
gay hosts and entertainers moved out of basement saloons and into
some of the district's better nightclubs. Gloria Swanson was perhaps the
most prominent gay club host; Gladys Bentley was the most visible lesbian. "Huge, voluptuous [and] chocolate colored," according to one fan,
Bentley was as famous for her tuxedo, top hat, and girlfriends as for her
singing. Although she sang the blues, she was best known for ad-libbing
popular ballads, show tunes, and the like, to give them a salacious
edge—and for encouraging her audience to join in singing the now
"filthy lyrics." As Eric Garber reports, she turned two Broadway tunes,
"Sweet Georgia Brown" and "Alice Blue Gown," into an "ode to the
joys of anal intercourse":

And he said, "Dearie, please turn around"
And he shoved that big thing up my brown.
He tore it. I bored it. Lord, how I adored it.
My sweet little Alice Blue Gown.

After a series of one-night stands at rent parties, buffet flats, and cellar clubs, Bentley landed steady jobs at two clubs in "Jungle Alley" on 133rd Street, including Hansberry's Clam House, which attracted an interracial audience of literati and entertainers, including many gay men and lesbians. She made her lesbianism and "bulldagger" looks part of her show-business persona at each of these clubs. When she finally moved on to the Ubangi Club, she toned down her lyrics to the merely risqué, wore "flashy men's attire," and headed a revue that included a pansy chorus line composed entirely of female impersonators.[77]

The visibility of bulldaggers and faggots in the streets and clubs of Harlem during the late 1920s and early 1930s does not mean they enjoyed unqualified toleration throughout Harlem society. Although they were casually accepted by many poor Harlemites and managed to earn a degree of grudging respect from others, they were excoriated by the district's moral guardians. Many middle-class and churchgoing African-Americans grouped them with prostitutes, salacious entertainers, and "uncultured" rural migrants as part of an undesirable and all-too-visible black "lowlife" that brought disrepute to the neighborhood and "the race." Like other black Northern communities—and like white New York—Harlem was rent by deep class and cultural divisions. An old elite of merchants, entrepreneurs, and professionals and an emerging middle class of teachers, artisans, and salaried employees struggled to steer the destiny of their neighborhoods and to exert control over the huge numbers of poor southern migrants flooding in. As the cultural historian Hazel Carby has shown, they organized homes to protect—and police—young single migrant women, called on the police to close brothels and buffet flats, and denounced dance halls and cabarets as a threat to the advance of the race and to their position as a respectable class of blacks.[78]

Sexuality became one of the critical measures by which the black middle class differentiated itself from the working class and constituted itself as a class. As Carby shows, the figure of the sexually irresponsible woman became one of the defining tropes of middle-class African-American discourse, a symbol of the dangerous social disintegration that urbanization could bring. Many white middle-class New Yorkers regarded the single woman in similar terms, but black middle-class women found it particularly crucial to attack—and distinguish themselves from—images of black female sensuality because racist ideology used those images so effectively to stigmatize all black women as morally debased.[79] Similarly, the "womanish-acting man" became a special threat to middle-class black men because their masculinity was under constant challenge by the dominant white ideology. As in white middle-class discourse, the attacks on homosexuals were usually but a part of a wider attack on men and women who threatened the social order by standing outside the family system.

Harlem's leading churchmen periodically railed against the homosexual "vice" growing in the neighborhood. Churches were major political forces and centers of social life in Harlem, their ministers' statements commanding close attention from the press and political leaders. The visibility of gay people and the tolerance afforded them in Harlem— even in some of its churches—was a particular concern of Harlem's most powerful minister, Adam Clayton Powell, the pastor of the Abyssinian Baptist Church from 1908 to 1937 and perhaps the most famous African-American clergyman in the nation. A champion of civil rights and an early leader of the Urban League and National Association for the Advancement of Colored People, Powell was also a tireless campaigner against "immorality" in African-American society. As the influential leader of one of the city's most prestigious black congregations, he used his political ties to drive prostitutes and gambling dens from the streets around his church. By his own account, he developed a close relationship with the African-American press after an editor of Harlem's *New York Age* supplied him with information about buffet flats run by churchwomen in his own congregation and promised to publish any sermon he gave denouncing them. "I have not known a more helpful ally than the Negro press," Powell later claimed, and through the years it magnified the power of his anti-vice crusades by giving them extensive publicity.[80]

The press outdid itself, however, when Powell launched a sensational attack on homosexuality in the African-American community—and particularly in the rectory. "DR. A. C. POWELL SCORES PULPIT EVILS" a banner headline across the front page of the *New York Age* proclaimed on November 16, 1929. The pastor "delivered a scathing and bitter denunciation of perversion as practised by many moral degenerates who not only are men and women of prominence in the secular world, white and colored, but many of whom fill the pulpits of some of the leading churches of the country," the paper announced. Charging that sexual perversion was "steadily increasing" in large American cities, Powell claimed that perversion among women "has grown into one of the most horrible, debasing, alarming and damning vices of present day civilization, and is . . . prevalent to an unbelievable degree."[81]

A week later, Powell claimed his office had been inundated with information revealing that the problem was even more extensive than he had believed. He implicitly blamed much of the problem on young people's "contact and association" with homosexuals in the world of dance halls, cabarets, and rent parties when he warned that "the seeking for thrills of an unusual character by the modern youth" led many to experiment with homosexuality. Homosexuality, he seemed to say, was simply the last step down the road to ruin for morally weak youth. Moreover, personal degeneration had wider social consequences, for the spread of homosexuality threatened the Negro family, the bedrock of social stability, "causing men to leave their wives for other men, wives to leave their husbands for other women, and girls to mate with girls instead of marrying."[82] The homosexual, like the heterosexual single woman, was a sign of the social disorganization that accompanied urbanization. Powell's emphasis on the dangerous extent of lesbianism in the black community suggests that he saw women's refusal to marry as posing the most insidious threat to the black family.

Other ministers joined the assault in the following weeks, preaching sermons or writing letters to the papers in support of Powell's denunciation of homosexual vice. A white philanthropist who funded programs for the moral reformation of African-American life signaled his approval of the campaign, condescendingly calling it "one of the most cheerful signs we have respecting the great advance that has been made among this ten per cent of our population, who have had every conceivable drag put upon their efforts to be . . . Christians in spirit and in truth."[83]

Powell took special umbrage at the ministers who continued to preach despite being publicly accused of homosexual assaults on boys in their churches, and even more at the congregations that supported them despite full knowledge of such charges. He was particularly concerned, he later explained, about preachers "who had been publicly accused of abnormal sex practices" and about the churches that "with a full knowledge of [their] sins called [them] to its pulpit."[84] Although neither Powell nor the other ministers publicly named the offenders they had in mind, they described some of the cases in sufficient detail that knowledgeable parishioners would have been able to recognize the targets. Powell presumably hoped to hound such ministers from their posts, and it is likely that rumors about the identities of the offenders began to spread at the social hour following the service and washed through Harlem for weeks thereafter.

The results of such whisper campaigns are uncertain. Nonetheless, the intensity of Powell's denunciation suggests the lack of a consensus supporting his position within the black church. Although no one spoke up publicly to defend gay pastors from Powell's attack, some congregations appear to have been willing to accept gay pastors and choirmen so long as they observed a degree of discretion—and even, in some cases, when their homosexuality was well known or had resulted in legal trouble.

"The only reason a church keeps a rotten minister is because it is rotten," Powell charged. The very vehemence of his attack suggests how "rotten"—or tolerant—certain churches may have been.

Many African-American newspapers joined church leaders in attacking homosexuals, as Powell's press coverage shows. This was consistent with their general editorial policy, for many papers took on the role of policing their community as well as boosting it. In the wake of the Great Migration, black newspapers regularly exhorted Southern newcomers to assimilate into Northern society by leaving their "uneducated" rural ways behind. They lectured migrants on how to carry themselves properly on buses, what to wear, and how to behave in public, all for fear that disreputable behavior would bring disgrace to the whole community.[85] Some of them policed the lives of Harlem's working people by reporting on arrests—and policed the lives of middle-class men and women as well by publishing gossip columns. Gossip about purported homosexuality posed one of the gravest threats to a man's reputation; the press magnified that threat immensely by taking it into the public sphere. The *Amsterdam News* often published the names, addresses, ages, and occupations of men arrested for female impersonation or homosexual solicitation, thus multiplying the consequences of the arrest. The *Inter-State Tattler*, an East Coast black society and gossip sheet, lived up to its name by including news of gay relationships in its gossip columns. Along with engagement announcements, rumors of love triangles, and reports of divorces, the paper included accounts of gay romances and broken hearts such as this:

> Louis W—, who is so temperamental that he changes friends as often as Peggy Joyce changes husband, has secretly leased an apartment in 141st Street with Kenneth S—. They have a not too bad "joint" with soft lights, incense, and everything. And poor William is singing "How about me?" [Full names appeared in the original.]

The next item announced: "Theodore H—, you don't act like yourself nowadays. Do tell us who the lucky man is!"[86] It is possible that these men were already well known as gay in the community and enjoyed seeing their names in the paper. The light-hearted tone suggests this interpretation. But the paper had a negative reputation among gay men. "The *Tattler* went after people who were arrested," one black gay man recalled. "Anyone who was important, anyone who was gay."[87] Such items were not that common, but they were common enough to serve as a warning. In 1932 one of the paper's columnists launched a broadside against Harlem as a whole in the course of explaining why he had been unable to attend the previous weekend's social affairs. He had briefly "deserted Harlem where men are 'that way,' to spend a week in the wide open spaces where men ARE men."[88]

The Hamilton Lodge Ball

Nothing reveals the complexity—and ambivalence—of the attitudes of the black press and Harlem as a whole toward gay men and lesbians more than the Hamilton Lodge ball, the largest annual gathering of lesbians and gay men in Harlem—and the city. (A more thorough discussion of the internal organization and cultural significance of the city's drag balls appears in chapter 10.) The organizers of the ball, Hamilton Lodge No. 710 of the Grand United Order of Odd Fellows, officially called it the Masquerade and Civic Ball, but by the late 1920s everyone in Harlem knew it as the Faggots Ball. Precisely when it acquired that name is not certain. Some observers writing in the late 1930s, when its reputation was well established, thought the ball, held annually since 1869, had always been a female impersonators' event. Somewhat more reliable sources, however, suggest the gay element became prominent only in the 1920s, perhaps after a new group of organizers within the lodge took charge of the ball in 1923. Although some drag queens had almost certainly attended the ball before 1926, a newspaper report that year was the first to note the presence of a sizable number of "fairies"—about half of all those present. "Many people who attend dances generally declare that the . . . ball was the most unusual spectacle they ever witnessed," the paper noted with some understatement.[89] A decade later, one observer summarized the common wisdom when he explained matter-of-factly that the ball drew together "effeminate men, sissies, 'wolves,' 'ferries' [sic], 'faggots,' the third sex, 'ladies of the night,' and male prostitutes . . . for a grand jamboree of dancing, love making, display, rivalry, drinking and advertisement."[90]

Although whites attended the ball as both dancers and spectators, most of the guests were black. Lesbian "male impersonators" and straight masqueraders attended as well as gay men, but the latter constituted the vast majority of dancers and the focal point of attention. Although some upper-middle-class men showed up in drag, most of the drag queens—like the majority of "flaming faggots"—were young workingmen. The seventeen men arrested for homosexual solicitation at the 1938 ball included two laborers, two unemployed men, a dishwasher, a domestic servant, an elevator operator, a counterman, a handyman, an attendant, a clerk, and a nurse, along with a musician, an artist, and an entertainer. More than half were under thirty, and only one was over forty years old.[91]

The ball's popularity grew steadily in the late 1920s and peaked in the early 1930s, when a "pansy craze" (discussed in chapter 11) seized the city. About eight hundred guests attended the 1925 ball and fifteen hundred in 1926. But as the event became known as the Faggots Ball, growing numbers of spectators attended not to dance but just to gawk at "Harlem's yearly extravaganza—'The Dance of the Fairies.'" "Four thousand citizens, numbering some of Harlem's best, elbowed and shoved each other aside and squirmed and stepped on one another's toes and snapped at each other to obtain a better eyeful," the *Amsterdam News* reported in 1934.[92] Three thousand spectators gathered to watch two thousand "fairies" dance in 1929, and during the following three years, at the height of the ball's popularity, up to seven thousand dancers and spectators attended. Attendance hovered around four thousand for the rest of the decade, but leapt to eight thousand in 1937.[93]

Harlemites turning out to see the balls included celebrities, avant-garde writers, society matrons, prostitutes, and whole families who sometimes brought their suppers.[94] At the beginning of her career, the singer Ethel Waters not only attended the balls but boasted about the prizes won by drag queens (fans from a local club) to whom she had loaned her gowns. The singer Taylor Gordon "call[ed] up everyone I thought hadn't been to one" to urge them to attend a ball where he would serve as a judge. "That night the hall was packed with people from bootblacks to New York's rarest bluebloods," he recalled.[95] In February 1930 the young white writer Max Ewing attended the ball, where "all the men who danced . . . were dressed as women, wearing plumes and jewels and decorations of every kind." He observed several wealthy spectators, black as well as white, who had taken boxes to view the display, and watched the dancers do "special exhibition dances" in front of the boxes of the two most prominent black women present, the heiress A'Leila Walker and the singer Nora Holt.[96] Two years later an alderman served as a judge at the costume contest.[97]

Those who did not attend the Hamilton Lodge ball could read about it every year from the mid-1920s until the end of the 1930s in Harlem's largest paper, the *Amsterdam News*, and often in the *New York Age*, Baltimore's *Afro-American*, and the *Inter-State Tattler*. In the 1930s the black press paid more attention to the Hamilton Lodge ball than to any other ball held in Harlem, regularly publishing photographs or drawings of the winning contestants, interviewing them and describing their costumes, and listing the dozens of society people in attendance—almost all in the news section on the first or second page, not buried in the society pages where the balls thrown by other social clubs got briefer notices. Its coverage reflected the growing interest of straight Harlemites in these affairs in the late 1920s and 1930s—and the ambivalence with which they viewed them.

In the 1920s the papers were likely to deride the dancers as "subnormal, or, in the language of the street, 'fairies.'"[98] By the early 1930s, though, as the number of society people and ordinary Harlemites attending the ball approached seven thousand, most papers adopted the more positive (or at least bemused) attitude of those spectators. Some accounts delighted in parodying the camp tone of the dancers. "GRACIOUS ME! DEAR, 'TWAS TO-OO DIVINE," ran the 1936 *Amsterdam News* headline, in imitation of the dancers' arch chatter; the following year its headline reported familiarly: "PANSIES CAVORT IN MOST DELOVELY MANNER AT THAT ANNUAL HAMILTON LODGE 'BAWL.'" All the reporters expressed genuine admiration for—and astonishment at—the extravagance and creativity of the costumes. Even the sneering 1929 reference to subnormal fairies appeared under a headline citing the "GORGEOUS COSTUMES."

Even the relatively conservative *New York Age* changed its tune as the ball's popularity grew. "Clubs would do well to ask this body for the secret of their success," its 1932 account began.

To one of the largest gatherings that has ever graced this hall [Rockland Palace] came the all-conquering Hamilton Lodge, resplendent in all the panoply of pomp and splendor, to give to Harlemites who stood in wide-eyed astonishment at this lavish display a treat that shall never be forgotten. The usual grand march eclipsed in splendor all heretofore given by them, and women screamed full-throated ovation as the bizarre and the seeming impossible paraded for their approval. . . . [We] say 'All Hail, Hamilton.'"[99]

Another column reporting on the weekend's social events reluctantly admitted that "All those who were missing from Friday night's club affairs were located . . . up at the Rockland Palace at the 'Fairies' ball. Oh, yeah!," it added. "We will never understand that."[100] But where their readers went, the papers followed.

The complex spectacle of the drag balls allowed observers to position themselves in a variety of ways. They were all careful, though, to distinguish themselves from the queers who organized and participated in the affairs, often by casting aspersions on the Hamilton Lodge itself. "Say, Jack, in case you didn't know, this function was given by the Odd Fellows," a 1936 account reminded its readers in the most common and most obvious pun. A 1933 account made it even more obvious by referring to "The Grand United Order of (Very) Odd Fellows," and in 1937, an unusually mean-spirited promotional piece for the ball called the lodge a "society of strange fellows," a "wigged fraternity," and a "famed, effete and ubiquitous society of . . . Odd Fellows."[101]

While many black middle-class men—like white middle-class men—found the drag queen a disquieting figure, he also served as a foil whose utter effeminacy confirmed the manliness of other black men. Male columnists sometimes used jocular, man-to-man terms to describe the affairs. "Jack, the chicks were ready at the Hamilton Lodge toe-warming ball at Rockland Palace last Friday night," one columnist reported in 1936. He described the drag queens in the same dismissive terms he might have used for other "chicks": "The 'girls' proved to be a temperamental lot. They fussed and squabbled all over the joint. . . . When one of the 'girls' had her train stepped on she promptly cussed out the other 'girl' . . . and accused the 'low-down huzzy' of trying to steal the show." But he also evinced a remarkable degree of manly interest in the "girls": "Some of the contestants were luscious looking wenches. . . . Others were gloriously clad. . . . Many pranced like thoroughbred women. . . . Every one of them was notoriously effeminate."[102] A typical 1929 account used the "notorious effeminacy" of the female impersonators—their near-perfect rendition of stereotypical feminine demeanor—to ridicule women who did not perform the role of women as successfully. "One could learn a great deal (meaning the female of the species) on how to deport one's self when on parade" by observing the impersonators, it advised.[103]

The interracial character of the ball provoked varying responses. In the 1920s some black observers openly expressed hostility toward the whites who attended and virtually blamed the presence of homosexuals and female impersonators in Harlem on bohemian whites from Greenwich Village. The issue exploded in April 1926 when the well-known party impresario James Harris organized a benefit for the Fort Valley Industrial School, a school in Georgia that often received the support of respectable black charitable organizations. Advertised as a "Benefit Costume Ball . . . [where] The Village and Harlem . . . Will Meet," it drew attention from the black press around the country when dozens of female and male impersonators showed up. The *Chicago Defender* described it as "one of the gayest affairs that the night life of New York has yet been able to furnish . . . weirdly and grotesquely dressed men and women of both races revelled till the wee hours of morn."[104] But another paper denounced the "disgraceful antics of the male women and female men who are said to have attended the benefit by the scores" for sullying the name of the "splendid" school, which "stood for the making of manly men and womenly women, for thrift, industry and christian [sic] character among the colored people." Homosexual whites were the last people to whom blacks seeking respectability should turn, it argued, warning: "The discarded froth of Caucasian society cannot lift them or their race in the respect and confidence of the Caucasian world."[105] In 1929 the *Amsterdam News*'s report on the Hamilton Lodge ball still took umbrage at the presence of "some of the most notoriously degenerate white men in the city" who "seized the opportunity of a masquerade to get off some of their abnormality in public." The *New York Age* seems to have found the dancers' willingness to cross racial lines in their coupling at the 1926 ball no less disquieting than their cross-dressing.[106]

Many Harlemites found the participation of whites to be intriguing rather than disturbing, however, and the press began to reflect this perspective in the 1930s. The presence of white drag queens at the balls reversed the racial dynamic usually at work in interracial encounters in Harlem, presenting whites as an object of spectacle for blacks. An *Amsterdam News* cartoonist drew attention to this reversal in his 1936 depiction of black men in the audience watching a white drag queen on stage (see figure 9.2). Some spectators also took delight in watching the transgression of racial boundaries that seemed to accompany the transgression of gender and sexual boundaries—and in watching white gay men forced to transgress them by their entry into a space controlled by black gay men. As one bemused Harlem observer, Abram Will, noted of the Hamilton Lodge ball:

> There were corn fed "pansies" from the deep South breaking traditional folds by mixing irrespective of race. There were the sophisticated "things" from Park Avenue and Broadway. There were the big black strapping "darlings" from the heart of Harlem. The Continent, Africa and even Asia had their due share of "ambassadors." The ball was a melting pot, different, exotic and unorthodox, but acceptable.[107]

For a moment, moreover, the *racial* differences between black and white spectators, although hardly forgotten, were overshadowed by their common positioning as "normal" bystanders who were different from the queer folk on the ballroom floor. In a city where racial boundaries were inscribed in the segregation of most public accommodations (integrated buses notwithstanding), the difference between normal spectators and abnormal dancers was inscribed in the differentiation of the balcony and other viewing areas from the dance floor. Each zone was racially integrated, but marked as sexually different from the other.

Racial divisions were hardly erased at the balls, however. Drag queens mixed across racial lines but never forgot them, as Abram Will's careful delineation of European- , African- , and Asian-American participants made clear. Moreover, racial iconography was central to many of

Figure 9.2 Harlem's leading newspaper, the *Amsterdam News,* regularly carried pictures of the winning contestants in the costume competition at the Hamilton Lodge ball, New York's biggest drag ball. In 1932, the paper's illustrator pictured the "girls," and in 1936 he poked gentle fun at the rivalry, glamour, drunkenness, and gender ambiguity of the annual affair. He also poked fun at straight Harlem's response: note the expressions of desire and confusion on the faces of the two black men looking at the white drag queen. (*From the* Amsterdam News: *"The Artist Pictures the 'Girls,'" March 2, 1932; "And, Girls, How They Carried On!" March 7, 1936.)*

the dancers' costumes. "Among the outstanding costumes" at the 1932 ball, according to the *Inter-State Tattler*,

> were a pair of Flora Dora girls in sweeping Empire gowns of red velvet trimmed in black velvet . . . an African chieftain, his tribal marks in gold, the sacred bull's horn on his head and ropes of wooden beads around his neck; . . . an oriental dancer with long hair; a belle of the gay '90's—parasol and all; . . . a bare foot east Indian in colorful flowing robes; a black and red be-ruffled Spanish senorita; . . . [and] no end of . . . Colonial dames."[108]

The balls became a site for the projection and inversion of racial as well as gender identities. Significantly, though, white drag queens were not prepared to reverse their racial identity. Many accounts refer to African-American queens appearing as white celebrities, but none refer to whites appearing as well-known black women. As one black observer noted, "The vogue was to develop a 'personality' like some outstanding woman," but the only women he listed, Jean Harlow, Gloria Swanson, Mae West, and Greta Garbo, were white.[109]

The pageantry of the balls sometimes exacerbated the racial divisions in the gay world. The costume competition became a highly charged affair, with all sides watching to see whether a black or white queen would be crowned. The Harlem press took considerable interest in the racial aspect of the competition, taking special note in 1931 when a black contestant, Bonnie Clark, was awarded the grand prize for the first time.[110] He won again in 1932, but after losing in 1933 he denounced the racial injustice of the city's drag competitions. "There is a conspiracy afoot," he told the black press. "I participated in seven of these masquerades last year and except for the one here [sponsored by the Hamilton Lodge], they are always arranged for the white girls to win. They never had no Negro judges."[111] "Considerable rivalry exists between the ofay chicks and the Mose broods," a columnist for the *Amsterdam News* declared after attending the ball in 1936. "Last year an ofay won the costume prize. This year a Mose 'girl,' Jean La Marr, won the $50."[112] While much of the black press used a mocking tone to distance itself from both the black and white contestants, it nonetheless often took the side of black contestants, regarding them as Harlem's representatives in the competition and thus granting them a place in black society.

The Price of Respectability

As the response of Harlem's press and public to the drag balls suggests, drag queens and other gay men could earn the grudging respect

—and even the awe—of many Harlemites. But they could not achieve respectability. "While youth will have its fling," the newspaper attack on the 1926 Fort Valley Industrial School Benefit had warned, "there is a special need for the colored graduates of northern Universities to emulate the solid and substantial characters of their forefathers." Harlem's social elite and intelligentsia made it clear that the open expression of one's homosexuality precluded participation in respectable society. As noted in chapter 7, W. E. B. Du Bois fired the managing editor of *The Crisis* upon learning that he had been arrested for homosexual solicitation in a public washroom. Whatever Du Bois's personal response to the revelation of the man's homosexual interests, it seems clear he believed it necessary to dismiss the man to safeguard the reputation of the journal.[113]

Gay members of Harlem's middle class were well aware of this injunction and felt obliged to exercise greater discretion than many workingmen did. This was the case even among the most avant-garde of Harlem's middle class, the writers and poets of the Harlem Renaissance, the flowering of black literary arts in the 1920s that transformed the American literary landscape. Indeed, the contours and constraints of middle-class gay life are exemplified by the problems faced by this group of avant-garde writers. (A full survey of the role of lesbians and gay men in the Harlem Renaissance is beyond the scope of this social history.)

Gay social networks played a key role in fostering the Renaissance. Two of its major patrons, Howard University professor Alain Locke and Carl Van Vechten, were gay men who took more than a purely literary interest in the young writers they championed and brought to the attention of publishers and benefactors. As cultural historians such as Eric Garber, David Levering Lewis, Amitai Avi-ram, and Alden Reimonenq have begun to show, many of the leading male poets and novelists of the Renaissance were gay-identified or sexually active with men as well as women, including Countee Cullen, Wallace Thurman, Bruce Nugent, Claude McKay, and possibly Langston Hughes. They regularly socialized with each other in gay settings and discussed the affairs they were having with other men. A gay artist from France who was immediately drawn into their circle when he visited New York in the late 1920s recalled that "there was a whole small crowd of rather nice gay blacks around Countee Cullen. They used to meet practically every evening at Caska Bonds' and sit by the hour playing cards there." They were also involved in broader gay social circles, attending the gay parties thrown by Bonds, Clinton Moore, Eddie Manchester, and other black gay men, and the extravagant "mixed" parties thrown by the millionaire heiress A'Leila Walker and Van Vechten.[114]

Several of their novels depicting the Harlem scene included gay and lesbian characters, including Claude McKay's *Home to Harlem* (1927) and Wallace Thurman's *The Blacker the Berry* (1929) and *Infants of the Spring* (1932). As Avi-Ram, Reimoneng, and other critics have noted, the poetry of Countee Cullen and possibly other Renaissance figures can be read as offering critiques of heterosexism as well as racism and odes to homosexual love as well as to black solidarity.[115] In their boldest collective move, in 1926 they published *Fire!!*, an avant-garde literary journal that included Bruce Nugent's "Smoke, Lillies, and Jade," an extraordinary homoerotic story (or prose poem) celebrating his cruising and consummating an affair with a Latin "Adonis."[116] Their flamboyance was instantly denounced by Harlem's leading intellectuals and social figures, including Alain Locke, who considered such flamboyance unacceptable.

Although these gay social networks played an important role in the construction of the Harlem Renaissance, they were carefully hidden. Most of its writers, like most other middle-class African-Americans, endeavored to keep their homosexuality a secret from the straight world. Even Bruce Nugent, the most audacious of the circle, published his story under the name Richard Bruce to avoid embarrassing his parents. Countee Cullen, who had begun to identify himself as gay before he turned twenty and was involved in several long-term relationships with men, twice married women in search of respectability. His first wedding, to Yolande Du Bois, daughter of W. E. B. Du Bois, was one of the major social events of 1928, but their marriage quickly foundered. Yolande appears to have cooperated in making sure that the Harlem press reported Cullen was infatuated with another woman, but she confided to her father that Cullen's homosexuality was the problem. Cullen married again twelve years later, even though he was romantically involved with another man. As Reimoneng has shown, Cullen became increasingly concerned in the 1930s and 1940s to hide his homosexual liaisons, using codes to refer to them in his letters to friends and signing letters to his beloved with a pseudonym. Cullen had quickly become one of the most celebrated poets of the Harlem Renaissance and had no illusions about what the revelation of his homosexuality could do to his career.[117]

Another bright star of the Renaissance, the novelist Wallace Thurman, also spent years worrying that his homosexuality would be used against him. He had been arrested within weeks of arriving in the city for having sex with a white hairdresser in a 135th Street subway washroom. Although he gave police a false name and address and a minister bailed him out, word of the arrest began to spread. Four years later, having established himself as an editor and leader of young black writers, he still felt dogged by rumors of the arrest and wondered anxiously whether others had heard of it. His fears were exacerbated when his wife, after a short and unsuccessful marriage, threatened to use his homosexuality as grounds for divorce. "You can imagine with what relish a certain group of Negroes in Harlem received and relayed the news that I was a homo. No evidence is needed of course beyond the initial rumor," he wrote a friend in 1929, denying that the rumors were true.[118]

The organization of the Hamilton Lodge ball codified the differences between the public styles of middle-class and working-class gay men. Middle-class men passing as straight sat in the balcony with other members of Harlem's social elite looking down on the spectacle of workingmen in drag. Although the newspapers regularly noted the appearance of Caska Bonds, Harold Jackman, Edward G. Perry, Clinton Moore, Eddie Manchester, Jimmie Daniels, and other middle-class gay men at the balls, they simply included them in the lists of other celebrities and society people in attendance, all presumed to be straight.[119] Some of the society people they joined to watch the queers must have known of their involvement in the gay life, and undoubtedly some of the reporters and readers of the papers knew as well. But all concerned seem to have agreed not to say anything.

The differences between the social worlds and public styles of middle- and working-class gay men should not be exaggerated, however. Men often interacted across class lines, gathering at the same speakeasies and sharing some of the same pleasures. And they negotiated their way through the neighborhood in not altogether dissimilar ways. Workingmen and men who had migrated to Harlem without their families were more likely than middle-class men to present themselves as gay men in the public sphere, but even they might choose to keep their participation "in the life" distinct from their family life. Many workingmen moved between two worlds, appearing as drag queens at the balls and as dutiful sons in their parents' apartments. Adopting a camp name helped them keep the two lives separate. "John Smith" could become "the sepia Mae West" at a drag ball, and even be quoted in the papers as Mae West, without drawing attention to John Smith. One man who had attended the Hamilton Lodge ball in drag recalled his panic when a neighbor asked him about it at a family dinner the next day. His brother and a friend, who were wise to the situation, immediately covered for him to protect his parents from the embarrassment of learning—or seeing a guest learn—that their son was a drag queen. "Nobody wanted their parents to know," he insisted.[120] Another man participated actively in the gay life for years without telling his sister, even though he shared an apartment with her. When he brought a man home, he simply told her that it was a friend who couldn't get home that night. She probably knew the score, but she never asked, and he never told. It seemed a fine arrangement to him, since it allowed him to take part in gay life while also continuing an important family relationship.[121] The "open secret," widely known but never spoken, governed many working-men's relations with their families, just as it governed some middle-class men's relations with the larger social world.

PART III

The Politics of Gay Culture

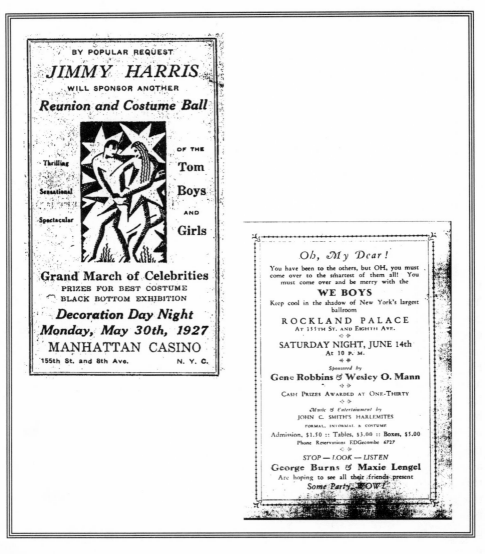

Figure 10.1. Attended by celebrities and thousands of onlookers, drag balls were held throughout the year. The biggest were held at Harlem's Manhattan Casino, later renamed the Rockland Palace. Invitations made it clear that a ball would be gay by making suggestive references to "Tom Boys and Girls" and the like. *(From Yale Collection of American Literature, Beinecke Rare Books and Manuscripts Library, Yale University.)*

Chapter 10

THE DOUBLE LIFE, CAMP CULTURE, AND THE MAKING OF A COLLECTIVE IDENTITY

IN 1927, NINETEEN-YEAR-OLD GENE HARWOOD DECIDED TO MOVE TO NEW York City from his small hometown in upstate New York after an older gay friend, who had already moved there, returned to tell him about the gay life possible in the city. The friend encouraged Harwood to join him and offered to help him make the move. Persuaded to give it a try, Harwood initially stayed in the apartment his friend shared with two actors, who "showed me around a little bit and gave me an idea of what life [in the city] would be like." Hardwood met other gay men through his roommates and at the parties his friend regularly threw in the apartment and eventually moved in with one of them when his roommates' parties became too frequent for his taste. At a party at another friend's apartment, he met Bruhs Mero, who would become his lover. Together they developed a large circle of gay friends and lived together for more than fifty years. Years later George Sardi had a similar experience. He first visited New York to attend a New Year's Eve party given by some gay friends from home. He so liked what he saw in the city that he decided to stay, moved into his friends' fourth-floor walk-up, and soon got a job at the gay bar in the ground floor of the building. He worked for more than thirty years in bars and other gay businesses.[1]

The migration to New York of both these men—like that of many others—was encouraged and facilitated by gay friends who had gone before them, who sent them word about the gay life to be found there, and who assisted them in making the move by providing them initial accommodations and, in some cases, contacts that might lead to employment. Both Harwood and Sardi built on those initial contacts to develop extensive gay social networks that were central to their lives. Historians writing about other migrant groups have described this process as "chain migration."[2]

Whether they migrated to Manhattan's gay world from the small towns of America or Europe, from the city's outer boroughs or suburbs, or from the straight world of their families and social convention in Manhattan, many gay men adapted to the urban environment in ways remarkably similar to those of other migrant groups. They developed extensive social networks on the basis of their sexual ties and shared experience of marginalization, just as immigrants elaborated social networks on the basis of their kinship and regional ties. Gay men expanded those ties and invested them with new meaning because, like other immigrants, they needed them in order to adapt to the city, to find housing, work, and emotional support in a hostile society. Although men were not integrated into the gay world by their families of origin, gay men developed methods to incorporate newcomers into it. Within that world they created a distinctive culture that enabled them to resist, on an everyday basis, their social marginalization: tactics for communicating with one another in hostile settings, ways of affirming, transmitting, and celebrating their communal ties, and resources for subverting the ideology that marginalized them as "unnatural."

Some men who migrated to the city with no other connections there developed almost entirely gay social worlds, as did other men who kept their contact with "normal" people to a minimum in order to avoid their scorn and rejection. A doctor who studied homosexuals in the early 1920s noted that most of the men he interviewed "associate[d] primarily with [other] homosexuals"; as one gay man explained, he felt more at ease in the company of other homosexuals, with whom he could "talk and act in a freer manner."[3] Another man announced to a second doctor in the late 1930s: "I have no contact with heterosexual people." He had built a life for himself that revolved entirely around other gay men, and claimed he would no longer "feel comfortable with [heterosexuals] and I would rather be with people of my own type."[4]

Such men found jobs, living arrangements, and meeting places that kept them involved almost exclusively in the gay world. In 1936 a psychiatry student described a man who had worked as a female impersonator at a Long Island hotel, performed in a "pansy chorus" in a nightclub, frequented gay "gathering places like S . . . in the 'Village,' . . . reads Oscar Wilde, Dorian Grey [sic] and other authors of this type. . . . After an extensive interview with the psychiatrist," he reported, "it was clearly indicated that the patient had fully rationalized his condition and his tendencies, and prefers continuing to function on the overt homosexual level."[5] In 1922 a twenty-year-old gay man imprisoned on degenerate-disorderly-conduct charges in the New York City Jail on Welfare Island explained what his daily routine had been in Manhattan:

> [I] got up around noon. . . . Had breakfast and went to work [as an entertainer at a Greenwich Village restaurant]. After work had my dinner most always at B———, 49th Street between Sixth and Seventh Avenues, where I ate because lots of fags hang out there. . . . After performance usually [went] to F———. This was my routine for week-days. Saturday nights, however, after the theatre, I always went to ———[,] one of the places for homosexuals. After eating, I usually went to a place called the ———, where I met both male and female homosexuals. About 2:30 in the morning, we used to go to ———. On Sunday I always went to [Paul and Joe's, in the Village], which is the main rendezvous for homosexuals.[6]

His life, in short, revolved around constant interactions with gay men (and sometimes lesbians) at restaurants and speakeasies that were well established as homosexual rendezvous. He not only spent his leisure time almost exclusively within gay society, but also held a job in which he could be openly gay.

GAY LIVES, DOUBLE LIVES

Some men lived primarily in the gay world; other men, especially fairies, presented themselves as gay in both gay and straight settings. But most queer men led a double life. They constantly moved between at least two worlds: a straight world in which they were assumed to be straight and a gay world in which they were known as gay. Managing two lives, two personas, was difficult for some men. But it did not necessarily lead them to denigrate their necessarily compartmentalized gay persona. Most men regarded the double life as a reasonable tactical response to the dangers posed by the revelation of their homosexuality to straight people. As one man active in gay life since the 1930s reflected in the early 1960s, "All my life I had had to wear a rigid mask, a stiff armour of protection, not necessarily to pretend to be what I was not—heterosexual—but not to be identified as homosexual. Not that I was ashamed of so being, but to defend against insults, humiliations and mockery, [and] also to make a living and do the sort of work I wasn't wanted to do."[7]

Managing a double life was relatively easy for many men because they did not consider their homosexual identity to be their only important identity. Identities are always relational, produced by the ways people affiliate themselves with or differentiate themselves from others—and are marked as different *by* others.[8] All men managed multiple identities or multiple ways of being known in the many social worlds in which they

moved, because they had to present themselves in different ways in different contexts. They might be workers on the job; brothers, uncles, or
fathers with their families; African-Americans or Italian-Americans when
participating in an ethnic street festival or dealing with abusive Anglo-
Americans. While they might also think of themselves as gay in each of
those settings—while talking with a gay co-worker, or hearing a brother
tell an anti-gay joke—often they did not.

The gay world was only one of the worlds in which most gay men
moved, a richly supportive and engaging world for many, but not their
only source of identity. Although many men received crucial practical
and emotional support from other gay men, they were also likely to be
enmeshed in similar relations of mutual dependence with their natal families, workmates, or other nongay associates. Even within the gay world,
they were constantly reminded of their other identities, as the epithets
"rice queen," "dinge queen," and the like made clear. Although a black
gay man might find himself scorned as a "faggot" in a straight black
social milieu, he could find himself equally marked as a "nigger" in a
white gay milieu.

One reason many men at this time found it easier to "pass" in the
straight world than their post-Stonewall successors would was that they
found it easier to manage multiple identities, to be "gay" in certain social
milieus and not others. "We weren't gay when we were shaving,"
remarked one man, impatient with the claims of a later generation.
"Why would you even want to tell your parents?" another asked. "For
some people it was your whole life, your soul," another man explained.
"For others it was what you did on the weekend."[9]

The degree to which men participated in the gay world depended in
part on their jobs. Some occupations allowed men to work with other
gay men in a supportive atmosphere, even if they had to maintain a
straight facade in dealing with customers and other outsiders. Men who
worked in the city's restaurants, department stores, hotels, and theater
industry, among other occupations, often found themselves in such a
position.[10] One man who joined the Denishawn dance company when he
moved to the city in the 1920s recalled that he "had never heard the
word homosexual until I came to New York," but in the dance company
"becoming homosexual just seemed the most natural thing to me. I saw
that other boys were attracted to me and I accepted their advances." He
and another man in the company soon realized they were both gay and
became fast friends.[11] In about 1928, when he was sixteen, another man
got a job as an usher at a theater where most of the other ushers hired
by the gay manager were good-looking young gay men. "There was
much open knowledge and conversation of sodomy among the boys who
worked in this theater," he recalled, and "I found myself in compatible

company."[12] A man who worked at Macy's in the early 1930s found that stories were rife among the workers about affairs between senior officers and stockboys. After the Second World War, Macy's "got a goodly share of the servicemen who were gay," through whom he was introduced to the gay bars of Greenwich Village.[13]

Some men were even able to use their gay contacts to find jobs, particularly in those occupations in which many gay men worked or that tolerated a relative degree of openness on the part of their gay workers. Roger Smith, for instance, got a job as a window designer at a major department store through his friendship with another designer. David Hearst lost his job at the New York Public Library after being arrested for cruising in Central Park, but got a job at another library with the assistance of two gay librarians.[14]

Although some jobs allowed men to meet other gay men and to be fairly open with their coworkers, other occupations discouraged such interactions, as Tom R. discovered. Tom had made only limited forays into the gay world when he took a job as a guide at the NBC studios at Rockefeller Center at the beginning of the Second World War. But the other guides there quickly "psyched me out," he recalled, and started discussing opera and other "gay subjects" in front of him in an effort to elicit a reference to his homosexuality. After he began discussing the gay life with some of them, they invited him to parties where he met other gay men, and he quickly became a part of an extensive gay social circuit. Working at Rockefeller Center "opened my eyes and showed me how great the gay world could be," he recalled. Once he finished his schooling and took a job as a professional medical writer, however, he found he had moved into a work environment in which his homosexuality would not have been tolerated. He never made reference to it at work and began to strictly segregate his work and nonwork lives.[15]

Although Tom had to suppress any intimation of his gay life at his new job, this was relatively easy to do because discussion of *any* aspect of one's nonwork (or "private") life was eschewed at his new workplace. Indeed, many middle-class gay men sought to preclude their colleagues' questions about their "private" lives by insisting that they strictly observe the separation of private and public spheres that theoretically governed the culture of the professional workplace. Most heterosexuals observed that separation in theory more than in practice, since they often adorned their fingers with wedding rings and their offices with family photos and peppered their conversation with talk about family outings. Nonetheless, the ideological separation between work and home and between public and private spheres existed as a resource middle-class gay men could call on to protect their privacy. One broker thought he had managed to do quite well on Wall Street because it observed such a strict division between public and private life that questions simply were not asked about his private life. That division protected him, he said, and it was what protected many gay men of his generation.[16]

Many in a later generation of gay men considered it a betrayal of their identities not to be "out" to their straight associates at work and in other social settings, but the salient division between gay men in the prewar years tended to be between men who covertly acknowledged their homosexuality to other gay men and those who refused to do even that. Most middle-class men believed for good reason that their survival depended on hiding their homosexuality from hostile straight outsiders, and they respected the decision of other men to do so as well. Indeed, a central requirement of the moral code that governed gay life and bound gay men to one another was that they honor other men's decisions to keep their homosexuality a secret and do all they could to help protect that secret from outsiders. But they disagreed about whether a man was morally obliged to reveal his homosexuality to other *gay* men. Some men felt no such obligation, but they were bitterly resented by others who considered them hypocrites and cowards for not acknowledging their membership in "the club" to other members. "What was criminal was . . . denying it to your sisters," one man in the latter camp declared. "Nobody cared about coming out to straights."[17]

Such debates hinged on men's different perceptions of the boundaries of the gay world and the requirements of "membership" in it. They reflected the fact that most men's double life was not strictly divided between a straight work world and a gay social world. Men could participate in—and more important, *create*—the gay world in almost any setting. Many men in "straight" workplaces discovered other gay coworkers with whom they were able to communicate without drawing the attention of others. They could interact with some people in an office as "normal," unmarked colleagues, but they were able to interact sub rosa with other gay colleagues as gay men. In a single evening a man might adopt several different personas, as he moved from work, where he was known as straight but enjoyed bantering discreetly with a gay colleague down the hall, to a gay cocktail party, where he unleashed his camp wit before an all-gay crowd, to dinner in a "straight" restaurant, where most of the other diners assumed he was straight (if they bothered to label him at all), but he nonetheless flirted with the gay waiter and waved to gay acquaintances at the corner table, to a Village speakeasy, where most people thought he was gay—and the fellow he tried to pick up was sure he was.

Most men learned the skills that enabled them to maintain a double life through their participation in the gay social world that took shape in predominantly gay social settings. Not all men experienced the easy entrée into the gay social world that Harwood and Sardi did. Some had heard of New York's gay scene because of its reputation in the homosexual circles they moved in elsewhere, but still had to locate it once they arrived. One man who had "mingle[d] in male homosexual society" in Boston, for instance, reported that he had moved to New York with a friend around 1930 because of "the tales I [had] heard of the freedom and lively times to be had" there.[18] Many men arrived in the city with only a vague understanding of what they might find, but, fearful they would never fit in in their hometowns, were drawn simply by the city's reputation as a center of "nonconformist" or bohemian behavior. Some of those men discovered the gay world almost by chance, through the contacts they made in their rooming houses or in the streets; others found it by looking for places such as the Life Cafeteria (or the Village in general) they had heard their heterosexual associates mention scornfully.

Whatever the route by which men made their initial contact with New York's gay world, they usually needed guidance in their exploration of it. They often received the counsel of men they met in their first forays into gay clubs or neighborhoods. Those men, often older and better established in both the straight and gay worlds, became their mentors—and in some cases their lovers as well. They introduced the newcomers to the institutions of the gay world that had been hidden to them before, showed them how to find others, and, if they needed such help, assisted them in coming to terms with their homosexuality and crafting new ways of understanding themselves. They also taught newcomers gay slang and folklore and how to survive in a hostile world. "I was a gawky, sissy boy with plucked eyebrows and loud clothes," one man said of his youth in the 1920s. A "teacher took pity on me, taught me how to dress, warned me against any appearance of effeminacy." Another man recalled of the same era that an older gay man had taken a nonsexual interest in him and had "initiated me into the dialect and the conventionalities [of gay society]."[19]

On his first visit to a New York gay bar, Frank McCarthy met an older man who became his mentor in the gay world. They quickly became lovers, and in the six months that followed, McCarthy's new friend introduced him to gay life, the concept of which had been "incomprehensible" to him before. "He brought me around," McCarthy recalled, "taught me the language, if you will, took me to places. I found out that there were gay restaurants, that there were gay clubs, that there was a gay beach, that there was a *gay world*." His new friend treated him to outings McCarthy never could have afforded himself, and he was also a "buffer" for a young man new to the gay scene. "I probably wouldn't have gone to all these places by myself, even if I'd found out about them," McCarthy reflected years later. "I would have been too frightened." While taking McCarthy to gay bars and parties, his mentor also imparted to him some of the skills valued in gay culture by teaching him "how to dress," furnish an apartment, and the like, and introduced him to aspects of the cultural life cherished by middle-class gay men: art, ballet, opera, theater.[20]

Perhaps most important, mentors introduced men new to the gay world to their circle of friends. Many men aware of homosexual desires had spent years thinking they were the only ones to feel as they did, or fearing that their desires meant they would become the sort of flamboyant street fairies they saw being ridiculed in their own communities. The gay world they discovered reassured them that they were not alone, and that there were a variety of ways to be gay. One man told a researcher in the late 1930s that before moving East, "I had thought that homosexuality was something that struck just one or two people. I soon learned that it was prevalent. . . . On every holiday or on the slightest excuse I went to some large city where I could make new contacts among my own type."[21]

Young men often found themselves swept up in a dizzying sequence of gay parties, which quickly placed them in the midst of a gay social world more immense than they had ever imagined existed. Parties provided many men with an entrée into New York's gay society and a vehicle for expanding their networks of gay friends. When one scion of a wealthy Boston family moved to New York in the 1940s, he knew only one gay man in the city. He quickly met many more when the friend took him to a number of cocktail parties, and he realized that the best way to meet people and establish himself socially would be to give parties himself. He did so every weekend for three months. His small circle of new acquaintances came and brought their friends, who brought their friends, and after three months "my address book was filled with names."[22]

Because gay men found their behavior highly regulated in most commercial institutions by managers concerned about police surveillance, they flocked to parties, where they could dance, joke in a campy way, and be affectionate without fear. To men who traveled in both the straight and gay worlds in the 1930s and 1940s, apartment parties seemed to be both more common and more significant events in the gay world than in the straight. Many of the men interviewed by the medical researcher George Henry in the 1930s described parties as central to their social lives and a major way to meet other men. "Homosexuals seem to be drawn together by these [cocktail] parties," commented one man, who himself threw parties every week. "Homosexuals are more interested in cocktail parties than other men [are]," another, more dissaffected man sneered. "Homosexuals have an exaggerated sense about these parties. . . . They're on the go all the time."[23]

Most parties were hosted on a reciprocal basis among friends, or on a grander scale by men of exceptional means. But they were such a significant meeting place that some people were able to support themselves by organizing them. "Rent parties," at which guests were asked to make a contribution to the rent, were regular events in Harlem in the 1920s and Depression years; lesbians and gay men were welcome at many of those given by straight people, and also threw their own.[24] During the Depression, some wealthier men and women began giving such parties on a grander scale, in order to keep their estates. An older friend (and mentor) took Frank Burton to a party that lasted all weekend at a grand home in New Jersey, whose owners, a banker and theatrical agent, needed to rent out its numerous rooms on the weekend in order to supplement their suddenly reduced incomes.[25] Many such parties were small, invitational affairs, but others were immense and became regular events on gay men's calendars. In the early 1940s, Frank Thompson followed a regular party circuit every Saturday night. He and his lover started the evening at a cocktail party in a basement apartment on West Seventieth Street just off Central Park West. For 75 cents, guests could drink as much as they wished, dance, and meet friends. As Thompson recalled with special fondness, couples could hold hands in the garden, something few would dare try in public. When that party ended around midnight, many of the guests moved on to a second, more intimate party in a small, dimly lit apartment in the West Twenties, where men could kiss as well as dance to slow music.[26]

Parties, whether held in palatial penthouses or tiny tenement flats, constituted safe spaces in which a distinctive gay culture was forged. A doctor studying homosexuals in the 1930s commented on the ability (and, one might add, determination) of one man to "avoid being conspicuous with [non-gay] men," but to engage in camp behavior when in a group of gay men, or, as the doctor put it, to give "his effeminacy freer play to the extent of being one of the gayest of the 'queens.'"[27] The empowerment some lesbians and gay men felt in such an environment was indicated by the behavior of people attending a "woman's party" (as it was called) in a Harlem tenement on West 137th Street in 1928—and by the response an investigator got to his interrogation of a lesbian (or "bull dagger") there. Fifteen lesbians and five gay men were in attendance, all African-American. "The men were dancing with one another," the investigator reported, "and the women were dancing with one another and going through the motions of copulation . . . and a number of the women had their dresses pulled up to their thighs." Asked by the investigator to explain the character of the party, the

hostess, a thirty-five-year-old woman who sold drinks to the partygoers, explained matter-of-factly that it was a "freakish party, everybody
in here is supposed to be a bull dagger or a c—." Exclaiming that he
was "neither" and that "I like mine in a normal way," the investigator
approached one woman, demanding "Are you one of these so-called
things here or are you a normal, regular girl?" The woman, he reported
with some amazement, defiantly pointed out: "Everybody here is either
a bull dagger or faggot and I am here," to which the investigator could
only reply, "Some logic." One of the men then tried to pick him up.[28]

Although private parties were largely free from interference by police
and social-purity forces, they did occasionally encounter difficulties. In
the summer of 1922, the police, apparently at the instigation of the
Society for the Suppression of Vice, raided a private "degenerate 'party'"
thrown by a forty-seven-year-old male housekeeper in the West Ninety-
third Street apartment of his employer. The host and his four guests, a
forty-five-year-old theater manager and three male nurses in their twenties, were arrested, and all but one were sentenced to sixty days in the
workhouse. The police also raided a party Frank Thompson gave in his
apartment in the early 1940s and arrested the men they found dancing
there on charges of engaging in "lewd and lascivious behavior." The
charges were dismissed the next morning, after the partygoers had spent
the night in jail. As a result of such dangers, as well as concerns about
what neighbors might see, the hosts of parties often took precautions.
When Gene Harwood and Bruhs Mero organized the Nucleus Club, a
small group of lesbian and gay male friends who regularly partied at
their home in the Village during the war, they pulled the blinds and were
careful to have men and women leave the apartment in mixed pairs.[29]

Gay Folklore

As the defiance of the woman at the Harlem party suggests, the world
created by homosexuals in the city's streets, cafeterias, and private apartments became the crucible in which they forged a distinctive gay culture.
That culture helped them to counteract the negative attitudes about
themselves pervasive in their society, develop strategies that enabled them
to survive outside of gay enclaves, and establish a collective identity.

In a society that denigrated homosexuality and imposed severe sanctions against its expression, it was no easy task for gay men to affirm
themselves. Social hostility and the resulting need of most men to lead
double lives imposed enormous strains on them. Many men interviewed
by a doctor in the 1930s understandably expressed their unhappiness at
being "abnormal." One man explained that he wanted to "overcome" his
homosexuality because "it had made me more nervous [and made] . . . me
a social outcast. At work I try to act as a normal person. I don't think the

double life is good." Another man simply commented, "I would much prefer to be normal [because] it would be a lot easier in life." Many men who could not bring themselves to marry missed sharing in the family life they had been raised to expect, and many were particularly unhappy at the prospect of not having children. For others, the genuine desire for children—as well as the desire for respectability—led to the decision to marry, although that did not always end their participation in gay life. One man believed homosexuals had an admirable "sensitiveness that usually doesn't go with the average normal [man, which he] . . . would regret los[ing]." Nonetheless, as he bluntly put it, "I like respectability and some time I might marry for the sake of having it."[30]

Although some men did internalize the anti-homosexual attitudes promulgated by their doctors, clergymen, and neighbors, gay culture was more successful in helping men resist others' negative judgments than is generally imagined. In this regard, the medical literature on homosexuality usually conveyed far more than it intended. For while it was devoted to the medicalization and denigration of homosexuals, it is full of disruptive subtexts, of moments of gay resistance, which can be heard in its dismissive—and disconcerted—accounts of gay people's "shameless behavior," their stubborn and "immature" failure to accept the doctors' authority, their "pathetic" claims that their homosexuality was not the problem the doctors thought it was.[31] In 1917, for instance, Dr. R. W. Shufeldt reported that a man he had interviewed, a "loquacious, foul-mouthed and foul-minded 'fairy,'" was "lost to every sense of shame; believing himself designed by nature to play the very part he is playing in life." In 1912 another New York doctor noted that a twenty-six-year-old chorus boy (generally referred to as "Rose"), who had been forced to flee his hometown for New York when his family discovered his homosexuality, was "very busy in arraigning society for its attitude toward those of his type, and was prepared to ethically justify his characteristics and practices." Many of the gay men and women George Henry interviewed in the 1930s announced they considered their homosexuality "natural."[32]

Indeed, it became the reluctant consensus among doctors that most inverts considered their homosexuality perfectly acceptable. The medical director of the National Committee for Mental Hygiene told New York's anti-vice societies in 1921 that "well known facts" sustained the view among doctors that "the pervert" did "not deem his acts unnatural."[33] Dr. William J. Robinson, the noted birth-control advocate, had presented a different view in 1914, claiming that *his* homosexual patients were dissatisfied with their condition, but that he argued his position so strenuously is some measure of the prevalence of the opposing view. Moreover, he fully anticipated that critics of his position would claim that only homosexuals unhappy with their "abnormality [would] go to the physician, while those who are satisfied with their condition do not invoke medical aid," an argument that evidently predominated, even though Robinson believed his own experience contradicted it.[34]

The extent to which some people were persuaded of the "naturalness" of their homosexuality was indicated even more strikingly by an article Robinson wrote eleven years later. A number of lesbians and gay men apparently considered it strategically useful to state their case before so prominent a sex reformer as Robinson. According to Robinson, many of the homosexuals who talked with him not only rejected the view that they were "degenerate" but claimed that "they stand on a *higher* level than those normally sexed, that they are the *specially favored* of the muses of poetry and the arts." Robinson ridiculed their claims and indicated he still thought there was "something 'not quite right'" with them, but he admitted that the conversations had led him to take a "broader, more tolerant, perhaps even more sympathetic [attitude]."[35] The fact that they had approached him at all demonstrated the self-confidence some gay people had developed.

Robinson's contacts were not the only gay people to defend homosexuality. Fairies did so regularly on the streets, both by their mere presence and by their efforts to limit straight men's ridicule of them. Other gay men and women took on the press, writing letters to newspapers to protest anti-gay articles that had been published. Several gay men and their supporters wrote to *Broadway Brevities* in the mid-1920s, in response to that tabloid's "exposing" the institutions of "fairyland." The editors reported that "a back-load of correspondence, part in protest, part in applause, has reached us in the wake of our exposé of Broadway perversion." They received letters from the supporters of homosexuals as well as gay people themselves. "God made them," wrote one man who said his son was homosexual. "They did not choose their status. . . . It is not a medical matter. . . . You know there are quite as many able people among them as among your so called 'normal.' . . . Let your campaign be to remove the penal laws which make these 'diseased' people a prey for blackmailers. Give them recognition and let them live their lives."[36] Henry Gerber, writing in 1932 under the pseudonym Parisex, responded to an article in *The Modern Thinker* that condemned homosexuality. "Is not the psychiatrist again putting the cart before the horse in saying that homosexuality is a symptom of a neurotic style of life?" he insisted. "Would it not sound more natural to say that the homosexual is made neurotic because his style of life is beset by thousands of dangers?"[37]

Gay men were able to counteract negative images largely because their constant association with other gay men reassured them of the counter-stereotypical variety and diverse personal qualities of homosexuals. But they also developed cultural resources and subcultural strategies that allowed them to undermine the authority of the dominant culture more directly and to create more affirmative conceptions of themselves. One prime way they did this was to create gay histories, and in particular to claim that heroic figures from the past were gay. As one novelist who argued that Shakespeare was an invert wrote in 1933, "All I want is to show people we're not monsters any more than Shakespeare was."[38] Claiming that respected historical figures—ranging from Julius Caesar, Michelangelo, and Shakespeare to Walt Whitman and Oscar Wilde—were homosexuals helped enhance the usually maligned character of gay men.

Several gay scholars working at the turn of the century sought to construct a gay historical tradition, in part as an effort to refute the influential arguments of late-nineteenth-century sexologists such as Richard von Krafft-Ebing that homosexuality represented a form of social and biological degeneration. John Addington Symonds, the esteemed British classicist, was the most notable of these scholars writing in English. He endeavored to dispel the association of homosexuality with degeneration by demonstrating that it had been tolerated and had flourished in the ancient Greek culture that most educated Anglo-Americans had begun to regard as the zenith of Western civilization. Symonds's work ultimately influenced a generation of scholars, but it did not receive widespread public attention in his lifetime. In the 1880s Symonds dared print only ten copies of his major essay on the subject. Before his death he agreed to have it appended to Havelock Ellis's *Sexual Inversion*, but his estate bought out the first English edition of *Sexual Inversion* in 1897 and withdrew permission for inclusion of his essay in the second edition, which, in any case, was promptly suppressed by the British government.[39]

As the fate of Symonds's study suggests, the project of historical reclamation was a difficult one for gay men, for it faced formidable obstacles from scholars and the government alike. Moreover, the history of homosexuality was omitted in formal history instruction and had no place in the family-centered oral traditions available to other disenfranchised groups. Having no access to a formal body of scholarship, gay men needed to invent—and constantly reinvent—a tradition on the basis of innumerable individual and idiosyncratic readings of texts. They also had to embed its transmission in the day-to-day social organization of their world. The folklore was typically passed on in bars and at cocktail parties, from friend to friend, from lover to lover, and from older men serving as mentors to younger men just beginning to identify themselves as gay.

A few gay intellectuals were more successful than Symonds in publishing works that introduced gay folklore to a wider audience. Edward Carpenter, the most notable among those writing in English, published several treatises on the "intermediate sex" in the early years of the century. His 1917 anthology of writings on male "friendship," *Ioläus*, was a more popular-oriented effort (booksellers reportedly called it "the bugger's bible"), whose contents suggest the outlines of the cultural tradition early gay intellectuals sought to construct. Among other selections, Carpenter included poetry by Shakespeare, Whitman, Goethe, Tennyson, and Byron, and an extensive selection of the "poetry of friendship among [the] Greeks and Romans." While his compilation, like most, imagined a gay cultural universe that was distinctly white and Western in its contours, he also included quasi-ethnographic accounts of non-Western customs of male friendship by Western anthropologists, explorers, and travel writers. He paid particular attention to Herman Melville's "interesting and reliable accounts of Polynesian customs" of the early 1840s, which Melville based on his observations as a traveler in the Pacific. *Ioläus* was published before Bronislaw Malinowski and other anthropologists had established the singular authority of their own brand of fieldwork-based ethnographies, and thus travelers' accounts, such as Melville's, were taken more seriously than they would be in later years.[40] Carpenter relied so heavily on Melville's work that it seems likely that *Omoo*, *Typee*, and some of Melville's other stories of the South Pacific were already widely regarded by gay men as ethnographies of homosexuality. If this was not the case, Carpenter, by dutifully citing them all, provided interested readers a guide for further study.[41]

The anthology's depiction of the nobility of male affection and love helped readers affirm their own love for men by encouraging them to identify it—and themselves—as part of an honorable tradition. Alain Locke, the gay professor of philosophy at Howard University who served as the mentor to many of the Harlem Renaissance's young writers, recommended *Ioläus* to Countee Cullen soon after they met. Cullen found it electrifying: "I read it through in one sitting," he wrote Locke in 1923, "and steeped myself in its charming and comprehending atmosphere. It opened up for me soul windows which had been closed; it threw a noble and evident light on what I had begun to believe, because of what the world believes, ignoble and unnatural. I loved myself in it."[42]

Other gay authors used less direct means than Carpenter to popularize the idea of a gay historical tradition. Few gay men heard their teachers discuss the possible significance of homosexuality in Plato, Whitman, or Shakespeare, but they could find it mentioned in almost every gay novel published in the early 1930s. In his 1933 novel *Better Angel*, Richard Meeker directly attacked "the professors" as "fools . . . [for] manufactur[ing] all sorts of shifts and silly dodges to avoid calling Shakespeare an invert." Meeker announced to his readers that Shakespeare "loved the boy actor [the object of many of Shakespeare's sonnets], and he celebrated his love in the finest . . . poetry of his whole career." His novel also asserted that Marcel Proust, André Gide, and Thomas Mann were part of a gay canon and were valuable guides in their own right to the literature of homosexuality.[43] Similarly, in *Strange Brother* (1931), author Blair Niles provided her readers with an extensive list of books to read by having her protagonist discover Whitman's *Leaves of Grass*, Carpenter's *Love's Coming of Age*, Plato's *Symposium*, Ellis's *Psychology of Sex* volumes, and Auguste Forel's *The Sexual Question*, among other books. She also identified Caesar, Michelangelo, Leonardo da Vinci, Shakespeare, Francis Bacon, and James I of England, along with numerous other historical figures, as homosexual. "You find them all the way back," one character explained, "among the artists and intellectuals of their time. . . . Kings and Emperors [are] in the list, too."[44] The regular appearance of such comments in the novels of the 1930s suggests both the currency of such ideas among gay intellectuals and their allies and their determination to disseminate them among gay readers.

Such ideas had become part of the folklore of the gay world by the 1910s—ideas used by men to legitimate and even exalt their identities as homosexuals. One well-educated gay prisoner interviewed by a prison doctor in the early 1920s listed "Shakespeare, Coleridge, De Quincey, Rosa Bonheur, Joan of Arc, Beethoven, Wagner and Napoleon [as] homosexuals," in order to buttress his contention that "most of the world's genius can be traced directly to the homosexual."[45] Apparently most of the gay men and lesbians who talked with the sex reformer Dr. William Robinson made such claims, for he took time to note (and dismiss) the "pathetic eagerness" of "almost all homosexuals . . . to claim . . . as homosexuals people whose homosexuality is extremely doubtful. . . . Thus they speak of Shakespeare, Byron and Whitman as belonging to their class, as if their homosexuality . . . were a well-established historical fact."[46] One man told yet another doctor in the mid-thirties that he "had read Freud, Jung, and Havelock Ellis and I had a feeling that I belonged to the elect. I didn't see any reason for being hypocritical about it."[47] Simon Karlinsky, a Russian émigré to the United States who first discovered the gay world in the 1930s, recalled years later "the excitement of joining a fascinating secret brotherhood that . . . included some of the admired actors, artists, writers and dancers of the present and the past."[48]

As Karlinsky's comment suggests, claiming certain historical figures was important to gay men not only because it validated their own homosexuality, but because it linked them to others. One of the ways groups of people constitute themselves as an ethnic, religious, or national community is by constructing a history that provides its members with a shared tradition and collective ancestors. This was a central purpose of the project of gay historical reclamation as well. By constructing historical traditions of their own, gay men defined themselves as a distinct community. By imagining they had collective roots in the past, they asserted a collective identity in the present.[49]

DOUBLE ENTENDRE AND CAMP CULTURE

Gay men developed a variety of other cultural strategies that helped them manage a double life and resist the dominant culture's contempt. While offering them practical assistance in dealing with a hostile world, such strategies also affirmed their cultural distinctiveness and solidarity. Perhaps most significantly, gay men developed a rich language of their own, which reflected the complex character and purposes of gay culture generally. Much gay argot had its origins in the banter of the fairies who stood at the center of gay culture; many words were adopted by self-identified queers only later, after the fairies had made them a part of gay culture. While a few words used by gay men were made-up terms that had no meaning in standard English or slang, most gave standard terms a second, gay meaning. Many were derived from the slang of female prostitutes. *Gay* itself referred to female prostitutes before it referred to gay men; *trade* and *trick* referred to prostitutes' customers before they referred to gay men's partners; and *cruising* referred to a streetwalker's search for partners before it referred to a gay man's. Other terms, such as *coming out*, burlesqued the rituals of society women. And a host of terms vividly described gay sexual practices: *browning* referred to anal intercourse, 69 described mutual oral sex.[50]

By giving common words a second meaning that would be readily recognized only by other gay men, gay argot allowed gay men to communicate with one another in hostile surroundings without drawing attention from others. Indeed, double entendre made the double life possible. It allowed men to construct a gay world in the midst of but invisible to the straight world—to identify themselves as gay to other gay men and to communicate as one gay man to another in settings where outsiders identified them only as workers, sight-seers, or something else. Donald Vining vividly illustrated how gay men used double entendre in an essay recalling his life as a gay man in the 1940s:

> "I adore seafood. Gorge myself whenever the fleet's in. But I can't abide fish," [a gay man] might say, and any gay man would instantly know that the speaker was turned on by sailors and turned off by women, while the puzzled Mr. and Mrs. Readers Digest, listening in, would assume this was a discussion about food preferences.[51]

When discussing their dates or relationships in the presence of outsiders, gay men often referred to their male partners with feminine pronouns. One man used this tactic when talking with another gay clerk at the travel agency where he worked, assuming his gay meaning would be unintelligible to the straight woman who shared their office. As he recalled, though, "Once I made a big mistake. I was describing a hot new guy I had just met, and told my friend that 'she' was this and 'she' was that, and then I exclaimed, 'She even buys her suits at Brooks Brothers!'" The woman coworker said nothing, "but I was mortified."[52]

Men's use of gay argot fostered their sense of collective identity. The very fact that men could understand a common code emphasized their membership in a group to whose codes they alone were "wise," and became a sign by which they distinguished themselves from outsiders. Indeed, it made *them* the insiders in a world that normally cast them as outsiders, and many men treasured the sense it gave them of participating in a secret society.

But gay codes also allowed men to see themselves as participants in the dominant culture by enabling them to see themselves in the interstices of that culture. As the literary theorist Harold Beaver observed in an influential essay, "The homosexual . . . is a prodigious consumer of signs—of hidden meanings, hidden systems, hidden potentiality. Exclusion from the common code impels the frenzied quest: the momentary glimpse, the scrambled figure, the chance encounter, the reverse image, the sudden slippage, the lowered guard."[53] Some gay men and lesbians in the early twentieth century left a remarkable record of such gay interpretations by filling scrapbooks with newspaper clippings that they read this way: a photo of Greta Garbo and her companion, Mercedes D'Acosta, walking together in pants; an article about two boys filing suit to claim a portion of the estate of the gentleman who had "kept" them; stories about women suing for divorce because their husbands wanted longtime male companions to share their homes. They also preserved pictures that gave them a special gay pleasure: West Point cadets and fraternity boys decked out in drag for a school play, basketball players and other handsome young men performing various tasks in various states of undress. Carl Van Vechten kept a Boston Navy Yard visitor's pass in his scrapbook, probably because of the delight its last line gave him: "This pass does not allow you to discuss or to engage in any business or trade while in the Navy Yard." Men also learned how to read the paper for news of gay men murdered by the tough young men they had picked up and taken home to their apartments. Although the stories almost never explained how the murderers got into the men's apartments and never identified the murders as gay-related, gay men read them as accounts of anti-gay violence, as the profusion of such newspaper clippings in their scrap-books demonstrate.[54]

Some men even placed carefully coded classified ads in newspapers and magazines in order to contact other gay men. Two such ads appeared in the New York Herald in April 1905, although the doctor who discov-ered them considered them unusual. A quarter-century later, Broadway Brevities claimed that romance magazines with correspondence depart-ments ran messages in every issue designed to put homosexuals in touch with one another. "Want to correspond with temperamental artist, musi-cian, writer or actor who is interested in the better things of life," ran their parody of the typical ad.[55] According to Donald Vining, some gay men ran ads for "roommates" in the Sunday New York Times in the 1940s in order to meet other men. The men could make new friends or at least spend a pleasant afternoon with the men wise to the system who stopped by "to see the apartment"—and simply tell those who called gen-uinely looking for a room that it had already been taken.[56]

Numerous artists of the 1920s and 1930s, some of them widely known to be gay within the gay world if not beyond it, produced work that fairly bristled with gay meanings. "Noël Coward was the Mount Everest of double entendre," recalled one gay fan of the gay playwright, and Cole Porter's songs were mainstays in gay culture.[57] Some perform-ers were so well known for the gay-tinged double entendre of their lyrics that their performances drew large audiences of gay men. Whether or not the other members of the audience noticed them, they were aware of their numbers in the audience and often shared in the collective excite-ment of transforming such a public gathering into a "gay space," no matter how covertly. Judy Garland's concerts would take on this charac-ter in later years; Beatrice Lillie's concerts were among the most famous such events in the early 1930s. "The Palace was just packed with queers, for weeks at a time, when Lillie performed," remembered one man who had been in the audience. One of her signature songs, "There Are Fairies at the Bottom of Our Garden," was a camp classic in the gay world, and twenty years later Lillie noted that she still "always" got requests for it from her audience. Her rendition of "I'm a Campfire Girl" was also always a hit.[58]

Gay men, in other words, used gay subcultural codes to place them-selves and to see themselves in the dominant culture, to read the culture against the grain in a way that made them more visible than they were supposed to be, and to turn "straight" spaces into gay spaces. When they read the classified ads, watched films starring Greta Garbo or Bette Davis, or listened to Cole Porter's songs, they appropriated them for the gay world and thus extended the boundaries of the gay world far beyond those officially tolerated.

While gay argot allowed gay men to communicate secretly in straight settings, its most important effect was to help men mediate the contradictions produced in their lives by their stigmatization as non-men. By foregrounding the idiom of sexual inversion that was central to gay representation, gay argot served both to mark gay men's sense of themselves as feminized and to challenge the social order that had feminized and marginalized them. The slang expressions used by gay men to describe the social situations in which they revealed their homosexuality are particularly telling in this context, for such expressions often hinged on (and thus emphasized) the difference between the "masculinity" of the personas they normally presented in public and the supposed "femininity" of the inner homosexual self, which expressed a "womanlike" sexual desire for men. Most of the expressions played on the image of gay men as "long-hairs" to graphically represent the gay self as a woman, whose femininity was revealed when "she" stopped hiding her hair. Men commonly described one gay man's efforts to drop hints to another man that he was gay, often in an effort to determine whether the second man was also, as "dropping [hair] pins" or—calling on a different but related image—as "dropping beads all over." Calling on the same imagery, men also spoke of "letting their hair down" when they abandoned the pretense of their masculine, heterosexual personas. In 1946, for instance, one man recorded the reaction among his friends when a man who had long claimed to be straight had "let his hair down completely and [made] no bones about his being as queer as anyone else. . . . Last night he was 'high,' and the hair was all over the pavement, to everyone's amusement."[59]

The phrase was one of many gay men had appropriated from women's culture. By the late 1930s "letting one's hair down" (with the general meaning of letting one's guard down) appears to have been unselfconsciously adopted by nongay men as well, for whom, however, it did not have same peculiar cultural resonance. It nonetheless continued to be useful, in the right context, as a coded homosexual reference. A story recounted in 1945 by Donald Vining makes this clear, and also accentuates the phrase's camp origins. Vining was with a group of gay men who had befriended a woman despondent over her unhappy marriage (and who did not realize that her new friends were gay): "Bob's smooching was just what she needed and she flitted from the arms of one [man] to another and said, 'It's wonderful to be the only girl here with all these boys.'" "'You just think you're the only girl,'" one of the men snapped, which brought a dirty look from Bob, the host, and "the remark 'If you don't keep your hair up, I'm going to kick you.'"[60]

The banter Vining recorded also illustrates the ease with which most men switched back and forth between a straight persona and a gay one, and the sort of repartee typical of camp culture and sensibility. The idiom of sexual inversion invoked by "letting one's hair down" was the central aspect of camp, the name gay men as early as the 1920s had given their most distinctive, and characteristic, cultural style. ("You are a camp" was a common gay expression meaning "You are a riot, very witty," one man explained around 1922.)[61] Camp represented a critical perspective on the world—or, more accurately, a stance in relation to the world—that derived from gay men's own experience as deviants.

Camp was at once a cultural *style* and a cultural *strategy*, for it helped gay men make sense of, respond to, and undermine the social categories of gender and sexuality that served to marginalize them. As the anthropologist Esther Newton argued in her pathbreaking study of 1960s female impersonators, camp was a style of interaction and display that used irony, incongruity, theatricality, and humor to highlight the artifice of social convention, sometimes exaggerating convention to the point of burlesquing it, sometimes inverting it to achieve the same end.[62] The drag queen thus epitomized camp, and any verbal play that questioned gender categories, such as the man's quip, recorded by Vining, that questioned whether the woman was the only "girl" present, embodied it.

By playing on the artificiality of social roles and mocking the conventions of gender, camp helped many men mediate the contradictions they had to confront between their status as males socialized to be men and the status ascribed to them by the dominant culture as non-men or pseudo-women. Camp humor represented one way men expressed their anger at the marginalization and loss of gender status that followed from their being grouped with women. But camp also represented some gay men's recognition of the artificiality of social roles—of the cultural contingency and radical "unnaturalness" of the social order—that grew out of their personal struggles with those contradictions and their recognition that conventional "masculine" roles were "unnatural" to them. It resulted as well from their acute awareness of the artificiality of the roles they regularly played in the many social settings in which they needed to "pass" as straight.[63] Such a realization had highly subversive implications at a time when the social order represented itself as natural and preordained, for it allowed gay men to question the very premise of their marginalization. The social order denounced gay men as "unnatural"; through camp banter gay men highlighted the unnaturalness of the social order itself.

Often disowned when they revealed their homosexuality to their natal families, gay men also used camp culture to undermine the "natural" categories of the family and to reconstitute themselves as members of fictive kinship systems. Many gay men adopted the idiom of kinship to delineate their relationships with other gay men. The use of such terminology was hardly universal, and, like most aspects of camp culture, was more common among fairies than queers, but it also cropped up occasionally and playfully in the banter of more conventional men. Most commonly, gay men called each other "sisters," thereby signaling their identification with and allegiance to other men like themselves. Men involved in relationships sometimes called themselves "friends" or "lovers," but men involved in relationships in which they enacted—to widely varying degrees—the gendered division of labor and sexual roles characteristic of "normal" families, often defined themselves as "husbands" and "wives." Gay culture also used the idiom of kinship to map the boundaries of social relationships, replicating the injunctions against "incest" and defining endogamous and exogamous relationships. "Sisters" were never "married" to each other; "wives" were usually not involved with other "wives"; and in the world of fairies and trade, "men" were not even involved with "men." Moreover, elderly men in the community were often called "aunties" (and, less commonly but more respectfully, "mothers"), which signaled their seniority, their presumed wisdom and social authority, and sometimes their removal from the field of potential sexual partners. The use of such terminology inverted and thus undermined the "natural" categories of the family, but by reinvesting them with meaning it also confirmed their significance. Like other aspects of gay culture, gay men's use of the idiom of kinship struck a delicate balance between violating and reaffirming the conventions of the dominant culture.[64]

BUILDING A COLLECTIVE IDENTITY: DRAG BALLS AND GAY CULTURE

Gay men created cultural institutions and rituals that fostered a sense of collective identity, much as the ethnic theater and dances of immigrant groups did. The most prominent of these were the drag (or transvestite) balls, some of which drew thousands of participants in the 1920s. The balls, the largest and most significant collective events of gay society, were highly representative of the organization of the gay subculture and its relationship to the dominant culture. Although drag balls, at which gay men dressed in women's clothes and danced together, were quintessential gay institutions, they were not the unique creations of gay men. Like most social practices of the gay subculture, they were patterned on—but gave new meaning to—the practices of the dominant culture that gay men had observed and participated in.

Masquerade balls had a centuries-long tradition and were common events at the turn of the century. In the vice districts of the 1880s and 1890s, masquerades were major affairs, known for the promiscuous intermingling they encouraged among people from different classes. "Every patron is in disguise, with a mask covering at least the upper third of the face," reported Ralph Werther, who often attended the balls in drag, "and the millionaire and the thief dance and flirt together."[65] The most infamous of these events was the French Ball, held annually from 1866 to 1901 and frequently denounced by moral reformers during the Lexow Commission's investigation of police corruption.[66] More restrained versions of masquerade were immensely popular throughout New York society. They captured the fancy of the city's social elite, and even men's fraternal orders sponsored masquerades, which the organizers sometimes invited their lady friends to attend in male garb while they dressed as women.[67] Youth clubs in the tenement districts, which organized dances on a regular basis, also organized occasional masquerade balls at which dancers competed for prizes for the best costumes.[68] They were important fund-raisers for the clubs, as well as festive social occasions in themselves, and they most likely served as the model for the balls the Liberal Club and other bohemian groups began to organize in the Village in the 1910s. The police issued licenses for 173 masquerade balls in 1931 alone, and it is certain that many more unlicensed balls were held as well.

Like Halloween parades and certain other street festivals and carnivals, masquerades created liminal cultural spaces in which people could transgress—and, simultaneously, confirm—the social boundaries that normally divided them and restricted their behavior. Inversions of race, class, and gender status were central to the conceit of the balls, where participants wore masks and clothing inappropriate to their status. As the *New York Herald Tribune* reported in its account of a 1934 Greenwich Village ball:

> Blonds equipped themselves with dark hair. Caucasians came disguised as Orientals. Mongoloid individuals blackened their faces and appeared as Ethiopians. Negroes powdered their skins and dressed as Scandinavian villagers. College boys masqueraded as hoboes. Waitresses and soda clerks wore full evening dress. Men danced with women in men's clothes. Women danced with men in women's clothes. And strange androgynous couples careened about the floor oblivious to the workings of society and nature.[69]

As the last sentence suggests, gay men and lesbians participated in some of the masquerade balls. Gay men attended the scandalous Lower East Side balls in drag, and the balls held in Greenwich Village and Harlem in the 1920s attracted growing numbers of gay participants. They were able to attend some balls because the setting made it difficult to distinguish them from other participants. They were tolerated—and even welcomed—at other balls precisely because their presence contributed to the conceit of inversion already central to the affairs. But homosexuals were harassed at still other balls, perhaps because, as the *Herald Tribune*'s hostile tone suggests, *their* cross-dressing seemed less a masquerade than an expression of their genuine perversion of "the workings of society and nature."

Gay men thus drew on a long tradition when they began organizing their own masquerades—or drags, as they usually called them—in the late nineteenth century. Like most gay institutions, gay drag balls did not emerge *sui generis* in the gay world, but were subcultural adaptations of the institutions and social practices of the dominant culture. Like most of the establishments frequented by gay men, originally they were neither organized by them nor exclusively homosexual in patronage, but rather were places that for some reason tolerated their presence. Gay men first carved out space for themselves in institutions dominated by other groups, and only re-created them as their own as their numbers grew and as cultural and political conditions permitted or required.

Gay men had begun organizing their own drags by the 1890s. A North Carolina medical student visiting New York around 1890, it will be recalled, visited a ball at the Lower East Side's Walhalla Hall, where he found some five hundred same-sex male and female couples "waltzing sedately to the music of a good band." In 1896 a doctor reported being told that "'the Fairies' of New York," a group he thought must be a secret society, organized balls like those in Europe where "men adopt the ladies' evening dress."[70] In the 1910s and 1920s, one group of gay men sponsored an annual drag at the Little Beethoven assembly room in the rear of a saloon on East Fifth Street near the Bowery, and another held an annual affair at a hall near Columbus Circle. By the mid-1920s the Village's Webster Hall was the site of an annual gay and lesbian drag ball as well as numerous other masquerades attended by homosexuals. Smaller drags were sponsored in the late twenties and early thirties by the proprietors of out-of-the-way dives, such as Frank's Place in Brooklyn, where gay civilians in drag danced with sailors from the nearby Navy Yard at dances held every two weeks.[71]

In the 1910s and early 1920s, Thanksgiving was the occasion for one of the most significant—and largest—of the annual balls. Since the mid-nineteenth century, Thanksgiving had been celebrated by children and youths from the tenement districts of New York with "ragamuffin parades." As the white novelist William Dean Howells observed in 1907, "The poor recognize [Thanksgiving] as a sort of carnival. They go about in masquerade on the eastern avenues, and the children of the foreign races who populate the quarter penetrate the better streets, blowing horns, and begging of the passers." The African-American novelist Alice Dunbar-Nelson witnessed the "quaint New York custom" in 1928: "The streets are full of 'Ragamuffins'—kids dressed in ridiculous Hallowe'en costumes, begging for pennies." By dressing in outlandish costumes and invading middle-class neighborhoods to beg for treats, poor children inverted the meaning of a holiday that "respectable" Americans devoted to the consecration of American identity and the giving of thanks for prosperity. By holding an annual drag ball on Thanksgiving, gay men both built on the day's tradition of masquerade and expanded the inversion it implied. On a day that celebrated the family, they assembled to celebrate their membership in a gay family.[72]

The popularity and social cachet of the drags grew tremendously during the 1920s, when the general cultural ethos engendered by Prohibition and the laissez-faire attitude of the police under the administration of Mayor Jimmy Walker tended to sanction such flouting of convention. By the late 1920s, six or seven enormous affairs were staged every year in some of the city's largest and most reputable halls, including Madison Square Garden and the Astor Hotel in midtown, the Manhattan Casino (later renamed the Rockland Palace), the Alhambra, and the Savoy Ballroom in Negro Harlem, and the New Star Casino in Italian Harlem. As we have seen, the Hamilton Lodge ball held every February in Harlem drew thousands of dancers and spectators and was the largest and best-known such event in the city. By the beginning of the thirties some observers remarked that New York's drag balls had surpassed those of Chicago and New Orleans in size and opulence, and that the city rivaled Berlin in its tolerance of such affairs.[73]

One observer described the scene at a 1933 ball:

On the floor of the hall, in every conceivable sort of fancy dress, men quaver and palpitate in each other's embrace. Many of the "effeminates" are elaborately coiffured, in the powdered head dresses of the period of Madame Pompadour. They wear the billowy, ballooning skirt of that picturesque pre-guillotine era. . . . [O]thers wear the long, tight-fitting gowns which were a recent vogue . . . [while] still others wear the long, trailing skirts and the constricting corsets of the 1880's—yards of elaborately furbelowed material, frou-frouing behind them, when space permits.[74]

Like the cafeterias, speakeasies, and cabarets frequented by homosexuals, the drag balls organized by lesbians and gay men were subject to raids and other forms of police harassment, since the police and the courts construed the disorderly-conduct statute in ways that criminalized any public gathering of homosexuals. The drags faced special legal difficulties as well, because a New York State law prohibited people from appearing in public in disguise or masquerade. The law had been enacted in 1846 to control farmers protesting rural land rents who sometimes disguised themselves to elude the authorities, but by the turn of the century the police used it primarily to harass cross-dressing men and women on urban streets.[75] The police were swift to raid unauthorized drag balls, sometimes arresting everyone in attendance. Smaller drags were especially likely to be targeted. The police raided Frank's Place near the Brooklyn Navy Yard one night in the summer of 1931, for instance, ending its series of drags for good. And although men were safer at drag parties held in private homes, even these were subject to raids. In 1938 a gay man called Mona showed an undercover investigator a picture of himself in a gown that had been taken at a party he said was later raided, resulting in the arrest of nine or ten "fairies."[76]

Nonetheless, gay organizers were often able to secure police authorization for their balls. One provision of the law prohibiting disguise permitted people to appear in masquerade so long as they were going to a masquerade ball licensed by the police, and gay men seized the opportunities provided by this exemption. The organizers of gay drags secured the official sponsorship of fraternal or neighborhood groups in which they had influence, such as the Hamilton Lodge, or simply created their own. These groups applied for the licenses that made drag balls legal.[77]

The resulting arrangement was anomalous indeed. On almost every score the drags should have been illegal and subject to constant harassment. But their licenses allowed them to become quite public affairs, advertised in the press and by invitations distributed up and down Broadway (see figure 11.1), and held in some of the city's most respectable ballrooms and hotels. At the largest of them, uniformed policemen provided security, keeping the crowds that gathered outside the hall from harassing (or simply overwhelming) the dancers as they arrived, and circulating within the hall to ensure order.[78]

The presence of the police within the halls was a mixed blessing. Some of them seem genuinely to have enjoyed attending the affairs and interacting with the drag queens there (one man remembered being flattered when a policeman earnestly urged him to compete in the fashion contest at a drag held around 1930).[79] But other officers were determined to impose their own sense of order on the festivities, enforcing standards of behavior different from those the organizers would have established. The legal fiction that permitted gay balls to receive police protection—their masquerade, as it were, as conventional masquerade balls—was fragile, fraught with tension and curious paradoxes. The drag organizers could allow men to dance together, for instance, so long as one (or both) of them wore a dress, but if both of them were wearing pants the police might force the organizers to stop them. (This also happened at the predominantly heterosexual masquerades at Webster Hall. At one dance held in 1917, an undercover agent saw the dance's organizer, Bobby

Edwards, censure two gay men for "being indecent," but later overheard Edwards assure them that he had done so only at the insistence of the police.)[80] As in many other settings, two men could publicly interact in a sexually charged manner so long as one of them made it clear he was playing the woman's part.

Dancers surrounded by other gay men in a gay-organized setting often tested the limits placed on their behavior, however, forcing the drags' sponsors into the difficult position of mediating between them and the police. Two of the last big drags of the 1930–31 season were called off after mounting tensions with the police (due in part to the growth of such same-sex dancing, as well as broader shifts in the Depression-era political climate) led the organizers to fear that the police might raid them.

As the growth of same-sex dancing suggests, many men found attending the balls to be an intoxicating experience, their "one-night-a-year freedom." Some were emboldened by the thrill of gathering with hundreds of other openly gay men at an event celebrating their style and grace, and they left the balls unwilling, at least for a moment, to accept the usual constraints on their behavior. Rather than hide on their way home from the balls, some refused to bundle into cabs but marched daringly through the streets. In 1929 two twenty-five-year-old hotel telephone operators leaving a ball sauntered up Broadway to a restaurant near their apartment on Seventy-second Street. Attired in a "Spanish shawl and beautiful red flaming dress" and other women's clothes, according to *Variety*, they attracted a crowd, which turned hostile and followed them into the restaurant, "almost causing a small riot." They had to be "rescued" by a patrolman who took them to a police station, where they almost caused another riot by asking a newspaper reporter for a powder puff.[81]

Men who stopped in restaurants after a ball were often refused service or harassed by other customers, and frequently protested their treatment. After leaving the 1931 Hamilton Lodge ball, a nineteen-year-old ballet dancer walked into Drake's restaurant on West Forty-second Street attired in "a long lavender gown, hennaed wig, a large black velvet cape and silver slippers," according to *Variety*, which added that "his boy friend was attired in mufti." When the management refused to serve him he was "indignant" and "demanded an explanation, stamping his silver slippers on the floor." A passing patrolman tried to defuse the situation by suggesting that the dancer simply "go home with [his] friend." Adamant that he had the right to be served at the restaurant, the dancer refused to leave—which resulted in his being arrested and sentenced to fifteen days in the workhouse.[82] These incidents highlight the official and extralegal repercussions facing gay men who dared to be visible on the streets, but also illustrate the sense of entitlement to a place in the world that they took from the balls.

Not surprisingly, the balls and their organizers occupied an honored place in gay culture. "For weeks beforehand he plans and prepares his costume for one of these balls," a researcher commented about one man who was "a constant attendant at the drags" of the thirties. "The happenings at such a function serve him as a topic of conversation for weeks afterward."[83] Every gay novel published in the early 1930s paid homage to the drags,[84] and the men who organized them were among the major personalities of gay society: H. Mann in the Village in the 1910s, Jackie Mason in the Village and midtown in the 1920s and 1930s, and Phil Black in Harlem from the 1930s through the 1960s.

The balls were a particular source of pride for the fairies who were ordinarily derided by "normals" and "normal"-looking queers alike. "They admired us—they were *dazzled* by us," exulted one black man who frequented Harlem's balls in the twenties. Word had it, he recalled, that the onlookers filling the balconies and crowding the entryways included numerous downtown fashion designers who had come up to see the gowns. "What we wore to the ball one year," he claimed, "you'd see offered in the best shops the next season." Whether or not this was the case, his conviction that it was shows the pride with which he regarded the affairs.[85]

The theater of the drag balls enhanced the solidarity of the gay world and symbolized the continuing centrality of gender inversion to gay culture, much as ethnic parades and festivals helped establish the solidarity of the ethnic community by bringing people together and constructing a sense of common culture.[86] The "drag queens" or "fairies" on display at the balls embodied camp culture in their inversion (and often burlesque) of gender conventions. The organized program of the drags served to emphasize even further the role of the "queen" as the symbolic embodiment of gay culture. The central event of the largest drags was the "parade of the fairies," followed by a costume contest offering cash prizes and often judged by a delegation of literary or stage celebrities. At the appointed hour, a hundred or more contestants paraded through the crowd and then marched down a long elevated runway in the center of the hall to the applause and delighted screams of spectators. "Some [men] in a trailing cloud of feathers," one observer recorded, "rival birds of paradise or peacocks. Great plumed head-dresses nod and undulate from their shapely heads." Another mentioned "their gorgeous and daring gowns shimmer[ing] beneath the glaring lights." Some costumes used different (but still quintessentially camp) techniques to achieve the same dramatic effect. At one drag at the Savoy Ballroom, Carl Van Vechten joined the writer Muriel Draper and the wealthy painter Bob Chanler in awarding first prize to a young man almost "stark naked, save for a decorative cache-sex and silver sandals, and . . . painted a kind of apple green."[87] The balls literally put the queens in the spotlight.

Many queer-identified men were appalled by the dominant public image of homosexuals created by the audacious behavior of fairies on the streets, of course. Not surprisingly, some of them were aghast at the "flagrant" displays at the balls. As one man insisted to a doctor in the 1930s, "I went to a drag in Harlem once but it made me sick."[88]

But the balls also evoked more complex responses from queer men. Many men who would never have considered wearing feminine clothing in other settings put on a bit of makeup or a somewhat unconventional costume to attend. Other men who rejected the style of the fairies for themselves nonetheless attended the balls as spectators (something rarely acknowledged by press accounts, which assumed that the only queers at the balls were on the dance floor in costume). In the gay cultural space the balls created, queers could acknowledge their affinity, however contested, with the fairies in a culture in which all gay men were stigmatized as non-men, and they often applauded the audacity and skill of the "queens." Their response to the balls was not unlike that of many second-generation immigrants to the ethnic festivals and theater organized by their parents' generation, for it involved a complex mixture of self-recognition, embarrassment, and defiant pride. The drags, like ethnic theater for other groups, represented a "purer" (or exaggerated), but still familiar, expression of the everyday culture of most gay men. They simultaneously evoked embarrassment at the failure to assimilate they highlighted, and pride at the resistance to the conventions of the dominant culture they celebrated.[89]

The number and size of New York's drag balls in the 1920s and 1930s indicates the cohesion and scale of the gay world in those years. The very fact that hundreds (and sometimes thousands) of gay people attended them provides singular evidence of the vigor and extent of the social ties that bound gay men, since such large-scale events simply could not have been organized without the existence of the elaborate social networks that constituted the gay subculture. The fact that participants traveled hundreds of miles to attend the balls, and that others could compare New York's balls to those of Chicago, New Orleans, and Berlin shows that New York's gay world was part of a larger gay subculture.

While the balls reflected the existence of an extensive gay subculture, they also extended the reach of that subculture. Although many of the gay friendship circles in which individuals were involved were overlapping, others were wholly separate, and none were large enough to bring more than a fraction of the city's gay men into contact with one another.

The innumerable gay social networks based in restaurants and private party circuits constituted gay society, but they linked men to a collective gay world in only an abstract way. The balls made the existence and scope of that world manifest. In a culture hostile to gay men, the balls confirmed their numbers by bringing thousands together. In a world that disparaged their culture, it was at the drag balls, more than any place else, that the gay world saw itself, celebrated itself, and affirmed itself.

Figure 11.1. Gay life became extraordinarily visible in the late 1920s and early 1930s, as these 1931–32 banner headlines from the front page of *Broadway Brevities* indicate. Possibly written by a gay man (using various sexually tinged pseudonyms), the headlines display a remarkable familiarity with gay slang. *(From* Broadway Brevities, *various dates, 1931–32.)*

Chapter 11

"PANSIES ON PARADE": PROHIBITION AND THE SPECTACLE OF THE PANSY

GAY MEN HAD BEEN VISIBLE IN THE STREETS OF NEW YORK AND IN SOME OF its nightspots at least since the end of the nineteenth century. But in the Prohibition years of 1920–33, they acquired unprecedented prominence throughout the city, taking a central place in its culture. As a "pansy craze" swept through New York, they became the subject of newspaper headlines, Broadway dramas, films, and novels. The drag balls they organized attracted thousands of spectators, and the nightclubs where they performed became the most popular in the city. Visible gay life moved from the margins of the city—from the waterfront and the Bowery, Harlem, and Greenwich Village—into Times Square, the city's most prestigious cultural center.

The development of the pansy craze and the complex cultural politics of homosexuality during the era of jazz and Prohibition can be traced most clearly in Times Square, the central stage of New York nightlife and high culture alike and the city's major tourist attraction. The Square's theaters and nightclubs made it the "crossroads of the world" and the preeminent symbol of the city to the rest of the nation.[1] It was in the Square that the city's boosters, its cultural elite, and its political leaders saw the city represent itself to itself. The role given gay culture in such a setting reveals much about its status in the city's culture as a whole and offers illuminating new perspectives on the cultural upheavals wrought by Prohibition.

THE GROWTH OF A GAY ENCLAVE IN TIMES SQUARE

A gay enclave had quietly developed in Times Square before the 1920s because the theater and the district's other amusement industries attracted large numbers of gay men who worked as chorus boys, actors, stagehands, costume designers, and publicity people; waiters and club performers; busboys and bellhops.* Gay men did not enjoy unalloyed acceptance in this work environment, to be sure, but the theatrical milieu did offer them more tolerance than most workplaces. As one man who had been a theatrical writer in the mid-1910s observed, "The New York theatrical world [of that era was] . . . a sort of special world . . . with its own standards of fellowship [and] sexual morals."[3] Homosexuality, along with other unconventional sexual behavior, was regarded in an unusually open-minded way by people who were themselves often stigmatized because of the unconventional lives they led as theater workers. Some men could be openly gay among their coworkers, and many others were at least unlikely to suffer serious retribution if their homosexuality were discovered.†

As in the Village, the eccentricity attributed to theater people and "artistic types" in general provided a cover for many men who adopted widely recognized gay styles in their dress and demeanor. "The neighborhood is full of theatrical boarding houses . . . with their scandals, their romances, their literary discussions," the *Sun* observed in a 1903 description of the Square's black theater workers that pointed to the same signs that would have been used to identify homosexuals. "In no other quarter of New York can there be found such elaboration of manners and of the picturesque combination of colors in dress as are to be found in the boarding house parlors."[5] Even the most "obvious" gay men stood out less in Times Square.

Many men working in the amusement district lived there as well, and they were joined by other gay men who appreciated the advantages of the

---

*It is impossible to trace the involvement of gay men in any industry with precision, of course, given the absence of the census records historians normally use for such purposes, and I offer no estimates of the rate of their participation. My claim is not that gay workers predominated in the theater, hotel, or restaurant industries, but simply that disproportionately large numbers of gay men worked in them, and that many of them enjoyed greater tolerance in them than they would have elsewhere. This assertion is based primarily on the accounts I gathered in my interviews with men who worked in the industry or were otherwise familiar with it.[2]

†Although a single letter should not be given too much weight, it is striking that in a review of some one hundred sodomy cases heard between the 1880s and 1930s, the only letter found from an employer to a judge in support of an employee convicted of sodomy was from the manager of a theater company, in the case of an actor convicted in 1914. The employer professed "surprise at the charge," to which the actor had already pleaded guilty, and asked for the court's mercy in sentencing in the terms most likely to be persuasive, "because this experience will be indelibly impressed in his life, and because I believe he will prove himself worthy of mercy shown to him."[4]

transient housing the district offered. Times Square and, to the west of Eighth Avenue, Hell's Kitchen together formed one of the major centers of housing for single adults in the city, and in many respects constituted a prototypical furnished-room district, the sort of neighborhood dominated by a nonfamily population in which, as the Chicago sociologists discovered in the 1920s and historians such as Mark Peel and Joanne Meyerowitz have more recently remarked, unconventional sexual behavior was likely to face relatively little community opposition.[6] One gay man who had migrated to New York from his rural North Carolina home as a teenager in 1922 recalled that in "the theatrical district [then] . . . they wasn't too hinkty about who rented a room, and they was kinda bohemian and minded their own business. They were more liberal, more tolerant."[7] The district offered rooming houses, theatrical boardinghouses, and small residential and transient hotels serving theater workers, as well as most of the city's elegant bachelor apartments.[8]

Middle-class men tended to live to the north and east of the Square in the West Forties and Fifties, where many of the city's fashionable apartment hotels designed for affluent bachelors were clustered, and where many of the elegant old rowhouses between Fifth and Sixth Avenues had been converted into rooming houses as the intrusion of commerce resulted in the departure of their original residents.[9] The theater district bustled to the west, the fashionable, expensive East Side was taking shape to the east, and the streets of the East and West Fifties, "once given over to the homes of New York's wealthiest families," one observer noted in 1932, were "now filled with smart little shops, bachelor apartments, residential studios and fashionable speakeasies."[10] The men who lived there included some of the more successful of the writers and artists who had fled Greenwich Village in the wake of the commercialization and "decline" of that neighborhood in the early twenties. They were "the *Smart Set* and *Vanity Fair* people," fellow literatus Max Eastman recalled of the literati who moved to this neighborhood, "the writers and artists who, while leading an unconventional life, were financially successful, and in whose aspirations present-day success played a major though unacknowledged part."[11] By the twenties, the presence of such artists, intellectuals, and theatrical folk gave the West Fifties "something of the Greenwich Village atmosphere, minus the night life," according to a 1925 guide, and led some to refer to the neighborhood as "Uptown Bohemia."[12]

Another, poorer group of men lived to the west of the Square in the tenements of Hell's Kitchen and the cheaper hotels and rooming houses to be found in the Fifties west of Seventh Avenue and Broadway. Many gay men, for instance, lived in the Men's Residence Club, a former YMCA hotel at West Fifty-sixth Street and Eighth Avenue; a number of the theatrical boardinghouses in the area housed gay men; and some tenement apartments served as collective homes for the poorest of gay theater workers.[13] Groups of theater and restaurant workers were joined by gay teenagers forced out of their natal homes by hostile parents, gay migrants from the American heartland, hustlers, gay bartenders, and men who had more conventional jobs elsewhere in the city but who valued the security and convenience such housing offered. The district also included numerous transient hotels and rooming houses where male (or heterosexual) couples who had met in a bar or on the street could rent a room for an hour.[14]

The men who lived and worked in the district formed the core of a social world—or several social worlds, really—in which men who both lived and worked elsewhere could participate. Times Square served as the primary social center for many such nonresidents, the place where they met their friends, built their strongest social ties, "let their hair down," and constructed public identities different from those they maintained at work and elsewhere in the straight world. They built a gay world for themselves on the basis of the ties they developed in the commercial institutions entrepreneurs had developed to serve the needs of the theater workers rooming in the district and the tourists who flocked there.

Many gay men patronized the speakeasies located in the Fifties just west of Fifth Avenue, and the small, moderately priced restaurants, mostly Italian, that lined the West Forties and that served the large population of single men living in the area.[15] So many gay men visited or lived in the area that a man who had worked as a hustler in New York since the mid-twenties claimed in the mid-thirties that "all [the] restaurants and barrooms between Forty-third and Fifty-ninth, east and west, are just packed with [homosexuals]," and estimated that "one out of four [men] in these places is a homosexual."[16] As he suggested, gay men mingled with other customers in most of the area's restaurants and bars, rather than clustering in a few, exclusively gay places; although a few restaurants, such as Louis' and the Jewel, and numerous cafeterias and Automats became known as gay meeting places in the 1920s and 1930s (see chapter 6). Even if he overstated the case considerably, the very fact that he perceived such a pervasive homosexual presence in the area's restaurants is telling. People often referred to the hectic streets of the theater district as the "Frenzied Forties," but *Broadway Brevities,* the one paper that delighted in identifying the haunts of even the most discreet gay men, went on to nickname the residential area just north of it as the "Faggy Fifties."[17]

PROHIBITION AND THE PANSY CRAZE

Gay life in Times Square remained largely invisible to outsiders until the 1920s, when the area changed dramatically, in ways that made its gay

world larger, more secure, and more visible. In the eyes of many contemporaries, Prohibition and the decline of the theater industry combined to transform the Square in the 1920s from a genteel theater district to a "tawdry" amusement district, a development only hastened by
the onset of the Depression.[18] Although the theater industry appeared to
thrive through most of the prosperous twenties, with entrepreneurs
building new theaters in the blocks north of Forty-second Street and
Broadway enjoying its most successful season ever in 1927–28, when
264 new shows opened in the district, the boom masked the worsening
structural problems of the industry. The burgeoning movie business was
offering competition to stage shows throughout the country in the
twenties, undermining New York's own theater industry by precipitat-
ing a collapse in the national theatrical road circuits in which New
York–based companies had played the central role. The crisis con-
fronting the industry became evident in 1929, when a fifth of Times
Square's theaters stood empty during the Christmas season, normally
the busiest time of the year. While the district's newest theaters continued to do well, some of the oldest and most vulnerable of them—particularly those clustered on Forty-second Street between Seventh and
Eighth Avenues—managed to stay open in the twenties only by convert-
ing themselves into cheap "grind" movie houses. In 1931, in the midst
of the Depression, several of them even became burlesque theaters. Both
kinds of theaters catered to an almost exclusively male and "rough"
audience, and some went so far as to let themselves be used as gay meeting grounds (as noted in chapter 7).

The effects of Prohibition on the Square's economy and moral tone
were both more abrupt and more pervasive, and helped make it possible for the gay presence in the Square to grow. The Prohibition
Amendment had been ratified in 1919 (and began being enforced
under the Volstead Act in January 1920) in large part to control public
sociability—and in particular to destroy the autonomous working-class
male culture of the immigrant saloon, which seemed so threatening to
middle-class and rural Americans. But in cities such as New York,
Prohibition resulted instead in the *expansion* of the sexual underworld
and undermined the ability of the police and anti-vice societies to control it. The economic pressures Prohibition put on the hotel industry by
depriving it of liquor-related profits, for instance, led some of the sec-
ond-class hotels in the West Forties to begin permitting prostitutes and
speakeasies to operate out of their premises.[19] Prohibition also drove
many of the district's elegant restaurants, cabarets, and roof gardens
out of business, for such establishments had depended even more heavily on liquor sales for their profitability. They were replaced, on the
one hand, by cheap cafeterias and restaurants whose profits depended

on a high turnover rate rather than a high liquor-based profit margin, and, on the other hand, by nightclubs and speakeasies whose profitability depended *wholly* on illegal liquor sales. The change was emblematized when Murray's, a famous Forty-second Street restaurant, closed in 1924, only to be replaced by Hubert's Museum, a cheap dime museum and freak show. "Forty-second Street, . . . the place where New York's Broadway sector begins, is going to seed," *Variety* warned in 1931. "More and more [it] is getting to look like 14th. No one thinks this is an accomplishment."[20]

The criminalization of liquor not only drove many respectable middle-class establishments out of the restaurant business, but resulted in the virtual criminalization of nightlife. This had far-reaching implications for the culture of the city, but one of its most immediate consequences was to undermine the policing of the city's nightlife in ways that benefited gay meeting places. The proliferation of illegal speakeasies and nightclubs after Prohibition led to the wholesale corruption of policing agencies, the systematic use of payoffs, and the development of crime syndicates that offered protection from the police. All of these measures made it easier for establishments where gay men gathered to survive, because they made them stand out less. All speakeasies—not just gay speakeasies—had to bribe the authorities and warn their customers to be prepared to hide what they were doing on a moment's notice.

Prohibition did more than contribute to the corruption of the agencies charged with policing the city's moral life. Even more distressingly, from the perspective of the city's moral guardians, the popular revolt in New York against the aims and tactics of Prohibition undermined the moral authority of such policing altogether. By 1931, the Committee of Fourteen, for one, was reduced to pleading that it had never "been interested in regulating the conduct of individuals," an objective by that time evidently in some disrepute, but had only been concerned to attack the parties "who make money out of the exploitation of girls." The onset of the Depression only exacerbated the problem. In 1932, the Committee, which had effectively prodded the police to pursue "moral criminals" since 1905, was forced to terminate its work when its traditional backers were unable or unwilling to support it any longer.[21] Mayor Jimmy Walker's popularity, by contrast, resulted in part from his highly visible participation in the city's nightlife and his implicit repudiation of Prohibition through the tacit approval he and Tammany Hall gave to the city's illegal nightclubs, including his support for the end of local enforcement of the Volstead Act.[22] Indeed, popular resistance to Prohibition seemed to undermine the respect for all forms of the law. Instead of purifying the nation by drawing a strict boundary between the acceptable and unacceptable, it threatened to blur those boundaries by encouraging many normally law-abiding citizens to break the law, to regard the police as their enemies, and to question the law's moral authority.

Although Prohibition was designed to reduce the cultural influence of immigrants, it only increased it in New York by forcing "legitimate" middle-class entrepreneurs out of business and giving effective control of middle-class nightlife to immigrants. Ethnic "gangsters" not only supplied liquor to illegal speakeasies but operated many of them, where they introduced their patrons to the "low-life" world of prostitutes, gamblers, and "coarse" working-class entertainers. Visiting speakeasies brought middle-class Anglo-Americans into close—and unexpectedly favorable—contact with Jewish, Irish, and Italian immigrants and with a criminal underworld they previously would have shunned.

Indeed, it was precisely the participation of middle-class men and (especially) women in the "immoral" and disreputable world of the speakeasies—and their apparent vogue among New Yorkers—that most concerned the city's moral guardians. "Speakeasies lend an atmosphere of apparent respectability to prostitution," the Committee of Fourteen warned in 1928. "They are attracting young women and men of a type who never would have visited the [vice resorts] which led to the organization of the Committee of Fourteen, 25 years ago; yet conditions in these speakeasies are becoming no less terrible than in those earlier [resorts]."[23] The speakeasies, they feared, were dissolving the distinctions between middle-class respectability and working-class licentiousness that had long been central to the ideological self-representation of the middle class.

The culture of the speakeasies did not mark so significant a break in the city's middle-class entertainment habits as the Committee warned in its public statements, which the Committee's senior officers well knew. Many middle-class men, at least, had frequented the resorts located in working-class neighborhoods at the turn of the century. More significant is that the conventions of middle-class sociability had been changing for more than a generation with the expansion of commercial entertainments. If the middle class had once restricted its social life to private clubs, homes, and exclusive restaurants or to formalized promenades in selected city boulevards, it had steadily moved into "public" due to the development of lobster palaces, cabarets, amusement parks, and other sites where men and women could interact more freely.[24] While much of the middle class continued to constitute itself as a class and distinguish itself from the working class, in part, through its different use of urban space, its sociability was less privatized than it had been before.

Nonetheless, the organization and culture of the speakeasies did encourage middle-class men and women to interact even more casually and to experiment further with the norms governing acceptable public sociability. Usually smaller, more informal, and more intimate than the prewar cabarets and cafés—and less extravagant in decor, given the possibility that they might be shut down at any time—the speakeasies filled the basements of the brownstones lining the side streets of Times Square; a fifth of the city's speakeasies were said to be clustered there. Many of the clubs tried to capitalize on their setting by creating an intimate and freewheeling atmosphere. Even some of the larger clubs tried to enhance their appeal by using the personalities of their hosts and hostesses, such as Texas Guinan, Helen Morgan, and Harry Richman, to create a highly individualized, almost familial atmosphere.

The speakeasies eroded the boundaries between respectability and criminality, public and private, and between commercial space and home life, for the hosts welcomed patrons into their basement hideaways as if into their homes, and encouraged them to mingle with the other guests and to spurn the conventions that normally governed their public behavior. By speaking the password and entering a "speakeasy," patrons entered an intimate theater in which each was expected to play a role; the most notable sign of this to most observers was the degree to which single men and women were encouraged to interact with each other.

Clubgoers' participation in the criminalized demimonde of the speakeasies introduced them to new social worlds and encouraged them to test the limits of social convention in other ways as well. As the historian Lewis Erenberg has remarked, speakeasies encouraged a sense of rebellion—and were regarded by the authorities *as* rebellious—because of the way they encouraged behavior that flouted public morality.[25]

It was in this context that the flamboyant gay men known as fairies (or more commonly, in the 1920s, as pansies) began to play a more prominent role in the culture and reputation of the city as whole and the Square in particular. Part of the attraction of amusement districts, after all, was that they constituted liminal spaces in which visitors were encouraged to disregard some of the social injunctions that normally constrained their behavior, allowing them to observe and vicariously experience forms of behavior that in other settings—particularly their own neighborhoods—they might consider objectionable enough to suppress. This aspect of Times Square's appeal was only enhanced by the cultural developments of the Prohibition era. The popular revolt against the moral policing of Prohibition, the transformation of the Square into a "tawdry" amusement district, and the incitement to transgression generated by the speakeasies themselves fomented a rejection of convention and an interest in the outré that both generated interest in pansies and made space for them.

Over the course of the decade, gay men became more visible in almost every setting the Square provided, including its streets, burlesque halls, theater roof gardens, and nightclubs, as well as the "legitimate" stage. Each of those settings was governed by different conventions, had different performance traditions, and provided a different sort of platform for pansies. A detailed analysis of those differences and of the role of the pansy in every aspect of the Square's culture is beyond the scope of this study. I offer instead only a preliminary map of them here. Even this brief sketch of what came to be known as the pansy craze, though, should demonstrate that gay men became a highly visible part of New York's Prohibition culture and that while they were often turned into a spectacle, some of them made this an unsettling spectacle indeed.

The Square already had something of a gay reputation in the early 1920s. One 1924 account, for example, bemoaned the number of "impudent sissies that clutter Times Square."[26] (The wording is significant, suggesting, as it does, the "shameless" or "brazen" manner—other favorite formulations—in which such men carried themselves in the face of social opprobrium.) As the Square became more of a "tawdry" amusement park, visiting the Square became more of a theatrical experience in itself, and pansies increasingly became part of the exotic spectacle clubgoers and tourists expected to see there. Thus when *Vanity Fair*'s "intimate guide to New York after dark" noted in 1931 that the tourist could see "anything" on Broadway at night, it included "pansies" among the sights along with the more predictable "song writers, college boys, . . . big shots, [and] bootleggers."[27] A New York tabloid noted the same year: "The latest gag about 2 A.M. is to have your picture taken with one or two pansies on Times Square. The queens hang out there for the novel racket."[28]

The pansies soon made their way onto the stages of Times Square as well. The district's impresarios were constantly searching for new angles that might attract a crowd, and the growing competition among the theaters, cabaret revues, nightclubs, and speakeasies encouraged them to vie with one another in challenging the conventional limits placed on entertainment and satisfying their customers' appetite for new and ever more sensational thrills, a tendency only accentuated at the end of the 1920s when the Depression devastated their industry.

The efforts of nightclub impresarios to cultivate and respond to the growing fascination of white middle-class clubgoers with African-American jazz and performance is the best-known aspect of this phenomenon, and in many ways the "Negro vogue" of the mid-twenties set the stage for the pansy craze that soon followed it. As white fascination with the burgeoning African-American world of Harlem grew in the 1920s, entrepreneurs opened clubs featuring black entertainers in Times Square as well as Harlem, including the Everglades, the Club Alabam, and the Plantation. The existence of such clubs ensured that "slummers" would not even need to leave the security of a white neighborhood or sit in an integrated audience to witness the spectacle of black "primitivism."[29] The clubs thus played on their customers' desire to feel they were transgressing the conventional boundaries of race while they resolutely confirmed them. Most of the district's restaurants refused to serve African-Americans and the police made sure few of them lingered on the district's streets, but their role in the clubs made them part of the spectacle of the Square.

Similar Prohibition-era economic pressures and cultural dynamics resulted in the pansy becoming part of the show. If whites were intrigued by the "primitivism" of black culture, heterosexuals were equally intrigued by the "perversity" of gay culture. As the gay world of Greenwich Village and Harlem grew and became more visible in the wake of World War I and the imposition of Prohibition, it evoked growing curiosity on the part of slummers, just as the black social world of Harlem did.

The growing popularity of the city's drag balls revealed the heterosexual public's growing fascination with gay culture. Hundreds of slummers had attended the Greenwich Village balls during the 1910s to catch a glimpse of "Homosexualists," but the popularity and social cachet of the drags grew tremendously during Prohibition. "During the height of the New Negro era and the tourist invasion of Harlem [in the 1920s and early 1930s]," Langston Hughes recalled a decade later, "it was fashionable for the intelligentsia and the social leaders of both Harlem and the downtown area to occupy boxes at this ball and look down from above at the queerly assorted throng on the dancing floor." The Vanderbilts, the Astors, and other pillars of respectability were often there, along with Broadway celebrities popular in the gay world, such as Beatrice Lillie, Clifton Webb, Jay Brennan, and Tallulah Bankhead.[30] By most accounts, thousands of spectators gathered to watch the biggest balls in the late 1920s and early 1930s. "FAG BALLS EXPOSED" screamed a headline in *Broadway Brevities* in 1932. "6,000 CROWD HUGE HALL AS QUEER MEN AND WOMEN DANCE."[31] (See figures 5.1 and 11.1.) By the early 1930s, they were even being staged in Madison Square Garden and the Astor Hotel in midtown.[32]

Seizing on the public's fascination with this new phenomenon, Times Square entrepreneurs began to evoke the flamboyant image of the pansy to generate business. "Pansy" acts began to appear on the stage, in the press, and in the clubs, but at this point they usually were the gay equivalent of blackface: straight actors putting on drag or stereotypical mannerisms to mimic and ridicule gay men, to the hoots and jeers of an anti-gay audience. This buffoonery became a standard feature in burlesque and high-class cabaret revues alike, which reinforced the dominant public images of homosexuals. By the 1920s, burlesque had been reduced to little more than a showcase for strippers and comedians who relentlessly played to salacious interests. A doctoral student at New York University who claimed he had attended a thousand burlesque performances in the mid-1930s to research his thesis reported that "homosexual situations [were] found in almost every performance—one man making advances to another, kissing him, 'goosing' him, etc."[33] "Queer doings" were also regularly given the spotlight in revues designed for higher-class audiences such as *The Ritz Revue* and *Artists and Models,* according to several observers, including one who went on to ask why "the public enjoy[s] seeing [such queer doings] portrayed in some of the most expensive and exclusive productions" if they "are as disgusting as [people] say they are." Such high-class revues, typically produced on the stage of theater roof gardens, focused as much as burlesque did on the spectacle of barely clothed women's bodies, but they "elevated" that spectacle, as the historian Robert T. Allen notes, by connecting it "not with the working-class sexuality of burlesque but with the cosmopolitan worldliness of Paris." Its comedians engaged in a more "sophisticated," connotative humor, which often included considerable homosexual innuendo. One reviewer wryly complained in 1924 that *The Ritz Revue,* a typical amalgam of singing, dancing, and semi-nudity, included so "many references . . . to topics so disorderly that one suspects Kraft-Ebbings [sic] to be hidden among the librettists," and he pointed especially to a sketch about the "'The Four Horse-Women' [a slang term for lesbians] and the impish 'fairy' tales that are told in the Ritz Revue" as requiring clarification for the "innocent majority of the playgoers."[34] Two years later another reviewer complained about the number "of 'third sex' species that has been seen around town of late."[35]

Homosexuality became so much a part of the cultural landscape that several plays ventured to address the topic in the mid-twenties. The Shuberts decided in 1926 to produce *The Captive,* which was regarded as a serious depiction of the "social problem" of lesbianism, and the following year Mae West attempted to bring to Broadway a farcical representation of pansy life, *The Drag.* Edouard Bournet's *Captive* was a controversial enough venture, attracting large audiences (including many young women and female couples) and provoking widely varying responses. The critic George Jean Nathan regarded it as "the most subjective, corruptive, and potentially evil-fraught play ever shown in the American theater . . . nothing more or less than a documentary in favor of sex degeneracy."[36] But many Broadway powers defended the play's effort to deal seriously with a timely issue. *Variety* hailed it as "the most daring play of the season . . . and one of the best written and acted in years."[37] The controversy generated by *The Captive* took on added significance when the newspaper magnate William Randolph Hearst turned the play into the center-piece of his campaign for a state stage censorship law.

The controversy was brought to a head in 1926 when Mae West opened *Sex,* a play she wrote and starred in, on Broadway, and announced her plan to bring a second play, *The Drag,* to New York after a series of try-outs in Connecticut and New Jersey. *The Drag* promised to offer a vigor-ous defense of the right of homosexuals to lead their lives as they saw fit. It opened with a doctor denouncing the criminalization of homosexuality. "Are we going to declare these unfortunates who through no fault of their own have been born with instincts and desires different from ours? Are we . . . going to force them into secrecy and shame, for being what they can-not help being, by branding them as criminals . . . ?" Even in the course of disagreeing with the doctor, a judge announced: "There are approximately five million homo-sexuals in the United States, and of these the great per-centage are born sexual inverts." It soon unfolded that the judge's own son was an invert, who had long hidden his homosexuality from his father. The play also highlighted the problem of police harassment. Full of references to police raids ("It was a great party but the place was raided and when they backed up the wagon, they got all but one and she jumped out the window"), the play ended with a raid on a drag ball.[38]

While reflecting the dominant culture's conception—one widely shared in the gay world—that gay men were half-women who desired "normal" men, the play also included constant references to taxi dri-vers, sailors, and other "rough trade" who found gay men sexually desirable. "I was born a male, my mind has been that of a female," one character explained. "I'm the type that men prefer," another declared. "I can . . . go through the navy yard without having the flags drop to half mast." "Listen, dearie," added yet another. "I'm just the type that men crave. The type that burns 'em up. Why, when I walk up 10th Avenue, you can smell the meat sizzling in Hell's Kitchen." When one queen told another that he had seen "your husband" the other day, the second had to ask, "Which one, dearie, which one?" The dialogue was also full of gay slang, campy repartee, and descriptions of luxurious drag gowns ("You should see the creation I'm wearing, dearie. Virginal white, no back, with oceans of this and oceans of that, trimmed with excitement in front"). The play drew much of its inspiration from its cast, about forty gay chorus boys whom West had apparently recruited at a Greenwich Village speakeasy and whom she encouraged to impro-vise on stage. Mae West had patterned much of her own stage persona on that of Bert Savoy, one of the first major female impersonators widely known to be gay. She had learned how to write this play (which she directed but did not perform in) from the gay men in her cast.[39] The play put gay men on stage to play gay men.

The play culminated with an unscripted drag ball, which lasted twenty minutes and allowed thirty of its performers to put on a "show" much as they might have at Mother Childs, at a Rockland Palace ball, or in a night-club revue. "In the playing it is exactly like a revue number, or the floor show of a nightclub," *Variety* reported in its review of the Bridgeport, Connecticut, opening; it took the sort of gay act that had become a part of Times Square's roof garden revues, dramatically expanded it, and trans-posed it to the legitimate stage. The problem was that this threatened the legitimacy of the Broadway stage. "The attempt to put the piece on at this particular juncture is the dumbest thing imaginable," *Variety* warned, clearly with Hearst's censorship campaign in mind. "If it ever gets to Broadway, it would be a calamity, just at this time, when, more than ever before, the subject of a Broadway play censor is under national agitation."[40]

Divided over whether to condemn *The Captive* or to defend it as a serious drama, Broadway united in attacking *The Drag* as a dangerous threat to the autonomy of the stage. But the police soon took the matter out of the theater industry's hands. On the night of February 9, 1927, they raided productions of *The Captive, Sex,* and a third play, *Virgin Man,* and arrested members of their casts, including Mae West herself. Most of the city's papers connected the raids to the threat of *The Drag*'s being brought to the city, as the theater historian Kaier Curtin has noted, and on the day after West's arrest, a municipal prosecutor in Bayonne, New Jersey, ordered that city's production of *The Drag* to be closed. Mae West promptly obtained a court injunction against police interfer-ence with *Sex,* and continued starring in it for six weeks before being convicted and sentenced to jail for ten days for "maintaining a public nuisance." *The Captive* also managed to secure an injunction and run for five more days before its producers decided to close it. But West never tried to bring *The Drag* to the city. Two months later, the state leg-islature amended the public obscenity code to include a ban on any play "depicting or dealing with the subject of sex degeneracy, or sex perver-sion." Four years after the state legislature had for the first time specifi-cally prohibited homosexual "lewdness" or cruising, it enacted the first law specifically banning the appearance of gay people or discussion of gay issues on the stage.[41]

Eliminating gay characters from the legitimate Broadway stage did not eliminate homosexuality from Broadway, however. Not only did homo-sexual innuendo delivered by straight performers continue to appear in cabaret revues and burlesque, but as the district began to reel from the effects of the Depression, pansies themselves began to become part of the draw in a number of the Square's best-known nightclubs. A series of arti-cles on the front page of *Variety* in 1930 and 1931 bemoaned the state of

"B'WAY'S DYING NITE CLUBS" and "BROADWAY'S LOST LURE," warning that clubgoers were deserting the clubs for cheaper and more freewheeling private parties.[42] As the clubs turned to ever more exotic acts in a desperate effort to attract a crowd in the face of this crisis, several entrepreneurs tried to imitate the success of a handful of Greenwich Village clubs in drawing tourists with "pansy shows." Not long after the onset of the Depression and end of the Negro vogue, a pansy craze seized Broadway. In 1930–31, clubs with pansy acts became the hottest in town.

Most of the gay club acts of Times Square originated in the mid-1920s in several Village clubs, which had initially offered gay-oriented entertainment to cultivate a gay following rather than to pander to tourists. Many of the entertainers were female impersonators. Jack (or Jackie) Mason, who was later to become a major impresario in professional female-impersonator circles, for instance, ran a club on Charles Street where female impersonators served as masters of ceremonies.[43] Other entertainers were simply gay men who exhibited a camp gay style on stage; as the sociologist Caroline Ware put it, demeaningly but accurately, the "favorite entertainer" at another Village speakeasy was "a 'pansy' whose best stunt was a take-off on being a 'pansy.'"[44] The Rubaiyat, a "queer Greenwich Village dive" that was the best known of the clubs, seems to have been the first to try to cultivate an uptown audience by featuring such pansy acts; it may have hoped to duplicate the success of the Greenwich Village balls in drawing slummers with the allure of homosexual exotica. The Rubaiyat began as something of a gay club—or as one hostile 1931 account stated, it catered originally to "boys with falsetto voices and girls who sang in basso profundo," who "gathered there nightly." But, the account continued, it soon began to expand its audience, attracting "the night riders and the gadabouts," sated with normal entertainments, who were "seeking new thrills." As a result, it also attracted the attention of the police, who raided it in 1930, but not before midtown producers had noticed the success of its strategy and it had started a trend.[45]

The career of Gene Malin, who starred at the Rubaiyat before it was raided and who led the movement of gay acts into midtown, illustrates the complex cultural politics of the pansy craze. Born in Brooklyn in 1908 to Polish and Lithuanian parents, Malin was a precocious teenager and took New York by storm in his early twenties. Victor Eugene James Malin took the name "Jean" Malin upon his entry into New York's gay world and when in drag also used the name of Imogene Wilson, one of the most famous of the Ziegfeld Follies showgirls. He competed for prizes at the city's drag balls while still in his mid-teens, and was said to have won prizes for an outfit of black velvet and silver lace and for several other more exotic creations consisting entirely of pink or gold feathers.

Malin worked as a chorus boy in several Broadway shows, but, after losing several jobs because he was considered too effeminate, decided to become a professional female impersonator. In the mid-1920s, while still a teenager, he began working in gay clubs in the Village, moving from Paul and Joe's to Jackie Mason's Charles Street speakeasy and eventually to the Rubaiyat. There he appeared under his drag name, probably attracted some of the people who knew him from the balls, and earned the meager sum of ten to fifteen dollars a week. His luck changed in the spring of 1930 when several Broadway columnists who saw him perform there liked his act, and one of them persuaded Louis Schwartz, part owner of the Club Abbey, to see it. Schwartz, as one columnist later explained, "saw in Malin a distinct novelty for a Broadway that was tiring of the customary masters-of-ceremonies." Deciding to give "Broadway its first glimpse of pansy night life," another columnist reported, Schwartz booked Malin at his elegant uptown club and had an immediate success, which other clubs soon imitated.[46]

By the time Malin moved his act from the Village to the Club Abbey, he had transformed his stage role from that of a female impersonator to that of a pansy. A large and imposing man, he strolled about the club, interacting with the patrons and using his camp wit to entertain them (and presumably scandalizing them with his overtly gay comments). The club's master of ceremonies and central attraction, he introduced other performers and was assisted, for a time, by Helen Morgan, Jr., a female impersonator who had taken the name of the well-known torch singer and club hostess (and gay favorite) Helen Morgan (see figure 11.2). Malin's "act" was simply to bring the camp wit of the gay subculture from Greenwich Village to the floor of one of the city's swankiest clubs, although virtually no evidence remains concerning the precise content of that act. He "wore men's clothes," one paper explained, "but [he] talked and acted like women." Some newspapers continued to call him a female impersonator, even though he wore men's clothes; others called him a male impersonator, as if his men's clothes were the only manly thing about him. In a glowing account of Malin's success at the Abbey, *Daily Mirror* columnist Mark Hellinger explained: "Standing on the floor for an hour at a time and making no bones about earning his living as a professional pansy, Malin intrigued those customers who did not resent this type of thing."

As Hellinger's account suggests, Malin was widely thought to be a pansy playing a pansy. When Malin married Christine Williams in January 1931, the *Daily News* ran the headline "JEAN MALIN MARRIES GIRL!" The article went on to remind readers that Malin was a "horticultural lad"—a common and readily understood allusion to the sort of man nicknamed

Figure 11.2. In 1931, when the pansy entertainer Jean Malin was the toast of Broadway, *Vanity Fair* published this drawing of him at the Club Abbey, where he was master of ceremonies. Malin is shown with Helen Morgan, Jr., a female impersonator. *(From* Vanity Fair, *February 1931. Courtesy* Vanity Fair. *Copyright ©* 1931 [renewed 1959] by Conde Nast Publications Inc.)

"pansy" and "buttercup"—"whose boast is 'I wear a rose in my lapel because it won't stay in my hair.'" Within a few months the papers reported that Malin and his wife had slept in twin beds on their honeymoon, and when they subsequently filed for divorce the papers called it a "one-night marriage" and agreed that the reason given for the divorce— incompatibility—"was a good one." Only *Broadway Brevities* and the *Daily Mirror* explicitly stated that Malin was a pansy, but the other papers did not need to. One column in the *Daily News* went so far to ask of Malin, "Is he —?"; it did not need to fill in the blank with the word *homosexual* or *pansy* since the editors were confident that the public presumed he *was.*

Malin, in other words, was regarded as a gay man whose nightclub act revolved around his being gay, not as a "normal" man scornfully mimicking gay mannerisms or engaging in homosexual buffoonery, as was the case in most vaudeville and burlesque routines. And although he had been imported to midtown by impresarios keen to exploit the nightclub public's fascination with sexual perversity, Malin did not abide by the conventions of pansy impersonation. That he was not isolated on a stage was significant in itself, for the conventional spatial arrangement would have served to reinforce the cultural distance between him, as a performer, and a clearly demarcated audience.[47] More significantly, his act included ridiculing the men in the audience who heckled him. Or, as one newspaper put it, his act was simply to "infuriate [the] red-blooded he-men who visited his club with their sweeties."

His very presence on the club floor elicited the catcalls of many men in the club, but he responded to their abuse by ripping them to shreds with the drag queen's best weapon: his wit. "He had a lisp, and an attitude, but he also had a sharp tongue," according to one columnist. "The wise cracks and inquiries of the men who hooted at his act found ready answer." And if hostile spectators tried to use brute force to take him on after he had defeated them with his wit, he was prepared to humble them on those terms as well. "He was a huge youth," one paper reported, "weighing 200, and a six footer. Not a few professional pugilists sighed because Jean seemed to prefer dinner rings to boxing rings." Although Malin's act remained tame enough to safeguard its wide appeal, it nonetheless embodied the complicated relationship between pansies and "normal" men. His behavior was consistent with their demeaning stereotype of how a pansy should behave, but he demanded their respect; he fascinated and entertained them, but he also threatened and infuriated them.

This was an astonishing reversal of gay men's usual fate on the stage, and it electrified segments of the gay world as well as the straight. *Broadway Brevities,* a tabloid more explicit about gay matters than other papers were, reported that after his nightclub success "the pansies hailed La Malin as their queen!," and we can well imagine that even while he dismayed those gay men who would have preferred a more conventional-seeming and respectable representative, he earned the admiration of others. Rather than hide his inclinations, he proclaimed proudly in his best-known quip that he would "rather be Spanish than mannish," a line whose significance as a parody of masculine gender imperatives was evident to all. It seems likely that many men who had been subjected to catcalls on the streets felt he stood up for *them* as much as for himself when he took on the hecklers in his audience.

A story told about Malin highlights the image he developed as a street-smart defender of his dignity as a gay man and the degree to which his fans thought his stage and offstage personas were one and the same. Published in the *Daily Mirror* after he had become famous, and presumably circulating in the gay world before then, the story explained that after winning a prize for being the "best dressed woman" at a Greenwich Village drag ball, he had wandered into a cafeteria without having bothered to change his clothes. This was, as noted in chapter 10, a common step for a man to take after experiencing the heady solidarity of a drag ball, and the heckling he started to receive from some of the other customers at the cafeteria was also fairly routine. But what happened next was not. "When a party of four rough looking birds tossed a pitcher of hot water at him as he danced by," the columnist reported, "he pitched into them. After beating three of them into insensibility, the fight went into the street, with two taxi drivers coming to the assistance of the surviving member of the original foursome." The story portrayed Malin as claiming his right to move openly through the city as a drag queen. Still, it ended on a suitable camp note. When the fight was over, Malin was said to have had tears in his eyes. Yes, he'd won the fight, he told another man, "but look at the disgraceful state my gown is in!"[48]

This sort of hostile encounter was an everyday occurrence on the streets of the city: Malin elevated it to an art in his club act, and, not the least of his successes, he briefly became the darling—and top earner—of Broadway. Given the inequalities of power in the Times Square club world and in the culture at large, it was inevitable that he would be turned into a spectacle and his act exploited for the amusement and profit of the straight world. More remarkable, however, given that context, was Malin's determination to challenge his marginalization as a gay man and his success in creating more space for the gay members of his audience and for gay culture at large.

The success of Malin's club act quickly led other clubs to hire imitators. "Before the main stem knew what had happened, there was a hand on a hip for every light on Broadway," one columnist recalled. "He established a new fashion in masters of ceremonies," declared another paper more sedately, by "creat[ing] a vogue for effeminacy" in 1930 and 1931. In September 1930, *Variety* reported in a businesslike manner that Malin's success the previous spring had inspired plans for several "nite places with 'pansies' as the main draw," and noted that Berlin and Paris, like Greenwich Village, already featured "similar night resorts, with the queers attracting the lays."[49] By November, one of *Variety*'s reviewers was complaining about the number of "fast-tempoed, 'pansy' dominated, mid-town spots."[50] The Argonaut began to feature a gay act (even Malin appeared there after leaving the Abbey), and the Club Calais opened, featuring Arthur ("Rose") Budd and Jackie Maye, "the male soprano."[51] The degree to which the pansy craze was patterned on—and temporarily supplanted— the Negro vogue was indicated when even the Everglades, which previously had featured a Southern-inflected "colored show," briefly got into the act. In December its featured performer was Francis Renault, one of the country's best-known female impersonators.[52]

The pansy craze may have reached its zenith on December 19, 1930, when a new club calling itself the Pansy Club opened across the street from the Everglades. Featuring another of the nation's best-known female impersonators, Karyl Norman, the "Creole Fashion Plate," the club sent out opening-night invitations printed in lavender ink to the "regular list of first nighters."[53] Its newspaper advertisement announced that it would feature "'something different' entitled 'PANSIES ON PARADE'" (see figure 11.3). The floor show's title was an allusion, which would have been easily recognized at the time, to the central event of the city's biggest drag balls, the "parade of the fairies" that preceded the costume contest. In announcing its intention to put "pansies on parade" the club promised to offer its patrons a safely contained, but still titillating, version of the subcultural practices of a marginalized group brought into the heart of the city's most prestigious entertainment district. Much as the old Everglades had offered its Times Square patrons an easily digestible taste of Harlem, the Pansy Club (as well as the new Everglades) offered them a palatable taste of the Village.

While pansies were featured at several of the district's nightclubs that attracted an affluent audience of society people (as well as well-heeled criminal figures, such incongruous intermingling being characteristic of Prohibition-era nightlife), they also appeared in Times Square clubs attracting a "rougher" audience of single men and women. Their different role in such clubs highlights the continuing class differences in the place of gay men in such social settings. For example, the Coffee Cliff, a nightclub on Forty-fifth Street near Broadway, just three blocks south of the Pansy Club, featured "normal" male entertainers and female singers, but at the

Figure 11.3. At the height of the pansy craze in 1930–31, a nightclub calling itself the Pansy Club opened in the heart of Times Square. The club featured a pansy chorus line and host Karyl Norman, one of the nation's best-known female impersonators. *(Advertisement in unidentified New York newspaper, December 19, 1930. From Yale Collection of American Literature, Beinecke Rare Book and Manuscripts Library, Yale University.)*

height of the pansy craze in December 1930, the management also employed a "man attired in woman's clothes, apparently a fairy, [who] was dancing with men." The master of ceremonies, who told "many indecent jokes . . . which the audience appeared to enjoy," according to an investigator, highlighted the sexual aspects of the female impersonator's character (and the association of gay men with prostitutes) by bringing him onto the floor and cracking, "How does she look? Don't she look like Polly Adler [a well-known madam]?" The club was *not* a "fairy hangout"; it catered to single men by offering them a risqué floor show, hard liquor, and the opportunity to mingle freely with the "unescorted" women, many of them prostitutes, who could be found there. Malin's appearance in an elite social setting was an unprecedented development, brought about in part by the cultural ethos of Prohibition, and it is unsurprising that the Club Abbey received the attention of the press, since the appearance of fairies in such a setting was anomalous. But the fairy's appearance in the Square's rougher clubs drew on a long history of gay visibility in such social settings. The fairy employed at the Coffee Cliff, moreover, interacted with the men there even more assertively than Malin did with his patrons. While Malin *talked* with his patrons, the fairy *danced* with his, the most intimate behavior possible in such an environment.[54]

When the pansy craze in the city's nightclubs was at its height in the winter of 1930–31, two of Times Square's three most successful clubs "depended upon 'pansy personalities' for their main draw," according to *Variety*. In its New Year's Eve review of the state of Broadway that season, *Variety* concluded that "the horticultural touch added to the gay spots this year [is] the most significant development in nite club floor shows."[55] It already detected signs, though, that the "pansy floor shows . . . are beginning to . . . [lose] their drawing power"; just the week before, the Everglades and the D'Orsay had "discontinued the boys doing male imitations, substituting conventional girl revues and manly m.c.'s."[56]

While the pansy craze lasted only a bit longer in Times Square, for reasons to be discussed in the following chapter, it quickly spread to other parts of the nation. Several of the pansy acts that had taken root in New York soon blossomed in other cities as well.* Jean Malin, for one, took his act to Boston after the Club Abbey closed, and then went on to

---

*More research needs to be conducted on other cities to determine the scope, chronology, duration, and causes of the craze, as well as its broader cultural meaning. A handful of articles in *Variety* suggests, however, that while it was centered in large cities and resort towns, it nonetheless took hold in places as disparate as Chicago, Arizona, and Colorado. A handful of pansy clubs drawing a mixed or largely straight audience survived in cities in the 1940s, '50s, and '60s, including the Club 181, its successor the Club 82, the Club Capri in New York City, and Finocchio's in San Francisco.

Hollywood, where he became the toast of the town before dying in a car accident in the summer of 1933 at age twenty-five (he drowned when his car careered off a pier). By September 1932, Hollywood had four pansy clubs, three of them starring pansy performers or female impersonators who had headlined at clubs in New York the year before: Malin in a club bearing his name, Karyl Norman at La Boheme, and Francis Renault at Clarke's. Rae Bourbon starred at Jimmy's Back Yard, and B.B.B.'s featured a line of ten "boys." "Several oo-la-la entertainers are figuring on opening spots here," *Variety* reported, "believing the craze will build up, and hold at least over the winter." A month later, city authorities launched a "drive on the Nance and Lesbian amusement places in town," but the clubs survived for another two seasons before the authorities discovered, or began enforcing, an ordinance prohibiting "the appearance of anyone in a cafe in drag unless employed in the cafe." Apparently enough drag queens and other gay men had been patronizing the clubs that banning them was enough to kill "the lavender spots."[57] Rae Bourbon promptly took his "Boys Will Be Girls" revue to San Francisco, where for two weeks he headlined "Frisco's first pansy show" at Tait's café before it succumbed to a series of raids. (Since a radio station had decided to broadcast the show, the first raid was carried live on the local airwaves.)[58] The mayor of Atlantic City reacted as negatively to the spread of pansy acts as San Francisco officials had; he banned such acts in January 1933 after becoming enraged by the "adverse advertising" the resort was getting because the only two clubs still open that winter, the Pansy Club and the Cotton Club, both featured pansy acts.[59]

PANSIES IN THE MEDIA

Although the pansy craze peaked in New York's nightclubs in 1930–31, a flurry of novels, films, and newspaper reports kept pansies in the public eye for several more years. In the summer of 1932, the New York tabloid *Broadway Brevities* announced that "queens are very much the fashion just now. From the comic pansy-baiting in vaudeville to serious works, called 'of art,' like Blair Niles' [new novel] 'Strange Brother,' your queen is held up to the humorous tolerance, and even the soulful admiration, of the great public."[60] *Brevities* was right, and in its own breathless style it had both paid homage to and helped generate that fashion by providing extensive coverage of the gay scene in its pages. The first edition of *Brevities* appeared as a monthly in the mid-twenties, and, like its weekly successor, it included numerous features on gay life, including an astonishing yearlong series of articles in 1924 on "Nights in Fairyland," which described some of the major institutions of the gay world, from Louis' Restaurant on Forty-ninth Street to Mother Childs at Columbus Circle (see figure 6.1). This edition of *Brevities* appears to have been suppressed by the authorities, although the exact circumstances of its demise are uncertain. It reappeared in 1931, in any case, billing itself as "America's First National Tabloid Weekly" and offering even more extensive coverage of the gay scene. Usually twelve to sixteen pages, it included a plethora of gay items in its general survey of Broadway gossip and regularly devoted its entire first or last page to stories on the gay world.[61] Cartoons detecting a sexual subtext in virtually every kind of interaction between men and women ran side by side with cartoons lampooning the efforts of pansies of pick up men on Riverside Drive (see figure 7.1), their desire for sailors and policemen (see figure 3.1), and their supposed insistence on claiming the status of women (see figure 2.1).[62]

Many of the gay-related cartoons and humorous sketches published in the paper lent themselves to divergent readings. They often made fun of gay men or lesbians, but some of them could easily have represented a jaded gay insider's view of his milieu. Indeed, the paper's political perspective on the gay world is curiously difficult to determine. The difficulty is revealing, for the multiple readings possible of its stories and cartoons that are possible (and the now obscure internal politics that may have produced such complexity) suggest the complex ramifications for gay life of the sudden attention paid pansies. As the pages of Brevities illustrate, the pansy craze made the gay world more visible—to itself and those seeking to become a part of it, as well as to curious outsiders—even as it subjected it to considerable exploitation. The paper's coverage was often abrasive and demeaning, but it provided a good deal of information about meeting places, prominent figures in the gay world such as Jean Malin and Jackie Mason, drag balls, police activity, and the like, which gay readers would have found useful. Many of the cartoons ridiculed gay men and lesbians, but no more than they ridiculed the interactions of presumptive heterosexuals, and some of them showed lesbians in positions of relative power over the men desperately pursuing them. "I love you with all my heart and want you for my wife," begs one man on his knees at the foot of Eve, smartly dressed in a skirt and tuxedo jacket and surrounded by paintings of buxom women. Oh, says Eve, "who up until then had taken no part in the conversation . . . have you a wife?" Another cartoon portrayed two beautiful women wearing ties and short hair, leaving the club Doo Dike Inn arm in arm. Glancing back at the man beginning to follow them, the "First Ikeday" says to the other: "Let's be nice to him Billie; maybe he has a sister."[63]

The paper's articles were so well informed and accurate in their coverage of the gay scene that many of them were almost surely written by lesbians or gay men. In its 1924 "Nights in Fairyland" series, Brevities referred to gay meeting places dating back to the turn of the century, such as Columbia Hall (better known as Paresis Hall) and the Black Cat, as well as to raids on the Ariston, Lafayette, and Everard baths back to 1903.[64] In the 1930s it also provided remarkably thorough and accurate histories of the gay and lesbian speakeasies of the previous decade, as well as comments on more current personalities and clubs. It published biting depictions of gay life (as well as articles that seem to offer an arch—or "bitchy"—insider's camp commentary on gay foibles), but it also published letters from gay readers and their supporters that criticized such coverage and propounded a more positive view (such as the letter from the father of a gay man quoted in chapter 10). While it overtly construed its writers and readers as straight, the paper was almost certainly read and written, in part, by gay people.

Part of the reason *Brevities* was so well informed about the gay scene was that it hired the columnist Billy Scully away from the *Greenwich Village Weekly News,* where, as noted in chapter 9, he had written knowledgeable and generally positive notices of gay events and personalities.[65] In October 1931, Scully announced in the *Weekly News* that he was leaving the Village paper for *Brevities,* and although his name never appeared on the latter's masthead, it seems likely that he was the author who began writing stories for *Brevities* the next month under pseudonyms whose homosexual innuendo was blatant: "John Swallow Martin," "Stephen O'Toole," and "Buddy Browning." His extensive articles on the gay scene, which often took up the entire first or back page, appeared under banner headlines reveling in their knowledge and use of gay argot (see figure 11.1). Although his articles in *Brevities* were generally more mocking in their coverage of the gay scene than those in the *Weekly News,* their tone seems to have served as a legitimizing ruse for articles that were, on the whole, extremely informative. For example, the front page of the November 9, 1931, issue was devoted to an article titled "Sapphic Sisters Scram!," which traced the history of lesbian clubs in the city and included an extended discussion of Eve Addams's club, which Scully had discussed a few weeks earlier in a *Weekly News* column. The author was listed as "Connie Lingle."

Brevities was only one of the city's newspapers to increase its coverage of the gay scene in the early 1930s. The *Broadway Tattler,* introduced at about the same time as *Brevities,* adopted a similar tone, and devoted a double column in most issues to the "Pansy Bugle," which reported "fictitious but typical homosexual exploits in a heavy satirical style."[66] Even more established papers increased their coverage of the gay world in the 1920s and 1930s, although none matched *Brevities*'s detail, volume, or explicitness. Most of the press accounts of the gay scene focused on the Village and took a sensationalist, outsider's perspective. Bernarr Macfadden's short-lived tabloid, the *New York Evening-Graphic* (nicknamed the *Evening-Pornographic* by some), reported on the gay scene using the rhetoric of moral outrage. In the summer of 1931, for instance, Paul Yawitz began his *Evening-Graphic* series on the depravity of the Village with a scornful look at the gay clubs of MacDougal Street, which he called "the innermost stations of Greenwich Village's sex, pollution and human decay."[67]

Even *Vanity Fair* provided some limited coverage of the pansy craze. In a survey of New York nightlife, it included a sketch of Jean Malin and Helen Morgan, Jr., at the "'smart' Club Abbey" (see figure 11.2), which it described as one of "the growing pains of our metropolitan culture."[68] *Variety*, the New York–based trade publication of the entertainment industry, in which many gay men worked, regularly covered the gay scene from the mid-1920s until 1931. Most of the articles concerned the role of homosexuality in show business—the spread of pansy acts, the censorship of homosexual innuendo in vaudeville, the controversy over *The Captive*—but the paper also published articles with less obvious connections to its bailiwick, about gay men in a Coney Island beauty contest, arrests of men in drag, and the like. Its gay coverage was never extensive, but for several years it seems to have presumed, or acknowledged, that its theater-industry readership might be interested in such things.[69]

The early thirties also saw book publishers race to satisfy the public's growing interest in the gay scene, for a flurry of gay-themed novels appeared between 1931 and 1934. Several of them depicted New York's gay world. As their titles suggest, most focused on the flamboyant fairy: *Strange Brother* by Blair Niles (1931), *Twilight Men* by Andre Tellier (1931), *A Scarlet Pansy* by Robert Scully (1932), *Goldie* by Kennilworth Bruce (1933), *Better Angel* by Richard Meeker (1933), and *Butterfly Man* by Lew Levenson (1934). The arrival of such novels suggests the extent to which social convention had been undermined by the 1930s, for publishers had previously been unwilling to broach the subject of homosexuality. Just a few years earlier, in 1929, the New York publisher Covici-Friede had been taken to court and convicted for obscenity for daring to publish Radclyffe Hall's lesbian novel, *The Well of Loneliness*, a conviction only overturned on appeal.[70] More important, the novels suggest that a few authors were able to seize the possibilities created by the pansy craze to depict the gay world and publicly articulate a gay sensibility. The writing in some of the novels was wooden, although a few fairly sparkled with camp repartee. Some portrayed the gay world in unflattering terms, but several provided remarkably detailed descriptions and defenses of gay speakeasies, drag balls, and other institutions. Most ended with the death or suicide of the gay protagonist, but only a few made this end seem inevitable; in the other novels the ending is obviously nothing but an obligatory bow to convention, transparently intended to disarm the moralists who might otherwise have tried to suppress the books. The novels were widely discussed by gay men, and a few received attention in the straight press.[71]

The Prohibition-era preoccupation with pansies made its way into the movies as well. A handful of films on gay subjects appeared, along with many more that included gay images. Two gay films shown in New York received particular attention: *Mädchen in Uniform* (*Girls in Uniform,* 1931), a German release depicting lesbian love at a boarding school as a form of resistance to authoritarianism, and *Chained,* a study of "a male captive," its ads declared, in a testimony to the notoriety the play *The Captive* had achieved (see figure 11.4) Many more movies included incidental gay characters or had their protagonists engage in homosexual buffoonery, particularly as vaudevillians began to move into films and create a new genre of vaudeville-inflected film comedy. Laurel and Hardy movies, for instance, regularly depicted one of the duo goosing the other, pulling down his pants, or engaging in obscene poses. In one early feature, *Their First Mistake* (Roach, 1932), Laurel and Hardy decide to adopt a child, without consulting Ollie's wife. When she walks out, they proceed to establish a household and raise the child themselves. Before long they are sleeping together (with the baby) in Hardy's marriage bed and Laurel is sucking the bottle Hardy holds; in another scene Hardy holds the bottle in his lap and strokes it so hard that the milk spurts out of it. Soon they receive a court notice announcing that Hardy's wife is suing for divorce and naming Laurel as the co-respondent.[72] Such films caricatured pansies but also destabilized gender categories and implied that any man might sexually desire another man.

The flavor of the old vaudeville and burlesque pansy routines is preserved in the Bugs Bunny cartoons produced for movie theaters in the 1940s and 1950s, which drew on many of those routines but were able, as cartoons, to avoid the censorship imposed on other films by then. Along with the exaggerated physical blows and falls and even more exaggerated misunderstandings of the old stage forms, the cartoons regularly depicted Bugs putting on drag and giving Elmer a big, wet kiss. In the duo's very first meeting in *A Wild Hare* (1940), Bugs gives Elmer a kiss after stroking the man's rifle repeatedly; in *What's Cookin', Doc?* (1944) Bugs dresses as Carmen Miranda and puts on a drag show extravaganza.[73] In doing so the cartoons drew directly on the vaudeville and burlesque traditions of homosexual buffoonery and pansy caricature.

By the late 1920s, gay men had become a conspicuous part of New York City's nightlife. They had been visible since the late nineteenth century in some of the city's immigrant and working-class neighborhoods, and since the 1910s in the bohemian enclave of Greenwich Village. But in the 1920s they moved into the center of the city's most prestigious entertain-

ALL NEW YORK

IS TALKING

All New York is talking about and reading an unusual novel which has been called "the finest handling of this important theme yet attempted . . . better than *The Well of Loneliness*." The talented Andre Tellier, who wrote it, has achieved "a beautiful handling of a delicate subject." The title of the book is

TWILIGHT MEN

It is on sale at $2.50 at all bookstores. Published by GREENBERG, 160 Fifth Ave., New York.

ALREADY IN ITS 3RD LARGE PRINTING

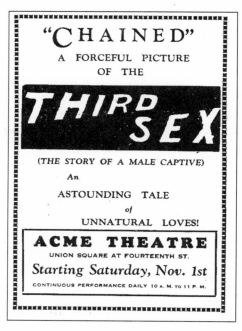

"CHAINED"

A FORCEFUL PICTURE
OF THE

THIRD SEX

(THE STORY OF A MALE CAPTIVE)

An

ASTOUNDING TALE

of

UNNATURAL LOVES!

ACME THEATRE

UNION SQUARE AT FOURTEENTH ST.

Starting Saturday, Nov. 1st

CONTINUOUS PERFORMANCE DAILY 10 A. M. TO 11 P. M.

Society had made him ashamed of what he was. The law had made him afraid of what he was. To the woman who opened her arms to him he could not return man's real love.

STRANGE BROTHER

A brave and daring story about the dilemma of an intermediate man in modern society, ranking with *The Well of Loneliness* as a pioneering novel. The reality of *Strange Brother* has been attested by many confidential letters.

3rd edition, $2.50

By BLAIR NILES

HORACE LIVERIGHT INC. WEST 47TH STREET NEW YORK

Figure 11.4. It seemed that all of New York was talking about homosexuality in the early 1930s, when a host of novels and films dealing with gay topics appeared. (*Advertisements from unidentified New York newspapers, 1931–33. From Yale Collection of American Literature, Beinecke Rare Books and Manuscripts Library, Yale University.*)

ment district, became the subject of plays, films, novels, and newspaper headlines, and attracted thousands of spectators to Harlem's largest ballrooms. "All New York is talking," an ad for a gay novel published in 1931 proclaimed (see figure 11.4). The ad made its claim in typically hyperbolic fashion—but in fact much of New York *was* talking about the pansy phenomenon.

The pansy craze highlights the cultural upheaval wrought by Prohibition. By criminalizing much of New York City's nightlife, Prohibition gave control of that nightlife to men and women from the "lower classes" who introduced middle-class audiences to "coarse" forms of entertainment previously restricted to working-class neighborhoods. Fairies were a part of the culture of those neighborhoods, and they moved with the gangsters to Times Square and other centers of middle-class nightlife.[74] By driving middle-class men and women to break the law if they wanted to socialize where they could have a drink and bringing them in contact with "low-life" figures, Prohibition encouraged them to transgress other social boundaries as well. By impinging on middle-class as well as working-class life, Prohibition led many middle-class New Yorkers to question the moral agenda of the social-purity forces for the first time.

The reaction of middle-class clubgoers to the moral agenda of the Prohibitionists was consonant with the sense of disillusionment that followed World War I.[75] The nation's leaders had promoted it as the most noble, selfless, and just of wars, but its moralistic pretensions had been shattered for many Americans by the power-brokering at the Versailles peace conference and by the massive strikes, the race riots, and the Red scare that convulsed the nation in the year following the armistice. Many people came to reject the moral certainties that had fueled both the war and the Prohibition campaign. One sign of this was that the old fear of "overcivilization" gave way to a new appreciation of "sophistication." Displaying sophistication became one of the ways many New Yorkers distinguished themselves from the "narrow-minded" folk whom they blamed for the passage of Prohibition and whose moral fervor now seemed dangerously constraining. New Yorkers could demonstrate their sophistication, in part, by their knowledge and appreciation of the very transgressive social practices that so horrified the social-purity forces—be it the rhythms of African-American jazz or the double entendre of gay male repartee. *Vanity Fair* hinted at this when it described "Jean Malin's 'smart' Club Abbey, where, through a lavender mist somewhat bewildered clientele smirk with self-conscious sophistication at the delicate antics of their host." Keen to assert its superiority over host and clientele alike, the magazine was hardly enthusiastic about Malin's "wilted postures and tense warbling"; it concluded that clubs with pansy acts were simply "the growing pains of our metropolitan culture."[76] But even though the magazine thought the "bewildered" members of Malin's audience were unable to understand him, it recognized they thought it was important that they *appear* to understand him. At that moment in the development of "metropolitan culture," having the daring to see and the ability to appreciate the sophisticated double-entendre and camp antics of a gay man seemed to some the pinnacle of sophistication.

The *Vanity Fair* article suggests the complex origins and multiple meanings of the pansy craze and its similarities to the "Negro vogue" that preceded it. Both fads allowed members of the dominant culture to shore up their identities and solidarity by contrasting themselves with the otherness of the African-American and the homosexual. At a time of bitter white ethnic rivalries, which resulted in the resurgence of anti-Semitism and the passage of exclusionary immigration laws in the early 1920s, the spectacle of black "primitivism" allowed whites to express their solidarity with other whites by distinguishing themselves from blacks. At a time when the culture of the speakeasies and the 1920s' celebration of affluence and consumption might have undermined conventional sources of masculine identity, the spectacle of the pansy allowed men to confirm their manliness and solidarity with other men by distinguishing themselves from pansies. But each spectacle provoked a wider range of responses than this. Malin's courage in "standing on the floor for an hour at a time and making no bones about [being] a professional pansy" elicited respect as well as ridicule. Jazz appealed because it seemed primitive, and camp because it seemed perverse; but each had a utopian appeal as well, for each seemed to offer a path to freedom from the constraints of the bourgeois moral order under which men and women self-consciously chafed. The Negro and pansy vogues each revealed only a fraction of a vibrant urban subculture to the dominant culture, but those fractions pointed to worlds that seemed to some New Yorkers to offer alternatives to the constraining forms of that dominant culture.[77]

The changing organization of middle-class sociability and the peculiar cultural ethos generated by World War I and Prohibition help explain how the pansy craze became possible, but in themselves they cannot account for it. Lesbians and gay men also made it happen, by starting their own speakeasies and performing at clubs in the Village and Harlem, by organizing drag balls in the city's ballrooms, and by carrying themselves openly in the city's streets and putting on "shows" for the other customers at the city's Automats, cafeterias, and speakeasies. The fascination they provoked led entertainment entrepreneurs to put homosexuals on their own stages. At first pansies were simply mimicked and ridiculed by "normal" comics who made gay men and lesbians the objects of their jokes or included homosexual buffoonery in their stage routines. They were caricatured by cartoonists in *Broadway Brevities* and sneered at by columnists in the

Evening-Graphic. While this dismissive ridicule set the predominant tone of the pansy craze, even it betrayed a fascination with the gay subculture and a nervousness about the questions its visibility raised regarding the inevitability of heterosexual arrangements. By the late 1920s and early 1930s, gay men had moved to center stage themselves. Jean Malin and his imitators spoke for themselves and forced their audiences to contend with them directly in unequal verbal contests that left the audiences alternately charmed, bewildered, dazzled, and outraged. The clubs put the "pansies on parade" in order to profit from the curiosity provoked by the pansies' own willingness to parade openly throughout the city. But at least some gay performers seized the opportunities Prohibition culture provided to expand the space available for gay self-representation and to challenge the conventions of ridicule and disdain that governed the straight world's response to them.

Figure 12.1. Drag queens and other easily recognized gay men were the first targets of the crackdown on gay life in the 1930s. But Weegee's photograph of a drag queen stepping out of a police van in 1940 also points to the continuing determination of such men to make a place for themselves. The queen exuberantly posed for the camera, while the more conventional looking man sitting behind him hid his face. *("The Gay Deceiver," 1940. Copyright © Weegee/Magnum Photos.)*

Chapter 12

THE EXCLUSION OF HOMOSEXUALITY FROM THE PUBLIC SPHERE IN THE 1930s

"THE SUDDEN FEATURING OF THE HORTICULTURAL YOUNG MAN AS A NIGHT-club feature" was noted with distress by a New York nightclub insider at the height of the pansy craze in 1931. He quickly reassured his readers, though, that "recurrent though the vogue is for this type of entertainer, its popularity is short."[1] The vogue in New York, however, had little time to run its course. After a decade in which gay men and a smaller number of lesbians had become highly visible in clubs, streets, newspapers, novels, and films, a powerful backlash to the Prohibition-era "pansy craze" developed. The anti-gay reaction gained force in the early to mid-thirties as it became part of a more general reaction to the cultural experimentation of the Prohibition years and to the disruption of gender arrangements by the Depression. As the onset of the Depression dashed the confidence of the 1920s, gay men and lesbians began to seem less amusing than dangerous. A powerful campaign to render gay men and lesbians invisible—to exclude them from the public sphere—quickly gained momentum.

Early in 1931 several of the city's newspapers began a campaign against clubs featuring female impersonators and "m.c.'s who boast of a lavender tinge in their make-up." The campaign gathered momentum when gunfire broke out at Jean Malin's venue, the Club Abbey, on the night of January 25, which sent its gangster proprietor, Dutch Schultz, into hiding, and his assailant, Charlie (Chink) Sherman, into a hospital. Although the Abbey managed to reopen the following night, it closed for good a few days later. Rumors abounded that the shootout marked the beginning of a long-feared war between rival gangs to control the Broadway liquor trade, and pressure built for the police to restore order.[2]

The police responded by launching a campaign of harassment against the remaining Times Square clubs featuring pansy acts. On the night of January 28, 1931, they raided the Pansy Club on West Forty-eighth Street and the Club Calais at 125 West Fifty-first Street. They charged both with liquor violations, even though city authorities had stopped enforcing the Volstead Act several years earlier. Police Commissioner Edward Mulrooney announced the next day: "There will be a shake-up in the night clubs, especially of those which feature female impersonators." True to his word, he sent plainclothesmen to the pansy clubs to make sure their paperwork was in order and that they had secured the proper cabaret licenses and certificates of occupancy. He also stationed uniformed officers at the door of each club, with orders to make sure it closed promptly at 3 A.M.—a curfew commonly violated—and he threatened to impose a 1 A.M. curfew. The policemen also endeavored to disturb the relaxed atmosphere and illegal liquor trade that were crucial to the clubs' profitability. "Cops spotted at the door of nite clubs are more inquisitive than ever," Variety reported. "All seekers after synthetic joy [that is, illegal liquor] are getting a Hawkshaw glance that is guaranteed to throw cheaters into a panic. This is scaring away the better wine-buyers." Two men entering a club "without a female in tow," the paper added, were subject to even greater scrutiny and intimidation. While the pansy acts had already begun to lose some of their popularity, the strict enforcement of the curfew and steady barrage of harassment left the clubs with no choice but to end their flirtation with such acts. "The 'temperamentals' who held sway on the main stem for a year," Variety reported in early February, "are about ready to concede they are slipping as nite draws."[3]

Later that year the police moved to crack down on the city's drag balls as well. They forced the organizers to cancel one planned for September 26 at the New Star Casino at Park Avenue and 107th Street, where several had been held the previous year, and half a dozen policemen appeared the following week to prevent a smaller drag from being held in its stead at a West 146th Street hall.[4] The suppression of Harlem's drag balls, at least, was short-lived. Within a few months, the police, having made their point, backed down and permitted the annual Hamilton Lodge ball, the largest drag ball of the year, to be held at the Rockland Palace. This ball continued to be held every February until the late 1930s and to receive extensive coverage from Harlem's leading paper, the Amsterdam News.* But no more drag balls were held in

*In 1939, in the wake of a panic over sex crimes (discussed in the epilogue), the police even brought the Hamilton Lodge balls to an end. The police appear to have warned the Lodge before the 1938 ball that it would receive special scrutiny. While

Madison Square Garden or midtown hotels, just as no more pansy acts were produced there.

The retreat of the drag balls from Times Square was telling. "If the cops have their way," *Variety* reported as the campaign against pansy acts got under way, "the effeminate clan will hereafter confine its activities to the Village and Harlem."[6] Prohibition culture had allowed gay visibility to move into the center of New York's most prestigious entertainment district, but in the early thirties, the authorities were determined to return it to the city's periphery. In addition to ending the Times Square pansy acts and drag balls, the police tried to eradicate pansies from the streets of the Square. In September 1931, for instance, they launched a "round-up . . . of apparent homosexualists" who gathered on Forty-second Street near Bryant Park. Their efforts were only partially successful. "The degenerates . . . gradually returned," as one social-hygiene society observed, "and [could be] seen in that section almost nightly." Bryant Park, portions of Forty-second Street and Sixth Avenue, and the streets of the Hell's Kitchen neighborhood to the west of the Square continued to serve as gathering places for young "painted queens," as well as for soldiers, seamen, hustlers, and the gay men who were attracted to them. But over the course of several years the police succeeded in forcing the majority of the most "obvious" gay men out of the rest of Times Square, especially the more "respectable" area north of Forty-second Street where the district's remaining theaters and night-clubs clustered. It was a commonplace among gay men that after Fiorello La Guardia, a man known for his moralism as well as his reformism, was elected mayor in 1933, he had issued orders forbidding the appearance of drag queens anywhere between Fourteenth and Seventy-second Streets. Whatever the cause, the disappearance of the "painted queens" from Times Square was noted by the less overt gay men who remained there. One of the Square's habitués remarked at the beginning of World War II that things had "changed since the decade of 1925–1935 when the flaming homosexual was a common sight on the streets of mid-town New York, and they are seldom to be encountered [there] nowadays."[7]

The timing of the initial crackdown, in 1931, seems to have been

---

the *Amsterdam News* ads for the balls in previous years had promised "a night of phenomenal excitement" and "a sight . . . never to be forgotten," the 1938 ad warned that "mode of costumes must be in conformity with good taste, scant clothing will not be permitted." Plainclothesmen kept dancers under closer surveillance than usual and arrested seventeen for homosexual solicitation. "Pandemonium broke loose" among the five thousand guests at the Palace when news of the arrests and rumors that the police were going to raid the ballroom began to circulate. The Lodge chose not even to try sponsoring a ball in 1939, abruptly ending a seventy-year-old tradition.[5]

determined only partially by the shooting at the Club Abbey. The declining political fortunes of Jimmy Walker's mayoral administration were more salient. An investigation into corruption in New York City's magistrates' courts and police force directed by the distinguished Tammany Hall foe Samuel Seabury had begun to pose a serious threat to Mayor Walker; his newly appointed police commissioner, Edward Mulrooney, launched a highly publicized war on vice in an effort to divert attention from the investigation.[8] The fact that the drag balls had become chic events for the social elite to attend doubtless had contributed to the inclination of the police under the laissez-faire Walker administration to tolerate them, but this provided tenuous security indeed. The prominence of the drags—along with gay club acts, burlesque, and other highly visible "moral evils"—made them an inviting target once the mayor needed to demonstrate his resolve to clean up New York.

Although the 1931 crackdown was precipitated by the newspaper campaign, the shooting at the Club Abbey, and the mayor's political crisis, it signaled a more fundamental shift in the cultural and political climate and was soon followed by more enduring measures that pushed "fairies" out of the clubs and back into the periphery of the city. Many Americans—including many New Yorkers—were appalled by the lawlessness of the speakeasies and nightclubs, and their fears only grew in the wake of the Depression, as battles broke out in the clubs between gangs struggling to claim a share of declining profits. Some worried that the cultural developments of the late Prohibition period had somehow contributed to the Depression by replacing a productionist ethic with a consumerist one, a regard for traditional American moral values with the flaunting of illicit desires.[9] By the early thirties, a general revulsion had set in against the "excesses" of Prohibition, and the celebration of sexual perversity on the stages of the premier cultural district of the American cultural capital seemed the most galling expression of such excess. New York had been denounced as the Sodom and Gomorrah of the nation throughout the twenties, but Jean Malin's pansy act must have provided a more vivid demonstration of the accuracy of that charge than most critics could have anticipated. As many Americans came to believe that such excesses could no longer be tolerated, a more enduring campaign against the visibility of the gay world was launched in New York and cities throughout the nation.

The most significant step in the campaign to exclude the gay world from the public sphere was a counterintuitive one: the repeal of Prohibition. For rather than initiating a new era of laissez-faire tolerance in urban life, as is often imagined, Repeal inaugurated a more pervasive and more effective regime of surveillance and control. Repeal made it possible for the state to redraw the boundaries of acceptable sociability that seemed to have been obliterated in the twenties. This had enormous consequences for gay life, for those boundaries were drawn in a way that marginalized and literally criminalized much of gay sociability. Repeal resulted in the segregation and isolation of the gay social world from the broader social life of the city, in which it had played such a significant role in the 1920s. This new isolation, in turn, established the conditions that made it possible for gay men and the gay world to be demonized in the even more hostile climate of the postwar period.

THE NEW SEGREGATION: REDRAWING THE BOUNDARIES OF ACCEPTABLE SOCIABILITY IN THE POST-REPEAL ERA

Prohibition had been a failure in New York. It had criminalized much of the city's nightlife, driven many entrepreneurs out of business, and resulted in the closing of numerous restaurants and several well-known hotels, as well as most of the city's saloons. But it had not stopped people from drinking or socializing in unrespectable ways. Instead, it had resulted in the growth of an underground economy controlled by criminal gangs, and it had precipitated a popular revolt against Prohibition enforcement that was so widespread it seemed to undermine the authority of the law itself. It had also created a speakeasy-based demimonde in which the boundaries of acceptable public sociability were significantly reconfigured by the "promiscuous" and unregulated intermingling of the classes and sexes.

The tendency of Prohibition to foster the flouting of social convention was particularly ironic because it was the social settings of drinking—rather than alcohol consumption per se—that had been the chief target of the most effective advocates of Prohibition. Temperance campaigners had long attacked the saloon, in particular, as a center of male disorder, where workingmen drank away their paychecks, leaving their wives and children destitute, and where gambling, prostitution, and even worse criminal activities and vices flourished. More broadly, the saloon had been feared by middle-class reformers as the central institution of an autonomous, urban, immigrant, working-class male culture, free from the supervision of the normal agencies of social control, and in the heady nativist days surrounding the Great War this fear had been an important factor in mobilizing support for the enactment of Prohibition.[10]

By the early 1930s, however, many public officials were convinced that Prohibition had wrought greater evil than it had remedied. Four hundred political, civic, and business leaders surveyed in 1933 cited "bootlegging, racketeering, . . . defiance of law, . . . hypocrisy, the breakdown of governmental machinery, [and] the demoralization in public and private life" as being among the most dangerous consequences of

Prohibition. Above all, popular resistance to Prohibition seemed to have undermined the hegemonic authority of the law itself, and this was so intolerable to the guardians of that authority that they resolved to end the "noble experiment." But the architects of Repeal were nonetheless determined to prevent a return to the conditions that had led to Prohibition in the first place. This was, no doubt, in part a moral decision, but it was also in part a practical political judgment: only if the most undesirable conditions associated with the saloon were eliminated, they calculated, would the demands for a return to Prohibition be defused and the enduring controversy over alcohol finally be stilled. President Franklin D. Roosevelt thus coupled his announcement of Repeal with a call for a nationwide effort to prevent a "return to the saloon either in its old form or some modern disguise," and this became one of the major concerns of state legislators as they designed new administrative mechanisms for regulating the sale of liquor.[11]

The alcoholic beverage control laws promulgated after Prohibition were designed, then, not only to control the consumption of liquor per se but also to regulate the public spaces in which people met to drink. Officials intended them to help reestablish the boundaries of respectable public sociability that had been eroded by the Prohibition ethos. To this end, state legislatures throughout the country enacted stringent rules to govern the conduct of taverns and put powerful new regulatory agencies in place to enforce them. The cornerstone of the power of the administrative agency established in New York, the State Liquor Authority (SLA), was its exclusive authority to license the sale of alcohol. If liquor would once again be sold legally, the state sought to ensure that it would be sold only by those duly licensed on the basis of their acquiescence to state regulations governing their behavior and that of their patrons. Licenses became a privilege, which the state could revoke if an establishment failed to conform to state standards.[12] By offering state sanction and all the privileges it entailed to those drinking establishments that conformed to SLA regulations, the law severely discouraged proprietors from risking violations of them.

The genius of the licensing mechanism lay in the way it expanded the state's ability to survey and regulate public sociability. The SLA had only a small staff of plainclothes agents to investigate the compliance of bars. But by threatening proprietors with the revocation of their licenses if its agents discovered that customers were violating the regulations, it forced proprietors to uphold those regulations on behalf of the state. Turning such proprietors into deputy enforcement agents expanded the reach of state surveillance into every establishment serving liquor in the state. Since not only bars but also most restaurants, nightclubs, and cabarets depended on liquor sales to make a profit, the strategy allowed the state to police most of the most common sites of urban sociability. It made that policing at once invisible and pervasive.[13]

As historian Lewis Erenberg has argued, Repeal was essential to the relegitimization of nightlife in the 1930s because it enabled reputable entrepreneurs to reenter the business and create sanitized forms of entertainment.[14] But the obverse was equally significant: Repeal served to draw new boundaries between the acceptable and the unacceptable, and to impose new sanctions against the latter. The most general rule designed to effect this project of normalization (or to "prevent a return to the conditions of the saloon") required that licensed establishments not "suffer or permit such premises to become disorderly."[15]

The requirement that establishments be "orderly" proved to have a profound impact on gay bars. For while the legislature did not specifically prohibit bars from serving homosexuals, the SLA made it clear from the beginning that it interpreted the statute to mandate such a prohibition.[*] The simple presence of lesbians or gay men, prostitutes, gamblers, or other "undesirables," it contended, made an establishment disorderly. An owner who tolerated their presence risked losing his or her license.

The SLA took this policy seriously and devoted significant resources to enforcing. The Liquor Authority usually depended on the police to report possible violations of the liquor law, because its staff was too small to supervise all the bars in the city itself, but upon receiving a complaint, the SLA assigned investigators to the bar in question.[17] The investigators acted in an independent, clandestine manner, remarkably similar to that of their predecessors from the Committee of Fourteen. One investigator, Walter R. Van Wagner, reported in 1939 that he went to the SLA office only on Mondays, to receive his instructions, and spent the rest of the week on his own, checking out the bars he had been assigned. During the week, he normally made twenty-five to thirty-five visits to bars, where he bought drinks, talked with the other customers and the bartender, kept his eyes open for actionable violations of SLA regulations, and took care to remain incognito. He normally visited a bar several times before writing a report on it, and sometimes went with a second agent.[18] In 1939 another SLA agent claimed that in his first four years of work, he had conducted "hundreds" of such investigations of bars suspected of tolerating homosexual patrons.[19]

The implications of the SLA's anti-gay policy for gay bars and gay sociability were made clear by its closing of Gloria's, a bar on Third

---

[*]The state legislature deliberately left the definition of disorderliness vague, fearful, the State Liquor Authority repeatedly noted, "'lest the craft of man evade the definition,'" and it granted the SLA broad discretionary authority to interpret the restriction.[16]

Avenue at Fortieth Street, in 1939. The owners had made it apparent they wanted to run it as a gay bar by hiring Jackie Mason as its manager. Mason was a well-known figure in gay circles, who had run a gay speakeasy on Charles Street in the mid-1920s (where Jean Malin once worked), had organized the Madison Square Garden drag ball in 1930, and since then had regularly arranged drag shows for both gay and straight clubs. As one SLA investigator put it, Mason was "a fag and a leader of that element . . . where Jackie Mason is, fags are"; he was a popular man and a sure draw as a host. Gloria's was part of a gay bar circuit that included Benny's, a block to the south; Will Finch described both bars in the spring of 1939 as "very crowded, almost exclusively with homosexuals." Men felt free to camp it up at Gloria's. They "gabbed around in feminine voices," it seemed to one SLA investigator. "Some called others by feminine names. [They] acted, walked, and impersonated females, and [female] attitude and gestures."[20]

It was precisely this openness that aroused the ire of the police and SLA. The SLA warned Gloria's management that they had endangered their license by "permit[ting] the premises to become disorderly in permitting homosexuals, degenerates and undesirable people to congregate on the premises." As the SLA indicated at a hearing, it based this judgment on its investigators' reports that the bar had hired Mason to attract a gay following and that the men they had seen at the bar behaved in a campy (or "feminine") manner. The SLA also specified two particular incidents of disorderly conduct witnessed by its agents: a man the agents had invited to the bar had, after a two-hour conversation in a booth, caressed (or "fondled," as they put it) one of the agents under the table; and the management had permitted two heterosexual couples to goose several homosexual men who had passed by them in the crowded bar. The SLA also alleged that two men had solicited the investigators and that one had offered to arrange a date between an investigator and two "degenerates." The SLA initially agreed to renew Gloria's license on the condition that it ban homosexuals from the premises. When the management failed to evict its homosexual patrons, the Authority not only revoked the owner's license, but prohibited the licensing of the premises to anyone else for a year, thus making it virtually impossible for the owner to recoup his original investment by selling his equipment.[21]

Unlike most bars, Gloria's took the SLA to court and offered an exceptionally forthright challenge to the revocation of its license. It first tried to protect its license by denying that it had violated the SLA regulation. The SLA had not proved that homosexuals had been present at the bar, it argued, and, moreover, the investigators' lack of scientific training about homosexuality rendered them incompetent to identify homosexuals. But having implicitly acquiesced to the SLA's anti-gay policy as a safeguard, the bar then challenged the policy itself. So long as homosexuals were neither diseased nor engaging in conduct it agreed would be disorderly, such as making noise, soliciting, or the "annoying or accosting of people," the bar contended, the Liquor Authority could not require a bar's management to "refuse to serve such people." "There is no rule or regulation of the State Liquor Authority nor any section of the Alcoholic Beverage Control Law," Gloria's insisted, "which provides that a sex variant may not be served at a licensed premises."[22*]

The Liquor Authority successfully countered both arguments. It stood by the testimony of its investigators and insisted that it would be improper for the court to second-guess the Authority's own finding of fact. More significant is that while it continued to maintain that numerous specific acts of disorderly conduct had occurred, it argued that even if no such acts had taken place, it still had the power to close the bar simply because "lewd and dissolute" people such as homosexuals had congregated and been served there.[23] In a brief order, the Appellate Division (the state's second-highest court) affirmed the decision of the Liquor Authority.[24] It did not explain its reasoning and thus did not address the arguments made by either party, but the effect of its ruling was to uphold the Authority's policy of closing bars that served homosexuals.

The SLA made full use of that power. In the two and a half decades that followed, it closed literally hundreds of bars that welcomed, tolerated, or simply failed to notice the patronage of gay men or lesbians. As a result, while the number of gay bars proliferated in the 1930s, '40s, and '50s, most of them lasted only a few months or years, and gay men were forced to move constantly from place to place, dependent on the grapevine to inform them of where the new meeting places were.

---

[*]Gloria's remarkably forthright defense of the right of homosexuals to assemble was made more remarkable by its use of the latest "scientific" research on sex variation to bolster its case. The bar had obtained a prepublication summary of the findings of a research study conducted by George Henry, a psychiatrist at the Payne Whitney Clinic, for the New York–based Committee for the Study of Sex Variants (eventually published in 1941 as *Sex Variants: A Study of Homosexual Patterns*). The bar's use of the material before its publication suggests a measure of cooperation with the Committee, a group of distinguished psychiatrists and other professionals interested in studying the situation of homosexuals, or with the lesbians and gay men working with the Committee (see the epilogue). The bar used the research findings in a somewhat disingenuous way, however. While Henry had argued that, contrary to popular stereotypes, not all male homosexuals were effeminate, he still believed there was a deep connection between effeminacy and homosexuality in men. But the bar emphasized Henry's statement that there was "no necessary relationship between effeminacy and [homosexuality]," and argued that it provided scientific evidence that the SLA had been wrong to claim that Gloria's patrons were homosexual simply on the basis of their effeminacy.

When the SLA launched a campaign against bars serving homosexuals as part of its effort to "clean up the city" in the months before the 1939 World's Fair opened, it quickly discovered just how effective that grapevine could be. The authorities were particularly concerned about the Times Square area, which remained a major tourist attraction and showcase for the city despite its rapid "deterioration" under the impact of the Depression. After closing several bars in the area patronized by homosexuals, including the Consolidated Bar & Grill on West Forty-first Street, the Alvin on West Forty-second, and more distant bars that were part of the same circuit, the SLA's investigators discovered that many of the patrons of those bars had simply converged on the Times Square Garden & Grill on West Forty-second Street and turned it into their new rendezvous. In late October 1938 an SLA investigator, sent to the bar after a police report that "about thirty . . . fairys [sic] and fags" had been noticed there, noted that several of the gay men he had previously noticed at the other bars were "now congregating" there, along with a large number of soldiers. The owner himself insisted that "we never looked for . . . this kind of business. . . . [The police] close some places; [the fairies] come over here. . . . It was the neighborhood—[the fairies] know what places . . . are [open to them]. The word passes so fast. They knew [when a bar] is a degenerate place."[25]

The fate of the Times Square Garden & Grill is worth detailing, for it illustrates even more effectively than Gloria's the range of agencies involved in the regulation of bars and the steps they were willing to take to rid commercial establishments of homosexuals. The owner of the Times Square, Morris Horowitz, had not sought a gay patronage, even though his bar was located on a block (Forty-second Street between Seventh and Eighth Avenues) that by the mid-thirties had become a major center of gay bars and male prostitution. But his experience on the Square had alerted him to the risk posed by the gay men who suddenly appeared in his bar. He had seen the SLA close the Barrel House and numerous other neighborhood bars, and he knew that the advent of the World's Fair threatened to precipitate even greater police vigilance at the same time that it promised huge profits to the businesses able to cater to the tourist trade. "You know what it means," he later pleaded before the State Liquor Authority, "if I should [lose] that place? . . . I know what it means to be on 42 Street in the World's Fair. Would I take a chance for that?"[26] He thus quickly contacted the police and military, who he doubtless suspected were already aware of the situation, for assistance in ridding his bar of the homosexuals. A member of the police vice squad who had frequently dealt with "fag cases" visited the bar on two occasions and advised him to try to discourage the gay men's patronage by putting salt in their drinks or refusing to serve them altogether. But the police and SLA also put the bar under surveillance. An undercover SLA agent who visited the bar filed reports noting that while he had overheard both the manager and bartender indicate their desire to rid the bar of "fags," they had not in fact done so. The plainclothes policemen who visited the bar used their usual methods to secure definitive evidence that the bar was frequented by "degenerates": they struck up conversations with the other patrons, made arrangements to go home with several of them, and then arrested them as they left the bar, charging them with "degenerate disorderly conduct." (Five patrons were arrested and convicted; some had their sentences suspended, others spent sixty days in the workhouse.)

A week later, while the bar was still under surveillance by the police and SLA, army officers inspected the premises at the request of the manager and were sufficiently alarmed by the mixing of soldiers and "fairies" there that they raided the bar the following evening (again with the cooperation of the manager) and ordered every soldier to leave. The owner may have thought that this drastic tactic had solved his problem, but he then somehow discovered that the authorities had put his bar under surveillance, despite his efforts to cooperate with them, and he began to panic. After identifying one of the plainclothesmen in the bar, he warned several gay patrons to avoid him, a fact duly noted by the plainclothesman he had not recognized. In retaliation, the police raided the bar, evicted its patrons, and forced it to close. They agreed to let it reopen only on the condition that a uniformed policeman be stationed on the premises to maintain order.

Not surprisingly, the policeman's presence, the two raids, the eviction of the soldiers, and the arrests of patrons by plainclothesmen had the intended effect on the bar's gay customers: they went away. Nonetheless, the Liquor Authority still decided to revoke the bar's license on the grounds that it had allowed homosexuals and other people of "questionable character" to congregate on the premises. As a last-ditch effort to save his investment, the owner appealed the revocation to the courts, but his appeal did not question the SLA's policy against bars that catered to homosexuals. Both the SLA and the bar focused their arguments on whether the manager had engaged in a "good faith [effort] to eliminate this condition and . . . cooperate with the police authorities," and the bar owner lost.[27]

The Times Square Garden & Grill case illustrates the full range of forces that could be brought to bear against gay bars in the city, the extent of the SLA's commitment to its anti-gay policy, and the futility of most defense strategies available to such bars. It served to warn bar owners that they did not need to *cultivate* a gay patronage in order to suffer the SLA's wrath: any bar that so much as *tolerated* the presence of a single homosexual risked losing its license. And in conjunction with the Gloria's case, it demonstrated that bars had no legal defense against this policy because the SLA had the full support of the courts. As a result, the SLA faced few legal challenges to its campaign against gay bars for the next fifteen years. It regularly closed both bars that had sought a gay clientele and bars that had served a single gay patron.

A short survey of the state regulation of bars where gay men and lesbians congregated in the following three decades, while moving beyond the purview of this book, makes the full implications of this anti-gay policy clear. Police and SLA harassment of gay bars escalated in the postwar decades. But it was only in 1954, fifteen years after the Times Square case, that the courts began to worry that the SLA had become so zealous in its punishment of bars serving the occasional gay man or lesbian that it posed a threat to the stability of the retail liquor business itself. Ironically, the case that led the courts to begin limiting the SLA's powers involved the Fifth Avenue Bar, part of the enormous Stanwood Cafeteria complex on Broadway at Seventy-first Street, which was well known among white working-class gay men as a rendezvous for "painted queens" from the Upper West Side, Brooklyn, and the Bronx, some of them effeminate prostitutes there along with their johns.[28] It would have been easy for the SLA to build a strong case against the bar, given its tolerance of gay patrons, but it had revoked the bar's liquor license on the basis of slender evidence indeed: a single report from a plainclothes policeman that on a single visit to the bar, beginning at 3:15 one morning and lasting less than half an hour, he had seen fifteen men he believed to be homosexuals and had arrested one man who had invited him home.[29] The SLA's ruling indicates both its growing antipathy toward bars that served homosexuals (since, unlike in the prewar cases, it offered the bar no opportunity to correct the situation before it took action) and its confidence, given the earlier court rulings, that it had virtually unassailable authority to close them.

In this case the SLA's confidence was misplaced. The stature given the bar by its association with the Upper West Side's largest cafeteria weighed too heavily with the court. Citing "the excellent reputation of the licensed premises running over a period of many years, [and] the large investment which petitioner has in the business," the court rebuked the Authority for revoking the cafeteria's license on the basis of such inadequate evidence of such minor misconduct. It affirmed its support for the Authority's efforts to revoke the licenses of bars that "suffer or knowingly permit such misconduct to exist or to continue," by which it meant bars whose management deliberately cultivated or permitted a gay clientele. But the court cautioned that any bar might inadvertently serve someone whose homosexuality had not been recognized, and it made it more difficult for the Authority to show that a proprietor had knowingly allowed his bar to became a gay rendezvous. In the future, the court ruled, the Liquor Authority would be required to prove either that "more than a single [disorderly] event" had occurred *or* that the management had witnessed and acquiesced in the single event.[30]

The court's ruling limited the SLA's authority to define what constituted a "disorderly" bar. Heretofore, the SLA had decreed that the simple presence of a homosexual at a bar made it disorderly; henceforth, it could be required to demonstrate both that the gay men or women present had engaged in disorderly conduct *and* that the management had acquiesced in that conduct.

Nonetheless, two factors limited the practical effect of the ruling. First, neither the Liquor Authority nor the police paid much attention to it, since they anticipated, correctly, that most bars would not challenge their rulings. Second, the court's reasoning undermined its technical ban on the closing of bars where homosexuals were merely present, even when those bars took the SLA to court. In effect, the ruling allowed bars to be patronized by homosexuals, but only so long as they did nothing to *indicate* they were homosexuals, because it allowed the Liquor Authority to rule that any behavior coded as homosexual was ipso facto disorderly.

What evidence of homosexuality constituted disorderly conduct? As at the Times Square Garden & Grill, where five men were arrested for solicitation, one man picking up another man at a bar provided the clearest such evidence, since "homosexual solicitation" had been classified as a form of "degenerate disorderly conduct" in the penal code since 1923. Moreover, it was usually reported (and always brought as a criminal charge) by a presumably impeccable source, the plainclothes policeman whom the gay man had "solicited" and whose word was usually confirmed by the gay man's conviction or failure to contest the charge, and it was likely to occur even at bars where men were quite circumspect in their behavior.[31] It is impossible to determine from police and court records how many arrests for solicitation originated in bars, but the number was large: in 1964, a gay lawyer who had defended men charged with solicitation since the 1930s identified gay bars as one of the two most common places where entrapment occurred.[32] The arrest usually had calamitous effects: a fine or jail term for the man entrapped, an SLA investigation of the bar where he had met the officer, and either a letter of warning to the bar, the revocation or suspension of its license, or its designation as a "raided premises."[33] An arrest for solicitation could also lead to a bar's loss of its lease if the police decided to report the incident to its landlord.[34]

The definition of disorder encompassed more than simply solicitation, however. The State Liquor Authority and courts alike continued to use a wide range of cultural practices to mark men as both gay and disorderly, much as they had in the case of Gloria's. They continued to classify men as queer on the basis of the same gender-inflected signs used by lay observers to identify such men: their campy behavior (or, as the agents called it, their "effeminacy"), their use of rouge or lipstick, their practice of calling each other by camp or women's names, the way they talked or the fact that they talked about the opera or other suspect topics, or other aspects of their dress or carriage.[35] In 1960, for instance, the state's highest court upheld a ruling by the SLA that the owner of the Fulton Bar in Brooklyn had permitted the bar to "be used as a gathering place for homosexuals and degenerates who conducted themselves in an offensive and indecent manner" because "the majority of the patrons were . . . wearing tight fitting trousers. . . . 3 male patrons walk[ed] to the rear of the premises with a sway to their hips, . . . [and two of them spoke] in high pitched effeminate tones and . . . gesture[d] with limp wrists."[36] Three years later, in an upstate case frequently cited by New York liquor authorities, the courts allowed the SLA to close a bar in Albany where it alleged that the disorderly conduct consisted of men calling each other "her," "sweetheart," and "dearie"; speaking in "high-pitched voices" and commenting on each other's hair and dress; "swagger[ing] their hips"; putting their arms about one another's waists; and, on one occasion, kissing. The Authority's investigators had also observed "two females, one mannish in appearance, [who was] holding the hands of the other female."[37] In effect, then, the Liquor Authority regarded campy gay male and butch lesbian cultural practices, as well as expressions of same-sex affection, as disorderly—indeed, as sufficiently dangerous disruptions of the normative social order to merit prohibition and the revocation of a liquor license.*

Technically, then, at least after the 1954 *Stanwood* ruling, the central issue in a liquor license revocation hearing was whether or not the homosexuals patronizing a bar had been disorderly, but in practice the SLA

---

*As the two cases just cited suggest, the courts continued to uphold the Liquor Authority's determination that such gay-coded practices were disorderly well into the 1960s. Not all judges agreed, though. Indeed, in the absence of unambiguous case law the prejudices of individual judges often settled the matter. In 1956, for instance, a municipal court judge dismissed a case in which a patrolman had charged the owner of Main Street, a popular Eighth Street bar, with running a disorderly premises, after the patrolman had reported seeing nothing more than "approximately forty male patrons at the bar, some [of] which were acting in an effeminate manner . . . [including] some of these men ["four, five or six of them" he later specified] walking back and forth with a sway of their hands and their hips."[38]

pointed to patrons' "disorderly" behavior only to show that they were homosexual, both before and after that ruling. A wide range of cultural practices were considered disorderly, in other words, only because they were coded as homosexual and thus "proved" that the patrons were actually homosexuals. Underlying the question of whether or not such behavior was disorderly, therefore, was the question of whether it could be used to identify the men or women at the bar as homosexuals.

Much of the examination and cross-examination of witnesses at Liquor Authority hearings consequently focused on the semiotics of homosexuality. Disputes over how homosexuals could be identified became fundamental to the legal strategies of both sides. The SLA sought to show that the men at a bar were recognizably gay in order to bolster their claim that the management must have recognized and tolerated their presence. The bars, on the other hand, tried to argue that their patrons' unconventional gender performances did not *necessarily* signify that they were homosexual, even if it did mean they were unconventional in some other respect. A defense attorney for the Stanwood Cafeteria bar itself used this tactic in 1953, for instance, when he pressed an officer to admit that he had "seen actors employed by the television studios [in the neighborhood] going out of the studios with pancake makeup on," so that the mere fact that some of the men seen at the bar wore such makeup was not evidence that "they are prima facie homo-sexuals."[39] Similarly, when an SLA attorney asked a bartender at the Big Dollar in 1960 if he hadn't seen a man wearing an earring at the bar, the bartender replied that there was but one: the actor who played "a character from television, Mr. Clean."[40] Some bars tried to use their bohemian reputation as a defense against the charge that their patrons were homosexual. The owner of the Salle de Champagne, a well-known Greenwich Village rendezvous for theatrical producers and performers, insisted in 1950 that the mannerisms of one of his patrons could be called "abnormal" only "if you call theatrical not normal . . . [because] the theatrical profession doesn't act in a normal manner." Even Milton Berle, the owner's attorney added, "sometimes affects certain mannerisms." The owner concurred: "Most of the theatrical profession do."[41]

The bars hoped such arguments would prove that the SLA's investigators had incorrectly identified their customers as homosexuals, or, at the least, that the bars themselves could be excused for not having recognized that their customers were gay and thus had not deliberately "suffered and permitted" homosexuals to congregate. The narrow logic of this defense was indicative of the legal constraints under which gay bars operated. Indeed, restrictive court rulings led the relatively few bars that fought the revocation of their licenses in the 1950s and early 1960s to adopt the safest defense strategy possible: denying the SLA's claim that homosexuals had been on the premises at all, and further asserting that, if any had been present, the management had been unaware of them. The bars' attorneys considered such denials the only defense possible in those years, a lawyer who represented several gay and lesbian bars in the 1950s recalled. "It was useless to raise other issues," he contended; "all you could do was deny that you'd seen anything happen."[42] Some bars sought to bolster this defense by showing they had prohibited strangers from talking with each other and taken other measures to discourage incidents of disorderly conduct.[43] But with few exceptions, such defenses failed. For more than three decades following the repeal of Prohibition, gay bars were stymied in their legal efforts to fight their own prohibition.

Gay bars were the primary targets of that prohibition, but the injunction against gay culture served as an injunction against any non-normative gender behavior. It codified the proper dress, speech patterns, modes of carrying one's body, and subjects of intellectual and sexual interest for any man or woman who wished to socialize in public. Since this administrative code only reinforced the more general cultural code that governed the gender organization of everyday life (a code less explicit but equally precise in its injunctions), it remained invisible to most bar patrons and city residents, whose behavior was already governed and normalized by that code. Only people who had not been successfully normalized by the dominant gender culture, such as gay men or lesbians (though not limited to them, but including, in different ways, for instance, certain working-class or minority men or women), were likely to face the more overt and brutal policing that occurred at the boundaries of the gender order, because only they came close to those boundaries. Nonetheless, the coding of a wide range of behavior as homosexual and its definition as disorderly served to establish and enforce the boundaries of the normative gender order in a way that affected the patrons of any bar, whether or not they identified as gay. Even Mr. Clean had to think twice about wearing an earring.

The enhanced role of the State Liquor Authority in the regulation of gay life marked an important transition in the policing of urban sociability. In the half-century before the Depression, the primary impetus for the policing of morality had come from private societies that organized to exert pressure on the metropolitan police to enforce moral codes and even used their influence at the state and federal level to acquire police powers for themselves. But the moral crisis generated by Prohibition had undermined their legitimacy, and the financial crisis generated by the Depression had undermined their private support. By 1931 the Committee of Fourteen, as noted before, had seen its cultural authority so diminished by the popular revolt against moral vigilantism that it was reduced to pleading to donors that it had never "been interested in regulating the conduct of individuals," an objective now evidently in some disrepute, but had only been concerned to attack the parties "who make money out of the exploitation of girls."[44] When it lost the support of its major financial backers the next year, the most effective social-purity society in the city's history was forced to terminate its work. The state legislature established the State Liquor Authority the following year, however, and its agents took up the task previously performed by the Committee's agents: surveying bars and other sites of public sociability, threatening the livelihoods of entrepreneurs who sanctioned public disorder, defining such disorder even as they searched for it.

While a number of historians have argued that the police (and, by implication, the state more generally) reduced their role in moral policing in the early twentieth century, the history reconstructed here demonstrates that such periodizations need to be revised. The role of private agencies declined and the state actually took *greater* responsibility for important aspects of such policing in the middle decades of the century. The state's reliance on the licensing mechanism made its policing less visible than before but allowed it to become even more pervasive. Indeed, the city and state increasingly relied on the licensing power to regulate public sociability, since it allowed them to circumvent the limits placed on police power. The extent and effectiveness of this form of regulation become evident as soon as its effects on lesbians and gay men are considered. SLA licensing restrictions prohibited lesbians and gay men from working in most restaurants, bars, and other businesses where liquor was served, and prohibited lesbians and gay men from gathering openly in such establishments. This served to exclude lesbians and gay men from the public sphere and amounted to a virtual ban on the public assembly of gay men and women.

The criminalization of bars serving homosexuals did not eliminate gay bars, however. They proliferated in the city in the postwar years, and at any given moment during most of the 1950s there were usually seventy or more bars serving gay men. A few bars were able to survive for years or even decades. But from the 1930s through the 1960s, most gay bars lasted only a few months or years before the police closed them and forced their patrons to move on to some other locale. They survived at all only by paying off the local patrolmen and policing the behavior of their own patrons. The vulnerability of even those bars that paid off the police made them too risky an investment for most small businessmen trying to go it alone. As a result, organized criminal syndicates, the only entities powerful enough to offer bars systematic protection, took over the gay bar business. The syndicates had been consolidated in the process of establishing control over the liquor traffic during Prohibition. After Repeal, their role in the business as a whole was diminished (though hardly eliminated), as state-sanctioned businesspeople tried to revive "legitimate" nightlife. But they continued to exert a particular power in those portions of the business still prohibited, and they played a pervasive role in the operation of gay bars.[45]

Rather than eliminating gay bars, in fact, SLA regulations ironically served to foster the creation of exclusively gay bars. Before Repeal, most gay men had gathered at saloons, restaurants, and speakeasies also frequented by straight people. Gay men remained "discreetly" invisible at some, but were quite open at others. Restaurants and saloons had always risked trouble with the authorities if they allowed gay men to gather on their premises, and their patrons were subject to arrest for disorderly conduct. Actual interference from the authorities, however, was rare. But after Repeal, bar owners risked losing their entire business if they served a single homosexual. Given this danger, most bars became reluctant to let *any* gay people mix openly with their other patrons and sought to protect themselves by excluding from their premises anyone they suspected of being gay. Lesbians and gay men continued to covertly patronize bars and restaurants throughout the city. But the anti-gay SLA regulations served, as intended, to exclude homosexuals from the public sphere by preventing them from socializing *openly* in "straight" bars. The same ban also resulted in the establishment of exclusively gay bars, however, where men could be openly gay. Bars that saw profit in serving gay men usually committed themselves to them, knowing their tenure would likely be brief. Exclusively gay bars, a relatively rare phenomenon before the 1930s, proliferated after Repeal. Thus, while gay life continued to thrive in the 1930s, '40s, and '50s, it was more hidden and more segregated from the rest of city life than it had been before.

The new policies of the police and SLA served to exacerbate the class and cultural chasms already dividing the gay world. Because the presence of "obvious" homosexuals or "fairies" in a bar invited the wrath of the SLA and the police, even many gay bars refused to serve them, and other gay men were encouraged in their hostility toward them. Moreover, SLA policy encouraged even those bars that welcomed the presence of homosexuals to try to suppress expressions of a homosexual sensibility, and reinforced the development of a hierarchy of gay bars in the city. The ranking depended in large part on the bars' relative safety, which was closely tied to their class character and cultural style, to how "gay" a bar—and what *kind* of gay bar—it was. As enforced, SLA policy favored bars whose customers were circumspect over bars whose customers were campy, bars whose clientele could afford to pay for "connections" over bars whose customers were less able to afford protection.

While many men patronized gay bars, others were unwilling to do so, at least during crackdowns, for fear of being caught in a raid, which might result in their being arrested or at least being forced to divulge their names and places of employment. This was an especially powerful threat to professionally successful men, since either police action carried the risk of further penalties if the police contacted their landlords or employers. Some of those who did go to the bars found their visits shrouded with fear. "I always expected the bar I was in to be raided," one Wall Street executive recalled. "It was a constant, deadening fear on the few occasions I went."[46] Nonetheless, they found other places to meet their friends and to continue their participation in gay society. Some of them retreated to their apartments, where they entertained their friends at small dinner parties and enormous cocktail parties. Other men sought to avoid the dangers inherent in entering a gay bar by covertly meeting their friends in commercial establishments not identified as gay. Not only were the police much less likely to raid such places, but a man's homosexuality would not necessarily be revealed if he happened to be seen there by a straight associate.[47] Some men of moderate means frequented restaurants and cafeterias operating without liquor licenses, but men of greater wealth and social status had access to more secure venues, where they faced even less risk of being arrested or recognized as homosexual.

Several of the elegant nightclubs that opened to the north and east of Times Square in the late twenties and thirties were available to these men. The clubs had been started by entrepreneurs who sought to appeal to a society and business clientele by offering a more socially exclusive rendezvous than the increasingly disreputable nightclubs run by immigrants, gangsters, and other "lower-class" impresarios along Broadway itself. Among the new, more elite entrepreneurs were the Rockefellers, who opened the Rainbow Room in a Rockefeller Center penthouse.[48] Several of these clubs were heavily—but covertly—patronized by gay men and lesbians. If the highly flamboyant working-class "painted queens" who gathered at Bryant Park represented one extreme of homosexual self-presentation, the highly circumspect, high-society lesbians and gay men who met at nightclubs like Tony's, described by the 1939 WPA guide as "a once famous speakeasy [on Fifty-second Street, and currently a] . . . culinary high spot where celebrities go to see and be seen," represented another. Although most patrons would not have guessed it, the bar at the entrance to Tony's was "crowded with homosexuals," according to one gay man in 1939, and others gathered at the tables in the back room, where Spivy, an enormous lesbian famous in the elite gay world, sang for her gay following. In 1940 Spivy opened her own nightclub, Spivy's Roof, in the penthouse of a building on Fifty-seventh Street at Lexington. Along with Spivy, the performers included Mabel Mercer and Thelma

Carpenter; Liberace and Paul Lynde both performed there early in their careers. According to a jazz pianist who worked for Spivy in the 1940s, her club welcomed small numbers of gay people, so long as they were "discreet." This policy encountered little opposition, for as successful businesspeople, many of Spivy's patrons had every reason to hide their sexual identities. Lesbians and gay men sometimes went to the club together as "couples." Nonetheless, Spivy still instructed her doorman to exclude homosexuals whenever their numbers or overtness began to threaten the club's reputation.[49]

A somewhat more varied group of men frequented the highly respectable businessmen's bars found in many hotels. Such bars had been popular rendezvous even before Prohibition. One man who had migrated to New York as an eighteen-year-old in 1917 recalled going with his "friends to the chic bars like the Astor, the bar in the Hotel Claridge or the Biltmore [and] the Knickerbocker. These bars were chic, and discreet, and adventuresome," he added. "I never liked the gay bars [in later years]; they seemed too common."[50] Another well-known rendezvous among gay men was the elegant Oak Room at the Plaza, where men were expected to dress well and carry themselves with great discretion. As one man recalled, "The Plaza Hotel, of course, was a choice place to conduct yourself with decorum and make a pretty good pickup."[51]

The longest-lived and most famous such bar was the one in the Astor Hotel, at the corner of Seventh Avenue and Forty-fifth Street. Although it had been a gay meeting place since the 1910s, it reached the zenith of its popularity during World War II, when it developed a genuinely national reputation among gay servicemen as a place to meet civilians when passing through New York. Gay men's use of the bar was carefully orchestrated—in both its spatial and cultural dimensions—to protect both their identities and its license. Gay men gathered on only one side of the oval bar, where the management allowed them to congregate so long as they did not become too "obvious." As one man who frequented the Astor during the war recalled, "The management would cut us down a little bit when it felt we were getting a little obvious. If you got a little too buddy, or too cruisy . . . too aggressive, they'd say cut it out, men, why don't you go somewhere else? You had to be much more subtle." Men on the other side of the bar, however, were allowed to "do anything they wanted," the man added; "they could put *their* arms around each other, *they* could touch, because it was very obvious that they were butch."[52] Gay men had to be "subtle" so that the straight men among them—including the occasional strangers who unknowingly sat down on the gay side of the bar—would not realize they were surrounded by queers. They used the same clues they had developed in other contexts to alert each other to their identities: wearing certain clothes fashionable among gay men but not stereotypically associated with them, introducing certain topics of conversation, or casually using code words well known within the gay world but unremarkable to those outside it (such as *gay*). Using such codes, men could carry on extensive and highly informative conversations whose significance would be unnoticeable to the people around them.

Gay men continued to covertly appropriate other kinds of public spaces for their own purposes, even in the context of the post-Prohibition clampdown. On a much larger scale than at the Astor, they regularly gathered en masse at the performances of entertainers who assumed special significance in gay culture, such as Beatrice Lillie and Judy Garland. Opera and dance performances also drew large numbers of gay men. The Metropolitan Opera, on Broadway at Fortieth Street, was "standard meeting place," according to one man. Another man whimsically recalled that "since there were no known instances of police raids on [such distinguished] cultural events, all stops were pulled out as far as costume and grooming. The hairdos and outlandish clothes many gays wore were not to be equaled until the punk rock era."[53] The cultural significance of such events had always been determined as much by the audience as by the performers on stage. But as their role in gay life suggests, such events were the site of multiple audiences and productive of multiple cultural meanings, many of them obscure to the class that nominally dominated them.

Such were the politics of public space in much of the city—and such was the legacy of the complicated relationship between "fairies" and "queers." Gay men and straight men often used the same spaces in entirely different ways, with the latter not suspecting the presence of the queers in their midst, in part because the queers did not look or behave like the fairies they saw at Bryant Park or on the stage. The Astor could maintain its public reputation as an eminently respectable Times Square establishment, while its reputation as a gay rendezvous and pickup bar assumed legendary proportions in the gay world.

Gay men continued to meet throughout the city, then, much as they had before the Repeal of Prohibition. The SLA regulations did not achieve their announced purpose of keeping gay men and lesbians from gathering in public. But they did make it more dangerous for them to gather in public and forced them to remain hidden. In an important sense, then, the regulations did exclude gay men from the public sphere, because they dramatically reduced the level of interaction between gay and straight people. Gay men hardly disappeared from the city, but for thirty years they became less visible to outsiders.

THE NEW CENSORSHIP

Whereas the State Liquor Authority regulations sought to prevent the public assembly of homosexuals, other regulations sought to eliminate the *representation* of homosexuality in the public sphere. New censorship regulations passed in the late 1920s and early 1930s were aimed at curbing both the discussion of homosexuality and even the simple depiction of homosexual characters in films, theaters, and cabarets. The padlock bill, passed by the New York state legislature in 1927 after the controversy over *The Captive* and *The Drag* (see chapter 11), was the first such measure. It prohibited any play from "depicting or dealing with, the subject of sex degeneracy, or sex perversion." In other words, it forbade any playwright to include gay and lesbian characters or even to address the subject of homosexuality.

The city extended this ban to nightclubs in the 1930s and 1940s. In order to restore a measure of control over the city's huge Prohibition-era nightclubs (or "cabarets") the city had begun requiring them to obtain licenses in 1926. (This had little effect on most of the city's speakeasies, which were either hidden or did not come under the rubric of "cabarets" since they did not provide dancing or musical entertainment.) In 1931 the city shifted the administration of cabaret licensing from the Department of Licenses to the police, who, as the lawyer Paul Chevigny has noted, "turned it into an instrument of control over the employees of the cabarets." In 1940 the police began to require cabaret employees to obtain identification cards, which were issued only after a fingerprint check to ensure that the applicant was of good character and had not been convicted of certain offenses, including degenerate disorderly conduct. New regulations prohibited the employment of people "who *pretended to be*" homosexuals as well as homosexuals themselves, which effectively banned pansy acts as well as gay staffers who might attract a gay clientele. The SLA also threatened to revoke the liquor license of any cabaret found violating the city's cabaret regulations. A handful of clubs featuring female impersonators or pansy acts, including the Club Richman, the Howdy Club, and the Club 181, managed to survive despite the regulations, but the police and SLA strictly enforced them in most cases. In 1950 they revoked the liquor license of the Salle de Champagne, a nationally known Greenwich Village restaurant cabaret popular among the theater crowd, because a black performer who, it turned out, had been denied a cabaret card on the basis of two prior convictions for homosexual solicitation had been permitted to sing several songs in a loosely organized amateur night, even though the restaurant had not hired the singer. Although the restaurant claimed that he had simply sung a "show tune . . . [perhaps by] Cole Porter," the SLA's investigators charged that "he acted like a degenerate" and sang "songs that had to do with fairies and lesbians."[54]

The new anti-gay vigilance quickly spread beyond New York. In February 1931, just as the police were shutting down the pansy clubs in Times Square, the R-K-O vaudeville circuit issued orders to the house managers in its nationwide chain of theaters prohibiting performers from even using the words *fairy* and *pansy* in their vaudeville routines.[55] When the female-impersonator and pansy acts forced out of New York tried to open in other cities, including Hollywood and San Francisco, they were promptly raided by local authorities (see chapter 11). In the next few years, numerous states passed laws prohibiting female impersonation on the stage.[56]

The most significant step to censor gay images nationally was taken in Hollywood. Demands for the censorship of films had arisen almost from the moment of their appearance at the turn of the century in cheap theaters in immigrant neighborhoods. Those demands had grown as movies had become one of the nation's preeminent forms of entertainment and as the Hollywood studios had sought competitive advantage by producing films dealing with a host of risqué topics. In response to the chaos created by the existence of a host of local censorship authorities, each with a somewhat different perspective on the boundaries of acceptable content, the Hollywood studios adopted a production code in 1930 designed to establish a single national standard for the production of morally unobjectionable films. The code allowed the depiction of adultery, murder, and a host of other immoral practices, so long as they were shown to be wrong, but it prohibited any reference whatsoever to homosexuality, or "sex perversion," along with a handful of other irredeemably immoral practices. The code initially had little effect on the studios, but in 1934, in response to the threat of a national boycott organized by the Catholic-led Legion for Decency, the studios established an independent Production Code Administration, which enforced the ban for another thirty years. After a generation in which films had depicted homosexuals and homosexually tinged situations, such images were prohibited altogether.[57]

The revulsion against gay life in the early 1930s was part of a larger reaction to the perceived "excesses" of the Prohibition years and the blurring of the boundaries between acceptable and unacceptable public sociability. But it also reflected the crisis in gender arrangements precipitated by the Depression. As many men lost their jobs, their status as breadwinners, and their sense of mastery over their own futures, the central tenets undergirding their gender status were threatened. A plethora of sociological studies of "The Unemployed Man and His Family" reflected a widespread concern that massive male unemployment and job insecurity had upset gender relations and diminished the status of men in the family. The reaction against the challenges posed to manhood by Depression conditions was widely evident in the culture, from the celebration of powerful male physiques in the public art of the New Deal to the attacks on married women for "stealing" men's jobs and the laws passed by several states requiring women to be dismissed from teaching jobs when they married.[58] Lesbians and gay men began to seem more dangerous in this context—as figures whose defiant perversity threatened to undermine the reproduction of normative gender and sexual arrangements already threatened by the upheavals of the thirties. The new laws forbidding gay people to gather openly with heterosexuals in licensed restaurants and bars and banning even the *representation* of homosexuality bespoke a fear that gender arrangements were so fragile, even a glimpse of an alternative might endanger them. The risk seemed so palpable that special attention was not even given to the threats such contact or images posed to impressionable young people—the usual vehicle for the expression of fears about social reproduction. Even the adults who patronized Times Square nightclubs needed to be protected from them.

THE STRANGE CAREER OF THE CLOSET

IN THE 1950S AND 1960S, WHEN THE GAY AND LESBIAN MOVEMENT BEGAN to challenge anti-gay regulations and customs, they seemed to be the residue of an age-old, unchanging social antipathy toward homosexuality. Openly gay meeting places and overt references to homosexuality were so rare as a result of them that it was hard to believe homosexuality had ever been visible in the public sphere. As the memory of the early decades of the century receded further, those regulations came to seem even more enigmatic, at once inevitable and inexplicable. If homosexuality had always been so invisible and homosexuals had always been confined to the closet, why were such rules even enacted?

As this book has shown, those regulations were not simply the inevitable elaborations of an age-old antipathy, nor did they simply ratify the invisibility and isolation of homosexuals. In the late nineteenth and early twentieth centuries, an extensive gay world took shape in the streets, cafeterias, saloons, and apartments of New York, and gay men played an integral role in the social life of certain neighborhoods. Fairies drank with sailors and other workingmen at waterfront dives and entertained them at Bowery resorts; "noted faggots" mixed with other patrons at Harlem's rent parties and basement cabarets; and lesbians ran speakeasies where Greenwich Village bohemians—straight and queer alike—gathered to read their verse. In the late 1920s, gay performers moved from the margins of the city into its most prestigious entertainment district and briefly became the darlings of Broadway.

The anti-gay laws of the 1920s and 1930s were enacted in response to the growing visibility of the gay world and to the challenge it seemed to pose to fragile gender and social arrangements. The Broadway run of *The Captive* and the imminent production of *The Drag* led the New York state legislature to pass a theater censorship law; the proliferation of gay images and homosexual buffoonery in film led national censorship forces to demand the prohibition of "sexual perversion" by the Hollywood film code; the pansy craze prompted states and municipalities around the nation to ban female impersonation; and the growing visibility of gay and lesbian patrons in speakeasies and restaurants led the New York State Liquor Authority to forbid their presence after Prohibition's repeal.

The new laws did not mark a complete break from the past. Although some gay men had risked harassment by boldly declaring their presence in the city's streets and restaurants, many more had kept their homosexuality hidden from outsiders. Indeed, before the 1930s much of gay life had been governed by an informal "understanding" fashioned through constant skirmishes over the uses of public sites, which allowed queer men to socialize in public only so long as they did nothing to draw attention to themselves as homosexuals. Restaurants, speakeasies, and even bathhouses patronized by gay men were able to flourish so long as they kept out of public view.

But the new regulations did mark a significant change, for they turned that informal understanding into an enforceable contract between unequal partners. Municipal authorities had already enforced the old arrangement by defining gay sociability as a kind of disorderly conduct, raiding commercial establishments they regarded as too visibly gay and arresting men they thought carried themselves too boldly on the streets. But such attacks on gay men were episodic, not continuous, and had an uncertain basis in the law. In 1920 the municipal court judge who heard the cases of the men arrested at the Hotel Koenig worried that their conviction for disorderly conduct might be overturned on appeal, since they had done nothing more than gather openly as homosexuals. He would not have had to worry after 1933, when state regulations upheld by the state's highest court explicitly prohibited gay men and women from gathering in licensed public establishments, and when a host of other regulations systematized the exclusion of homosexuality from the public sphere.

The new regulations not only codified the ban on gay visibility but raised the stakes for those who considered violating it. They threatened to destroy the business of any bar or restaurant proprietor who served a single drink to a single gay man or lesbian, to close any theater presenting a play with gay characters, and to prevent the distribution of any film addressing gay issues. They explicitly defined one man's trying to pick up another man as a criminal offense. Never before had gay life been subject to such extensive legal regulation.

The new regulations did not eradicate the gay world, for the gay subculture provided men with the resources they needed to circumvent them. The use of double entendre, virtually mandated by the regulations, still allowed gay men to communicate privately and to address gay issues more publicly. Even after the passage of the Padlock Law, for instance, some theatrical producers continued to present homosexual themes, although they did so more obliquely than before. The early thirties saw several Broadway plays implicitly refer to homosexuality, including Noël Coward's *Design for Living* (1933) and Mordaunt Shairp's *The Green Bay Tree* (1933), the latter depicting the relationship between an effete wealthy bachelor and his adopted working-class "son." As the historian Kaier Curtin has noted, many reviewers conspired to prevent the censorship of such plays by ignoring—or denying—the fact that they had anything to do with "queer" topics. A disgruntled critic complained in 1933: "My brothers of the First Night Garden, remembering the bad luck of 'The Captive,' are prone to pretend that Mr. Shairp's play . . . has nothing to do with the way of a man with a man. Well, if it has nothing to do with that it has nothing to do with anything."[1] Films such as Alfred Hitchcock's *Rope* (1948) and Vincente Minnelli's *Tea and Sympathy* (1956) portrayed homosexual characters and situations—though often without much sympathy—by using connotative rather than denotative codes that foiled the efforts of censors. Unabashed gay self-representation, let alone the direct defense of homosexuality that began Mae West's *Drag*, would not be allowed on the stage or screen again for more than a generation. But gay subtexts persisted, and the complex subcultural codes and semiotics of gay life continued to infuse popular culture through the lyrics of Cole Porter, the flamboyant costumes of Liberace, the campy antics of the comedian Paul Lynde, and the jokes and innuendo of the Jack Benny radio show.[2]

So long as gay men were "discreet," moreover, they continued to face relatively little harassment in the 1930s. Bathhouses remained relatively safe because they kept out of view. The Flamingo, a palatial gay bar on West Fifty-sixth Street, and other exclusively gay clubs were sometimes able to survive for years at a time. Tony's, Spivy's, and other elegant nightclubs continued to welcome gay men and lesbians so long as they remained invisible to outsiders. Late-night cafeterias and drugstore counters, not subject to SLA licensing, continued to serve as gay haunts. Forty-second Street continued to be a central meeting place for hustlers, sailors, and gay men interested in "rough trade," and the Barrel House, the Pink Elephant, and other bars for sailors and gay men operated in lower Times Square until extraordinary circumstances—such as the crackdown preceding the 1939 World's Fair—spelled their doom. New neighborhood enclaves took shape on the east and west sides of Manhattan, in Brooklyn Heights, and in Jackson Heights in Queens. Gay men who lived through the intense anti-gay campaigns of the post–World War II decade looked back fondly on the 1930s as a time of relative calm, just as many of the men who lived through the even more severe crackdowns of the early 1960s looked back on the 1950s as a golden age.

Although gay life continued to flourish, it became less visible to outsiders and was increasingly segregated from the broader life of the city. Forcing the gay world into hiding—or, to use the modern idiom, into the closet—was precisely the intention of the authorities. They sought to prevent the public display of homosexual styles and identities from disrupting the reproduction of normative gender and sexual arrangements that were already threatened by the crisis of moral authority and social hierarchy provoked by the Prohibition experiment and the gender upheavals of the Depression. A few pansy clubs managed to survive as tourist traps in the Village, but the gay subculture as a whole stopped being part of the spectacle of urban life.

The marginalization and segregation of the gay world set the stage for broader changes in that world and in American sexual culture. A brief survey of those changes suggests how the gay world and sexual culture of the 1930s—recognizable to the modern eye, but as alien as they are familiar—began to be transformed into those of the present era.

As we have seen, the ascendancy of *gay* as the primary self-referential term used by men within the gay world represented a subtle shift in the boundaries of the male sexual world. It reflected a reorganization of male sexual categories and the transition from a world divided into "fairies" and "men" on the basis of gender persona to one divided into "homosexuals" and "heterosexuals" on the basis of sexual object-choice. The transformation in gay culture suggested by the ascendancy of *gay* was closely tied to the masculinization of that culture. Jeans, T-shirts, leather jackets, and boots became more common in the 1940s, part of the "new virile look" of young homosexuals. Increasing numbers of conventionally masculine men identified themselves as gay, in part, because doing so no longer seemed to require the renunciation of their masculine identities. Many gay men still considered themselves "sissies," but it was no longer as necessary for them to do so, and growing numbers adopted a self-consciously masculine style.

Perhaps the most telling evidence of the new sexual and cultural patterns was that growing numbers of bars served homosexuals exclusively. This was in part a consequence of the intensified policing of commercial spaces instituted by the State Liquor Authority, which left most "regular" bars reluctant to let homosexuals mix with their other patrons. But the rise of exclusively gay bars also reflected the changing patterns of gay

sociability. As more gay men identified themselves as homosexuals interested in *other* men who were homosexuals, bars where they could meet
one another became more attractive than bars where they could meet
trade. At the same time, the sharpening of the boundaries between the
heterosexual and homosexual in working-class culture left fewer straight
men willing to become trade. Both sexual systems continued to coexist,
each influencing the terms by which the other was defined. But one was
ascendant, and it represented the future.

At the same time, the culture at large paid increasing—and increasingly hostile—attention to this new breed of gay man. Indeed, the homosexual hardly disappeared from public view after the early 1930s, for
police bulletins and press coverage continued to make him a prominent,
but increasingly sinister, figure. As Americans anxiously tried to come to
terms with the disruptions in the gender and sexual order caused by the
Depression and exacerbated by the Second World War, the "sex deviant"
became a symbol of the dangers posed by family instability, gender confusion, and unregulated male sexuality and violence. A number of children's murders in the late 1930s and the late 1940s, sensationalized by
the local and national press and interpreted as sexual in nature by the
police, fanned a series of panics over sex crime, which became the vehicle
for a wide-ranging discourse about the boundaries of acceptable sexual
and gender behavior.[3]

Beginning in the late 1930s, the panics over sex crimes and the "sex
deviants" who committed them recast the dominant public images of
homosexuals. The majority of cases of child "sex murders" reported by
the press involved men attacking girls. But the press used the murders of
little boys to demonstrate the danger of unsuppressed homosexuality.
Numerous articles warned that in breaking with social convention to the
extent necessary to engage in homosexual behavior, a man had demonstrated the refusal to adjust to social norms that was the hallmark of the
psychopath, and he could easily degenerate further. As an article in
Coronet put it in the fall of 1950, "Once a man assumes the role of
homosexual, he often throws off all moral restraints. . . . Some male sex
deviants do not stop with infecting their often-innocent partners: they
descend through perversions to other forms of depravity, such as drug
addiction, burglary, sadism, and even murder."[4] The press's representation of gay men assumed special cultural authority in the postwar period
because of the growing isolation of gay men from other social groups,
making it even less likely that heterosexuals would know openly gay
men whose complex lives and personalities might counter such images.

As a result of such press campaigns, the long-standing public image of
the queer as an effeminate fairy whom one might ridicule but had no reason to fear was supplemented by the more ominous image of the queer as

a psychopathic child molester capable of committing the most unspeakable crimes against children. The fact that homosexuals no longer seemed so easy to identify made them seem even more dangerous, since it meant that even the next-door neighbor could be one. The specter of the invisible homosexual, like that of the invisible communist, haunted Cold War America. The new image was invoked to justify a new wave of assaults on gay men in the postwar decade. As police efforts to control homosexual activity intensified, the number of reported "sex crimes" surged dramatically. This provoked yet greater public alarm and thus further escalation of police efforts. The number of men arrested for homosexual solicitation in Manhattan alone rose from about seven hundred a year in the 1930s to more than three thousand a year in the late 1940s.[5]

The growing attacks on gay men forged new bonds among them, as the historian John D'Emilio has argued in his study of the postwar gay rights movement.[6] Most gay people resisted such attacks through informal means, but even in the 1930s some of them began organizing to do so more formally. Around 1934 a group of lesbian and gay New Yorkers began meeting to plan a campaign on behalf of homosexuals. Deciding that they lacked the cultural authority to address the public or the legislature directly, they called on a group of psychiatrists and scientists to conduct a "scientific" investigation of homosexuality. Their efforts led to the establishment in the spring of 1935 of the Committee for the Study of Sex Variants, a group of distinguished psychiatrists and other professionals, and the publication six years later of a two-volume study, *Sex Variants*, written by Dr. George Henry, a psychiatrist associated with the Payne Whitney Clinic.[7]

The gay organizers, led by a lesbian using the pseudonym Jan Gay, helped Henry secure funding and arranged for him to interview forty gay men and an equal number of lesbians, who agreed to recount their life stories and submit to psychological and physical examinations in hopes that doing so would help the homosexual cause. Most of the people who had encouraged the study felt betrayed by Henry's handling of their life histories and bitterly disappointed by the failure of the Committee to further their goals. But their efforts represented the beginning of the complex relationship between lesbian and gay activists and psychiatric, religious, and juridical authorities that would be central to the next thirty years of gay organizing.[8]

Thus the dangers gay men faced increased rapidly in the postwar decades, even as the cultural boundaries of their world were changing. I take up the reconfiguration of the boundaries between queer and normal men, the reshaping of the gay world and the transformation of its public image, and the shifting modes of gay resistance in my next book, *The*

Making of the Modern Gay World, 1935–1975, currently in progress. Here it must be noted, though, that even as gay men adopted new strategies to claim space for themselves, many of them continued to rely on the stereotype of the fairy to protect them on an everyday basis. Far from being confined to marginalized locales, some of these invisible gay men claimed the most conventional and prestigious of cultural spaces as their own, even after they had been legally denied the right to associate. And far from remaining invisible, some men—albeit in smaller numbers— continued to use their dress, style, and audacious behavior to establish a high-profile gay presence in the streets of the city, even after "pansies" had been driven from its stages. Different groups of gay men continued to adopt different strategies for staking out and defending their widely differing worlds, and wealthier men continued to have access to safer meeting places. But even men hidden from the dominant culture were not hidden from one another. They still met at the Astor Hotel bar, they still danced at Phil Black's affairs in Harlem, and they still filled Carnegie Hall when Judy Garland performed.

Note on Sources

Notes

Index

NOTE ON SOURCES

THE METHODOLOGICAL PROBLEMS FACING THE HISTORIAN OF HOMOSEXUALITY APPEAR, at first glance, to be unusually daunting. With the exception of the fairies and lesbian butches who audaciously used their clothing and manner to identify themselves to others, most people sought to conceal their gay lives from the police and other outsiders. They were not identified by census takers, nor, with some notable exceptions, were they the focus of inquiry by social reformers or the press. It has been assumed generally that the sources needed to reconstruct the social and cultural history of gay men and lesbians did not exist. And until recently, most professional historians were told that it would be dangerous to their careers even to look for them.

The sources do exist, though, and the political barriers to their use are falling. Only a handful of books have been published on the social history of lesbians and gay men in the United States, most focusing on the years since the beginning of World War II; this is the first book devoted to the prewar years. But a growing number of graduate students and community historians are beginning studies of gay culture and the social organization and cultural meaning of same-sex relations in a wide range of contexts—in Midwestern cities, in small towns and rural areas, in communities of color; in the arts and other media; in diverse political settings. These studies will ultimately revise and make more complicated the periodizations based so far on national studies of coastal cities, and they will challenge our fundamental conceptual categories even more. In order to assist those historians—and to satisfy the curiosity of readers with less pressing interests—this note discusses the major sources used in this study that might be replicated in other locales.

The records of the public and private agencies that policed public sociability and sexual life in New York City were particularly useful. The New York Police Department, like most police departments, has refused to open its records to scholars, but various court records are available. The records of the Manhattan District Attorney and various magistrates' courts have been preserved by the diligent staff of the New York Municipal Archives. The Manhattan D.A. kept a file on every sodomy prosecution. Most files contain little more than a record of court dates and the deposition of the arresting officer describing the alleged facts of the case and the circumstances of the arrest, but some of them contain statements by witnesses, notes from trial lawyers, and memoranda providing a more detailed account of the background of the defendant and the alleged circumstances of the crime. A handful contain excerpts of trial testimony. Even the thinnest files helped make it possible to map the shifting geography of the city's cruising areas and gay meeting places, as well as the social contexts in which men were arrested and the changing organization of the policing of sexual behavior. Although providing crucial evidence for this study, in other words, the District Attorney's papers were not particularly rich or extensive. Since the case files were not indexed by charge, I had to search through thousands of cases in the D.A.'s annual docket books (which listed every case prosecuted by the D.A. in a given year in roughly alphabetical order by name of defendant) in order to find the papers concerning two hundred sodomy prosecutions between 1880 and 1950. The files then had to be retrieved from a warehouse in another borough by a member of the archive's dedicated but limited staff, a process which usually took a week. To make the project manageable, I surveyed the docket books for every fifth year from 1880 to 1950 (and for selected other years).

In addition to the D.A.'s case files (which contain the records of felony prosecutions for sodomy), the manuscript docket books of the city's magistrates' courts (which provide the name, age, address, and occupation of people arrested on less serious misdemeanor charges, including "degenerate disorderly conduct") are also available at the New York Municipal Archives. Although I surveyed the docket books for all twelve police districts in Manhattan for 1924 in an effort to analyze the patterns of cases, it proved more profitable to use them more selectively to secure information about men arrested in particular cases drawn to my attention by other sources (see my discussion of the 1916 Lafayette bathhouse raid below).

Only a handful of actual transcripts of sodomy trials have been preserved (primarily by the John Jay College Trial Transcript Project); transcripts usually were not even produced unless a case was appealed. But the few I located—particularly the transcripts of the eight sodomy trials resulting from the 1903 raid on the Ariston bathhouse—were invaluable.

The records of state and city licensing agencies, particularly the State Liquor Authority (SLA), were also useful. Although these records are often difficult to obtain, despite state freedom of information laws, they offer valuable insights into the regulation of urban sociability and the character of particular bars. Some of them include investigators' descriptions of bars, accounts of interactions with other patrons, and the like. When bars appealed the revocation of their licenses to the courts, they often produced court records that preserved the entire proceeding, from the initial police reports about a bar's homosexual patrons to the reports of SLA investigators, the hearing before the Authority, and relevant correspondence, as well as the legal briefs submitted by both the SLA and the bar's attorneys. The records often provide more evidence about the preconceptions of the police than about the people they were policing, but they offer the *only* evidence available about the social organization of many of the bars patronized by gay people and revealing evidence about the cultural codes used to identify homosexuals.

The records of investigative commissions established by reformers seeking to rationalize government or upstate politicians seeking to embarrass the city's Democratic administration also provide rare glimpses of the city's sexual underworld, since these commissions often sought to undermine the authority of the city's political leaders by drawing attention to the webs of corruption that protected illicit social practices, including gay meeting places. The records of the state commissions appointed in the 1890s by the Republican-controlled state legislature in order to investigate and embarrass New York City's Tammany Hall produced limited evidence about Paresis Hall and other "degenerate resorts."

Even though none of the social-purity societies established in the late nineteenth century in response to the police's failure to control urban "vice" focused on homosexual matters (with the exception of the Society for the Suppression of Vice during World War I), their records constituted one the richest sources for this book. Anti-prostitution societies modeled on the Committees of Fourteen and Fifteen were organized in more than one hundred American cities during the Progressive Era, and historians writing about gay life in other cities should consult their papers. Useful overviews of the anti-prostitution campaigns of the Progressive Era are provided by Allan Brandt, *No Magic Bullet: A Social History of Venereal Disease in the United States Since 1880* (1985), and Ruth Rosen, *The Lost Sisterhood: Prostitution in America, 1900–1918* (1982).

The most useful records were produced by the Committee of Fourteen, an anti-prostitution society whose investigators kept much of the city's nightlife and streetlife under surveillance from 1905 to 1932. Its agents filed thousands of one- to five-page reports on commercial establishments suspected of harboring vice (such as saloons, cabarets, movie theaters, and, during Prohibition, speakeasies) and on street corners and tenements where prostitutes plied their trade (see figure 5.1 for an example); they took special care to determine if local patrolmen and landlords were colluding in the trade. In the course of their search for prostitutes they regularly encountered gay men (and only rarely met women they thought were lesbians). The reports they filed about those encounters provide exceptionally rich evidence about the haunts of gay men, gay street culture, and the social conventions that governed gay men's interactions with other men and the reactions of the investigators themselves to them. Those reports, however, are dispersed—unreferenced—in other records primarily devoted to female prostitution; I had to read almost ten thousand typescript reports in order to find fewer than two hundred accounts of homosexual matters. This was a useful exercise, though, since the other reports painted a vivid portrait of the sexual culture and street culture of the city as a whole. Also useful were the bulletins sent irregularly by the Committee's general secretary to his board of directors, which include reports on homosexual cases and police activity of all sorts.

The Committee of Fifteen (founded 1900) conducted several surveys of prostitution in the city, and while their reports (at the New York Public Library) are less detailed than those of its successor, they include descriptions of "degenerate resorts." The papers of the Society for the Prevention of Crime, held at Columbia University, contain notes on a handful of gay-related cases.

The records of the Society for the Suppression of Vice (Comstock Society), at the Library of Congress, consist of little more than manuscript ledger books recording the bare details of cases the Society prosecuted. But since the Society was involved in the arrest of almost two hundred men for degenerate disorderly conduct during World War I and orchestrated three raids on the Everard and Lafayette Baths in 1916–19, its records provided me with useful data about the men arrested as well as brief notes about the places where they met.

Numerous published sources are also worth consulting. Some of the physicians and medical researchers who took up the subject of sexual inversion and homosexuality near the turn of the century published case histories in their local medical journals. These articles chart physicians' changing conceptualization of the "problem" of abnormal sexuality, but they also offer intriguing glimpses into the lives of the subjects and the ways in which doctors and gay subjects interacted (all, of course, from the perspective of the doctors). An extremely useful (but not exhaustive) guide to such publications is provided by the *Index-Catalog of the Library of the Surgeon-General's Office, United States Army* (several series, beginning 1880).

Articles in local law journals provide valuable information about the policing of homosexuality. A handful of books published by medical researchers contain transcripts of interviews with research subjects. Two were particularly useful to this study, although both must be used with caution. Samuel Kahn's *Mentality and Homosexuality* (1937) was written in the early 1920s while Kahn was a graduate student at New York University and on the staff of the New York City penitentiary on Welfare [Blackwell] Island, where he interviewed dozens of men incarcerated in the homosexual segregation unit. *Sex Variants* (1941) contains extensive transcripts of interviews with lesbians and gay men conducted in the late 1930s by George W. Henry, a psychiatrist at the Payne Whitney Clinic (described in the epilogue). Other books by lawyers and journalists, gay men's memoirs (particularly those by "Ralph Werther"), and guides to the city's nightlife are also useful sources. By the 1960s, a handful of anthropologists, ethnographers, and sociologists had begun studying gay life in urban America. Esther Newton's classic study of 1960s Midwestern female impersonators, *Mother Camp* (1972), is the finest example of such studies (and has influenced or offered confirmation for my thinking about a number of issues). Most were never published but are available as dissertations.

Many newspapers provided more coverage of gay-related matters than the myth of invisibility would lead one to suspect. The more respectable papers, such as the *New York Times*, were unlikely to think that news of homosexuality was "fit to print," but tabloids and some neighborhood newspapers were less reticent. A handful of gossip sheets, notably *Broadway Brevities*, devoted considerable attention to gay life (see chapter 11). Although its circulation was probably limited, it garnered considerable attention, and it is possible that similar papers existed in other cities in the 1920s and 1930s. Historians writing on other cities should look for them—and should not expect archivists to know whether they are in their collections. Neighborhood papers published in areas with gay enclaves were also more likely to report on gay matters than citywide papers. The Greenwich Village papers I consulted on a hunch turned out to be full of commentary, ranging from the hostile notices published in the conservative *Greenwich Village: A Local Review* to the extraordinarily informative—and sympathetic—reporting of columnists in the *Greenwich Village Weekly News*. Harlem's newspapers carried news of drag balls and arrests, and my limited survey of African-American newspapers in other cities suggests that at least some of them provided comparable coverage. *Variety*, the entertainment industry's trade journal, also reported on gay matters in the 1920s and 1930s; most but not all articles focused on New York. I do not mean to suggest that newspapers besides *Broadway Brevities* carried extensive news of gay matters; finding gay-related articles requires hours of microfilm research. But it is likely that newspapers in other cities carried enough articles, particularly during the pansy craze of the 1920s and early 1930s and the sex crime panics of the late 1930s, '40s, and '50s, to make them worth surveying. One has to *look* for such articles to see them, however; at the beginning of this project, several historians who had surveyed New York's papers assured me that none of them carried gay-related articles.

The records of policing agencies and other "outsiders" were crucial to this study, but sources left by gay men themselves were even more helpful since most men strove to hide their gay lives from the police. Several diaries, studies of homosexuality, and collections of letters provided a richly detailed insider's view of gay life from the 1910s to the 1950s. Three manuscripts at the Kinsey Institute Library were particularly useful: the two studies prepared by Thomas Painter in the late 1930s, "The Homosexual" and "The Prostitute" (dated 1941), which survey gay life in New York City, and the diary kept by the pseudonymous "Will Finch." The Beinecke Rare Books and Manuscripts Library at Yale University, the Harvey Ranson Library at the University of Texas, Austin, and the Library of Congress also have particularly useful collections, including the correspondence, diaries, and other papers of gay literary figures such as Tennessee Williams and Carl Van Vechten.

Many diaries and letters are still held privately by literary executors, surviving partners, and relatives. Donna Anderson, the literary executor of Charles Tomlinson Griffes, kindly let me examine portions of Griffes's diary; and Charles Boultenhouse, executor of the Parker Tyler estate, kindly gave me permission to examine and quote some of Tyler's letters. Such papers are immensely valuable and immensely difficult to locate; I beseech anyone reading this who might have such a diary—an aunt's, a great uncle's, a partner's—to consider donating it, or a copy of it, to an archive. A handful of diaries have been published. Donald Vining's four volumes of diaries, *A Gay Diary* (1979–83), are extraordinary rich sources for the reconstruction of New York gay life from the 1940s to 1970s. Glenway Wescott's diary, *Continual Lessons: The Journals of Glenway Wescott, 1937–1955*, edited by Robert Phelps with Jerry Rosco (1990), offers thoughtful reflections on gay life. Just as I was finishing this study Ina Russell published another treasure trove, *Jeb and Dash: A Diary of Gay Life, 1918–1945* (1993), a carefully edited selection of the diaries of her uncle, "Jeb Alexander," who spent most of his life in Washington, D.C.

Evidence from widely disparate sources sometimes allowed me to build a more comprehensive and multifaceted portrayal of early twentieth-century gay establishments and social patterns than I had imagined possible. Jonathan Katz's publication (in *Gay/Lesbian Almanac* [1983]) of a 1929 article from a gay German magazine about a police raid on the Lafayette Baths alerted me to the existence of the bathhouse, and prompted me to search the docket books of the appropriate magistrates' court for records concerning the raid, which provided not only the names, addresses, ages, and occupations of the men arrested but also the actual location of the bath (previously misidentified). References in a memorandum in the Committee of Fourteen papers to a police raid on the Lafayette in 1916 made it possible for me to track down the records of those arrests in the magistrates' court records. Since it turned out that the Society for the Suppression of Vice was involved in the 1916 raid, I was able to use its record book to garner additional data about the raid and the baths' patrons. The diary of Charles Tomlinson Griffes, who frequented the bath in the mid-1910s, provided a different—and much richer—perspective on the social world patrons created there. Charles Demuth's 1916 painting (see figure 8.1) provided yet another perspective.

As this survey should make clear, the problem for the historian is not the absence of sources but the dispersion of those sources and the absence of guides to them. Since virtually no organizations focused on homosexual matters before World War II, historians must spend hours—or, more precisely, years—looking for references interspersed in the papers of organizations preoccupied with other subjects, identifying individuals whose papers are preserved who might have been gay or had contact with gay people, scanning newspapers on microfilm. The exciting news is that the sources are there; the sobering news is that they are hard to find.

Ironically—and unexpectedly—the fact that social-purity forces focused on policing working-class districts means that more evidence about working-class than middle-class gay life has been preserved. It is easier to chart the meeting places and cultural styles of working-class "fairies" than of middle-class "queers." At the same time, though, the evidence produced by gay men themselves (except that filtered through medical or juridical authorities) was more likely to have been produced by middle-class men, who tended to be more literate (or whose writings, in any case, were more likely to have been preserved). No source is "unfiltered," of course; it is precisely the discursive conventions and categories that shape any source that are often of greatest interest. I want here only to draw the reader's attention to the significant variations in the texture of the evidence on which this study is based, and to note that their interpretation has required a variety of theoretical and methodological approaches.

Early in my research it became clear that oral histories would be the single most important source of evidence concerning the internal workings of the gay world, and I conducted approximately seventy-five interviews with gay men born between 1895 and 1935; lawyers who handled gay-related cases; and others with knowledge of New York's gay world. The interviews, almost all recorded, ranged in length: a few lasted less than an hour; most were one to three hours long; and several, conducted over the course of several days, took as long as seven hours. For particularly thoughtful commentaries on oral history methodology, see Elizabeth Kennedy and Madeline Davis, *Boots of Leather, Slippers of Gold: The History of a Lesbian Community* (1993), and Esther Newton, *Cherry Grove, Fire Island: Sixty Years in America's First Gay and Lesbian Town* (1993).

   While all of the interviews influenced my thinking about the the city's gay history, many of them focused on the post–World War II period, and I have listed here only the interviews cited in the notes of this study or those that directly bore on its development. The other interviews will be listed in my next book on the postwar gay world.

ORAL HISTORIES

The interviews listed below were conducted by the author in New York City unless otherwise indicated. Several interviews were conducted in Cherry Grove, a predominantly gay summer community near the city on Fire Island. Several interviews, as noted, were conducted by members of the oral history committee of Senior Action in a Gay Environment (SAGE), an agency serving gay seniors in New York. Many men requested anonymity, and I have indicated (in this list, not the notes) which names are pseudonyms.

Adams, Max (pseud.), Jan. 11, 15, and 27, 1988.
Addison, Dick, in Cherry Grove, July 11, 1987, July 16, Sept. 11, 1988.
Burton, Frank (pseud.), Dec. 19, 1984.
D., Richie, Feb. 21, 1986.
D., Robert, June 1, 1987.
Dewey, Sherwood, in Cherry Grove, Sept. 4, 1986.
Egan, Ed, Dec. 14, 1985, Jan. 5, 1986.
Emmet, Roger (pseud.), in Cherry Grove, Aug. 29, 1986.

F., Leo, Dec. 11, 1985.
Ford, Charles Henri, July 18, 1986.
Fowler, Nat, in Cherry Grove, Aug. 13, 15, 1986.
Frank, in East Lansing, Michigan, Oct. 4, 1983.
Frederickson, Jerome, in Cherry Grove, Sept. 10, 1988.
Friedrich, Hans (pseud.), May 17, 1988.
Gebhard, Paul, in Bloomington, Indiana, Feb. 11, Apr. 2, 1987.
George, George, May 4, 1987.
Goldberg, George, May 14, 1987.
Goodkin, Martin, in Fort Lauderdale, Florida, Nov. 21, 1987.
Gottfried, Jeffrey (pseud.), interviewed by SAGE.
Gross, Alfred, Dec. 15, 1985.
Hansen, Timothy (pseud.), Oct. 2, 1987.
Harwood, Gene, Nov. 21, Dec. 19, 1984.
Hay, Harry, in Los Angeles, Oct. 6, 1988.
Hearst, David (pseud.), Jan. 12, 1987.
Heffner, Ronald (pseud.), in Philadelphia, Apr. 17, 1987.
Hendricks, Wayne, in Cherry Grove, Aug. 19, 1986.
Honig, Joel, in Chicago, Oct. 28, 1992, Oct. 23, 1993.
Hubert, Rene (pseud.), Apr. 7, 1986.
Isaacs, Henry (pseud.), in Brooklyn, Nov. 19, 1987.
Johnson, Wendel (pseud.), May 15, 1985.
K., Al, in Cherry Grove, Aug. 17, 1986.
Lanton, Michel (pseud.), July 18. 1988.
Legg, Dorr, in Los Angeles, Oct. 4, 1988.
Leitsch, Dick, Aug. 13, Oct. 2, 1987.
Leo, interviewed by SAGE, Sept. 10, 1984.
Leonard, Martin (pseud.), in Cherry Grove, Aug. 29, 1986.
McCarthy, Frank, in Cherry Grove, Sept. 5, 1986.
McGree, Grant (pseud.), Oct. 18, Nov. 20, 1984.
McNamara, Frank, in Cherry Grove, Sept. 11, 1988.
Mason, Robert (pseud.), Nov. 20, Dec. 4, 1985.
Mero, Bruhs, Nov. 21, Dec. 19, 1984.
Mirell, Jack, in Cherry Grove, Sept. 11, 1988.
N., John, in Cherry Grove, August 1986.
Nugent, Bruce, in Hoboken, New Jersey, May 5, 1985.
Nusser, Chuck, in Cherry Grove, Sept. 12, 1986.
O'Connor, Joe, in Cherry Grove, Sept. 5, 1986.
Paulsen, Bob, Jan. 23, 1987.
Pennington, Edward (pseud.), Oct. 14, 1985.
R., Tom (pseud.), Mar. 24, 1986.
Raymond, Howard (pseud.), May 4, 1987.
Risicato, Sebastian, in Cherry Grove, Aug. 28, Sept. 11, 1988.
Roberts, Ronald (pseud.), Oct. 14, 1984.
Roditi, Edouard, interviewed by Ray Gerard Koskovich, May 23, 1983.
Romano, Mike (pseud.), in Cherry Grove, Sept. 8, 1986.
Rustin, Bayard, June 8, 1987.
Sardi, George, in Cherry Grove, Sept. 3, 1988.
Sarnoff, Harvey (pseud.), May 22, 1988.
Smith, Roger (pseud.), Mar. 1 and 8, 1986.
Stanley, Mark (pseud.), interviewed by SAGE, June 3, 1983.

Tashker, Frank, Aug. 7, 1987.
Thompson, Frank, June 1, 2, 1988.
V., Robert, Apr. 8, 1986.
Vining, Donald, Jan. 25, 1986.
W., Willy, in Cherry Grove, Sept. 2 and 5, 1986.
Winston, Robert (pseud.), Oct. 11, 1986.
Winters, Wystan (pseud.), Mar. 1 and 8, 1986.
Young, Richard, in Bloomington, Indiana, Feb. 9, 1987.

NOTES

Various archival sources and other organizations have been abbreviated as follows:

BSH   Bureau of Social Hygiene papers, Rockefeller Archives Center, North Tarrytown, N.Y.

CGS   Court of General Sessions, New York City

COF   Committee of Fourteen papers, New York Public Library

DAP   Manhattan District Attorney's papers, New York Municipal Archives

JJC   John Jay College of Criminal Justice Trial Transcript Collection, City University of New York

KIL   Kinsey Institute for Research in Sex, Gender, and Reproduction Library, Indiana University, Bloomington

MSNY Mattachine Society of New York

NYMA New York Municipal Archives, Department of Records and Information Services, New York City

NYHS New-York Historical Society

NYPD New York Police Department

NYPL Rare Books and Manuscript Division, The New York Public Library, Astor, Lenox, and Tilden Foundations

SCRBC Special Collections, Schomburg Center for Research in Black Culture, New York Public Library

SLA   New York State Liquor Authority

SSV   Society for the Suppression of Vice papers, Library of Congress, Washington, D.C.

Yale   Yale Collection of American Literature, Beinecke Rare Books and Manuscripts Library, Yale University, New Haven, Conn.

INTRODUCTION

1. Michael Denneny, "Chasing the Crossover Audience and Other Self-Defeating Strategies," *Out/look* 1:4 (Winter 1989): 18. Dennis Altman has argued

in a similar vein: "It is extraordinary to consider that with the possible exception of pre-Hitler Berlin, no city in the world had a gay communal life before the late sixties equivalent to that now found in Phoenix or any one of perhaps a hundred Western cities" (*The Homosexualization of America, The Americanization of the Homosexual* [New York: St. Martin's, 1982], 8).

2. George W. Henry and Alfred A. Gross, "The Homosexual Delinquent," *Mental Hygiene* 25 (July 1941): 429. By "enforced" withdrawal they referred to the segregation of homosexual prisoners in a special unit of the city prison, a prison policy that they criticized; as their remarks make clear, they believed such enforced segregation only reinforced the "voluntary" tendency of many homosexuals outside the prisons to withdraw into a social world of their own creation. On this point see also Maurice Leznoff and William A. Westley's landmark study of the Montreal gay male subculture, "The Homosexual Community," *Social Problems* 3 (1956): 257–63.

3. E. S. Shepherd, "Contribution to the Study of Intermediacy," *American Journal of Urology and Sexology* 14 (1918): 242, 245.

4. Altman, *Homosexualization of America*, 3.

5. James C. Scott, *Weapons of the Weak: Everyday Forms of Peasant Resistance* (New Haven, Conn.: Yale University Press, 1985). See also his *Domination and the Arts of Resistance: Hidden Transcripts* (New Haven, Conn.: Yale University Press, 1990). While Scott has offered a useful theorization of such tactics, they have been widely noted by a generation of historians of slaves, workers, and other subaltern groups. For only two of the many possible examples, see Eugene D. Genovese, *Roll, Jordan, Roll: The World the Slaves Made* (New York: Pantheon, 1971) and David Montgomery, *Workers' Control in America: Studies in the History of Work, Technology, and Labor Struggles* (New York: Cambridge University Press, 1979). For a creative recent application of Scott's theories to American history, see Robin Kelley, "'We Are Not What We Seem': Rethinking Black Working-Class Opposition in the Jim Crow South," *Journal of American History* 80 (June 1993): 75–112. In their important recent study, *Boots of Leather, Slippers of Gold: The History of a Lesbian Community* (New York: Routledge, 1993), Elizabeth Kennedy and Madeline Davis argue in a similar vein that the willingness of lesbian "butches" to claim their right to be visible on the streets of Buffalo, New York, in the 1950s and 1960s, often in the face of violent opposition, should be considered a form of "prepolitical" resistance. The position of gay male "fairies" was analogous in many respects to that of lesbian butches, since, like the butches, they announced their sexual character by visibly violating gender conventions (Elizabeth Kennedy and I analyzed some of the parallels and differences between the two groups in a panel discussion at the "Constructing Masculinities" conference at the Rutgers Center for Historical Analysis, Dec. 8–9, 1989). I argue further that the ability of other gay men to build a gay world covertly in the midst of a hostile straight world should also be considered a form of resistance, since it was their very ability to keep parts of the gay world invisible that allowed them to circumvent the prohibition of that world.

6. Samuel Kahn, *Mentality and Homosexuality* (Boston: Meador, 1937), 127, emphasis added. Kahn published this study in 1937 but wrote it in the mid-1920s on the basis of his research at the beginning of that decade. I discuss gay men's responses to the medical profession in chapter 10.

7. *Nowhere* is a strong word, and it is more difficult to find conclusive evidence of an absence than a presence; it is possible that references to the "closet" will be found in sources predating the 1960s. Still, a survey of the three "homophile" publications of the 1950s and early 1960s, *Mattachine Review*,

ONE, and *The Ladder,* revealed no use of the term, nor does it appear in gay or lesbian novels published before the 1960s or in any of the pre-sixties glossaries of homosexual argot, such as Gershon Legman's comprehensive study, "The Language of Homosexuality: An American Glossary," in George W. Henry, *Sex Variants* (New York: Paul B. Hoeber, 1941), vol. 2, appendix VII, or even in glossaries prepared in the early 1960s, such as Will Finch's unpublished 1963 study (at the KIL). The fact that a sociological study conducted in the mid-1950s in Montreal, which focused on the difference between what it called "secret" and "overt" homosexuals, did not use the term also seems to offer strong evidence that it was not current (Leznoff and Westley, "The Homosexual Community"). Arguably, a few earlier writers had used similar spatial metaphors (as, for instance, in the title and central image of James Baldwin's 1956 novel, *Giovanni's Room*), but that does not demonstrate that such metaphors were widely used. The origins of the gay use of "closet" are obscure. It may have been used initially because many men who remained "covert" thought of their homosexuality as a sort of "skeleton in the closet" (I thank Michael Sherry for that observation), or because other people, who are more likely to have initiated the derisive use of the word, thought such men treated their homosexuality that way. Although oral histories are poor sources for such retrospective reconstructions of terminology, on the basis of the casual use of the term by the men I interviewed I suspect that it was used initially by "fairies" (who made their homosexuality known by their dress and manner) to refer to men who were more covert: several self-identified "queens" referred derisively in interviews to "closet queens" who hid their homosexuality. It must be stressed, though, that they may well have applied that term retrospectively after it had become widespread in the post-Stonewall era.

8. These phrases are discussed in chapter 10. For examples of the use of "double life," see Ralph Werther ("it is natural for them to live a double-life"), *The Female-Impersonators* (New York: Medico-Legal Journal, 1922), 97; and Reginald M. ("I was very much amused at living a double life so successfully"), quoted in Henry, *Sex Variants,* 397. For "masks," see "The Tragedy of Masks," a poem by Doyle Eugene Livingstone published in *ONE* (February 1959): 6–7.

9. Eve Kosofsky Sedgwick's deservedly influential analysis of the *Epistemology of the Closet* (Berkeley: University of California Press, 1990) offers an illuminating approach to what might be called the epistemology of the double life, although it seems to me to conflate the conceptually distinct categories of the double life and the closet. While the isolation and invisibility connoted by the metaphor of the closet are sometimes presumed (implicitly or explicitly) by her analysis, they are not essential to it, for it focuses instead in highly productive and revealing ways on the problems of knowing and unknowing, of recognition and misrecognition, that were and are central to the everyday strategies necessary to maintain a double life. While the double life is predicated on the need for secrecy, hiding, and double entendre, which she analyzes, it does not connote the utter invisibility and aloneness of the closet: it recognizes the visibility of the gay world to gay men as well as its invisibility to the dominant culture. The closet has played a role in gay history similar in many respects to that played in women's history by another spatial metaphor, "woman's sphere." Both served for years to help organize historians' thinking, but both ultimately constrained that thinking. See Linda K. Kerber, "Separate Spheres, Female Worlds, Woman's Place: The Rhetoric of Women's History," *Journal of American History* 75 (1988): 9–39.

10. *Baltimore Afro-American,* Mar. 21, 1931. I discuss New York's drag balls in chapters 9 and 10.

11. Legman, "The Language of Homosexuality," 1159, 1161.

12. On this process, see John D'Emilio, "The Homosexual Menace: The Politics of Sexuality in Cold War America," in *Passion and Power: Sexuality in History,* ed. Kathy Peiss and Christina Simmons (Philadelphia: Temple University Press, 1989), 226–40; and my article "The Postwar Sex Crime Panic," in *True Stories from the American Past,* ed. William Graebner (New York: McGraw-Hill, 1993), 160–78.

13. For an introduction to the rapidly growing inquiry into and debate over the meaning of the public sphere, see Jurgen Habermas, "The Public Sphere: An Encyclopedic Article (1964)," *New German Critique* 5 (1974): 49–55; idem, *The Structural Transformation of the Public Sphere,* trans. Thomas Burger (Cambridge, Mass.: MIT Press, 1989); *Social Text* no. 25/6 (1990), special issue on "The Phantom Public Sphere."

14. Both D'Emilio and Berube have pointed to the postwar, Cold War anti-gay backlash that followed the explosive growth of the gay subculture during World War II: John D'Emilio, "The Homosexual Menace"; idem, *Sexual Politics, Sexual Communities: The Making of a Homosexual Minority in the United States, 1940–1970* (Chicago: University of Chicago Press, 1983), ch. 3; Allan Berube, *Coming Out Under Fire: The History of Gay Men and Women in World War Two* (New York: Free Press, 1990), ch. 10. See also Lillian Faderman, *Odd Girls and Twilight Lovers: A History of Lesbian Life in Twentieth-Century America* (New York: Columbia University Press, 1991), ch. 6. It is a sign of the youth of the field of lesbian and gay history that the massive Cold War reaction, now widely known to historians, was utterly unknown to them as recently as the early 1980s, when D'Emilio and Berube first identified it. It is a sign of the field's continuing marginalization that some Cold War historians still do not refer to it in their accounts of Cold War politics.

15. Numerous American academics did study homosexuality before the 1970s, but almost all their work was conducted under the rubrics of psychology, endocrinology, or allied disciplines, as part of a normalizing intellectual project designed to produce the knowledge regimes that would codify, contain, and otherwise enhance the social control of homosexuality. There were a few notable exceptions, however, including the work of the psychologist Evelyn Hooker and sociologists such as Howard Becker and John Gagnon.

16. Jonathan Katz, *Gay American History* (New York: Crowell, 1976); Joan Nestle, "Butch-Fem Roles: Sexual Courage in the 1950s," *Heresies* 12 (1981). For reflections on the history of the field by one of its academic pioneers, see the essays collected in Part II of John D'Emilio, *Making Trouble: Essays on Gay History, Politics, and the University* (New York: Routledge, 1992).

17. See, for example, the sociologist Tomas Almaguer's remark (in *Out/look* 2:1 [Summer 1989]: 83) that it was during World War II that "identifiable gay communities initially emerged [in the United States]. . . . Despite the opprobrium white gay men confronted during the period, their position in the social structure afforded them the opportunity to boldly create new gay institutions, communities, and a unique subculture."

18. This argument was developed by Allan Berube, "Marching to a Different Drummer," *Advocate,* Oct. 15, 1981; idem, *Coming Out Under Fire;* and John D'Emilio, *Sexual Politics, Sexual Communities,* ch. 2.

19. Most historians of mid- and late-nineteenth-century American cities have found that "at least half, often two thirds, of the adults present at one end of a decade had left ten years later, and rates based on shorter periods reveal a stream of people constantly flowing through nineteenth-century cities," as noted by Michael B. Katz, Michael J. Doucet, and Mark J. Stern, "Migration and the Social

Order in Erie County, New York: 1855," *Journal of Interdisciplinary History* 8 (1978): 669; see also, for example, Stephan Thernstrom, *The Other Bostonians: Poverty and Progress in the American Metropolis, 1880–1970* (Cambridge, Mass.: Harvard University Press, 1973), 222–23; Peter R. Knights, "Population Turnover, Persistence, and Residential Mobility in Boston, 1830–1860," in *Nineteenth-Century Cities: Essays in the New Urban History,* ed. Stephan Thernstrom and Richard Sennett (New Haven, Conn.: Yale University Press, 1969), 264; Clyde Griffen, "Workers Divided: The Effect of Craft and Ethnic Differences in Poughkeepsie, New York, 1850–1880," in ibid., 57; Kathleen Neils Conzen, *Immigrant Milwaukee, 1836–1860: Accommodation and Community in a Frontier City* (Cambridge, Mass.: Harvard University Press, 1976), 42–43; and the other studies cited in Katz et al., "Migration," 669 n. 1.

20. For a summary of the limited amount known about nineteenth-century lesbian and gay urban life, see John D'Emilio and Estelle Freedman, *Intimate Matters: A History of Sexuality in America* (New York: Harper & Row, 1988), 226–28. Numerous medical articles on homosexuality published in the early twentieth century include short accounts of gay life in American cities such as Chicago, Philadelphia, and St. Louis; see James Kiernan, "Classification of Homosexuality," *Urologic and Cutaneous Review* 20 (1916): 350 (references to New York, Chicago, and Philadelphia); Charles Hughes, "Homo Sexual Complexion Perverts in St. Louis: Note on a Feature of Sexual Psychopathology," *Alienist and Neurologist* 23 (1907): 487–88 (about interracial gay cafés in St. Louis); and the articles cited in James Burnham, "Early References to Homosexual Communities in American Medical Writings," *Medical Aspects of Human Sexuality* 7 (1973): 40–49.

21. While New York's prewar gay subculture has remained virtually unknown, the gay subcultures that flourished in Paris and Berlin before the rise of the Nazis have received more attention from historians. See, for example, Gilles Barbedette and Michel Carassou, *Paris Gay 1925* (Paris: Presses de la Renaissance, 1981), and, on the more highly developed culture in Berlin, the catalogs for two exhibitions: *Eldorado: Homosexuelle Frauen und Männer in Berlin 1850–1950: Geschichte, Alltag und Kultur* (Berlin: Froelich & Kaufmann, 1984), and *750 Warme Berliner* (Berlin: Verlag rose Winkel, 1987). One of the reasons Berlin's subculture is better known now is that it generated a mass-based homosexual emancipation movement, which had virtually no equivalent in the United States. Analyzing the reasons for this difference would be highly productive.

22. It may be that gay bars opened in numerous small cities for the first time during the war, as some historians have argued, but this cannot be assumed until further research is conducted into the prewar histories of those cities. In any case, gay bars may not be the most useful marker of the scale of a city's gay subculture: even in New York, "gay bars" per se appeared only after the repeal of Prohibition in 1933. Some revealing evidence about gay social networks in small towns in the mid-twentieth century appears in Berube, *Coming Out Under Fire,* particularly in the first chapter, which recounts how gay men in small towns gathered with their gay friends to contemplate the possible significance of Pearl Harbor. For two of the few published studies of prewar American urban gay subcultures, see Eric Garber, "A Spectacle in Color: The Lesbian and Gay Subculture of Jazz Age Harlem," in *Hidden from History: Reclaiming the Gay and Lesbian Past,* ed. Martin Duberman, Martha Vicinus, and George Chauncey (New York: New American Library, 1989), 318–31; and Gregory Sprague, "Chicago Past: A Rich Gay History," *Advocate,* Aug. 18, 1983, 28–31, 58.

23. Studies of male homosexuality in the early modern period include Mary

McIntosh, "The Homosexual Role," *Social Problems* 16 (1968): 182–92; numerous articles by Randolph Trumbach, including "London's Sodomites: Homosexual Behavior and Western Culture in the Eighteenth Century," *Journal of Social History* 11 (1977): 1–33, and "Sodomitical Subcultures, Sodomitical Roles, and the Gender Revolution of the Eighteenth Century: The Recent Historiography," *Eighteenth-Century Life* 9 (1985): 109–21; Alan Bray, *Homosexuality in Renaissance England* (London: Gay Men's Press, 1982); Michel Rey, "Parisian Homosexuals Create a Lifestyle, 1700–1750: The Police Archives," *Eighteenth-Century Life* 9 (1985): 179–91; idem, "Police et sodomie à Paris au XVIIIe siècle: du péché au désordre," *Revue d'Histoire Moderne et Contemporaine* 29 (1982): 113–24; Kent Gerard and Gert Hekma, eds., *The Pursuit of Sodomy: Male Homosexuality in Renaissance and Enlightenment Europe* (New York: Harrington, 1989); and the essays by James M. Saslow, Randolph Trumbach, and Arend H. Huussen, Jr., in *Hidden from History,* ed. Duberman, Vicinus, and Chauncey. For the earlier European period, see, especially, John Boswell, *Christianity, Social Tolerance and Homosexuality: Gay People in Western Europe from the Beginning of the Christian Era to the Fourteenth Century* (Chicago: University of Chicago Press, 1980).

24. G. Frank Lydston, "Sexual Perversion, Satyriasis and Nymphomania," *Medical and Surgical Reporter* 61 (1889): 254.

25. Or, as the sociologist Pierre Bourdieu puts it, "every established order tends to produce (to very different degrees and with very different means) the naturalization of its own arbitrariness, . . . thereby founding immediate adherence . . . to the world of tradition experienced as the 'natural world' and taken for granted" (*Outline of a Theory of Practice,* trans. Richard Nice [New York: Cambridge University Press, 1977], 164). The meaning and utility of the concept of hegemony have been subject to considerable inquiry and debate in recent years. In this study I use the term in the manner Jean Comaroff and John Comaroff have proposed in their masterly study, *Of Revelation and Revolution: Christianity, Colonialism, and Consciousness in South Africa* (Chicago: University of Chicago Press, 1991), 23, as "that order of signs and practices, relations and distinctions, images and epistemologies—drawn from a historically situated cultural field—that come to be taken-for-granted as the natural and received shape of the world and everything that inhabits it." On the history and utility of the concept, see, for example, Antonio Gramsci, *Selections from the Prison Notebooks* (New York: International Publishers, 1971); Raymond Williams, *Marxism and Literature* (New York: Oxford University Press, 1977), 108–14; T. J. Jackson Lears, "The Concept of Cultural Hegemony: Problems and Possibilities," *American Historical Review* 9 (1985): 567–93; Ernesto Laclau and Chantall Mouffe, *Hegemony and Socialist Strategy: Towards a Radical Democratic Politics* (London: Verso, 1985).

26. Legman, "The Language of Homosexuality," 1165, 1174–75.

27. Summary Report on Cabaret Investigations by J. A. S., n.d. [1917–18], box 31, COF.

28. Report by J. K., "Colored pervert, 125th St. & Lenox Ave. subway station," May 19, 1927, box 36, COF.

29. Report by R. A. C. on a Tenement (Colored), 108 W. 137th St., May 25, 1928, box 36, COF.

30. Report by R. A. C. on the Blue Ribbon Chile Parlor, 72 W. 131st St., May 16, 1928, box 36, COF.

31. Bruce Nugent, interviewed; Robert D., interviewed. Dick Addison (interviewed), a white man who frequented Harlem in the 1930s and 1940s, also considered the phrase a distinctive part of black gay argot.

32. *Broadway Brevities,* May 9, 1932, 2. This publication is described in chapter 11. For the use of some of these terms, see Legman, "The Language of Homosexuality," 1159, 1172, 1173, and their frequent appearance in the 1920s and 1930s in *Broadway Brevities.*

33. For more on the usage of *queer,* see chapter 4.

34. Dick Addison, interviewed.

35. Finch diary, Nov. 18, 1951, KIL.

36. For the first meaning, see Wayne Dynes, *Homolexis* (New York: Gay Saber Monograph No. 4, 1985), 58–59. See the Oxford English Dictionary (OED) for the second and third meanings. The OED's examples of *gay* used to refer to prostitutes are all from France and England, where the usage was most common, but there are also instances of such usage in the United States. See, for example, the investigator F. H. Whitin's references to "gay girls in the back-room" at 745 Sixth Avenue, and to a "bunch of gay common women with men in the back-room" at 272 Seventh Avenue, where he seems to use *gay* to mean "loose women" or "amateur prostitutes" (a term he also used frequently), in his report, Aug. 19, 1907, box 28, COF. See also Gershon Legman's explanation in 1941 that *gay* was an adjective "used almost exclusively by homosexuals to denote homosexuality, sexual attractiveness, promiscuity, . . . or lack of restraint, in a person, place, or party," in "The Language of Homosexuality," 1167.

37. Finch glossary notes, 1963, KIL.

38. Charles Henri Ford and Parker Tyler, *The Young and Evil* (Paris: Obelisk Press, 1933), 64.

39. Lew Levenson, *Butterfly Man* (New York: Macaulay, 1934), 159, 181. For another example of the ambiguous use of *gay* in such novels, see Andre Tellier, *Twilight Men* (New York: Greenberg, 1931), 17–18.

40. See, for example, John Boswell, *Christianity, Social Tolerance and Homosexuality,* 43n., and Vito Russo, *The Celluloid Closet: Homosexuality in the Movies* (New York: Harper & Row, 1981), 47.

41. Thomas Painter, "The Homosexual" (typescript, 1941, KIL), 170.

42. Finch diary, Oct. 22, 1946.

43. The speakeasy invitation is preserved in an unidentified lesbian's scrapbook, KIL. The Cyrano Restaurant ad appeared in a 1951 Cherry Grove Arts Council theater program, courtesy of Esther Newton.

44. Finch diary, Nov. 18, 1951. Numerous other sources provide evidence that *gay* became the preeminent term used in the postwar years. In 1951, for instance, the gay author of a book on homosexuality, explained to his "uninitiated reader" that *gay* and *straight* were the "words in common usage in the world in which I move" (Donald Webster Cory, *The Homosexual in America: A Subjective Approach* [New York: Greenberg, 1951], xiv).

45. *Gloria Bar & Grill, Inc., v. Bruckman, et al.,* 259 A.D. 706 (1st Dep't 1940), testimony of William Wickes, SLA investigator, contained in Record on Review, 296, and Walter R. Van Wagner, 234, 237.

46. *Loubor Restaurant v. Rohan, et al.,* 10 A.D. 2d 627 (1st Dep't 1960), testimony of Harry Watson, SLA investigator, contained in Record on Review, 148.

47. Jack Lait and Lee Mortimer, *New York: Confidential!* (New York: Crown, 1948; 1951 revised edition), 72.

48. Elliot Weems, "Why They Call Broadway the 'GAY' White Way," *Tip-Off,* April 1956, 40ff.

49. *Loubor Record on Review* (1960), 189, order of words separated by the ellipsis reversed. The defense attorney objected to this line of questioning: "Who says Greenwich Village is supposed to be the home of homosexuals?" "It used to

be," the SLA attorney insisted, but the objection was sustained.

50. A. A. Gross, "The Homosexual in Society," typescript of an address given before the seminar of the Brooklyn Division of the Protestant Council, June 20, 1947, box 62, Society for the Prevention of Crime Papers, Manuscript and Archives Division, Columbia University Library.

51. Dick Addison, interviewed.

52. Frank, interviewed.

53. I draw here on sociological theories of deviance that are no longer fashionable but still seem to me, in this case, to be insightful and useful. See, for example, Erving Goffman, *The Presentation of Self in Everyday Life* (Garden City, N.Y.: Doubleday, 1959); Howard Becker, *Outsiders: Studies in the Sociology of Deviance* (New York: Free Press, 1963).

54. I draw here on the concept of "tactics" developed by Michel de Certeau, *The Practice of Everyday Life*, trans. Steven F. Rendall (Berkeley: University of California Press, 1984), especially xviii–xx, 29–42. See Jeffrey Escoffier's discussion of such approaches in gay social analysis, "Sexual Revolution and the Politics of Gay Identity," *Socialist Review* 82–83 (1985): 119–53. For a historian's depiction of nineteenth-century New York as women construed it, see Christine Stansell, *City of Women: Sex and Class in New York, 1789–1860* (New York: Knopf, 1986).

55. In developing an ethnographic analysis of the changing social organization of male sexual relations in twentieth-century New York, I follow the lead not only of the French theorist Michel Foucault (best known in this regard for his influential study *The History of Sexuality. Volume I: An Introduction*, trans. Robert Hurley [New York: Pantheon, 1978]) but also of several Anglo-American historians and sociologists. Randolph Trumbach was the first scholar to offer a systematic account of the major patterns in which male–male sexual relations seem to have been organized (along lines of imaginary gender or age difference as well on the egalitarian, coeval model predominant in most contemporary Western societies), and a number of other historians and sociologists have examined this phenomenon, although debates persist about the timing of shifts from one pattern to the next and about the degree to which highly complex and disparate erotic arrangements can be categorized in terms of a handful of categories. See, especially, Trumbach, "London's Sodomites"; idem, "Gender and the Homosexual Role in Modern Western Culture: The 18th and 19th Centuries Compared," in *Homosexuality, Which Homosexuality?* ed. Dennis Altman et al. (London: GMP Publishers, 1989), 149–69; Jeffrey Weeks's many studies, including *Coming Out: Homosexual Politics in Britain from the Nineteenth Century to the Present* (London: Quartet, 1977) and *Sex, Politics and Society: The Regulation of Sexuality Since 1880* (London: Longman, 1981); John Marshall, "Pansies, Perverts and Macho Men: Changing Conceptions of Male Homosexuality," in *The Making of the Modern Homosexual*, ed. Kenneth Plummer (London: Hutchinson, 1981); S. O. Murray, *Social Theory, Homosexual Realties* (New York: Gay Academic Union, 1984); David Greenberg, *The Construction of Homosexuality* (Chicago: University of Chicago Press, 1988).

56. I draw here on an immense body of theory developed primarily by sociologists and historians associated with the Birmingham Center for Contemporary Cultural Studies. For a useful introduction to such approaches, see Dick Hebdige, *Subculture: The Meaning of Style* (London: Methuen, 1979), and Stuart Hall and Tony Jefferson, eds., *Resistance Through Rituals: Youth Subcultures in Post-war Britain* (London: Hutchinson, 1976).

57. This is, in effect, the classic deconstructionist observation: while the sub-

ordinate category B (the "queer") is overtly defined by its difference from the superordinate category A (the "normal"), A actually depends just as much for its definition on its differentiation from B. See Harold Beaver, "Homosexual Signs (In Memory of Roland Barthes)," *Critical Inquiry* 8 (1981): 99–119.

58. See N. Abercrombie and B. Turner, "The Dominant Ideology Thesis," *British Journal of Sociology* 29 (1978): 149–70.

59. In charting a map of the sexual categories and meaning systems operative in the early twentieth century, moreover, I do not mean to ascribe to those maps a regularity, clarity, and certainty they did not possess. As Bourdieu has argued (*Outline of a Theory of Practice,* 2, 37–38), the very act of drawing a map covers up irregularities in the terrain and implies a kind of predestination to the patterns of social relations that are constantly being negotiated, contested, and reformulated. The maps I sketch here seem to me to have guided the sexual practices of most men, but they sometimes took detours and forged their own paths, and different men followed different maps of sexual meaning. On maps of meaning, see also Stuart Hall, "Culture, the Media, and the 'Ideological Effect,'" in *Mass Communication and Society,* ed. James Curran et al. (London: Open University Press, 1979).

60. This argument is in keeping with the recent work of several social historians, who have identified the origins of sexual change in early-twentieth-century American culture in the subcultures of urban working-class youth rather than in middle-class culture or prescriptive literature. See, for example, Kathy Peiss, *Cheap Amusements: Working Women and Leisure in Turn-of-the-Century New York* (Philadelphia: Temple University Press, 1986), and D'Emilio and Freedman, *Intimate Matters.*

61. I initially developed this argument in an article on the American medical literature of 1890 to 1930, "From Sexual Inversion to Homosexuality: Medicine and the Changing Conceptualization of Female Deviance," *Salmagundi,* no. 58–59 (Fall/Winter 1982–1983), 114–46, and elaborated it in a second article, which emphasized the multiplicity of sexual discourses that coexisted in a small World War I–era community and the class variations in homosexual identities assumed by men there, "Christian Brotherhood or Sexual Perversion? Homosexual Identities and the Construction of Sexual Boundaries in the World War One Era," *Journal of Social History* 19 (1985), 189–211. The best-known historian advocating the alternative position is Lillian Faderman; see "The Morbidification of Love Between Women by Nineteenth-Century Sexologists," *Journal of Homosexuality* 4 (1978): 73–90; idem, *Surpassing the Love of Men: Romantic Friendships and Love Between Women from the Renaissance to the Present* (New York: Morrow, 1981); idem, *Odd Girls and Twilight Lovers.* Faderman is writing about women rather than men, but there is no reason to believe that women, especially working-class women, were more influenced by medical discourse than men were.

62. On the significance of the persisting tension between the two categories and analytic frameworks, see Eve Kosofsky Sedgwick's keen observations in *Epistemology of the Closet,* 46–48. I agree with her claim that no conclusive, unilinear narrative of change should be presumed, for it is clear that no single system of sexual classification obtains today. A multiplicity of sexual ideologies have always coexisted in ambiguous—and often uneasy—relationship to one another. Nonetheless, it is significant that particular ideologies have predominated at particular times. The fairy stood at the center of the dominant system of interpretation at the turn of the century, and deeply influenced the self-understanding and practices of even those men most anxious to distinguish themselves from him; he does not today.

63. Two groundbreaking studies of American lesbian history have recently appeared: Kennedy and Davis, *Boots of Leather, Slippers of Gold;* and Faderman, *Odd Girls and Twilight Lovers.* See also Joan Nestle, *A Restricted Country* (Ithaca, N.Y.: Firebrand Books, 1987). The differences in lesbian and gay male history are striking and deserve further study, in part because they highlight broader differences in the social history of women and men.

CHAPTER 1. THE BOWERY AS HAVEN AND SPECTACLE

1. Cornelius Willemse, *Behind the Green Lights* (New York, 1931), 24. Willemse was a bouncer at another Bowery resort at the time; he later became chief of police.

2. *Report of the Special [Mazet] Committee of the Assembly appointed to investigate the Public Offices and Departments of the City of New York and of the Counties Theirin Included* (Albany: J. B. Lyon, 1900), Joel S. Harris testimony, 1429. The Mazet Committee's investigation of Paresis Hall was first drawn to the attention of historians by Jonathan Katz's landmark collection of documents, *Gay American History* (New York: Crowell, 1976).

3. *Mazet Committee Report,* George P. Hammond, Jr., testimony, 1431.

4. *Mazet Committee Report,* 173–76, 1382–83, 1394–95, 1429, 1431, 5125–27; Frank Moss, *The American Metropolis* (New York: Collier, 1897), vol. 3, 163, 222.

5. Bulletin 1480, Nov. 12, 1921, box 88, COF; *Committee of Fourteen Annual Report for 1914* (New York: Committee of Fourteen, 1915), 12.

6. On the emergence of the Bowery as the center of a distinctive working-class public culture in the nineteenth century, see Peter G. Buckley, "To the Opera House: Culture and Society in New York City, 1820–1860" (Ph.D. diss., State University of New York, Stony Brook, 1984); Sean Wilentz, *Chants Democratic: New York City and the Rise of the American Working Class, 1788–1850* (New York: Oxford University Press, 1984), 257–71; Christine Stansell, *City of Women: Sex and Class in New York, 1789–1860* (New York: Knopf, 1986), 89–100; and Elliott J. Gorn, *The Manly Art: Bare-Knuckle Prize Fighting in America* (Ithaca, N.Y.: Cornell University Press, 1986), 132–35. On the Bowery's role in the lives of the "new immigrants" of the late nineteenth century and on the number of prostitutes on the Lower East Side, see the investigators' reports in boxes 5–7, Committee of Fifteen papers, NYPL; Timothy J. Gilfoyle, *City of Eros: New York City, Prostitution, and the Commercialization of Sex, 1790–1920* (New York: Norton, 1992), 210–18; Thomas Kessner, *The Golden Door: Italian and Jewish Immigrant Mobility in New York City* (New York: Oxford University Press, 1977), 128ff.; Irving Howe, *World of Our Fathers* (New York: Harcourt Brace Jovanovich, 1976), 96–98; Edward J. Bristow, *Prostitution and Prejudice: The Jewish Fight Against White Slavery, 1870–1939* (New York: Schocken, 1983), 146–50; Kathy Peiss, *Cheap Amusements: Working Women and Leisure in Turn-of-the-Century New York* (Philadelphia: Temple University Press, 1986); Susan A. Glenn, *Daughters of the Shtetl: Life and Labor in the Immigrant Generation* (Ithaca, N.Y.: Cornell University Press, 1990); and the memoirs of two men who grew up on the Lower East Side, both of whom note their parents' chagrin that they lived in or near the city's red-light district: Mike Gold, *Jews Without Money* (New York: Liveright, 1930), 14–15; and Samuel Chotzinoff, *A Lost Paradise* (New York: Knopf, 1955), 69–70.

7. Gold, *Jews Without Money,* 15, 58–60; *Mazet Committee Report,* Mr. Moss, 174, 177; Jimmy Durante and Jack Kofoed, *Night Clubs* (New York: Knopf, 1931), 50–55; Irving Drutman, *Good Company: A Memoir, Mostly*

Theatrical (Boston: Little, Brown, 1976), 5; David Nasaw, *Children of the City: At Work and at Play* (Garden City, N.Y.: Anchor Press/Doubleday, 1985), 140–44.

8. Lewis A. Erenberg, *Steppin' Out: New York Nightlife and the Transformation of American Culture, 1890–1930* (Chicago: University of Chicago Press, 1981), 5–29; Perry R. Duis, *The Saloon: Public Drinking in Chicago and Boston, 1880–1920* (Urbana: University of Illinois Press, 1983), 86–87, 113, 205–9; Roy Rosenzweig, *Eight Hours for What We Will: Workers and Leisure in an Industrial City, 1870–1920* (New York: Cambridge University Press, 1983), 51. Middle- and upper-class visiting, even promenading in Central Park, deliberately took more ritualized, carefully orchestrated form than the constant interactions of the stoop and the saloon. See David Scobey, "Anatomy of the Promenade: The Politics of Bourgeois Sociability in Nineteenth-Century New York," *Social History* 17 (1992): 203–27. On the contrast, for example, between the formality of the Easter Promenade and the "looseness" of a resort like Coney Island, see John F. Kasson, *Amusing the Million: Coney Island at the Turn of the Century* (New York: Hill and Wang, 1978), 41–44.

9. Peter T. Cominos, "Late Victorian Sexual Respectability and the Social System," *International Review of Social History* 8 (1963): 33, 238–40; Charles Rosenberg, "Sexuality, Class and Role in Nineteenth Century America," *American Quarterly* 25 (1973): 131–54; Carroll Smith-Rosenberg, "The Hysterical Woman: Sex Roles and Role Conflict in Nineteenth Century America," *Social Research* 39 (1972): 667.

10. John Modell and Tamara K. Hareven, "Urbanization and the Malleable Household: An Examination of Boarding and Lodging in American Families," in *The American Family in Social-Historical Perspective*, ed. Michael Gordon (2nd ed.; New York: St. Martin's, 1978), 51–68; Kessner, *The Golden Door*, 99–101; Elizabeth Ewen, *Immigrant Women in the Land of Dollars: Life and Culture on the Lower East Side, 1890–1925* (New York: Monthly Review Press, 1985), 119–21.

11. Mary Casal, *The Stone Wall: An Autobiography* (Chicago: Eyncourt, 1930), 184.

12. The general accounts of late-nineteenth-century slumming published in the 1920s and 1930s (when the destination of most slummers had shifted from the Bowery and Tenderloin to Harlem) are perhaps best characterized as guides for armchair slummers, since they offer the vicarious thrills of slumming in their descriptions of the resorts rather than a critical perspective on the activity itself. See, for example, Alvin Harlow, *Old Bowery Days* (New York: D. Appleton, 1931), 428ff., and Herbert Asbury, *The Gangs of New York* (New York: Knopf, 1928). See also Ivan Light, "From Vice District to Tourist Attraction: The Moral Career of American Chinatowns, 1880–1940," *Pacific Historical Review* 43 (1974): 367–94; idem, "The Ethnic Vice Industry, 1880–1944," *American Sociological Review* 42 (1977): 464–79; Neil Larry Shumsky, "Tacit Acceptance: Respectable Americans and Segregated Prostitution, 1870–1910," *Journal of Social History* 19 (1986): 665–79; Erenberg, *Steppin' Out*, 20–23; Gorn, *The Manly Art*, 182–85; and John D'Emilio and Estelle Freedman, *Intimate Matters: A History of Sexuality in America* (New York: Harper & Row, 1988), 183–86, 194–201, and, on the origins of this spatial and class division earlier in the nineteenth century, 130–38.

13. *People v. Schaumloeffel* (CGS 1904), testimony of Detective John M. O'Shea, 14–30.

14. Society for the Suppression of Vice record books, vol. 4, 100–101 (Oct. 5, 1900), SSV.

15. Asbury, *Gangs of New York,* 187–90; Edward Van Every, *Sins of New York, as "Exposed" by the Police Gazette* (1930; New York: Benjamin Blom, 1972), 215–17.

16. "Here, Mr. Nicoll, Is a Place to Prosecute," *New York Herald,* Jan. 5, 1892, 8. Similarly, the physical-culture advocate Bernarr Macfadden reported in 1904 that a detective had informed him that "recently there existed on Houston street in New York city a resort given over to the accommodation of the votaries of the vice. Slummers knew it well, together with its crowd of unsexed things that spoke in falsetto voices and called each other by girls names" (*Superb Virility of Manhood: Giving the Causes and Simple Home Methods of Curing the Weaknesses of Men* [New York: Physical Culture Publishing Co., 1904], 175).

17. *New York World,* Feb. 21, 1915.

18. Michael Schudson, *Discovering the News: A Social History of American Newspapers* (New York: Basic Books, 1978), 92–106; Daniel C. Hallin, "The American News Media: A Critical Theory Perspective," in *Critical Theory and Public Life,* ed. John Forester (Cambridge, Mass.: MIT Press, 1985), 121–46. For a masterly analysis of the development of the metropolitan press in London and its role in constructing the spectacle of that city, see Judith R. Walkowitz, *City of Dreadful Delight: Narratives of Sexual Danger in Late-Victorian London* (Chicago: University of Chicago Press, 1992).

19. *New York Herald,* Jan. 5, 1892, 8.

20. Charles Torrence Nesbitt memoir (1938), Charles Torrence Nesbitt papers, Duke University Library. Part of this manuscript has been published in Jonathan Ned Katz, *Gay/Lesbian Almanac: A New Documentary* (New York: Harper & Row, 1983), 218–22. All of Toto's quotes must be taken as paraphrases at best, of course.

21. Nesbitt memoir (1938), 106–7. On the use of Walhalla Hall for balls by other clubs, see Moss, *American Metropolis,* 171–73; Harlow, *Old Bowery Days,* 370, 426, 436; Asbury, *Gangs of New York,* 270. (I discuss the drag balls in chapter 10.)

22. On the saloon, see Raymond Calkins, *Substitutes for the Saloon* (Boston: Houghton Mifflin, 1919), 1–24; Duis, *The Saloon,* especially 113–25, 178–92; Rosenzwieg, *Eight Hours,* 35–64; and Jon Kingsdale, "The 'Poor Man's Club': Social Functions of the Urban Working-Class Saloon," in *The American Man,* ed. Elizabeth Pleck and Joseph Pleck (Englewood Cliffs, N.J.: Prentice-Hall, 1980), 255–83.

23. Report of J. Kreisworth, Sharon Hotel, 136 Third Ave., July 15, 1901, box 20, Committee of Fifteen papers, NYPL.

24. Reports on Billy's Place, 239 Third Ave., Apr. 19 and June 5, 1901, box 20; Apr. 22, 1901, box 23, Committee of Fifteen papers, NYPL.

25. Little is known about Werther because he took great care to disguise his own identity; "Werther" was a pseudonym, and no evidence concerning his later life has yet been discovered. A somewhat disguised account of his life appeared in his first book, *Autobiography of an Androgyne,* edited by and with an introduction by Alfred W. Herzog, editor of the New York–based *Medico-Legal Journal* (New York: Medico-Legal Journal, 1918). Werther also published "Studies in Androgynism" (*Medical Life* 27 [1920]: 235–46) and *The Female-Impersonators* (New York: Medico-Legal Journal, 1922), and claimed to have prepared a manuscript titled "The Riddle of the Underworld," which appears never to have been published. Werther also went by the pseudonyms Earl Lind and Jennie June; to avoid confusion, I have called him Ralph Werther throughout this study.

26. On the social clubs, see Peiss, *Cheap Amusements,* 59–62, 90–93; Asbury, *Gangs of New York,* 268–69.

27. Samuel Goodwin Gant, M.D., *Diseases of the Rectum and Anus* (New York: F. A. Davis, 1902), 653–54; idem, *Diseases of the Rectum, Anus, and Colon* (Philadelphia: W. B. Saunders, 1923), 2:201. I am grateful to the late Michael Lynch for the Gant references.

28. Werther, *The Female-Impersonators,* 157, 146–52. The role of the gay subculture in shaping men's lives and self-conceptions is discussed more extensively in the following chapters.

29. Ibid., 95, 158–59, 203. A sympathetic and unusually well informed doctor writing in 1918 confirmed the validity of such concerns, noting that in respectable society, "the accusation of perversity [homosexuality] . . . means ruin": E. S. Shepherd, "Contribution to the Study of Intermediacy," *American Journal of Urology and Sexology* 14 (1918): 242.

30. Werther, *The Female-Impersonators,* 97. On the meaning of *bisexual* in Werther's era, see the following chapter.

31. Werther, *The Female-Impersonators,* 202; see also 181, 90–95.

CHAPTER 2. THE FAIRY AS AN INTERMEDIATE SEX

1. *The Stone Wall: An Autobiography* (Chicago: Eyncourt, 1930), 184–85.

2. The fairy was a prominent figure in turn-of-the-century New York City, but I do not mean to suggest that he was a novel invention of that era. The historian Randolph Trumbach has subtly analyzed the culture and identities of effeminate "mollies," who had a well-developed network of meeting places and set of cultural conventions in early-eighteenth-century London and whose styles resembled those of New York's fairies in significant (but certainly not all) respects (see, for instance, "The Birth of the Queen: Sodomy and the Emergence of Gender Equality in Modern Culture, 1660–1750," in *Hidden from History: Reclaiming the Gay and Lesbian Past,* ed. Martin Duberman, Martha Vicinus, and George Chauncey [New York: New American Library, 1989], 129–40). London's mollies may have been the cultural ancestors of the fairies of late-nineteenth-century New York, although the threads of historical continuity that may connect them need to be reconstructed rather than assumed. The history of the figure of the fairy in the United States before the end of the nineteenth century has yet to be written, but sufficient evidence exists to establish that the fairy was recognized as a distinct cultural type by the 1870s. Note, for instance, Billy McGlory's decision to hire them at his Bowery dance hall (see chapter 1), and their depiction in a guide to the social geography of New York published in the 1870s (see figure 1.1). Some evidence indicates that certain homosexually active men were feminized in the 1850s, though that does not mean they were regarded as or imagined themselves to be "fairies"; see some of the comments in Philip Van Buskirk's diary, as reported in B. R. Burg, *An American Seafarer in the Age of Sail* (New Haven, Conn.: Yale University Press, 1994). Gayle Rubin suggested the term "sex/gender system" for the cultural matrix of sex, gender, and sexuality and outlined some of its components in her now-classic article "The Traffic in Women: Notes on the 'Political Economy' of Sex," in *Toward an Anthropology of Women,* ed. Rayna R. Reiter (New York: Monthly Review Press, 1975), 157–210.

3. Harriet Whitehead usefully describes this as the difference between the "leading edge" and the "trailing edge" of gender distinction in her analysis of the Native American berdache, whose gender position seems to have been analogous in some (though certainly not all) respects to that of the fairy: "Sexual object choice was very much the trailing rather than the leading edge of gender definition." ("The Bow

and the Burden Strap: A New Look at Institutionalized Homosexuality in Native North America," in *Sexual Meanings: The Cultural Construction of Sexuality and Gender,* ed. Sherry B. Ortner and Harriet Whitehead [New York: Cambridge University Press, 1981], 80–115.) Similar arguments about the relative significance of gender inversion have been made by historians of lesbianism: see, for example, Esther Newton, "The Mythic Mannish Lesbian: Radclyffe Hall and the New Woman," *Signs* 9 (1984): 557–75; and my article "From Sexual Inversion to Homosexuality: Medicine and the Changing Conceptualization of Female Deviance," *Salmagundi,* no. 58–59 (Fall 1982–Winter 1983): 114–46. On men, see the work of Randolph Trumbach, especially "Sodomitical Subcultures, Sodomitical Roles, and the Gender Revolution of the Eighteenth Century: The Recent Historiography," *Eighteenth-Century Life* 9 (1985): 109–21; John Marshall, "Pansies, Perverts and Macho Men: Changing Conceptions of Male Homosexuality," in *The Making of the Modern Homosexual,* ed. Kenneth Plummer (London: Hutchinson, 1981), 133–54; and my article "Christian Brotherhood or Sexual Perversion? Homosexual Identities and the Construction of Sexual Boundaries in the World War One Era," *Journal of Social History* 19 (1985): 189–211.

　　4. William Lee Howard, "Sexual Perversion in America," *American Journal of Dermatology and Genito-Urinary Diseases* 8 (1904): 10 (emphasis added).

　　5. For some of the medical accounts that conceptualize inversion in these broad terms rather than focusing more narrowly on homosexual object choice as the defining characteristic of the invert, see George M. Beard, *Sexual Neurasthenia,* ed. A. D. Rockwell (New York: E. B. Treat, 1884), 106; George F. Shrady, "Perverted Sexual Instinct," *Medical Record* 26 (1884): 70–71; James G. Kiernan, "Sexual Perversion and the Whitechapel Murders," *Medical Standard* 4 (1888): 170–72; Richard von Krafft-Ebing, "Perversions of the Sexual Instinct: Report of Cases," *Alienist and Neurologist* 9 (1888): 556–70, 579–81; Allan MacLane Hamilton, "The Civil Responsibility of Sexual Perverts," *American Journal of Insanity* 52 (1896): 505; William Lee Howard, "Effeminate Men and Masculine Women," *New York Medical Journal* 71 (1900): 686; Herbert J. Claiborne, "Hypertrichosis in Women: Its Relation to Bisexuality (Hermaphroditism): With Remarks on Bisexuality in Animals, Especially Man," *New York Medical Journal* 99 (1914): 1181; Douglas C. McMurtrie, "Manifestations of Sexual Inversion in the Female: Conditions in a Convent School, Evidence of Transvestism, Unconscious Homosexuality, Sexuality of Masculine Women, Masturbation Under Homosexual Influences, Indeterminate Sexuality in Childhood," *Urologic and Cutaneous Review* 18 (1914): 444–46; idem, "Psychology of a Tribadistic Uxoricide: A Lombrosian Case Record," ibid.: 480; J. Allen Gilbert, "Homosexuality and Its Treatment," *Journal of Nervous and Mental Disease* 52 (1920): 297–322. For a fuller review of the meaning of inversion in the turn-of-the-century American medical literature, see Chauncey, "From Sexual Inversion to Homosexuality"; Carroll Smith-Rosenberg, "The New Woman as Androgyne: Social Disorder and Gender Crisis, 1870–1936," in her *Disorderly Conduct: Visions of Gender in Victorian America* (New York: Knopf, 1985), 245–96; and Newton, "The Mythic Mannish Lesbian."

　　6. On Ulrichs, see Hubert Kennedy, *Ulrichs: The Life and Works of Karl Heinrich Ulrichs, Pioneer of the Modern Gay Movement* (Boston: Alyson, 1988). For a brief statement of Edward Carpenter's views, see his essay "The Intermediate Sex," in his *Love's Coming of Age* (London: George Allen and Unwin, 1906; 12th enl. ed., 1923), 130–49; on Carpenter, see Sheila Rowbotham and Jeffrey Weeks, *Socialism and the New Life: The Personal and Sexual Politics of Edward Carpenter and Havelock Ellis* (London: Pluto Press, 1977), 25–138. On Hirschfeld,

see James D. Steakley, *The Homosexual Emancipation Movement in Germany* (New York: Arno Press, 1975). Frederic Silverstolpe points out that the theories of the earliest German medical writers on the subject were significantly influenced both by homosexual crusaders and by the doctors' patients: "Benkert Was Not a Doctor: On the Nonmedical Origin of the Homosexual Category in the Nineteenth Century," paper presented at the International Scientific Conference on Gay and Lesbian Studies, Free University of Amsterdam, Dec. 15–18, 1987.

7. The term invariably had this meaning late in the nineteenth century. It usually did so early in the twentieth century (see, for example, James Kiernan, "Bisexuality," *Urologic and Cutaneous Review* 18 [1914]: 372–75; idem, "Sexual Perversion and the Whitechapel Murders," 129; Claiborne, "Hypertrichosis in Women," 1181) and frequently still did so in the 1930s (see, for example, Dr. La Forest Potter's definition of bisexuality as "partaking of both male and female sexual characteristics," in *Strange Loves: A Study in Sexual Abnormalities* [New York: National Library Press, 1933], 241), although the modern sense had begun to be employed by the 1920s.

8. *Report of the Special [Mazet] Committee of the Assembly appointed to investigate the Public Offices and Departments of the City of New York and of the Counties Therein Included* (Albany: J. B. Lyon, 1900), Joel S. Harris testimony, 1429.

9. The names cited are taken from Ralph Werther, *The Female-Impersonators* (New York: Medico-Legal Journal, 1922), 100, 118–19; idem, *Autobiography of an Androgyne* (New York: Medico-Legal Journal, 1918), 155; Samuel Kahn, *Mentality and Homosexuality* (Boston: Meador, 1937), 111, 126, 233; Jimmy Durante and Jack Kofoed, *Night Clubs* (New York: Knopf, 1931), 54–55; *Broadway Brevities,* Oct. 5, 1931, 10; ibid., Oct. 12, 1931, 5; George Chauncey, "Christian Brotherhood or Sexual Perversion?" 191.

10. On prostitutes' adoption of pseudonyms, see Ruth Rosen, *The Lost Sisterhood: Prostitution in America, 1900–1918* (Baltimore: Johns Hopkins University Press, 1982), 102–3.

11. Werther, *The Female-Impersonators,* 93–94; 100; 118–19. Jennie June was the pen name of Jane Cunningham Croly (1829–1901), who wrote for the *New York Tribune* and numerous other papers; see *Notable American Women, 1607–1950,* vol. I (Cambridge, Mass.: Belknap Press, 1971), 409–411.

12. Max Adams (whose real name was not Max, but who was occasionally called "Maxine" because of a facetious connection he had with a Max), interviewed; Henry Isaacs (who went by the pseudonym "Henry" and was occasionally called "Henrietta"), interviewed.

13. Werther, *The Female-Impersonators,* 150; Kahn, *Mentality and Homosexuality,* 234.

14. Werther, *The Female-Impersonators,* 104. Although the details varied between cities, the semiotics (or system of identifying signs) of homosexuality seems to have been generally similar throughout North America. See, for example, Elsa Gidlow's description of a gay man she knew in Montreal in 1916: "To his work on the newspaper he went perforce scrubbed and in tweeds; but at home among friends, at the theatre and concerts, he was delicately made up and elegantly dressed, wearing exotic jewelry and as colorful clothes as he dared. Receiving at home, he donned a bronze green robe of heavy silk" ("Memoirs," *Feminist Studies* 6 [1980]: 122). For the standard male fashions of the era, see Douglas A. Russell, *Costume History and Style* (Englewood Cliffs, N.J.: Prentice-Hall, 1983).

15. Thomas Painter, "The Prostitute" (typescript, 1941, KIL), 168–69.

16. Gershon Legman, "The Language of Homosexuality: An American Glos-

sary," in George W. Henry, *Sex Variants* (New York: Paul B. Hoeber, 1941), vol. 2, appendix VII, 1165–66.

17. James Kiernan, "Classifications of Homosexuality," *Urologic and Cutaneous Review* 20 (1916): 350.

18. Quoted in Havelock Ellis, *Sexual Inversion* (Philadelphia: F. A. Davis, 1915), 299–300. Red neckties still made their appearance at the Astor Bar in the late 1930s, according to Roger Smith (interviewed), but by the beginning of World War II they had generally lost their currency as a homosexual sign (Thomas Painter, "The Homosexual," [typescript, 1941, KIL], 167).

19. Finch diary, June 26, 1951, Apr. 26, 1952, KIL; John S. Wood, *Christ and the Homosexual*, 45. Some of the most interesting studies of the cultural politics of style in dress have focused on the meanings given the zoot suit, which was adopted by many Latino and African-American youths in the 1940s. See, especially, Stuart Cosgrove, "The Zoot-Suit and Style Warfare," *History Workshop Journal* 18 (1984): 77–91; Robin D. G. Kelley, "The Riddle of the Zoot: Malcolm Little and Black Cultural Politics During World War II," in *Malcolm X: In Our Own Image,* ed. Joe Wood (New York: St. Martin's, 1992), 155–82; and, for a more general analysis, Stuart Hall and Tony Jefferson eds., *Resistance Through Rituals: Youth Subcultures in Post-war Britain* (London: Unwin Hyman, 1976).

20. Sidney Skolsky's profile of Richman appeared in his "Tintypes" column, *New York Daily News,* Oct. 2, 1933; see also an article in *Broadway Brevities & Society Gossip,* January 1924, 14, which identified a fairy on the basis of his "absolutely beardless face, delicate features and flamboyant jewelry [which] proclaimed his avocation," and Louis E.'s recollection of the singular appearance of the first homosexual he met, c. 1920, when he was fourteen (quoted in Henry, *Sex Variants,* 194): "He was very, very feminine. He wore bracelets."

21. I draw here on the work of Suzanne J. Kessler and Wendy McKenna, *Gender: An Ethnomethodological Approach* (1978; Chicago: University of Chicago Press, 1985), especially ch. 5, "Gender Construction in Everyday Life: Transsexualism." However, while I agree with their argument that most people are not so concerned with displaying their gender status as those who are trying to "pass" as another gender, such as preoperative transsexuals (since the former take their gender for granted), it is nonetheless the case that people regularly measure themselves against the ideal gender types of their culture and deliberately seek to emulate them, through their dress, exercise, diet, and so on. See also Judith Butler, *Gender Trouble: Feminism and the Subversion of Identity* (New York: Routledge, 1990); idem, "Performative Acts and Gender Constitution: An Essay in Phenomenology and Feminist Theory," *Theatre Journal* 40 (1988): 519–31; and Kathy Peiss's masterly historical studies of the gendering of the body through cosmetics, including "Making Faces: The Cosmetics Industry and the Cultural Construction of Gender, 1890–1930," *Genders* 7 (Spring 1990): 143–69; and "Of Men and Makeup: The Gender of Cosmetics in Twentieth Century America," in *The Material Culture of Gender,* ed. Kenneth Ames and Katherine Martinez (New York: Norton, forthcoming).

22. Potter, *Strange Loves,* 184. According to Potter, the "platinum blond hair" worn by many gay men had been "made popular by one of our motion picture actresses a few years ago" (188). The title character of *Goldie,* a novel published the same year as Potter's study, who took his name from his bleached blond hair, constantly feared policemen would recognize him as a "degenerate" if they saw "the unusual hue of his hair"; he consequently wore a cap, taking it off "only to attract the attention of his prospect," who, presumably, would be

equally aware of the coloring's significance. (Kennilworth Bruce, *Goldie* [New York: William Godwin, 1933], 102, 119.)

23. For the visitors' comments, see, for example, "Here, Mr. Nicoll, Is a Place to Prosecute," *New York Herald,* Jan. 5, 1892, 8, and the other accounts of visits provided in chapter 1. Werther, *Autobiography,* 155.

24. Kahn, *Mentality and Homosexuality,* 217.

25. "The Neighborhood Credo," 23–24, in Frederic M. Thrasher, "The Use of the Superior Boy in Research," BSH, box 11, folder 229 ("NYU Boys Club Study, 1930"), microfilm reel 6. See also the gay writer Parker Tyler's comment in a 1929 letter to a gay friend, Charles Henri Ford: "My eyebrows now dear are perfect. They're a sight in themselves" (Dec. 16, 1929).

26. *Gloria Bar & Grill, Inc., v. Bruckman, et al.,* 259 A.D. 706 (1st Dep't 1940), testimony of Walter R. Van Wagner, contained in Record on Review, 229, 232. I analyze the government's efforts to discourage bars from serving homosexuals and to close those that did in chapter 12.

27. Werther, *The Female-Impersonators,* 151. See also his comment in describing another encounter: "From my dress and manners . . . any city-bred youth would have already judged my sexual status" (132).

28. Painter, "The Homosexual," 161. For the use of *swish,* see Legman, "The Language of Homosexuality," 1177, and the testimony of a witness before the State Liquor Authority in 1939, who asserted that *swish* was "show parlance," *Gloria Record on Review* (1940), testimony of William E. Wickes, 336.

29. Quoted in Chauncey, "Christian Brotherhood," 191–92. The sailor was questioned at the Newport, Rhode Island, naval training station, but had spent time in New York and was involved in a gay world not unlike that of the city.

30. Leo, interviewed.

31. Quoted in Kahn, *Mentality and Homosexuality,* 124 (emphasis added); a point also made by Legman, "The Language of Homosexuality," 1166.

32. For a pioneering analysis of the role of "social scripts" in the organization of sexual interactions and construction of sexual meanings, see John H. Gagnon and William Simon, *Sexual Conduct: The Social Sources of Human Sexuality* (Chicago: Aldine, 1973).

33. Report on speakeasy, 109 W. 136th St., basement, May 27, 1928, box 36, COF.

34. *Gloria Record on Review* (1940), testimony of Mr. McIlhargy, questioned by Atty. Goldberg, 373.

35. Such status-confirming status reversals were in the tradition of the European carnivals analyzed by Natalie Zemon Davis, "The Reasons of Misrule" and "Women on Top," in her *Society and Culture in Early Modern France* (Stanford, Calif.: Stanford University Press, 1975), 97–151.

36. Parker Tyler to Charles Henri Ford, Apr. 29, 1929. I discuss the significance of Tyler's refering to one of the men as a "wolf" in chapter 3. For similar accounts, see Ralph Werther's description of an encounter with a young man on a park bench in *The Female-Impersonators,* 132–36, and his *Autobiography,* 156.

37. Report on Dance Hall and Martin's Saloon, Aug. 15, 1912, box 28, COF. Similarly, another investigator reported that fairies had begun to gather at the Hotel Koenig on East Fourth Street in the spring of 1920, and that "most of the patrons paid more attention to the action of the fairies than to the cabaret performance" (F. H. Whitin to Insp. Thomas MacDonald, First I.D., June 2, 1920, box 5, COF). I discuss the Hotel Koenig at length in chapter 6.

38. Report on Jimmie's speakeasy, 344 W. 17th St., Jan. 5, 1928, box 36, COF. The "fairy hangout" was the Spaghetti House, in the basement at 207 W.

17th Street, where, two months earlier, a waitress had introduced two men interested in meeting "sporting girls" to a fairy instead (see chapter 3).

39. Durante and Kofoed, *Night Clubs,* 54–55.

40. Paul G. Cressey, "Preliminary Report of Motion Picture Study," as quoted in Frederic M. Thrasher, Ph.D., Director, Boys' Club Study of New York University, "Final Report on The Jefferson Park Branch of the Boys' Club of New York" (submitted to the Bureau of Social Hygiene, Oct. 21, 1935, in BSH, microfilm reel 7, box 12, unnumbered folder), 288; see also pp. 236–37 for discussion of boys meeting homosexuals in movie theaters. Several years earlier, Thrasher, a sociologist trained at the University of Chicago, published *The Gang: A Study of 1,313 Gangs in Chicago* (Chicago: University of Chicago Press, 1927).

41. Werther, *The Female-Impersonators,* 141; see also 132–45, 156–57, 163; Nesbitt memoir (1938), Charles Torrence Nesbitt papers, Duke University Library. For a powerful fictionalized account of such violence (which was widely discussed at the time of publication), in which the author recalls seeing a group of Italian youths attack a man who had approached one of them at Coney Island, see Robert M. Coates, "One Night At Coney," *American Mercury,* May 1934, reprinted in *The American Mercury Reader,* ed. Lawrence E. Spivak and Charles Angoff (Philadelphia: Blakiston, 1944), 191–96.

42. Report by K[ahan]., Mar. 2, 1920, box 34, COF.

43. Examples of this danger were provided by Tom R., interviewed; John N., interviewed; Sebastian Risicato, interviewed; see also Donald Vining, *A Gay Diary* (4 vols.; New York: Pepys Press, 1979–83), 1:347–48 (entries for Sept. 16 and 17, 1944), 1:384 (entry for Apr. 28, 1945); and Chauncey, "Christian Brotherhood," 176.

44. Werther, *Autobiography,* 78–79, 157–58.

45. On the highly complex conventions surrounding violence against women and the interactions of Bowery men and uptown slummers during an earlier period, see Christine Stansell, *City of Women: Sex and Class in New York, 1789–1860* (New York: Knopf, 1986), 95–99.

46. The association between fairies and prostitutes may have been of long standing. See Trumbach's analysis of a similar pattern in eighteenth-century London, in "The Birth of the Queen." On the "tough girls" of the Bowery and other working-class districts, see Kathy Peiss, *Cheap Amusements: Working Women and Leisure in Turn-of-the-Century New York* (Philadelphia: Temple University Press, 1986), 58–59, 65–66, 71, 106.

47. There are countless examples in the Committee of Fourteen papers of agents identifying women as "street walkers" on the basis of their being "all painted up." See, for example, David Oppenheim report on Ahneman Brothers, 772 Broadway, Brooklyn, Nov. 23, 1916, box 30, COF; and J. A. S., report on Reisenwebers, Jan. 23, 1917, box 31, COF; see also Rosen, *The Lost Sisterhood,* 107; and, more generally, Lois W. Banner, *American Beauty* (New York: Knopf, 1983), 42, 74–75, 133.

48. On the abhorrence of oral eroticism as "dirty" in the early twentieth century, particularly among working-class couples, see Alfred Kinsey, Wardell Pomeroy, and Clyde Martin, *Sexual Behavior in the Human Male* (Philadelphia: W. B. Saunders, 1948), 369–73. Kinsey also detected an increasing openness to the practice in the early decades of the century, however, for he reported that the incidence of women performing fellation on their husbands had doubled in the course of a generation, from 29 percent of the women born before 1900 to 57 percent of the women born in the 1920s (*Sexual Behavior in the Human Female* [Philadelphia: W. B. Saunders, 1953], 362).

49. Moreover, it was those women who refused to engage in "abnormal" sexual practices such as oral sex—not specifically those who rejected lesbian behavior—who were considered "straight." See, for example, the language used by an agent to report two prostitutes' response to his query about their willingness to provide oral sex: "I first asked [them] . . . if they were french (perverts); they replied, 'Straight only'" (report on 269 1/2 W. 22nd St., May 26, 1927, box 36, COF).

50. The association of male homosexuality with female prostitution was enshrined in the Wolfenden Report, published in Great Britain in 1957, which considered both phenomena in conjunction: *Report of the Committee on Homosexual Offenses and Prostitution, Sir John Wolfenden, Chairman* (1957; New York: Stein and Day, 1963). (For a further analysis of this association, see the following chapter.)

51. Quoted in Kahn, *Mentality and Homosexuality,* 127.

52. Parker Tyler to Charles Henri Ford, c. Feb. 18, 1931.

53. Quoted in Kahn, *Mentality and Homosexuality,* 155.

CHAPTER 3. TRADE, WOLVES, AND THE BOUNDARIES OF NORMAL MANHOOD

1. Report on Times Square Building by J. K., May 2, 1927, COF. "D—" in the original.

2. *Happy Hour Bar & Grill, Inc., v. Bruckman, et al.,* 256 A.D. 1074 (2nd Dep't 1939), reports on the Happy Hour Bar & Grill by investigators Tierney and Kirschenbaum, dated Oct. 10 and Oct. 17, 1938, contained in Record on Review, 47–48, 56.

3. E. S. Shepherd, for example, specifically referred to "fairies" as "the male prostitute of the streets" in "Contribution to the Study of Intermediacy," *American Journal of Urology and Sexology* 14 (1918): 245.

4. Richard Meeker, *Better Angel* (New York: Greenberg, 1933), 259; Kennilworth Bruce, *Goldie* (New York: William Godwin, 1933), 105.

5. Gershon Legman, "The Language of Homosexuality: An American Glossary," in George W. Henry, *Sex Variants* (New York: Paul B. Hoeber, 1941), vol. 2, appendix VII, 1176, quoting a study of prostitutes' slang; *Report and Proceedings of the [Lexow] Senate Committee appointed to investigate the Police Department of the City of New York* (Albany: J. B. Lyon, 1895), Captain Ryan testimony, 5591.

6. Charles W. Gardner, *The Doctor and the Devil; or, the Midnight Adventures of Dr. Parkhurst* (New York: Gardner & Co., 1894), 52.

7. R. W. Shufeldt, M.D., "Biography of a Passive Pederast," *American Journal of Urology and Sexology* 13 (1917): 451–60. Although the interview was reported in 1917, it took place in 1906. "Looping the loop" had become a generic slang expression for such amusement park rides in the 1900s; see Jane Addams's reference to "looping the loop" in *The Spirit of Youth and the City Streets* (New York: Macmillan, 1909), 69, as quoted in John F. Kasson, *Amusing the Million: Coney Island at the Turn of the Century* (New York: Hill and Wang, 1978), 100, who also discusses the ride on pp. 81–82.

8. Quoted in George Chauncey, "Christian Brotherhood or Sexual Perversion? Homosexual Identities and the Construction of Sexual Boundaries in the World War One Era," *Journal of Social History* 19 (1985): 195. The sailor was questioned at the Newport, Rhode Island, naval training station, but had spent time in New York and was involved in a gay world not far removed from that of the city.

9. R. E. Fay, C. F. Turner, A. D. Klassen, and J. H. Gagnon, "Prevalence and

Patterns of Same-Gender Sexual Contact Among Men," *Science* 243 (1989): 343–48; S. M. Rogers and C. F. Turner, "Male–Male Sexual Contact in the USA: Findings from Five Sample Surveys, 1970–1990," *Journal of Sex Research* 28 (1991): 491–519; J. O. G. Billy, K. Panfer, W. R. Grady, and D. H. Klepinger, "The Sexual Behavior of Men in the United States," *Family Planning Perspectives* 25 (1993): 52–60.

10. Alfred Kinsey, Wardell Pomeroy, and Clyde Martin, *Sexual Behavior in the Human Male* (Philadelphia: W. B. Saunders, 1948), 612, 614.

11. Ibid., 616.

12. The reputation of Italian men for trade in the gay world was noted by Frank Burton, Bruce Nugent, and Sebastian Risicato in interviews; see also the role of Italian men in Charles Henri Ford and Parker Tyler, *The Young and Evil* (Paris: Obelisk Press, 1933), which was based on Tyler's experiences in the Village, where he regularly encountered "straight" Italian men interested in sex with men. On Irish men, see the discussion of Charles Tomlinson Griffes and policemen in the following chapter. I have been unable to locate sufficient evidence concerning the sexual cultures of other immigrant groups in New York to propose even a tentative analysis of them. New York City's small Chinatown community, for instance, consisted almost entirely of bachelors as a result of restrictive immigration policies. While slender oral history evidence hints at homosexual activity among some of the bachelors, there is not a single gay-related reference (and virtually no reference of any kind) to Chinese men in the records of the Committee of Fourteen and Committee of Fifteen I have examined. The single sodomy case I have found concerns an unmarried twenty-four-year-old Chinese laundryman, who allegedly forced sex on two Jewish boys he enticed into the premises of a laundry on East Broadway one evening in 1898. He was acquitted, and the DAP case file contains no additional information (*People v. Ong*, DAP 22,086 [CGS 1898]).

13. Frederick H. Whitin, "Sexual Perversion Cases in New York City Courts, 1916–1921," bulletin 1480, Nov. 12, 1921, box 88, COF. My review of the backgrounds of the two hundred men arrested by the police (with the assistance of the Society for the Suppression of Vice) for degenerate disorderly conduct in 1920–21 suggests that almost twice as many Italians than Jews were arrested (see the eleven-page list, untitled, in "Homosexuality" folder, box 63, COF). Religious and national backgrounds for most (but not all) of the men arrested were supplied in the records of the Society itself, volumes 3–5 (SSV). These figures, of course, may reveal as much about the enforcement priorities of the police as about the actual incidence of homosexual conduct. I include them, however, as one piece of evidence for the pattern of ethnic differences suggested more conclusively by the greater visibility and institutionalization of gay life in the Italian than Jewish Lower East Side.

14. 207 Canal St. report, "Court of Special Sessions [cases]," box 65, COF. A judge ultimately refused to close the saloon on the basis of "disorderly conversation" alone.

15. Report of J. R., Mar. 22, 1901, box 7, Committee of Fifteen papers, NYPL.

16. Report of H. S. Conklin, Mar. 5, 1901, box 5; report of Salomon and Robinson, February 1901, box 7, Committee of Fifteen papers, NYPL. According to the typed transcript of the investigators' notes cited here, the five boys were known as "faniss," by which they may have meant "finocchio," the Italian-American term for fennel, used in the production of licorice, which Italian-Americans used synonymously with the English term cocksucker. (This presumably was the origin of the name of Finocchio's, a famous club in San Francisco featuring

a female-impersonation act in the 1940s and 1950s.) Other investigators' reports refer to such men as "fairies," as well as "perverts" and, most commonly, "cock suckers." "Pansy" did not become a common term for gay men until the 1920s.

17. Report of Captain Titus [to the Mayor], Dec. 20, 1900, box 9, Van Wyck papers, Mayors' Papers, NYMA. The same report notes that the police investigated rumors that 138 Chrystie St. was a disorderly house, but does not indicate what kind of "disorder" was said to occur there. I am indebted to Timothy Gilfoyle for this reference.

18. Kinsey, *Sexual Behavior*, 483. On Italian immigrants' response to church teachings, see Robert Orsi, *The Madonna of 115th Street: Faith and Community in Italian Harlem, 1880–1950* (New Haven, Conn.: Yale University Press, 1985), xvi–xviii, 219–21; Gary R. Mormino and George E. Pozzetta, *The Immigrant World of Ybor City: Italians and Their Latin Neighbors in Tampa, 1885–1985* (Urbana: University of Illinois Press, 1987), 210–32.

19. Kinsey also noted that many sexologists in Italy itself considered southern Italy "the most homosexual place in the world," although he continued to believe that homosexual behavior was more widespread in several countries in the Middle and Far East. See Wardell Pomeroy, *Dr. Kinsey and the Institute for Sex Research* (New Haven, Conn.: Yale University Press, 1972), 423–27. On the general openness of Italian men to sexual contacts with men, see also the letters from one of Kinsey's informants reprinted in Martin Duberman, *About Time: Exploring the Gay Past* (New York: Gay Presses of New York, 1986), 173–77. For one gay veteran's view of homosexual life in Italy, see John Hope Burns's postwar novel, *The Gallery* (New York: Harper, 1947). On instrumentalist approaches to the body, see Pierre Bourdieu's observations in "Sport and Social Class," *Social Science Information* 17 (1978): 819–40. Bourdieu argues that such attitudes are more characteristic of (French) working-class men than middle-class men, but unfortunately does not historicize that assessment. Although the homosexual culture on the Lower East Side bears a remarkable resemblance in many respects to the limited accounts we have of Mediterranean sexual patterns, the subtle variations in those patterns, both within the Mediterranean basin and between Europe and the United States, need to be studied with care. "Mediterranean" cultures are often represented as more homogeneous in such matters than they actually are. On the dangers of such homogenization, see, for example, Michael Herzfeld, "The Horns of the Mediterraneanist Dilemma," *American Ethnologist* 11 (1984): 439–54. See also John J. Winkler, *Constraints of Desire* (New York: Routledge, 1990).

20. On the different demographic patterns of Italian and Jewish immigration to New York, see Thomas Kessner, *The Golden Door: Italian and Jewish Immigrant Mobility in New York City* (New York: Oxford University Press, 1977), 26–32. On the unusually large number of single men who immigrated to the United States from Italy, see also Dino Cinel, *From Italy to San Francisco: The Immigrant Experience* (Stanford, Calif.: Stanford University Press, 1982), 162–72. For an analytic overview of the circumstances in Europe and the Americas that resulted in European emigration and of the significance of family networks to migration, see John Bodnar, *The Transplanted: A History of Immigrants in Urban America* (Bloomington: Indiana University Press, 1985), 1–84. Numerous historians have studied Italian and Jewish immigration to New York. See, for example, Moses Rischin, *The Promised City: New York's Jews, 1870–1914* (Cambridge, Mass.: Harvard University Press, 1962); Irving Howe, *World of Our Fathers* (New York: Harcourt Brace Jovanovich, 1976); Donna R. Gabaccia, *From Sicily to Elizabeth Street: Housing and Social Change Among Italian Immigrants* (Albany:

State University of New York Press, 1984); as well as the other studies cited elsewhere in this section.

21. Sophonisba Breckinridge, *New Homes for Old* (New York: Harper, 1921), 176–77. See also Susan A. Glenn, *Daughters of the Shtetl: Life and Labor in the Immigrant Generation* (Ithaca, N.Y.: Cornell University Press, 1990), 81–82, 159–66, 162, 215–16. On the greater degree of social interaction between men and women in Jewish than Italian neighborhoods, see also Kathy Peiss, *Cheap Amusements: Working Women and Leisure in Turn-of-the-Century New York* (Philadelphia: Temple University Press, 1986), 30, 68; Elizabeth Ewen, *Immigrant Women in the Land of Dollars: Life and Culture on the Lower East Side, 1890–1925* (New York: Monthly Review Press, 1985), 210–11; Elinor Lerner, "Family Structure, Occupational Patterns, and Support for Women's Suffrage," in *Women in Culture and Politics: A Century of Change*, ed. Judith Friedlander et al. (Bloomington: Indiana University Press, 1986); Gabaccia, *From Sicily*, 97.

22. Orsi, *The Madonna of 115th Street*, 21, 115–17, 135–43. On living arrangements, see Kessner, *The Golden Door*, 99–101; and Gabaccia, *From Sicily*, ch. 5–6. On the use of leisure time, see Perry R. Duis, *The Saloon: Public Drinking in Chicago and Boston, 1880–1920* (Urbana: University of Illinois Press, 1983), 146–48, Louise C. Odencrantz, *Italian Women in Industry: A Study of Conditions in New York* (New York: Russell Sage), 203–5, who noted that in such families "the mother had no recreation and [even] the father took his alone" (203), and Gabaccia, *From Sicily*, 97.

23. John H. Mariano, *The Second Generation of Italians in New York City* (Boston: Christopher Publishing, 1921), 140–43. For a fine analysis of such social clubs and gangs, see Leonard H. Ellis, "Men Among Men: An Exploration of All-Male Relationships in Victorian America" (Ph.D. diss., Columbia University, 1982), 1–60. Ellis assumes too readily that boys usually left such gangs for poolrooms and saloons once they reached the age of sixteen or eighteen, but he offers a thoughtful analysis of the role of all three such neighborhood-based all-male social groupings and spaces in the everyday lives of late-nineteenth-century men.

24. For a fascinating analysis of the origins and social organization of the Irish bachelor culture, see Richard Stivers, *A Hair of the Dog: Irish Drinking and American Stereotype* (University Park: Pennsylvania State University Press, 1976). For evidence of the concern the high rates of bachelorhood and spinsterhood provoked among Irish and Catholic leaders, see the articles cited by Stivers: James Walsh, "Catholic Bachelors and Old Maids," *America*, Aug. 12, 1922, 389–90; idem, "The Disappearing Irish in America," *America*, May 1, 1926, 56–57; idem, "Shy Irish Bachelors," *America*, Mar. 29 1930, 592–93; M. V. Kelly, "The Suicide of the Irish Race," *America*, Nov. 17 and 24, 1928, 128–29, 155–56.

25. The paintings by Cadmus and Demuth of sailors in homoerotic situations appear in many of the catalogs of their work. In addition to the Cadmus painting reproduced at the beginning of this chapter, see the paintings reproduced in the catalog for the Demuth retrospective at the Whitney Museum of American Art, *Charles Demuth* (New York: Abrams, 1987). For later pornographers, see almost any issue of *Tomorrow's Man, VIM, Physique Pictorial,* and the other gay-oriented "physique magazines" published in the 1940s–1960s.

26. On the decline of the transient workforce, see Nels Anderson, *Men on the Move* (Chicago: University of Chicago Press, 1940), 2–5, 12.

27. There were also ethnic, occupational, and generational differences among the men in the various male subcultures that collectively constituted the "bachelor subculture," but most of them shared its distinctive characteristics to some degree.

28. Ralph Werther, *Autobiography of an Androgyne* (New York: Medico-Legal Journal, 1918), 83–84, 88.

29. Report on the Subway Cabaret, Fourteenth St. near Fourth Ave., 10 P.M., Jan. 12, 1917, COF.

30. On the importance of what he calls "masculine conviviality" to such men, the character of the bachelor subculture, and the relationship between the culture of the "rough" working class and the respectable, see David Montgomery, *The Fall of the House of Labor: The Workplace, the State, and American Labor Activism, 1865–1925* (Cambridge: Cambridge University Press, 1987), 87–92; Roy Rosenzweig, *Eight Hours for What We Will: Workers and Leisure in an Industrial City, 1870–1920* (New York: Cambridge University Press, 1983), 57–64, 74–81; Elliott J. Gorn, *The Manly Art: Bare-Knuckle Prize Fighting in America* (Ithaca, N.Y.: Cornell University Press, 1986), 129–45, especially 140–45; Ned Polsky, *Hustlers, Beats, and Others* (Chicago: Aldine, 1967), 31–37, 90, 105, 109–10; Ellis, "Men Among Men," 1–60; and Peter Bailey, "'Will the Real Bill Banks Please Stand Up?' Towards a Role Analysis of Mid-Victorian Working-Class Respectability," in *Expanding the Past: Essays from the Journal of Social History,* ed. Peter N. Stearns (New York: New York University Press, 1988), 73–90.

31. For two distinct perspectives on the performativity of everyday life, see Erving Goffman's classic study, *The Presentation of Self in Everyday Life* (Garden City, N.Y.: Doubleday, 1959); and Judith Butler's splendid *Gender Trouble: Feminism and the Subversion of Identity* (New York: Routledge, 1990).

32. On the carnival, see Peter Stallybrass and Allon White, *The Politics and Poetics of Transgression* (Ithaca, N.Y.: Cornell University Press, 1986).

33. Antonio L., quoted in Henry, *Sex Variants,* 420.

34. Report on Italian Restaurant, 207 W. 17th St., Oct. 6, 1927, box 36, COF.

35. Frederick H. Whitin to Captain T. N. Pfeiffer, War and Navy Departments Commission, Washington, Apr. 3, 1918, box 25, COF.

36. J. A. S., Conditions about the Brooklyn Navy Yard, June 6, 1917, box 25, COF. See also, for example, Harry Benjamin's 1931 article arguing that "the suppression of prostitution [in New York] has probably increased and favored homosexual tendencies and practices" ("'For the Sake of Morality,'" *Medical Journal and Record* 133: 380–82).

37. For more on the sexual mapping of the city, see chapter 7.

38. On the magnitude of the business of prostitution in nineteenth- and early-twentieth-century New York City, and its decline after the 1910s, see Timothy J. Gilfoyle, *City of Eros: New York City, Prostitution, and the Commercialization of Sex, 1790–1920* (New York: Norton, 1992).

39. Kinsey, *Sexual Behavior,* 38; William Foote Whyte, "A Slum Sex Code," *American Journal of Sociology* 49 (1943): 24–31.

40. On the belief that men had to have regular orgasms to maintain their health, see Charles Rosenberg, "Sexuality, Class, and Role in Nineteenth-Century America," in *The American Man,* ed. Elizabeth H. Pleck and Joseph H. Pleck (Englewood Cliffs, N.J.: Prentice-Hall, 1980), 230–32, and E. Anthony Rotundo, *American Manhood: Transformations in Masculinity from the Revolution to the Modern Era* (New York: Basic Books, 1993), 121–22. Both accounts focus on the nineteenth century, but it is clear that the belief persisted into the twentieth. For examples of the term *satisfaction* used casually to mean orgasm, see, for example, Salvatore N., quoted in Henry, *Sex Variants,* 176; Victor F. Nelson, *Prison Days and Nights* (Boston: Little, Brown, 1933), 157–58.

41. Finch diary, Aug. 8, 1949, KIL.

42. "Social Contagion in the Pool-room," 14–15, in Frederic M. Thrasher, "The Use of the Superior Boy in Research," BSH, box 11, folder 229 ("NYU Boys Club Study, 1930"), microfilm reel 6.

43. Shufeldt, "Biography of a Passive Pederast," 457.

44. "Sex Practices and Stimuli," 12–13, in Thrasher.

45. Finch diary, Jan. 3, 1951. Committee of Fourteen investigators regularly reported that even prostitutes were unwilling to engage in oral sex; see, for example, the reports on 269 1/2 W. 22nd St., May 26, 1927; tenement, 756 Eighth Ave., Dec. 4, 1928; tenement, 2544 Eighth Ave., June 21, 1928; Navarre Hotel, Seventh Ave. and 38th St., Mar. 16, 1928, box 36, COF. Not all women rejected such requests, however; see the reports on tenement, 954 Eighth Ave., Sept. 20, 1927 ("I don't make a practice of it, but if you want it, I'll accommodate you"); tenement, 42 W. 46th St., July 22, 1927; and B&G Sandwich Shop, 140 Fulton St., Dec. 19, 1927 (the woman there said "the only way I do it is the French way," explaining that she did not want to risk pregnancy), all in the same file.

46. Allan M. Brandt, *No Magic Bullet: A Social History of Venereal Disease in the United States Since 1880* (New York: Oxford University Press, 1985), ch. 2–3, provides the best account of such campaigns. On men's fear of catching a disease from a prostitute, see, for example, Report on Maxim's, 108 W. 38th St., Sept. 25, 1916, box 31, COF. In significant respects such campaigns prefigured the AIDS education campaigns of the early 1980s, which often identified sex with a gay man or an IV-drug user, rather than sex without a condom, as the source of AIDS. Such campaigns led many people to fear that the most casual contact with certain categories of people was unsafe, while reassuring them, with deadly inaccuracy, of the safety of the most intimate contact with other categories of people.

47. Report on Hanover Lunch, 2 South St., June 12, 1931, box 35, COF. Gene Harwood and Frank Burton, in discussing their memories of the 1920s and 1930s in an interview with the author, also pointed to men's fear of getting venereal diseases from women as a reason for their willingness to have sex with gay men. The sociologist Nels Anderson also reported that hoboes argued they were less likely to catch a venereal disease from homosexual than from heterosexual intercourse (*The Hobo: The Sociology of the Homeless Man* [Chicago: University of Chicago Press, 1923], 134, 147–48), a view shared by the Chicago Vice Commission in its 1911 report, *The Social Evil in Chicago*, 296–97, cited in Anderson, 148. See also Samuel Kahn, *Mentality and Homosexuality* (Boston: Meador, 1937), 50–51. For indications that this belief was of long standing, see Randolph Trumbach, "The Birth of the Queen: Sodomy and the Emergence of Gender Equality in Modern Culture, 1660–1750," in *Hidden from History: Reclaiming the Gay and Lesbian Past*, ed. Martin Duberman, Martha Vicinus, and George Chauncey (New York: New American Library, 1989), 129–40.

48. Bulletin 1504, Mar. 24, 1922, box 88, COF.

49. Shufeldt, "Biography of a Passive Pederast," 459, 456.

50. Will Finch thought the latter, although he sometimes substituted the older Navy word *pogue* for the more generally used *punk*. As he commented of one young Norwegian sailor, an older sailor's "boy" who nonetheless ended up in bed with Finch one summer night in 1946 and made it clear he expected Finch to anally penetrate (or "brown") him: "I decided that he was either queer and *liked* to be browned or the big guy's pogue and *expected* to be browned" (Finch diary, July 14, 1946). On the widespread use of *pogue* by sailors in the World War I era to mean a man who desired to be browned, see Chauncey, "Christian Brotherhood or Sexual Perversion?" especially 192, 196. The evidence suggests that the young men to whom the term was applied fell into all three camps.

51. Alexander Berkman, *Prison Memoirs of an Anarchist* (New York: Mother Earth Publishing Association, 1912), 170, 172. Joseph F. Fishman, the first federal Inspector of Prisons and, in the late 1920s, the Deputy Commissioner of the New York City Department of Corrections, used the word *wolf* for the aggressive party in homosexual encounters in his description of prison homosexuality among non-homosexuals, in *Sex in Prison* (New York: National Library Press, 1934), 152, as did his critic, Louis Berg, *Revelations of a Prison Doctor* (New York: Milton, Balch, 1934), 120, 142. For evidence of the use of such terms among hoboes in the 1910s–1930s, see Anderson, *The Hobo*, 99, 101, 103, 144–48 (*wolf, jocker, lamb, kid, wife,* and *punk*), and *Broadway Brevities*, Nov. 9, 1931, 10. In the novel *Goldie,* a sailor approached the protagonist, who was hustling on Times Square, called himself "the slickest wolf in ther navy," and added, in reference to the hustler, "I guess I ought ter know a regular punk when I sees one" (116). The terms were also used in Los Angeles by the 1920s, according to Aaron J. Rosanoff, "Human Sexuality, Normal and Abnormal, from a Psychiatric Standpoint," *Urologic and Cutaneous Review* (1929), 528. *Punk* was also widely used in the criminal underworld beyond the prison walls, specifically to refer to the underlings in a criminal gang and more generally as an epithet; see, for example, its use in Cornelius Willemse, *Behind the Green Lights* (New York, 1931), 336–37. On the term's diffusion into general slang, see Legman, "The Language of Homosexuality," 1174. The terms were still used with similar sexual meanings in prisons in the 1970s; see Wayne S. Wooden and Jay Parker, *Men Behind Bars: Sexual Exploitation in Prison* (New York: Da Capo, 1982).

52. The distinction between "wolves" and homosexuals (or "queers") persisted. One hustler picked up in 1949 by a conventionally masculine queer, Will Finch, queried whether he were "'just queer or a wolf,'" adding that there was "no use in 'getting up there and finding out it's no use,'" which Finch took to mean that "he won't be pedicated" (Finch diary, May 20, 1949). The hustler, in other words, insisted on remaining the man in the encounter, which he could do if he were sexually serviced by a queer, and refused to be feminized by being pedicated by a wolf. Finch's response, that he was "not a wolf—unless [the hustler] wants me to be," suggests that, at least by the postwar period, *wolf* described a sexual role as much as a social or characterological "type."

53. Report on the Seamen's Church Institute and vicinity, July 15 and 16, 1931, COF.

54. Reports on the Seamen's Church Institute and vicinity, May 27, June 22, July 2, and July 15 and 16, 1931, COF.

55. Ibid.

56. Rev. Frank Charles Laubach, "Why There Are Vagrants: Based upon an Examination of One Hundred Men" (Ph.D. diss., Columbia University, 1916), 13–14, reported that twenty-four of the hundred men were perverts. A 1935 survey of ninety men housed in a Chicago shelter for the homeless noted that "7 percent stated they were engaging in homosexual practices" (Edwin J. Sutherland and Harvey J. Locke, *Twenty Thousand Homeless Men: A Study of Unemployed Men in the Chicago Shelters* [Chicago: Lippincott, 1936], 131). The 7 percent figure is almost surely low: not only does it report the number of men who "stated" they were homosexually active, something many such men would doubtless deny to people surveying them in a homeless shelter, but the figure was produced during the Depression, when a more diverse group of men had been made homeless.

57. Dean Stiff [pseudonym of Nels Anderson], *The Milk and Honey Route: A Handbook for Hobos* (New York: Vanguard Press, 1931), 161.

58. Anderson, *The Hobo,* 145.

59. Important early efforts to investigate such social worlds from this perspective include Susan Lee Johnson's "'The Gold She Gathered': Difference, Domination, and California's Southern Mines, 1848–1853" (Ph.D. diss., Yale University, 1993); B. R. Burg, *Sodomy and the Pirate Tradition: English Sea Rovers in the Seventeenth-Century Caribbean* (New York: New York University Press, 1984); Chad Heap, "The Melting Pot of Trampdom," unpublished seminar paper, University of Chicago, 1993.

60. Wooden and Parker, *Men Behind Bars.*

61. Berg, *Revelations of a Prison Doctor,* 137, 152–61; Kahn, *Mentality and Homosexuality,* 23–24, 129; see also Perry M. Lichtenstein, "The 'Fairy' and the Lady Lover," *Medical Review of Reviews* 27 (1921): 369–74.

62. *New York Herald Tribune,* Jan. 27, 1934, 2.

63. Berg, *Revelations of a Prison Doctor,* 161–63.

64. The raid has not received much attention from historians, but for La Guardia's appointment of Austin H. MacCormick as Commissioner of Corrections and his insistence that the Tammany influence be driven from the Corrections Department, see Lowell M. Limpus and Burr W. Leyson, *This Man La Guardia* (New York: Dutton, 1938), 378, 381, and Thomas Kessner, *Fiorello H. La Guardia and the Making of Modern New York* (New York: McGraw-Hill, 1989), ch. 8.

65. "M'Cormick Raids Welfare Island, Smashes Gangster Rule of Prison; Warden Relieved, Deputy Seized: Commissioner Discovers Top Notch Thugs Living at Ease in Hospital . . . Private Section Housing Degenerates Revealed in 'World's Worst' Bastille; Flare-Up Feared," *New York Herald Tribune,* Jan. 25, 1934, 1, 9; "McCann Admits 'Convict Rule,'" *Daily Mirror,* Jan. 26, 1934, 10. In yet another article in the same issue, "Welfare Milk Racket Bared," 3, the paper asked "why 'Greta Garbo,' alias 'Top and Bottom,' the drug-eaten former U.S. Navy gob, wears his hair to his waist." The *New York Times* also gave the prison raid extensive coverage. Although it paid less attention to the most scandalous elements, even it described the "altogether different line of contraband" found in the homosexual cell block, including "rouge, powder, mascara, perfume, even a woman's wig," and went on to describe how "several of the inmates of this cell block affected long hair. Silk undergarments were found in the cells" ("Welfare Island Raid Bares Gangster Rule Over Prison; Weapons, Narcotics Found . . . Vice Carried on Openly," Jan. 25, 1934, 3).

66. In addition to the studies already cited, see Joseph F. Fishman, *Sex in Prison: Revealing Sex Conditions in American Prisons* (New York: National Library Press, 1934). The growth of interest in homosexuality in prisons may account for the publication of Samuel Kahn's study, *Mentality and Homosexuality,* in 1937, even though it had been written more than a decade earlier.

67. Thomas Mott Osborne, *Prisons and Common Sense* (Philadelphia: Lippincott, 1924), 89–90. He also recognized a third category: "the degenerates, whose dual nature [combining male and female elements] has been a problem to the psychologist since the days of ancient Greece."

68. Nelson, *Prison Days and Nights,* 157–58. Note the assumption that male and female fellators were equally anomalous and virtually interchangeable.

CHAPTER 4. THE FORGING OF QUEER IDENTITIES AND THE EMERGENCE OF HETEROSEXUALITY IN MIDDLE-CLASS CULTURE

1. E. S. Shepherd, "Contribution to the Study of Intermediacy," *American Journal of Urology and Sexology* 14 (1918): 245.

2. Richard Meeker [pseud. of Forman Brown], *Better Angel* (New York: Greenberg, 1933), 259.

3. Salvatore N., quoted in George W. Henry, *Sex Variants* (New York: Paul B. Hoeber, 1941), 175–76, 178. Another man told Henry that as a child he had encountered a "very, very feminine" homosexual: "I told him that before I would become like him I would poison myself" (Louis E., 194).

4. Jonathan Ned Katz, "The Invention of Heterosexuality," *Socialist Review* 20 (January–March 1990): 7–34.

5. Dorr Legg, interviewed.

6. George George, interviewed.

7. Jeffrey Gottfried, interviewed.

8. "Jeb Alexander" (pseudonym), diary entry for Feb. 4, 1927, in *Jeb and Dash: A Diary of Gay Life, 1918–1945,* ed. Ina Russell (Boston: Faber and Faber, 1993), 90–91. See also his comment about a man at a gay party he attended three years later: "Junior tried to behave himself, but made offensive remarks and emitted shrieks in his effeminate manner that I detest" (Sept. 19, 1930, 189).

9. On the relative youthfulness of the men who attended the gay drag balls in women's clothes, see, for example, the remark of an older participant, Rudolph Von H., that "most of the [other] boys were twenty," quoted in Henry, *Sex Variants,* 495–96; and an investigator's observation that most men at a Greenwich Village ball "were younger men between 20 and 35 years of age," in his report on the Liberal Club Ball, Feb. 11, 1917, box 31, COF.

10. Irving T., quoted in Henry, *Sex Variants,* 338–39. Interviews with Nat Fowler and Frank Thompson; Ralph Werther, *Autobiography of an Androgyne* (New York: Medico-Legal Journal, 1918), 209; Samuel Kahn, *Mentality and Homosexuality* (Boston: Meador, 1937), 126.

11. Samuel M. Steward, in his introduction to the 1982 reissue of James Barr, *Quatrefoil* (1950; Boston: Alyson Press, 1982), ix–x.

12. Edward Maisel to author, Feb. 1, 1989, speaking of his interviews with the associates of the composer Charles Tomlinson Griffes, whose biography he wrote (*Charles T. Griffes: The Life of an American Composer* [1943; updated edition, New York: Knopf, 1984]).

13. Gene S., quoted in Henry, *Sex Variants,* 255.

14. Max Adams, interviewed.

15. Alexander diary, Jan. 16, 1924, *Jeb and Dash,* 73, and May 3, 1925, 82.

16. See, for example, the references to "obvious homosexuals" and "obvious types" cited above; as well as Will Finch's definition of the "swish" as "a homosexual of the extreme type," and his reference to the use of "she" and "Mary" by "the extreme homosexual," in his 1963 glossary, KIL.

17. Matthiessen to Cheney, Jan. 28, Feb. 7, 1925, reprinted in *Rat and the Devil: Journal Letters of F. O. Matthiessen and Russell Cheney,* ed. Louis Hyde (Hamden, Conn.: Archon Books, 1978), 69, 87.

18. Alexander diary, July 5, 1923, in *Jeb and Dash,* 65. For Alexander's other references to Whitman, see, for example, his diary entries for Nov. 14, 1922 (55), in which he invoked Whitman and Nietzsche to give him courage, and Aug. 25, 1930 (188), in which he recalled his first sexual experience, exactly ten years earlier, with a line from Whitman's Calamus poems: "That night I was happy."

19. On German Jews' concerns about the threat posed by the influx of Orthodox immigrants to "their hard-won respectability," and their efforts to minimize that threat by fostering the newcomers' assimilation, see, for example, Moses Rischin, *The Promised City: New York's Jews, 1870–1914* (Cambridge, Mass.: Harvard University Press, 1962), 95–103. On Northern blacks' concerns about the style of rural migrants and the development of programs to teach them to dress and behave "properly," see James Grossman, *Land of Hope: Chicago, Black*

Southerners, and the Great Migration (Chicago: University of Chicago Press, 1989), 123–60; William Tuttle, *Race Riot: Chicago in the Red Summer of 1919* (New York: Atheneum, 1970); Kenneth Kusmer, *A Ghetto Takes Shape: Black Cleveland, 1870–1930* (Urbana: University of Illinois Press, 1976), 251–54; and Peter Gottlieb, *Making Their Own Way: Southern Blacks' Migration to Pittsburgh, 1916–1930* (Urbana: University of Illinois Press, 1987), 187–90. See also Gilbert Osofsky, *Harlem: The Making of a Ghetto: Negro New York, 1890–1930* (New York: Harper & Row, 1966), 53–67.

20. Finch, glossary, addenda 1, 1963, KIL. Finch wrote this in 1963, but his diary makes it clear he had entertained such concerns about the fairy since the 1930s. See also the 1918 comment by E. S. Shepherd, a sympathetic doctor who seems to have been echoing the opinions of his gay acquaintances: "There is no more warrant for judging the intermediates by their lowest manifestations than for judging our womanhood by the lowest class of prostitutes" ("Contribution to the Study of Intermediacy," 242). There was, of course, a significant difference between gay men and the other groups: It was relatively easy for queer men to pass as straight, but few blacks were in the same position; middle-class and "assimilated" or not, most of them could not easily pass as white. (Enough did do so, however, that passing was a major subject of discussion among African-Americans. See, for example, Nella Larsen's extraordinary 1929 novel about black women, *Passing,* which, as Deborah McDowell has observed, also offers a subtextual exploration of lesbian passing; see her introduction to the edition she edited of Larsen's *Quicksand* and *Passing* [New Brunswick, N.J.: Rutgers University Press, 1986].) More middle-class Jews were able to—and did—pass as Christian, but not in the numbers or with the ease with which gay men passed as straight.

21. Interviews with Robert Winston and Joel Honig.

22. Noble Krieder to Edward Maisel, July 31, 1938; letter in possession of Professor David Reed, Muhlenberg College.

23. Krieder to Maisel, July 31, July 18, 1938. Part of the July 18 letter quoted here is also quoted in Maisel's biography of Griffes, p. 349. My account of Griffes's activities and attitudes is based on Maisel's fine biographical study as well as my discussions with Mr. Maisel. In the quotations from the diary that follow, I have generally followed the translations of German passages provided by Donna Anderson. I have translated several passages myself, however, and thank three native speakers of German, Hans Hengelein, Juergen Poppinger, and Moishe Postone, for advising me on the subtleties of several particularly delicate passages.

24. Glenway Wescott, *Continual Lessons: The Journals of Glenway Wescott, 1937–1955,* ed. Robert Phelps with Jerry Rosco (New York: Farrar, Straus & Giroux, 1990), 11. For examples of gay men's expression of interest in "real men" or "rough trade" as sexual partners, see the comments of several men interviewed in Henry, *Sex Variants:* Noel W., 270, 278; Walter R., 288; Dennis C., 310; José R., 346 ("I prefer men to fairies").

25. Griffes diary, May 27, 1915.

26. See, for example, Griffes diary, Apr. 24, 1915: "Conductor X said hello to me as I entered the train car, so he remembers me. This time I talked to him a lot during the trip, and find him very attractive. . . . I want to get to know him quite well."

27. Ibid., Apr. 27, May 9, Sept. 9 and 11, 1914; May 15, 1915; Apr. 1 and Apr. 27, 1914.

28. Ibid., Aug. 28, Dec. 31, 1915. For the development of their relationship, see Maisel, *Charles T. Griffes,* 155–58, 161, 242.

29. Griffes diary, July 17, 1916; Nov. 25, 1914; July 13, 1915 (emphasis

added). Note that F. must have told Griffes what M.'s name was, since Griffes did not identify him by street corner. It is likely, although not certain, then, that Griffes told M. he had been sent to him by F. If this was the case, the policeman would almost surely have surmised that Griffes was a gay man, sent to him by another gay man.

30. Alfred Kinsey, Wardell Pomeroy, and Clyde Martin, *Sexual Behavior in the Human Male* (Philadelphia: W. B. Saunders, 1948), 384.

31. A. A. Brill, "The Conception of Homosexuality," *Journal of the American Medical Association* 61 (1913): 335.

32. E. Anthony Rotundo, *American Manhood: Transformations in Masculinity from the Revolution to the Modern Era* (New York: Basic Books, 1993), 249; T. J. Jackson Lears, *No Place of Grace: Antimodernism and the Transformation of American Culture, 1880–1920* (New York: Pantheon, 1981), 60. My analysis of the turn-of-the-century masculinity crisis in the following paragraphs relies heavily on Rotundo's study and has also been informed by the work of Lears and several other historians: Gail Bederman, "'The Women Have Had Charge of the Church Work Long Enough': The Men and Religion Forward Movement of 1911–1912 and the Masculinization of Middle-Class Protestantism," *American Quarterly* 41 (1989): 432–65; Peter Gabriel Filene, *Him/Her/Self: Sex Roles in Modern America* (New York: Harcourt Brace Jovanovich, 1975), 77–95; Joe L. Dubbert, *A Man's Place: Masculinity in Transition* (Englewood Cliffs, N.J.: Prentice-Hall, 1979), 80–121; Elliott J. Gorn, *The Manly Art: Bare-Knuckle Prize Fighting in America* (Ithaca, N.Y.: Cornell University Press, 1986), 187–93; and Gerald F. Roberts, "The Strenuous Life: The Cult of Manliness in the Era of Theodore Roosevelt" (Ph.D. diss., Michigan State University, 1970). On the new corporate order, see Alfred D. Chandler, Jr., *The Visible Hand: The Managerial Revolution in American Business* (Cambridge, Mass.: Belknap Press, 1977); Alan Trachtenburg, *The Incorporation of America: Culture and Society in the Gilded Age* (New York: Hill and Wang, 1982); Olivier Zunz, *Making America Corporate, 1870–1920* (Chicago: University of Chicago Press, 1990).

33. Krieder to Maisel, July 31, 1938. On the gendering of the rhetoric that framed workplace and other class conflicts, see Ava Baron's important collection, *Work Engendered: Toward a New History of American Labor* (Ithaca, N.Y.: Cornell University Press, 1991).

34. "The Strenuous Life," speech to the Hamilton Club, Chicago (1899), in Theodore Roosevelt, *American Ideals* (New York: Review of Reviews, 1910), 20–21. For an excellent analysis of the gendering of turn-of-the-century political rhetoric, see Gail Bederman, "'Civilization,' The Decline of Middle-Class Manliness, and Ida B. Wells's Antilynching Campaign (1892–94)," *Radical History Review* 52 (1992): 5–30.

35. Maurice Thompson, "Vigorous Men, A Vigorous Nation," *Independent* 50 (Sept. 1, 1898): 609–11; see also Henry Childs Merwin, "On Being Civilized Too Much," *Atlantic Monthly* 79 (June 1897): 838–46; and Alfred T. Mahan, "The Possibilities of an Anglo-American Reunion" (1894), in his *The Interest of America in Sea Power, Present and Future* (Boston: Little, Brown, 1903), 107–34, especially 120–21. Mahan, the best-known advocate of American naval power, warned that the "peace prophets of to-day" advocated the same sort of degeneration "of the strong masculine impulse . . . into that worship of comfort, wealth, and general softness" that had condemned the Roman Empire to collapse, a reference apparently designed to evoke the well-known theory that Rome's decline could be explained by its embrace of sexual perversion. Gerald Roberts's disserta-

tion, "The Strenuous Life," provides an extensive survey of such rhetorical formulations.

36. Rotundo, *American Manhood*, 258, 247–62; David I. Macleod, *Building Character in the American Boy: The Boy Scouts, YMCA, and Their Forerunners, 1870–1920* (Madison: University of Wisconsin Press, 1983).

37. Merwin, "On Being Civilized Too Much," 842.

38. Gorn, *Manly Art*, 187; Donald J. Mrozek, *Sport and American Mentality, 1880–1910* (Knoxville: University of Tennessee Press, 1983), ch. 7, especially 209–25.

39. Rotundo, *American Manhood*, 223.

40. John Higham, "The Reorientation of American Culture in the 1890s," in his *Writing American History: Essays on Modern Scholarship* (Bloomington: Indiana University Press, 1970), 79.

41. Rotundo, *American Manhood*, 270–74, 278.

42. Eve Kosofsky Sedgwick, *Epistemology of the Closet* (Berkeley: University of California Press, 1990), 40–44, 82–90.

43. Bernarr Macfadden, *Superb Virility of Manhood: Giving the Causes and Simple Home Methods of Curing the Weaknesses of Men* (New York: Physical Culture Publishing Co., 1904), 176. I thank Doug Ischar for drawing my attention to this source. Editorial in *Physical Culture*, February 1903, 150, as quoted in Greg Mullins, "Nudes, Prudes, and Pigmies: The Desirability of Disavowal in Physical Culture," *Discourse* 15.1 (1992): 35. On the disavowal of the homoerotics of Macfadden's premier magazine, *Physical Culture*, published 1899–1942, see Mullins.

44. This process of cultural transformation has been widely studied in recent years. See, for example, Kathy Peiss, *Cheap Amusements: Working Women and Leisure in Turn-of-the-Century New York* (Philadelphia: Temple University Press, 1986); Christina Simmons, "Companionate Marriage and the Lesbian Threat," *Frontiers* 4 (Fall 1979): 54–59; Mary Ryan, *Womanhood in America: From Colonial Times to the Present*, 2d ed. (New York: New Viewpoints, 1979), 151–82; Nancy F. Cott, *The Grounding of Modern Feminism* (New Haven, Conn.: Yale University Press, 1987); Beth L. Bailey, *From Front Porch to Back Seat: Courtship in Twentieth-Century America* (Baltimore: Johns Hopkins University Press, 1988); Michael Gordon, "From an Unfortunate Necessity to a Cult of Mutual Orgasm: Sex in American Marital Literature, 1830–1940," in *The Sociology of Sex*, ed. James Henslin and Edward Sagarin (New York: 1978), 59–84. On the significance of family ties to the formation of the respectable middle class in the nineteenth century, see Mary Ryan, *Cradle of the Middle Class: The Family in Oneida County, New York, 1790–1865* (New York: Cambridge University Press, 1981).

45. Cott, *Modern Feminism;* Carroll Smith-Rosenberg, "The New Woman as Androgyne: Social Disorder and Gender Crisis, 1870–1936," in her *Disorderly Conduct: Visions of Gender in Victorian America* (New York: Knopf, 1985), 245–96; Estelle B. Freedman, "Separatism as Strategy: Female Institution Building and American Feminism, 1870–1930," *Feminist Studies* 5 (1979): 512–29; Bederman, "'The Women Have Had Charge of the Church Work Long Enough.'"

46. Kinsey, *Sexual Behavior*, 361. Kinsey explains his system for grouping occupations, based on the standard indexes of his day, on pp. 78–79.

47. John D'Emilio and Estelle B. Freedman, *Intimate Matters: A History of Sexuality in America* (New York: Harper & Row, 1988).

48. Kinsey, *Sexual Behavior*, 347–63, 383–84, 370–73. Depending on their age, workingmen were two to seven times more likely to play the "man's part"

than the "queer's part" in sexual relations with other men, whereas college-educated men were only about 1.5 times more likely to do so.

49. Rotundo, *American Manhood,* 77, 78, 82, 85, 278. See also Rotundo, "Romantic Friendship: Male Intimacy and Middle-Class Youth in the Northern United States, 1800–1900," *Journal of Social History* 23 (1989): 1–25, D'Emilio and Freedman, *Intimate Matters,* 121–30, 191–94, and the other articles cited in the following note.

50. "The lack of a word for homosexuality is closely tied to the fact that there was no concept of it, no model for sexuality other than heterosexuality," writes Rotundo (*American Manhood,* 83), as if there *were* a word for heterosexuality in the nineteenth century. But neither word—or concept—existed then. The literature on romantic friendship in the nineteenth century is vast. The pioneering studies concerned women: Carroll Smith-Rosenberg, "The Female World of Love and Ritual: Relations Between Women in Nineteenth-Century America," *Signs* 1 (1975): 1–29, and Lillian Faderman, *Surpassing the Love of Men: Romantic Friendship and Love Between Women from the Renaissance to the Present* (New York: Morrow, 1981). Articles on men's romantic friendships that try to heterosexualize men who passionately loved other men include Rotundo, "Romantic Friendship"; Donald Yacovone, "Abolitionists and the 'Language of Fraternal Love,'" in *Meanings for Manhood: Constructions of Masculinity in Victorian America,* ed. Mark C. Carnes and Clyde Griffen (Chicago: University of Chicago Press, 1990), 85–95; and Jeffrey Richards, "'Passing the Love of Women': Manly Love and Victorian Society," in *Manliness and Morality,* ed. J. A. Mangan and James Walvin (New York: St. Martin's, 1987), 92–122. One can agree with Yacovone that "Victorian men rested comfortably in the knowledge that their effusive and affectionate behavior was rooted in physiology as well as in centuries of Christian tradition" (95), but this gives historians no license to argue, as both he and Richards do, that the Victorians' relations should be understood as part of "a heterosexual tradition of affectionate male relations" (239 n.41). Useful correctives include Leila J. Rupp, "'Imagine My Surprise': Women's Relationships in Mid-Twentieth Century America," and Robert K. Martin, "Knights-Errant and Gothic Seducers: The Representation of Male Friendship in Mid-Nineteenth-Century America," both in *Hidden from History: Reclaiming the Gay and Lesbian Past,* ed. Martin Duberman, Martha Vicinus, and George Chauncey (New York: New American Library, 1989); and Katz, "The Invention of Heterosexuality," 7–34.

51. Charles Rosenberg and Carroll Smith-Rosenberg, "The Female Animal: Medical and Biological Views of Women," *Journal of American History* 60 (1973): 332. On the contemporary theories of sexual difference in intelligence and personality that guided and were reified by scientific inquiry, see Rosalyn Rosenberg, *Beyond Separate Spheres: Intellectual Roots of Modern Feminism* (New Haven, Conn.: Yale University Press, 1982); Cynthia Eagle Russett, *Sexual Science: The Victorian Construction of Womanhood* (Cambridge, Mass.: Harvard University Press, 1989); Thomas Laqueur, *Making Sex: Body and Gender from the Greeks to Freud* (Cambridge, Mass.: Harvard University Press, 1990); Sander Gilman, *Difference and Pathology: Stereotypes of Sexuality, Race, and Madness* (Ithaca, N.Y.: Cornell University Press, 1985); idem, "Black Bodies, White Bodies: Toward an Iconography of Female Sexuality in Late Nineteenth-Century Art, Medicine, and Literature," in *"Race," Writing, and Difference,* ed. Henry Louis Gates, Jr. (Chicago: University of Chicago Press, 1986) [*Critical Inquiry* 12 (1985)], 223–61.

52. See, for example, Herbert J. Claiborne, "Hypertrichosis in Women: Its Relation to Bisexuality (Hermaphroditism): With Remarks on Bisexuality in

Animals, Especially Man," *New York Medical Journal* 99 (1914): 1178-83; James Kiernan, "Sexual Perversion and the Whitechapel Murders," *Medical Standard* 4 (1888): 129; George Frank Lydston, "Sexual Perversion, Satyriasis and Nymphomania," *Medical and Surgical Reporter* 61 (1889): 254-55; idem, *The Disease of Society (The Vice and Crime Problem)* (Philadelphia: Lippincott, 1904).

53. James G. Kiernan, "Increase of American Inversion," *Urologic and Cutaneous Review* 20 (1916): 46.

54. Kiernan, "Bisexuality," ibid. 18 (1914): 375, commenting on Claiborne, "Hypertrichosis in Women."

55. William Lee Howard, "Effeminate Men and Masculine Women," *New York Medical Journal* 71 (1900): 687. For a fuller discussion of this point, see my article "From Sexual Inversion to Homosexuality: Medicine and the Changing Conceptualization of Female Deviance," *Salmagundi,* no. 58-59 (Fall 1982-Winter 1983): 114-46, and Carroll Smith-Rosenberg, "The New Woman as Androgyne."

56. Perry M. Lichtenstein, "The 'Fairy' and the Lady Lover," *Medical Review of Reviews* 27 (1921): 369-74.

57. Brill, "The Conception of Homosexuality," 336-37.

58. Sigmund Freud, *Three Essays on the Theory of Sexuality,* trans. James Strachey et al. (New York: Basic Books, 1962), 1-2.

59. Havelock Ellis, "Sexo-Aesthetic Inversion," *Alienist and Neurologist* 34 (1913): 156; for an earlier expression of similar views, see his article "Sexual Inversion in Men," ibid. 17 (1896): 142.

60. See, particularly, the influential work of Lillian Faderman, *Odd Girls and Twilight Lovers: A History of Lesbian Life in Twentieth-Century America* (New York: Columbia University Press, 1991), and "The Morbidification of Love Between Women by Nineteenth-Century Sexologists," *Journal of Homosexuality* 4 (1978): 73-90.

61. For the use of some of these terms, see Gershon Legman, "The Language of Homosexuality: An American Glossary," in George W. Henry, *Sex Variants* (New York: Paul B. Hoeber, 1941), vol. 2, appendix VII, 1159, 1172, 1173, and their frequent appearance in the 1920s and 1930s in New York tabloids. On the distinction between she-men (as queer) and he-men (as normal), see, for example, one gay character's comment in Richard Meeker's novel *Better Angel,* 180: "nobody ever accused them of being 'queer.' Oh no! They are normal—he-men."

62. On abortion, see James Mohr, *Abortion in America: The Origins and Evolution of National Policy, 1800-1900* (New York: Oxford University Press, 1978); on prostitution and venereal disease, see Allan M. Brandt, *No Magic Bullet: A Social History of Venereal Disease in the United States Since 1880* (New York: Oxford University Press, 1985); on the lack of medical influence over state and popular conceptions of homosexuality before World War II, see my article "Christian Brotherhood or Sexual Perversion? Homosexual Identities and the Construction of Sexual Boundaries in the World War One Era," *Journal of Social History* 19 (1985), 189-211, and on its growing influence during the war and postwar years, see Allan Berube, *Coming Out Under Fire: The History of Gay Men and Women in World War Two* (New York: Free Press, 1990), and my article "The Postwar Sex Crime Panic," in *True Stories from the American Past,* ed. William Graebner (New York: McGraw-Hill, 1993), 160-78.

63. "Sexuality," David Halperin has argued, is a distinctly modern production, which "defines itself as a separate, sexual domain within the larger sphere of human psychophysical nature" and which "generates sexual identity: it endows each of us with an individual sexual nature, with a personal essence defined (at

least in part) in specifically sexual terms [and] implies that human beings are individuated at the level of their sexuality . . . and, indeed, belong to different types or kinds of being by virtue of their sexuality." David M. Halperin, "Is There a History of Sexuality," in *The Lesbian and Gay Studies Reader,* ed. Henry Abelove, Michelle Barale, and David Halperin (New York: Routledge, 1993), 417. See also Michel Foucault, *The History of Sexuality. Volume I: An Introduction,* trans. Robert Hurley (New York: Pantheon, 1978); Arnold Davidson, "Sex and the Emergence of Sexuality," *Critical Inquiry* 14 (1987): 16–48.

64. Richard Parker, *Bodies, Passions, and Pleasure: Sexual Culture in Contemporary Brazil* (Boston: Beacon, 1991), 1–6.

CHAPTER 5. URBAN CULTURE AND THE POLICING OF THE "CITY OF BACHELORS"

1. Paraphrased in Ralph Werther, *The Female-Impersonators* (New York: Medico-Legal Journal, 1922), 200–201. It is entirely possible that Werther was the source of these sentiments, rather than the person to whom he attributed them, but that would not undermine my point that gay men viewed the city in these terms.

2. Erwin R. A. Seligman, ed., *The Social Evil: With Special Reference to Conditions Existing in the City of New York* (1902; New York: Putnam's, 1912), 8. On the Committee of Fifteen, see Jeremy P. Felt, "Vice Reform as a Political Technique: The Committee of Fifteen in New York, 1900–1911," *New York History* 54 (1973): 24–51.

3. C. Judson Herrick, note concerning his translation of Marc André Raffalovich, "Uranism, Congenital Sexual Inversion," *Journal of Comparative Neurology* 5 (March 1895): 65. G. Frank Lydston also commented in 1889 that there was "in every community of any size a colony of male sexual perverts; they are usually known to each other and are likely to congregate together" ("Sexual Perversion, Satyriasis and Nymphomania," *Medical and Surgical Reporter* 61 [1889]: 254); see also James Kiernan, "Classification of Homosexuality," *Urologic and Cutaneous Review* 20 (1916): 350.

4. Walter C. Reckless, "The Distribution of Commercialized Vice in the City: A Sociological Analysis," in *The Urban Community,* ed. Ernest W. Burgess (Chicago: University of Chicago Press, 1926), 192, 202.

5. The major proponent of this alternative view of urbanism is Claude Fischer, *To Dwell Among Friends: Personal Networks in Town and City* (Chicago: University of Chicago Press, 1982), especially 64–66; idem, *The Urban Experience* (New York: Harcourt Brace Jovanovich, 1976), especially 35–39.

6. Contributors to this debate include Fischer, *The Urban Experience,* 25–36, and Manuel Castells, "Is There an Urban Sociology?," *Urban Sociology: Critical Essays* (New York: St. Martin's, 1976). On the breakdown of social control in nineteenth-century cities upon the decline of artisanal modes of production and the increasing class segregation of cities, and the related decision of employers and reformers to establish professional police forces in New York and other cities in the 1840s–60s, see John C. Schneider, *Detroit and the Problem of Order, 1830–1880: A Geography of Crime, Riot, and Policing* (Lincoln: University of Nebraska Press, 1980), 83–86 and passim; for a detailed study of this process in New York City, see Sean Wilentz, *Chants Democratic: New York City and the Rise of the American Working Class, 1788–1850* (New York: Oxford University Press, 1984).

7. Robert Park, "The City: Suggestions for the Investigation of Human Behavior in the Urban Environment" (1916), as reprinted in *Classic Essays on the Culture of Cities,* ed. Richard Sennett (New York: Meredith, 1969), 126.

8. *People v. Galbert,* DAP 41,914 (CGS 1903), statement by A. D. A. Ely, 292–93, JJC.

9. George M. Beard, *Sexual Neurasthenia,* ed. A. D. Rockwell (New York: E. B. Treat, 1884), 102; A. A. Brill, "The Conception of Homosexuality," *Journal of the American Medical Association* 61 (1913): 335. For an account of a man forced to flee his home, see Douglas C. McMurtrie, "Some Observations on the Psychology of Sexual Inversion in Women," *Lancet-Clinic* 108 (1912): 488.

10. Martin Goodkin to author, Aug. 3, 1988; Maurice Leznoff, "The Homosexual in Urban Society" (master's thesis, McGill University, 1954), 40–49.

11. George W. Henry and Alfred A. Gross, "Social Factors in the Case Histories of One Hundred Underprivileged Homosexuals," *Mental Hygiene* 22 (1938): 602.

12. See, for example, Joanne J. Meyerowitz, *Women Adrift: Independent Wage Earners in Chicago, 1880–1930* (Chicago: University of Chicago Press, 1988).

13. "The Bachelors of New York," *New York Times Magazine,* Sept. 9, 1928. Although the *Times* was probably not thinking of gay bachelors in particular, some of its gay readers seem to have understood the article in such terms. Alexander Gumby, a black gay man who ran a famous salon frequented by Harlem's intellectuals, many of them gay, in the 1920s, clipped the article and put it in a scrapbook he titled "Odd, Strange and Curious," now a part of the Alexander Gumby papers at the Columbia University Library.

14. James Ford, *Slums and Housing: With Special Reference to New York City: History, Conditions, Policy* (Cambridge, Mass.: Harvard University Press, 1936), 336; *Twelfth Census of the United States Taken in the Year 1900, Vol. II, Population, Part II* (Washington, D.C.: United States Census Office, 1902), 254, 333; see also *1890 Census, Part I,* 883; *1910 Census, Vol. I,* 630; *1920 Census, Vol. II,* 504; *1930 Census, Vol. II,* 962; *1940 Census, Vol. IV, Part III,* 683.

15. *Thirteenth Census of the United States Taken in the Year 1910, Vol. I, Population 1910, General Report and Analysis* (Washington, D.C.: Government Printing Office, 1913), 948.

16. An immense number of historical studies document and analyze these trends. The major points are usefully summarized and argued in Paul Boyer, *Urban Masses and Moral Order in America, 1820–1920* (Cambridge, Mass.: Harvard University Press, 1978), 123–31; see also, to cite just three other studies, John Higham, *Strangers in the Land: Patterns of American Nativism, 1860–1925* (New Brunswick, N.J.: Rutgers University Press, 1955); Kenneth T. Jackson, *Crabgrass Frontier: The Suburbanization of the United States* (New York: Oxford University Press, 1985); Thomas Kessner, *The Golden Door: Italian and Jewish Immigrant Mobility in New York City* (New York: Oxford University Press, 1977).

17. A number of historians have analyzed this process. See, for example, Boyer, *Urban Masses;* Daniel M. Bluestone, *Constructing Chicago* (New Haven, Conn.: Yale University Press, 1991); David Scobey, "Empire City: Politics, Culture, and Urbanism in Gilded Age New York" (Ph.D. diss., Yale University, 1989).

18. For an overview of the role of the police, see Samuel Walker, *A Critical History of Police Reform* (Lexington, Mass.: Lexington Books, D. C. Heath, 1977).

19. My comments on the general character of the societies are based on my research in their organizational records (as described in the Note on Sources) and on Timothy J. Gilfoyle, "The Moral Origins of Political Surveillance: The Preventive Society in New York City, 1867–1918," *American Quarterly* 38 (1986): 637–52; idem, *City of Eros: New York City, Prostitution, and the Com-*

mercialization of Sex, 1790–1920 (New York: Norton, 1992), 185–96; Boyer, *Urban Masses;* Mary Ryan, *Women in Public: Between Banners and Ballots, 1825–1880* (Baltimore: Johns Hopkins University Press, 1990), ch. 3; John D'Emilio and Estelle Freedman, *Intimate Matters: A History of Sexuality in America* (New York: Harper & Row, 1988), ch. 7 and 9; and Linda Gordon, *Heroes of Their Own Lives: The Politics and History of Family Violence* (New York: Viking, 1988).

20. Kathy Peiss, "'Charity Girls' and City Pleasures: Historical Notes on Working-Class Sexuality, 1880–1920," in *Passion and Power: Sexuality in History,* ed. Kathy Peiss and Christina Simmons (Philadelphia: Temple University Press, 1989), 57–69.

21. W. E. B. Du Bois to the Committee, letter dated Sept. 23, 1911 (the actual year must have been 1912); Frederick H. Whitin to Du Bois, Oct. 11, 1912, Du Bois folder, box 11, COF. Du Bois wrote to protest the Committee's campaign against Marshall's, which had once been a popular nightspot when many of Manhattan's African-American residents had lived in the midtown area, because it was "about the only place where a colored man downtown can be decently accommodated." The Committee continued to worry that illicit sexual intentions offered the only explanation for the social mingling of blacks and whites; see, for example, their investigator's observation in 1928 that Small's Paradise, a famous Harlem nightspot on Seventh Avenue, "was rather crowded with white and colored people, dancing and drinking. . . . Mixed couples are allowed to enter this place," he noted ominously (report on Small's Paradise, 2294 1/2 Seventh Ave., basement, July 24, 1928, 2 A.M., box 36, COF).

22. Linda Gordon, *Woman's Body, Woman's Right: A Social History of Birth Control in America* (New York: Penguin, 1976); David J. Pivar, *Purity Crusade: Sexual Morality and Social Control, 1868–1900* (Westport, Conn.: Greenwood, 1973). I discuss the attacks on scientific books on homosexuality, lesbian plays and short stories, and the like in chapters 9, 11, 12.

23. I have not offered more precise figures here because the sources are dismayingly vague and contradictory. The number of sodomy cases between 1796 and 1873 is based on the comprehensive survey of the Manhattan district attorney case files conducted by Timothy Gilfoyle in the course of his research on prostitution in nineteenth-century New York, and is reported in Michael Lynch, "New York City Sodomy, 1796–1873," as cited in D'Emilio and Freedman, *Intimate Matters,* 123. The immense number of cases prosecuted in the twentieth century made a comprehensive survey of the case files impossible, so I have relied instead on published reports and a sampling of the manuscript case files. The annual reports of the Board of City Magistrates and Board of Police Justices give figures for the number of arrests and convictions for sodomy in New York for the late nineteenth and early twentieth centuries, but those numbers often conflict; one reports that thirteen men were arrested for the crime against nature in 1896, for instance, while the other reports thirty-eight arrests. (I have based my estimates on the lower figure given, so they should be taken as conservative estimates.) It is even more difficult to determine the percentage of cases in which the SPCC played a role, since that is not noted in the annual reports. My estimates are based on my review of actual district attorney case files concerning sodomy prosecutions from 1890 to 1940 (see the Note on Sources for more information about those files). Because the district attorney did not index cases by charge, I reviewed his alphabetical list of all cases prosecuted for every year surveyed and then ordered the cases identified as sodomy cases. Only a fraction of the sodomy cases were identified as such in the docket books, however, so my estimate could not be based on a full

survey of the sodomy prosecutions. There is no reason to believe that the two hundred sodomy cases I did review were unrepresentative, but given the limitations of the evidence I have not attempted to offer more precise or "definitive" figures for the percentage of cases initiated by the SPCC. It is clear that the SPCC played an active role and that men who had sex with boys were the primary targets of sodomy prosecutions, but precise figures are unavailable.

24. Superintendent's Report to the Board of Directors, n.d. [Apr. 9, 1917], and Minutes of a regular meeting of the Board of Directors, Apr. 9, 1917, box 13, Society for the Prevention of Crime papers, Rare Book and Manuscript Library, Columbia University.

25. My comments on the role of the moral-reform societies in policing homosexual matters are based on my review of the manuscript records of the Society for the Prevention of Crime (most of which are held at the Rare Book and Manuscript Library, Columbia University) and the Society for the Suppression of Vice (Library of Congress). The particular actions taken by the societies are documented later in this chapter and in subsequent chapters.

26. T. S. Settle to Raymond Fosdick, chair, War Department Commission on Training Camp Activities, Sept. 4, 1917, box 24, COF.

27. J. A. S., report on street conditions, Nov. 17, 1917, box 25, COF.

28. See the hundreds of reports submitted by Committee of Fourteen investigators during the war.

29. M. J. Exner, "Prostitution in its Relation to the Army on the Mexican Border," *Social Hygiene* 3 (April 1917): 205, as quoted in Allan M. Brandt, *No Magic Bullet: A Social History of Venereal Disease in the United States Since 1880* (New York: Oxford University Press, 1985), 57. My characterization of World War I discourse is based primarily on the accounts provided by Brandt's superb study, as well as David Kennedy's *Over Here: The First World War and American Society* (New York: Oxford University Press, 1980). I have, however, stressed the continuity between the Progressive Era depiction of urban immorality and wartime moral discourse more than these authors have.

30. Brandt, *No Magic Bullet*, 52; James H. Timberlake, *Prohibition and the Progressive Movement, 1900–1920* (Cambridge, Mass.: Harvard University Press, 1963), especially 57–66, 111–19, 144–45; Kennedy, *Over Here;* Robert K. Murray, *Red Scare: A Study in National Hysteria, 1919–1920* (Minneapolis: University of Minnesota Press, 1955).

31. On the efforts of social hygienists to protect American soldiers from prostitution, see Brandt, *No Magic Bullet*, ch. 2–3; Mark Thomas Connelly, *The Response to Prostitution in the Progressive Era* (Chapel Hill: University of North Carolina Press, 1980), ch. 7; Ruth Rosen, *The Lost Sisterhood: Prostitution in America, 1900–1918* (Baltimore: Johns Hopkins University Press, 1982), 33–36; Kennedy, *Over Here*, 185–87; and D'Emilio and Freedman, *Intimate Matters*, 211–13.

32. Frederick H. Whitin, "Sexual Perversion Cases in New York City Courts, 1916–1921," bulletin 1480, Nov. 12, 1921, box 88, COF; J. A. S., Conditions about the Brooklyn Navy Yard, June 6, 1917, box 25, COF. The scene is discussed at greater length in chapter 3. See also F. H. Whitin to Raymond B. Fosdick, Dec. 6, 1917; Whitin to O'Keefe and Cunningham, Jan. 14, 1918; Whitin to Pfeiffer, Mar. 5, 1918; report on Pennsylvania Depot and Streets in Vicinity, Apr. 28, 1918; report on Brooklyn Navy Yard, Jan. 3, 1919. The Committee wrote numerous brewers, warning them that civilians had been seen buying liquor for servicemen on premises they supplied and that they should ensure that such illegal practices cease; see, for example, Whitin to

Col. Jacob Ruppert, May 20, 1918; Whitin to George Ehret, Inc., May 20, 1918, box 25, COF.

33. Allan Berube, *Coming Out Under Fire: The History of Gay Men and Women in World War Two* (New York: Free Press, 1990), and John D'Emilio, *Sexual Politics, Sexual Communities: The Making of a Homosexual Minority in the United States, 1940–1970* (Chicago: University of Chicago Press, 1983), 23–39. My research in the records of the New York City anti-vice societies and the military persuades me that abundant sources exist for a study of the history of lesbians and gay men in World War I.

34. Unfortunately, no study of the gay subculture in Paris during the war yet exists, but for a review of the gay world there during the 1920s, which certainly could not have appeared full-blown without some precedent, see Gilles Barbedette and Michel Carassou, *Paris Gay 1925* (Paris: Presses de la Renaissance, 1981). On the more highly developed culture in Berlin, see the catalogs for two exhibitions: *Eldorado: Homosexuelle Frauen und Männer in Berlin 1850–1950: Geschichte, Alltag und Kultur* (Berlin: Froelich & Kaufmann, 1984), and *750 Warme Berliner* (Berlin: Verlag rose Winkel, 1987). On Griffes, see Edward Maisel, *Charles T. Griffes: The Life of an American Composer* (1943; updated edition, New York: Knopf, 1984), 344–46n, and my personal communication with Maisel; on Gerber, see Jonathan Katz, *Gay American History* (New York: Crowell, 1976), 385–97. Some work has now been done on the two major salons in Paris run by American lesbians, those of Gertrude Stein and Natalie Barney, but their influence on gay Americans upon their return deserves further scrutiny. On the salons, see Shari Benstock, *Women of the Left Bank: Paris, 1900–1940* (Austin: University of Texas Press, 1986), and "Paris Lesbianism and the Politics of Reaction, 1900–1940," in *Hidden from History: Reclaiming the Gay and Lesbian Past,* ed. Martin Duberman, Martha Vicinus, and George Chauncey (New York: New American Library, 1989), 332–46.

35. On the impact of World War I on African-American political consciousness, see, for example, David Levering Lewis, *When Harlem Was in Vogue* (New York: Knopf, 1981), ch. 1, and the long-running debate over the political significance of the African-American response to the war in *The Crisis,* the National Association for the Advancement of Colored People journal edited by W. E. B. Du Bois.

36. Parisex (pseudonym of Henry Gerber), "In Defense of Homosexuality," *Modern Thinker* (June 1932), as reprinted in Martin Duberman, *About Time: Exploring the Gay Past* (New York: Gay Presses of New York, 1986), 119.

37. George Chauncey, "Christian Brotherhood or Sexual Perversion? Homosexual Identities and the Construction of Sexual Boundaries in the World War One Era," *Journal of Social History* 19 (Winter 1985): 189–211; Lawrence R. Murphy, *Perverts by Official Order* (New York: Harrington Press, 1988).

38. About a third of the gay civilians arrested during the investigation were New Yorkers who had taken jobs as houseservants during Newport's social season (Chauncey, "Christian Brotherhood," 190).

39. See, for example, the report of one investigator in 1918: "Saw several fairies strolling about 3rth Street [sic: context suggests it was probably 34th] and B'way but was accosted by none of them" (J. A. S., Report on street conditions, n.d. [c. Sept. 12, 1918], box 31, COF), and an agent's report, Aug. 19, 1918, which suggests the Committee had reason to believe that "fairies" were soliciting soldiers on Broadway from Twenty-third Street to Fourteenth Street, although they were not there the night he looked for them: "I didn't find any fairies, only a few unescorted prostitutes soliciting."

40. Investigator's report, June 19, 1919; Report on 64 W. 11th St., June 30, 1919, box 34, COF.

41. Comstock commented on his dealings with men "of this character" during his testimony in *People v. Bushnell* (CGS 1900), JJC, 89–90.

42. My summary of the Society for the Suppression of Vice's campaign is based primarily on the records it kept of the legal cases in which it became involved (Society for the Suppression of Vice record books, vol. 4 [for 1916–22], SSV); see also John Sumner to Frederick Whitin, Oct. 31, 1921, letter in box 63, COF, and Whitin, "Sexual Perversion Cases." The number of actions against homosexuals cited in the record books of the Society dropped precipitously after 1921. Unfortunately, the Society record book contains only minimal information, which reveals more about the persons it prosecuted than about the Society's reasoning for the campaign. The Society's attacks on gay bathhouses and stage shows are detailed in the following chapters.

43. Whitin, "Sexual Perversion Cases"; and bulletin 1504, Mar. 24, 1922, box 88, COF. The figures given are for convictions, not arrests; according to Whitin, about 89 percent of the men charged with homosexual offenses were convicted, a percentage, as he noted, "much above the average of convictions for [other] offenses."

44. A modified version of the memorandum (which also reports on the discussion held at the meeting and forms the basis of my description of it here) survives as Whitin, "Sexual Perversion Cases."

45. Ibid.

46. On the disagreements between French and American military leaders, see Brandt, *No Magic Bullet,* 100–106.

CHAPTER 6. LOTS OF FRIENDS AT THE YMCA: ROOMING HOUSES, CAFETERIAS, AND OTHER GAY SOCIAL CENTERS

1. Willy W., interviewed.

2. George W. Henry and Alfred A. Gross, "The Homosexual Delinquent," *Mental Hygiene* 25 (1941): 426; idem, "Social Factors in the Case Histories of One Hundred Underprivileged Homosexuals," *Mental Hygiene* 22 (1938): 597. Each study surveyed 100 homosexuals. The figures for 1938 were roughly the same as those for 1940, but they showed a smaller percentage (49 percent) living in rooming houses and a higher percentage (39 percent) in tenements; the authors, however, considered the 1938 figures less reliable. The subjects of the studies had either been arrested on homosexual charges or been identified as homosexual once in the prison system. The findings should not be taken as entirely representative, since their subjects, like most men in prison, were relatively poorer than the average population from which they were drawn. In fact, it is likely that an unrepresentatively high percentage of the prisoners were found to be living in tenement apartments with families precisely because these men, who had the least privacy at home, were most likely to try to have sexual encounters in places where they might be apprehended by the police. Since the census data that historians customarily use to map the distribution of ethnic groups and classes in cities are unavailable for a study of gay men, most of the following analysis is necessarily based on literary rather than quantitative sources.

3. For examples, see *People v. Davis,* DAP 23,087 (CGS 1898), in which two men were charged with forcible sodomy by the man they had met in Madison Square Park and taken to the West Twenty-fifth Street room one of them had occupied for three days (the actual facts of the case are unclear, but the circumstances suggest that the complainant may have been carrying through with a blackmail

threat against the men he had gone home with, and the judge, perhaps for this reason, dismissed the charge); *People v. Mylott,* DAP 100,270 (CGS 1914), in which a man was assaulted by the man he had picked up and taken to his West Fifty-second Street room.

4. In my discussion of lodging houses and the social organization and implications of the housing market in general, I draw especially on Paul Groth's splendid study, *Living Downtown: The History of Residential Hotels in the United States* (Berkeley: University of California Press, 1994), which I read in manuscript. See also Albert Benedict Wolfe, *The Lodging House Problem in Boston* (Boston and New York: Houghton Mifflin, 1906); Harvey Warren Zorbaugh, *The Gold Coast and the Slum: A Sociological Study of Chicago's Near North Side* (Chicago: University of Chicago Press, 1929), 69–86; Joanne J. Meyerowitz, *Women Adrift: Independent Wage Earners in Chicago, 1880–1930* (Chicago: University of Chicago Press, 1988); idem, "Sexual Geography and Gender Economy: The Furnished Room Districts of Chicago, 1890–1930," in *Gender and American History Since 1890,* ed. Barbara Melosh (New York: Routledge, 1993), 43–71; and Mark Peel, "In the Margins: Lodgers and Boarders in Boston, 1860–1900," *Journal of American History* 72 (1986): 813–34.

5. Wolfe, *The Lodging House Problem,* 109–12.

6. Report on 53 W. 16th St., Sept. 27, 1928, box 36, COF; for other examples, see reports on 138 W. 49th St., Dec. 4, 1930, box 35; 52 W. 111th St., Jan. 19, 1927, box 36. Some proprietors did object, and others drew the line at women working as prostitutes on their premises; see, for example, 2272 Broadway, Jan. 27, 1932, box 35. The *Home News* began an editorial campaign against furnished-room houses as centers of vice and degradation in 1919; see, for example, the Mar. 5, 1919, issue. In the 1920s, after the Committee of Fourteen and other groups had succeeded in closing most of New York's brothels and pushing prostitutes off the streets, they discovered that prostitution had moved into such houses. Some were run as brothels, but most as smaller operations. Indeed, many hotels closed as disorderly houses were converted into furnished-room houses, since it was more economical for proprietors to reopen them as such than to convert them into tenements or business offices. In 1922, for instance, a prostitute took a vice squad officer to a furnished room in a building near Union Square which years earlier had been closed as a disorderly house: bulletin 1505, "A Hotel Problem," Jan. 17, 1922, box 88, COF; Committee of Fourteen, *Annual Report for 1922* (New York: Committee of Fourteen, 1923), 9–10.

7. Report on colored fairy, 63 W. 50th St., Aug. 2, 1919, box 34, COF.

8. *People v. Jagley and Walters,* DAP 31,547 (CGS 1900).

9. One gay man recalled living in the early twenties in a Milwaukee rooming house in which one of the other rooms was occupied by two middle-aged men who worked at the Gimbels department store. The other roomers suspected the nature of their relationship and joked about them behind their backs, but no one tried to have them evicted from their room, and no one suspected the observer, who lived alone (Leo, interviewed).

10. Such experiences were related by several men in interviews, including Roger Emmet and Bruhs Mero.

11. Wolfe, *The Lodging House Problem,* 111–12. The classic statement of the debilitating effects on young migrants of exposure to life in the cheapest of the city's lodging houses was provided by Jacob Riis in his chapters on the "Stale-Beer Dives" and "Cheap Lodging Houses" in *How the Other Half Lives* (1890; New York: Hill and Wang, 1957), 52–67.

12. Report on the Seamen's Church Institute and vicinity, July 15 and 16,

1931, box 35, COF. The incident is discussed at greater length in chapter 3.

13. Record of the arrests of Mills House residents appears in the entries for Mar. 9, 11, and 23, 1920, in the Society for the Suppression of Vice record books, vol. 4, 396–98, SSV. Robert A. M. Stern, Gregory Gilmartin, and John Montague Massengale, *New York 1900: Metropolitan Architecture and Urbanism, 1890–1915* (New York: Rizzoli, 1983), 272–79, includes floor plans for the Mills House.

14. Paul S. Boyer, *Urban Masses and Moral Order in America, 1820–1920* (Cambridge, Mass.: Harvard University Press, 1978), 108–19; David I. Macleod, *Building Character in the American Boy: The Boy Scouts, YMCA, and Their Forerunners, 1870–1920* (Madison: University of Wisconsin Press, 1983), 72–74, 127–28. The early history of the Y deserves further study with these questions in mind: Boyer notes that many of the early organizers of the Y were young, unmarried small businessmen and clerks.

15. On the construction of the first YMCA residential facilities in New York and the demographics of their residents, see "The Survey of the Young Men's Christian Association of the City of New York: June, 1925–July, 1926," Arthur L. Swift, Jr., director (published in mimeograph form by the Association Press, 1927), 172–209, especially 172–73, 177–85; and C. Howard Hopkins, *History of the Y.M.C.A. in North America* (New York: Association Press, 1951), 577–79.

16. Ronald Roberts, interviewed. *Yip, Yip, Yaphank* also included female impersonators trained by the vaudevillians Savoy and Brennan; see Anthony Slide, *Great Pretenders* (Lombard, Ill.: Wallace-Homestead, 1986), 33. As noted, this development was hardly unique to New York. Many gay men rented rooms at the Newport Army & Navy YMCA, took their meals there, and spent the evenings in the lobby, where they were widely recognized as "fairies"; see George Chauncey, "Christian Brotherhood or Sexual Perversion? Homosexual Identities and the Construction of Sexual Boundaries in the World War One Era," *Journal of Social History* 19 (Winter 1985): 190.

17. Louis E., quoted in George W. Henry, *Sex Variants* (New York: Paul B. Hoeber, 1941), 199–200. For other examples of men experimenting sexually or meeting other gay men at a YMCA in the 1920s and 1930s, see ibid., 298 (Archibald T.), 410 (Max N.), 471 (Peter R., about a man picking him up at a YMCA in Miami). Also see Perry M. Lichtenstein, "The 'Fairy' and the Lady Lover," *Medical Review of Reviews* 27 (1921): 370–71. Examples for the 1940s, 1950s, and 1960s were provided in interviews with Nat Fowler; Joe O'Connor; Al K.; Willy W.; and Grant McGree. In 1969, a Mattachine Society correspondent recommended that a prospective visitor to New York stay at the West Side Y, "if you would like a real, groovy place (gay)": Dick Griffo to A. V., Atlanta, Ga., Sept. 8, 1969, MSNY.

18. David Hearst, interviewed.

19. Grant McGree, interviewed; Joel Honig, interviewed.

20. Donald Vining, *A Gay Diary* (4 vols.; New York: Pepys Press, 1979–83), 1:231–34 (entries for Sept. 13, 14, 18, 23, 1942); 1:390 (entry for June 19, 1945); and passim.

21. Joel Honig, interviewed.

22. Vining, *Diary*, 1:274 (entry for June 28, 1943). On another occasion, Vining reported that the security office refused to intervene when a sailor complained that he was leaving because the man he had taken a room with had made a pass at him (1:372, entry for Jan. 16, 1945). The very fact that men took the risk of making such advances suggests the extent to which they regarded the Y as homosexual territory.

23. Elizabeth C. Cromley, *Alone Together: A History of New York's Early Apartments* (Ithaca, N.Y.: Cornell University Press, 1990); Richard Plunz, *A History of Housing in New York City: Dwelling Type and Social Change in the American Metropolis* (New York: Columbia University Press, 1990); Amy Kallman Epstein, "Multifamily Dwellings and the Search for Respectability: Origins of the New York Apartment House," *Urbanism Past and Present,* no. 10 (Summer 1980): 29–39; Gwendolyn Wright, *Building the Dream: A Social History of Housing in America* (New York: Pantheon, 1981), 135–51; and Stern, Gilmartin, and Massengale, *New York 1900,* 272–79. *New York 1900* includes photographs of the Hermitage Hotel and the Bachelor Apartments as well as floor plans for the latter.

24. *Broadway Brevities,* Apr. 25, 1932.

25. Donald Vining, for one, forced by poor finances and the wartime housing shortage to live in a single room, was acutely aware of the social advantages of an apartment. See, for instance, Vining, Diary 1:337 (entry for Feb. 11, 1945), and 1:419 (Oct. 13, 1945).

26. "Financial Success and Moral Failure," *Outlook* 67 (Apr. 27, 1901), 932–33; Committee of Fourteen, *Annual Report for 1910* (New York: Committee of Fourteen, 1911); Statement for publicity by the Chairman, n.d. [May 1907], box 86, COF; Timothy J. Gilfoyle, *City of Eros: New York City, Prostitution, and the Commercialization of Sex, 1790–1920* (New York: Norton, 1992), 243–48; Roland Richard Wagner, "Virtue Against Vice: A Study of Moral Reformers and Prostitution in the Progressive Era" (Ph.D. diss., University of Wisconsin, 1971), 117.

27. Or so suggested a Mr. Hoffman while questioning a witness before the Mazet Committee in 1899: *Report of the Special [Mazet] Committee of the Assembly appointed to investigate the Public Offices and Departments of the City of New York and of the Counties Therein Included* (Albany: J. B. Lyon, 1900), 5130.

28. This history is conveniently summarized in the Committee of Fourteen's *Annual Report for 1912* (New York: Committee of Fourteen, 1913), 1–5, in which the Committee explained its decision to reorganize. For a more extensive discussion of the two committees' origins and the background of their leaders, see Wagner, "Virtue Against Vice," 76–149.

29. John Peters, chairman, Committee of Fourteen, letter soliciting contributions, Oct. 27, 1909, box 86, COF. See also Wagner, "Virtue Against Vice," 119–22.

30. Unnumbered bulletin [no. 1164], "Prostitution Cases, Brooklyn, March 1918," Apr. 27, 1918, box 87, COF; F. H. Whitin to Lt. Timothy Pfeiffer, Washington, D.C., Mar. 5, 1918, box 25, COF. The arrests were made late in 1917: Whitin to Raymond B. Fosdick, chairman, War and Navy Departments Commissions, Washington, D.C., Dec. 6, 1917, box 25, COF. For a detailed explanation of the economics of saloon ownership and the role of brewers as suppliers and backers of individual proprietors, see Perry R. Duis, *The Saloon: Public Drinking in Chicago and Boston, 1880–1920* (Urbana: University of Illinois Press, 1983), 15–85.

31. Committee of Fourteen, *Annual Report for 1918* (New York: Committee of Fourteen, 1919), 32–40. The Committee took note of the hotels that allowed only unmarried couples, rather than professional prostitutes, to use their rooms, after reporting on arrests made in 1917 at four such hotels near Twenty-third Street, on Lexington Avenue and Third Avenue: the Lusitania, Bellwood, Knickerbocker, and Lee (bulletin 1078, "Assignation Hotel Cases," June 27, 1917, box 87, COF).

32. Report on the Seamen's Church Institute and vicinity, July 15 and 16, 1931, box 35, COF. On the lodging houses in the Chatham Square and Bowery area, see John C. Schneider, "Skid Row as an Urban Neighborhood, 1880–1960," *Urbanism Past and Present,* no. 17 (Winter–Spring 1984): 10–20, especially 11.

33. In the Battery Park area in August 1918, for instance, a fifty-two-year-old engineer who picked up an eighteen-year-old molder, who was apparently hustling, was able to hire a room at 64 Whitehall Street where they could spend an hour before the engineer returned to his home in New Jersey. The vice squad appears to have been watching the area, as one of its agents followed the couple to the room and burst in on them while they were having sex (*People v. Davis,* DAP 121,319 [CGS 1918]). See also *People v. Williams,* DAP 80,706 (CGS 1910); *Times Square Garden & Grill, Inc., v. Bruckman, et al.,* 256 A.D. 1062 (1st Dep't 1939), contained in Record on Review; and interviews with Bob Paulsen and Frank McCarthy.

34. Griffes diary, June 18, 1915; Mar. 24, 1916; and, especially, Oct. 2, 1915.

35. Report on male pervert, Hotel Shelton, Dec. 17 and 18, 1929, box 36, COF. Another man who lived in the Shelton in the 1930s and 1940s recalled that its residents included many gay men: "The Shelton Hotel where I lived became so darned gay that during World War II they suddenly closed the bar, overnight practically, because all these military guys were in there all the time. . . . All you had to do was just go down and get the one drink and bring someone upstairs with you if you wanted some company" (Leo, interviewed).

36. For similar readings of the meaning of leisure time for black people in the United States and Britain, see Robin D. G. Kelley, "'We Are Not What We Seem': Rethinking Black Working-Class Opposition in the Jim Crow South," *Journal of American History* 80 (June 1993): 84–86; Paul Gilroy, "One Nation Under a Groove: The Cultural Politics of 'Race' and Racism in Britain," in *Anatomy of Racism,* ed. David Theo Goldberg (Minneapolis: University of Minnesota Press, 1990), 274. The newspaper image is drawn from Carl Van Vechten's scrapbook (Van Vechten papers, Yale), and is discussed further in chapter 10.

37. Harvey A. Levenstein, *Revolution at the Table: The Transformation of the American Diet* (New York: Oxford University Press, 1988), 185–89.

38. Michael and Ariane Batterberry, *On the Town in New York: From 1776 to the Present* (New York: Scribner's, 1973), 187–89; Stern, Gilmartin, and Massengale, *New York 1900,* 225–26; George Chappell, *The Restaurants of New York* (New York: Greenberg, 1925), 125; Duis, *The Saloon,* 194–95; *The WPA Guide to New York City* (New York: Random House, 1939), 24.

39. Horn & Hardart, *Directory of Horn & Hardart Automats,* n.d. [1939?], NYHS; Jack Alexander, "The Restaurants That Nickels Built," *Saturday Evening Post,* Dec. 11, 1954, 22–23, 98ff.; *Saturday Evening Post,* Dec. 18, 1954, 30, 55ff; Batterberry, *On the Town,* 189. Using the advertising slogan "Less Work for Mother," the Automats also appealed to young women who had continued to work after marriage by establishing retail stores, beginning in 1924, where women could pick up meals to serve at home.

40. Richard Miller, *Bohemia: The Protoculture Then and Now* (Chicago: Nelson-Hall, 1977), 181.

41. Chappell, *Restaurants of New York,* 125.

42. Report on Taxi and Street Conditions, Broadway and 34th St., Nov. 1, 1917, box 25, COF; H. Kahan report, Sept. 30, 1921, and reports on Childs Restaurant, Columbus Circle, Jan. 12 and 19, 1919, and Aberdeen Hotel, Apr. 30–May 2, 1919, all in box 34, COF; report for June 27, 1924, 1924 Democratic National Convention folder, box 35, COF.

43. Whitin, "Sexual Perversion Cases in New York City Courts, 1916–1921," bulletin 1480, Nov. 12, 1921, box 88, COF.

44. Tyler to Charles Henri Ford, Oct. 15, 1929.

45. *Broadway Brevities,* Nov. 2, 1931, 2. Frank Thompson reported in an interview that this was still the case in the 1940s.

46. Dorr Legg, interviewed; Charles G. Shaw, *Nightlife:* Vanity Fair*'s Intimate Guide to New York* (New York: John Day, 1931), 66.

47. Report by H. Kahan, Sept. 14, 1926, box 35, COF; Jeffrey Gottfried, interviewed; *Broadway Brevities,* October 1924, 48–49; *Broadway Brevities,* Nov. 16, 1931, 10. Additionally, a twenty-year-old actor explained in 1922 that after work he "most always" had his dinner at a place on Forty-ninth Street between Sixth and Seventh Avenues, "where I ate because lots of fags hang out there" (Samuel Kahn, *Mentality and Homosexuality* [Boston: Meador, 1937], 183). *Brevities* (Dec. 28, 1931, 7) also referred to the more general phenomenon, in its usual tone, when a columnist reported that "THE GARDENIA BOYS [a relatively uncommon slang term for gay men] are in again. . . . Under the chaperonage of Frankie (Drag) Carroll, they hold 'Midnight Teas' at various and well-known eateries in this versatile city of New Yawp." In later years certain cafeterias in gay bar districts, such as a Bickford's on Lexington Avenue in the East Fifties, were whimsically nicknamed "The Last Chance" or "The Last Stand," a place for men to take a final stab at picking someone up after the bars had closed (David Hearst, interviewed; Willy W., interviewed; Jeffrey Gottfried, interviewed).

48. *Broadway Brevities,* January 1924, 16; investigators' reports dated Apr. 4, 1921; Dec. 13, 1920; June 4, 1921; and July 19, 1921, box 34, COF.

49. Mark Stanley, interviewed. His further comments provide additional evidence of how well known the Columbus Circle Childs must have been, for he added that it "was the only [gay meeting] place that I was aware of New York having at that time"; he rarely participated in the gay scene, went only occasionally to this Childs, and apparently remained ignorant of the other cafeterias and the tearooms on MacDougal Street.

50. *WPA Guide to New York City,* 140.

51. George Ross, *Tips on Tables: Being a Guide to Dining and Wining in New York* (New York: Covici-Friede, 1934), 238; *Broadway Brevities,* Nov. 2, 1933, 9.

52. "Degenerates of Greenwich Village," *Current Psychology and Psychoanalysis,* December 1936, reprinted in Martin Duberman, *About Time: Exploring the Gay Past* (New York: Gay Presses of New York, 1986), 132–34, at 132 and 133. The author mistranslated "jam" as "young boy (. . . virgin)." He was almost certainly describing the Life, given the other descriptions available of the Life and of its location on the Square. If not, his description would still confirm my point about the openness with which gay men could carry on in such cafeterias and their role in attracting other customers, and would simply indicate that there was yet another cafeteria in the Village that had adopted the same strategy that the Life and Childs had.

53. Dick Addison, interviewed.

54. Tyler to Charles Henri Ford, July 22, 1929; on other reprimands, Mar. 11 and Apr. 2, 1929.

55. Tyler to Ford, May 6, 1929. It is unclear whether Tyler's friends reacted so strongly because they found his carrying himself as if he were "heterosexual" an affront (and were, in effect, trying to police his sexual behavior and prohibit any indication of bisexuality) or because they wanted to prevent the woman from being hurt by his deception. It is also unclear whether Tyler was embarrassed because his

friends had discovered his masquerade as a heterosexual or because they had publicly identified him as a homosexual.

56. Report on Fairies' hangout in basement, Times Square Bldg., 42nd St. and Broadway, Mar. 2, 1927, box 36, COF.

57. This account of the Koenig raid is based on the following sources: F. H. Whitin to Insp. Thomas MacDonald, First I.D., June 2, 1920, box 5, COF; investigator's reports for Apr. 30, June 12, and June 21, 1920, box 34, COF; bulletin 1391, "Police Action, East Side," Aug. 3, 1920, box 88, COF; bulletin 1438, "Finger Print Report, 1920," Mar. 15, 1921, box 88, COF; and bulletin 1480, "Sexual Perversion Cases in New York City," Nov. 12, 1921, box 88, COF. The COF bulletins do not give the date of the raid, which I determined by searching the Essex Market police court's record book for a record of arrests matching the description provided by the bulletins, that is, an arraignment of thirty men charged with degenerate disorderly conduct on a Saturday night in July (actually Sunday morning, Aug. 1, as it turned out), and given the penalties reported by the Committee: City Magistrates' Courts Record Book, Third Police Court, vol. 47 (July 26, 1920–Jan. 10, 1921), docket numbers 9242–73, NYMA.

58. *Cahill's Consolidated Laws of New York, Being the Consolidated Laws of 1909, as amended to July 1, 1923,* ed. James C. Cahill (Chicago: Callaghan, 1923), 1416. The legislative history of the statute's revision is obscure, since few records remain of New York State legislative deliberations of any sort from this period. One very short newspaper account of the legislation suggests that one of its prime advocates was the United Real Estate Owners' Association, which intended to use the law against tenants who damaged their property, were "noisy and boisterous, . . . and [made] insulting, quarrelsome, and threatening remarks and actions." The article made no reference to the law's provisions restricting other forms of public "disorder" (*New York Times*, June 10, 1923, sec. 9, p. 1). Nonetheless, it seems likely that the moral-reform societies played some part in the legislature's decision to include homosexual solicitation in the measure, given their role in the development of legislation concerning related matters. On the significance of the shift from legislation criminalizing sodomy to that criminalizing a more amorphous "lewdness" (as the New York statute put it) or "gross indecency" (as the British statute, the subject of his article, put it), see Ed Cohen's insightful essay, "Legislating the Norm: From Sodomy to Gross Indecency," *South Atlantic Quarterly* 88 (1989): 181–217.

59. *Broadway Brevities,* Nov. 16, 1931, 10.

60. Ibid. "After much ado," the account added, "they were all released, but for a time the place was closed."

61. *Gloria Bar & Grill, Inc., v. Bruckman, et al.,* 259 A.D. 706 (1st Dep't 1940), testimony of Frederick Schmitt, contained in Record on Review, 4th Division office, NYPD, 249. The official testified in this 1939 case, heard on appeal in 1940, about an incident that had occurred several years earlier.

62. H. Kahan, Report on Jack's Restaurant, 763 Sixth Ave., Dec. 27, 1921, box 34, COF. Kahan's phrasing—particularly his reference to "men chang[ing] tables and talk[ing] to men who called them over"—was strikingly similar to the language used by investigators to describe the social interaction between men and women at restaurants the Committee considered too "loose."

63. Griffes diary, for example, June 27, July 4, 9, 19, 30, Aug. 7, 14, 1915.

64. Ronald Heffner, interviewed. On the nongay aspects of the second Jack's reputation as a famous theatrical rendezvous, see William Laas, *Crossroads of the World: The Story of Times Square* (New York: Popular Library, 1965), 130;

Herbert Asbury, *The Great Illusion: An Informal History of Prohibition* (Garden City, N.Y.: Doubleday, 1950), 195.

65. Investigator's reports for June 1, 1925, and Oct. 5, 1926; annotated list of suspicious places, Oct. 2, 1926, box 35, COF; *Broadway Brevities,* December 1924, 34; *Broadway Brevities,* Nov. 16, 1931, 10; Ross, *Tips on Tables,* 146–47. Louis' may already have been a gay rendezvous in the mid-1910s; Charles Tomlinson Griffes, who had an apartment nearby, frequently took meals with gay friends at a place called Louis', although it is not certain that he was referring to the same restaurant: see the diary entries cited in note 63. Louis' moved from 41 West 49th St. to 43 West 48rd St. late in 1926.

66. *Broadway Brevities,* October 1924, 50.

67. Investigator's report for June 1, 1925, box 35, COF.

68. Chappell, *Restaurants of New York,* 127.

CHAPTER 7. "PRIVACY COULD ONLY BE HAD IN PUBLIC": FORGING A GAY WORLD IN THE STREETS

1. Bernarr Macfadden, *Superb Virility of Manhood: Giving the Causes and Simple Home Methods of Curing the Weaknesses of Men* (New York: Physical Culture Publishing Co., 1904), 175–76; E. S. Shepherd, "Contribution to the Study of Intermediacy," *American Journal of Urology and Sexology* 14 (1918): 242, as also quoted in this book's introduction.

2. Tyler to Charles Henri Ford, July 9, 1929; see also his letter of July 4, 1929.

3. On the middle-class ideology of parks and the class conflict generated over their use, see the masterly study of Roy Rosenzweig and Elizabeth Blackmar, *The Park and the People: A History of Central Park* (Ithaca, N.Y.: Cornell University Press, 1992); Daniel Bluestone, *Constructing Chicago* (New Haven, Conn.: Yale University Press, 1991), 7–61; and Roy Rosenzweig, "Middle-Class Parks and Working-Class Play: The Struggle over Recreational Space in Worcester, Massachusetts, 1870–1910," *Radical History Review* 21 (1979): 31–48.

4. Leo, interviewed.

5. Jeffrey Gottfried, interviewed. Rene Hubert, also a gay immigrant German Jew, had a similar experience ten years later, when he arrived in New York with no job and knowing no one. While sitting in Central Park, he was approached by a man who subsequently invited him to a series of parties where he met other gay men. Within a year he had developed an extensive network of friends, and learned of a number of other places where gay men met (Rene Hubert, interviewed).

6. Parker Tyler to Charles Henri Ford, July 1929.

7. Glenway Wescott, *Continual Lessons: The Journals of Glenway Wescott, 1937–1955,* ed. Robert Phelps with Jerry Rosco (New York: Farrar, Straus & Giroux, 1990), 81 (diary entry for Apr. 13, 1941).

8. Sebastian Risicato, interviewed.

9. Henry Isaacs, interviewed. Isaacs was a regular at Prospect Park in the 1940s and 1950s; for a brief account of gay friends meeting in the park in the 1920s, see Samuel Kahn, *Mentality and Homosexuality* (Boston: Meador, 1937), 216–17. For more on Battery Park, see chapter 3 of this book; for Riverside Park, see Jeffrey Gottfried's story (note 5) above and note 58 below.

10. *People v. Matthews* (CGS 1896); *People v. Koster,* DAP 21,728 (CGS 1898); *People v. Carlson,* DAP 20,546 (CGS 1898); *People v. Frerer,* DAP 20,950 (CGS 1898); *People v. Meyer and Ward,* DAP 43,369 (CGS 1903); *People v. Franc and Hurley,* DAP 154,475 (CGS 1924); *People v. Hartwich,* DAP 156,909 (CGS 1924); *People v. Coree,* DAP 160,472 (CGS 1925); all cases from NYMA. For gay

men's own stories of picking up men in Central Park in the late 1920s and early 1930s, see accounts in George W. Henry, *Sex Variants* (New York: Paul B. Hoeber, 1941), by Thomas B., 105, Eric D., 153, and Daniel O'L., 432.

11. "N.Y.'s Central Park Greatest Circus Without Canvas Anywhere in U.S.," *Variety,* Oct. 23, 1929, 61. The article also noted, "Many arrests are made among the nance element."

12. Thomas Painter, "The Prostitute" (typescript, 1941, KIL), 32–35; see also Wescott, *Continual Lessons,* 81 (diary entry for Apr. 13, 1941); Rosenzweig and Blackmar, *The Park and the People,* 479, 405; interviews with Dick Addison, Sebastian Risicato, Donald Vining, and Jeffrey Gottfried, who also commented that when he moved to New York in 1927, "I went to Central Park and certainly at that time the Goldman Band Festivals were the ideal meeting spots." The popularity of the southeastern corner of the park by the end of World War I is indicated by the large number of arrests made by the two officers assigned to the nearby Central Park zoo cages in the first half of 1921: Frederick H. Whitin, "Sexual Perversion Cases in New York City Courts, 1916–1921," bulletin 1480, Nov. 12, 1921, box 88, COF. "Vaseline Alley," a nickname assigned to several streets and alleys where men had sex, alluded to the use of Vaseline petroleum jelly as a lubricant.

13. Donald Vining, *A Gay Diary* (4 vols.; New York: Pepys Press, 1979–83), 1:284–85 (entry for Aug. 31, 1943); Vining suspected, probably correctly, that the police were simply seeking to meet their arrest quotas. Milk would later be elected as an openly gay candidate to the San Francisco Board of Supervisors; see Randy Shilts, *The Mayor of Castro Street: The Life and Times of Harvey Milk* (New York: St. Martin's, 1982), 3–4.

14. Interviews with Mike Romano, David Hearst, and Joel Honig. For examples of men cruising at Coney Island and meeting men there, see Antonio L., quoted in Henry, *Sex Variants,* 422; Victor R., ibid., 443. Unfortunately, I have been unable to learn more about the group of deaf gay men or to interview anyone who was a member of it. It seems likely that it existed, though, since it was recalled independently by three different men in separate interviews. On the development of a gay beach community near New York City, see Esther Newton, *Cherry Grove, Fire Island: Sixty Years in America's First Gay and Lesbian Town* (Boston: Beacon, 1993).

15. "Floozies Forgotten in Male Beauty Contest," *Variety,* Aug. 14, 1929, 47. As striking as the existence of a male beauty contest is the humorous, tongue-in-cheek tone with which *Variety* reported it. It gently ridicules the contestants, but it ridicules even more the "Coney Island dowagers" serving on the jury who hadn't a clue about what the sophisticated reporter saw transpiring, and seems to take glee in the exasperation of the chief judge, who did know what was going on.

16. *People v. Williams,* DAP 80,706 (CGS 1910). The fate of the younger man is uncertain.

17. The evidence concerning the organization of the vice squad's anti-homosexual activities before the 1940s is limited, but it is clear that the squad continued to assign officers to homosexual cases. In the 1930s, for instance, another plain-clothes officer in the vice squad explained that "at one time my job was to arrest degenerates," and that he had arrested "degenerates from the parks known as bushwackers . . . [and] degenerates from the park for annoying children . . . [and] a number of degenerates in toilets and subways" (*Gloria Bar & Grill, Inc., v. Bruckman, et al.,* 259 A.D. 706 [1st Dep't 1940], testimony of Frederick Schmitt, contained in Record on Review, 243–50). The squad also periodically shifted its primary focus from prostitution to homosexuality, and back again (see, for exam-

ple, the report that the squad, after stepping up its efforts to arrest homosexuals immediately following World War I, had decided to redirect its primary attention to prostitutes [bulletin 1504, Mar. 24, 1922, box 88, COF]). On the organization of the policing of homosexuality in later years, see, for example, William Wolfson, "Factors Associated with the Adjustment on Probation of One Hundred Sex Deviates" (M.S.E. thesis, City College of New York, 1948).

18. In the fall of 1919, he followed a Swedish longshoreman and Italian printer he had seen meet at Union Square to the home of the printer on East Twenty-first Street, where he arrested them (Society for the Suppression of Vice record books, vol. 4, 386–87, cases 108–9, Oct. 6, 1919, SSV). See also the description of the elaborate ruses he used in a case in which he became involved concerning a dentist who had approached a Committee of Fourteen investigator at the Childs Cafeteria at Columbus Circle: bulletin 1484, "A Perversion Case," Nov. 28, 1921, box 88, COF; H. Kahan reports, June 11 and July 19, 1921, box 34, COF. Officer Harvey arrested 88 (30 percent) of the 293 men convicted of degeneracy in the first half of 1921; given his specialized skills, his arrests resulted in an exceptionally high conviction rate (Whitin, "Sexual Perversion Cases").

19. Although some 89 percent of the men charged with degenerate disorderly conduct were convicted, less than half of the indictments for sodomy (and in some years less than a quarter) resulted in conviction. This calculation is based on the figures provided for sodomy prosecutions, 1900–1920, in the memorandum "Extract from Annual Reports of the Chief Clerk of the District Attorney's Office," COF.

20. This observation is based on my review of the manuscript docket books of the magistrates' courts in Manhattan in the 1910s. By 1915, the annual report of the magistrates' court confirmed that such records were kept when it specified the number of men arrested for degeneracy, even though no such offense had yet been specified by the legislature (*Annual Report, City Magistrates' Courts [First Division] [Manhattan and the Bronx], 1915*, 106).

21. Penal Law, Chap. 41, Article 70, Section 721, sub-section 8, as cited in *Cahill's Consolidated Laws of New York: Being the Consolidated Laws of 1909, as amended to July 1, 1923*, ed. James C. Cahill (Chicago: Callaghan, 1923), 1416.

22. See Whitin's description in his memorandum, "Sexual Perversion Cases." It should also be noted that although prostitution and homosexual solicitation were criminalized in different sections of the Code of Criminal Procedure, the police grouped them together as "crimes against chastity" in their annual reports.

23. The figure given for the average number of men convicted of degenerate disorderly conduct is based on the statistics published in the annual reports of the New York Police Department and of the City of New York Magistrates' Court, 1920–1940; the 1921 study was prepared by Frederick Whitin of the Committee of Fourteen, and reported in his memorandum "Sexual Perversion Cases."

24. J. A. S., Report on street conditions, n.d. [c. Sept. 12, 1918], box 31, COF; Gene Harwood, interviewed; Parker Tyler to Charles Henri Ford, [August] 1930. Tyler's account of his encounter with the sailors formed the basis of a scene in the novel he coauthored with Ford, *The Young and Evil* (Paris: Obelisk, 1933), 181–91. Ironically, a social worker who began working with men arrested on homosexual charges in the 1930s commented that it was usually not the fairy who was arrested, but the average-looking man, because fairies had learned how to avoid the police (Alfred A. Gross, "The Troublesome Homosexual," *Focus* 32 [January 1953]: 16). Although Gross did not explain his finding, he implied that it was because fairies were likely to be more deeply involved in the gay world and attuned to the political dynamics of the streets. "It is the unwitting, employed, mid-

dle-class individual," he added, "who usually gets picked up [by the police]."

25. T. Griswold Comstock, PH.D., M.D., "Alice Mitchell of Memphis," *New York Medical Times* 20 (1892): 172. He added: "Instances have been authenticated to me where such perverts when meeting another of the same sex, have at once recognized each other, and mutually become acquainted and have left in company with each other to practice together their unnatural vices." See also, for example, William Lee Howard, "Sexual Perversion in America," *American Journal of Dermatology and Genito-Urinary Diseases* 8 (1904): 11 ("by some subtle psychic influence these perverts recognize each other the moment they come in social contact"); James Kiernan, "Insanity: Sexual Perversion," *Detroit Lancet* 7 (1884): 482 ("these patients claim to be able to recognize each other"); G. Adler Blumer, "A Case of Perverted Sexual Instinct (Contraere Sexualempfindung)," *American Journal of Insanity* 39 (1882): 25. Krafft-Ebing made a similar observation of German "inverts" in "Perversions of the Sexual Instinct: Report of Cases," *Alienist and Neurologist* 9 (1888): 570.

26. The various gay magazines published in the 1950s periodically published articles with titles such as "Can Homosexuals Be Recognized?" One particularly insightful article by that title, although written by Donald Webster Cory twenty-five years after the period under discussion here, noted several of the same signs used by gay men a generation earlier, and it was wryly, but appropriately, illustrated with pictures of men staring into each other's eyes, men walking in peculiar ways, and articles of clothing and adornment fashionable among gay men: certain kinds of shoes and sandals, large rings, scarves, and the like. ("Can Homosexuals Be Recognized?" *ONE Magazine* 1 [September 1953]: 7–11.) (For an extended discussion of the semiotics of inversion, see chapter 2.)

27. Wystan Winters, interviewed.

28. Thomas Painter, "The Homosexual," (typescript, 1941, KIL), 25; Ewing, *Going Somewhere* (New York: Knopf, 1933), 182.

29. James Duncan, "Men Without Property: The Tramp's Classification and Uses of Public Space," *Antipode* 10 (March 1978): 24–34.

30. Susan Porter Benson, *Counter Cultures: Saleswomen, Managers, and Customers in American Department Stores, 1890–1940* (Urbana: University of Illinois Press, 1986), 18. Note that the incident in Ewing's novel *Going Somewhere* took place at a shop window.

31. Natalie D. Sonnichsen report, Nov. 27, 1913, box 39, COF. Sonnichsen heard this story from a saleswoman she had befriended while secretly investigating allegations of immorality among department store workers on behalf of the Committee of Fourteen. Third Avenue in the East Fifties would become one of the city's premier gay bar strips and cruising areas in the years following World War II.

32. Whitin, "Sexual Perversion Cases." There were thirty-three arrests at both the Union Square and Bloomingdale's stations, sixteen at Herald Square, ten at Times Square, and twenty at other subway stations, including a number at Grand Central. The subway arrests accounted for 38 percent of all arrests studied. The figures do not cover all arrests for homosexual solicitation made during the first six months of 1921, but only those heard before four of the eight relevant magistrates' courts in Manhattan. Those four courts, however, accounted for 86 percent of all such arraignments. The subway station at Bloomingdale's was also, at least occasionally, a place where men could go to meet female prostitutes; in 1927 a newsboy who sold his papers in the station served as a go-between for prostitutes working out of a nearby cafeteria, and arranged for an investigator to meet one there at 2:15 one morning (Report on Barney, newsdealer, underneath Bloomingdale's, Dec. 22, 1927, box 36, COF). Whitin had discovered in one of his earliest studies

of the geography of prostitution in New York that such vice was not confined to a single neighborhood, but tended to be found in the vicinity of the city's several retail shopping districts (Frederick Whitin to the Rev. Calvin McLeod Smith, Buffalo Federation of Churches, Oct. 22, 1920, box 59, COF).

33. Ralph Werther, *The Female-Impersonators* (New York: Medico-Legal Journal, 1918), 104–6, quote at 106; Timothy J. Gilfoyle, *City of Eros: New York City, Prostitution, and the Commercialization of Sex, 1790–1920* (New York: Norton, 1992), 210–12; Lloyd Morris, *Incredible New York: High Life and Low LIfe of the Last Hundred Years* (New York: Random House, 1951), 181–93.

34. Werther, *The Female-Impersonators,* 98.

35. Magnus Hirschfeld, *Die Homosexualität des Mannes und des Weibes* (Berlin: Louis Marcus, 1914), 547. As noted above, in the first half of 1921 thirty-three men were arrested for homosexual solicitation at the Union Square subway station, more than at all but one other site (Whitin, "Sexual Perversion Cases"). On the Rialto as a center of female prostitution, see Gilfoyle, *City of Eros,* 210–12; as a center of male prostitution, see Painter, "The Prostitute," 20–21. Painter's comments on Union Square are less reliable than most of his information, since they are based on his reading rather than his own experience (which dated from the mid-1930s) or interviews with older gay men. Court cases suggesting the well-established role of Union Square as a center of gay male cruising, as well as of both casual and professional male prostitution, include *People v. Casteels,* DAP 76,910 (CGS 1910), in which a silversmith hired a room at the Union Square Hotel, then went out and returned with a youth, whom he presumably had met in the neighborhood; *People v. Oreste,* DAP 79,786 (CGS 1910), in which a watchman followed two men who walked from Union Square to a building on East Seventeenth Street, where they hid themselves under the stoop to have sex before the watchman seized them; *People v. DeMatti,* DAP 126,271 (CGS 1919); *People v. Wilson,* DAP 129,057 (CGS 1920); *People v. Ismail Solomon,* DAP 178,147, (CGS 1929).

36. Dorr Legg, interviewed; *St. EOM in the Land of Pasaquan: The Life and Times and Art of Eddie Owens Martin,* ed. Tom Patterson (East Haven, Conn.: Jargon Society, 1987), 146 (Martin hustled on Forty-second Street before shifting to Fifth Avenue, where he could make more money); Daniel O'L. (an Irish fairy who hustled Greeks on Eighth Avenue), quoted in Henry, *Sex Variants,* 431–32; and Painter, "The Prostitute."

37. Margaret Mary Knapp, "A Historical Study of the Legitimate Playhouses on West Forty-second Street Between Seventh and Eighth Avenues in New York City" (Ph.D. diss., City University of New York, 1982), 389–90.

38. Tennessee Williams recalled cruising Times Square with Donald Windham in the early 1940s, where he made "very abrupt and candid overtures [to groups of sailors or GIs], phrased so bluntly that it's a wonder they didn't slaughter me on the spot. . . . They would stare at me for a moment in astonishment, burst into laughter, huddle for a brief conference, and, as often as not, would accept the solicitation, going to my partner's Village pad or to my room at the 'Y.'" (Tennessee Williams, *Memoirs* [1975; New York: Bantam, 1976], 66; see also 123, 172.) Some verification of their activity in Times Square is offered by a letter Williams wrote Windham on Oct. 11, 1940, while he was visiting his family in Missouri: "Have to play jam [straight] here and I'm getting horny as a jack-rabbit, so line up some of that Forty-second Street trade for me when I get back. Even Blondie would do!" (*Tennessee Williams' Letters to Donald Windham, 1940–1965,* ed. Donald Windham [New York: Holt, Rinehart and Winston, 1977], 17); see also Donald Windham, *Lost Friendships: A Memoir of Truman Capote, Tennessee Williams, and Others* (New York: Morrow, 1987), 114. *Broadway Brevities,* Nov. 2, 1931,

referred to gay men and servicemen making the block bounded by Broadway, Seventh Avenue, and Forty-second and Forty-first Streets "their special hangout."

39. The social and regional backgrounds of Depression-era hustlers are impossible to determine with certainty—no census-taker made note of them—but the ones cited here were reported by the normally reliable Painter on the basis of his interviews with a sample of sixty-seven of them in the mid- and late 1930s: "The Prostitute," 125–27.

40. Will Finch, notes on peg-houses (male brothels), dated Apr. 24, 1962, KIL.

41. Painter, "The Prostitute," 110, 115, recounting the histories of two hustlers.

42. This mapping and that of the following paragraph are based primarily on Painter, "The Prostitute," 22–23, 30; Finch, "Homosexual Resorts in New York, as of May 1939," Finch papers, KIL, and Broadway Brevities, July 4, 1932, 12; Nov. 2, 1931.

43. Report on Fairies' hangout in basement, Times Square Bldg., 42nd St. and Broadway, Mar. 2, 1927, box 36, COF.

44. See Will Finch, autobiographical notes, 1935, KIL.

45. John Nichols, "The Way It Was: Gay Life in World War II America," QQ Magazine 7 (August 1975): 54.

46. Finch diary, for example, Oct. 29, 1947, KIL.

47. I say "reputed" to be such rendezvous because the Committee of Fourteen investigator H. Kahan visited both places "looking for fairies and pimps" in 1920, which suggests he had heard they would be there, but he was unable to "make any connections with any of them," possibly because both places were almost empty at the time of his visit: report, Apr. 28, 1920, box 34, COF. See also the investigator's report, Apr. 27, 1921, box 34, COF.

48. Broadway Brevities, Nov. 2, 1931, 2. In his interview, Frank Thompson reported this was still the case in the 1940s.

49. Kathy Peiss, Cheap Amusements: Working Women and Leisure in Turn-of-the-Century New York (Philadelphia: Temple University Press, 1986), 145–53, especially 151; Robert Sklar, Movie-Made America (New York: Random House, 1975), ch. 2.

50. For reports of ushers acting as go-betweens between male patrons and female prostitutes, see H. Kahan's reports on the Olympic Theater, East 14th St., Mar. 18, 1919, and on B. F. Kahn's Union Square Theater, 56 E. 14th St., June 23, 1919, box 33, COF.

51. Magistrate J. E. Corrigan to Mayor John F. Hylan, Dec. 14, 1920, "Dept. of Licenses, 1920" folder, box 218, Mayor Hylan papers, NYMA. Corrigan urged the mayor to permanently revoke the license of the theater (which had already lost its license temporarily several times in the previous two years), and the mayor ordered his license commissioner to do so (Secretary to the Mayor to Commissioner John G. Gilchrist, Dec. 15, 1920, same folder), but the theater was still open the following year, when the forty-five men were arrested there (Whitin, "Sexual Perversion Cases"). The name of the theater is not given.

52. Kahn, Mentality and Homosexuality, 197–98. This man was recounting his experiences as a youth in London, where he began visiting theaters around 1905, but men had similar experiences in New York: for example, Martin Goodkin, interviewed. An NYU doctoral student, though more hostile, reported the same phenomenon in the burlesque theaters on 14th, 42nd, and 125th Streets: David Dressler, "Burlesque as a Cultural Phenomenon" (Ph.D. diss., New York University, 1937), 161, 204, 210.

53. See, for example, Vining, *Diary,* 1:260 (entry for Mar. 8, 1943); 263 (Apr. 4, 1943: he accompanied someone home from the Selwyn and "we talked a blue streak of theatre, ballet, music, personalities, etc. and I'd have enjoyed the conversation alone" [that is, without sex]); 270 (May 27, 1943); 271 (June 6, 1943: "another dull fruitless night" at the New Amsterdam); 276 (July 7, 1943).

54. See, for example, Vining, *Diary,* 1:371 (Jan. 10, 1945: "[Friends] warned me against theater cruising because of the plainclothesmen"); 374 (Jan. 26, 1945: "There was a policeman by the Selwyn box office so I wasn't surprised to find no standees row.") A civilian, he also complained that the danger posed by plain-clothesmen made servicemen, always a desirable catch, "rely more on [other] service men since they're sure they're not detectives."

55. *People v. Duggan and Malloy* (CGS 1889) (covered wagon); *People v. Jerome* (CGS 1896) (ice wagon); *People v. Nicols* (CGS 1896) (doorway); *People v. Dressing and Doyle* (CGS 1896) (loading platform); *People v. Schimacuoli,* DAP 22,087 (CGS 1898) (vacant lot); *People v. Vincent,* DAP 16,430 (CGS 1897) (out-house); *People v. Ranson,* DAP 21,292 (CGS 1898) (several youths in the base-ment of a building); *People v. Viggiano,* DAP 46,835 (CGS 1904) (two Italian youths on the roof of their building); and *People v. Heartstein,* DAP 125,604 (CGS 1919) (a thirty-nine-year-old Hungarian laborer and a Jewish teenager, in the com-mon toilet room of a rooming house and a few nights later on the roof of a tene-ment).

56. Report by H. Kahan, Aug. 27, 1920, box 34, COF. "Many girls were here with sailors and later on the girls were seen walk out from park alone. . . . A few white girls were also seen going in Park escorted by Japanese or Chinese," he added.

57. Reports on Van Cortlandt Park, Aug. 22, Sept. 19, 20, 1917, box 25, COF.

58. For cases of men caught in City Hall Park, see *People v. Clark and Mills,* DAP 10,481 (CGS 1896); *People v. Johnson and Weismuller,* DAP 6362 (CGS 1896); for Tompkins Park, see *People v. Stanley* (CGS 1896); for Battery Park, see *People v. Adams and Dawson,* DAP 11,476 (CGS 1896); *People v. Lang and Meyer,* DAP 32,264 (CGS 1900); for Mount Morris Park, see *People v. Burke and Ginn,* DAP 20,366 (CGS 1898); *People v. Abbey,* DAP 162,316 (CGS 1925); for Riverside Park, see *People v. Mohr,* DAP 11,497 (CGS 1896); *People v. Morton,* DAP 11,498 (CGS 1896); *People v. Pendergrass and Serpi,* DAP 110,748 (CGS 1916); for Washington Square Park, see *People v. Carrington and Rowe* (CGS 1910). Other sources corroborate the trial evidence; one imprisoned hustler told a doctor in 1922, for instance, that he had had his first homosexual experience in Central Park, apparently in the 1910s, and had "been earning a livelihood in the parks and hotels through homosexual acts, etc." (Kahn, *Mentality and Homosexuality,* 67; see also 77, 171, 216–17).

59. Stanley H. Howe, *History, Condition and Needs of Public Baths in Manhattan* (New York: New York Association for the Improvement of the Condition of the Poor, publication no. 71, n.d. [1911]), 10; *R. L. Polk & Company's General Directory of New York City,* vol. 134 (1925), 39.

60. *People v. Johnson and Weismuller; People v. Clark and Mills.* The men in the first case were discharged; in the second case, the cook was discharged and the porter sentenced to two years in the state penitentiary. For Battery Park, see, for example, *People v. Adams and Dawson,* concerning a fifty-year-old cook from East 109th Street found with a twenty-seven-year-old laborer; and *People v. Lang and Meyer,* concerning two Germans, one a ship's steward, the other a porter who lived on Canal Street.

61. Although the term was still in use in the 1970s and 1980s, its origins had long since been forgotten; not even the sociologist Laud Humphreys, author of the well-known study of homosexual encounters in such locales, could explain its etymology: *Tearoom Trade: Impersonal Sex in Public Places* (Chicago: Aldine, 1970), 2n. For examples of the casual use of the term "toilet room," see *People v. Vincent*, DAP 16,430 (CGS 1897), and *People v. George Weikley* (CGS 1912). A 1929 glossary of homosexual slang defined "tea house" as "a public lavatory frequented by homosexuals": Aaron J. Rosanoff, "Human Sexuality, Normal and Abnormal, From a Psychiatric Standpoint," *Urologic and Cutaneous Review* 33 (1929): 528. On the comfort station at Longacre [Times] Square becoming known as the "Sunken Gardens," see Louis E., quoted in Henry, *Sex Variants*, 196. On Beatrice Lillie's song, see chapter 10.

62. See Humphreys, *Tearoom Trade*, 1–15; and Edward William Delph, *The Silent Community: Public Homosexual Encounters* (Beverly Hills, Calif.: Sage, 1978), based on the author's fieldwork in New York in the 1970s. I am also indebted to the analysis of the social dynamics of tearoom encounters provided by two men on the basis of their own experiences in them in the 1940s and 1950s: Grant McGree, interviewed; and Martin Goodkin, interviewed.

63. *People v. Martin*, DAP 13,577 (CGS 1914). Most men apprehended in subway tearooms were charged with disorderly conduct, but a few were prosecuted for sodomy, and the more extensive records of their cases provide details about police methods unavailable in the records of the magistrates' courts. See, for example, *People v. Bruce and Clark*, DAP 118,852 (CGS 1918), which indicates two officers were stationed in the closet of the subway tearoom at the 135th Street and Lenox Avenue station of the IRT in Harlem; *People v. Chapman and Tamusule*, DAP 156,845 (CGS 1924), two officers stationed at the Stone Street entrance to the BMT line; and *People v. Murphy and Tarrence*, DAP 156,956 (CGS 1924), police at the 125th and Lenox Avenue station of the IRT. For the Pennsylvania Railroad case, see *People v. George Weikley (aka Wallis)* (CGS 1912). The agents cut the hole in the ceiling after discovering that men had drilled holes in the partitions between booths to facilitate sexual encounters. Also see James D., quoted in Henry, *Sex Variants*, 264.

64. Whitin, "Sexual Perversion Cases." For other evidence from the 1920s and early 1930s of men having encounters in subway washrooms, see the accounts in Henry, *Sex Variants*, by Michael D., 135, 137, and Eric D., 154. Such encounters in later years were described by Martin Goodkin and Willy W. in their interviews.

65. Augustus Granville Dill entry in *The Harlem Renaissance: A Historical Dictionary for the Era*, ed. Bruce Kellner (Westport, Conn.: Greenwood, 1984), 100–101.

66. George W. Henry and Alfred A. Gross, "The Homosexual Delinquent," *Mental Hygiene* 25 (1941): 426; idem, "Social Factors in the Case Histories of One Hundred Underprivileged Homosexuals," *Mental Hygiene* 22 (1938): 597. It should be noted, though, that wealthier men were less likely to be imprisoned (and thus less likely to appear in the survey) because they were more likely to be able to pay a fine (or pay off the arresting officer). Indeed, it was widely believed in the gay world that men caught by the police in tearooms were subject to police extortion: a man arrested by the Pennsylvania Railroad's agents at the Cortlandt Street ferry station in 1912 charged that company detectives had tried unsuccessfully to blackmail him before turning him over to the police (*People v. George Weikley [aka Wallis]*), although his accusation, while plausible, cannot, of course, be taken at face value, since he may have fabricated it simply to undermine the testimony of

the detectives against him. A generation later, at the height of the postwar anti-gay crackdown in 1948, Will Finch reported that "three first hand sources" had informed him that "the police are now in the midst of a 'drive' to clean out doings in public toilets, and spy on them through holes specially made, or gratings for ventilators, then rush in and nab them when they get going. . . . The police try to shake them down themselves. Only if they haven't enough money on them to pay off the police do [the police] take them into the court" (Finch diary, Mar. 7, 1948).

67. Howard Raymond, interviewed.

68. See the letters reprinted in *Rat and the Devil: Journal Letters of F. O. Matthiessen and Russell Cheney,* ed. Louis Hyde (Hamden, Conn.: Archon Books, 1978), for example, Cheney to Matthiessen, Feb. 2, 1925, 76.

69. Martin Goodkin, interviewed; Martin Leonard, interviewed; Roger Smith, who worked at a nearby department store, remembered finding the overtness of the sexual scene at the Herald Square tearoom so astonishing that he took his lover, Wystan Winters, to see it; Smith, interviewed.

70. Whitin, "Sexual Perversion Cases." This figure is derived not from Whitin's study of the cases heard in magistrates' court in the first six months of 1921, but from his study of the two hundred arrests in which the Society for the Suppression of Vice was involved from January 1920 to October 1921, which accounted for some 15 percent of the total number of arrests made during this period. Fifty of the two hundred men arrested with the Society's participation were married, as were a large (but unspecified) number of the men convicted in the first half of 1921. It should be noted, of course, that some married men participated quite fully in gay life, but many more kept their distance from it.

71. Whitin, "Sexual Perversion Cases."

72. Kahn, *Mentality and Homosexuality,* 135–36.

73. Martin Goodkin to author, May 16, 1987; Goodkin, interviewed. For a set of thoughtful reflections on the construction and meaning of this sort of process of identification, see Samuel R. Delaney, *The Motion of Light in Water: Sex and Science Fiction Writing in the East Village, 1957–1965* (New York), 173, and Joan Scott, "The Evidence of Experience," *Critical Inquiry* 17 (1991): 773–97.

74. Samuel Chotzinoff, *A Lost Paradise* (New York: Knopf, 1955), 81–82. The same point about the lack of privacy in the tenements was made by Elsa Herzfeld in her study of families in Hell's Kitchen, *Family Monographs: The History of Twenty-four Families Living in the Middle West Side of New York City* (New York: Kempster, 1905), 33–35. On the efforts of men living in rooming houses to spend time outside them, see Perry R. Duis, *The Saloon: Public Drinking in Chicago and Boston, 1880–1920* (Urbana: University of Illinois Press, 1983), 86–87 (although he does not deal with sexual matters or with gay life, I have found Duis's discussion of the class differences in the organization and use of urban space quite helpful, especially ch. 3), and Roy Rosenzwieg, *Eight Hours for What We Will: Workers and Leisure in an Industrial City, 1870–1920* (New York: Cambridge University Press, 1983), 56–57.

75. Russell Sage Foundation, *West Side Studies, vol. I: Boyhood and Lawlessness* (New York: Survey Associates, 1914), 21, 155. The study also emphasized the lack of privacy available in the tenements, given their thin walls and the usual absence of closed doors between rooms, 57–58. See also recollections of men and women who grew up in the pre–World War II middle west side about the widespread use of movie theater balconies and tenement hallways for sexual encounters, recorded in Jeff Kisseloff, *You Must Remember This: An Oral History of Manhattan from the 1890s to World War II* (New York: Harcourt Brace Jovanovich, 1989), 564–65.

76. Kathy Peiss, *Cheap Amusements,* 54–55, 106; idem, "'Charity Girls' and City Pleasures: Historical Notes on Working-Class Sexuality, 1880–1920," in *Passion and Power: Sexuality in History,* ed. Kathy Peiss and Christina Simmons (Philadelphia: Temple University Press, 1989), 57–69; Joanne J. Meyerowitz, *Women Adrift: Independent Wage Earners in Chicago, 1880–1930* (Chicago: University of Chicago Press, 1988), 101–6.

77. Russell Sage Foundation, *Boyhood and Lawlessness,* 21, 76. See also Cary Goodman, *Choosing Sides: Playground and Street Life on the Lower East Side* (New York: Schocken Books, 1979), and David Nasaw, *Children of the City: At Work and at Play* (Garden City, N.Y.: Anchor Press/Doubleday, 1985).

78. Russell Sage Foundation, *Boyhood and Lawlessness,* 155.

CHAPTER 8. THE SOCIAL WORLD OF THE BATHS

1. I have found Allan Berube's history of the baths in San Francisco, "The History of Gay Bathhouses," *Coming Up!,* December 1984, 15–19, very useful as I have thought through the history of New York's baths. His argument about the sexual culture promoted by the bathhouses is especially illuminating. My research suggests that exclusively gay bathhouses developed much earlier in New York than in San Francisco.

2. Stanley H. Howe, *History, Condition and Needs of Public Baths in Manhattan* (New York: New York Association for the Improvement of the Condition of the Poor, publication no. 71, n.d. [1911]), 6, 10, 16; Marilyn Thornton Williams, "New York City's Public Baths: A Case Study in Urban Progressive Reform," *Journal of Urban History* 7 (1980): 49–82; idem, "The Municipal Bath Movement in the United States, 1890–1915" (Ph.D. diss., New York University, 1972), 96–102.

3. Moses Rischin, *The Promised City: New York's Jews, 1870–1914* (Cambridge, Mass.: Harvard University Press, 1962), 87.

4. *People v. Downing and Goehle,* DAP 77,986 (CGS 1910). The incident occurred on June 15, and Downing was sentenced on June 28. The younger man's sentence was suspended.

5. "Fags Tickle Nudes: Pashy Steam Rooms Pander to Pansies[,] Joyboys on Make for Lurid Lushes," *Broadway Brevities,* Nov. 23, 1933, 1.

6. Quoted in Magnus Hirschfeld, *Die Homosexualität des Mannes und des Weibes* (Berlin: Louis Marcus, 1914), 551.

7. Of the McAlpin Hotel, for instance, an investigator evidently under orders to investigate rumors of homosexual activity reported that "I saw or heard nothing for which I particularly went there except that in the sleeping place the lounges are drawn up in pairs close together instead of being separated as they should be," J. A. S., Report of Investigation, Jan. 20, 1917, box 31, COF. See also the report on the Luxor Baths, which found it to be "frequented by the underworld" and female prostitutes, Investigator's Report, Oct. 6, 1926, box 35, COF. Hans Friedrich, interviewed.

8. Jeffrey Gottfried, interviewed; Thomas Painter, "The Prostitute" (typescript, 1941, KIL), 65.

9. Painter, ibid., 65–66, 97. The manuscript does not name the baths in this passage, but other passages make it clear that he was referring to Stauch's.

10. Interviews with Frank McCarthy and Joe O'Conner; Finch diary, June 17, 1954, KIL. In 1948 Finch complained there were "too many faggots" at Stauch's, calling it "Times Square in Coney Island" (diary, July 8, 1948). He also spent time sunbathing nude on the sundeck at Coney Island's Washington Baths (diary, July 5, Aug. 7, 1953).

11. Xavier Mayne (pseudonym of Edward Prime Stevenson), *The Intersexes: A History of Similisexualism as a Problem in Social Life* (privately printed in Rome, 1908), 440. Although printed in 1908, the manuscript had been finished by about 1901, according to the preface.

12. District Attorney William Travers Jerome to the Governor, Mar. 21, 1905 (regarding William Bennett's application for executive clemency), filed with *People v. Galbert,* DAP 41,914 (CGS 1903), JJC.

13. For accounts of the raid and police tactics, see the *World,* Feb. 22, 1903, 1; *New York Sun,* Feb. 23, 1903, 9; *New York Times,* Feb. 23, 1903, 14.

14. *People v. Casson,* DAP 41,913 (CGS 1903), JJC, testimony of Robert Hibbard, 4th Inspection District, NYPD, 3–6; Richard W. Abbott, 22nd Precinct, 24; Harry McCutcheon, 22nd Precinct, 34; and Exhibit A (a police diagram of the Ariston's layout); *People v. Galbert,* JJC, testimony of George Galbert, 193, and Berth Fiedler, 184. Note: All trial records cited below are in the NYMA, unless specified as in the JJC.

15. See, for example, *People v. Galbert,* JJC, testimony of Thomas Phelan, 22nd Precinct, 88–89.

16. *People v. Casson,* JJC, testimony of Robert Hibbard, 5–13, and Richard Abbott, 18–23. For another pairing, see *People v. Schnittel,* DAP 41,921 (CGS 1903).

17. See *People v. Rogers,* DAP 41,910, 42,021–28; *People v. Beck,* DAP 41,949; *People v. Brown,* DAP 41,945; *People v. Casson; People v. Johnson,* DAP 41,911; *People v. Kregal,* DAP 41,916; *People v. Lawrence,* DAP 41,909; *People v. Shanyo,* DAP 41,912; *People v. Torn,* DAP 41,946; *People v. Williams,* DAP 41,922, all indicted Mar. 4, 1903, in the CGS.

18. *People v. Galbert,* JJC, testimony of Thomas Phelan, 127, and Norman Fitzsimmons, 4th Inspection District, NYPD, 152–53. Galbert's defense attorney considered such public sexual activity so inconceivable to respectable sensibilities that he challenged the police account as precisely that: incredible. The prosecution had charged that "shameless to the witnesses there, to the officers, to everybody in that room, the defendant walks in, and the sheet comes off of him, . . . and he stands before those officers, watching him, with his penis erect. Is it true?" the defense attorney demanded. "Is it credible? That is what I want to ask you" (statement by Attorney LeBarbier, 238).

19. *People v. Galbert,* testimony of George Galbert, 191–92.

20. *New York Sun,* Feb. 23, 1903, 9; *People v. Casson,* JJC, testimony of Richard W. Abbott, 24–25; *People v. Galbert,* testimony of George Galbert, 193. For other accounts of the raid, see the *World,* Feb. 22, 1903, 1, and *New York Times,* Feb. 23, 1903, 14.

21. *People v. Casson,* judge's charge to the jury, 69–71.

22. The assistant district attorney prosecuting one of the cases referred to both the "character and importance of the case, [and] the fact that the subject matter of the indictment has been widely commented upon," *People v. Kregal,* DAP Brief Upon the Application for a Special Jury under the provisions of Chapter 602 of the Laws of 1901, by James R. Ely, A.D.A., n.d. [May 1903]. For the disposition of the sodomy cases, see DAP 41,909–16, 41,921–22, 41,945–46, 41,949, 41,967, 42,021–28 (especially 42,025); for the other cases, see the Manhattan Seventh District Magistrates' Court Docket Book, unnumbered volume covering Oct. 16, 1902–Apr. 18, 1903, 235–36, NYMA.

23. F. K., "Der Bericht aus Amerika," *Blätter für Menschenrecht* 7 (May 1929): 8–9; translated by James Steakley and published in Jonathan Ned Katz, *Gay/Lesbian Almanac* (New York: Harper & Row, 1983), 452–53 (order of first two sentences reversed).

24. Society for the Suppression of Vice record books, vol. 4, 356–57, case 117, Oct. 24, 1916, SSV. On the raid, see also *Society for the Suppression of Vice Annual Report for 1916* (New York: Society for the Suppression of Vice, 1917); bulletin 1016, "Finger Print Reports, October–November 1916," Dec. 29, 1916, box 87, COF.

25. *World,* Feb. 22, 1903, 1; Superintendent's Report to the Board of Directors, n.d. [Apr. 9, 1917], and Minutes of a regular meeting of the Board of Directors, Apr. 9, 1917, Society for the Prevention of Crime papers, box 13, Rare Book and Manuscript Library, Columbia University.

26. See, for example, Hirschfeld, *Homosexualität, 550*–52, as well as the reference to the "several" baths existing in New York at the turn of the century in Stevenson, *The Intersexes,* 440.

27. *New York Times,* May 26, 1977, B-9; Committee of Fourteen, *Annual Report for 1914* (New York: Committee of Fourteen, 1915), 10–14; Timothy J. Gilfoyle, *City of Eros: New York City, Prostitution, and the Commercialization of Sex, 1790–1920* (New York: Norton, 1992), 203–10.

28. Society for the Suppression of Vice record books, vol. 4, 374–75, cases 1–10, Jan. 5, 1919, SSV; Manhattan Second District Magistrates' Court Docket Book, unnumbered volume covering Feb. 19, 1920–Oct. 3, 1920, 16–17, docket numbers 2032–42, 2046–49, NYMA. The docket book actually indicates that ten of the men, or two-thirds, went to the workhouse instead of paying the fine, but, according to a subsequent Committee of Fourteen bulletin, only two of them, at most, ultimately did so (bulletin 1367, "Finger Print Bureau, February and March 1920," box 88, COF). The fact that the bulletin made a point of recording the judge's justification for the fines indicates that its report, not the magistrates' record, was accurate (the Committee considered jail a greater deterrent than fines in the case of homosexuals, as in the case of prostitutes, but noted that in this instance the judge "thought the city needed the money").

29. Emlyn Williams, *Emlyn* (London: The Bodley Head, 1973), 54.

30. On the Lafayette, see below; on the Produce Exchange, see the records in Charles Griffes's diary of his visits on, for example, July 25, 1914 ("nothing going on"); Nov. 18, 1916 (he went with a friend and found the bath "somewhat interesting—especially *one* man"); Nov. 29, 1916 ("found noone there," so he and the man he had gone with [whom he had originally met at the Lafayette] had "a long time together" and "a lot of fun"); Dec. 9, 1916 (when he picked someone up there).

31. F. K., "Der Bericht aus Amerika." The analysis of the Lafayette's clientele is based on the information provided in the Society for the Suppression of Vice record books, vol. 4, 352–57, cases 80–115, Oct. 22, 1916, SSV; the Manhattan Third District Magistrates' Court Docket Book, unnumbered volume, 1916, docket numbers 14,354–89; ibid., unnumbered volume, 1929, docket numbers 1590–1618, both at NYMA.

32. Nat Fowler, interviewed; Leo, interviewed; Martin Goodkin, interviewed. The *New York Times* reported District Attorney Robert Morgenthau's denial of the rumor, "said to be 'gay-community lore,'" that the Police Athletic League, which he headed, owned the baths, in its report on the 1977 fire, May 27, 1977, A-22.

33. The Penn Post Hotel's role as an assignation hotel persisted for decades; in 1923 the Committee of Fourteen discovered men could easily take women guests to their rooms, and in 1965 a police deputy inspector was demoted and fined for impeding a police investigation of homosexual activities at the hotel: Report on the Penn Post Hotel, 304 W. 31st St., Apr. 27, 1923, box 34, COF; *Mattachine Newsletter* 10 (March 1965): 12.

34. Interviews with Willy W., Nat Fowler, Edward Pennington, and Leo F.

35. *New York Post,* Feb. 11, 1957, 38; interviews with Willy W., Nat Fowler, Martin Goodkin, and Harvey Sarnoff.

36. Quoted in Hirschfeld, *Homosexualität,* 551–52.

37. Interviews with Nat Fowler, Mike Romano, and Harvey Sarnoff.

38. *People v. Galbert,* JJC, testimony of Norman Fitzsimmons, 142, and Thomas Phelan, 91–93; District Attorney William Travers Jerome to the Governor, Mar. 21, 1905. In the mid-1930s a man explained that it was "a common thing at the baths" for men to have mutually responsive sexual encounters in groups (Sidney H., quoted in George W. Henry, *Sex Variants* [New York: Paul B. Hoeber, 1941], 55).

39. Griffes diary, Aug. 8, 9, 1916; Oct. 21, 1914; Robert T. and Sidney H., quoted in Henry, *Sex Variants,* 215, 55.

40. Painter, "The Homosexual" (typescript, 1941, KIL), 186; idem, "The Prostitute," 66; Hirschfeld, *Homosexualität,* 551; Nat Fowler, interviewed.

41. Society for the Suppression of Vice record books, vol. 4, 352–57, cases 80–115, Oct. 22, 1916, and 374–75, cases 1–10, Jan. 5, 1919, SSV. Griffes frequently visited the Lafayette with a married friend (see, for example, diary entries for Mar. 7, July 10, Oct. 3, 1914; June 19, 1915; and Jan. 8, 1916) and met other married men there; on one occasion he was "astonished" to learn that a man he had picked up at the bath and seen several times since was married (diary, Aug. 31, 1915). The pattern continued; several men commented in interviews on the number of married men they met in the baths in the 1940s and 1950s: Martin Goodkin, interviewed; Harvey Sarnoff, interviewed.

42. Griffes diary, July 25, 1914. An employee at the St. Mark's in the 1960s recalled the number of clergymen and Hasidic Jews who frequented the bath in the evenings. The terror such men felt at the prospect of being discovered there was emphasized for him one night when a Jesuit priest had a heart attack and, before losing consciousness, begged the staff to remove his body so that it would not be known he had died there. He survived only because the frightened manager and floorman dressed him and drove him to nearby Bellevue Hospital, where they said they had found him "on the street" (Harvey Sarnoff, interviewed).

43. Williams, *Emlyn,* 55–56.

44. District Attorney William Travers Jerome to the Governor, Mar. 21, 1905.

45. F. K., "Der Bericht aus Amerika"; interviews with Nat Fowler, Willy W., Leo, and Harvey Sarnoff.

46. Griffes diary, Sept. 19, Oct. 3, 1914 (he made an appointment with M. R., a Swede, which M. R. did not keep); Apr. 21, 24, 28, May 5, 8, June 7, 1915 (he met and developed a friendship with C. L., a German); Aug. 6, 7, 10, 1915 (he made contact with M. M., whom he had met at the baths, by writing him, even though he was not sure he had the right address); July 15, 17, 1916 (met J., who visited his apartment); Dec. 9, 10, 1916 (met V. B., whom he visited in Brooklyn the next day).

47. See, for example, Griffes diary, Sept. 13, Nov. 15, 18, 29, 1916.

48. Ibid., Jan. 16, Apr. 21, June 19, 20, 24, 1915; Jan. 8, 1916. "Very happy about the matter," he said of this latter visit to the bath, which also resulted in a pleasant sexual encounter.

49. Letter to the author, Dec. 30, 1987.

50. *Broadway Brevities,* December 1924, 36.

CHAPTER 9. BUILDING GAY NEIGHBORHOOD ENCLAVES: THE VILLAGE AND HARLEM

1. Stephen Graham, *New York Nights* (New York: Doran, 1927), 114; *Broadway Brevities*, Apr. 11, 1932, 5.

2. Malcolm Cowley, *Exile's Return: A Literary Odyssey of the 1920s* (1934; New York: Viking, 1956), 48; Caroline F. Ware, *Greenwich Village, 1920–1930: A Comment on American Civilization in the Post-War Years* (New York: Houghton Mifflin, 1935), 18–22; Allen Churchill, *The Improper Bohemians* (New York: Dutton, 1959), 22. See also the interesting discussion of the multiple (and often simultaneous) rises and falls of bohemia (and of the Village in particular) in Russell Jacoby, *The Last Intellectuals: American Culture in the Age of Academe* (New York: Basic Books, 1987), ch. 2.

3. The sociologist Caroline Ware emphasized the extent to which becoming an artist or writer, particularly a poor one who rejected the genteel tradition, made one a deviant in early-twentieth-century middle-class society; see Ware, *Greenwich Village*, 239.

4. *Greenwich Village: A Local Review*, April 1929, n.p.

5. Ellen Kay Trimberger, "Feminism, Men, and Modern Love: Greenwich Village, 1900–1925," in *Powers of Desire: The Politics of Sexuality*, ed. Ann Snitow, Christine Stansell, and Sharon Thompson (New York: Monthly Review Press, 1983), 131–52; Leslie Fishbein, *Rebels in Bohemia: The Radicals of The Masses, 1911–1917* (Chapel Hill: University of North Carolina Press, 1982).

6. Cowley, *Exile's Return*, 52.

7. Curiously, Dell described the encounter with Sumner but did not mention the raid in his memoirs, *Homecoming* (New York: Farrar & Rinehart, 1933), 278. Case 68, Aug. 31, 1916, vol. 4, 350–51, SSV. The September 1916 issue of *The Masses* carried a display ad for the Forel book on p. 43, as had several previous issues. Sumner also prosecuted the book's publisher, or possibly distributor, and, the following May, a Brooklyn bookshop selling the book. The latter case was dismissed; the first two cases were sent to the Court of Special Sessions, with unrecorded results, except that the two defendants were "paroled"; case 67, Aug. 30, 1916, vol. 4, 350–51, and case 40, May 23, 1917, vol. 4, 364–65, SSV. The cartoon satirizing Comstock appeared in *The Masses*, September 1915, 19, and is reproduced in Rebecca Zurier, *Art for* The Masses: *A Radical Magazine and Its Graphics, 1911–1917* (Philadelphia: Temple University Press, 1988), 97. On Dell's theory that homosexuality was a "patriarchal institution," representing "a permanent state of emotional childishness," see *Love in the Machine Age* (New York: Farrar & Rinehart, 1930), especially 23ff.

8. *The Masses*, November 1916, 11.

9. Judith Schwartz, *Radical Feminists of Heterodoxy: Greenwich Village, 1912–1940* (Lebanon, N.H.: New Victoria Publishers, 1982).

10. Louis Sheaffer, *O'Neill, Son and Playwright* (London: J. M. Dent, 1969), 352–53; idem, *O'Neill, Son and Artist* (London: Paul Elek, 1974), 242.

11. Ware, *Greenwich Village*, 16–22.

12. Ibid., 15–17, 56–58. See also the comments on the passing of the old Greenwich Village in the memoirs of Floyd Dell, *Love in Greenwich Village* (New York: Doran, 1926), 16–17, 320–31; and Malcolm Cowley, *Exile's Return*, 66.

13. Churchill, *The Improper Bohemians*, 270–76. Julius' became a gay bar thirty years later, but did not attract a noticeable gay clientele in the twenties.

14. Ware's critique of the "pseudo-Bohemians" of the twenties suffuses her chapter on their social world, revealingly titled "Art and Sex as Avenues of Escape," and is made sharpest on pp. 238–40.

15. On New York's image as the nation's Sodom and Gomorrah and on the role generally of the rural–urban cleavage in American politics and rhetoric during the twenties, see David Burner, *The Politics of Provincialism: The Democratic Party in Transition, 1918–1932* (1967; New York: Norton, 1975), especially 76ff.

16. He added, though, that there was much he disapproved of in Village gay society—"they use entirely too much powder and perfume, and I don't think I ever could like people that paint their cheeks and eyelids"—and he was sometimes "sorry I ever became one myself," although he had met one man he "like[d] immensely . . . [and] thought we would make a wonderful match," if only he could get his attention (letter to the editor, dated Nov. 15, 1924, published in *Broadway Brevities,* December 1924, 16).

17. *Evening-Graphic,* Aug. 28, 1931, 6.

18. "In the Village they dance together unashamed to a murmurous chorus of 'fairies, fairies'" (Graham, *New York Nights,* 114).

19. *Evening-Graphic,* Aug. 25, 1931, 3.

20. Bruce Rogers, "Degenerates of Greenwich Village," *Current Psychology and Psychoanalysis,* December 1936, 29ff.

21. This description of the film is based on Vito Russo, *The Celluloid Closet: Homosexuality in the Movies* (New York: Harper & Row, 1981), 42–43, which also reproduces a still from the scene in the gay club.

22. Ware, *Greenwich Village,* 96, 238.

23. Ibid., 253. Lillian Faderman uncritically accepts Ware's analysis in her own analysis of "lesbian chic" in the 1920s Village, *Odd Girls and Twilight Lovers: A History of Lesbian Life in Twentieth-Century America* (New York: Columbia University Press, 1991), ch. 3.

24. *Greenwich Village Quill,* August 1926, 44.

25. Dell, *Love in Greenwich Village,* 299. See also Cowley, *Exile's Return,* 49–50.

26. "The dance was purely a money making affair as are most of those being given now by the so-called Villagers. . . . They are all stimulated by the great financial success of the Liberal Club's annual dance," J. A. S., Report on the Saraband of Apes Dance at Webster Hall, Mar. 23, 1917, box 31, COF.

27. J. A. S., Summary Report, "Greenwich Village Affairs," n.d. [1917–18], box 31, COF.

28. Ibid. He also noted the presence of "the usual crowd of homosexualists . . . some dressed in female attire, others in more or less oriental costumes," at the Saraband of Apes Dance (see note 26).

29. J. A. S., Report on the Greenwich Village Carnival [organized] by Glenn Coleman, Webster Hall, Apr. 6, 1917, box 31, COF. The balls were not the only places in the Village slummers went in order to see homosexuals. Frank Ortloff (interviewed), a Quaker lawyer who would begin representing men arrested on homosexual charges in the 1940s, recalled visiting with his fiancée the Village clubs where gay men gathered in the 1930s; he did it just for the fun of it, and because his friends did so.

30. J. A. S., Report of Investigation, The Liberal Club Ball, Feb. 11, 1917, box 31, COF.

31. *Greenwich Village Quill,* May 1922, 23.

32. In 1917 the Committee of Fourteen, apparently responding to such a reputation, sent an investigator to gather information about the "men perverts" said to be gathering in the tea shops around Washington Square, particularly along West Fourth Street (investigator's report, Dec. 11, 1917, box 31, COF). Thus Allen Churchill was incorrect when he suggested that lesbians and homosexuals began

congregating in the MacDougal Street nightclubs opposite the Provincetown Theater only after the end of Prohibition; they had actually made that strip their own at least a decade earlier (Churchill, *The Improper Bohemians*, 321).

33. Report on the Golden Eagle, June 18, 1919, box 34, COF (emphasis added).

34. "Village 'Joints' Out or Tame," *Variety*, May 6, 1925, 19 (I thank Lewis Erenberg for this reference); "Sapphic Sisters Scram!" *Broadway Brevities*, Nov. 16, 1931, 1, 10.

35. H. Kahan's report on The Jungle, 11 Cornelia St., July 4, 1922, box 34, COF.

36. "Village 'Joints' Out or Tame"; "Sapphic Sisters Scram!"

37. Ware, *Greenwich Village*, 252–55; on Polly's, see Bernardine Kielty Scherman, *Girl from Fitchburg* (New York: Random House, 1964), 64–67, and Churchill, *The Improper Bohemians*, 33.

38. Ware, *Greenwich Village*, 18–19, 237.

39. The Committee of Fourteen's agents reported in 1926 that it was "a well known hang out for fairies and lady lovers." Reports on the Greenwich Village Mill, Sept. 10 and 17, 1918, box 31, COF; Report on Paul and Joe's, 62 W. 9th St., n.d. [1919], box 34, COF; Report re Padlock List, [October–November?] 1926, box 35, COF. See also *Broadway Brevities*, October 1924, 50; December 1924, 16; Nov. 16, 1931, 1, 10; *Greenwich Village Quill*, July 1924, 34; April 1925, 33; Samuel Kahn, *Mentality and Homosexuality* (Boston: Meador, 1937), 183, 127.

40. The account of Eve's Place in this and the following two paragraphs is based on the following sources: "'Eve's Tea Room' Boss Ran Into Policewoman: Result, Arrest on Two Charges—Had Immoral Book Called 'Lesbian Love,'" *Variety*, June 23, 1926, 35; "Evelyn Addams, 1 Yr. and Deportation: Boss of Eve's in Village Sold 'Dirty' Book—Man-Hater Besides," ibid., July 7, 1926, 33; "Eve Addams' Ring of Rich Cultists," ibid., July 28, 1926, 37; *Greenwich Village Weekly News*, Oct. 10, 1931, 8; *Broadway Brevities*, Nov. 16, 1931, 1, 10; Edwards's comments appeared in the *Greenwich Village Quill*, June 1926, 28; July 1926, 8, 46, 60; August 1926, 44; September 1926, 57. The Society for the Suppression of Vice took note of the case (Society for the Suppression of Vice record books, vol. 5, 50–51, Kotchever case, June 17, 1926, SSV), thus supplying me with the date of the raid, but gave it no case number, instead marking it a "police case," which suggests that the SSV played no role in the raid but had simply been advised of it because of the twelve "objectionable" books and manuscripts possessed by Kotchever at the time of her arrest, which the police confiscated and the Society inventoried.

41. "Queer Show Quits Before Cops Cop It," *Variety*, Feb. 6, 1929, 1.

42. *Greenwich Village Weekly News*, Oct. 17, 1931, 8; *Broadway Brevities*, Nov. 16, 1931, 10.

43. *New York Evening-Graphic*, Aug. 25, 1931. The original announcement cards for the Left Bank and Fullhouse Restaurant are included in an unidentified scrapbook, apparently kept by a lesbian in New York in the early 1930s, now held by the KIL.

44. *Greenwich Village: A Local Review*, April 1929, n.p.

45. See, for example, the ad for *The Psychology of Homosexuality* by Doctor A. Hesnard in the July 1, 1933, issue, 4; and homosexual references in the issues of Aug. 1, 1–3; Aug. 15, 2; Dec. 1, 1933, 3; February 1934, 14; and, possibly, July 15, 1934, 1.

46. *Greenwich Village Weekly News*, Oct. 17, 1931, 1; ibid., Oct. 10, 1931, 8.

47. Ibid., Oct. 28, 1931, 10; see also Oct. 17, 1931, 8.

48. Ibid., Nov. 21, 1931, 4.

49. See, for example, Kathy Peiss, *Cheap Amusements: Working Women and Leisure in Turn-of-the-Century New York* (Philadelphia: Temple University Press, 1986); John D'Emilio and Estelle Freedman, *Intimate Matters: A History of Sexuality in America* (New York: Harper & Row, 1988); and Joanne J. Meyerowitz, *Women Adrift: Independent Wage Earners in Chicago, 1880–1930* (Chicago: University of Chicago Press, 1988).

50. Edouard Roditi, interviewed.

51. Robert Brennan, interviewed by Gregory Sprague, Jan. 28, 1984, Gregory Sprague papers, Chicago Historical Society.

52. On the development of Harlem as a black neighborhood, see Gilbert Osofsky, *Harlem: The Making of a Ghetto: Negro New York, 1890–1930* (New York: Harper & Row, 1966).

53. On the Great Migration, see James Grossman, *Land of Hope: Chicago, Black Southerners, and the Great Migration* (Chicago: University of Chicago Press, 1989); Kenneth Kusmer, *A Ghetto Takes Shape: Black Cleveland, 1870–1930* (Urbana: University of Illinois Press, 1976); Peter Gottlieb, *Making Their Own Way: Southern Blacks' Migration to Pittsburgh, 1916–1930* (Urbana: University of Illinois Press, 1987); Joe W. Trotter, Jr., *Black Milwaukee: The Making of an Industrial Proletariat, 1915–45* (Urbana: University of Illinois Press, 1985); Trotter, ed., *The Great Migration in Historical Perspective: New Dimensions of Race, Class, and Gender* (Bloomington: Indiana University Press, 1991).

54. Simon Williamson, "Sports and Amusements of Negro New York, Part II, Amusements," Federal Writers Project New York, Negroes of New York, 1936–1941, sports section, reel 5, SCRBC. (I thank Eric Garber for drawing my attention to the significance of the FWP papers.) On Harlem's cultural life in the 1920s, see David Levering Lewis, *When Harlem Was in Vogue* (1981; New York: Vintage, 1982); Nathan Irvin Huggins, *Harlem Renaissance* (New York: Oxford University Press, 1971); and Jervis Anderson, *This Was Harlem: A Cultural Portrait, 1900–1950* (New York: Farrar, Straus & Giroux, 1982). On Harlem in the 1930s, see Cheryl Greenberg, *"Or Does It Explode?" Black Harlem in the Great Depression* (New York: Oxford University Press, 1991), and Mark Naison, *Communists in Harlem During the Depression* (Urbana: University of Illinois Press, 1983).

55. Abram Hill, "Ed Smalls," Federal Writers Project New York, Negroes of New York, SCRBC.

56. Bricktop, with James Haskins, *Bricktop* (New York: Atheneum, 1983), 75.

57. *Variety*, Oct. 16, 1929, as reprinted in *Amsterdam News*, Oct. 23, 1929, in *Harlem on My Mind: Cultural Capital of Black America, 1900–1968,* ed. Allon Schoener (New York: Random House, 1968), 80.

58. George Chappell, *The Restaurants of New York* (New York: Greenberg, 1925), 119–20. For further analysis of the interest in African-American culture, see Lewis, *When Harlem Was in Vogue;* Anderson, *This Was Harlem;* Lewis A. Erenberg, "Impresarios of Broadway Nightlife," in *Inventing Times Square: Commerce and Culture at the Crossroads of the World,* ed. William R. Taylor (New York: Russell Sage, 1991), 158–77.

59. Although this lack of external moral regulation reduced some of the obstacles to the development of a gay world in Harlem, it also, ironically, meant a less extensive record of gay life was preserved for Harlem than for the Village.

60. Committee of Fourteen, *Annual Report for 1928* (New York: Committee

of Fourteen, 1929). This assessment is based primarily on a review of the investigators' reports submitted to the Committee and its other internal documentation. For the decision to launch a special investigation of Harlem, see bulletins 1977 [Jan. 26, 1928] and 1994 [Jan. 24, 1929], box 89, COF.

61. Eric Garber, "A Spectacle in Color: The Lesbian and Gay Subculture of Jazz Age Harlem," in *Hidden from History: Reclaiming the Gay and Lesbian Past,* ed. Martin Duberman, Martha Vicinus, and George Chauncey (New York: New American Library, 1989), 318–33.

62. Twenty-two percent of Negro men in Manhattan aged thirty-five to forty-four were single in 1930, compared to 6.8 percent in South Carolina, 9.4 percent in North Carolina, 14.1 percent in Virginia, and 13 percent in the United States as a whole: *Fifteenth Census of the United States: 1930 Population, vol. 2, General Report, Statistics by Subjects* (Washington, D.C.: Government Printing Office, 1933), 962, 891, 890, 888, 843. More work needs to be done on the social organization and acceptability of homosexual relations in rural black and white communities alike. The reflections of the black feminist theorist bell hooks on the relative tolerance afforded gay men (though not lesbians) in her hometown offers a thoughtful starting point. See "Homophobia in Black Communities," in her *Talking Back: Thinking Feminist, Thinking Black* (Boston: South End, 1989), 120–26.

63. "Negro Amusements," Federal Writers Project New York, Negroes of New York, 21, SCRBC.

64. Report on speakeasy, 109 W. 136th St., basement, May 27, 1928, 1 to 1:30 A.M., box 36, COF.

65. Report on Blue Ribbon Chile Parlor, 72 W. 131st St., 1:35 to 2:35 A.M., box 36, COF.

66. "On Seventh Avenue," *Baltimore Afro-American,* Dec. 27, 1930, 9.

67. *Amsterdam News,* Feb. 15, 1928, 1.

68. "Two Eagle-Eyed Detectives Spot 'Pansies on Parade,'" *Inter-State Tattler,* Mar. 10, 1932, 2.

69. "'She' Turns Out to Be a 'He' in Court: Fur-Coated 'Woman' Gives Cop Liveliest Chase of His Life," *Amsterdam News,* Feb. 8, 1928, 16.

70. "Fear of Arrest May Claim Life," *Amsterdam News,* Mar. 23, 1932, 3. For other accounts of female impersonators arrested on the streets, see "Bass Voiced 'Girl Friends' Sentenced—Alas! and Only Because 'She' Turned Out to Be He," ibid., Aug. 28, 1929, 2; "Male 'Lady' Jailed," ibid., June 4, 1930, 19.

71. Interview with Ruby Smith by Chris Albertson, 1971, as quoted by Garber, "Spectacle," 323.

72. Eric Garber, "Gladys Bentley: The Bulldagger Who Sang the Blues," *Out/look* (Spring 1988): 52–61; see also Hazel V. Carby, "'It Jus Be's Dat Way Sometime': The Sexual Politics of Women's Blues," *Radical America* (1986): 9–22; Chris Albertson, *Bessie* (New York: Stein and Day, 1972).

73. Songs are quoted in Garber, "Spectacle," 320. For further analysis of the songs, see Faderman, *Odd Girls,* 76–79.

74. Bruce Nugent, "Gloria Swanson" study, Federal Writers Project New York, Negroes in New York, reel 1, biographies section, SCRBC.

75. Ibid.

76. Garber, "Spectacle," 324; idem, "Gladys Bentley"; "On Seventh Avenue," *Baltimore Afro-American,* Dec. 27, 1930, 9; "Is This Really Harlem?," *Amsterdam News,* Oct. 23, 1929, in Schoener, ed., *Harlem on My Mind,* 79–81.

77. I rely heavily here on Garber's article "Gladys Bentley," the best study of the singer. See also Gladys Bentley, "I Am a Woman Again," *Ebony,* August 1952,

92–98; Wilbur Young, "Gladys Bentley," Federal Writers Project New York, Negroes of New York, reel 1, biographies section, SCRBC; and Faderman, *Odd Girls,* 72.

78. Hazel V. Carby, "Policing the Black Woman's Body in an Urban Context," *Critical Inquiry* (1992): 738–55. Lillian Faderman's assertion of "the manifest accept[ability] of bisexuality among the upper classes in Harlem" is based on the heiress A'Leila Walker's acceptance of it (*Odd Girls,* 75–76). Walker did have many gay and lesbian friends who attended her parties, but she was never accepted by Harlem's social elite and her attitudes cannot be taken as evidence of the elite's. On Walker's exclusion from Harlem's elite, see Lewis, *When Harlem Was in Vogue,* 165–69, and Bruce Nugent, "A'Leila Walker," Federal Writers Project New York, Negroes of New York, reel 1, biographies section, SCRBC. Several historians have recently offered subtle analyses of the construction of class divisions within Northern black communities: Grossman, *Land of Hope;* Kusmer, *A Ghetto Takes Shape;* Gottlieb, *Making Their Own Way;* and Trotter, *Black Milwaukee.*

79. Hazel V. Carby, "'On the Threshold of Woman's Era': Lynching, Empire, and Sexuality in Black Feminist Theory," in *"Race," Writing, and Difference,* ed. Henry Louis Gates, Jr. (Chicago: University of Chicago Press, 1986), 301–16; Carby, *Reconstructing Womanhood: The Emergence of the Afro-American Woman Novelist* (New York: Oxford University Press, 1987).

80. Adam Clayton Powell, *Against the Tide: An Autobiography* (New York: Richard R. Smith, 1938), 57–59.

81. "Dr. A. C. Powell Scores Pulpit Evils: Abyssinian Pastor Fires a Broadside into Ranks of Fellow Ministers, Churches . . . Denounces Sex Degeneracy and Sex-Perverts," *New York Age,* Nov. 16, 1929, 1.

82. Powell, *Against the Tide,* 216.

83. "Dr. Powell's Crusade Against Abnormal Vice Is Approved: Pastors and Laity Endorse Dr. Powell's Denunciation of Degeneracy in the Pulpit: Chorus of Commendation Is Heard as Eminent Men Express Approval and Give Promises of Their Support," *New York Age,* Nov. 23, 1929. The *Amsterdam News* did not cover Powell's sermon, but a month later it published a supportive column by Kelly Miller, "Corruption in the Pulpit" (Dec. 11, 1929, 20). See also Powell's account of the crusade, *Against the Tide,* 209–20.

84. Powell, *Against the Tide,* 216.

85. Several historians have insightfully analyzed the role of newspapers in the acculturation of Southern migrants to Northern cities, including Grossman, *Land of Hope,* and William Tuttle, *Race Riot: Chicago in the Red Summer of 1919* (1970; New York: Atheneum, 1985).

86. *Inter-State Tattler,* May 24, 1929, 10.

87. Howard Raymond, interviewed.

88. Billy Rowe, "Week-End Affairs," *Inter-State Tattler,* Jan. 28, 1932, 11. See also the Feb. 22, 1929, issue, p. 10.

89. Abram Hill, "The Hamilton Lodge Ball," Aug. 30, 1939, Federal Writers Project New York, Negroes of New York, 1936–41, reel 4, "New York City and Its People," SCRBC; *Broadway Brevities,* Mar. 14, 1932, 12; "Hamilton Lodge Ball an Unusual Spectacle," *New York Age,* Mar. 6, 1926, 3.

90. Hill, "Hamilton Lodge Ball."

91. "17 'Odd Fellows' Wind Up Before Tough Judge," *Amsterdam News,* Mar. 5, 1938, 1.

92. "Snow and Ice Cover Streets as Pansies Blossom Out at Hamilton Lodge's Dance," *Amsterdam News,* Feb. 28, 1934, 1.

93. The number of guests is impossible to ascertain with precision, since estimates varied widely from paper to paper (three papers put the attendance at the 1932 ball, for instance, at variously 5,000, 6,000, and 7,000 people). My estimates of the size of the gatherings and the relative ratios of gay men, lesbians, and straight people attending in costume are based on a review of the coverage of the balls each year in the *Amsterdam News, New York Age,* and *Inter-State Tattler.*

94. Sydney H., quoted in Henry, *Sex Variants,* 56; Report on tenement, 2612 Broadway, Apt. 4-S, Feb. 25, 1928, box 36, COF.

95. Ethel Waters, *His Eye Is on the Sparrow* (New York: Bantam, 1959), 149–50; Taylor Gordon, *Born to Be* (New York: Covici-Friede, 1929), 228. Gordon may not have been describing the Hamilton Lodge Ball, since he remembered the drag being held at the Savoy rather than the Rockland Palace; his account still suggests the popularity of Harlem's drag balls. For another account of Harlem's fascination with the balls, see Langston Hughes, *The Big Sea: An Autobiography* (1940; New York: Thunder's Mouth Press, 1986), 273–74.

96. Max Ewing to his parents, Feb. 17, 1930, Ewing papers, Yale.

97. *Amsterdam News,* Mar. 2, 1932, 2.

98. "Masquerade Ball Draws 5,000 People: As Usual, Feministic Males Turn Out in Gorgeous Costumes," *Amsterdam News,* Feb. 20, 1929, 2. Other headlines took a similar approach: "Mere Male Blossoms Out in Garb of Milady at Big Hamilton Lodge Ball: Coy Imitators Simper Sweetly at Affair Attended by 7,000," *Amsterdam News,* Feb. 19, 1930, 3.

99. "The Social Club World" column, "Hamilton Lodge, No. 710" report, *New York Age,* Mar. 5, 1932, 9.

100. "The Gang Says" column, ibid.

101. The three references appeared in the *Amsterdam News,* Mar. 7, 1936; Mar. 1, 1933, 2; Feb. 27, 1937, 1.

102. Roi Ottley, "Hectic Harlem" column, *Amsterdam News,* Mar. 7, 1936.

103. *Inter-State Tattler,* Feb. 22, 1929, 7.

104. "The Village Meets Harlem," *Chicago Defender,* Apr. 16, 1927, clipping in Carl Van Vechten scrapbook, Yale. The advertising flyer for the ball is also in the scrapbook.

105. "The Fort Valley Spectacle," unidentified newspaper editorial in the Van Vechten scrapbook. Presumbably referring to Van Vechten's novel *Nigger Heaven* (1926), it added: "The venomous attack made by a recent and perverted writer upon the morals of Harlem society in his salacious novel would be justified if the Fort Valley Industrial Benefit at the Renaissance should be taken as a criterion."

106. *Amsterdam News,* Feb. 20, 1929, 2. The 1926 report noted that "many Bohemians from the Greenwich Village section took the occasion to mask as women for this affair. . . . Although Hamilton Lodge is a colored organization, there were many white people present and they danced with and among the colored people" (*New York Age,* Mar. 6, 1926, 3).

107. Hill, "Hamilton Lodge Ball."

108. "Hamilton Lodge Costume Ball Marks Gayest Night of Season: Thousands Storm Rockland for Midnight Jamboree," *Inter-State Tattler,* Mar. 3, 1932, 5. Note that *gay* does not denote homosexual in this headline, although the headline writer may have been aware of its homosexual connotation.

109. Hill, "Hamilton Lodge Ball"; Roi Ottley, "Hectic Harlem" column, *Amsterdam News,* Mar. 7, 1936.

110. "Hamilton Lodge Clears $5,000 From Its Annual Ball," *New York Age,* Mar. 7, 1931, 6.

111. "3,000 Attend Ball of Hamilton Lodge: Bonnie Clark, Last Year's Prize

Winner, Disgruntled as Another 'Sweet Young Thing' Is Chosen for First Place," *Amsterdam News,* Mar. 1, 1933, 2.

112. Ottley, "Hectic Harlem" column.

113. Du Bois's personal response is difficult to discern, in part because he wrote an editorial disguising the reason for the editor's departure and wishing him a fond farewell: "Augustus Dill," *The Crisis,* March 1928, 36.

114. On the writers, see Lewis, *When Harlem Was in Vogue;* Garber, "Spectacle," 326–28; Amitai F. Avi-Ram, "The Unreadable Black Body: 'Conventional' Poetic Form in the Harlem Renaissance," *Genders* 7 (1990): 32–45; Alden Reimonenq, "Countee Cullen's Uranian 'Soul Windows,'" *Journal of Homosexuality* 26 (1993): 143–65; Henry Louis Gates, Jr., "The Black Man's Burden," in *Fear of a Queer Planet: Queer Politics and Social Theory,* ed. Michael Warner (Minneapolis: University of Minnesota Press, 1993), 230–38; Roditi, interviewed. Arnold Rampersad disputes assertions that Hughes was gay in *The Life of Langston Hughes,* Vol. I: *1902–1941: I, Too, Sing America* (New York: Oxford University Press, 1986). On Walker, see Garber, "Spectacle," 322; Lewis, *When Harlem Was in Vogue,* 165–69, and Nugent, "A'Leila Walker." On Van Vechten, see Lewis; Garber; and Bruce Kellner, *Carl Van Vechten and the Irreverent Decades* (Norman: University of Oklahoma Press, 1968).

115. Avi-Ram, "The Unreadable Black Body"; Reimonenq, "'Soul Windows.'"

116. Richard Bruce [Nugent], "Smoke, Lillies and Jade, A Novel, Part I," *Fire!!: A Quarterly Devoted to the Younger Negro Artists* 1 (1926): 33–39. On Nugent, see Charles Michael Smith, "Bruce Nugent: Bohemian of the Harlem Renaissance," in *In the Life: A Black Gay Anthology,* ed. Joseph Beam (Boston: Alyson, 1986), 209–20; Garber, "Spectacle," 327, 330; idem, "Richard Bruce Nugent," *Dictionary of Literary Biography* 51 (Detroit: Gale, 1986), 213–21; and my interview with Nugent.

117. Reimonenq, "'Soul Windows.'"

118. Thurman to William Rapp, May 7, 1929, box 1, folder 7, Wallace Thurman papers, James Weldon Johnson Memorial Collection, Yale. See also Lewis, *When Harlem Was in Vogue,* 278–79.

119. See, for instance, "'Pansies'—Men in Women's Gowns Dance for N.Y. Society," *Baltimore Afro-American,* Mar. 7, 1931, 1, 7; "Men Step Out in Gorgeous Finery of Other Sex to Vie for Beauty Prizes," *Amsterdam News,* Mar. 2, 1932, 2.

120. Howard Raymond, interviewed.

121. Robert D., interviewed.

CHAPTER 10. THE DOUBLE LIFE, CAMP CULTURE, AND THE MAKING OF A COLLECTIVE IDENTITY

1. Gene Harwood, interviewed; George Sardi, interviewed.

2. On the role of chain migration in the formation of migrant communities, see John S. and Leatrice D. MacDonald, "Chain Migration, Ethnic Neighborhood Formation, and Social Networks," *Milbank Memoral Fund Quarterly* 17 (1964): 82–97, and John Bodnar, *The Transplanted: A History of Immigrants in Urban America* (Bloomington: Indiana University Press, 1985), 57–71. In an important essay, Stephen O. Murray argued that the institutional infrastructure of Toronto's gay community in the 1970s was so well developed that it should be considered a quasi-ethnic community: "The Institutional Elaboration of a Quasi-Ethnic Community," *International Review of Modern Sociology* 9 (1979): 165–77.

3. Samuel Kahn, *Mentality and Homosexuality* (Boston: Meador, 1937), 135–36, 65. Kahn's study was researched and written in the early 1920s.

4. Daniel O'L., quoted in George W. Henry, *Sex Variants* (New York: Paul B. Hoeber, 1941), 435.

5. Dawson F. Dean, "Significant Characteristics of the Homosexual Personality" (Ph.D. diss., New York University, 1936), 459, 461, 463.

6. Kahn, *Mentality and Homosexuality.* Names deleted in the original.

7. Will Finch, autobiographical notes, n.d. [c. early 1960s?], KIL.

8. On the construction of identities, see Stuart Hall, "Ethnicity: Identity and Difference," *Radical America* 23 (1989): 9–20; Jeffrey Weeks, "Questions of Identity," in *The Cultural Construction of Sexuality,* ed. Pat Caplan (New York: Tavistock, 1987), 31–51; Werner Sollors, ed., *The Invention of Ethnicity* (New York: Oxford University Press, 1989).

9. Interviews with Richard Young, Max Adams, and Joel Honig.

10. The role of work-related contacts is particularly difficult to assess systematically, given the absence of the census data historians normally depend on for such studies. My comments in this section thus remain tentative, relying on significant anecdotal evidence from oral histories, arrest records, and other sources. The relationship between what Allan Berube has called queer work and queer identities needs to be put on the agenda of social historians, for it offers a crucial vantage point for analyzing the gendering and racializing of work. See Berube's pioneering efforts to address this issue in *Coming Out Under Fire: The History of Gay Men and Women in World War Two* (New York: Free Press, 1990), 57–66, and his paper "Dignity for All: The Role of Homosexuality in the Marine Cooks and Stewards Union, 1930s–1950s," presented at the Reworking American Labor History: Race, Gender, and Class Conference, University of Wisconsin, Madison, April 1992.

11. Mark Stanley, interviewed.

12. Malcolm E., quoted in Henry, *Sex Variants,* 165.

13. Leo, interviewed. For other examples of men who met other gay men through their jobs, see the accounts recorded in Henry, *Sex Variants,* by Tracy O. (as a musical accompanist), 68; Malcolm E. (who met men while working as an usher), 165; Julius E. (as an interior decorator), 528.

14. Roger Smith, interviewed; David Hearst, interviewed.

15. Tom R., interviewed.

16. John R., personal communication; Joel Honig, interviewed. For an impressive survey of how gay male professionals use such ideological camouflage today, which adopts a different perspective on such tactics than that developed here, see James D. Woods with Jay Lucas, *The Corporate Closet: The Professional Lives of Gay Men in America* (New York: Free Press, 1993). More work needs to done on how the boundaries between public and private life are negotiated in everyday interactions at different kinds of workplaces.

17. This assessment is based on my interviews with many older gay men; interviews with Joel Honig (quoted) and Martin Goodkin were particularly helpful. Other historians have reached similar conclusions. See Allan Berube, *Coming Out Under Fire,* 104, and John Grube's paper, "'No More Shit': Toronto Gay Men and the Police," presented at "La Ville en Rose," the First Quebec Lesbian and Gay Studies Conference, University of Quebec at Montreal and Concordia University, Nov. 12–15, 1992.

18. Daniel O'L., quoted in Henry, *Sex Variants,* 431.

19. Dennis C., quoted in Henry, *Sex Variants,* 309; Louis E., ibid., 196. Dennis C. also reported that his teacher advised him "to go with girls." It is unclear whether the teacher was advising him to forsake homosexual relations (a possibility, although the teacher did have a sexual encounter with him) or simply to

make a show of going with women to deflect suspicions. For an excellent analysis of the role of mentors, see John Grube, "Queens and Flaming Virgins: Towards a Sense of a Gay Community," *Rites* 2:9 (1986): 14–17.

20. Frank McCarthy, interviewed. Several other men described the importance of mentors as they began to explore the gay world: George George, Mike Romano, and Martin Goodkin, all interviewed.

21. Reginald M., quoted in Henry, *Sex Variants,* 396–97.

22. Max Adams, interviewed.

23. Walter R., quoted in Henry, *Sex Variants,* 288; Paul A., ibid., 227. Comments on the significance of parties or recollections of meeting men at them occur repeatedly in Henry's study; see, for example, the comments of Eric D., 154 ("I meet [homosexuals] at parties where I am introduced"); Louis E., 196; Paul A., 227 ("At a party I met a boy with whom I afterward lived for nearly two years"); Archibald T., 298; Reginald M., 398; and Julius E., 530.

24. See the depiction of a Harlem rent party in Wallace Thurman's roman à clef, *Infants of the Spring* (New York: Macaulay, 1932), 184; Eric Garber, "A Spectacle in Color: The Lesbian and Gay Subculture of Jazz Age Harlem," in *Hidden from History: Reclaiming the Gay and Lesbian Past,* ed. Martin Duberman, Martha Vicinus, and George Chauncey (New York: New American Library, 1989), 321–23; and chapter 9 of this book.

25. Frank Burton, interviewed. A typically sensationalist account of the Depression-era phenomenon of wealthy homeowners opening their country estates to weekend guests appeared in *Broadway Brevities,* Aug. 1, 1932, 1, 12: "Week-End Love Holes!"

26. Frank Thompson, interviewed.

27. Henry, *Sex Variants,* 303.

28. Report on Tenement (Colored), 108 W. 137th St., May 25, 1928, 2:45 to 3:40 A.M., box 36, COF. The woman eventually did agree to have sex with him, though only if he would pay five dollars, a very high price at the time.

29. Society for the Suppression of Vice record books, vol. 5, 30–31, cases 52–56, SSV; Frank Thompson, interviewed; Gene Harwood and Bruhs Mero, interviewed.

30. Leo S., quoted in Henry, *Sex Variants,* 365; Robert T., ibid., 216; Archibald T., 300. For another example of men who told Henry they might marry to achieve respectability, see Michael D., 13.

31. I follow and paraphrase here the description by Jean Comaroff and John Comaroff of the interpretive methodology deployed in their study *Of Revelation and Revolution: Christianity, Colonialism, and Consciousness in South Africa* (Chicago: University of Chicago Press, 1991), 37.

32. R. W. Shufeldt, M.D., "Biography of a Passive Pederast," *American Journal of Urology and Sexology* 13 (1917): 457, referring to an interview conducted in 1906; Douglas C. McMurtrie, "Some Observations on the Psychology of Sexual Inversion in Women," *Lancet-Clinic* 108 (1912): 488; Walter R., quoted in Henry, *Sex Variants,* 289; Julius E., ibid., 531.

33. Quoted in Frederick H. Whitin, "Sexual Perversion Cases in New York City Courts, 1916–1921," bulletin 1480, Nov. 12, 1921, box 88, COF. One doctor, probably James Kiernan, observed that the great majority of the inverts whose case studies were included in Havelock Ellis's study "were emphatic in their assertion that their moral position is precisely that of the normally constituted individual" (K., "Review of Havelock Ellis, *Studies in the Psychology of Sex, vol. 2: Sexual Inversion,*" *Alienist and Neurologist* 23 [1902]: 111).

34. William J. Robinson, "My Views on Homosexuality," *American Journal of Urology* 10 (1914): 551.

35. William J. Robinson, "Nature's Sex Stepchildren," *Medical Critic and Guide* (December 1925): 475 (emphasis added).

36. "A Father," *Broadway Brevities,* January 1924, 20–22; see also the other letter in that issue, and the letters in the December 1924 issue, 16–17, 31, 53.

37. Parisex [pseud. of Henry Gerber], "In Defense of Homosexuality," *Modern Thinker,* June 1932, reprinted in Martin Duberman, *About Time: Exploring the Gay Past* (New York: Gay Presses of New York, 1986), 119.

38. Richard Meeker, *Better Angel* (New York: Greenberg, 1933), 228.

39. Richard von Krafft-Ebing, *Psychopathia Sexualis* (numerous editions; the standard English translation is of the 12th, revised German edition, and was published in the United States in 1906); John Addington Symonds, *A Problem in Greek Ethics: Being an Inquiry into the Phenomenon of Sexual Inversion* (privately printed, 1883, 1901). On the fate of Symonds's study, see Jeffrey Weeks, *Coming Out: Homosexual Politics in Britain Since the Nineteenth Century* (London: Quartet, 1977), 59–60.

40. On the emergence of the "science" of ethnographic anthropology in the early twentieth century, and its subsequent crisis of authority, see James Clifford, "On Ethnographic Authority," in *The Predicament of Culture: Twentieth-Century Ethnography, Literature, and Art* (Cambridge, Mass.: Harvard University Press, 1988), 21–54, and George E. Marcus and Michael M. J. Fischer, "Ethnography and Interpretive Anthropology," in their *Anthropology as Cultural Critique: An Experimental Moment in the Human Sciences* (Chicago: University of Chicago Press, 1986), 17–44.

41. Edward Carpenter, ed., *Ioläus: An Anthology of Friendship* (New York: Mitchell Kennerley, 1917; Pagan Press, 1982). For a succinct statement of Carpenter's views, see his essay "The Intermediate Sex," in his *Love's Coming of Age* (London: George Allen and Unwin, 1906; 12th enl. ed., 1923), 130–49; for a more general discussion of Carpenter, see Sheila Rowbotham and Jeffrey Weeks, *Socialism and the New Life: The Personal and Sexual Politics of Edward Carpenter and Havelock Ellis* (London: Pluto Press, 1977), 25–138. On Melville's stories, see Robert K. Martin, *Hero, Captain, and Stranger: Male Friendship, Social Critique, and Literary Form in the Sea Novels of Herman Melville* (Chapel Hill: University of North Carolina Press, 1986). On the cultural significance for gay men and women of travel writing in the late nineteenth and early twentieth centuries, see the brief but highly suggestive comments offered by Martin in his review of Paul Fussell's *Abroad: British Literary Traveling Between the Wars,* in *Gay Studies Newsletter* 10 (July 1983): 13.

42. Countee Cullen to Alain Locke, Mar. 3, 1923, as quoted in Alden Reimonenq, "Countee Cullen's Uranian 'Soul Windows,'" *Journal of Homosexuality* 26 (1993): 144.

43. Meeker, *Better Angel,* 228, 246.

44. Blair Niles, *Strange Brother* (1931; New York: Avon, 1952), 49, 101, 120–21, 133, 150, 170, 191–201.

45. Kahn, *Mentality and Homosexuality,* 157. He also discussed Oscar Wilde's *The Picture of Dorian Gray* as a gay novel (p. 158).

46. Robinson, "Nature's Sex Stepchildren," 475.

47. Louis E., quoted in Henry, *Sex Variants,* 196.

48. Simon Karlinsky, "Gay Life in the Age of Two Josephs: McCarthy and Stalin," *Advocate,* Apr. 28, 1983.

49. See Benedict Anderson, *Imagined Communities: Reflections on the Origin and Spread of Nationalism* (New York: Verso, 1983), and Eric Hobsbawm and Terence Ranger, eds., *The Invention of Tradition* (New York: Cambridge University Press, 1983). On the cultural significance of gay historical imagination, see also the insightful work of Scott Bravmann, "Telling (Hi)stories: Rethinking the Lesbian and Gay Historical Imagination," *Out/look* 8 (Spring 1990): 68–74, and Murray, "Institutional Elaboration," 171–72.

50. The best evidence of the scope of gay argot is provided by several glossaries developed by homosexual and heterosexual researchers; the most useful are Gershon Legman, "The Language of Homosexuality: An American Glossary," in Henry, *Sex Variants,* vol. 2, appendix VII; and Aaron J. Rosanoff, "Human Sexuality, Normal and Abnormal, From a Psychiatric Standpoint," *Urologic and Cutaneous Review* 33 (1929): 528. On the use of *cruising* by nineteenth-century prostitutes, see Amy Stanley, "The Prostitute as Criminal," paper presented at the Eighth Berkshire Conference on Women's History, Douglass College, Rutgers University, June 7–10, 1990.

51. Donald Vining, *How Can You Come Out If You've Never Been In?* (Trumansburg, N.Y.: Crossing Press, 1986), 55. See also Dennis Altman, *The Homosexualization of America, the Americanization of the Homosexual* (St. Martin's, 1982), 150–52.

52. Roger Emmet, interviewed.

53. Harold Beaver, "Homosexual Signs (In Memory of Roland Barthes)," *Critical Inquiry* 8 (1981): 104.

54. Numerous such articles appear in Carl Van Vechten's scrapbooks, Yale; Will Finch's diary, KIL; the scrapbook of an unidentified lesbian New Yorker, KIL; and the scrapbook marked "Odd, Strange and Curious," Alexander Gumby papers, Columbia University Library. A fascinating medical article published in 1941 explained to doctors how to decode newspaper articles about gay murders: F. A. McHenry, "A Note on Homosexuality, Crime and the Newspapers," *Journal of Criminal Psychopathology* 2 (1941): 533–48.

55. Paul Nacke, "Der homosexuelle Markt in New-York," *Archiv für Kriminal-Anthropologie und Kriminalistik* 22 (1906): 277, as quoted in Jonathan Katz, *Gay American History* (New York: Crowell, 1976), 48; *Broadway Brevities,* Aug. 1, 1932, 4.

56. Donald Vining, interviewed.

57. Joel Honig, interviewed.

58. Interviews with Dorr Legg and Joel Honig; "An Evening with Beatrice Lillie," reviewed by John Mason Brown, *Saturday Review* (n.d. [1952?]); article on Lillie by T. B. F., *Town and Country,* December 1952 ("And, inevitably, the fairies at the bottom of her garden are once more revisited. They are, she admits, '. . . growing elderly but people simply adore them. They always ask for them.'"), both in Lillie clipping file, Billie Rose Theater Collection, Lincoln Center, NYPL. See also Berube, *Coming Out Under Fire,* 115–16.

59. Finch diary, Oct. 22, 1946; for an earlier use of the phrase in a homosexual context, see *Broadway Brevities,* Aug. 1, 1932, 4. Legman identified "letting down one's hair" as a common expression in both homosexual and general slang (although without explaining why it had become a homosexual expression), and posited that its use in common American slang to mean dropping all pretenses had originated in its homosexual usage ("The Language of Homosexuality," 1168).

60. Donald Vining, *A Gay Diary* (4 vols.; New York: Pepys Press, 1979–83), 1:374–75 (entry for Jan. 30, 1945). See also 1:368 (entry for Dec. 31, 1944).

61. Kahn, *Mentality and Homosexuality,* 184.

62. Esther Newton, *Mother Camp: Female Impersonators in America* (Englewood Cliffs, N.J.: Prentice-Hall, 1972).

63. Richard Dyer describes "camp" as "a characteristically gay way of handling the values, images and products of the dominant culture through irony, exaggeration, trivialisation, theatricalisation and an ambivalent making fun of and out of the serious and respectable" (*Heavenly Bodies: Film Stars and Society* [New York: St. Martin's, 1986], 178); I have also been helped in thinking about camp by Newton, *Mother Camp;* Jack Babuscio, "Camp and the Gay Sensibility," in *Gays and Film,* ed. Richard Dyer (London: British Film Institute, 1977), 40–57; Jeffrey Escoffier, "Sexual Revolution and the Politics of Gay Identity," *Socialist Review* 82/83 (1985): 140–41; Allan Berube, *Coming Out Under Fire* (New York: Free Press, 1990), 86–91; Altman, *Homosexualization,* 152–55; and Susan Sontag, "Notes on Camp" (1964), reprinted in *A Susan Sontag Reader* (New York: Farrar, Straus & Giroux, 1982), 105–19.

64. This analysis of gay men's use of kinship idiom is based on my reading of sources from the early twentieth century, including gay novels and studies of homosexuals in which they are quoted, as well as my interviews with numerous older gay men, who either specifically addressed the use of such terms or unselfconsciously used them in the course of conversation. For a few examples of the uses of the terms, see Ralph Werther, *The Female-Impersonators* (New York: Medico-Legal Journal, 1918), 13, 158; Kahn, *Mentality and Homosexuality,* 148–51; Henry, *Sex Variants,* 214, 255, 268, 477. For an insightful study by an anthropologist of the construction of lesbian and gay kinship today, see Kath Weston, *Families We Choose: Lesbians, Gays, Kinship* (New York: Columbia University Press, 1991).

65. Werther, *The Female-Impersonators,* 183.

66. See *Report and Proceedings of the [Lexow] Senate Committee appointed to investigate the Police Department of the City of New York* (Albany: J. B. Lyon, 1895), for example, testimony on 3118–26, 4577–81, and Timothy J. Gilfoyle, *City of Eros: New York City, Prostitution, and the Commercialization of Sex, 1790–1920* (New York: Norton, 1992), 232–36.

67. See, for example, the description of the Sappokanican's Thanksgiving Masque in a neighborhood newspaper, the *Greenwich Village American,* Dec. 1, 1913, 1. "While the 'Duchess of Houston Street' was romping joyfully around in the full capacity of her royalistic nibs," the reporter related in a style indicative of the levity with which he regarded the whole proceeding, "something broke, and Charles Heckworth couldn't retain the jolly disguise any longer." See also Alvin Harlow, *Old Bowery Days* (New York: D. Appleton, 1931), 434–36, and Lloyd Morris, *Incredible New York: High Life and Low Life of the Last Hundred Years* (New York: Random House, 1951), 17–19, 29–30, 239–42.

68. Elsa G. Herzfeld, *Family Monographs: The History of Twenty-four Families Living in the Middle West Side of New York City* (New York: Kempster, 1905), 18; Frank Moss, *The American Metropolis* (New York: Collier, 1897), 171–77.

69. "2,500 Revelers Do It Up Brown at Village Ball: All Teachings of Anthropology Count for Naught at Interracial Hoopla," *New York Herald Tribune,* Jan. 28, 1934, 12.

70. Colin A. Scott, "Sex and Art," *American Journal of Psychology* 7 (1896): 216. For Charles Torrence Nesbitt's account of the ball he witnessed in 1890, see chapter 1.

71. *Broadway Brevities,* Oct. 5, 1931, 1; Hans Friedrich, interviewed; Edward B. Marks (as told to A. J. Liebling), *They All Sang* (New York: Viking, 1935), as quoted in Anthony Slide, *Great Pretenders* (Lombard, Ill.: Wallace-Homestead,

1986), 31. The Little Beethoven Hall was probably the hall opened on East Sixth Street in 1889, near the original Beethoven Hall built on East Fifth Street by the Beethoven Männerchor in 1870; see Harlow, *Old Bowery Days,* 370.

72. William Dean Howells, *Through the Eye of the Needle* (New York, 1907), 308, as quoted in William Leach, *Land of Desire: Merchants, Power, and the Rise of a New American Culture* (New York: Pantheon, 1993), 331 (Leach provides an excellent account of the ragamuffin parade, which was the inspiration for the Macy's Thanksgiving Day parade, 331–32); *Give Us Each Day: The Diary of Alice Dunbar-Nelson,* ed. Gloria T. Hull (New York: Norton, 1984), 279: entry for Nov. 29, 1928. On the Thanksgiving drag ball, see Kahn, *Mentality and Homosexuality,* 126–27, 184, and my interview with Dick Addison, who mentioned the ragamuffin connection.

73. *Broadway Brevities,* Oct. 5, 1931, 1; Oct. 12, 1931, 5; Nov. 16, 1931, 2.

74. La Forest Potter, M.D., *Strange Loves: A Study in Sexual Abnormalities* (New York: National Library Press, 1933), 188.

75. Penal Law, Chap. 41, Article 68, Sections 710–11, as cited in *Cahill's Consolidated Laws of New York: Being the Consolidated Laws of 1909, as amended to July 1, 1923,* ed. James C. Cahill (Chicago: Callaghan, 1923), 1415; on the law's origins, see *Newsletter of the Mattachine Society of New York,* January–February 1967, 5–7; David Maldwyn Ellis, *Landlords and Farmers in the Hudson-Mohawk Region, 1790–1850* (Ithaca, N.Y.: Cornell University Press, 1946), 271–72; Henry Christman, *Tin Horns and Calico: A Decisive Episode in the Emergence of Democracy* (New York: Henry Holt, 1945), 132. I thank Reeve Huston for informing me of the Ellis and Christman studies.

76. Jack Mirell, interviewed; Dick Addison, interviewed; *Broadway Brevities,* Oct. 5, 1931, 1, 10; *Gloria Bar & Grill, Inc., v. Bruckman, et al.,* 259 A.D. 706 (1st Dep't 1940), testimony of Walter R. Van Wagner, contained in Record on Review, 233–34, 189. One gay man told a researcher that after being arrested along with twenty other men at such an affair in the early 1930s, he had been careful to attend only "those [drags] which have a permit" (Daniel O'L., quoted in Henry, *Sex Variants,* 433).

77. Dick Addison, interviewed; Sebastian Risicato, interviewed.

78. *Broadway Brevities,* Oct. 12, 1931, 5; Dick Addison, interviewed; Howard Raymond, interviewed; Andre Tellier, *Twilight Men* (New York: Greenberg, 1931), 205; Potter, *Strange Loves,* 185–86.

79. Rudolph Von H., quoted in Henry, *Sex Variants,* 495–96. "Most of the [other] boys were twenty," he added, so "it flattered me. In women's apparel I have 'it.'" "It," of course, was the term for sex appeal popularized by the Clara Bow movies of the twenties.

80. Report on "The Bal Primitive" by Bobby Edwards and "Bobby" Brown, Webster Hall, Oct. 12, 1917, box 33, COF.

81. "'Boys' Powder Puff Missing—Dismissed," *Variety,* Dec. 4, 1929, 47 (I thank Ron Gregg for this reference).

82. "Ballet Dancer Wore a Dress—But She's a He, And She Can Prove It!," *Variety,* Feb. 23, 1931, 46; "Wore Dress; Workhouse," ibid., Mar. 11, 1931, 52. In 1930 a thirty-four-year-old food checker caused a sensation when he showed up at a Harlem restaurant in a "crimson evening gown with long gloves, wig, and pumps." The other customers began jeering at him, and he only increased their wrath by shouting that his purse had been stolen. When the customers started throwing cups, dishes, and cutlery at him, he threw a sugar bowl at them before fleeing to the street ("Girlie Beaned by Badly Fired Bowl of Impersonator's," ibid., Apr. 16, 1930, 65). For an excellent analysis of a similar dynamic among young

African-Americans in the Jim Crow South, see Robin Kelley, "'We Are Not What We Seem': Rethinking Black Working-Class Opposition in the Jim Crow South," *Journal of American History* 80 (June 1993): 75–112.

83. George Henry, commenting on Daniel O'L., *Sex Variants,* 425.

84. Tellier, *Twilight Men,* 204–5; Robert Scully, *A Scarlet Pansy* (New York: Nesor, 1932), 245ff; Max Ewing, *Going Somewhere* (New York: Knopf, 1933), 100; Meeker, *Better Angel,* 183–84; Charles Henri Ford and Parker Tyler, *The Young and Evil* (Paris: Obelisk Press, 1933), 151–55, 166–67; Lew Levenson, *Butterfly Man* (New York: Macaulay, 1934), 196–204.

85. Howard Raymond, interviewed.

86. On the role of ethnic parades and festivals in constructing a sense of collective ethnic identity, see, for instance, Kathleen Neils Conzen's "Ethnicity as Festive Culture: Nineteenth-Century German America on Parade," in *The Invention of Ethnicity,* 44–76.

87. Potter, *Strange Loves,* 190–91; *Broadway Brevities,* Mar. 14, 1932, 12; Carl Van Vechten, as quoted in Bruce Kellner, *Carl Van Vechten and the Irreverent Decades* (Norman: University of Oklahoma Press, 1968), 201; Rudolph Von H., quoted in Henry, *Sex Variants,* 495–96.

88. Gene S., quoted in Henry, *Sex Variants,* 255.

89. For a thoughtful analysis of the response of nontransvestite homosexuals to female impersonators, see Newton, *Mother Camp,* a pioneering anthropological study based on the author's fieldwork in the Midwest in the late 1960s. Although Newton studied professional stage impersonators rather than participants in drag balls, her insights have confirmed and help me develop my own interpretation of the drag balls.

CHAPTER 11. "PANSIES ON PARADE": PROHIBITION AND THE SPECTACLE OF THE PANSY

1. On the emergence of Times Square as the city's preeminent entertainment center and symbol in the 1920s, see the essay collection *Inventing Times Square: Commerce and Culture at the Crossroads of the World,* ed. William R. Taylor (New York: Russell Sage, 1991).

2. Interviews with Max Adams, Harry Hay, and Martin Goodkin. See also Samuel Kahn, *Mentality and Homosexuality* (Boston: Meador, 1937), who commented that the gay men he interviewed in prison in the 1920s tended to work as "cooks, waiters, hotel bellboys, sailors, hospital orderlies, laundry employees, elevator operators, male and female impersonators, and stage workers in other capacities"—that is, in the restaurant, hotel, and theater industries (at 55; see also 53, 182); Irving Drutman, *Good Company: A Memoir, Mostly Theatrical* (Boston: Little, Brown, 1976), 51–53; and Esther Newton, *Cherry Grove, Fire Island: Sixty Years in America's First Gay and Lesbian Town* (Boston: Beacon, 1993), 21.

3. Harold E. Stearns, *The Street I Know* (New York: Lee Fuerman, 1935), 92.

4. Theodore Kingsbury to the Honorable C. T. Crain, June 30, 1914, letter enclosed in the Manhattan District Attorney's file concerning *People v. Mylott,* DAP 100,270 (CGS 1914).

5. "New York's Rich Negroes," *Sun,* Jan. 18, 1903, as quoted in Jervis Anderson, *This Was Harlem: A Cultural Portrait, 1900–1950* (New York: Farrar, Straus & Giroux, 1982), 30.

6. For general accounts of the culture of lodging and furnished-room houses and the character of the districts in which they predominated, see chapter 6 of this book; Albert Benedict Wolfe, *The Lodging House Problem in Boston* (Boston and

New York: Houghton Mifflin, 1906); Harvey Warren Zorbaugh, *The Gold Coast and the Slum: A Sociological Study of Chicago's Near North Side* (Chicago: University of Chicago Press, 1929), 69–86; Mark Peel, "In the Margins: Lodgers and Boarders in Boston, 1860–1900," *Journal of American History* 72 (1986): 813–34; and Joanne J. Meyerowitz, "Sexual Geography and Gender Economy: The Furnished Room Districts of Chicago, 1890–1930," in *Gender and American History Since 1890,* ed. Barbara Melosh (New York: Routledge, 1993), 43–71; Meyerowitz, *Women Adrift: Independent Wage Earners in Chicago, 1880–1930* (Chicago: University of Chicago Press, 1988).

7. *St. EOM in the Land of Pasaquan: The Life and Times and Art of Eddie Owens Martin,* ed. Tom Patterson (East Haven, Conn.: Jargon Society, 1987), 147.

8. James Ford, *Slums and Housing: With Special Reference to New York City: History, Conditions, Policy* (Cambridge, Mass.: Harvard University Press, 1936), 341–44; Robert A. M. Stern, Gregory Gilmartin, and John Montague Massengale, *New York 1900: Metropolitan Architecture and Urbanism, 1890–1915* (New York: Rizzoli, 1983), 275–78; Charles Lockwood, *Bricks and Brownstone: The New York Row House, 1783–1929* (New York: Abbeville, 1972).

9. Stern et al., *New York 1900,* 275–78. On the conversion of upper-middle-class brownstones into middle- and lower-middle-class rooming and lodging houses, see Ford, *Slums and Housing,* 341–42; Lockwood, *Bricks and Brownstone.*

10. Helen Worden, *The Real New York: A Guide* (Indianapolis: Bobbs-Merrill, 1932), 289. The blocks in this district bounded by Fifth and Sixth Avenues between Forty-eighth and Fifty-first Streets were destroyed by the construction of Rockefeller Center in the 1930s, an omen of things to come.

11. Max Eastman, *Love and Revolution: My Journey Through an Epoch* (New York: Random House, 1964), 252.

12. George Chappell, *The Restaurants of New York* (New York: Greenberg, 1925), 24, 126–29.

13. Daniel O'L., for instance, reported that he and a gay friend took a room in a theatrical boardinghouse when they moved to New York from Boston around 1931, in George W. Henry, *Sex Variants* (New York: Paul B. Hoeber, 1941), 431–32. C. A. Tripp, who observed New York's gay scene in the 1930s, has written that "in New York during the depression of the early 1930's, young homosexuals (especially those aspiring to the theater) often lived in groups, saving rent by sharing a single large apartment" (*The Homosexual Matrix* [New York: McGraw-Hill, 1975], 184–85). See also my interview with Donald Vining; *The WPA Guide to New York City* (New York: Random House, 1939), 170, 179.

14. Remarkably little has been written about the theater district as a residential district, but two pieces of evidence generated by police actions indicate its residential significance. The three chorus girls arrested when the police raided a burlesque show at the Gaiety Theater in 1935 all lived in hotels and rooms in the upper West Forties between Sixth and Eighth Avenues ("Burlesque Dancers Held," *New York Times,* Apr. 5, 1935). Similarly, all of the men arrested for homosexual solicitation by plainclothes members of the vice squad who were investigating a Forty-second Street bar in 1938 lived in the area or made use of its transient hotels. Several of them invited the plainclothesmen home to their apartments or furnished rooms in the West Forties and Fifties between Seventh and Ninth Avenues. Others, whose homes were more distant or unavailable for homosexual trysts, or who had no homes in the city at all, hired rooms in the area for prices ranging from 60 cents to $2 at the Hotel Fulton on West Forty-sixth Street between Seventh and Eighth

Avenues, another hotel on Eighth Avenue and Fortieth Street, and a rooming house on Eighth at Forty-fourth Street. See *Times Square Garden & Grill, Inc., v. Bruckman, et al.,* N. Kirschenbaum report to the SLA, Nov. 30, 1938, contained in Record on Review, 24–28; Memo, Commanding Officer, 3rd Division [vice squad], to Police Commissioner, "Recommending revokation [sic] of ABC license issued to Times Square Garden & Grill, 259 West 42 St.," Dec. 13, 1938, ibid., 31–37; Memo, Commanding Officer, 18th Precinct, to Police Commissioner, "Arrests in premises licensed by the New York State Liquor Authority," Dec. 5, 1938, ibid., 38–39.

15. Chappell, *Restaurants of New York,* 92–93, 128; *Broadway Brevities,* Sept. 14, 1931.

16. Leonard R., quoted in Henry, *Sex Variants,* 1941), 458; Leo, interviewed.

17. See, for example, *Broadway Brevities,* June 27, 1932, 12.

18. On Times Square in the 1920s, see Jack Poggi, *Theater in America: The Impact of Economic Forces, 1870–1967* (Ithaca, N.Y.: Cornell University Press, 1968); Drutman, *Good Company,* 1–74; Lewis A. Erenberg, "From New York to Middletown: Repeal and the Legitimization of Nightlife in the Great Depression," *American Quarterly* 38 (1986): 761–78; idem, "Impresarios of Broadway Nightlife," in *Inventing Times Square,* 158–77; Brooks McNamara, "The Entertainment District at the End of the 1930s," in ibid., 178–82; Herbert Asbury, *The Great Illusion: An Informal History of Prohibition* (Garden City, N.Y.: Doubleday, 1950), 192–96; Margaret Mary Knapp, "A Historical Study of the Legitimate Playhouses on West Forty-second Street Between Seventh and Eighth Avenues in New York City" (Ph.D. diss., City University of New York, 1982).

19. Asbury, *Prohibition,* 193, 197.

20. "'Round the Square," *Variety,* Feb. 18, 1931, 53.

21. Bulletin 2023 [c. Oct. 31, 1930]; bulletin 2030 [c. Jan. 27, 1931], box 89, COF. The Committee terminated its operations in May or June 1932: bulletin 2046 [May 1932], ibid. The Committee's desperate appeals for funds to John D. Rockefeller, long a major financial backer for moral-reform efforts, are documented in the records of the Bureau of Social Hygiene. Rockefeller's advisers counseled against continuing to fund the Committee, because they no longer trusted its claims and believed it had lost public support. See file memorandum, "Meeting Held by the Committee of Fourteen, Jan. 12," Jan. 12, 1932, and L. B. Dunman memoranda to Colonel Woods, May 27, June 2, 1932, box 16, folder 269, BSH, Series 3:4.

22. George Walsh, *Gentleman Jimmy Walker: Mayor of the Jazz Age* (New York: Praeger, 1974).

23. Bulletin 1975 [Jan. 21, 1928?], box 89, COF.

24. Lewis A. Erenberg, *Steppin' Out: New York Nightlife and the Transformation of American Culture, 1890–1930* (Chicago: University of Chicago Press, 1981).

25. My analysis of the nightclubs is much indebted to Erenberg, "Impresarios of Broadway Nightlife," although he does not treat the issues of public–private distinctions or the development of gay acts in clubs. See also Asbury, *Prohibition,* 193, 197; Erenberg, *Steppin' Out.* In one article *Variety* warned that the heterosocial freedom of the speakeasies threatened the business of licensed nightclubs ("Class Speaks Where Sexes Meet to Drink and Dine [are] Killing Off Club Life," Mar. 25, 1931).

26. *Broadway Brevities,* December 1924, 33.

27. Charles G. Shaw, *Nightlife:* Vanity Fair's *Intimate Guide to New York After Dark* (New York: John Day, 1931), 22. This was also the guide that noted

that "a touch of lavender" made the Childs cafeteria in the district's Paramount Building particularly interesting (see chapter 6 of this book).

28. *Broadway Brevities,* Dec. 14, 1931, 2.

29. Chappell, *Restaurants of New York,* 119–20. For further analysis of the interest in African-American culture, see Erenberg, "Impresarios of Broadway Nightlife"; Anderson, *This Was Harlem;* David Levering Lewis, *When Harlem Was in Vogue* (New York: Knopf, 1981).

30. Langston Hughes, *The Big Sea: An Autobiography* (1940; New York: Thunder's Mouth Press, 1986), 273; *Broadway Brevities,* Oct. 5, 1931, 1.

31. *Broadway Brevities,* Mar. 14, 1932, 1, 12. For similar estimates of the size of the crowd at a different ball, see Report on Commercialized Amusement, Manhattan Casino, Feb. 24, 1928, box 36, COF (figure 5.1), and chapter 9 of this book. It is difficult to determine how many of those in attendance were dancers in drag and how many were spectators.

32. *Broadway Brevities,* Oct. 5, 1931, 1; Oct. 12, 1931, 5; Nov. 16, 1931, 2. The Madison Square Garden drag, held in mid-May, 1930, apparently drew most of its participants and 2,500 spectators from the Broadway show world. Given the expense of renting the Garden, it lost money. Its organizer was apparently Jack Mason, impresario of the Rubaiyat (discussed above) in the early 1930s and of Gloria's (discussed in chapter 12) in the late 1930s. *Variety* gave his name, but was not sure who he was. "Madison Sq. Garden's 'Drag' Financial Bust—Navy Sends Two S.P.'s," *Variety,* May 21, 1930, 41.

33. David Dressler, "Burlesque as a Cultural Phenomenon" (Ph.D. diss., New York University, 1937), 59, 77–80, 160–61, and passim; on female impersonation and representations of the fairy in burlesque, see also Irving Zeidman, *The American Burlesque Show* (New York: Hawthorn, 1967), 169, 201–5; Morton Minsky and Milt Machlin, *Minsky's Burlesque* (New York: Arbor House, 1988), 52, 90.

34. Robert C. Allen, *Horrible Prettiness: Burlesque and American Culture* (Chapel Hill: University of North Carolina Press, 1991), 245. Percy Hammond's review of *The Ritz Revue* appeared in the *Tribune,* Sept. 18, 1924. The newspaper reviews of the annual *Artists and Models* show organized by the Shuberts are less explicit, but one in the *Post,* Oct. 16, 1924, claimed that one scene involved a male comedian whose "suggestive lines, . . . actions and gestures" were so "objectionable" as to deserve elimination from the production. A letter published in the generally more explicit *Broadway Brevities,* December 1924, 31, was more explicit. It noted "the queer doings in such reviews as 'The Ritz Review [*sic*],' 'Artists and Models,' also in the play 'Ashes,'" and asked why the public enjoyed them. Richard von Krafft-Ebing, one of the era's most famous sexologists, was best known for his monumental study of "perversion," *Psychopathia Sexualis* (1886).

35. "Cabaret Reviews: Everglades," *Variety,* Feb. 17, 1926, 49.

36. George Jean Nathan, "Theater," *American Mercury,* March 1927, 373, as quoted in Kaier Curtin, *"We Can Always Call Them Bulgarians": The Emergence of Lesbians and Gay Men on the American Stage* (Boston: Alyson, 1987), 62.

37. *Variety,* Oct. 6, 1926, 80.

38. All quotes from the play are from Mae West, *The Drag,* typescript, 1927, Manuscripts Division, Library of Congress.

39. George Eells and Stanley Musgrove, *Mae West: The Lies, The Legend, The Truth* (London: Robson Books, 1984), 64–68; Pamela Robertson, "'The Kinda Comedy That Imitates Me': Mae West's Identification with the Gay Male Camp," *Cinema Journal* 32 (1993): 57–72.

40. *Variety,* Feb. 2, 1927, 49.

41. I have not described the controversy over *The Captive* and *The Drag* at length because it has already received attention from several historians. My account of the controversy relies heavily on Curtin, *Bulgarians,* as well as my own reading of *Variety's* account of the controversy. See also Robertson, "'The Kinda Comedy That Imitates Me'"; Allen, *Horrible Prettiness,* 276–79; and June Sochen, *Mae West: She Who Laughs, Lasts* (Arlington Heights, Ill.: Harlan Davidson, 1992), 37–47.

42. *Variety,* Jan. 7, 1931; Sept. 24, 1930. Both were banner headlines on the front page.

43. *Broadway Brevities,* Nov. 16, 1931, 10.

44. Caroline F. Ware, *Greenwich Village, 1920–1930: A Comment on American Civilization in the Post-War Years* (New York: Houghton Mifflin, 1935), 253. Other Village clubs, such as Paul and Joe's and the Jungle, also featured such entertainment; see chapter 9 above.

45. Jack Kofoed in Jimmy Durante and Jack Kofoed, *Night Clubs* (New York: Knopf, 1931), 34; the Rubaiyat is also referred to as an "obscure" or "queer" "Greenwich Village dive" in the course of the articles about Gene Malin cited below.

46. The second columnist, unfortunately, is unidentified; a clipping of his undated column, published shortly after Malin's death in August 1933, appears in an unidentified New York lesbian's scrapbook, KIL. His account is substantially confirmed and elaborated by a profile of Malin in Sidney Skolsky's "Tintypes" column, *New York Daily News,* Apr. 2, 1931, and several other articles on Malin: *Broadway Brevities,* Oct. 5, 1931, 10; *New York Daily News,* Jan. 31, 1931; *Boston Daily Record,* Aug. 12 and 14, 1933; and an undated (1930) column by Mark Hellinger in the *New York Daily Mirror,* enclosed in an undated letter from Parker Tyler to Charles Henri Ford, 1930. These seven articles form the basis for most of the following account of Malin's career. I have quoted from them extensively in order to convey the tenor of the pansy craze, but have not cluttered the notes with repetitive citations to the articles for each quote.

47. On the cultural significance of such spatial arrangements generally, see Erenberg, *Steppin' Out,* ch. 4.

48. Mark Hellinger reported the story in his "People I've Met" column in the *Daily Mirror,* n.d. The column was sent by Parker Tyler to Charles Henri Ford along with an undated letter written sometime in 1930. Tyler drew Ford's attention to the story of the fight and signaled his excitement about it by putting two exclamation marks next to it. Tyler's several references to Malin in his letters to Ford give some indication of the interest Malin generated among gay men, and suggest that he had Malin's willingness to be openly gay in mind as he and Ford planned their gay novel, *The Young and Evil.* "i mean the moral victory of behaving like that without making money out of it like jean malin is just too luxurious like a fur coat," Tyler wrote Ford, c. Feb. 22, 1931, at the height of Malin's fame. See also Tyler's letters of Oct. 5, 1930; February 1931 (which mentions *Vanity Fair's* drawing of Malin [figure 11.2]); and c. Mar. 28, 1931 (which includes a newspaper clipping announcing Malin's appearance at the Argonaut, 151 W. 54th St.; it promised he would offer "sophisticated entertainment").

49. "'Pansy' Places on Broadway," *Variety,* Sept. 10, 1930, 1.

50. "Barney's New York," review, *Variety,* Nov. 5, 1930, 65.

51. *Broadway Brevities,* Oct. 5, 1931, 10.

52. *Variety,* Dec. 17, 1930, 57; Dec. 31, 1930, 31.

53. *Variety,* Dec. 17, 1930, 57. *Variety's* headline conveyed its assessment of the situation: "'Pansy Club' Now . . . Racket Getting Bolder."

54. Report on the Coffee Cliff, 45th Street, just east of B'way, 1:15–2:55 A.M., Dec. 2, 1930, box 35, COF. Polly Adler's memoir concerning her life as a madam was published as *A House Is Not a Home* (New York: Rinehart, 1953).

55. "The Dying Nite Clubs," *Variety*, Dec. 31, 1930. Note that *gay* here does not imply homosexual.

56. "'Pansy' Stuff Slipping," ibid., 31.

57. "Hollywood Adds Two New Nightery Spots," *Variety*, Sept. 27, 1932, 58; "Coast Raid on Panze Joints," ibid., Oct. 4, 1932, 52; "Hollywood Goes Beer Quaffing, A La Singing, Hirsuted Waiters," ibid., Nov. 21, 1933, 59.

58. "Transplanted," *Variety*, May 16, 1933, 57; "Rough Frisco Cops Send Pinched Boys to Women's Court," ibid., May 30, 1933, 1; "Rosenberg Minus Pansies, But Gets Beer Permit," ibid., June 6, 1933, 56.

59. "A.C. Clubs All Dark; Mayor Bans Pansies," *Variety*, Jan. 17, 1933, 55.

60. *Broadway Brevities*, July 4, 1932, 12.

61. *Brevities* is not listed in the *Union Serial Catalog*, the Library of Congress does not hold it, no American library appears to have a full run of it, and its history is obscure. I have assembled an extensive collection of issues and copies of issues from the 1930s by visiting used-book stores and several private and public collections in New York, Boston, and Bloomington, Indiana. I own two issues from 1924 and am grateful to Leonard Finger and Laurence Senelick for supplying me with a photocopy of the October 1924 issue from Mr. Finger's collection. My inability to locate more of the 1924 issues, however, means that I unfortunately have been able to see only three articles from the yearlong series on "Nights in Fairyland." The Kinsey Institute Library holds an extensive run of the paper; a note from the (unidentified) dealer who supplied it to them, apparently in the 1950s, claimed that it had been suppressed twice and suggested that it was most "risqué" in 1932–33. The exact relationship between the *Broadway Brevities and Society Gossip* published monthly in the 1920s (and possibly the teens) and the *Broadway Brevities* published weekly in 1931–35 (?) is unclear.

62. See also the cartoons reproduced in Jonathan Ned Katz, *Gay/Lesbian Almanac* (New York: Harper & Row, 1983), 486–87.

63. *Broadway Brevities*, Oct. 5, 1931, 1; Nov. 30, 1931, 1.

64. Ibid., December 1924, 36. This is only one example (although a telling one, I think) of the paper's accuracy, but the reader may be assured that I have come to regard *Brevities* as a generally reliable source only on the basis of a more comprehensive survey. As the footnotes throughout this study suggest, I have been able to verify a large number of *Brevities*' reports by reference to other sources. *Brevities* often described people and places that were described by the police or investigators working for the Committee of Fourteen as well, and to the extent possible I have checked each such reference against other sources. See, for example, my discussion of Louis' Restaurant, Gene Malin, and the drag balls in this and earlier chapters. *Brevities*' language and general style are befitting a tabloid and off-putting to a historian, but this should not be allowed to undermine its remarkable utility as a source.

65. See the discussion in chapter 9; for some examples of Scully's coverage of Village lesbian and gay clubs, see *Greenwich Village Weekly News*, Oct. 10, 1931, 8; ibid., Oct. 17, 1931, 1.

66. Thomas Painter mentions the column in "The Prostitute" (typescript, 1941, KIL), 183. Virtually no issues of the *Tattler* seem to have survived. The Harvey Ranson Library at the University of Texas, Austin, holds just three issues (October–December 1933), which may be the only ones extant. I thank Allen Drexel for reviewing them on my behalf.

67. *New York Evening-Graphic,* Aug. 25, 1931.

68. *Vanity Fair,* February 1931, 69.

69. All the articles mentioned here are discussed and cited elsewhere in this book. The amount of gay coverage in *Variety* declined sharply after 1931. I thank Chad Heap for surveying several years of *Variety* on my behalf.

70. For an account of the trial, see Jonathan Katz, *Gay American History* (New York: Morrow, 1977), 397–405.

71. Another gay novel set in New York, *The Young and Evil* by Charles Henri Ford and Parker Tyler (1933), was not published in the United States but in Paris. It was recently reprinted, with an introduction by Steven Watson (New York: Gay Presses of New York, 1988). An extended discussion of the novels is unfortunately beyond the scope of this study, but for an introduction see Roger Austen, *Playing the Game: The Homosexual Novel in America* (Indianapolis: Bobbs-Merrill, 1977), 57–92, and James Levin, *The Gay Novel: The Male Homosexual Image in America* (New York: Irvington, 1983), 29–82. Both books are useful guides to the novels (and Austen's study is truly groundbreaking), but they unfortunately provide little more than plot summaries. The novels deserve more study.

72. An immense amount of work still needs to be done to identify and analyze the large number of gay characters and images in early film, but excellent introductions are provided by Vito Russo's pioneering *The Celluloid Closet: Homosexuality in the Movies* (New York: Harper & Row, 1981); Richard Dyer, *Now You See It: Studies in Lesbian and Gay Film* (New York: Routledge, 1990); and Andrea Weiss, *Vampires and Violets: Lesbians in Film* (New York: Penguin, 1993).

73. For a good introduction to the gay semiotics of Bugs Bunny cartoons, see Hank Sartin, "Bugs Bunny: Queer as a Three-Dollar Bill," *Windy City Times,* June 24, 1993, sec. 2, 79.

74. Columnists occasionally commented on the presence of gay men in the social milieu of the gangsters. While their intention may have been to undermine the manliness of the gangsters in the minds of middle-class readers, their comments may well have had some basis in the presence of fairies in rough working-class male culture. After the crime-syndicate boss Dutch Schultz was wounded in a shootout at the Abbey, according to one paper, he "was harbored and nursed by a whole colony of nice boys, whose ministrations were more tender than those of the most tender female nurse." The paper added that "Schultz was all man, but he enjoyed surrounding himself with those whose masculinity was not so pronounced." ("Tragedy over Girl Impersonators," *Boston Daily Record,* Aug. 12, 1933.)

75. On postwar disillusionment, see Thomas C. Leonard, *Above the Battle: War-making in America from Appomattox to Versailles* (New York: Oxford University Press, 1978), and David Kennedy, *Over Here: The First World War and American Society* (New York: Oxford University Press, 1980).

76. *Vanity Fair,* February 1931, 86.

77. Eric Lott's study of nineteenth-century minstrelsy points to the mulitiple readings possible of such a performance: *Love and Theft: Blackface Minstrelsy and the American Working Class* (New York: Oxford University Press, 1993). See also David R. Roediger, *The Wages of Whiteness: Race and the Making of the American Working Class* (New York: Verso, 1991).

CHAPTER 12. THE EXCLUSION OF HOMOSEXUALITY FROM THE PUBLIC SPHERE IN THE 1930s

1. Jack Kofoed in Jimmy Durante and Jack Kofoed, *Night Clubs* (New York: Knopf, 1931), 34.

2. "Different Causes Are Given for Club Abbey Mix-up by Bad Men," *Variety,* Jan. 28, 1931, 63; *Boston Daily Record,* Aug. 12, 1933; unidentified Malin clipping in NYPL Malin file. It was a week after the shootout that Malin married a woman he had known since his days at the Greenwich Village haunt, the Rubaiyat (*New York Daily News,* Jan. 31, 1931).

3. "Clubs Raided," *New York Herald Tribune,* Jan. 29, 1931, 4; "Two Clubs Raided," ibid., Jan. 30, 1931, 36; "Different Causes Are Given for Club Abbey Mix-up by Bad Men," *Variety,* Jan. 28, 1931, 63; "1 A.M. Curfew Would Be Final Washup on B'way Clubs; 'Pansy' Stuff Dying," *Variety,* Feb. 4, 1931, 84; "Police O-Oing Unlicensed Niters," *Variety,* Feb. 11, 1931, 77. See also "Broadway Chatter," *Variety,* Feb. 4, 1931, 59. Among the other clubs visited by plainclothesmen checking on cabaret licenses was the Argonaut Club at 151 W. 54th St., where Texas Guinan was the hostess and a pansy act was briefly featured.

4. *Broadway Brevities,* Oct. 12, 1931, 5.

5. "17 'Odd Fellows' Wind Up Before Tough Judge," *Amsterdam News,* Mar. 5, 1938, 1. The ads quoted appeared in the *Amsterdam News,* Feb. 3, 1932, 6; Feb. 12, 1938, 17.

6. *Variety,* Feb. 4, 1931, 84.

7. Thomas Painter, "The Prostitute" (typescript, 1941, KIL), 183. On the 1931 crackdown, see American Social Hygiene Association, "Progress Report, Commercialized Prostitution Conditions in New York City, Aug. 2–Dec. 12, 1931," typescript, Dec. 15, 1931, 7, 11, BSH, box 7, folder 165, Series 3. As always, *Broadway Brevities* was more extreme in its account of the continuing presence of gay men in the area in the early 1930s. The front-page headline of its May 15, 1933, issue announced: "B'WAY QUEERS BRAZEN! THIRD SEX RAMPANT ON MAIN STEM."

8. George Walsh, *Gentleman Jimmy Walker: Mayor of the Jazz Age* (New York: Praeger, 1974), 260–61; Gerald Astor, *The New York Cops: An Informal History* (New York: Scribner's, 1971), 129–42; *Broadway Brevities,* Oct. 12, 1931, 5.

9. Lewis A. Erenberg, "From New York to Middletown: Repeal and the Legitimization of Nightlife in the Great Depression," *American Quarterly* 38 (1986): 761–78.

10. On the saloon, see chapter 1. On the concerns of the advocates of temperance and Prohibition, see James H. Timberlake, *Prohibition and the Progressive Movement, 1900–1920* (Cambridge, Mass.: Harvard University Press, 1963), especially 57–66, 111–19, 144–45. Tellingly, one of the most important organizations advocating prohibition called itself the Anti-Saloon League.

11. Roosevelt quoted in *Annual Report of the State Liquor Authority, 1960* (Albany: J. B. Lyon, 1961), 7; Raymond B. Fosdick and Albert L. Scott, *Toward Liquor Control* (New York: Harper & Brothers, 1933), 13–19, especially 15; Mark H. Moore and Dean R. Gerstein, eds., *Alcohol and Public Policy: Beyond the Shadow of Prohibition* (Washington, D.C.: National Academy Press, 1981), 61–66, 75.

12. For the history of the establishment of the SLA, see *Annual Report of the State Liquor Authority, 1933–34* (Albany: J. B. Lyon, 1935), 5–8; for a rationale and explanation of its revocation authority, see *Annual Report of the State Liquor Authority, 1937* (Albany: J. B. Lyon, 1938), 6.

13. In effect, such policing embodied the strategies of modern power Michel Foucault enunciated in his analysis of Bentham's Panopticon; see *Discipline and Punish: The Birth of the Prison* (New York: Pantheon, 1977), 195–228, especially 214.

14. Erenberg, "From New York to Middletown," 761–78.

15. Alcoholic Beverage Control Law, section 106, subdivision 6; *Annual Report of the State Liquor Authority, 1933–34,* 8–9 (outlining steps taken "to prevent the return of the saloon"); Leonard V. Harrison and Elizabeth Laine, *After Repeal: A Study of Liquor Control Administration* (New York: Harper & Brothers, 1936), 4–9, 42–95.

16. See, for example, *Salle de Champagne, Inc., v. O'Connell, et al.,* 259 A.D. 706 (1st Dep't 1951), Brief of Respondents Constituting the State Liquor Authority, 13, quoting *Shonfeld v. Shonfeld,* 260 N.Y. 477, 479.

17. On the SLA's need for the cooperation of the police, see its *1936 Annual Report,* 8; *1937 Annual Report,* 8–9; *1948 Annual Report,* 8–10.

18. Testimony of Walter R. Van Wagner, *Gloria Bar & Grill, Inc., v. Bruckman, et al.,* 259 A.D. 706 (1st Dep't 1940), contained in Record on Review, 211–13, 116. Wagner's account is confirmed by the testimony of numerous investigators, who reported on their undercover visits to bars at the hearings called to consider the revocation of the bars' licenses.

19. *Gloria Record on Review* (1940), testimony of William E. Wickes, SLA investigator.

20. Report of Investigation No. 9852, submitted Nov. 20, 1939, in *Gloria Record on Review* (1940), 65; and W. R. Van Wagner, testimony, ibid., 96, 238, 148, 158; Finch, "Homosexual Resorts in New York, as of May 1939," manuscript notes, Finch papers, KIL.

21. Notice from the State Liquor Authority to the licensee, dated Dec. 13, 1939, quoted in the [Gloria's] Brief in Support of Motion for Leave to Appeal to Court of Appeals, 2–3; [SLA's] Brief in Opposition to Motion for Leave to Appeal to the Court of Appeals, 4–5; and Wagner testimony, *Gloria Record on Review* (1940), 151, 174.

22. Brief for Petitioner, 8–20, *Gloria Record on Review* (1940), quotes at 16.

23. "[T]o permit premises to become a resort of intemperate, lewd and dissolute characters is sufficient under a prosecution for maintaining a disorderly house or a nuisance," [SLA's] Brief in Opposition to Motion for Leave to Appeal to the Court of Appeals, 22, and passim.

24. *Gloria Record on Review* (1940), which unanimously confirmed the determination of the SLA, and 259 A.D. 813 (1st Dep't 1940), which denied leave to appeal to the Court of Appeals.

25. Testimony of Morris Horowitz, *Times Square Garden & Grill, Inc., v. Bruckman, et al.,* 256 A.D. 1062 (1st Dep't 1939), contained in Record on Review, 245. William I. Cohen, the attorney who represented the Times Square in its appeal of the revocation of its license, later told a longtime associate, George Goldberg, that the city "wanted, quote, to clean up the city before the tourists came in to the World's Fair" (Goldberg, interviewed), an observation also made in the Petitioner's Brief he drafted in the case.

26. Testimony of Morris Horowitz, *Times Square Record on Review* (1939), 246.

27. This history of the Times Square's interaction with the police is drawn from the testimony heard at the SLA hearing, the reports filed by police plainclothesmen and SLA investigators, and the briefs submitted by both sides, all included in *Times Square Record on Review* (1939).

28. Interviews with Frank McNamara and Jack Mirell.

29. The SLA did not always act so precipitously in the postwar period, it should be added; but, as the Fifth Avenue bar case shows, it was prepared to.

30. In January 1954, a split Court of Appeals upheld the ruling in a 4–3 vote,

explicitly affirming the Appellate Division's reasoning that the outstanding reputation of the premises and the absence of evidence that its manager had witnessed any indecent acts outweighed the minimal evidence produced of such acts: *Stanwood United v. O'Connell,* 283 A.D. 79 (1st Dep't 1954), 82; 306 N.Y. 749.

31. As chapter 7 explains, the state legislature had specified "frequent[ing] or loiter[ing] about any public place soliciting men for the purpose of committing a crime against nature or other lewdness" as a form of disorderly conduct in 1923 (P.L. 722, subdiv. 8).

32. *Mattachine Newsletter,* March 1964, 11. William Duffy recounted a (possibly apocryphal) case of entrapment originating in a bar in the first article of his nine-part series on the vice squad in the *New York Post,* May 19, 1958.

33. Newspaper reports, the recollections of gay bar patrons, the internal records of the SLA, and the records of several appellate reviews of SLA license rulings indicate how regularly entrapment was used to obtain evidence against gay bars. According to SLA records, plainclothesmen arrested men they met at the Pink Elephant (later called the Silver Rail), on Sixth Avenue at Forty-third Street, on Aug. 25, 1943; Apr. 28 and Sept. 2, 1944; May 17, 1945; Apr. 13, 1946; June 1 and 13, 1947; June 11 and Aug. 20, 1949; July 13, 1951; June 20, 1953; and Feb. 10, Mar. 14, and Mar. 28, 1954 (history card for premises licensed at 1123 Sixth Avenue, SLA Archive, New York Office). They also arrested four patrons at the Builders' Club in the course of three evenings in early February 1951; six men at McCann's Bar & Grill in November 1950; two men at Diamond Jim's on Forty-second Street in April 1953; and other men at the Fifth Avenue Bar on Broadway in February 1954; at the Big Dollar in July 1955 and again in November 1958; and at the Ekim Bar on Broadway at 103rd Street in September 1961 (Appellant's Brief to the Court of Appeals [in the *Lynch's* case], Sept. 14, 1951, 36; *Thomas Giovatto v. O'Connell,* 278 A. D. 371 [1st Dep't 1951]; *People v. Pleasant,* 23 Misc 2d 367; *Loubor Restaurant v. Rohan, et al.,* 10 A.D. 2d 627 [1st Dep't 1960], testimony of Det. Walter F. Ruger, 270, and Patrolman Harry Eginton, 286–88, contained in the Record on Review; testimony of Patrolman Vincent Leonardo, *Ekim Broadway Record on Review* [1961], 30–33).

34. In 1950, for instance, the police reported the arrests of several men at McCann's Bar on lower Third Avenue to its landlord, who then initiated dispossess proceedings based on those arrests. In this case, however, the bar resisted the landlord in municipal court, which ultimately ruled there was no evidence that the tenant, the licensee, had any knowledge of the criminal activity (that is, the solicitation), and refused to invalidate the lease (*Giovatto [McCann's] Record on Review* [1951], 12).

35. In addition to the examples previously cited, see, for example, the testimony of Agent Wickes (that half a dozen patrons used rouge and lipstick), 314, and Wagner (that the suspect was "very, very soft spoken and a bit effeminate in his actions"), 98, in *Gloria Record on Review* (1940); Patrolman George Roche (noting that customers wore pancake makeup and eye shadow), in *Stanwood United Record on Review* (1954), 33–35; Harry Watson, SLA, (citing customers with peroxided hair, high-pitched voices, and tight pants), 45–51; Jack Eisenberg ("they raised their arms and broke their wrists in gestures, the high pitched voices, effeminate terms"), *Fulton Bar & Grill v. State Liquor Authority,* 11 A.D. 2d 771 (2d Dep't 1960), contained in Record on Review, 40; and Patrolman Vincent Leonardo (noting that men called each other "Lois" and "Betty"), in *Ekim Broadway Record on Review* (1961), 30–33.

36. *Fulton Bar & Grill v. State Liquor Authority,* SLA Hearing Officer's

Report, Feb. 16, 1960, Exhibit "G" Annexed to Answer, Papers on Appeal from an Order, 67–74, at 68.

37. *Gilmer v. Hostetter,* 20 A.D. 2d 586, 587 (3rd Dep't 1963), and Respondent's Brief. The decision in this case may reflect the greater conservatism of the Third Department of the Appellate Division, which had jurisdiction in part of upstate New York, compared to the courts based in New York City. In determining that the simple presence of homosexuals in the bar violated the law (it used their campiness to prove their presence rather than to prove their disorderliness), it actually returned to pre-*Stanwood* standards. Although the decision was not technically binding on the courts hearing New York City cases, it was often cited by the SLA to support its position in those cases.

38. *Ptl. James O'Brien v. Leslie Barrett,* City Magistrates' Court of the City of New York, Borough of Manhattan, Dec. 12, 1956. I thank Frank Tashker, the Main Street's defense counsel, for supplying me with a copy of the stenographer's minutes of this trial.

39. *Stanwood United Record on Review,* direct examination of Capt. Elbert Harrison by Attorney Joseph G. Gubman, 72–73. In this case, of course, the tactic ultimately paid off. The Appellate Division cited this exchange in ruling that the SLA had not proved the presence of gay men at the bar (or at least the management's knowledge of their presence). The Liquor Authority hearing officer had not accepted the argument, however, and it rarely worked.

40. Testimony of Warren Meyer, *Loubor Record on Review* (1960), 172.

41. *Salle de Champagne Record on Review* (1951), testimony of Bernard Israel and comment by his lawyer, 79–80.

42. Frank Tashker, interviewed. Thus bars that served homosexuals claimed before the Liquor Authority that they did not, even when the evidence was manifestly the opposite. To cite but one example, a bartender at the Big Dollar Bar and Grill, which was closed in a 1959–60 crackdown and had been, by all accounts, heavily patronized by gay men, insisted at a hearing that his manager had instructed him not to serve "queers": "That is definitely out" (*Loubor Record on Review* [1960], testimony of Warren Meyer, 169). Martin Duberman mentioned visiting the Big Dollar in his diary on Dec. 20, 1957, reprinted in his article "Gay in the Fifties," *Salmagundi,* no. 58–59 (Fall 1982–Winter 1983), 72.

43. See, for example, *F&C Holding Co., v. State Liquor Authority,* 27 A.D. 2d 806 (1st Dep't 1967), testimony of William B., contained in Record on Review, 62.

44. Bulletin 2030, n.d. [c. Jan. 27, 1931], box 89, COF.

45. On the role of organized crime in running New York City's gay bars in the 1960s, see Martin Duberman, *Stonewall* (New York: Dutton, 1993).

46. J. C., personal communication.

47. As one man who frequented the Astor in the 1930s and 1940s recalled, it was his favorite bar "because it wasn't a gay bar. People didn't know you were gay. It was never raided." Martin Leonard, interviewed.

48. On this development in general, see Lewis Erenberg, "Impresarios of Broadway Nightlife," in *Inventing Times Square: Commerce and Culture at the Crossroads of the World,* ed. William R. Taylor (New York: Russell Sage, 1991).

49. On Tony's, see *WPA Guide to New York* (New York: Random House, 1939), 179; Will Finch, "Homosexual Resorts in New York, as of May 1939," KIL. On Spivy, see Irving Drutman, *Good Company: A Memoir, Mostly Theatrical* (Boston: Little, Brown, 1976), 208–11; James Gavin, *Intimate Nights: The Golden Age of the New York Cabaret* (New York: Grove Weidenfeld, 1991), 36–46; and my interview with Jerome Frederickson.

50. Ronald Heffner, interviewed. Years later, the former manager of the Knickerbocker recalled that "we had difficulty with them ["homosexual men, perverts"]" during his tenure in the late 1910s: *Times Square Record on Review* (1939), Edward T. Moriarty testimony, 182.

51. Leo, interviewed.

52. Nat Fowler, interviewed. Other accounts of the Astor were provided by Robert Mason, Wayne Hendricks, Frank McCarthy, and Willy W. in their interviews. The Astor was so famous in the gay world that upon the demolition of the hotel in 1966, a gay magazine published in Philadelphia ran a tribute to it: Paul Forbes, "Mrs. Astor's Bar," *Drum*, no. 20 (1966): 11–12. See also Allan Berube's account of the Astor during the war in *Coming Out Under Fire: The History of Gay Men and Women in World War Two* (New York: Free Press, 1990), 114–15.

53. Dore Legg, interviewed. Donald Vining, *How Can You Come Out If You've Never Been In?* (Trumansburg, N.Y.: Crossing Press, 1986), 57.

54. The employment of homosexuals and people who pretended to be homosexuals was prohibited by the Alcoholic Beverage Control Law, section 102, and Cabaret Regulations 5(a) and 18, as discussed in Edward J. McCabe, Deputy Commissioner in Charge of Licenses, NYPD, to Albert J. deDion, President, MSNY, Dec. 19, 1960, Dick Leitsch papers (in Leitsch's possession). The prohibition against gay people meeting or working in cabarets was ended only in 1971. See the testimony by Maxwell Grant (61–62) and Frank McDonagh (21–23) in *Salle de Champagne Record on Review* (1951); Paul Chevigny, *Gigs: Jazz and the Cabaret Laws in New York City* (New York: Routledge, 1991), 57–58; and "City Acts to Let Homosexuals Meet and Work in Cabarets," *New York Times,* Oct. 12, 1971. On New York clubs featuring female impersonators in the early 1930s and late 1940s, see Phil Black, "I Live in Two Worlds," *Our World*, October 1953, 12–15.

55. "Can't Call 'Em Pansies, And Take Your Thumb Away From Your Nose," *Variety,* Feb. 4, 1931, 47. The very need for an order is further evidence of the frequency with which such terms had been used before.

56. On the raids on the shows in other cities, see chapter 11. On the state laws, see Erenberg, "From New York to Middletown." They deserve more study.

57. See Vito Russo, *The Celluloid Closet: Homosexuality in the Movies* (New York: Harper & Row, 1981), 31; Robert Sklar, *Movie-Made America: A Cultural History of American Movies* (New York: Random House, 1975), 173–74; Leonard J. Leff and Jerold L. Simmons, *Dame in the Kimono: Hollywood, Censorship, and the Production Code from the 1920s to the 1960s* (New York: Grove Weidenfeld, 1990); and Francis G. Couvares, ed., *Hollywood, Censorship, and American Culture,* special issue of *American Quarterly* 44:4 (December 1992). Film historians are just beginning to examine the records of the Production Code Administration, whose papers were opened in the mid-1980s, with these questions in mind. One purpose of the national production code was to create a single, national censorship agency in place of the numerous state and local censorship bodies that Hollywood studios had found so difficult to deal with. No film historian has tried to study how those local censorship bodies defined, identified, and responded to "perversion" in film. Someone should.

58. The gender upheavals of the 1930s have been studied by a number of women's historians. See, for instance, Susan Ware, *Holding Their Own: American Women in the 1930s* (Boston: Twayne, 1982); Barbara Melosh, *Engendering Culture: Manhood and Womanhood in New Deal Public Art and Theater* (Washington, D.C.: Smithsonian, 1991); Mary Ryan, *Womanhood in America* (New York: Franklin Watts, 1979); Winifred Wandersee, *Women's Work and*

Family Values, 1920–1940 (Cambridge, Mass.: Harvard University Press, 1981); and Lois Scharf, *To Work and to Wed: Female Employment, Feminism, and the Great Depression* (Westport, Conn.: Greenwood, 1980). For contemporary studies of the effects of unemployment on men's status in their families, see Roger Angell, *The Family Encounters the Depression* (New York: Scribner's, 1936); Ruth Shonle Cavan and Katherine Howland Ranck, *The Family and the Depression* (Freeport, N.Y.: Books for Libraries Press, 1938); Mirra Komarovsky, *The Unemployed Man and His Family* (New York: Institute of Social Research, 1940); and E. Wright Bakke, *Citizens Without Work* (New Haven, Conn.: Yale University Press, 1940).

EPILOGUE. THE STRANGE CAREER OF THE CLOSET

1. *World-Telegram*, Oct. 28, 1933; Kaier Curtin, *"We Can Always Call Them Bulgarians": The Emergence of Lesbians and Gay Men on the American Stage* (Boston: Alyson, 1987), 154–89.

2. For an analysis of the use of connotative codes to signify homosexuality rather than denotative codes, see D. A. Miller, "Anal Rope," in *Inside/Out: Lesbian Theories, Gay Theories,* ed. Diana Fuss (New York: Routledge, 1991), 119–42. On the importance of historicizing such readings by interpreting film codes in relation to historically specific systems of codes, see Chon Noriega, "Something's Missing Here: Homosexuality and Film Reviews During the Production Code Era, 1934–1962," *Cinema Journal* 30:1 (1990): 20–41. For one example of such historically specific readings, see my paper on *The Band Wagon* (1953), "The Boys in the Bandwagon," presented at the Centennial Symposium on Canons in the Age of Mass Culture, University of Chicago, Feb. 10, 1992. On the Jack Benny show, see Margaret T. McFadden, "'America's Boyfriend Who Can't Get a Date': Gender, Race, and the Cultural Work of the Jack Benny Program, 1932–1946," *Journal of American History* 80 (1993): 113–34.

3. The following account of the panics is based on my article "The Postwar Sex Crime Panic," in *True Stories from the American Past,* ed. William Graebner (New York: McGraw-Hill, 1993), 160–78; Estelle Freedman, "'Uncontrolled Desires': The Response to the Sexual Psychopath, 1920–1960" [1987], in *Passion and Power: Sexuality in History,* ed. Kathy Peiss and Christina Simmons (Philadelphia: Temple University Press, 1989), 199–225; John D'Emilio, "The Homosexual Menace: The Politics of Sexuality in Cold War America," in ibid., 226–40; Gayle Rubin, "Thinking Sex: Notes for a Radical Theory of the Politics of Sexuality," in *Pleasure and Danger: Exploring Female Sexuality,* ed. Carole Vance (Boston: Routledge, 1984), 269–70; and Allan Berube, *Coming Out Under Fire: The History of Gay Men and Women in World War Two* (New York: Free Press, 1990).

4. Ralph H. Major, Jr., "New Moral Menace to Our Youth," *Coronet* 28 (September 1950): 104.

5. Arrest figures for New York taken from the annual reports of the New York City Magistrates' Court.

6. John D'Emilio, *Sexual Politics, Sexual Communities: The Making of a Homosexual Minority in the United States, 1940–1970* (Chicago: University of Chicago Press, 1983).

7. *Sex Variants* consists primarily of transcriptions of Henry's interviews with the lesbian and gay volunteers, introduced and then analyzed (in a remarkably unsophisticated manner) by Henry. While I have quoted the interviews throughout this study, I have generally disregarded Henry's comments and have not used the interviewees' statements when there was reason to doubt the veracity of their transcription. The historian is fortunate, however, that Henry was so confident of his professional authority that he made no effort to disguise his prejudices or to

rework those comments of his subjects that directly contradicted his characterizations of them.

8. Several historians have begun to analyze Henry's *Sex Variants* and the work of the Committee for the Study of Sex Variants. See, especially, Henry L. Minton, "Femininity in Men and Masculinity in Women: American Psychiatry and Psychology Portray Homosexuality in the 1930s," *Journal of Homosexuality* 13 (1986): 1–21, and Jennifer Terry, "Lesbians Under the Medical Gaze: Scientists Search for Remarkable Differences," *Journal of Sex Research* 27 (1990): 317–40. Both articles report the preliminary findings and analyses of larger studies still in progress, which promise to illuminate the cultural implications of the Committee's project. I will also discuss the Committee more extensively in my next book.

INDEX

Abyssinian Baptist Church, 254–256
A'Costa, Mercedes de, 287
Addams, Eve (Eva Kotchover), 240–241, 242–243, 323
Addison, Dick, 16–17, 21–22, 167–168
African-American culture, 10, 11, 105, 172, 328; and bachelor subculture, 76; bathhouse, 218; and color of clothing, 53; and Great Migration, 245, 246, 256; and male prostitutes, 72; middle class, 253–257, 260, 263–267; newspapers in, 7, 10, 254–263, 266; sexual classification in, 14; and sodomy laws, 140–141; wolf-punk relationships in, 91; working class, 248–257, 266–267; and World War I servicemen, 144. *See also* Harlem
Age: in wolf-punk relationships, 88–96. *See also* Inter-generational sex
AIDS, 9, 396n46
Alcoholic beverage control laws, 19–20, 57, 66, 336–348, 351, 356, 358–359. *See also* Prohibition
Alexander, Jeb, 101, 103, 104–105, 105
Alhambra, 294

Allen, Robert T., 311
Allen Street, 35
American Social Hygiene Association, 143, 147
Amsterdam News, 256, 258, 259, 261–263, 332, 333n
Anal penetration, 81, 84–85, 252, 286; browning, 286, 396n50. *See also* Inter-generational sex
Anderson, Margaret, 232
Anderson, Nels, 90–91
Androphobia, 122
Anglophilia, 106
Anti-gay policing, 21, 25–26, 249–250, 331–332, 337–349; and bathhouses, 146–147, 209, 210–217, 218, 221, 223, 323; during the Cold War, 8–9, 358, 360; during the Depression, 331–354, 355–358; and street harassment, 155, 158–159, 183, 184–187, 195–196; during World War II, 125n, 350–351. *See also* Legal restrictions; Police; Social-purity societies
Anti-prostitution campaign, 82, 130, 131–132, 134, 138–149, 159–163
Anti-Saloon League, 139, 143

Anti-Semitism, 75, 105, 328
Apartment hotels and houses, 158–159, 303
Apartment parties, 207, 278–280, 349
Ariston Baths, 134, 211–216, 217, 219, 222, 223, 323
Armory Hall, 37
Assignation hotels, 35, 42, 151, 159–163
Astor Hotel, 7, 294, 310
Astor Hotel bar, 201, 350–351, 361
Atlantic City, 321
Aunties, as term, 291
Automats, as gay meeting places, 164–166, 174, 193, 304, 328–329
Avenues. *See* Streets and avenues
Avi-ram, Amitai, 264, 265

Bachelor Apartments, 158
Bachelor subculture, 75, 76–86, 139; causes of, 76–78, 135–136; characteristics of, 78–80; ethic of male solidarity in, 79–80; fairies' place in, 79–86; and female prostitutes, 80–86; and male-female relationships, 80–86; manliness in, 79–81, 89, 112; and rise of gay subculture, 135–137. *See also* Housing
Baltimore Afro-American, 7, 10, 258
Bankhead, Tallulah, 310
Bara, Theda, 51
Barrel House, 193, 340, 357
Bars: hotel, 201, 350–351, 361; hustler, 192–193. *See also* Gay bars; Saloons; Speakeasies
Bathhouses, 134, 207–225, 357; Ariston Baths, 134, 211–216, 217, 219, 222, 223, 323; Claridge's, 210; Everard, 146, 216–217, 218, 220, 223, 323; gay, 206, 211–225; Jewish ritual bath (*mikvah*), 208–209; Lafayette Baths, 146, 206, 215, 216, 217, 220–223, 323; mixed, 207, 209–211, 219, 220; Mount Morris Baths, 218; Penn

Post Baths, 218; Produce Exchange Baths, 217, 221; public, 208–209; raids on, 146–147, 209, 210–217, 218, 221, 223, 323; Russian and Turkish baths, 208, 209–225; St. Marks, 218, 222; as sexual and social center, 219–223; Stauch's, 210–211
Battery Park, as cruising area, 89–90, 142, 162, 182, 196
Beaches, as cruising areas, 183–184
Beard, George, 135
Beardsley, Aubrey, 230
Beaver, Harold, 287
Belvedere Castle, Central Park, 182
Benny, Jack, 357
Benson, Susan Porter, 189
Bentley, Gladys, 251, 252–253
Berkman, Alexander, 88
Berle, Milton, 345
Berlin: gay subculture in, 12, 107, 144, 318, 377*n*21, 409*n*34. *See also* Germany
Berlin, Irving, 155
Berube, Allan, 9, 10, 144
Better Angel (Meeker), 284–285, 324
Big Dollar, 345
Billy's Hotel, 42, 132
Bisexuality, 13, 65, 96; bisexual, as term, 44, 49
Bitches' Walk, Central Park, 182, 204
Black, Phil, 297, 361
Black Cat, 322
Blacker the Berry, The (Thurman), 265
Black Rabbit, 34, 37, 241, 323
Blacks. *See* African-American culture
Bleached hair, 3
Bleecker Street, 34, 37, 155, 243
Bloomingdale's, 190
Blues, 250–251
Boardinghouses, 36, 76, 164, 202, 303–304
Bodybuilding, 114, 116, 121, 179
Bonds, Caska, 264–265, 266
Boston, 153, 277, 278, 320
Bourbon, Rae, 321

Bournet, Edouard, 311
Bow, Clara, 234
Bowery, 2, 4, 11, 33–45, 162, 187, 227; as center of commercialized vice, 34–37; dance halls, 33–34; fairy resorts, 33–34, 36–45, 47, 67–68, 138, 149, 162; as gay male enclave, 136; Hobohemia, 78, 91; Paresis Hall (Columbia Hall), 33, 34, 35, 42–44, 50, 55, 67–68, 69, 132, 141, 160, 322–323; as red-light district, 35, 36, 39, 40; saloons, 33–34, 54, 59; slumming and, 36–41, 44
Boyer, Paul, 137
Boys. *See* Children
Brandt, Allan, 143
Bray, Alan, 12
Breckinridge, Sophonisba, 75–76
Brennan, Jay, 310
Bricktop, 246
Brill, A. A., 123–124, 135
Broadway: as cruising area, 146; Tenderloin, 35, 36, 138, 179, 204, 216
Broadway Brevities, 167*n*, 223, 282, 288, 300, 449*n*61, 449*n*64; and pansy craze, 304, 310, 316, 317, 321–323, 328–329
Broadway Tattler, 323
Bronx Park, 181
Brooklyn, 137; Childs cafeterias in, 165, 169; dance halls in, 58; Frank's Place, 293, 295; Navy Yard, 143, 145, 161–162; Prospect Park, 68–69, 69, 181–182; St. George Hotel, 151, 162
Broom (magazine), 230
Brothels, 35, 68, 89, 190, 216; and anti-prostitution campaign, 139, 143; in Harlem, 247, 253. *See also* Prostitutes, female
Browning, 286, 396*n*50
Bruce, Kennilworth, 67, 324, 388–389*n*22
Bruce, Richard, 265

Bryant Park, 68, 165; as cruising area, 181, 183, 192, 194, 201, 333
Budd, Arthur ("Rose"), 318
Buffet flats, 250–251, 253
Bugs Bunny cartoons, 325
Bulldaggers (lesbians), 15; Harlem, 251–253, 279–280
Bungalow, The, 241–242
Bureau of Social Hygiene, 143
Burlesque houses, 147, 171, 190–195, 305, 311, 313
Burton, Frank, 279
Businessmen's bars, 350–351
Butler, Judith, 80
Buttercups, 125, 315–316
Butterfly Man (Levenson), 324

Cabarets, 352; and anti-prostitution campaign, 139; as gay meeting places, 170–173, 313
Cadmus, Paul, 54, 64, 78
Cafeterias, as gay meeting places, 136, 150, 164–170, 174, 193, 304, 305, 317–318, 328–329, 342–345, 349, 357
Call Her Savage (film), 234
Camp culture, 7–8, 290–291; and cafeteria society, 164–176, 193, 317–318, 328–329, 342–345, 357; and double entendre, 17–19, 286–290, 327, 357; and gay social world, 276–280. *See also* Pansy craze
Camp names, 40–41, 50–51, 56–57, 105, 251, 252, 266, 314, 315
Captive, The (play), 311–312, 313, 324, 325, 352, 356
Carby, Hazel, 253
Carpenter, Edward, 49, 107, 144, 231, 284, 285
Carpenter, Thelma, 349–350
Cartoons, 46, 178, 226, 322, 325, 328–329
Casal, Mary, 36, 47
Censorship, 8, 9, 311–313, 324–325,

Censorship *(continued)*
    352–353, 356, 357
Central Park, as cruising area,
    182–183, 189, 191, 196, 204, 275
Central Park West, as cruising area,
    146, 189
Cercle Hermaphroditis, 43
Chain migration, 271–273
Champion, Billy, 242
Chanler, Bob, 297–298
Chatham Square, 90, 162, 196, 198
Cheney, Russell, 104, 199
Chicago, 12, 144
Chicago Defender, 260
Chicanos, wolf-punk relationships
    among, 91
Children: ragamuffin parades,
    293–294; sex murders, 359–360;
    Society for the Prevention of Cruelty
    to Children, 138–139, 140–141. *See
    also* Inter-generational sex
Childs, William and Samuel, 164
Childs cafeterias, 164–167, 169, 174,
    176, 182, 183, 321
Chotzinoff, Samuel, 202
Circuses, 37
City Club, 160
City Hall Park, 196
City Vigilance League, 33, 141
Claridge's baths, 210
Clark, Bonnie, 263
Class. *See* Middle-class culture;
    Working-class culture
Classification. *See* Sexual terminology
Closet, metaphor of, 6–7, 358. *See also*
    Coming out
Clothing: color of, 52–53; of fairies,
    37, 40, 42, 44, 51–54, 68–69, 92,
    94–95; of queers, 3, 52, 54, 64, 105,
    106, 108, 187–188, 350–351; red
    ties, 3, 52, 54, 64. *See also*
    Transvestites
Club 181, 320*n,* 352
Club Abbey, 315, 316, 320, 324,
    327–328, 331, 334
Club Calais, 332

Club Richman, 352
Cocksuckers, as term, 85
Cock Suckers Hall (Sharon Hotel), 42
Coffee Cliff, 319–320
Cold War: anti-gay policing during,
    8–9, 358, 360; and censorship of
    inquiry into gay culture, 9
Color, of clothing, 52–53
Columbia Hall. *See* Paresis Hall
Columbus Circle Childs, 166, 176,
    182, 183, 321
Coming out, 8*n,* 168; concept of, 7,
    286; and drag balls, 7–8; and World
    War II, 10–12
Coming out flaming, 102
Committee for the Study of Sex
    Variants, 339*n,* 360
Committee of Fifteen, 134, 160; estab-
    lishment of, 131–132, 143
Committee of Fourteen, 138, 141,
    165*n,* 337; and bathhouses, 210;
    decline of, 346–347; establishment
    of, 132, 160; and Greenwich Village
    vice, 236, 240; in Harlem, 247, 248;
    and homosexual activity, 145–149,
    170–172, 176; and prostitution,
    130, 139, 141, 143, 160–162; and
    Times Square area, 306, 307
Comstock, Anthony, 37, 138, 146,
    230–231
Condoms, 85–86, 396*n*46
Coney Island, 35, 59, 68; bathhouses
    of, 210–211, 220; as cruising area,
    183; and male beauty contests, 184,
    324
Cory, Donald Webster, 188
Cott, Nancy, 118
Cotton Club, 247, 252, 321
Coward, Noël, 288, 357
Cowley, Malcolm, 229, 230, 231
Cruising, 18*n,* 142, 146, 180–184, 202;
    arrests for, 9; as term, 180, 286. *See
    also* Parks *and specific parks*
Cullen, Countee, 264, 265, 284
Cult of muscularity, 114, 116, 121,
    179

Curtin, Kaier, 313, 357
Cyrano Restaurant, 19

Daily Mirror, 94, 315, 316, 317
Daily News, 54, 315, 316
Dance halls: Bowery, 33–34; Brooklyn, 58; Lower East Side, 40–41, 43; same-sex dancing, 168–169, 173, 173*n*, 234, 248, 279–280, 295–296. *See also* Drag (transvestite) balls *and specific dance halls*
Daniels, Jimmie, 252, 266
Davis, Bette, 288
Degeneracy, 15, 170–173, 185–186, 213, 216, 337–346
Dell, Floyd, 231, 236
D'Emilio, John, 9, 10, 360
Demuth, Charles, 78, 206, 217, 232
Depression, 9, 11, 192, 359; anti-gay backlash during, 331–354, 355–358; Automats in, 164–166; and Times Square, 305, 306, 313
Design for Living (Coward), 357
Dickerman, Don, 233
Dill, Augustus Granville, 198
D'Orsay, 320
Double entendre, 17–19, 286–291, 327, 357
Double lives, 6–7, 24, 273–280; of fairies, 44, 50–51, 54, 58; and gay social world, 3*n*, 276–280; need for, 133–135; and work, 134–135, 274–276
Drag, The (play), 311, 312–313, 352, 356, 357
Drag (transvestite) balls, *xii*, 2, 4, 8, 25, 102, 130, 291–299, 301; and anti-gay backlash, 332–334; and coming out, 7–8; Hamilton Lodge Ball, 130, 227–228, 245, 252, 257–264, 266, 294, 295, 296, 332–333; Liberal Club, 235–237, 244–245, 292; Walhalla Hall, 40–41, 293; Webster Hall, 235–237, 293, 295–296
Drag queens, *xii*, 4, 51, 290, 330, 333.

See also Drag (transvestite) balls; Fairies; Female impersonators; Pansy craze
Draper, Muriel, 297
Du Bois, W. E. B., 139, 198, 264, 265
Du Bois, Yolanda, 265
Dunbar-Nelson, Alice, 293–294
Durante, Jimmy, 35, 59

Eastman, Max, 303
Edwards, Bobby, 240–242, 295–296
Effeminacy, 23, 102–106, 115–116, 125, 277; and gay bars, 339*n*, 344. *See also* Fairies
Elizabeth Street, 37, 68, 72–73
Ellis, Havelock, 104, 124, 283, 285
Employment. *See* Work
England, 12, 145, 188
Enrico's, 146
Erenberg, Lewis, 308, 337
Everard, James, 216
Everard baths, 146, 216–217, 218, 220, 223, 323
Everglades, 247, 310, 318, 320
Ewing, Max, 188, 258
Exhibition, and gay male bathhouses. *See also* Gay male subculture, spectacle of
Exhibitionism, and gay bathhouses, 212–213, 218
Eye contact, in cruising, 188–189

Faderman, Lillian, 9
Faggots Ball. *See* Hamilton Lodge Ball
Fags/faggots, 66–67, 274; flaming, 15–17, 18, 104, 106, 257; Harlem, 228, 253, 257–264; pride of, 6; in prisons, 6, 92–95; as term, 15–17, 18, 20, 101
Fairies, 32, 385*n*2; and bachelor sub-culture, 79–86; in Bowery resorts, 33–34, 36–45, 47, 68, 138, 149, 162; carriage, demeanor, and speech of, 54, 55–56, 187; clothing of, 37,

Fairies *(continued)*
40, 42, 44, 51–54, 68–69, 92,
94–95; compared with female prostitutes and tough girls, 50–51, 61,
80–86; as cultural type, 106; double
lives of, 44, 50–51, 54, 58; and gender inversion, 13, 15–16, 20–23,
47–63; "husbands" of, 86–96, 291;
identification of men as, 47–48,
102–103, 125–126, 282; and jockers, 88–96; and male beauty contests, 184, 324; and male prostitution, 66–76, 191, 192; as members
of third (intermediate) sex, 48, 49,
57, 121, 122–123, 125; middle-class
attitude toward, 44, 45, 51–59,
99–111, 115–116; as model of
female "inner nature" of men,
49–50, 55–57, 99–100, 104; and the
new journalism, 37–40, 41, 94–95;
as pejorative category, 115–116;
personal grooming of, 37, 40, 42,
50, 54–55, 58, 62, 64, 68–69, 92,
94–95; in prisons, 92–95; as pseudo-
women, 56–58, 60–61, 103; queers
versus, 100, 101–107; relationships
with "normal" men, 50, 61–62,
100, 122–123, 147–148; and sailors,
54, 64, 82–83, 143, 145; as term,
13–24, 27, 67, 101; violence
toward, 59–60; and wolves, 88–96;
and women's names, 40–41, 50–51,
56–57, 105, 251, 252, 266, 314,
315. *See also* Drag queens; Female
impersonators; Gay male subculture,
spectacle of; Pansy craze; Sexual terminology; Tactics, of gay men;
Transvestites
Fairy resorts, 115; Bowery, 33–34,
36–45, 47, 68, 138, 149, 162; in
Harlem, 250; Hotel Koenig,
170–173, 174, 176, 186, 356;
Lower East Side, 68, 138; Paresis
Hall (Columbia Hall), 33, 34, 35,
42–44, 50, 55, 68, 69, 132, 141,
160, 323

Fellation, 52, 71, 85, 95, 119, 390*n*48;
as perversion, 61, 85
Female impersonators, 47, 239, 250,
251–252, 256, 290. *See also* Drag
queens; Fairies; Pansy craze;
Transvestites
Fifth Avenue, as cruising area, 146,
166, 180*n*, 189
Fifth Avenue Bar, 342–343, 344–345
Films. *See* Movies
Finch, Will, 17, 18–19, 84*n*, 211, 338
Fishbein, Leslie, 230
Flaming faggots, 15–17, 18, 104, 106,
257
The Fleet's In (painting), 54, 64
Flint, Austin, 98
Flower Pot, The, 237
Ford, Charles Henri, 181, 191*n*
Forel, Auguste, 231, 285
Fort Valley Industrial School, 260,
264
Forty-second Street, 18*n*, 68, 97,
191–195, 306; Bryant Park, 68, 165,
181, 183, 192, 194, 201, 333; as
cruising area, 333; movie and bur-
lesque theaters, 194–195; Times
Square Building, 66, 70, 97, 120.
See also Times Square
Foucault, Michel, 27, 126
Fourteenth Street. *See* Rialto
(Fourteenth Street)
France, sexual mores of, 12, 144, 145,
148. *See also* Paris
Frank's Place, 293, 295
Free love, in Greenwich Village, 233,
234, 236
French Ball, 292
French Madam's, 216
Freud, Sigmund, 123–124
Fruited Plain, Central Park, 182,
204
Fullhouse Restaurant, 241
Fulton Bar, 344
Furnished-room districts, 136,
152–154, 229, 303

Gang rapes, 60, 84
Gangs: Italian, 76; sanctions on gay street behavior, 186–187
Garber, Eric, 247, 250, 252, 264
Garbo, Greta, 263, 287, 288
Garland, Judy, 288, 351, 361
Garvey, Marcus, 246
Gay, as term, 14–21, 24, 25, 286, 358
Gay bars, 11, 18, 275, 359; hustler bars, 192–193; legal restrictions on, 19–20, 25, 57, 337–349, 358–359; and lesbians, 344, 346, 347
Gay folklore, 280–286
Gay liberation movement, 2, 3, 20, 22, 360
Gay male subculture, 10, 17; advocacy groups of, 5, 360; bathhouses, 206, 211–225; components of, 2–3, 4–5; gay folklore in, 280–286; historical tradition, 283–286; history of, study of, 9–10, 27–28; and integration into mainstream culture, 3–4; and myth of isolation, 2–3, 47; relationship between dominant culture and, 25; strength of, 5–6; and urbanization process, 132–136; World War II impact on, 10–12, 144. See also Drag (transvestite) balls; Fags/faggots; Fairies; Pansy craze; Queers; Tactics, of gay men; Sexual terminology
Gay male subculture, spectacle of: and bathhouse raids, 212–215; at beaches, 183–184; cafeterias in, 166–170; and male acceptance of fairies, 80–81; and new journalism, 37–40, 41, 94–95; in raid on New York City Jail, 93–95. See also Drag (transvestite) balls; Pansy craze; Slumming; Transvestites
Gender inversion, 15, 27–28, 116; centrality to fairies, 13, 15–16, 20–23, 47–63; and concept of third (intermediate) sex, 48–49, 57, 71; homosexuality versus, 13, 22–23, 26–28, 48–49, 71, 124–126, 345–346; and lesbians, 27–28, 49, 124; medical

treatises on, 5–6, 48–49, 98, 121–126, 132, 135, 281–282. See also Fairies; Transvestites
Gerber, Henry, 144–145, 282
Germany: homosexual emancipation movement in, 107, 144, 145, 231; immigrants from, 53, 137. See also Berlin
Gerry, Eldridge, 138
Gershwin, Ira, 221, 221n
Gide, André, 107, 285
Gilfoyle, Timothy, 140
Gloria's, 337–339, 340, 342, 344
Goffman, Erving, 80
Going Somewhere (Ewing), 189
Gold, Mike, 35
Golden Rule Pleasure Club, 68
Goldie (Bruce), 67, 324, 388–389n22
Goldman, Emma, 231
Goodkin, Martin, 201, 223
Gordon, Linda, 138–139
Gordon, Taylor, 258
Gorn, Elliot, 114
Grant, Cary, 18
Grant's Tomb, 182
Great Depression. See Depression
Great Migration, 245, 246, 256
Green Bay Tree, The (Sharp), 357
Greenwich Village, 2, 4, 57, 142, 227, 228–244; cafeterias in, 166–170, 174, 183, 277; drag balls in, 235–237, 310, 317–318; and free love, 233, 234, 236; gay and lesbian personality clubs in, 237–244, 314; gay subculture in, 10, 20, 136, 226, 229–244, 302, 310, 325–327; housing in, 228, 229, 232–233; as lesbian enclave, 228, 229–230, 232, 234, 235, 237–242; newspapers, 242–243, 323; pansy craze in, 314–315; police crackdowns in, 238, 239–241; in Prohibition, 233–234, 310; restaurants in, 237–240, 241; slumming in, 233–234, 236, 314; speakeasies, 233, 237–238, 240, 241–242, 315,

Greenwich Village (continued)
338; tearooms in, 233, 237–238,
240; World War I and changes in,
232–235, 310
Greenwich Village: A Local Review,
242
Greenwich Village Quill, 240, 242
Greenwich Villager, 242
Greenwich Village Weekly News,
242–243, 323
Griffes, Charles Tomlinson, 107–110,
112, 118, 144, 162, 175, 217,
220–223, 224
Gross, Alfred, 21
Guinan, Texas, 308

Hall, Radclyffe, 324
Hamilton Lodge Ball, 130, 227–228,
245, 252, 257–264, 266, 294, 295,
296, 332–334
Happy Hour Bar & Grill, 70, 97
Harlem, xii, 2, 4, 15, 187, 227–228,
244–267; black migration to,
245–246; brothels, 247, 253, 254;
class and cultural divisions in, 198,
253–257, 263–267; clubs, 246–249,
252–253, 309–310, 318–319, 320,
321; as cruising area, 189; as gay
enclave, 15, 136, 244–245,
247–253, 279–280; Hamilton Lodge
Ball, 130, 227–228, 245, 252,
257–264, 266, 294, 295, 332–334;
and Harlem Renaissance, 227, 232,
246, 264–266, 284; housing in, 245,
247–248, 250–251, 253; as lesbian
enclave, 136, 247–248, 251–253,
279–280; Manhattan Casino
(Rockland Palace), 7, 259, 260, 270,
294; Mount Morris Baths, 218;
newspapers, 261–263; pansy craze
in, 309–310; slumming in, 246–247,
248, 310; speakeasies in, 56–57,
244, 246, 247, 248, 250; violence
toward fairies in, 59–60. See also
African-American culture

Harlem Renaissance, 227, 232, 246,
264–266, 284
Harlow, Jean, 263
Harris, James, 260
Hartley, Marsden, 232
Harvey, Terence, 185
Harwood, Gene, 271–272, 280
Haymarket, 216
Heap, Jane, 232
Hearst, David, 275
Hearst, William Randolph, 39, 312,
313
Hellinger, Mark, 315
Hell's Kitchen, 159, 191, 202, 203,
303–304, 333
He-men, 125
Henry, George, 278–279, 281, 339n,
360
Herald Square, 187, 189, 190
Hermaphrodites, 37, 49, 121, 123
Hermitage Hotel, 158
Heterodoxy, 231–232
Heterosexuality: concept of, absence of,
12–13, 100, 120, 125; emergence of,
in middle-class culture, 111–126;
homo-heterosexual binarism, 12–16,
20, 22, 26–27, 48, 71, 96–97, 100,
119–121, 124–126, 358, 359
Higham, John, 114–115
Hirschfeld, Magnus, 49, 107, 144, 190,
231
Historical imagination, 283–286
Hitchcock, Alfred, 357
Hoboes: and bachelor subculture, 75,
76–86; wolf-punk relationships
among, 88, 90–91
Hobohemia, 78, 91
Holladay, Paula, 238
Hollywood, 321, 353, 356
Holt, Nora, 258
Home to Harlem (McKay), 265
Homosexuality, 7, 65; bohemian opinions of, 230–232; concept of,
absence of, 12–13, 100, 120, 125;
gender inversion versus, 13, 22–23,
26–28, 48–49, 71, 124–126,

345–346; homo-heterosexual binarism, 12–16, 20, 22, 26–27, 48, 71, 96–97, 100, 119–121, 124–126, 358, 359; as term, 101. *See also* Gay male subculture; Lesbians; Sexual terminology *and specific categories*

Horn & Hardart, 164–165. *See also* Automats, as gay meeting places

Horowitz, Morris, 340–341

Horticultural gents or lads, 15, 249, 315. *See also* Pansy craze

Hotel bars, 201, 350–351, 361

Hotel Koenig, 170–173, 174, 176, 186, 356

Hotel Longacre, 162

Hotels: Bowery, 35; and Prohibition, 335; Raines Law, 160–161, 305; Times Square, 305. *See also* Housing *and specific hotels*

Hotel Shelton, 162

Housing, 136, 151–163; apartment hotels and houses, 158–159, 303; assignation hotels, 35, 42, 151, 159–163; boardinghouses, 36, 76, 164, 202, 303–304; buffet flats, 250–251, 253; furnished-room districts, 136, 152–154, 229, 303; Greenwich Village, 228, 229, 232–233; in Harlem, 245, 247–248, 250–251, 253; railroad flats, 151–152, 159; residential hotels, 138, 151, 154–158, 303–304; rooming houses, 76, 136, 151, 152–154, 164, 202, 303; tenement, 140, 152, 159, 202, 208, 303; in Times Square area, 303–304, 445–446n14

Howard, William Lee, 48–49, 122

Howdy Club, 352

Howells, William Dean, 293

Hubert's Museum, 306

Hughes, Langston, 264, 310

Humphreys, Laud, 197

Hunter, Alberta, 251

Husbands, of fairies, 86–96, 291

Hustlers: in bathhouses, 220; as term, 19; Times Square, 191–193

Immigration: to cities, 135–136, 245, 246, 256, 271–273; exclusionary laws, 328; and homosexuality, 10, 11, 132n; patterns of, 75; and Prohibition, 307; and sex ratios, 78; and sexual classification, 13, 14; trends in, 137. *See also specific immigrant groups*

Infants of the Spring (Thurman), 265

Inter-generational sex, 43, 84–85, 88–96, 140–141

Intermediate sex. *See* Third (intermediate) sex

Internalization, myth of, 4–6

Inter-State Tattler, 256–257, 258, 263

In the life, as term, 15, 251

Inversion. *See* Gender inversion

Invisibility, myth of, 3–4, 47

Ioläus (Carpenter), 284

Irish immigrants, 10, 137, 172; and bachelor subculture, 76–86; and color of clothing, 53; and male prostitutes, 72; relationships with queers, 108–110; and violence toward fairies, 59–60

Isolation, myth of, 2–3, 47

Italian immigrants, 10, 137, 228; and all-male social world, 75–76; and bachelor subculture, 75, 76–86; and color of clothing, 53; double lives of, 54, 58, 81; and male prostitutes, 72–76; and violence toward fairies, 59–60

Jackman, Harold, 266

Jack's Restaurant, 174–175

Jazz, 327, 328

Jewel Restaurant, 175, 304

Jewish immigrants, 105, 137, 202; anti-Semitism, 75, 105, 328; cruising by, 181; and Jewish ritual bath (*mikvah*), 208–209; and male prostitutes, 72, 73–75

Judge, Dolly, 237, 238–239

Julian's, 241

Julius', 233
Jumbo, 34, 161
Jungle, 238, 241

Karlinsky, Simon, 285
Katz, Jonathan, 9, 100
Kinsey, Alfred, 70–72, 74, 110, 118, 119
Kinship system, gay, 290–291. *See also* Marriage
Koenig, George, 170–171
Kotchover, Eva (Eve Addams), 240–241, 242–243, 323
Krafft-Ebing, Richard von, 283, 311

Lady lovers. *See* Lesbians
Lafayette Baths, 146, 206, 215, 216, 217, 220–223, 323
La Guardia, Fiorello, 92–93, 182, 183, 333
Lait, Jack, 20
La Marr, Jean, 263
Laurel and Hardy, 325
Law, Jackie, 239
Lears, Jackson, 111
Leaves of Grass (Whitman), 105, 285
Left Bank, 241–242
Legal restrictions, 2, 4–5; on alcoholic beverages, 19–20, 57, 66, 336–348, 351, 356, 358–359; and anti-vice societies, 15; censorship, 8, 9, 311–313, 324–325, 352–353, 356; during the Cold War, 8–9; on degenerate disorderly conduct, 72, 170–173, 185–186, 213, 216, 337–346; on gay assembly, 170, 173–176, 347, 351, 354; on gay bars, 19–20, 25, 57, 337–349, 358–359; on male prostitution, 172–173; on public obscenity, 313; on sodomy, 134, 140–141, 185, 195, 302n, 407n23; on transvestism, 43, 51, 239–240. *See also* Police
Legman, Gershon, 8n, 14, 52

Lesbians, 175, 360; advocacy groups of, 5; bulldaggers, 15, 251–253, 279–280; and disorderly conduct, 173n; enclaves of, 136, 228; and gay bars, 344, 346, 347; and gender inversion, 27–28, 49, 124; in Greenwich Village, 227–230, 231–232, 234, 235, 237–242; in Harlem, 136, 247–248, 251–253, 279–280; history of, study of, 9–10, 27–28; in literature and film, 324, 325; as members of third sex, 49, 122; and nightclubs, 349–350; pseudo- , 235; and spectacularization, 168–169; and World War II, 10–11. *See also* Women
Levenson, Lew, 324
Lewis, David Levering, 264
Lexow Commission, 292
Leznoff, Maurice, 135n
Liberace, 350, 357
Liberal Club ball, 235–237, 244–245, 292
Lichtenstein, Perry, 123, 125
Life Cafeteria, 166–168, 174, 183, 277
Liggett's, 170, 192
Lightbody, Cyril, 249
Lillie, Beatrice, 288, 310, 351
Lincoln, Abraham, 120
Line-ups, 84–85
Literature, gay and lesbian, 6, 8, 9–10, 241–243, 283–286, 324–325
Little Beethoven Assembly Hall, 293
Little Bucks, 34
Little Review, 232
Live sex shows, 37, 250
Locke, Alain, 264, 265, 284
London, 12, 188
Loop-the-loop, 68–69, 84, 87, 96
Lorenzo, Vito, 72–73
Los Angeles, 12
Louis' Luncheon, 241
Louis' Restaurant, 175–176, 304, 321
Love in the Machine Age (Dell), 231
Love's Coming of Age (Carpenter), 231, 285

Lower East Side, 202; cabarets, 170; dance halls, 40–41, 43; fairy resorts, 67–68, 138; and female prostitution, 35, 68, 72–73; homosexual behavior, 72–76; Italian neighborhoods of, 76; saloons, 41–45; social clubs in, 43. See also Bowery
Luhan, Mabel Dodge, 232
Lynch, Michael, 140
Lynde, Paul, 350, 357

Mabley, Jackie, 252
McCarthy, Frank, 277–278
McCarthy, Joseph, 8
MacCormick, Austin H., 93–94
MacDougal Street, 142, 240–244, 324, 431–432n32
Macfadden, Bernarr, 116, 179, 204, 323–324
McGlory, Billy, 37
McGree, Grant, 156
McKay, Claude, 264, 265
Macy's, 275
Madison Square Garden, 7, 294, 310, 333, 338
Male beauty contests, 184, 324
Male-female relationships: and fairies, 80–86; and family values, 75–76, 83–84
Male prostitutes. See Prostitutes, male
Malin, Gene (Jean), 239, 314–318, 320–321, 322, 324, 327–328, 329, 331, 334, 338
Malinowski, Bronislaw, 284
Manchester, Eddie, 264, 266
Manhattan Casino (Rockland Palace), 270, 294
Manilla Hall, 34, 35
Mann, Horace, 237, 297
Mann, Thomas, 285
Mariano, John, 76
Marine Bar & Grill, 193
Marriage, 136n; companionate, 117; and gay bathhouses, 220–221; homosexual, 68–69, 86–96, 232, 251, 291; lesbian, 232, 251; and nonmarital sexual behavior, 119
Marsden, Charles, 232
Marshall's Hotel, 139
Masculinity, 358; and bohemianism, 229, 230; and cult of muscularity, 114, 116, 121, 179; in middle-class culture, 111–126; in working-class bachelor subculture, 79–81, 89, 112
Mason, Jack (Jackie), 237, 297, 314, 315, 322, 338
Masquerade balls. See Drag (transvestite) balls
The Masses (magazine), 230–231
Masturbation, 84–85
Matthiessen, F. O., 104, 199
Maye, Jackie, 318
Medical discourse, 5–6, 48–49, 98, 121–126, 132, 135, 188, 281–282
Meeker, Richard, 284–285, 324
Melville, Herman, 284
Men's Residence Club, 156–157, 303
Mentors, gay, 277–278
Mercer, Mabel, 349–350
Mero, Bruhs, 271, 280
Metropolitan Opera, 351
Meyerowitz, Joanne, 202–203, 303
Middle-class culture, 10, 99–127; attitude toward fairies, 44, 45, 51–59, 99–111, 115–116; attitude toward queers, 106–111; attitude toward working-class culture, 36–41, 44, 57–59; black, 253–257, 260, 263–267; and bourgeois ideology, 35–36, 106–107; and class hostilities, 36–41, 44, 60; emergence of masculine heterosexuality in, 111–126; and housing, 36, 158–159; and Prohibition, 307–308, 327; sexual classification in, 14; and speakeasies, 307–308; street culture, middle versus working class, 179–204. See also Slumming
Migration: to cities, 135–136, 245, 246, 256, 271–273; Great Migration,

Migration (continued)
    245, 246, 256. See also Immigration
    and specific immigrant groups
Milk, Harvey, 183
Mills, Darius O., 154
Mills Houses, 154–155
Minnelli, Vincente, 357
Modernity (play), 241
Modern Thinker, The (magazine), 145,
    282
Molly houses, 12
Moore, Clinton, 264, 266
Morgan, Helen, Jr., 308, 315, 316, 324
Mortimer, Lee, 20
Mother Childs (cafeteria), 166, 176,
    182, 183, 321
Mount Morris Baths, 218
Mount Morris Park, as cruising area,
    196
Movies, 8; censorship of, 325, 353,
    356, 357; Greenwich Village gay
    scene in, 234–235; as meeting
    places, 194–195; and pansy craze,
    325
Mulrooney, Edward, 332, 334
Murray's, 306
Myths of gay life, 2–6; internalization,
    4–6; invisibility, 3–4, 47; isolation,
    2–3, 47

Nance, 125, 182, 183; as term, 15
Nathan, George Jean, 311
National Committee for Mental
    Hygiene, 147
Nesbitt, Charles, 40–41, 59
Nestle, Joan, 9
New Deal, 354
New Negro era, 310
Newport, Rhode Island, 145, 155
Newspapers: African-American, 7,
    10, 254–263, 266; coded classified
    ads in, 288; Greenwich Village,
    242–243, 323; and pansy craze,
    304, 310, 315–324, 329,
    332–334; and spectacularization,

    37–40, 41, 94–95. See also specific
    newspapers
New Star Casino, 294, 332–334
Newton, Esther, 290
New York Age, 254, 258, 259, 261
New York Association for the
    Improvement of the Condition of
    the Poor, 208
New York City Jail, 189; study of
    inmates in, 152, 201, 272–273;
    wolf-punk relationships in, 91–96,
    123. See also Prisons
New York Evening-Graphic, 323–324,
    329
New York Herald, 37–40, 41, 288
New York Herald Tribune, 292–293;
    and raid on New York City Jail,
    93–95
New York Public Library, 181, 201,
    275
New York Sun, 213
New York Times, 10, 135–136, 288
Nickelodeons, 194
Nigger Heaven (Van Vechten), 246
Nightclubs, 349–350, 352, 357
Niles, Blair, 285, 321, 324
Normal (straight) men, 120–121;
    fairies passing as, 7, 103; and homo-
    sexual marriage, 86–96; and Lower
    East Side saloons, 42–45; and male
    prostitution, 66–76; relationships
    with fairies, 50, 61–62, 100,
    122–123, 147–148; relationships
    with queers, 100, 107–108; and tea-
    room trade, 200; as term, 13–16,
    19–22, 24–25, 26; wolves versus,
    95–96
Norman, Karyl, 319, 321
Nucleus Club, 280
Nudity: of body builders, 114, 116. See
    also Bathhouses
Nugent, Bruce, 251–252, 264, 265

O'Neill, Eugene, 232
Oral sex, 61. See also Fellation

Orsi, Robert, 76
Osborne, Thomas Mott, 95

Padlock Law, 312, 313, 352, 356, 357
Painter, Thomas, 52, 188, 210–211, 220
Palace, 288
Palm Club, 34
Pansy, 48, 53, 125; as term, 15. *See also* Fairies; Pansy craze
Pansy Club, 318–319, 321, 332
Pansy craze, 239, 257–258, 301, 314–321, 352, 356; backlash to, 331–334, 353; in Harlem, 309–310; and the media, 321–329; origins of, 309–313; rise of, 314–315; in Times Square, 301, 315–321, 332–333
Paresis Hall (Columbia Hall), 33, 34, 35, 42–44, 50, 55, 67–68, 69, 132, 141, 160, 322–323
Paris, gay subculture in, 12, 144, 318, 377n21, 409n34
Parisex, 282
Park, Robert, 134
Parker, Jay, 91
Parker, Richard, 126
Parkhurst, Charles, 33, 68, 138, 160
Parks: Battery Park, 89–90, 142, 162, 182, 196; Bryant Park, 68, 165, 181, 183, 192, 194, 201, 333; Central Park, 182–183, 189, 191, 196, 204, 275; as gay social centers, 180, 181–183, 196; Mount Morris, 196; and Progressive Era reforms, 203–204; Prospect Park, 68–69, 181–182; Riverside Park, 142, 182, 196; Union Square, 141, 142, 162, 185, 189, 190
Passing, 7, 103, 273–280
Paul and Joe's, 239–240, 315
Peel, Mark, 303
Peiss, Kathy, 139, 202–203
Penn Post Baths, 218
Pennsylvania Railroad, and tearoom trade, 198

Perry, Edward G., 266
Perverts, as term, 14–15, 122–123, 147
Physical Culture, 116
Pink Elephant, 193, 357
Pirate's Den, 233, 237
Plato, 285
Plaza Hotel, 350
Police: and anti-gay raids, 249–250, 331–332, 337–349; and cruising areas, 183, 184–185, 186; and drag balls, 294–296; in Greenwich Village, 238, 239–241; in Harlem, 253, 254–257; and hustler scene, 193; patrolling of parks by, 195–196; raids on bathhouses, 146–149, 209, 210–217, 218, 221, 223, 323; raids on private parties, 280; relationships with queers, 108–110; and tearoom trade, 197–198, 199, 264–266; and urban reform efforts, 138–149. *See also* Legal restrictions
Polly's Restaurant, 238–239
Porter, Cole, 288, 352–353, 357
Powell, Adam Clayton, 254–256
Princess Toto, 40–41
Prisons: homosexual segregation in, 92–95, 123, 125; wolf-punk relationships in, 88, 91–96. *See also* New York City Jail
Privacy: and apartment houses and hotels, 151–152, 158–159; and roominghouses, 153–154; in streets and parks, 195–196, 201–203; and tearoom trade, 195–201; at YMCAs, 156–158. *See also* Parks; Public spaces; Streets and avenues
Prizefighters, 113–114
Produce Exchange Baths, 217, 221
Production Code Administration, 353
Prohibition, 9, 117, 143, 148; in Greenwich Village, 233–234, 310; impact of, 8–9, 164, 304–321, 327–328, 335–336; and pansy craze, 301, 309–329; repeal of, 173, 193, 207, 334–337, 347–348, 356;

Prohibition *(continued)*
    in Times Square, 306–309. *See also*
    Speakeasies
Prospect Park, as cruising area, 68–69,
    181–182
Prostitutes, female, 17, 35, 125*n*,
    139, 140; anti-prostitution cam-
    paign, 82, 130, 131–132, 134,
    138–141, 143, 147, 159–163; and
    bachelor subculture, 80–86; fairies
    compared with, 50–51, 61, 80–86;
    in Harlem, 247, 253, 254; and
    line-ups, 84–85; Lower East Side,
    35, 68, 72–73; and Raines Law
    (1896), 160–162, 305; and sailors,
    64, 66–67, 161–162; streetwalk-
    ers, 36, 160; in theaters, 194;
    Times Square, 305, 307; and vene-
    real disease, 85–86, 125*n*, 142,
    143
Prostitutes, male, 18*n*, 66–76; and anti-
    gay campaign, 147–149; anti-prosti-
    tution campaign, 141–149,
    159–163; and bathhouses, 220; fairy
    prostitutes, 66–76, 191, 192; hus-
    tlers, 19, 191–193, 220; in Italian
    neighborhoods, 72–76; in Jewish
    neighborhoods, 72, 73–75; legal
    restrictions on, 172–173; and line-
    ups, 84; Lower East Side, 33, 40,
    42, 50; police surveillance of,
    185–186; punks as, 89–90
Proust, Marcel, 49, 285
Pseudo-lesbians, 235
Psychology of Sex (Ellis), 285
Public spaces, 195–201; and hetero-
    sexual couples, 195–196, 201–203;
    public-private, contested bound-
    aries of, 34–36, 138–149,
    201–204; washrooms, 83, 146,
    185, 195–201, 264–266. *See also*
    Parks; Privacy; Slumming; Streets
    and avenues
Puerto Ricans, 53, 141
Pulitzer, Joseph, 39
Punks: in prison, 88; sexual character

of, 88; as term, 88, 396*n*50; in wolf-
    punk relationships, 88–96
Pussy-foot, 114

Queens, as term, 16, 101
Queers, 101–111; double lives of,
    273–280; dress and demeanor of, 3,
    52, 54, 64, 105, 106, 108, 187–188,
    350–351; fairies versus, 100,
    101–107; in Greenwich Village,
    243–244; in middle-class culture,
    106–111; as term, 13–22, 24–25,
    101, 125; in working-class culture,
    106–111. *See also* Gay male subcul-
    ture; Sexual terminology; Tactics, of
    gay men

Ragamuffin parades, 293–294
Railroad flats, 151–152, 159
Rainbow Room, 349
Raines Law (1896), 160–162, 305
Rainey, Ma, 251
RCA Building, eighth-floor restroom,
    197*n*, 201
Real man, as term, 16
Reckless, Walter, 132
Red Mask, 237
Red ties, 3, 52, 54, 64
Reimonenq, Alden, 264, 265
Religious communities, 354–356
Remembrance of Things Past (Proust),
    49
Renault, Francis, 318, 321
Residential hotels, 138, 151, 154–158,
    303–304
Restaurants: as gay meeting places, 11,
    19, 146, 150, 163–164, 165, 166,
    174–176, 238–240, 349; in
    Greenwich Village, 237–240, 242;
    Times Square, 304, 305
Retail shopping districts, as cruising
    areas, 189–190
Rey, Michel, 12
Rialto (Fourteenth Street), 33–35, 52,

68, 79; and emergence of gay sub-culture, 142, 190–191; and female prostitution, 35. *See also* Union Square

Richman, Harry, 54, 308

Riis Beach, as cruising area, 184

Ritz Review, The, 311

Riverside Drive, as cruising area, 52, 68, 146, 178, 181, 187, 189, 322

Riverside Park, 142, 182, 196

Rivington Street, 155

Robinson, William J., 281–282, 285

Rockefeller Center, 197n, 201, 275, 349

Rockland Palace (Manhattan Casino), 7, 259, 260, 270, 294

Roditi, Edouard, 244

Rooming houses, 76, 136, 151, 152–154, 164, 202, 303

Roosevelt, Franklin D., 336

Roosevelt, Theodore, 113

Rope (film), 357

Rosenberg, Charles, 121

Rotundo, Anthony, 111, 115, 120

Rough sports, 113–114, 116

Round Table, 168–169

Rubaiyat, 314–315

Russell, Lillian, 223

Russell Sage Foundation, 203

Sadomasochism, 220

Sailors: and bachelor subculture, 76–86; and fairies, 54, 64, 82–83, 143, 145; as gay icon, 54, 64, 78, 113; and prostitutes, 64, 66–67, 161–162; wolf-punk relationships among, 88, 89–90, 91n

St. George Hotel, 151, 162

St. Marks bath, 218, 222

Salle de Champagne, 345, 352

Saloons, 164, 190; anti-prostitution campaign, 82, 130, 131–132, 139, 140, 160–162; back rooms of, 37, 42, 68; Bowery, 33–34, 54, 59; in Coney Island, 35, 59; Lower East Side, 41–45; mixed, 42–45, 348; and Prohibition, 335; raids on, 146; and Raines Law (1896), 160–162; as social centers for gay men, 42–43, 72–73; and Temperance, 112, 112n, 160–162, 335. *See also* Bars; Gay bars; Speakeasies

Same-sex dancing, 168–169, 173, 173n, 234; at apartment parties, 279–280; and drag balls, 295–296; in Harlem, 248

Samuel Bickard's Artistic Club, 34

Sandow, Eugene, 114

San Francisco, 321, 353

Sardi, George, 271–272

Savoy, Bert, 312

Savoy Ballroom, 7, 252, 294, 297

Scarlet Pansy, A (Scully), 324

Schultz, Dutch, 331

Schwartz, Louis, 315

Schwarz, Judith, 231–232

Scott, James, 5

Scully, Billy, 242, 323

Scully, Robert, 324

Seabury, Samuel, 334

Seamen. *See* Sailors

Seamen's Church Institute, 89, 90, 154

Second Avenue, 35

Secrecy, 4–5, 6–7

Sedgwick, Eve Kosofsky, 116, 375n9, 381n62, 402n42

Self-hatred, 4, 43–44, 56–58, 121–126, 280–281

Servicemen. *See* Sailors; World War I; World War II

Seventh Avenue, 189, 246

Sex (play), 313

Sex crimes, 332n, 359–360

Sex deviant, 19, 332n, 359–360

Sexual aim, 124

Sexual Behavior in the Human Male (Kinsey), 70–72

Sexual Inversion (Ellis), 283

Sexual Question, The (Forel), 231, 285

Sexual terminology, 12–23; bull dagger (lesbian), 15; fag/faggot, 15–17, 18,

Sexual terminology *(continued)*
20, 101; fairy, 13–24, 27, 67, 101;
flaming faggot, 15–17, 18; gay,
14–24, 25, 286, 358; heterosexual,
12–13, 14, 15, 16, 22, 26; homosexual, 12–13, 14, 15, 16, 20, 22,
26–27, 101; hustlers, 19; nance, 15;
normal (straight), 13–16, 19–22,
24–25, 26; pansy, 15; queer, 13–22,
24–25, 101, 125; real man, 16; she-
man, 15; sissy, 15, 114; sister, 43,
291; swish, 16; trade, 16, 19,
20–22, 69–70, 100, 286. *See also*
Bisexuality; Heterosexuality;
Homosexuality; Lesbians *and spe-
cific categories*
*Sex Variants: A Study of Homosexual
Patterns* (Henry), 339*n,* 360
Shairp, Mordaunt, 357
Sharon Hotel, 42
Sheaffer, Louis, 232
She-man, 15, 121, 125
Sherman, Charlie (Chink), 331
Shufeldt, R. W., 87, 281
Shuffle Along (play), 246
Simmons, Christina, 117
Sissy, 125, 251, 358; as term, 15, 114
Sisters, as term, 43, 291
Situational homosexuality, 91
Sixth Avenue, 194; as cruising area,
189; Tenderloin, 35, 36, 138, 179,
204, 216
69 (club), 286
Slide, 37–40, 68, 155, 243
Slumming: in Bowery and Lower East
Side, 36–41, 44; in Greenwich
Village, 233–234, 236, 314; in
Harlem, 246–247, 248, 310. *See
also* Gay male subculture, spectacle
of
Small's Paradise, 252
Smith, Bessie, 250, 251
Smith, Roger, 275
Smith, Ruby, 250
Smith-Rosenberg, Carroll, 121
Social clubs, 41–45; Bowery, 44–45;

Italian, 76; Lower East Side, 43
Social Evil, The, 160–161
Social-purity societies, 15, 37, 79,
138–149, 170–173; and anti-gay
attitudes, 281–282; and Bowery
clubs and halls, 33, 34, 41, 50; in
Harlem, 254–257; and homosexual
vice, 146–149; rise of, 138–141; and
rooming houses, 153–154; and
World War I, 141–149. *See also spe-
cific organizations*
Society for Human Rights, 144
Society for the Prevention of Crime,
138, 141, 148–149, 215
Society for the Prevention of Cruelty to
Animals, 138
Society for the Prevention of Cruelty to
Children, 138–139, 140–141
Society for the Suppression of Vice,
138, 139, 146–147, 148, 165*n,* 210,
215–216, 230–231, 280
Sodomy, laws against, 134, 140–141,
185, 195, 302*n,* 407*n*23
Soldiers and Sailors Monument, 181,
182
Spanish-American War (1898), 113
Speakeasies, 117, 304, 352; as gay
meeting places, 19, 57–58, 323,
328–329; in Greenwich Village,
233, 237–238, 240, 241–242, 315,
338; in Harlem, 56–57, 244, 246,
247, 248, 250; in Times Square,
304, 306–309. *See also* Prohibition
Spectacularization. *See* Gay male subculture, spectacle of
Spivy's Roof, 349–350, 357
Sporting houses (tenement brothels),
68, 89
Stanwood Cafeteria, 342–343,
344–345, 352
State Liquor Authority (SLA), 19–20,
57, 66, 336–348, 351, 356,
358–359; and Gloria's, 337–339,
340, 342, 344; and Stanwood
Cafeteria, 342–343, 344–345, 352;
and Times Square Garden & Grill,

340–341, 343
Stauch's, 210–211
Stead, Joshua, 120
Stein, Gertrude, 176
Stevenson, Edward Prime, 211
Stevenson, Frank, 37
Steward, Samuel M., 103
Stewart's, 166–167, 174
Stonewall rebellion (1969), 2, 3, 6, 11
Straight men. See Normal (straight)
    men
Strange Brother (Niles), 285, 324
Streets and avenues: and anti-prostitu-
    tion campaign, 140; Bleecker Street,
    34, 37, 155, 243; Broadway, 35, 36,
    138, 146, 179, 204, 216; Central
    Park West, 146, 151, 155, 156, 189;
    as central to gay life, 179–180,
    184–195; Elizabeth Street, 37, 68,
    72–73; Fifth Avenue, 146, 166,
    180n, 189; Forty-second Street, 18n,
    66, 68, 70, 97, 120, 191–195, 306,
    333; Fourteenth Street (Rialto),
    33–35, 52, 68, 79, 142, 190–191;
    MacDougal, 142, 240–244, 324,
    431–432n32; raids on, 146–147;
    Riverside Drive, 52, 68, 146, 178,
    181, 187, 189, 322; Seventh
    Avenue, 189, 246; Sixth Avenue, 35,
    36, 138, 179, 189, 194, 204, 216;
    Third Avenue, 42, 68, 151, 159,
    185, 189, 190. See also Bowery;
    Cruising
Streetwalkers, 36, 160
Studio Club, 239
Subway Cabaret, 79
Subway washrooms, 83, 146, 185,
    197–201, 265–266
Sumner, John, 146–147, 230–231
Sunken Gardens, 197
Swanson, Gloria, 51, 263
Swanson, Gloria (Winston), 251–252
Swish, 104
Symonds, John Addington, 283
Symposium (Plato), 285

Tactics, of gay men, 187–190; camp
    culture, 7–8, 164–176, 193,
    286–291, 317–318, 327–329,
    342–345, 357; camp names, 40–41,
    50–51, 56–57, 105, 251, 252, 266,
    314, 315; clothing cues, 3, 4, 5,
    52–54, 64; coded words, 14–18,
    20–21, 24, 286–291, 351; double
    entendre, 17–19, 286–291, 327,
    357; double lives, 6–7, 24, 44,
    50–51, 54, 58, 133–135, 273–280;
    eye contact, 188–189; other codes,
    4–5, 55–56, 188–189, 344–346,
    350–351, 456n2
Tea and Sympathy (film), 357
Tearooms, in Greenwich Village, 233,
    237–238, 240
Tearoom (washroom) trade, 83, 146,
    185, 195–201, 264–266
Tecumseh Hall & Hotel, 37
Tellier, Andre, 324
Temperance, 112, 112n, 160–162, 335.
    See also Prohibition
Tenderloin, 35, 36, 138, 179, 204, 216;
    slumming and, 36–41
Tenements, 140, 152, 159, 202, 208,
    303
Terminology. See Sexual terminology
Thanksgiving ball, 293–294
Theaters, 8, 191–195; burlesque
    houses, 147, 170, 190–195, 305,
    311, 313; and Depression, 305; gay
    and lesbian, 241, 311–313, 356,
    357; and homosexuality, 301–302,
    345; raids on, 146–147
Their First Mistake (film), 325
Third Avenue, 42, 151, 159, 185; as
    cruising area, 68, 189, 190
Third sex (intermediate sex), 49, 284;
    fairies as members of, 48, 49, 57,
    121, 122–123, 125; lesbians as
    members of, 49, 122
Thompson, Battling, 241
Thompson, Frank, 279, 280
Thompson's Lunch Room, 193

Three Essays on the Theory of
  Sexuality (Freud), 124
Thurman, Wallace, 264–266
Times Square, 2, 11, 19, 67, 142, 162,
  191–193; burlesque theaters, 305,
  311; cafeterias, 305; as gay male
  enclave, 136, 142, 301–304, 357;
  hotels, 305; housing in, 303–304,
  445–446n14; pansy craze in, 301,
  315–321, 332–333; Prohibition
  impact on, 305–321; restaurants,
  304, 305; revues, 309, 311;
  speakeasies, 304, 306–309; subway
  washrooms in, 197; theater,
  311–313; theater roof gardens, 309,
  311; transformation of, as entertainment district, 304–321
Times Square Building, 66, 70, 97, 192
Times Square Garden & Grill,
  340–341, 343
Tompkins Square Park, as cruising
  area, 196
Tony's, 349, 357
Tough girls, fairies compared with,
  50–51, 61, 80–86
Trade: bachelor subculture in, 76–86;
  and male prostitution, 66–76,
  191–193; rough trade, 21, 191–193,
  220; tearoom (washroom), 83, 146,
  185, 195–201, 264–266; as term,
  16, 19, 20–22, 69–70, 100, 286
Train conductors, and queers, 108, 109
Tramps. *See* Hoboes
Transient workers. *See* Hoboes
Transvestites, 124; in the Bowery, 40,
  44; laws against, 43, 51, 249–250;
  in Lower East Side saloons, 42; in
  prisons, 92, 94–95; and prostitution,
  18n. *See also* Drag queens; Drag
  (transvestite) balls; Fairies; Gay male
  subculture, spectacle of; Pansy craze
Trick, as term, 286
Trilby's, 237
Trimberger, Ellen Kay, 230
Trumbach, Randolph, 12,
  377–378n23, 380n55,

385–386n2–3, 390n46
Turkish Bath (painting), 206
Twilight Men (Tellier), 324
Tyler, Parker, 57, 62, 87, 88, 165, 166,
  168–169, 180n, 181, 187, 191n,
  242–243

Ubangi Club, 253
Ulrichs, Karl Heinrich, 49, 231
Union Hall, 73
Union Square, 141, 162; as cruising
  area, 185, 189, 190; and emergence
  of gay subculture, 142. *See also*
  Rialto (Fourteenth Street)
Urbanization: and anonymity,
  132–134; and emergence of gay subculture, 132–136; and family values,
  131, 132, 134; and migration to
  cities, 135–136, 245, 246, 256,
  271–273

Van Cortlandt Park, 196
Van Der Meer, Theo, 12
VanDerZee, James, *xii*
Vanity Fair, 166; and pansy craze, 309,
  316, 324, 327–328
Van Vechten, Carl, 101, 175, 189, 232,
  246, 264, 287, 297
Van Wagner, Walter R., 337
Variety, 182, 184, 241, 246, 296, 306;
  and pansy craze, 311, 313–314,
  318, 320, 321, 332, 333
Vaseline Alley, Central Park, 182, 204
Vaudeville circuit, 305, 311, 313, 353
Venereal diseases, 85–86, 125n, 142,
  143
Village. *See* Greenwich Village
Vining, Donald, 156–157, 183,
  286–290
Violence: gang rape, 60, 84; sex crimes,
  332n, 359–360; toward fairies,
  59–60
Virgin Man (play), 313
Volstead Act, 305, 306, 332

Voyeurism: and gay bathhouses, 212–213, 218; and slumming in New York, 36–41, 44, 60, 68. *See also* Gay male subculture, spectacle of

Walhalla Hall, 40–41, 293
Walker, A'Leila, 258, 264
Walker, Jimmy, 294, 306, 334
Ware, Caroline, 233, 235, 239, 314
Washington Baths, 184
Washington Square Park, as cruising area, 196
Waterfront, 10, 11, 41; Brooklyn Navy Yard, 143, 145, 161–162; as cruising area, 142, 145, 189
Waters, Ethel, 251, 258
Webb, Clifton, 310
Webster Hall, 235–237, 293, 295–296
Welfare Island. *See* New York City Jail
Well of Loneliness, The (Hall), 324
Werther, Ralph, 42–44, 51, 52, 54, 55, 59–60, 62, 77, 79, 110, 118, 187, 190, 291–292
Wescott, Glenway, 108, 181
West, Mae, 51, 61, 263, 266, 311, 312, 313, 357
Whitin, Frederick, 147, 165n
Whitman, Walt, 104–105, 285
Wilde, Oscar, 54, 107, 230, 272
Will, Abram, 261
Williams, Christine, 315
Williams, Emlyn, 217, 220–221
Wives, as term, 291
Wolves, 58, 88–96; marked masculinity of, 89; in prison, 88; as term, 88; in wolf-punk relationships, 88–96
Woman's Christian Temperance Union, 112
Women: bohemian, 229–232; differentiation of men from, 111–115; employment of, 111–112, 117–118, 121–122, 354; fellation by, 61, 85, 390n48; middle-class, 253–254; and venereal disease, 85–86. *See also*
Lesbians; Male-female relationships; Marriage; Prostitutes, female
Wooden, Wayne S., 91
Work: and double lives, 134–135, 274–276; as male sphere, 111–112; and male unemployment, 354; and tearoom trade, 198, 264; and urbanization process, 133n; and women, 111–112, 117–118, 121–122, 354
Working-class culture, 10, 27, 33–97; acceptance of gay culture in, 3–4, 32, 34, 41–42, 44–45, 57–59, 80–86, 106–111, 118–119, 243–244; and anti-vice and social-purity societies, 138–141; bachelor subculture in, 75, 76–86; black, 248–257, 266–267; and boardinghouses, 36, 76, 164, 303–304; and cafeteria society, 163–176; fairies in, 106–107; and fancy-dress balls, 41; gender identity versus sexual identity in, 48; in Harlem, 248–257, 266–267; housing in, 151–158, 159–163, 202; as immigrant culture, 137; labeling of homosexual behavior in, 13; and male prostitution, 66–76; manliness in, 79–81, 89, 112, 113–114; plasticity of gender assignment in, 50–51, 56–58, 62–63, 65–66, 80–97, 118–119; and Prohibition, 327; queers in, 106–111; research on imprisoned homosexuals, 3, 6; and saloons, 41–45, 160–162; and social clubs, 41–45; and speakeasies, 307–308; street culture, working class versus middle class, 179–204; and tearoom trade, 83, 146, 195–201; viewed as depraved by middle class, 36–41, 44, 57–59. *See also* Immigration *and specific immigrant groups;* Slumming
Workingmen's clubs, 41–45
World's Fair (1939), 182, 340, 357
World War I: anti-prostitution campaign during, 82, 142–144; cam-

World War I *(continued)*
paign against venereal disease,
85–86; and changes in Greenwich
Village, 232–235, 310; and urban
moral reform movement, 141–149
World War II, 74, 195, 333, 358;
effects on gay subculture, 10–12,
144; restrictions on homosexuality
during, 125*n*, 350–351

WPA Guide to New York City, 167
Yacavone, Donald, 120, 403*n*50
Yawitz, Paul, 324
Young and Evil, The (Ford and Tyler),
17, 191*n*, 242–243
Young Men's Christian Association of
New York (YMCA), 138, 155–158;
Sloane House, 155–157; West Side
Y, 151, 155, 156